Chuckchi

Ostyak

apps

Ainu

Mongols

atsani

Taiwanese

Paharis   Lepcha
          Katchin

Muria   Yao
Hindu   Thai Montagnards

Darfur

Nuer   Nayar
Dinka   Danakil   Nambudiri   Semang
Azande   Somali
         Amhara

Pygmies   Karamojong   Manus
          Kipsigis Masai   Arapesh   Tolai
Nyoro   Arusha   Asmat Tchambuli Solomon Islanders
                                              Mundugamor Trobriand Islanders
Bakuba   Kamba   Balinese   Papuan   Dobuan
         Swahili   Alorese
Bena
Kombe

Pende   Yir Yoront
          Yao
shmen   Arunta

Thonga
Swazi
Zulu

Tasmanians

Maori

Anthropology Today

CRM BOOKS Del Mar, California

Anthropology Today

Every society depends on other societies,

and with every advance in technology the interdependence increases. A nation whose citizens are generally ignorant of other peoples in the world must to that degree be impeded in achieving its own goals, for we are at the stage in human history when national affairs cannot be separated from world development. Anthropology tells us about people everywhere—about their daily life as well as their high achievements, about the anonymous villager's sense of history as well as the succession of kings. It gives us a broad view of time, and place, and circumstance. It brings into focus the long-range workings of human society, and it projects, in their broadest perspective, the possibilities for man. It is in search of man's future, as well as his past, that we turn to anthropology today.

Richard L. Roe, Publisher, Social Sciences

Contents

THE EVOLUTION OF MAN III

THE ARCHAEOLOGICAL RECORD IV

EMERGENCE OF CONTEMPORARY SOCIETY V

THE STUDY OF SOCIETY AND CULTURE VI

CULTURE IN ITS INFINITE VARIETY VII

Anthropology Today

HORIZONS IN THE STUDY OF MAN

The Science of Man

1 Anthropology is the comparative study of mankind. *Comparative* is the key word here, for although man represents one single biologically unique and functionally uniform species, his range of physical and behavioral characteristics is dramatic and diverse. In other animals, each species follows its own fixed and largely instinctive behavior patterns. But the single interbreeding species of man has not only quite marked local genetic varieties but also a wide range of local behavioral patterns that change, moreover, both in geographic space and in historic time. Man is a paradoxical animal, in that his physical variations have little to do with his biologically more important adaptations—his varying cultures. The proper study of mankind therefore demands a whole interrelated collection of specialized sciences, some of them historic and documentary or descriptive, some of them biological, some sociological, and some applicable to man alone.

THE UNIQUE NATURE OF ANTHROPOLOGY

It is the specifically comparative method that sets anthropology apart from other social and behavioral sciences. When a sociologist talks about society or culture, he almost invariably, perhaps without realizing it, uses Western society as his tacit model. The insights and the hypotheses of sociology are therefore bound to Western culture, inasmuch as propositions will be chosen that are considered "common sense" in the West.

Perhaps political scientists are less prone to construct their theories from one perspective. Since the time of Aristotle they have been accustomed to dealing with comparative political systems; but the anthropologist nevertheless would like them to cast their inductive net more widely over all societies of the world. In fact, anthropology has recently developed its own specialty, called political anthropology, that takes a more systematically comparative approach. Meanwhile the anthropologist listens, with some dismay, to the daily news of some new international catastrophe viewed only in terms of Western sociopolitical and cultural preconceptions. The point is that then we really quite misunderstand what is actually happening, because in other societies men may have different implicit expectancies of government and of themselves.

Or consider the economist. In concentrating his inquiries on modern industrialized societies, he tends to have fixed notions concerning a supposedly universal profit motivation in economic affairs. But many societies have economic systems in which the profit motive as we know it does not even enter. In the potlatch of the Northwest Coast Indians, for example, property is not collected for purposes of profit but is competitively given away to gain prestige for a lineage. Curiously, the prestige value of native "coppers" is increased by breaking them, of slaves by killing them, and of boats by chopping them up. Again, a Trobriand Islander in Melanesia works hard to grow as many yams as possible—not to eat them but to gain prestige by displaying them in front of his sister's house (not his wife's), after which they may be left to rot. In the Melanesian *kula* ring, two sets of ceremonial objects—necklaces and arm bracelets—are exchanged around a ring of islands, the necklaces moving one way and the bracelets moving the other. This exchange promotes exciting interisland travel, incidental culture diffusion, enlargement of the peace group, and psychologically valued trade friendships or whatever, rather than profit, while the value of the commodities themselves does not depreciate with wear and use but increases with age and accretion of trade lore. In short, the economic exchange of goods can be based on a number of motivations other than profit. Indeed, one of the hotly argued present-day issues is whether or not the principles and "laws" developed from studying a market economy are of any use at all to economic anthropology.

Much of modern psychology is limited to neurophysiology or animal psychology because of moral strictures against experiments on human beings and the greater number of laboratory controls possible with animals. And this is as it must be, as long as psychology aspires to be a manipulative experimental science and not merely an observational natural science. Can more be learned about man by manipulating him or by merely observing him? In any case, many psychological generalizations about mankind at large are in fact only local and contemporary ethnography. Consider, for example, a simple question that has vexed man since the early Greeks: Is the human male more urgently sexed, or is the female? Given the sample responses from American society alone, it is not surprising that Alfred Kinsey discovered the local folklore that he did. If we are sure the male is the more urgently sexed, then what about the alternative notion implicit in the story of Adam and Eve? Certainly in the medieval Merovingian and Carolingian epics the female is presented as being more aggressive than the male, a notion that some modern Scandinavian people are also said to believe.

To anthropologists, a social psychology questionnaire is not the proper device to settle the matter. In fact, to some observers social psychology seems nothing more than a sort of experimental linguistics or applied lexicography—the choosing of some noun "entity" and then asking for some adjectival judgment about it—and is thus only a statistical measure of the semantic overlap in the unconscious connotation and denotation of the two parts of speech.

In all these concerns of other social scientists, the anthropologist is uneasily aware that they reckon without *culture*—the widely varying covert assumptions of which influence the behavior of every individual—and that this critical dimension cannot be ignored. Worse yet is the layman's improvised ethnography: "Some primitive tribes (unspecified) do such-and-such (in order to prove my momentary point)"—to which the anthropologist retorts, "But the Pukapukans do otherwise!" Anthropologists have been busy the first half of this century in battering down each absolutism that would grind some theoretical ax, for they are convinced that no generalization can be made about man at large unless it applies to all his cultural varieties. Modern anthropologists, having perhaps gained in their battle against such loose generalization by their aggressive relativism, have somewhat tired of the game.

Figure 2. Making the red feather money that is used in Solomon Island ceremonial exchanges. Socially motivated exchange where profit is not the main objective occurs throughout the world.

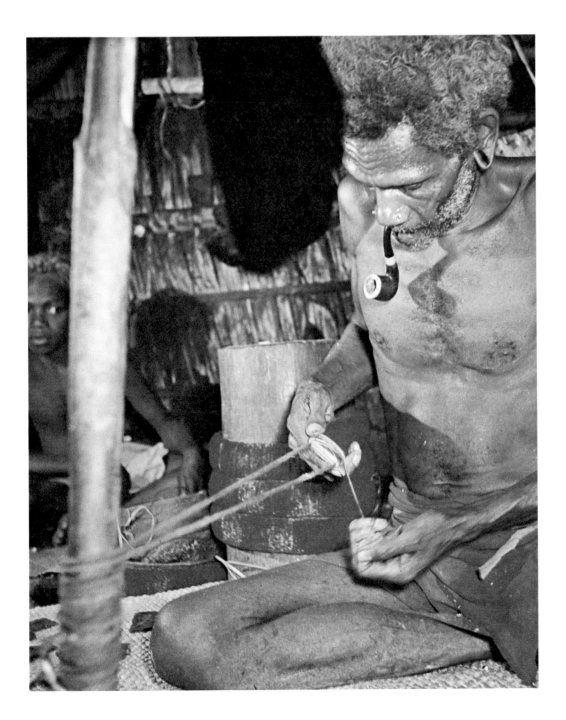

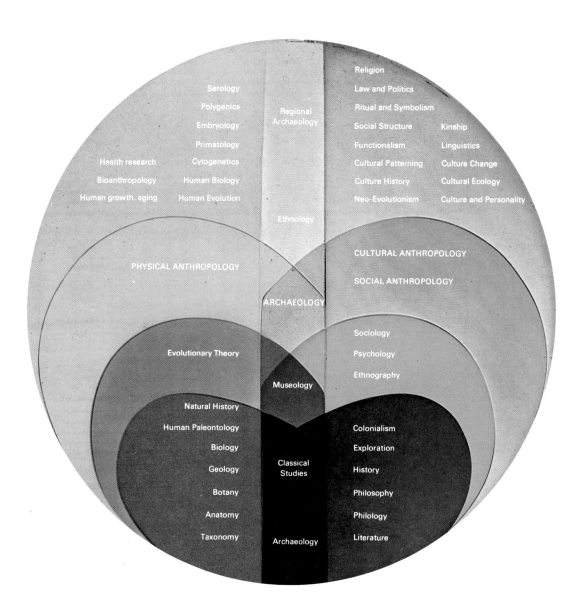

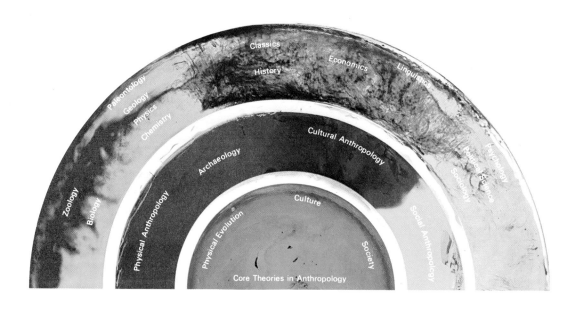

Figure 3. Overview of anthropology, showing some factors giving impetus to general growth as well as areas of interdisciplinary concern. Below are the major subfields of anthropology and the sciences that impinge on them. The charts roughly indicate the way the subfields of anthropology unfolded, although the more general, earlier concerns continue through. Ethnography, for instance, gave rise to culture and personality studies as a result of its interaction with psychology. Figure 4. The comparative ethnography of child rearing practices throws light on the effect of culture on adaptive personality.

Given man's infinite cultural variety, the search has now turned to the discovery of what features, after all, are truly human, a trend that has invaded even the study of the notorious variables in languages.

If history be counted a social science, history perhaps comes closest of all to the comparativist position. Culture inexorably changes through time, and good history long ago abandoned the simple chronicle of events to become in fact a painstaking and sophisticated culture history, the microethnography of the Western social tradition. When the historian labors mightily to convey just what Renaissance men were like, the anthropologist is apt to admire and sympathize with him, because he knows how difficult it is to describe an exotic culture through the haze of complacent assumptions we make about man. And some documented cultural events—for example, the educational system of the classic Greeks—may require explanation from not only the historian and the ethnographer but the psychiatrist as well. For that matter, who has ever adequately sketched the character and personality of that enigmatic and pivotally significant man Julius Caesar? Having much the same difficult problems, historians and cultural anthropologists understand one another. Ironically, anthropologists question whether ethnology is, like history, *idiographic* (describing the unique event) or whether it is, like science, *nomothetic* (discovering valid scientific generalizations). Historians as a group seem to have settled on being idiographic and on suppressing each maverick nomothete (such as Vico, Spengler, and Toynbee) who arises among them. If ethnographers aspire to be historians, it appears they must be satisfied with being idiographic. On the other hand, some students believe that anthropology is neither history nor science but *par excellence* another one of the humanities.

In any event, anthropologists must concern themselves with man in all times and places if they are to maintain the thoroughgoing comparative approach that has come to characterize their investigations. This focus places fundamental reliance on anthropological *field work*. Although subtle and profound insights are obtainable from investigations in the laboratory, the basic material of the science is generated by trained specialists working in the field, whether that field be the savanna of East Africa, the tundra of the Arctic Circle, or the megalopolis called Los Angeles. And field work today holds even greater promise of yielding insights into the paradoxical aspects of man because of the growing sophistication in research techniques and analytical methods.

THE NEW PRECISION IN RESEARCH

In the present century, elegant and ingenious new techniques have greatly increased the methodological precision of anthropology. In archaeology, for example, the radioactive carbon 14 found in all organic remains has extended mere relative dating through stratification to a more absolute dating in time, so that it can now be stated definitively whether a manuscript of Isaiah dates from 200 B.C. rather than A.D. 200 and thus constitutes a critical source and not just a late derivative manuscript. Again, by counting the unique pattern of tree rings set by a local climatic succession of wet and dry years and by matching this ring pattern along a master chart established by overlapping examples, it is possible to state that a particular wooden beam was a sapling in A.D. 1312 and was cut to build a now-ruined pueblo in the southwestern United States about A.D. 1348.

Potassium argon and other analysis techniques can be used for delineating larger expanses of time. A study of the almost indestructible pollen grains present in archaeological layers can reveal, for example, that the winter deer hunting camp at Star Carr in Yorkshire was made during a cool Mesolithic birch forest period contemporary with Mag-

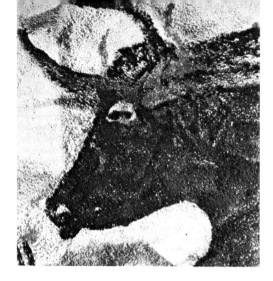

Figure 5. Cave painting at Lascaux, France. Such prehistoric art may provide clues about the conditions in which early man lived, because the animals that were portrayed are known to have been adapted to specific environments.

lemosian finds across the English Channel in Denmark. Indeed, this conclusion was confirmed when a peat fragment containing a classic Maglemosian harpoon point was fished up from an ancient marsh that now lies beneath the English Channel. Or consider the bones of long-dead animals. Because animals are physiologically and anatomically adapted to exact if complex environments, an assemblage of lion, hippopotamus, and rhinoceros bones in the caves of southern France can give a number of broad hints about details of the environment in which they lived. And if one primitive man painted a now-extinct aurochs bull on a cave wall and another painted a hairy mammoth, the anthropologist can be certain that the two men lived in two very distinct climatic periods.

The physical anthropologist has also developed precision techniques. Because man is an organism whose parts are functionally related, the expert can study a single thighbone and the posture it implies and be able to tell a great deal about the rest of the body of which it was part. Some anthropologists never did accept the seductively plausible idea that the famous Piltdown man represented a "missing link" with mixed ape-human features, because the tooth that was part of the assemblage implied a jaw quite incompatible with areas of muscle attachment on the braincase. Their doubts were justified when the questionable find was subjected to fluorine and other analyses, which proved the tooth to be a modern ape's and not of the same age and origin as the ancient human braincase.

In linguistics, by carefully searching for the plant, animal, and artifact names still spoken in all the daughter languages— "beech," "salmon," "turtle," and "iron" are key words here—the anthropologist can safely make several statements about our Indo-European linguistic ancestors. He can say that they lived around 2000 B.C. or earlier in the present area of Lithuania or Po-

land; that they had cattle, some agriculture, and wheeled wagons; that they possessed bronze artifacts but none of iron; and that they worshiped a sky god whose name meant "the shining one"—because all the descendant Indo-European dialects or languages have these systematically related words (for example, the *th* of English mother, father, brother is equivalent to the *t* of Latin mater, pater, frater).

There is not a scrap of written evidence from these ancient people because they were prealphabetic and lacked any kind of writing system. But it is known that in the climate of that period, beech trees did not grow east of a line drawn from the Baltic to the Caspian seas. Thus, if all the daughter languages still have a name for beech in common, then the ancestral Indo-Europeans must have lived west of this line. Turtles did not live north of the latitude of southern Schleswig-Holstein, so the now-scattered people could hardly have come from Scandinavia because they have a common word for turtle. As to salmon, in Europe these were confined to the Oder and Elbe, and other linguistic considerations lead to the selection of the easternmost river. A northern region is confirmed by the fact that the daughter languages contain a common word for wolf but not for lion or tiger or elephant. There is a common word for bronze (or copper) but different words for iron, implying that these earlier people had bronze in common but later the now dialectically divided groups borrowed the use of iron from others. It can even be proved that they could count to one hundred (because *hundert* and others are related words) but not to one thousand (because *mille* is a different word from *tausend*, and so on).

So rigid and consistent is linguistic behavior even today that a dialect expert can tell not only where an individual was born but also where his mother and father came from and where he went to college. The procedure is fairly simple, although exact. By present-

Figure 6. A few of the techniques used to probe the distant past. Above, dendrochronology can be used to give absolute dating in parts of the world where certain species of trees are found. These show broad climatic fluctuations, and the sequence can be matched against master sequence charts that already have been constructed for particular areas. Bottom left, by determining the relationship of potassium to argon in a rock sample, the geophycisist can establish its age. An isotopic "spike" is added to the specimen to provide a known standard for analysis in the mass spectrometer. Below right, using a centrifuge to separate pollen grains from deposits, the palynologist can classify and count the grains to determine the relative frequency of species, thus giving insights into the environment of early man.

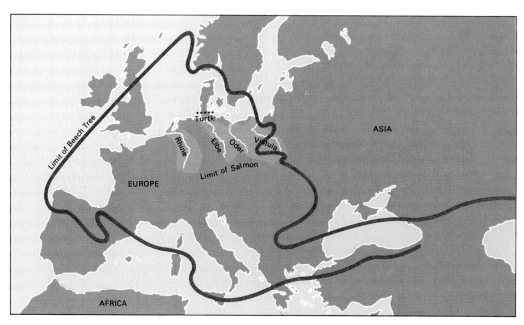

ing a picture of an object and asking an individual what it is called (for example, skillet, spider, or frying pan), broad regional hints are given. The pronunciation of *r* in the United States must be watched especially: north of a line drawn due east from Pittsburgh there is a North Atlantic dropping of the *r* (as in southern Atlantic) but also a false insertion between vowel sounds as in "lawr of the land"—but west of a line drawn north and south through Pittsburgh there is a strong sounding of the *r* in the "Westerrrn dialect." Terms for domestic utensils used in the kitchen would tend to indicate the mother's speech; terms for tools used by males give hints about the father's area of origin; technical terms used in college courses can help in placing the individual's educational origins.

Of course, dialect-forming contexts do change over time. In medieval England, travel and communication were so poor that neighboring counties developed mutually unintelligible dialects. But in eighteenth-century America, travel and communication had so improved that the United States today has only three major dialect regions, and only a backwoods Vermonter and a Georgia mountaineer might find themselves on the verge of mutual unintelligibility. Nowadays radio, television, movies, and popular records exert a leveling or standardizing effect on speech, as does wide travel on the part of many Americans. Nevertheless, to take a wider dialectical scale, just as a Frenchman can instantly spot an American who is speaking French (the American saying *tête* puts his tongue higher behind the upper teeth than the Frenchman thinks proper, does not waggle

his uvula on his *r* sounds, and hopelessly diphthongizes or glides his *e* sounds), so also can the American spot a French accent (the French tend to make the *i* in words like *"it"* identical with the *i* in *"police,"* have trouble with English *th* sounds and substitute *z*, and have an entirely different sentence melody or intonation). But French and English remain mere "dialects," mutually unintelligible now, of their common ancestor, Indo-European speech.

The same general principles apply elsewhere, even though the precise phonetic rules may differ. No written records are needed, only speech. Careful linguistic study reveals that Navajo hunters came to the American Southwest from western Canada east of the Rockies, separating from the Apache tribes only after they arrived, and that they borrowed the technique of growing corn from their new Pueblo neighbors. It can even be shown, by painstaking comparison of such features as the sing-song "pitch accent" of modern Navajo (and related Canadian Indian languages) with archaic proto-Chinese (reconstructed from Tibeto-Burman and Chinese regional dialects), that the ancestors of the Navajo came from eastern Asia over 10,000 years ago. By contrast, Susque*hanna* and Rappa*hannock* are river names from Algonkian tribes that separated dialectically only in relatively recent times. These conclusions are not wild surmises but the result of rigorous technical methods.

Other branches of anthropology have developed similarly precise and intellectually beautiful methods. Ancient and distant vistas are opened in cultural anthropology when, for example, conical tipis and wigwams are

Figure 7 (left). A look at linguistic behavior. By mapping out the words that are either common or unique to descendant Indo-European languages, we can extrapolate about the life of our Indo-European ancestors even though they left no written record of their culture. Figure 8 (right). An element common to many cultures — the Pawnee sweat vapor bath, an eighteenth-century steam bath used in England for the head, torso, and arms, and an Aztec version of the sweat bath.

found spread around the world almost continuously from Lapland to Labrador and sweat baths are found from Finland to Newfoundland. Even such intangibles as religion can be reconstructed. The bear ceremonialism that is found clear around the world in regions to the far north and southward among historic tribes in both Old and New worlds is quite probably related to a Middle Paleolithic bear cult once practiced in caves of the eastern Alps. The Orpheus legend of the shaman visiting the land of spirits was part of the folklore of both the Old World and North America, and the magic shamanistic tricksters of ancient northern Asia such as Raven are the same as those among American Indians. The eagle as thunderbird, sky god of lightning, and source of rain was spread from Mesolithic Eurasia into North America and southward; the eagle was also the bird of Zeus the Thunderer and of Jupiter Pluvius, both rain makers. It is in fact large collections of such mutually consistent racial, linguistic, cultural, and archaeological evidence that convince Americanist experts the Indians of the New World came from Northeast Asia.

THE HOLISTIC APPROACH

By mapping the universals in basic North and South American Indian cultures, experts can draw a fairly complete picture of the prehistoric Indian culture. The Mesolithic proto-Indian was a hunter who had dogs but no other domesticated animals. He had the spear thrower and the bow and arrow, fire but no metallurgy (and pottery perhaps later), and no agriculture but a highly developed interest in edible wild plants, especially hallucinogenic ones. He used ritual masks to scare children in puberty rites, and he ceremonially whipped the initiates. Spearheads, basket weaves, snowshoes, body armor, tailored clothing, certain art forms, and language families also help place in time the successive waves of hunters who came from Siberia to Alaska and thence to the rest of

the New World. Primitive "Paleo-Siberians," not Columbus, discovered America. There is even a substantial list of traits, spottily distributed in western regions of the Americas, that suggests minor movements of boatloads of people *from* the South Seas, and not the reverse as popular fantasy has it. But in all these inquiries, it is the use of *combined* forms of evidence that is both significant and overwhelming.

Although the subdisciplines of anthropology use different methods, their conclusions are profitably studied together. Ideally, societies should be studied *holistically*—that is, as wholes, and from all points of view. Recently, a curious and hitherto unknown neurological disease called *kuru* was discovered in the remote New Guinea mountains, open to anthropological study only since World War II. Cultural comparisons used alone would suggest that, seen behaviorally and psychiatrically, *kuru* might be related to the well-known "Vailala madness" because of certain peculiar traits of Melanesian culture and personality. Or *kuru* might be the same kind of phenomenon as the seasonal "mushroom madness" of Melanesian mountain tribes that eat a narcotic fungus. The question was raised as to whether it was caused by a recessive gene, established by long inbreeding. Certainly the disease occurred only within a limited geographic area. It was shown through a brilliant lexicostatistic study of a group of neighboring dialects that breeding isolation might indeed be a possibility. However, it was finally proved that an unusually slow-acting virus was responsible—spread by cannibalism, especially of uncooked brains. But who would have thought that linguistic, botanical, and cultural evidence would all help solve what appeared at first glance to be entirely a medical problem?

It is this kind of unpredictable situation that makes field work so fascinating. The anthropologist never knows just what he might encounter. One field worker on the

Figure 9 (left). Events that seem trivial to us may be critical in other cultures. The way a veil is draped in Western apparel may be shrugged off as being purely decorative; in the Sahara it provides an essential social signal. Figure 10 (right). Genes and culture traits may influence one another by placing different selective demands on the human body.

Lake Titicaca plateau in South America had hurriedly to learn as much botany as he could because the tribe he was studying turned out to have hundreds of plant medicines and some 400 named varieties of potato. Another anthropologist, working in the Pacific, had to brush up quickly on his knowledge of astronomy in order to understand the native custom of navigating long distances from island to island by using stick maps to give angles on the stars. A laughing outsider once said that anthropology is only an excuse for not specializing; a humanist remarked that a good anthropologist was the last Renaissance man. All the study of anthropology requires is a nimble and flexible mind—and an infinite curiosity about everything.

The anthropologist's mind had best not be dogmatic, either. In the field, he is almost like a child, needing to learn everything "from scratch." One well-meaning anthropologist repeatedly made mistakes in the technique of handing a piece of jaggery-sugar candy to babies in India. The same anthropologist also accidentally "ruined" the native crops of a South American tribe by innocently cleaning an excavated skull in the open air (the members of the tribe exposed the bones of their ancestors on hills, unknown to him then, as a way to influence the rains). Another ethnographer wrote a scientific paper on how to ask for a drink of water from a member of a tribe he had studied, and still another described in useful detail how to interpret the mood of fierce Saharan Tuareg warriors by the way they drape their veils.

The theory and practice of how to dunk doughnuts in North Africa, in order to avoid grave insults, has also been described carefully and serves as still another example of how apparently trivial events can be critical in unfamiliar places. The anthropologist can never depend on his own unconscious cultural assumptions but must always maintain an alert and open mind. In their private convocations anthropologists are full of stories about funny situations or even dangerous misunderstandings they have stumbled into, but these never get into their staid scientific reports. What those reports often fail to make clear is that field work is not passive, like a tourist's vacation, but instead a complicated and demanding activity requiring the mastery of an immense store of knowledge and the investigative talents of a crack journalist or, very often, of an ace detective.

RELATING BIOLOGY TO CULTURE

Although the special fields in anthropology have grown staggeringly complex, the anthropologist must always remain ready to use seemingly disparate branches of the science in order to solve the intricate problems confronting him. For example, from the anthropological point of view, there are two quite distinct types of heredity: *genetic heredity*, by which physical traits are passed from one generation to the next; and *social heredity*, the process by which one generation teaches its cultural inheritance to the next. It might therefore seem reasonable to suppose that physical anthropology and cultural anthropology should be completely separate and distinct disciplines. But genes and culture traits may affect one another. It has been suggested, for example, that the invention of the spear, replacing the club, may set entirely different conditions for survival to which the genes that control physical structure must adapt. Spear users' physiques would be selected for the leverage of broad shoulders and long limbs, whereas club users would be better off with ruggedly compact physiques.

In turn, the "environmental" factors that select for an archer's physique in areas where the bow and arrow are used would be greatly changed with the invention of agriculture, which requires long-enduring labor rather than quick accuracy of control. Thus new cultural inventions change the effective

Figure 11. Anthropology brings into focus the interrelated cultural and biological traits of man—the hunting and tool making adaptations, for instance, that possibly led to changes in face, teeth, and skin and to a steady increase in brain size. The brain and its functions, intelligence and intellect, were themselves directly responsive to the selective pressures that rewarded increased learning capacity, but the process may have stabilized when culture could be used to transmit the wisdom of the generations. Man's goal at first was survival; his means were in part the magically protected fertility of his body and mind with which he populated the earth and projected his goals upon the universe.

environment to which genes must newly adapt. Is it possible that civilized man has less need for "adrenal rage" than did the Paleolithic mammoth hunter? Is the aggressiveness necessary in frontier life less adaptive in dense population conditions? If, in fact, new conditions were to select for less active adrenal glands, then man's facial bones might also change, for it is known that intentional selection for docility in domestic animals incidentally causes glandular changes that affect skull bones.

This holistic culture-cum-biology viewpoint in anthropology became popular in the 1950s, and in the 1960s it flourished so vigorously that a number of physical anthropologists have edited or written books to show the evolution of man's biological capacity for culture and to underline the mutual influence of his genes and culture traits. Culture, especially as represented by the massive use of tools and symbol systems, may well constitute the *basic adaptive technique* of man. But adaptation is an ongoing evolutionary process. Although culture proper is unique to *Homo sapiens*, it is nevertheless the biologically adaptive technique of this particular animal, built physically and functionally as he is. The use of fire and weapons has certainly affected man's dentition and jaws, eyebrow ridges, and skull in general. But even more subtly and drastically, cultural adaptation has altered the basic biology of man.

Consider, for example, the intensified and pervasive *nonseasonal sexuality* of man—quite unlike that of other animals and not needed for the reproduction of better-protected and longer-lived offspring, and now even threatening man's future through excessive population growth. Does this nonseasonal sexuality have anything to do with the rise of the uniquely and universally human *family*, larger kin aggregates, and the incest tabu, universal in human societies but nonexistent among other animals? Is the biologically unfinished and long-dependent infantile state of human children related to the fact that man is a largely instinctless learning animal with culture? In this labile animal, the cultural past is as ever-looming as his evolutionary past as an animal. Cultural man is embodied past time.

The anthropologist who keeps the past in perspective is grateful that the study of man remains holistic in the United States, an untidy ragbag of sciences that seem unrelated but all of which help to illuminate what man is and how he behaves. It is probably true that, because of the phenomenal explosion of modern knowledge about man, no one individual can ever again be a "complete anthropologist" in the manner of the late Alfred Kroeber, equally at home with cultural, linguistic, physical anthropological, and archaeological data and competent in handling them all. But even if such universality is no longer possible, the anthropologist cannot afford the tunnel vision imposed by an exclusive enthusiasm for his specialty alone. However much it grows in scope, physical anthropology will remain the specifically human biology of a culture-bearing animal, just as archaeology will remain the record of the only animal with a cultural past. And, sooner or later, formal linguistics must deal with cultural content and meaning, and with what language is about and for.

INTERDISCIPLINARY DETECTIVE WORK

Soma is familiar to readers of Aldous Huxley's *Brave New World* as the drug of the future that virtually all people will use to escape the realities of their existence. It is also a word whose origins are so ancient as to antedate Sanskrit. In fact, *soma* has been the center of a millennia-old mystery that has only recently been solved through the application of the holistic approach that can prove so valuable to problems involving man.

Soma has been described in ancient writings as a powerful hallucinogen brought to earth through divine powers related to thunder and lightning, to the sources of life and

Figure 12. A Mavaca Indian from the Upper Orinoco in Venezuela smokes the narcotic *joppo* in the manner customary to his tribe. Use of plant hallucinogens is a cultural phenomenon that can be traced back many thousands of years.

immortality, and to the prehistoric discovery of fire. The question of what this *soma* plant could be has now been answered through the combined efforts of specialists in several different areas, and the story of this scientific and intellectual achievement is an intricate and fascinating one.

The *Rig Veda*, the earliest work in Indo-European literature, is full of ecstatic hymns of praise directed to the mysterious vision-evoking plant called *soma;* and for the past two centuries botanists and Sanskritists have argued over the identity of the sacred narcotic plant. In fact, many centuries ago the voluminous *Brahmanas*, or early priestly commentaries, were already trying to establish from the Vedic hymns just what this *soma* could possibly be that was so extravagantly praised. The priestly commentators had evidently lost direct knowledge of *soma*, which grew neither in the dry plains west of Delhi nor in the wet Ganges Valley to the east. *Soma* had last been known to the north in the holy Himalayas, through whose high passes the Aryan invaders had entered India well before 1500 B.C.

How would it be possible to identify a narcotic plant, known only prehistorically, and from some unidentified and unknown land? The quest for *soma* is an absorbing story. Before the search was over, archaeology, linguistics, ethnology and folklore, physiology, ethnobotany, prehistory, plant ecology, and philology had all been called upon to contribute pieces to the puzzle. The hunt logically began with the *Avesta*, sacred book of the Iranians, where the drink *haoma* (a word dialectically related to *soma*) was mentioned. But the substitute plant from which *haoma* was made in Iran did not match the Indian Vedic descriptions of *soma*. Nevertheless, the fact of an Indo-Iranian word relationship hinted at still older Indo-European origins and further suggested comparisons with the sweet nectar and odorous ambrosia of the (also Indo-European) Greeks: Brahman priests drank *soma* to become living

gods, and Greek gods took nectar and ambrosia to remain immortal. What were these rare and desirable substances? Nectar was probably the honey-based alcoholic drink *mead* (linguistically pan-Indo-European), but what was ambrosia? *"Ambrosia"* could be another name for *soma*, but ambrosia is linguistically related to another Vedic term, *amrita*. Could *soma* be an alcoholic drink? But why would priests drink *soma* when they already drank mead to achieve the divine intoxication? And why could not alcohol be made from any of a large number of new plants in India, not only the indispensable *soma*? Besides, alcohol has no place in Indic religious tradition; quite the contrary. If Indo-European in use, was *soma-ambrosia* perhaps the substance Norse shamans and warriors took for religious inspiration and to prepare for battle? Hardly, because physiologically *soma* produced quietly blissful ecstasy, not "berserker rage."

Still, what clues there were pointed irresistibly to lands north of the Himalayas. At this point, early modern ethnology became useful, for travelers in Siberia since the eighteenth century had found certain "Paleo-Asiatic" tribes still using a narcotic substance in their shamanistic seances. By studying the unrecorded Uralic dialects comparatively and discovering regularities among them, it soon became clear that the narcotic substance was known by a very old Uralic name pronounced *pangx*, a word widely diffused among several distinct language families of ancient Eurasia (Ugric *pong*, Ostyak *pangx*, Ob *pongx*, and Chukchi *pong*). This interfamily linguistic borrowing took place so long ago that the word has undergone all the proper dialectic sound shifts in daughter languages in each of the separate language families. But this same old Asiatic word was also primordial Indo-European, and the most eminent linguists now accept the identity of Ugric *pong* with a group of Indo-European words represented by Greek *sphóngos*, *spóngē*, Latin *fungus*,

Figure 13. Prometheus being punished by the eagle of Zeus. This legend is but one cultural manifestation of the widespread complex of beliefs about fire that provided an important clue in the search for the identity of *soma,* the source of divine inspiration to Siberian tribes.

and Germanic *spunk* and *punk* (perhaps also German *Funke*). The early Germanic form would suggest that, at one time, *fungus-punk* was used to catch the spark, *Funke,* in fire making with flints.

Comparative folklore now opened new vistas in this detective story. In Europe and elsewhere, Paleolithic flint hand axes have been widely regarded as "thunderstones," the lightning bolts flung by a sky god and still containing the secret spark man needed to make fire. A very old shrine to Zeus Feretrius in Rome, for example, had as the cult object a flint (*silex*). Prometheus, who "stole" fire from heaven, must therefore have been the first man who struck fire from flint, and for this theft his liver was eaten by the ancient sky god's bird, the eagle of Zeus. Another widespread notion in folklore is that toadstools are produced by lightning bolts during thunderstorms and appear after the rain. Toadstools contain violent poisons that kill men or produce strange divine spiritual derangements or madness. The English word "toadstool" is itself interesting, for toad skins contain a powerful hallucinogen (bufotenin), which is probably why toad skins were used in medieval witches' brews; and the French word for toadstool, *crapaudin,* comes from *crapaud,* a toad.

Through these miscellaneous clues, the trail became hotter. Evidently some ancient god-produced *fungus* was the source of both fire and a divine madness. The Vedic *soma* was repeatedly called *fire* in poetic metaphors and was associated with *red* and Surya, the Sun, the trickster Agni (Latin *ignis*), and the sky god Indra, who brings rain. Rain-lightning produces fire-flints; toadstools and toads also appear mysteriously after rain. *Punk-fungus,* like flint, holds hidden fire. And *spunk* is the essential soul-stuff or spark of life from the male, the divine fire or logos of Heraclitus.

Just what was the *fungus* that Siberian tribes were still eating in historic times to produce divine inspiration or contact with

the supernatural? The use must have had very ancient roots, because the aboriginal religion of Taoism in distant China mentions a mysterious *ling-chih* or "mushroom of immortality" that even the great emperor Shih Huang-ti searched for in vain. The Chinese also, in a twelfth-century text, referred to Manicheans who *eat red mushrooms.* Manicheism is an ancient Eurasiatic religion, the influence of which was felt historically over a dozen centuries from southern France to China. The divine principle of Manicheism was fire, the "shining one" and sky god of old northern Eurasia. And in the fourth century, Saint Augustine had bitterly censured the heretic Manicheans of the Old Religion for

Figure 14 (right). The deer-horned sorcerer from the Trois Frères cave in France. **Figure 15.** *Amanita muscaria,* the hallucinogen said to have been brought to earth by divine powers related to sources of life and immortality, and to the prehistoric discovery of fire.

their ritual fungus eating. Henceforth, the reasoning in the quest becomes densely logical.

Why not ignore all the false clues in the long theological discussions of the *Brahmanas,* whose writers plainly did not know what *soma* was? Why not treat as straightforward ethnobotany, and not mere poetic metaphors, the many references in the Vedic hymns as if they were literal descriptions of the *soma* plant? When the comparative description is carefully and exhaustively followed, *soma* turns out to be the fire-colored fungus *Amanita muscaria* of the botanists, the same fly-agaric still referred to by the Chinese name "toad-mushroom." And fly-agaric toadstools, of course, were the narcotic mushrooms still being eaten by eighteenth-century Siberian tribes. The closure is complete.

The reason that *soma* could not be found in the hot subtropic plains of India is now evident. In ecological terms, *Amanita muscaria* grows only in birch and pine forests in northern Europe and Asia and in the Himalayan heights (also in the birch and pine forests of North America and in the mountains of Mexico). Plainly, *soma* was a northern narcotic mushroom eaten long ago by Indo-European and Uralic shamans, the same fly-agaric still eaten by the Christian-persecuted Manicheans and by historic Paleo-Siberians. *Soma* could not be cultivated, but always appeared mysteriously god-engendered after rain, a divine gift of the sky gods. Toadstools, like flints, were thunderbolts containing divine fire, mind-stuff, life.

But what of the other *punk-fungus* used in making fire with flints? Evidence from archaeologically uncovered pollens shows that the Mesolithic deer hunters of Star Carr in Yorkshire lived in a cool birch-pine climatic phase; they also associated fertility and hunting magic with the ritual wearing of horned-deer frontlets (as indicated by the Dancing Sorcerer of the Trois Frères cave, the Celto-Roman deer-horned god Cernunnus, and the deer-horned god shown on the late Celtic silver Gundestrup Cauldron found in a Jutland bog actually not far from Mesolithic Maglemose). And the Star Carr bog dwellers apparently used the bracket fungus as tinder in fire making. At least, large quantities of *Fomes fomentarius* or European tinder-punk were found at the Mesolithic flint makers' camp at Star Carr—with some specimens still attached to fragments of birchwood.

The dramatic rediscovery of the prehistoric mushroom-narcotic and the Paleolithic *punk-fungus* is a good object lesson in how interrelated knowledge now marks anthropological research. Anthropology, in the past few decades, has taken on new practical functions also. Before World War II it was pursued, on the whole, in museums and taught only in the relatively few departments of anthropology in the oldest universities. But during the war, anthropologists were called upon to answer a wide variety of practical questions. They were asked to provide the standard range in uniform sizes; to give advice on how to parachute Allied airmen down to remote Montagnard tribes, to persuade these tribes to take only enemy heads and not those of Allied aviators flying over the Himalayas to China; and to suggest the use of lightweight foods (such as frost-dried potatoes) found in primitive cultures. After the war, anthropology also became far more popular as an academic discipline and today its popularity is so great that the demand for anthropologists to teach in universities has far outpaced the supply. In a post-colonial world grown ever smaller, the opportunities for the anthropologist seem almost endless.

Anthropology is a liberating science that frees one from the prison of the tribal and the intellectual tyranny of the contemporary. But one can never "learn anthropology," much less become an anthropologist by approaching it passively as an irreducible minimum of fixed truths. In the creative and scientifically imaginative practice of anthro-

pology one can never know enough. Anthropology is already a vast and still-expanding pursuit, the study of the most interesting animal on earth. Admittedly, it can only be said that "anthropology is what anthropologists do." But the catch is this: the authentic anthropologist cannot afford a self-limiting, prejudged notion of relevance. He must have an open, pure-scientific, questing love of everything human and a willingness to discipline himself to the exact and difficult—from pollen counts and tree rings and carbon 14 measurements to blood groups and trochanters, and genes and gorillas to phonemes and tagmemes and philology, to tipi distribution, myth motifs, and the spread of corn growing —indeed anything that might aid him in this pursuit—and to have an enduring scientific passion for the whole rich past of mankind.

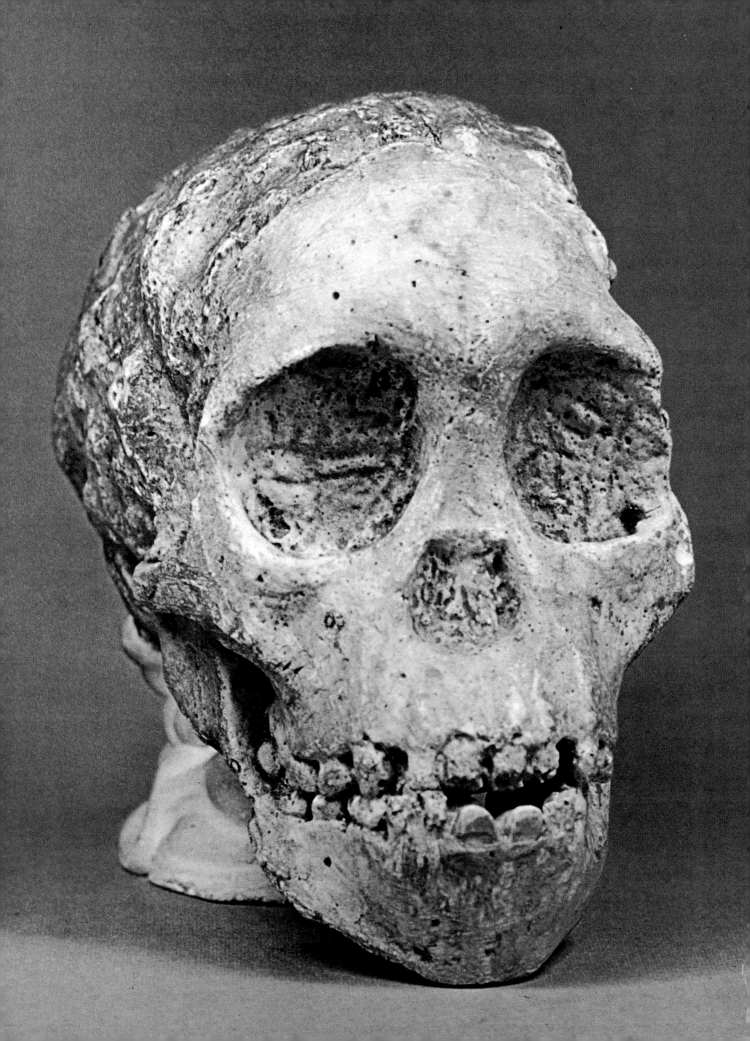

Studies of Man the Animal

2 Physical anthropology has had a relatively short history as a scientific discipline. It is possible to trace the history of thought and speculation about the physical origins and variations of the human species back to classical antiquity, when Aristotle and a few other Greek and Roman philosophers sketched out the notion that man is an animal and must be studied as such. For the most part, however, these thoughts and speculations about humans centered almost exclusively on the idea of special creation—that man appeared on this planet as the result of a special divine act and that his history could not be equated with that of the rest of the animal kingdom. Even the social philosophers of the Enlightenment generally held this view and, as a result, little progress was made in the development of what may be termed a truly scientific physical anthropology until almost the beginning of the modern era.

In the late eighteenth and early nineteenth centuries, the Linnean classification system and an increasing awareness on the part of geologists and prehistorians of the fact that the Biblical limitations on natural history were scientifically untenable stimulated criticism of the idea of special creation. The suggestion—at first it was only a suggestion —that our species might have a natural history came to have some currency. Georges Buffon, Johann Blumenbach, Jean Baptiste de Lamarck, even Johann Goethe contributed to this development, which culminated in the brilliant achievement of Charles Darwin in 1859. But of all those concerned with the antiquity of man in the decades prior to the publication of *On the Origin of Species*, perhaps the most important were Charles Lyell and the French customs-official-turned-prehistorian Jacques Boucher de Perthes. Lyell was the principal architect of the concept of *uniformitarianism*, which cleared the way for the development of geology and provided the means for surmounting the Biblical barrier. The basis of Lyell's concept was the idea that, unless there is evidence to the contrary, events that occurred in the past will have happened in the same way similar events happen now. He studied sequences of fossilized plants and animals extending back over tens of thousands of years, which showed him there was a record of changes in their forms as one geologic era succeeded another. This record was invaluable in estab-

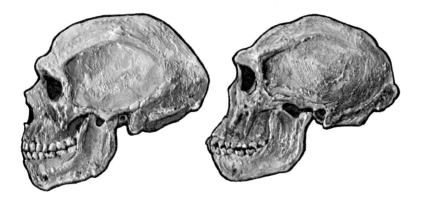

lishing comparisons among the remains in distinct strata, and the idea of progressive changes in fossilized representatives of known families, genera, and species ultimately came to be applied to the human fossil record.

It was Boucher de Perthes who, in the period between 1837 and 1846, first demonstrated that man must have inhabited Europe far longer than had previously been suspected. Although his evidence was cultural rather than biological—it consisted of crude stone tools of the sort classed as Lower Paleolithic by contemporary archaeologists—the French prehistorian's discovery established without doubt the extreme antiquity of the species. But only a few of his contemporaries accepted the evidence, despite the related work of such museum scholars as Christian Thomsen, because a fundamental problem remained. If man had been in Europe (and, by extension, on earth) for longer than had been suspected, and if it were to be assumed that man had undergone a slow but steady change in physical appearance like the plants and animals whose ancestors Lyell had found preserved in fossil sequences, where was the evidence? Where were the bones of those who had made the hand axes that Boucher de Perthes had so carefully examined at Abbeville?

THE EVOLUTIONARY RECORD

The first answer to the question of man's antiquity was supplied accidentally in 1856 by some quarriers who, while working in a cave in the valley of the Neander River near Düsseldorf, Germany, uncovered some curiously archaic albeit obviously human bones. The remains eventually reached the laboratory of Hermann Schaafhausen, professor of anatomy at the University of Bonn, who concluded that they represented an ancient form of our species.

The remains in question came to be known as Neanderthal man, but their antiquity was by no means universally and immediately accepted by the scientific community.

Thomas Huxley, Darwin's staunchest supporter, refused for many years to accept the authenticity of the find; even the eminent pathologist Rudolf Virchow suggested that the bones were those of a contemporary man disfigured by some horrible disease. It was even suggested that the Neanderthal fossil was that of a Mongolian soldier who had been captured during Napoleon's abortive invasion of Russia in 1812 and had died on the way back to a French prison camp. Many scholars were reluctant to accept the remains as evidence of a premodern human type, because in the years immediately following their discovery other Ice Age fossil men came to light, including those of the Cro-Magnon rock shelter in southwestern France, and none of them exhibited the characteristics of the Neanderthal specimens. All appeared quite modern, despite the fact that they were frequently found in association with Paleolithic (Old Stone Age) tools. The Neanderthal remains had not been found in association with a tool making tradition (or industry), and there was thus no real basis for assuming that they were necessarily older than the modern-appearing types found at Cro-Magnon and elsewhere.

In 1886, however, another Neanderthal-like skeleton was unearthed in the Belgian district of Spy, and these remains were found in association with a tool industry. This Mousterian tradition, as it was labeled, was demonstrably older than the Paleolithic industries associated with the Cro-Magnon types, and a strong case could be made for the greater antiquity of the Neanderthalers. Thus, Schaafhausen's initial suggestion was at last proved correct: Neanderthaler represented an earlier and perhaps immediately ancestral form of *Homo sapiens*, or modern man, and was thus a true hominid.

In the early 1890s, Eugene Dubois discovered teeth, a femur, and a skullcap belonging to a creature that appeared far older than the Neanderthalers. The remains were found in Java in a stratum that dated from the Second Interglacial period—400,000 to 600,000

Figure 4. From left to right, Pierre Teilhard de Chardin, Henri Breuil, and Max de Bégouin. Chardin was associated with the discovery of the Piltdown canine in 1913 but was not connected with the hoax. For years Piltdown was argued as proof that modern man did not descend from small-brained ancestors. Figure 5. No one was uneasy about the Cro-Magnon finds in Les Eyzies: Cro-Magnon looked comfortably like modern man. Figure 6. G. H. R. von Koenigswald in Java, where in 1941 he found a form of very early pithecanthropine that is somewhat reminiscent of australopithecines. Figure 7. The search for fossil man continues. Here, Louis Leakey and Phillip Tobias examine a *Homo erectus* skull from Olduvai Gorge.

years ago. Dubois named his discovery *Pithecanthropus erectus* (or erect ape-man), a taxonomic label borrowed from the evolutionist Ernst Haeckel, who had predicted that such a creature would be found. Once again the controversy erupted, although this time there was no argument about whether the remains were modern. Instead, many scholars believed that his Java man, as the specimen was popularly labeled, was really an anthropoid ape and not a hominid. Neanderthaler, despite his prognathism, pronounced brow ridges, thick cranial walls, and teeth with enlarged pulp cavities, did indeed have a cranial capacity of about 1,450 cubic centimeters, which is equal to that of modern man. The cranial capacity of the Java specimen was approximately 1,000 cubic centimeters, and in all other respects he appeared much more primitive, or apelike, than the Neanderthalers. Nevertheless, after several fossils of the same type were uncovered in central Java, it became apparent that Dubois' *Pithecanthropus erectus* was indeed a human, albeit a most primitive sort of human. Dubois' discoveries pushed back the antiquity of man half a million years, and a true fossil sequence had begun to appear.

In the first decade of the present century, that sequence was to be augmented considerably. In 1907, at the German village of Mauer near Heidelberg, one of the most significant of all fossil men was discovered by Otto Schoetensack. The remains were scanty—amounting to a mandible and its associated teeth—but the stratum in which they were found was equivalent to that of the site where Dubois' Java man had been discovered, proving that humans must also have lived in Europe half a million years ago. But the true significance of the find lies in the teeth. Although the mandible is massive, the dentition is surprisingly modern. The dental arch is short and evenly rounded. There are no missing teeth as might be expected in a specimen of this antiquity, and the whole assemblage indicates that this fossil man chewed his food in the same way his modern de-

Figure 5. Comparison of Java and Heidelberg
dentition. Figure 6. In 1925, Raymond Dart
stirred up controversy with his report of a
manlike ape in Africa. Eventually his
Australopithecus was accepted as a truly
ancient hominid; in fact, the most recent
australopithecine finds may date from about 5
million years ago. Figure 7 (right). Known
locations of *Homo erectus* (sites marked in
blue) and Neanderthalers (sites marked in red).
Figure 8. The controversial Steinheim and
Swanscombe fossils, whose roles in hominid
evolution continued to be debated.

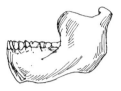

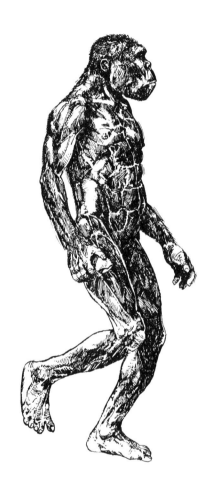

scendants do. On the basis of the teeth alone,
Shoetensack suggested that the hominid was
advanced enough to qualify for the generic
taxon *Homo* and proceeded to label him
Homo heidelbergensis.

Since then, however, the label *Homo* has
also been deemed appropriate for *all* hominids belonging to the pithecanthropine stage
of human evolution. It seems certain that all
the creatures who inhabited the Heidelberg
region some 400,000 years ago, together with
their counterparts in Java, China, and Africa,
belong to this overall stage, and today all are
considered to be regional variations or subspecies of a single genus and species: *Homo
erectus*.

The next really important discovery of humanlike remains pushed the history of
human evolution back even further. Between
1921 and the 1950s, several discoveries of
fossil remains of a very early hominid—designated *Australopithecus africanus*—were
made at scattered sites in South Africa and
Central Africa. They belong to several varieties of the same species that tentative new
evidence from Lothagan indicates may have
lived from about 5 million to 600,000 years
ago. The australopithecines, as these hominids are popularly called, were exceedingly
primitive in that their cranial capacity varied between 400 and 600 cubic centimeters.
But the general configuration of the cranium
proves that they walked erect, and the dentition is basically human rather than apelike.

Where the australopithecines belong in the
human evolutionary sequence has been and
still is a thorny question. Some scholars have
argued that they were an abortive offshoot of
the evolutionary sequence, and others have
stated that they represent a general phase in
hominid evolution; still others suggest that
certain varieties, such as *Australopithecus
africanus*, stood on the main line of human
evolution but that other varieties did not.

Meanwhile, other major discoveries were
being made in northern China that significantly extended the range of the pithecanthropines. The first examples of *Sinanthro-*

pus pekinensis, as these Far Eastern
specimens of *Homo erectus* came to be
termed, were uncovered by Davidson Black
in 1927 at Choukoutien, some forty-two
miles west of Peking. Eventually, the remains of approximately forty individuals
were discovered. Although they lived somewhat later in time—about 350,000 to 400,000
years ago—and were slightly more modern
in appearance than their Javanese and European counterparts, the resemblances are
close enough to verify that they belonged to
the same genus and quite probably the same
species as the rest of the pithecanthropines.
These fossils seem to have been the Far
Eastern representatives of *Homo erectus*,

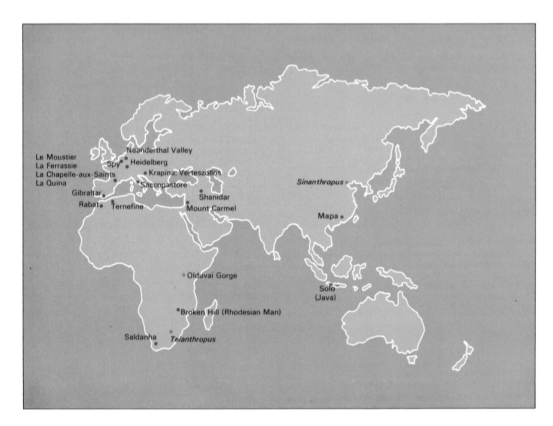

and the anatomical differences that separate them from the rest of the pithecanthropines would appear to be the result of an adaptation to environmental conditions in the Far East.

In the early 1930s, two fossils were found that partially bridged the timespan, in Europe at least, between the pithecanthropines and the Neanderthalers. These two specimens, designated Steinheim and Swanscombe, seem to represent an intermediate stage between Heidelberg man and the oldest Neanderthalers. From Palestinian sites excavated in 1931 and 1932, some important evolutionary evidence came to light in the form of two finds of the Neanderthal type. One was a complete skeleton of a woman identical in almost every respect to the European Neanderthalers, and the other included a group of ten individuals who exhibited a combination of the features of Neanderthalers and modern men. Since these discoveries, most physical anthropologists have divided the Neanderthalers (or at least the European and Near East Neanderthalers) into two broad categories: the Mousterian types, primarily found in Europe and represented in the Near East by the Palestinian woman; and the progressively more modern types. The distribution of Neanderthalers was further extended when a skullcap belonging to what must have been a Neanderthal-like individual was found at Mapa near

Canton in southern China. As a result of additional finds, it now seems likely that the range of the Neanderthalers stretched from Europe to the southern tip of Africa and from Indonesia to southern China.

By the end of the 1950s, enough information about the stages of human evolution was available for several scholars to suggest that the practice of assigning separate generic labels to each new find merely confused otherwise clear biological relationships, and that some overall categories, such as *Homo erectus*, should be developed. While this new taxonomic approach was being developed, however, some spectacular discoveries were being made by Louis and Mary Leakey in Tanzania and in Kenya.

Since the early 1930s, discovery of an extremely ancient tool industry in the lowest strata at Olduvai Gorge had held the promise that this cleft in the now arid plains of northeast Tanzania might hold the remains of some truly ancient specimens of humanity. It was not until 1959, however, that the first such specimen was recovered. Almost by accident, Mary Leakey discovered a fragmented skull in what appeared to be clear association with a *working floor*, a place where pebble tools had been made. The then newly discovered potassium-argon dating technique indicated the find to be approximately 1,750,000 years old. With the discovery in 1960 of an Olduvai pithecanthropine,

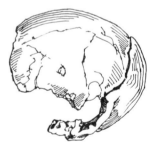

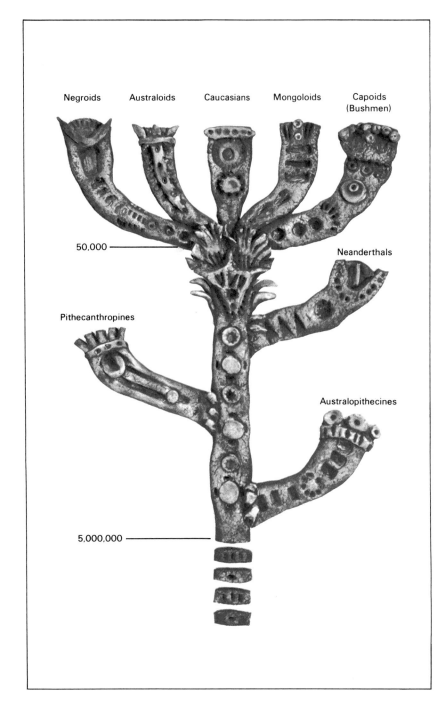

Negroids Australoids Caucasians Mongoloids Capoids (Bushmen)

50,000

Neanderthals

Pithecanthropines

Australopithecines

5,000,000

the Leakeys seemed to have found direct evidence of an evolutionary sequence connecting *Australopithecus* to the pithecanthropines.

The Leakeys intensified their search for early man, both at Olduvai Gorge and in neighboring regions of Tanzania and in Kenya. They soon began to discover some even more ancient specimens, and most recently at East Rudolf in Kenya Richard Leakey found signs of tool use that may date from about 2,500,000 years ago.

PHYLOGENETIC TREE OR TRELLIS?

The Leakeys' finds raised questions about the course of human evolution. Until the late 1950s, it was generally held that man as a distinct biological entity was about 1 million years old. The most acceptable explanation of his evolution was one based on the phylogenetic tree model, which has been depicted as a main trunk with a great many side branches, culminating about 50,000 years ago in the emergence of the modern races of *Homo sapiens* (Figure 9). Some recent discoveries have brought about reappraisal of the tree model. For one thing, the newly revealed antiquity of the hominids—an existence of perhaps 5 million years—allows for a far greater period of early development than was previously suspected. Second, and perhaps more importantly, it would appear that mankind initially evolved in a rather restricted geographic region—the high plains of east Central Africa—and that his presence in other areas of the world ultimately resulted from a migration out of Africa.

The tree model suggests that the bulk of the fossil evidence from later periods—the late australopithecines, the pithecanthropines, the Neanderthalers—cannot be assigned to the assumed main trunk but rather must be assigned to abortive side branches. This configuration, if correct, would mean that since the discovery of the original Neanderthal fossil in 1856, anthropologists have for the most part been discovering our collateral kinsmen rather than our direct ances-

Figure 9 (left) and Figure 10 (below) depict some of the issues concerning the course of human evolution. Figure 9 shows the earlier hominid forms as collateral, dead-end branches rather than direct ancestors of man. A more current view would assign these forms to the main stem. The races of modern man are shown as a relatively recent branching of the tree, taking place within the past 50,000 years. Figure 10 shows a different interpretation. A trellis with parallel lines of development in different geographic regions is interwoven by lines of genetic communication between population areas, which maintained the genetic unity of the human species. Following some theories, the initial branching is carried back to the migration of man's pithecanthropine ancestors out of Africa into differing adaptive zones.

tors. But to an increasing number of physical anthropologists, including Frederick Hulse and C. Loring Brace, this model is unacceptable and must be replaced by a trellis model, one that encompasses several main lines of development reflecting the several basic environmental zones—Central Africa, South Africa, western Eurasia, southern Asia, and the Far East—to which man has become adapted since his initial appearance in Africa. This model does not have an extended main trunk. The fossil men found in Europe, Indonesia, Africa, and elsewhere must all be thought of as our immediate ancestors. This does not mean, however, that the fossil types found in an area are the specific progenitors of the modern populations of that area. The continuity and the point of branching of the modern races from older forms are still problematic, as the two models indicate. Throughout this long period of parallel development, humanity managed to remain a single species, for there must have been lines of genetic communication between the several regions.

Differences in physical characteristics among men today must be the result of natural selection for traits that were most adaptive to a given environment. Skin pigmentation, for example, may have increased in tropical regions to counteract the intense ultraviolet rays from the sun, just as it may have decreased in cold climates where there is less sunlight and where the clothing needed for warmth would further prevent exposure.

TRENDS IN PHYSICAL ANTHROPOLOGY

In addition to the study of the manner in which modern man developed from ancient forms of animal life, physical anthropologists are concerned with the study of living human populations. Research is being conducted into the variation in physical traits and into man's biological adaptations to differing environments.

Human variation has long been the concern of physical anthropologists, but in the

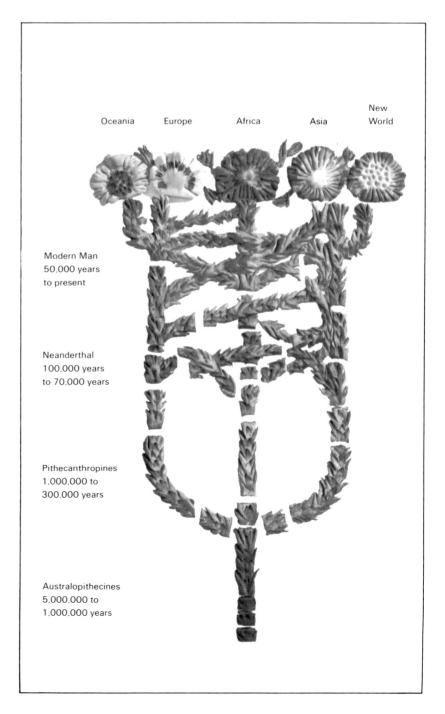

Oceania   Europe   Africa   Asia   New World

Modern Man
50,000 years
to present

Neanderthal
100,000 years
to 70,000 years

Pithecanthropines
1,000,000 to
300,000 years

Australopithecines
5,000,000 to
1,000,000 years

Figure 11. One of the greatest contributions of anthropology has been to refute the pretensions of racists that their theories have scientific validity. Contrary to theories of genetic determination, anthropology shows that culture reaches deep into the very structure of human behavior and intellect. To a far greater extent than is true of any other animal, man's nongenetic variation may be extreme in comparison to the genetic. Many anthropologists such as C. Loring Brace and Frank Livingstone are urging that we abandon the term "race" altogether and simply define human populations in terms of their positions on the continuous spectrum of human variation.

past their studies centered on the classification of various human "types" into discrete categories—stature, measurements of the head, skin, hair, and similar visible characteristics. Now, however, much research has been extended to include the internal mechanisms of the human body, as are involved in embryology and serology, and one branch of physical anthropology has become a highly specialized field related to genetics and medical science. Studies of blood types, for example, are yielding significant data on the patterns of genetic inheritance. Other subjects of interest include the measurement of body composition and the observation of growth rates in populations, which encompass studies of nutrition and physiological adaptability.

Another aspect of physical anthropology is the study of nonhuman primate behavior, or primate ethology. Recently, George Schaller's work among the mountain gorilla and Jane van Lawick-Goodall's field studies of chimpanzees have added to our understanding of man's closest living relatives, whose adaptations and social behavior in general may be used as points of departure for speculations about our own evolutionary beginnings.

Earlier in the history of the discipline, the two fields of physical and cultural anthropology were not as distinct as they are today. In the last several decades, due in large measure to the spectacular growth of knowledge in both physical and cultural anthropology, the two branches have become increasingly specialized; rarely does one find a contemporary scholar who does significant work in both fields. Yet even today the fields necessarily overlap. One example of this interdisciplinary nature is seen in the anthropological view that man's biological evolution cannot be understood apart from the evolution of his culture; indeed, the increase in cranial capacity, the development of upright posture, and the eventual reduction in the size of the teeth are all undoubtedly related to an increase in cultural complexity. Still another example of the interdisciplinary application of physical and cultural anthropology can be provided by tracing the development of the enigmatic question of race.

PERSPECTIVE ON THE THEORY OF RACE

Two rather appealing ideas lie behind the view that race plays an important role in bringing about cultural and psychological differences between groups. First, if people have obvious physical differences, how can they fail to have "mental" differences? After all, dogs that look differently from other dogs—say, Dobermans as opposed to dachshunds—do usually act differently as well. Second, in an overall sort of way, observation shows that people who look alike do act alike or at least have the same basic customs. Europeans are light-skinned and have complex industries, high religions, and well-developed governments, whereas dark-skinned people do not have these things until they get them from the Europeans. At least that is how these ideas go.

The difficulty with them comes when we begin to examine them closely. What, after all, are "obvious" physical differences? It is fairly easy to get Dobermans or dachshunds, which have been carefully bred, to look very much like one another. But it does not work that way with people. Human groups are just not that homogeneous. In fact, modern anthropologists have almost entirely abandoned the concept of "race" as a theoretical tool and use instead the ideas behind the term "breeding population." This shifts the focus of attention away from the notion that there are categories of people recognizable by external physical signs to a focus instead on the changing group that contributes the hereditary material over the generations from which all members of the group draw. In other words, striking physical features such as skin color are not the most useful basis for classifying people into different groups even with respect to heredity, inasmuch as it is known that people with the same skin color can come from groups with very different supplies of genes and that people with different-colored skins can have fairly similar genes. Unlike dogs and livestock, human populations are not kept separate, and finding even relatively homogeneous groups is a much more difficult task than it seems even when only a few bodily characteristics are considered.

Leaving the problems of how to classify people into groups that are uniform from the standpoint of heredity, we are still left with the difficulties involved in determining what parts of behavior can be explained by physical inheritance. It is not known how much of an *individual's* character and ability can be attributed to his genes. And the problem is much greater when we try to understand differences in the cultures of whole *groups* of individuals when physical variation within one group may be greater than the physical differences between the groups we are comparing. A long time ago, Franz Boas showed that physically different groups have very similar cultures and that physically similar groups have quite different cultures. Whatever the contribution of heredity to behavior, the contribution of learning—that is, of culture—is enormous, and in reviewing the entire human record, all anthropologists agree that we can account for the differences on cultural grounds whereas appeals to racial explanations are without scientific value. Usually, racial explanations of group differences are mixed together with ethnocentric judgments that take it for granted that the society from which an individual comes is more "advanced," "civilized," or—more generally—"wonderful," but the belief, say, that one's own religion is "true" and the religion of another group is "superstition" does not strengthen the explanatory power of the concept "race" however appealing it may be on emotional grounds. Even if the completely unfounded assertion that Europe (or anywhere else) is the sole source of "civilization" were not dismissed as the ethnocentric conceit it is, we still could not explain the differences between Europeans and others on the basis of differences in heredity.

Developing Sociocultural Views

3 According to Thomas Hobbes, writing in the mid-seventeenth century, man's life in a state of nature was "solitary, poore, nasty, brutish, and short." With every man and woman totally selfish and concerned exclusively with furthering their own interests, any kind of organized social life was impossible. Only under the firm hand of an authoritarian government could people hope to enjoy even a tolerable existence, free from the constant danger of burglary, rape, and murder.

About a hundred years later, Jean Jacques Rousseau, protesting against the miseries imposed by the grip of the French monarchy, was proclaiming the virtues of the state of nature. "Man is born free, but everywhere he is in chains," ran the famous opening of his *Social Contract*, published in 1762, in which he compared the sufferings of civilized man to the joys of the noble Indian savage, who appeared to be simple, honest, and uncorrupted by civilization and its attendant evils.

Are people naturally evil? Are they naturally good? Are they naturally neither but instead merely raw material to be molded by society and culture? What kind of life ways do other people follow, and what makes them live the way they do? It is possible that men have asked questions such as these ever since cultural patterns began to emerge in prehistoric times. The nature of the early inquiries can only be guessed at, however, for the first evidence of attempts to explain variations in the human condition comes from the historic Greco-Roman world.

ETHNOCENTRISM AND THE NOBLE SAVAGE

The oldest known description of a human culture—that of the Scythians—was written in 450 b.c. by the Greek philosopher Herodotus. He organized his data under the basic categories used for most modern ethnographies, including kinship, marriage, economics, technology, and religion. Yet ethnocentrism—a preoccupation with one's own culture, which usually leads to a judging of all groups but one's own as inferior—colored this otherwise systematic description. To the Greeks, the world was inhabited by two sorts of people, Greeks and barbarians, and the barbarians were not important enough to be taken seriously. Thus, the generalizations that might have emerged from an objective comparison of Greek and Scythian cultures never materialized.

Some 600 years later, the Roman historian Tacitus wrote the *Germania*, a description of

Figure 2 (left). Representative of the "noble savage" concept prevalent during the late eighteenth century is this romanticization of prehistoric man. Figure 3 (lower left). Herodotus, called the Father of History, and Tacitus, the Roman historian. Although their accounts of other cultures contain fascinating details, their culture-bound attitudes tended to distort their presentations.

the way of life of the Germanic tribesmen. Although this account is relatively free of the ethnocentrism characteristic of most of the Greek ethnographies, it does suffer from what might be termed the other extreme. Looking back over the events of the previous century, Tacitus was distressed by what seemed to be a progressive moral and spiritual decay in Roman society, and he saw in the relatively simple Germanic culture a model that could be drawn upon for the rejuvenation of his own society. To the Roman, the Germanic tribesman was a "noble savage," an idea implying that all things lacking the polish and complexity of highly developed societies are somehow the essence of nobility.

Ethnocentrism and its equally distorting opposite did not go away with the passing of the early Greeks and Romans any more than it began with them. In every society, people begin to learn their own culture from the time they are born, and part of this culture is a set of standards for judgment. Among these are standards that guide the individual in deciding what is important and what is not, what is good and what is bad, what is moral and what is wicked. It is probably necessary for the continuation of a society that a certain proportion of its members judge its main activities as important and good. If they did not, they would either cease to participate in these activities or be so full of psychological conflict about them that their participation would not be very useful in continuing the society as it is.

In other words, in most societies at most of the time, people will be positively inclined toward what they do and how they do it, and this inclination will lead them to take a negative view of people who do not do what they themselves do or who do it in some other way. Although such ethnocentrism is a socially useful psychological consequence of learning the culture of the group to which one is born, it can lead to failures to understand other people. It can even bring about

sharp conflicts between different groups when one or both decides it must "civilize" —or make like themselves—the other.

In this respect, the history of anthropology has been the history of a struggle to achieve greater objectivity by obtaining greater understanding of other societies and cultures. With the rediscovery of classical antiquity in the fourteenth and fifteenth centuries, the Renaissance, and the voyages and conquests of the Portuguese and the Spaniards, the amount of information available to Europeans about the non-European world by the end of the seventeenth century had grown considerably. But it was the twin revolutions of the eighteenth century—the political revolt in France and in America and the economic transformation brought about by the industrial revolution—that provided the impetus for the growth of anthropological thought. Suddenly it became obvious that a new socioeconomic order was at hand, one very different from anything that had ever gone before. In almost every sphere of activity, it became evident that the human condition could not be understood in static terms. Change, in particular, came to be recognized as a prime ingredient of that condition, and recognition of its importance led to the development of the first major theoretical system in anthropology: classical evolutionism.

CLASSICAL EVOLUTIONISM

The belief that evolutionary theory began with Charles Darwin is widespread but incorrect. Jean Baptiste de Lamarck developed an evolutionary scheme of biological development as early as 1809, although it was based on the subsequently disproved notion that acquired characteristics can be inherited. In 1748, Charles Louis de Secondat Montesquieu proposed that all societies must progress through three stages of development: savagery, barbarism, and civilization. In 1836, Christian Thomsen theorized that mankind must have progressed through a sequence of what he termed Stone, Bronze, and Iron

Figure 4. Three factors influencing the emergence of anthropological thought were the spread of the concept of biological evolution (above, the voyage of Darwin); the industrial revolution, which made it obvious that cultures were not static but were subject to forces of change; and political revolution (below, in France), with its challenge to the traditional order of European society.

ages, as indicated by the sequential levels of ancient artifacts being turned up in the pastures and quarries of Scandinavia. He used his three-age system to catalogue the Copenhagen museum's collection of northern artifacts. When the system was translated into English in 1848, the idea of prehistory became a cornerstone of classical evolutionism.

But it was only after Darwin's *On the Origin of Species* was published in 1859 that evolutionism moved into high gear. By that time, two newly emphasized concepts in European ideology—imperialism and progress—had become popular. The flags of the major European powers had been planted in almost every part of the non-Western world by the middle of the nineteenth century. At home, technological progress continued unabated. And both of these developments exerted a profound influence on the men who were shaping the discipline of anthropology.

Johann Jakob Bachofen

Johann Jakob Bachofen was a nineteenth-century Swiss jurist who was interested in Greco-Roman antiquity. In the course of his research, which was based on reports on a number of societies in Africa and the New World as well as on the early Greco-Roman accounts, he became convinced that matrilineal descent, in which property and membership in large groups is traced to a female ancestor and handed down from mother to daughter, had preceded all other systems of descent because the first humans were promiscuous and therefore could be sure only of who their mothers were. Like most of his contemporaries, Bachofen assumed that all societies passed through the same stages (beginning with complete promiscuity), thought the same thoughts (including an early interest in tracing descent but an ignorance of who their fathers were), and ultimately arrived at the same solutions to the same problems (beginning with matrilineality). This notion, first articulated in *Psychologie* by Adolf Bastian, is generally referred to as the

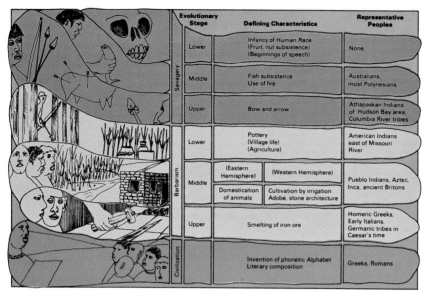

Evolutionary Stage		Defining Characteristics		Representative Peoples
Savagery	Lower	Infancy of Human Race (Fruit, nut subsistence) (Beginnings of speech)		None
Savagery	Middle	Fish subsistence Use of fire		Australians, most Polynesians
Savagery	Upper	Bow and arrow		Athapaskan Indians of Hudson Bay area, Columbia River tribes
Barbarism	Lower	Pottery (Village life) (Agriculture)		American Indians east of Missouri River
Barbarism	Middle	(Eastern Hemisphere) Domestication of animals	(Western Hemisphere) Cultivation by irrigation Adobe, stone architecture	Pueblo Indians, Aztec, Inca, ancient Britons
Barbarism	Upper	Smelting of iron ore		Homeric Greeks, Early Italians, Germanic tribes in Caesar's time
Civilization		Invention of phonetic Alphabet Literary composition		Greeks, Romans

Figure 5. Morgan's idea of social evolution, showing a unilineal sequence of cultural levels that was modified after later workers amassed data that did not fit into his theoretical framework. Figure 6 (lower left). Lewis Henry Morgan and Edward Burnett Tylor. Figure 7 (right). Tylor thought that the belief in spirit beings originated in man's dreams of life and death, which seemed to transcend the limitations of the physical world and, to some peoples, to become a form of reality.

"psychic unity" of the species. Today, anthropologists would readily agree that there are no significant differences in mental capacity among men and that substantially the same ability curve will occur in *any* group, regardless of culture or race. Nevertheless, they do not accept the idea that some "psychic unity" causes all societies inevitably to proceed through the same sequence of stages, for they now recognize that a combination of environment, history, immediate social and economic conditions, and cultural borrowing affect each society at least somewhat differently, leading to different sequences and rates of development in different societies.

Lewis Henry Morgan

Lewis Henry Morgan is credited with being the founding father of American anthropology. Although a New York lawyer by profession, he was deeply interested in the Iroquois Indians, and his studies of their culture led to his first book, *The League of the Ho-de-no-sau-nee or Iroquois* (1851), which remains one of the best early ethnographies of an American Indian community. It was not his ethnographic work that gave impetus to the growth of anthropology, however, but his achievements as an evolutionary theorist and a student of kinship and marriage. Echoing Montesquieu, Morgan in *Ancient Society* (1877) divided human history into three basic stages—savagery, barbarism, and civilization—and then further subdivided the first two stages into upper, middle, and lower substages. He assigned both contemporary and historically known people to one of these stages and substages on the basis of rigid criteria, many of which were based on property relationships. Savagery, he suggested, was characterized by "primitive com-

munism," in which all goods and property were held in common. At the level of barbarism, property rights began to emerge. Finally, at the level of civilization, the concept of private property reached full development and all goods and land were concentrated in private hands.

Morgan speculated that a final stage was to evolve in which a form of communism would reappear. The existing family structure would disappear and most goods would be held in common by the community. Although he was by no stretch of the imagination a revolutionist, his ideas came to the attention of Friedrich Engels, collaborator of Karl Marx, who saw in them verification of one of the central concepts of Marxist doctrine. The timid and thoroughly capitalistic attorney from New York ultimately became something of a Marxist saint, and to this day he remains one of the few Western scholars habitually cited by Soviet anthropologists.

Although Morgan's ideas about social evolution per se have been discredited by subsequent generations of anthropological critics (although their influence is to be seen in the work of Leslie White and his followers), his fundamental ideas about kinship constitute a step forward in the history of the discipline. His *Systems of Affinity and Consanguinity*, published in 1871, is firmly grounded in empirical data. Supported in part by the newly founded Smithsonian Museum and the Bureau of American Ethnology, Morgan personally interviewed numerous missionaries, consuls, and explorers and sent questionnaires to hundreds of others around the world. He asked his informants to describe the pattern of kin relations among the people they knew, and the end result was the first massive and generally systematic collection of cross-cultural data about a particular aspect of human behavior, family and marriage.

Edward Burnett Tylor

If Morgan can be designated the founding father of American anthropology, one of his

contemporaries, Edward Burnett Tylor, must be credited with being the first professional anthropologist. In 1865, he published the first of his major works, *Researches Into the Early History of Mankind and the Development of Civilization.* On the basis of extensive data collected from almost every culture then known, he attempted to establish the general similarity of men everywhere.

Tylor later conceived of an evolutionary pattern in the development of human thought about the supernatural, a progression beginning with animism (a belief that spirit beings inhabit most natural objects), extending through ancestor worship and polytheism, and finally reaching monotheism. In

many respects, Tylor was also a *diffusionist,* believing that certain aspects of a society could change as a result of the borrowing of beliefs and practices, which results from contact between different cultures. In his work with religious phenomena, for example, he suggested that a society might well be affected by the belief systems of neighboring societies and thus move from one stage of religious "development" to another.

Possibly Tylor's greatest achievement was his articulation of the concept of culture—the single most important concept in anthropological theory. In *Primitive Culture,* published in 1871, he observed that "Culture or civilization, taken in its wide ethnographic

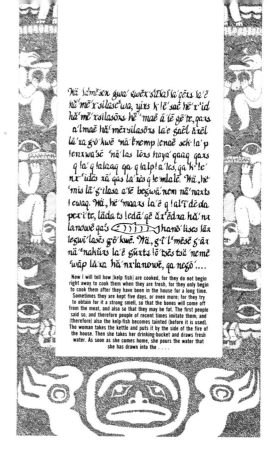

Figure 8 (below). Franz Boas, who led the American critique on classical evolutionism in the early twentieth century. He was also a leader in the intellectual attack on racism during this era. Figure 9. The extent of Boas' knowledge is indicated by his painstaking accumulation of even such seeming trivia as hundreds of Kwakiutl recipes.

Now I will tell how [kelp fish] are cooked, for they do not begin right away to cook them when they are fresh, for they only begin to cook them after they have been in the house for a long time. Sometimes they are kept five days, or even more; for they try to obtain for it a strong smell, so that the bones will come off from the meat, and also so that they may be fat. The first people said so, and therefore people of recent times imitate them; and (therefore) also the kelp-fish becomes tainted (before it is used). The woman takes the kettle and puts it by the side of the fire of the house. Then she takes her drinking-bucket and draws fresh water. As soon as she comes home, she pours the water that she has drawn into the . . . .

sense, is that complex whole which includes knowledge, belief, art, morals, law, custom, and any other capabilities and habits acquired by man as a member of society." Although the concept has been modified many times in the last hundred years—in 1951, Alfred Kroeber and Clyde Kluckhohn listed twenty-eight pages of definitions of culture—Tylor's remains the fundamental definition, the one on which, in some degree, all subsequent definitions of this key term are based.

BOAS AND THE EMPIRICAL REACTION

By the end of the nineteenth century, enough ethnographic data had been accumulated so that many of the generalizations of the evolutionists could be challenged successfully. This empirical approach—one based on actual observation and experience—is symbolized by the work of Franz Boas, who, more than any other single scholar, was responsible for the decline of classical evolutionism in anthropology. Boas' objections to classical evolutionism were first articulated in 1896 in *The Limitation of the Comparative Method of Anthropology*, which exposed the shortcomings of the existing evolutionist reconstructions of universal, ongoing stages of human society.

His efforts were not limited to his attack on cultural evolution. In fact, his most influential book, *The Mind of Primitive Man* (1911), has become almost the charter of the modern antiracist position. In it, he demonstrated that the differences among men arise from cultural characteristics rather than from any inherent racial characteristics. Indeed, *The Mind of Primitive Man* has figured in almost every contemporary attack on racism in the United States and was cited extensively in the 1954 Supreme Court decision that ended—in theory at least—racial segregation in American schools.

Boas was interested in more than one aspect of his discipline. He did some excellent work in physical anthropology and pioneered in the field of descriptive linguistics, especially in the languages of North American Indians. He was actively engaged in archaeological field work, and in his later years he became interested in culture and personality studies. No contemporary anthropologist has contributed to and influenced so many fields.

Yet there is controversy over Boas' position in the history of the discipline. Some anthropologists have downgraded his importance, suggesting that, if anything, his insistence on fact gathering in the absence of theory caused a thirty-year hiatus in the development of general theory; other anthropologists have been enthusiastic in their praise. The truth would seem to lie somewhere between the two extremes. The history of science in general seems to move in a kind of dialectic. First come the ground breakers, the high-order theorists. Then a reaction begins—new knowledge is obtained that is used to criticize and modify the preceding theories. Finally, out of the expanded knowledge, new theories arise only to be challenged by the empiricists, and the cycle begins again. In this sense, Boas played a vital role in the history of anthropology, for he challenged the ground breakers and, in his turn, provided the foundation for further development of the field.

Culture Analysis

One of Boas' earliest students, Alfred Kroeber, came to believe that culture could be analyzed on a distinct level of its own, one

separable from individual human behavior. Borrowing the term *superorganic* from the nineteenth-century English sociologist Herbert Spencer, Kroeber suggested that there are three levels of phenomena in the universe: the inorganic, the organic, and the superorganic, the latter being the sphere of culture. Each of these levels is dependent on the others but operates independently of them. Thus he believed that culture, once developed, operates on its own inherent principles, unexplainable by reference to biology or the idiosyncrasies of human personality. Culture, for Kroeber, was an "emergent" phenomenon that could be understood only in its own terms and could not be reduced to biological or psychological explanations. Although he came to modify this early idea, other anthropologists, notably White, have expanded upon it.

Kroeber later became concerned with the geographic distribution of culture traits such as pottery styles, kinship systems, and religious beliefs. He used the analysis of these distributions in the reconstruction of historic sequences. His major theme was the *culture-area concept*, developed initially by Clark Wissler for categorizing Indian artifacts on display in the American Museum of Natural History. Kroeber thought that cultures adapted to a certain environmental region— for example, the Great Plains—would share many social and material features, and that patterns of adaptation, once defined, would hold great potential for historic reconstruction. Together with Wissler, he developed the *age-area theory*, which holds that new ideas flow evenly and in a wavelike pattern from an assumed culture center or focus within a culture area. The only place that the age-area theory seems to work, however, is Australia, where the focus or innovating area seems to be located in the center of the continent. But unlike almost all other culture areas, Australia is relatively flat and has no major barriers to movement. Moreover, it has been almost totally isolated from the rest of the

world for thousands of years, and the factor of cultural borrowing, which upsets so many other distribution schemes, has thus been minimal.

From 1940 on, Kroeber concentrated on civilization's overall cultural processes and development. To some extent, he returned to the theories of the superorganic, but his main concern was in the cyclic patterns in civilization. In *Configurations of Culture Growth*, he suggested that cultures as well as individuals have a life cycle, being marked by growth, decline, and death. The laws governing these matters related to the superorganic or culture as a whole, but Kroeber did not believe they were completely separable from individual human action.

In 1958, he and the eminent American sociologist Talcott Parsons published what re-

mains one of the most influential contemporary statements of the relationship between the concept of culture and of society. Society, to Kroeber and Parsons, constitutes the *structure* of social relationships, whereas culture is the *content* of those relationships —the material items and behavioral characteristics and symbolic meanings that emerge from the relationships that constitute the structure. Neither culture nor society can exist without the other, but they can vary independently in that there may be more than one culture in a single society, and a single culture can exist in more than one society.

Cultural Patterning

One of Boas' most prominent students was Ruth Benedict. Drawing on her field work among the Zuñi and other southwestern American Indian groups, as well as on published accounts of the Northwest Coast Indians and the people of Melanesia, Benedict hypothesized that the central characteristics of a culture will be manifest in the personality characteristics of its members. Her position is summed up in her well-known statement: "Culture is personality writ large." By this, she did not mean that all the members of the same culture have the same personalities, but rather that the *type* of personalities found in a group dictates the type of culture that group has. Thus, for example, a group whose members tended to be personally suspicious and lacking in trust would have a culture whose fundamental pattern was paranoid.

From the anthropological view, there are some problems with this approach. First, it necessarily involves cutting and pruning the data to fit the theory, because exceptions to generalizations of the sort given in the example are easy to find. Second, and perhaps more importantly, it appears to be impossible to reduce the many aspects in culture to a single overriding pattern. No culture is without complexity or even without internal

Figure 13. Art is a form of expressive culture that has been examined by anthropologists who are concerned with the integration of culture and personality. The intricate decoration of this ceremonial house in New Guinea reflects the complex interweaving of totemic emblems and ancestral images from the many small and fragmentary social groupings.

contradictions, and personalities are not accurately summarized by a single tendency. Any integrative scheme must take into account these difficulties, however appealing sweeping generalizations may be. Nevertheless, Benedict's theory has proved important in the recent history of the discipline in that it stimulated further research into the processes involved in the integration of culture and personality.

CULTURE AND PERSONALITY STUDIES

Before the 1920s culture was largely treated in the abstract, as a list or assemblage of traits associated with whole, historic societies. There was little interest in the place of the individual in culture or in the role of culture in the life and personality of the individual. In the 1920s, however, a highly productive encounter began between anthropology and the psychoanalytic theories of Sigmund Freud and other psychoanalysts who followed him. The initial reaction of anthropologists (perhaps first signaled by Kroeber's review of Freud's *Totem and Taboo* in 1920) was critical, for it challenged the universality of such formative, interpersonal constellations as the Oedipus complex by pointing to cultural variants in the basic family constellation. At the same time, anthropologists were stimulated to bring these questions to their field research. They thus acquired what Milton Singer in 1961 termed a "bifocal" view of the cultural process. In other words, they began to perceive the individual as personality formation, and culture as standardized patterns of interpersonal relations among individuals and groups that are in process of cultural continuity, strain, change, and evolution. Bronislaw Malinowski's field work in the Trobriand Islands and the work of the psychoanalyst Geza Roheim in Australia, Somaliland, and the Normanbe Islands were forerunners of the many studies that followed in the search for cross-cultural validation or for modification of psychodynamic hypotheses. The prodigious field research and writings of Margaret Mead from 1925 to the present explored in many ways the question of the plasticity of human nature to cultural patterning in such areas as differentiation of sex roles and child development. As her own studies extended through time, they turned increasingly to the interlocked questions of personality formation and cultural transmission, or continuity and discontinuity, under conditions of rapid and radical culture change.

Much of the work that followed turned to characterizing whole populations in terms of psychological types and the well-functioning or psychopathology of typical personalities. One approach to this task was to try to delineate the so-called "basic personality structure" of a group by looking at its culture, its institutions, and its standardized projections of itself in fantasy, religion, and art. This integration of culture and personality was then accounted for by using the socialization of the individual in the family, which in turn was placed in the context of

Figure 14. This Canadian Indian girl must adapt to the standards of two cultures, those of her ancestral tradition and those of the dominant white culture. Some psychological anthropologists have been studying the interaction between the personalities of the members of a society and the often drastic changes resulting from culture contact, particularly between Western and non-Western cultures.

its society and its subsistence activities. A succession of cultures were analyzed by the psychoanalyst Abram Kardiner and anthropologists who brought their field data to his seminars, most notably Ralph Linton and Cora DuBois.

The alternative to delineating personality on the basis of culture is to attempt to arrive statistically at a group characterization through the analysis of data on individuals, individual documents, behavior, interviews, and psychological tests. This approach, called "modal personality structure" by DuBois in 1944 and methodologically developed by Anthony Wallace in 1952, helped to balance anthropological attention between the common features of a culture's "typical" personality and the very considerable individual variation within the range of a society. Culture also was found to require modal analysis. Generally, the position arrived at is that personality is not something unique to the individual and that culture is not something uniformly common to the group. Rather, both are distributed within a society in a complex structure of commonality and difference, integrated, as Wallace puts it, as an "organization of diversity."

THE RISE OF FUNCTIONALISM

While Boas and his students were reshaping anthropology in the United States, another tradition was emerging, especially in France and Britain, that was to influence all the social sciences, including anthropology. This was the functionalist tradition, founded by the French sociologist Emile Durkheim and developed further—although in different ways—by A. R. Radcliffe-Brown and Malinowski.

In *The Division of Labor*, published in 1893, Durkheim developed his concept of *social fact*, the idea referring to a power over members of society that functions to unify and control individual behavior. This power becomes manifest when it takes the form of coercion exercised over an individual through certain sanctions or when it is used to suppress individual efforts to violate these sanctions.

Durkheim viewed social facts as they affect and are affected by the evolution of social unity, or solidarity. The sources of this unity, he suggested, are to be found in the nature of the legal and moral codes every society has. He thought that the earliest type of unity is one of *mechanical solidarity*, a sort of solidarity based on what he termed a "repressive" legal and moral code. This type is found among the simplest tribal societies, where there is a simple division of labor based primarily on age and sex differences, and all members of the community subscribe to the same set of social facts. Briefly put, unity in these societies stems from the fact that everyone does the same kinds of work and lives the same sort of life; they are all subject to the same standards and the same sanctions. All members are participants in what he termed the "collective conscience."

As society becomes more complex, repressive legal and moral codes evolve into what Durkheim called "restitutive" codes, leading to an *organic solidarity* based on complementary relationships, much as human organs complement one another in the functioning of the human body. Solidarity here results from the interdependence of different parts of society, not from the homogeneity of the whole. In the more complex societies, legal and moral codes affect only certain segments of the community, and they inevitably affect each segment in a somewhat different fashion at any one time. Thus, in this case there is no unitary body of social facts.

In short, a society characterized by organic solidarity and restitutive law is a functionally integrated one. It is in *The Division of Labor* that Durkheim earned his reputation as the founding father of functionalism, for he was the first to show systematically that all societies are functionally integrated wholes, with the needs of the various parts

Figure 15. When all members of a society do basically similar work and conform in life styles and beliefs, individual variation is of narrow scope. This uniformity is called mechanical solidarity (above). Below, organic solidarity emerges when specialists depend on one another economically but, because of population density and work differences, tolerate and accept different life styles. Here, solidarity is based on interdependence of diverse social parts. (After Emile Durkheim, *The Division of Labor in Society*. New York: Macmillan, 1933.)

of a whole society being satisfied by other parts of the same society. He stressed the view that the needs of a society and its parts as such are related to but are on a different level from the needs of the society's individual members.

Radcliffe-Brown expanded on Durkheim's work but he did not agree with Durkheim's evolutionary theories. He believed social anthropology must be based on actual observations of behavior in the field; only then could it uncover the laws and principles that order social relationships. He thought conjectural reconstruction of history could only lead to the false understandings he attributed to the evolutionists.

His celebrated analysis of "joking relationships" is an example of his approach. These relationships, which have been observed among in-laws in many societies, involve an exaggerated amount of horseplay. Because relationships among people linked only by marriage can be potentially disruptive—the persisting cycle of mother-in-law jokes in American culture is a good case in point—the cause of functional integration is best served by setting the participants in these relationships apart in one of two ways that reduce the likelihood of conflict. First, society can stipulate that the parties concerned must never meet face-to-face (the Navajo, for example, prescribe such a pattern of total avoidance for a man and his mother-in-law). Second, society can turn the potentially tense relationship into one based on familiarity and horseplay. Although avoidance relationships and joking relationships would at first seem totally disparate, Radcliffe-Brown was able to demonstrate that they share a common functional goal: the reduction of tension between in-laws and, through this, the promotion of social unity.

Malinowski was another eminent functionalist. In his field work, he pioneered the *participant observation* approach, living among the people he studied and coming to experience their world view. Like Radcliffe-

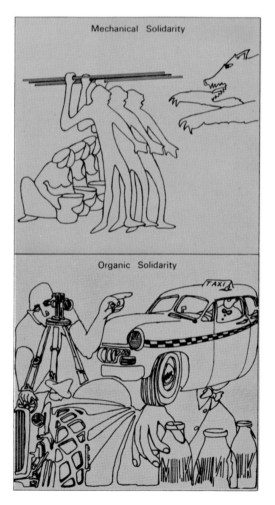

Mechanical Solidarity

Organic Solidarity

Brown, Malinowski rejected the historic approach in the study of society, asserting that functional analysis must be based on first-hand observation. But unlike Radcliffe-Brown, he focused on the individual and his immediate needs, ultimately arriving at a definition of culture that reflected this emphasis. He believed that culture emerged to satisfy the human needs that extended beyond direct adaptation to the environment. He viewed functionalism as a means to analyze the ways in which social institutions

Figure 16. How cultural and social phenomena are affected by the process of change is one focus of anthropological research. Adherence to traditional heritages and a concurrent adoption of elements of contact cultures present one such aspect of change, as manifest among these Tuareg of the Sahara.

interrelate to serve the primary and secondary needs of the individual. Primary needs were rooted in biological drives for nourishment, reproduction, and shelter; secondary needs were derived from the manner in which the primary needs were satisfied. For example, all men must eat, but in a given culture men will habitually eat only certain foods. Although secondary needs are one step removed from the immediate demands of biology, they are nevertheless just as crucial to the individual.

NEO-EVOLUTIONISM

In the 1930s, partly as a reaction to the ahistoricism engendered by Radcliffe-Brown and Malinowski and Boasian insistence on treating each society as a unique development, evolutionism began to reemerge. In large measure purged of its adherence to the comparative methods and the idea of progress, this neo-evolutionism, as it is usually termed, is still very much a part of contemporary anthropology. To date, its three most important advocates have been V. Gordon Childe, Leslie White, and Julian Steward.

Childe suggested that the evolution of technology is the key to understanding the social and cultural stages through which the species has passed. Perhaps his most important concept is that of revolution within an overall evolutionary pattern. To illustrate, in his two principal works on the subject (*What Happened in History* and *Man Makes Himself*), he stated that when men began to domesticate plants and animals some 9,000 years ago, they initiated a sociocultural revolution. Domestication created a food surplus,

Figure 17. Julian Steward views the cultural core of a society as its set of technologically mediated adaptations to the environment. The level of technology available to this Micronesian fisherman, for instance, exerts a profound influence on the social, political, and economic arrangements of his society.

which in turn permitted a rapid rise in population. Sedentary villages emerged, invention followed invention, and craft specialization became more elaborate. Within a very short timespan, a whole new social order emerged. He maintained that this phase in the evolution of human culture occurred late in eastern Europe and elsewhere as domestication diffused outward from the Near East.

Many of Childe's theories have been questioned, especially since the recent recovery of archaeological evidence indicating plant and animal domestication evolved independently in Europe and in the Near East. Nevertheless, his concept of this so-called "Neolithic revolution" and the forces that brought it about influenced several anthropologists, including White.

White developed what may be termed a general evolutionary theory. He has explicitly rejected the term "neo-evolutionism," asserting that there is a direct continuity from Morgan's evolutionism to his own concepts. He has stated that the main problem with Morgan's theory was Morgan's lack of adequate data, a problem now largely solved. White sees *energy* as the key factor in evolutionary development, with the amount of energy available per capita per annum determining the overall level of cultural evolution at any given time and place. He divides social and cultural phenomena into three major orders. The most basic is the technological order, where the process of change inevitably begins. The second is the sociological order, which includes groups and institutions such as the family and the state. Finally, there is the ideological order, which includes values, attitudes, and belief systems. Changes in the available energy level begin with the discovery or invention of some new item of technology. Such changes eventually affect the other two orders, and in the end a new evolutionary level is achieved.

Unlike Childe and White, Steward does not seek to revitalize classical evolutionism or to attempt a general synthesis of the evolution of culture. He has termed himself a "multilinear" evolutionist, concerned primarily with specific lines of development in specific cultures.

In his major work on the subject, *Theory of Culture Change* (1955), Steward suggests that each major environmental zone (arid, riverine, high altitude, tropical forest, and so on) tends to produce in the cultures of those who exploit it a common ecological adaptation. Multilinear evolution is concerned with tracing sequences of cultural development that are shaped by such ecological adaptations. For example, Steward suggests that cultures evolving in riverine valleys surrounded by arid regions, such as the Nile, the Tigris-Euphrates, and the Indus valleys, will share a common culture core, displaying such traits as irrigation agriculture (given the presence of plant and animal domestication), city-states, and a temple-centered religious system. Although they may differ in

Figure 18. Much of culture, including language, consist of the ways in which each society distinguishes, groups, and codes the stimuli of its physical and social environment. In doing this, it imposes a classification that determines the perceptual and response values of the stimuli themselves. For example, English speakers distinguish a series of voiced sounds from unvoiced sounds made at the same position in the mouth. The Manus and other Melanesians do not, and they would have difficulty in distinguishing the pairs of words shown unless they were preceded by the corresponding nasal sounds (mb, nd, and ng) of the voiced consonants.

English		Manus
VOICED	VOICELESS	VOICED VOICELESS
b [big]	p [pig]	{ b / p } ig
d [dug]	t [tug]	{ d / t } ug
g [gill]	k [kill]	{ g / k } ill

specifics, these cultures will tend to follow the same evolutionary sequence, whereas cultures evolving in tropical forest zones or in central deserts will have different sequences because their ecologically based cores will differ. A culture may thus follow any one of several distinct lines of development rather than a single sequence of prescribed universal stages. That it is the least controversial and at the same time most operational of the three approaches considered here is seen in the fact that Steward has greatly influenced the present generation of American anthropologists.

LINGUISTICS AND ANTHROPOLOGY

Anthropologists have long regarded language as part of culture. Through language, the symbols or representations that man forms within his mind are translated into communicable forms. Because communication is central to all cultures—indeed, culture could not exist without it—men historically have been concerned with the nature of language and its structure. As early as 400 B.C., the Indian scholar Patanjali created a grammar of the structure of Sanskrit from his study of the sacred Vedas, and linguistic investigations were carried out by the Greco-Roman grammarians.

Although early scholars were probably aware of culture as well, its systematic study and description did not begin until the nineteenth century, and even now linguistic analysis in some respects retains the lead. The

difference in the systematic achievements of linguistics and cultural anthropology is partly attributable to the nature of the thing studied. Languages could be written and graphically manipulated into unit representations that would be recognizably distinct in the semantic sense. Moreover, detailed information could be elicited systematically from individual informants. Such manipulation seemed only partially realizable in other aspects of culture, where events were often observed as natural occurrences, taken as they occurred, and where it proved more difficult to separate significant variation from the mere physical variability of events.

Patanjali's grammar directly influenced European scholars such as William Jones, who compared Sanskrit, Greek, Latin, Celtic, and Germanic and demonstrated not only that these languages were of a single family but that language change was constant and systematic. Others such as Franz Bopp in 1816, Jakob Grimm in 1819, and Karl Brugmann in 1886 established the comparative grammar and phonology of the Indo-European languages.

The comparative interest of early linguists led to a later descriptive phase that illuminated with increasing rigor and comprehensiveness the structure of particular languages. Good structural description in terms of units, relations, and levels of meaning was needed for comparative reconstructions of nonextant languages. Ferdinand de Saussure developed a systematic theory of the structure of language. Linguists such as Baudouin de Courtenay, Nikolai Trubetskoi, and Roman Jakobson, bridging the nineteenth and early twentieth centuries, developed the now-familiar units of structural description that include phonemes and morphemes. In addition, these linguists developed the concept of distinctive features of variation and contrast by which sounds are differentiated from one another. In the United States, the study of the unwritten American Indian languages also stimulated a strong descriptive development in linguistics. Two of the most outstanding scholars and theorists of American linguistics, Franz Boas and Edward Sapir, were anthropologists whose approach to the study of language was firmly embedded in a general anthropological background. The work of the linguist Leonard Bloomfield, as represented in his 1933 text *Language*, provided a synthesis of this comparative-descriptive development that appeared to be an adequate basis for elaboration in the next two decades.

Although linguistic analysis has been *structural* from the start, it has become much more so as investigators go increasingly beneath the surface variation of speech to the psychological and abstract categories, classifications, and contrasts underlying speech behavior in order to better understand the meanings and intention of the language speakers. Stemming in part from the work of Zelling Harris, the concepts of this so-called *transformational* or *generative grammar* have been extended vigorously by Noam Chomsky in the 1950s and 1960s into a kind of depth structuralism and critique of descriptive linguistics. Chomsky and others seek to explain why the speaker-hearer can create and comprehend a potentially infinite set of sentences—most of them novel, meeting the needs of new experience—from a relatively limited and fixed set of elementary forms. These investigators seek the rules governing the combination of these underlying forms and their subsequent translation into the overt or surface patterns of speech. The approach aspires to a theory of the structure of language, or perhaps of the human mind, through the study of how language expresses thought.

The development of semantics (the study of meaning) has moved roughly from discrete, "dictionary" definitions of morphemes or words to a systemic approach in which entire semantic fields or "domains" of related words—all the kinship terms of a language, for example, or all the color names—

are treated as mutually defining in terms of the way they divide some range of phenomena, such as kin relationships or the color spectrum. The eighteenth-century theorist Wilhelm von Humboldt and his successors in Germany were ahead of their time in developing the notion of semantic fields, but the concept was not consolidated until the present century in the work of Sapir, Jakobson, Harris, and others. It eventually led to the development of *ethnosemantics* by contemporary linguists and anthropologists.

Aside from the idea of semantic domains that segment or classify phenomena, linguistic investigators became interested in semantic dimensions that distinguish among the terms of a domain. With this approach, an entire domain of words can be defined against a range of phenomena, once the few select dimensions on which those phenomena vary have been identified. For example, although English kinship terms refer to a range of genealogical positions relative to ego, all these terms can be mutually defined on the same four dimensions. Thus, the term "father" may be applied to an individual who is related by blood rather than by marriage to ego; who is in ego's line rather than a collateral one; who is male rather than female; and, on the generational dimension, who is in the first ascending generation from ego. All the other basic English kinship terms—aunt, uncle, brother, grandfather—can be defined within the same four dimensions of this semantic field.

Through their work in the *componential analysis* of kinship terminologies (components = semantic dimensions = distinctive features), Ward Goodenough and Floyd Lounsbury in the 1950s initiated a strong development of ethnosemantics as a method of culture analysis. Many others have since made original contributions that extend this method to other domains, and their generalizations of the linguistic model have been applied to the analysis of behavioral events, such as rituals, and of narratives, such as

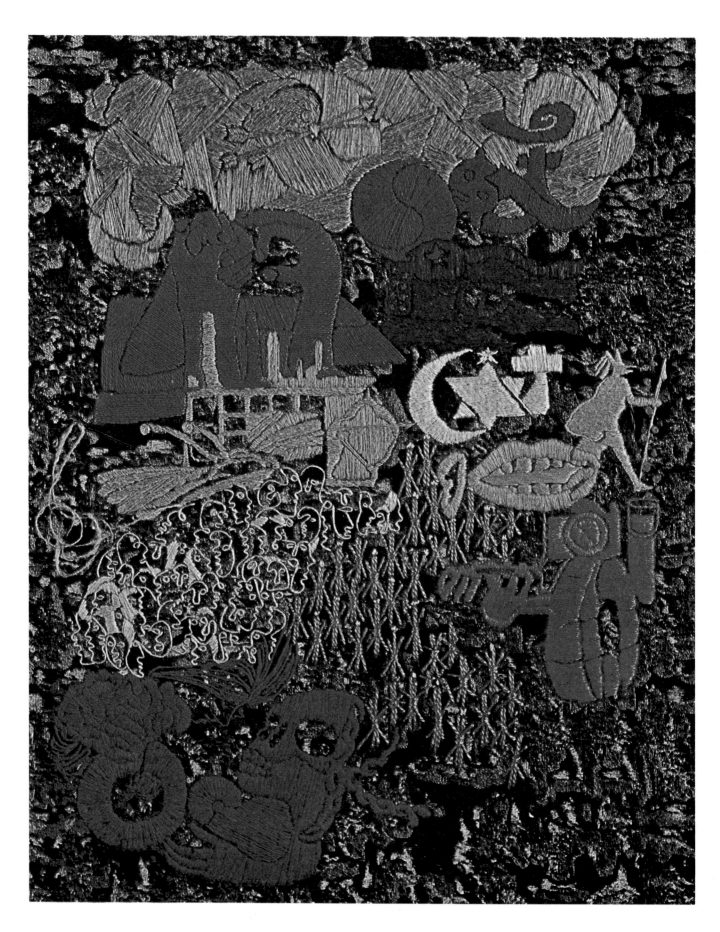

Figure 19. A tapestry of culture, portraying the interwoven yet distinct aspects of human life. Relationships are shown symbolically, as between the biological base (lower left) and population, environment, and technology, or through the language link (middle right) to religion, ideology, and world view. Far from being complete, the weaving of culture is an ongoing process in any direction, including the tracing of threads that lead to awareness of man's evolutionary past. Figure 20 (right). By piercing the shell of semantics, the psycholinguist seeks to define the universal bases of understanding that underlie all of the world's languages.

myths. This analytic development in anthropology is directly emulative of linguistics, partly on the assumption that the kind of structuring found in language is, in a broader sense, the structure of culture.

Like the studies of language, studies of culture have also gone through a comparativist phase of historic reconstruction that has stimulated more rigorous, more comprehensive description of cultures. And, like linguistic analysis, the analysis of culture has now reached a phase of depth structuralism in which, as stated by Goodenough and Claude Lévi-Strauss, the aim is to discover the underlying structures that generate the physical variability of behavior and give to this behavior (in our perception of it) its familiarity and formal unity over time. Goodenough defines adequate cultural description as Chomsky defined grammar: as an analysis of the competence of a member of a society to behave as his culture requires, within the limits of variation that it allows, and to interact effectively with others of that culture. For Lévi-Strauss, as for Chomsky, cultural differences are greatest at the surface level, but in their deeper structures they converge toward the structure of the human mind itself.

The ethnosemantic and structuralist development in anthropology has not been without a critical countertrend. Derived in part from evolutionist concerns, there has been continuing research and theoretical development in the study of man's external relations to his social and physical environment as mediated by culture—particularly by technology. Such studies of the consequences of adaptation to diverse environments have been particularly stimulated by the work of Steward, mentioned earlier. Scholars in this field take the function of ecological adaptation as the bedrock of culture and seek in ecology, with its quantification of environmental variables as correlates of cultural variables, the scientific rigor that others seek in structuralism. Marvin Harris in 1968 criti-

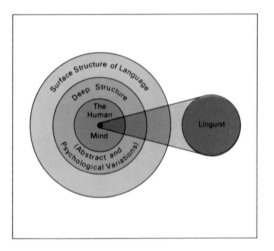

cized the structuralist approach as overly preoccupied with internal states of the mind. From the "neomaterialist" point of view, as he terms it, anthropology should be more concerned with behavior and its material setting and with comparative studies based on universally applicable descriptors, because attempts to describe each culture internally sacrifice comparability. Anthropology should aim at discovering cultural laws—the invariant relations that are predictive and therefore capable of being tested.

These two approaches—the structuralist and the nomothetic (from Greek *nomos*, "law")—are not antithetical, although they do compete for the time and resources of anthropologists. Some investigators, such as Harold Conklin, are practicing what amounts to "structural ecology" in their study of the cultural conceptualization of the environment in relation to the technological-ecological adaptation of members of particular societies. Culture, it seems, rests on a dual foundation in two equally important and pervasive but radically different ways. In one respect, the base is provided by language and symbolic processes and, in another respect, by the technological and organizational adaptation of people to their physical and social environment.

WHAT THE ANTHROPOLOGIST DOES ▌▐

Case Study: Digging Up the Past

4 Man has been littering the landscape of this planet for well over 2 million years, and the debris he has left behind is both varied and plentiful. One of the aims of the archaeologist is to bring order to this mélange once it has been removed from the ground and, following systematic analysis, make statements concerning the broader life ways of the people who left it behind. At the archaeological site, the material objects that have withstood the passage of time are but fragmentary evidence of what was once a rich and varied culture. Yet even with these few fragments it is possible to reconstruct such nonmaterial aspects of past cultures as social customs, religious behavior, and economic practices. The archaeologist pursues his business in all parts of the world, exploring sites in the arctic tundra, in the tropical forests of Africa, under the streets of major urban centers, and even under water. Whatever the site, however, he must address himself to the task of systematically recovering the maximum amount of material, ordering this material in some logical manner so that it can be described and also compared to other material excavated by other archaeologists, and finally making his generalizations about human behavior in the past.

How an archaeologist works, what the nature of his data is, and which methods he uses to recover and classify the information may be illustrated by an account of an actual excavation that was made under the direction of anthropologist James Deetz. Such an account may also clarify basic concepts and terms in use in archaeology and point out some of the more current practices being used to create imaginative reconstructions of life in the past.

CLASSIFICATION OF THE SITE

A three-component Arikara Indian village in central South Dakota was excavated by archaeologists in 1957 and 1958. This particular site had been occupied sequentially between 1700 and 1780 by members of the Arikara tribe, although in all probability by different communities representing this larger group. The term "component" is used to indicate how many times the same site has been

Figure 2 (below left). Artist's conception of an Arikara Indian. Figure 3. Map showing the location of the Medicine Crow site in the American Midwest. Figure 4 (right). Excavations in progress. Notice the control pit in the upper right corner of the photograph.

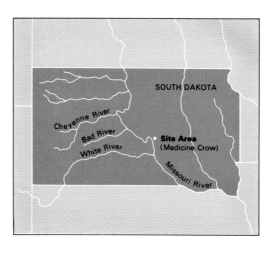

move first toward the major river drainages in that area and subsequently up the Missouri River in the direction of central South Dakota. Their northward migration continued during the eighteenth century, and by the nineteenth century they were located in North Dakota on a reservation with Mandan and Hidatza Indians. European trade material was introduced into the central Missouri River area about 1700, and early traders, trappers, and explorers in the upper Missouri River Valley had recorded that all the Arikara had moved north of the Medicine Crow site by the latter part of the eighteenth century. Therefore, the occupation of this site can be bracketed between 1700 and 1780.

TECHNIQUES OF EXCAVATION

The Arikara followed the village farming way of life. There was a mixed and somewhat seasonal variation in subsistence activity, with periodic bison hunts carried on by most members of the village. The meat derived from these hunts supplemented a diet based on corn, beans, and squash—the three major crops cultivated by the American Indian.

Their relatively stable and permanent villages were made up of a number of circular earth lodges, which were typical of the Indians of the Great Plains. The Arikara prepared the foundation for these lodges by digging a circular pit approximately eighteen inches in depth. A framework of willow poles was then erected over the pit and covered with sod, which gave the dwelling the appearance of a large dirt igloo. The size of the domestic lodges ranged from twenty to sixty feet in diameter. Lodges of this type have been found that are as large as 100 feet in diameter, but these structures were usually reserved for ceremonial purposes.

One of the most common questions asked of archaeologists is how they know where to dig. In the case of the Plains Indian, this question is easily answered. The large earth lodges along the grasslands bordering the

occupied. For instance, if a site had been occupied successively by three different groups of people or by the same people in three separate and also archaeologically separable periods, each occupation would be called a single component (A, B, and C).

The location of this archaeological excavation is known as the Medicine Crow site. In the official record of the Smithsonian Institution, the organization that sponsored the dig, it is designated as 39BF2. The number "39" refers to the alphabetical position of the state of South Dakota in a list of forty-eight states, exclusive of Hawaii and Alaska, which were added later. The letters "BF" indicate Buffalo County and the number "2" signifies that this particular site was the second one recorded during a site survey in the Missouri River area of that county. Thus the label "39BF2" indicates that Medicine Crow was the second site discovered and recorded in Buffalo County, South Dakota. This trinomial site-labeling method is universal in federal government site designating systems and is also used by a number of state organizations.

Assigning a date to the three components of this site was relatively easy. Arikara Indians were originally located in northern Nebraska. Late in the sixteenth century, severe drought conditions may have forced them to

Figure 5 (left). This aerial view of the Medicine Crow site shows the darker rings of the lodge foundations, the result of the organic debris that accumulated during settlement and encouraged heavy plant growth. Figure 6 (right). A central hearth, characteristic of all dwellings of this type.

Missouri River are quite conspicuous. Viewed from the air, the villages appear as a series of dark green circles against a lighter green or brown background. Organic debris in the foundations of the lodges has provided a rich soil in which vegetation flourishes and thus causes the dark green effect. The land surrounding the site and the spaces between the dwellings are not covered with this rich soil and do not support heavy growth of plant material.

The remains of the earth lodges are visible as dish-shaped depressions in the soil, the centers of which are somewhat lower than the surrounding ground. In a certain number of these lodge pits there is, in fact, a raised ring surrounding the lodge pit depression. This ring was formed when the sod that originally covered the lodge slid or was washed down from the framework and piled up around the periphery of the dwelling.

Work at Medicine Crow began with the creation of a scale map on which all visible lodge depressions were located and numbered. Lodge pits that were not visible from the surface, however, were not included in the original mapping but were later given numbers in the sequence.

The first excavation on the site was carried out by digging a *control pit*, about five feet square, well away from the surface indications of previous structures. This pit was dug in order to determine the normal undisturbed cross-sectional form of the soil deposits on the site. Thus, any excavation in areas that had in fact been disturbed by human activity could be measured against the constant control provided by this excavation.

Excavation began in one of the earth lodge depressions. A test pit was dug in the center of the remains to locate the central fire pit or hearth, typically found in all dwellings of this type. Eighteen inches below the surface, the archaeologists found the hearth and identified the floor of the dwelling in the surrounding area. Because the earth that filled the depression was filled with charcoal and other burned material, they concluded that the house had been consumed by fire. The resulting dark soil contrasted markedly with the white and light brown soil of the house floor. To locate the wall, a narrow trench was then dug along the floor near the edge of the lodge pit. The wall was found at a point where the consistency of the soil changed and became both harder and lighter in color. Trenching was then carried out along the circular edge of the pit. The wall was found to be continuous except for a break that indicated the entrance passage. Finally, the fill and whatever artifacts it contained were carefully removed.

When this site had been completely excavated, it became clear that there were three different types of lodges. A number of them were relatively small, between twenty-five and thirty feet in diameter. All the smaller lodges had very hard, apparently sun-baked floors, indicating a possible lapse of time between the excavation of the pits and the construction of the superstructures. The small dwellings also shared another feature. Just inside and to the left of the entrance passage, a pit was located in which a wooden mortar was found that had been used for the preparation of corn.

The second type of lodge was somewhat larger, ranging from thirty-five to forty feet in diameter. In contrast to the smaller houses, they had very soft floors, which were rather difficult to detect in some cases because of the fill material on top of them. Unlike the smaller houses, the larger structures had a number of small, bell-shaped storage pits depressed in the floors, and all lacked the mortar pit characteristic of the smaller dwellings.

A third type of lodge was seen in only two cases, but pottery was found that was similar to pottery found in a number of large, bell-shaped storage pits outside the lodge area. These dwellings were the largest of all, reaching a diameter of sixty feet. They had dimly defined floors, with storage pits similar to those of the medium-size structures.

A few small lodges had been dug into the medium-size houses, and portions of the two large houses were found beneath the medium-size structures. This overlap indicated that three components were represented on the site and that over time the diameter of lodges had been reduced from sixty feet to twenty-five feet. A reduction of approximately half the diameter of a circular lodge results in a fourfold decrease in the amount of usable living space. In fact, allowing space for storage pits, hearths, mortar pits, and support posts, the amount of usable living space had been even more seriously curtailed.

RECORDING ARCHAEOLOGICAL DATA

In archaeological excavation, it is extremely important to record the precise location of all the materials that have been recovered.

Later, when the material is being analyzed, its location may enhance inferences about the life ways of the inhabitants. When there are structural remains on a site, such as those of the lodge pits, the remains themselves form the most logical categories by which the artifacts and other materials may be segregated and recorded. In cases where archaeologists cannot find visible evidence of a structure, they superimpose a standard grid over the site. The grid consists of five-foot square units laid out in north-south, east-west directions. All artifacts from each grid pit are kept separate from artifacts found in other grid pits. *Vertical controls* are exercised by carefully digging through visibly distinct layers present in the soil, because each layer might reflect a different component occupation. In the absence of visible layering, arbitrary levels three or six inches in thickness are used.

Vertical segregation in the earth lodges at Medicine Crow was based on one unit, desig-

Figure 8 (left). One of the pottery samples found at the site and later restored. Figure 9. Some of the artifacts recovered. These were organized into type categories for comparison with materials excavated from other sites in the same general area.

nated *fill*. This unit was composed of the sod from the roof of the lodge, which had fallen in when the dwelling had burned, plus some material that may have drifted in on the top following the burning and subsequent abandonment of the house. The fill was recorded separately from materials located directly on the floor, with the latter being designated *floor material*.

Material from the sod roof contained artifacts representing an earlier occupation of the site. The earth piled on the roof by the builders of the lodge contained debris scattered about the site by earlier inhabitants. The artifacts directly on the floor were assumed to relate to the inhabitants of the lodge and to the activities that went on during the time the lodge was occupied. Such a relationship is actually a reversal of the expected time relationship, inasmuch as the older layers are normally found below the layers closer to the surface. In this instance, earlier material was added atop the superstructure and the expected order was thus reversed.

All told, sixteen lodges were excavated and the recovered artifacts were segregated according to the vertical categories that had been established. Materials found in the lodges included quantities of broken pottery, projectile points (probably arrowheads), small and delicately worked chipped stone points used in the hunting of bison, various types of stone and shell beads, red pipestone pipes, needles, bone awls, bone reamers for skins, chipped stone scraping tools, and stone knives. In addition, there was a considerable collection of European trade goods that included glass beads, metal wire, gun parts, iron nails, and miscellaneous unidentified fragments of iron and brass.

ANALYSIS OF THE ARTIFACTS

All the materials recovered were sent to the laboratory to be cleaned and catalogued according to their field location. The artifacts were then classified so that the excavated material could be compared with the data of other archaeologists working on similar sites.

One of the basic concepts at this stage of operation is the *type concept*, which consists of organizing the artifacts according to general categories—for instance, "chipped stone implements," "pottery," "bone tools"—and then placing them in smaller groups based on shared traits. Thus, a "pottery" type category might contain an artifact that is a pottery ware, gray-brown in color, with an inverted lip decorated by chevron incisions

along the rim and incised, decorated shoulders. Another type might have a direct vertical rim with cord-impressed, parallel horizontal decorations running along the lip and no shoulder decoration. By describing any class of artifact in this manner, formal type categories are created and other workers can then describe their data in terms of previously defined type categories. This process is useful in comprehensive comparisons among the material recovered from a series of sites in a general geographic area. The various traits that constitute a given type category, such as the form of a rim, the shape of the decoration, or the method by which the decoration was achieved, are referred to as *attributes*. A standard type category is usually based on the sharing of a number of attributes.

When analysis was begun on the Medicine Crow pottery, one interesting tendency became apparent early in the organizing process. The pottery fragments from vessels, called *potsherds*, that were found in component C (the earliest component) fell readily into distinct type categories. Potsherds from the component B sample were less easily

segregated, and potsherds from the most recent group, component A, almost defied clear classification into discrete type categories. This progressive reduction of the tendency of attributes to cluster consistently and create clearly defined types demanded an explanation.

Because of the presence of European trade goods in all three components, the archaeologists first thought that contact with incoming Europeans during the eighteenth century might have led to a breakdown in design tradition, but this answer seemed too vague to be acceptable. A computer was therefore used to help determine the nature and degree of reduction in attribute clustering. The material for computer analysis had to be prepared, and a card, punched according to a code that listed all attributes belonging to each class, was completed for each potsherd. For example, one class included every possible cross-sectional shape of a pot rim, and another class consisted of every design placed on the rim of a pot.

The descriptive code for the pottery was developed through a process of actually describing each potsherd. Each time a new attribute was discovered, it was added to the class to which it properly belonged. The pottery from each component was thus described potsherd by potsherd—one card for each vessel. About 2,000 potsherds were excavated from all three components, and they had been distributed almost equally among the three. A program was then prepared for the computer in order to determine the percentage of times any given attribute occurred with any other attribute in the entire sample from each component. Once all the material had been processed, it was easy to state, for example, that 37 percent of all cord-impressed rims in component A pottery samples occurred in conjunction with an outflaring lip on the vessel.

Distribution graphs were then prepared for each component, showing the degree of association between all attributes of all

potsherds in each component. Close examination of these graphs confirmed what attempts at typological sorting had previously suggested. Beginning with the earliest component C material and progressing to the latest component A material, there was a strong, steady reduction in the degree to which attributes tended to combine with one another in a patterned way. In component C, there were numerous attributes that were associated one with another 100 percent of the time. But the component A material was characterized by a virtually random mode of distribution, with the probability of a given attribute occurring with any other attribute in any other class being almost equal.

After the computer confirmed the suspected trend in attribute association, it was necessary to seek some cultural explanation of this change. After all, the combination of any set of attributes on a given piece of pottery is, in the final analysis, a product of a set of decisions made by the potter—who, among the Arikara and all other agricultural Indians of this time period in North America, was female. If the potter used the same patterns repeatedly, her products would be similar. If she changed the attributes she used from one pot to another, the expected result would be a more random mode of attribute combination.

The progressive reduction in house size from component C through component A seemed to indicate a change in the size of the social unit, and it seemed likely that this reduction might be related in some way to the observed and recorded change in attribute patterning of the pottery. Accordingly, a study was made of the historically recorded changes in Arikara culture, particularly in the area of social organization.

GENERALIZATION ABOUT LIFE WAYS
The earlier Arikara, residing in northern Nebraska before they moved into South Dakota, were probably organized along much the same lines as their nearest relatives, the

Pawnee. The Pawnee had *matrilocal extended families*, which lived together in large earth-covered lodges. Such families consist of a set of related females—grandmothers, mothers, and daughters—residing under the same roof who, upon marriage, bring their husbands to live with them. Ethnographic studies have demonstrated that matrilocality is a common institution in some parts of the world among sedentary, relatively permanent farming societies in which females are the primary participants in subsistence activities. And the contents of deep refuse deposits found on Arikara sites in Nebraska indicate permanent occupation of these sites over periods of perhaps several centuries. One reason for the length and permanence of settlement was the abundance of timber in the area, which satisfied all possible needs for firewood, lodge construction, and the manufacture of various implements.

When the Arikara left their Pawnee neighbors and moved north along the Missouri River, however, they entered a somewhat different environment that was characterized by a less plentiful supply of wood. Early explorers have recorded that the Arikara, residing along the middle portion of the Missouri River in South Dakota, were forced to move their villages at five- to ten-year intervals because of the depletion of wood. Continual movement of this nature tends to disrupt the pattern of matrilocality. Thus, the Arikara probably developed a somewhat different form of social organization later in the eighteenth century.

Encroachments by European settlers caused a second disruptive change. During the increasing trade in horses and guns between such nomadic groups as the Dakota Sioux, Blackfeet, Cheyenne, Arapaho, and Crow during the eighteenth and nineteenth centuries, the Arikara, along with other river village groups, acted as middlemen—horses from the south went to groups in the north in exchange for the guns that were flowing south. As middlemen, they became involved

Figure 12. Reconstruction of life at the site. Through his careful analysis of artifacts and other material remains, the archaeologist has contributed to our understanding of the nonmaterial aspects of this past way of life.

in a set of activities quite new to them, activities that gave more emphasis to the role of the male in the society. The shift from male-to-female and female-to-male roles is thought to work against consistent matrilocal residence. Warfare also contributed to this breakdown. Because they were middlemen in the horse and gun trade, the Arikara found themselves in conflict with their surrounding nomadic neighbors as well as with European settlers in the area.

A fourth factor was disease of European origin. A smallpox epidemic decimated the Arikara population during the eighteenth century. Under the conditions of extreme depopulation, matrilocality tends to break down rapidly and the mode of residence after marriage becomes primarily a matter of expedience rather than cultural tradition.

Given all these factors, a strong case can be made for a collapse of a consistent matrilocal residence and co-resident extended families. This breakdown would appear to be reflected quite strongly in the progressive reduction in house size evidenced at the Medicine Crow site. The larger lodges probably housed fragments of the matrilocal extended families, whereas the smaller houses apparently sheltered only nuclear family units—the husband, the wife, and their children.

What factors, then, affected the potter's choice of designs? In a society organized around consistent matrilocality and having female potters, the fairly large group of women living together in each matrilocal extended family would be strongly inclined to maintain a consistent set of designs that would differ to a considerable extent from other design configurations produced by the women of other matrilocal extended families. However, a breakdown of these family units and a greater mobility of women between what had earlier been matrilocal extended families could easily correspond to a weakening in the degree of coherence in pottery design: the now more mobile women could mix with one another and bring to-

gether the designs of their various families. This is precisely the pattern seen at Medicine Crow.

The archaeologists were thus able to see a directional and marked change in the nature of attribute patterning in pottery of the females of a given culture. And they deduced that the breakdown occurred at a time when marked changes were taking place in the social organization of the same people. This study concentrated on only two aspects of the total material culture recovered from the Medicine Crow site—the lodges and the pottery—but similar questions can be asked of other portions of the assemblage, whether it be chipped stone, bone tools, or whatever. The important point is that there are *patterns of culture*, patterns that can be used in tracing the developments and changes in the behavior of its possessors.

Because artifacts are the products of patterned behavior, it follows that the patterning exhibited by the Medicine Crow artifacts is a reflection of the patterning of the behavior that led to their production. This consideration is basic to all archaeological inference, for it provides the vehicle by which statements can be made concerning the intangible aspects of the culture. No one has ever unearthed a religious belief or a political system. Yet archaeologists do excavate objects that hold, in the patterning of the attributes, a reflection of nonmaterial aspects of the culture producing them. It is through the delineation of these linkages between the material and nonmaterial aspects that the archaeologist contributes to the larger task of the anthropologist: that of understanding the ways of mankind. One has only to look at the immense store of literature produced by archaeologists over the past half century to realize that meaningful and important insights are gradually being gained into the immense timespan occupied by men before us. And the future holds promise for even greater and more precise understanding of our total culture history.

Case Study: Primates in the Field

5

A significant number of primatologists—students of the zoological order of man and his relatives—are beginning to observe monkeys in the tropical forest habitat, the regions popularly but incorrectly known as jungles. The largest expanses of intact virgin forest are found in Central America and South America, and some sixty species of monkeys inhabit them. Although these New World monkeys are not closely related to man, they offer some interesting perspectives on specific evolutionary issues.

The first comprehensive study of primates in their natural setting was made in the early 1930s by C. R. Carpenter, who observed a population of howler monkeys that had been isolated on an island formed by the construction of the Panama Canal. Despite this excellent start, recent field research has centered on Old World monkeys and apes, particularly the terrestrial or semiterrestrial variety. One reason for this one-sided emphasis has been the relative remoteness of the New World monkeys from man's lineage. Another reason lies in the difficult working and observational conditions in tropical forests. Some of these

unique obstacles are described in the following account of a project carried out by an anthropologist and his wife, Lewis and Dorothy Klein, who went to Colombia, South America, to study spider monkeys.

FORMULATION OF RESEARCH OBJECTIVES
The spider monkey, one of the largest of the South American primates, had been observed briefly in its natural habitat by Carpenter in Panama and by J. Eisenberg and H. O. Wagner in different parts of Mexico. The reports of these investigators were conflicting and posed some interesting viewpoints. It was on the basis of these reports that the anthropologist formulated certain questions about the social life of the spider monkey that he believed could be answered by a longer study in a different location. What, for example, was the precise nature of the spider monkey's social group—were there "insiders" and "outsiders" or just shifting alliances of temporarily compatible individuals? What did these animals eat, and did they compete for food on an overt or covert level with members of the same species or with other kinds of monkeys, mammals, birds, or even

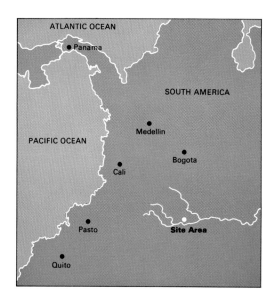

insets? What was their sexual and reproductive life like—were there breeding seasons, were sexual relations free and open or restrictive and secretive, and were the animals promiscuous, monogamous, or bigamous? Who cared for the infants and for how long, and at what age did they become independent travelers and eaters? How did the animals keep in contact with one another in this typically dense habitat—were unique vocal, visual, or olfactory signals used? And were specific signals used by specific age-sex classes in specific adaptive contexts—sexual, aggressive, parental, and territorial defense? How far did the animals travel in a day, a month, or a year? Did males and females travel over the same areas, and were their ranges related in any obvious way to weather conditions, food supply, and the presence or absence of enemies?

Other unanswered questions about the spider monkey concerned the unique anatomical characteristics of these animals. Of all the New World monkeys, only the spider monkeys possess shoulders and forelimbs that look and function like those of man and the apes. Their behavioral similarities to gibbons and young orangutans and chimpanzees are especially pronounced. But spider monkeys are only remotely related to man and the apes, for their genetic divergence probably occurred about 50 million years ago. What pattern of selective forces had oriented the ancestors of the spider monkey in a direction similar to our own? Were they the same forces that may have affected our own zoological family? The anthropologist could not hope to find direct answers to these questions, but he could find evidence for and against the several possibilities. As a start, he intended to note the manner and frequency of the movement of the monkey's

forelimbs and, in particular, whether they were used independently of the hind limbs to support the animal's weight beneath the branches.

The prehensile tail of the spider monkey was another source of curiosity. The anthropologist planned to obtain precise and accurate descriptions of the manner and situations in which this tail was used and then to compile rough frequency data for each of its functions. He and his wife planned to compare the spider monkeys with other primates in the forest—the howler, wooley, and capuchin monkeys, which also have prehensile tails, and the squirrel, owl, and titi monkeys, which do not. Not only would this comparison facilitate the process of describing and analyzing uniquely patterned behavioral activities and rhythms, but competitive advantages between types of monkeys could be assessed on the basis of ecological preferences.

FINDING THE MONKEYS

The initial task was to look over possible study sites and to locate, count, and determine sex and probable age of all spider monkeys and any other primates, mammals, or birds encountered. The first two months in the field were disappointing and frustrating. The field workers began by surveying specific areas recommended by Colombian and American citizens and scholars, but most of these sites were unsuitable for this project because all were relatively accessible to man. The sites were relict forests, contained and limited by frequent fires and felling. The extent to which individuals or groups of primates would range in their daily and yearly activities—which was one of the anthropologist's main questions—was more likely to be limited by the size of the forests than by the monkey's own behavioral inclinations. Moreover, population density and competitive interrelationships were being affected by several factors that had not been a part of the evolutionary past of the New World primates but had been introduced recently by man.

Figure 2 (left). The location of the study site in Colombia, South America. Figure 3 (right). One of the critical factors rarely mentioned in reports on anthropological field work is the securing of adequate transportation into remote regions. A good portion of the funds for this project had to be allocated for travel and thus affected the researchers' choice of the study site.

Several of the most promising places that were surveyed in the early and rainy months were eliminated because of the unassailable evidence that animal and forest destruction had been going on in the past and was obviously going to continue. Although the researchers observed six types of primates in these small, partially destroyed forests, they did not see any spider monkeys.

They realized that if their study was going to be successful, they would have to leave as far behind as possible the amenities of even a frontier town. They had heard about an area called La Macarena, which the Colombian government was attempting to set aside as a forest reserve. Through some well-timed assistance from a Colombian professor, they were able to contact the head of the national bureau responsible for park administration, and after presenting their credentials and a plan of the work, they received permission to enter the park boundaries as well as a generous offer of transportation assistance. This trip turned out to be another frustrating event, for the promised transportation turned out to be sick or unbroken mules or broken outboard motors. During this sojourn, the researchers spent twenty-one days waiting for transportation and about four days doing what they had come to do: looking for and at monkeys. Besides, the more accessible areas of the projected park were undergoing colonization, and the only source of nourishment and cash for the colonizers was what the forest could provide—and a good portion of that was monkeys.

The anthropologist and his wife later visited a southern section of the projected park that was still relatively untouched by colonists because of the presence of rapids upstream and downstream on the Rio Guayabero. When they arrived, one large Indian family and several Indians living with them were the only inhabitants on the park side for about a hundred miles along the river. Here the anthropologist and his wife encountered many spider monkeys as well as other primates, undoubtedly owing to the fact that,

with the exception of the Indians' twenty-five-acre clearing, the entire area was virgin forest. The time spent waiting for the government boat to pick them up (which, incidentally, it never did) was put to profitable use. The researchers negotiated and traded for a boat, selected and hired a boatman-mechanic, and began to adjust to the usual Indian menu of fish, dried tapir, and an occasional paca or peccary, invariably accompanied by manioc or cassava. In time, most of these items became the basis of their own diet.

For the next three months, surveying progressed smoothly. The purchase of an outboard motor and boat required all the funds the researchers had available for travel, however, and they now had to find a suitable study site within or near the southern portions of the projected forest reserve.

METHODS OF SURVEY
During the survey, the anthropologist and his wife used three complementary procedures. First, they made long daily treks from either a base camp or a point on a river or creek leading directly into the forest, following natural landmarks or a consistent compass

direction for as long as the terrain would permit them to do so. Moving and fleeing animals could often be spotted because the researchers could hear and see systematically rebounding and shaking branches as far away as 100 yards. Nevertheless, it was almost impossible to keep fleeing spider monkeys in sight for more than five minutes at a time.

The second procedure was to spend rest periods beneath large fruiting trees, especially those with signs of having been visited recently by monkeys. Dropped and partially eaten fruit, particularly those with tooth impressions, as well as fresh feces were useful indicators. During this period, the desire of the researchers to settle down to work was paradoxically hampered by another desire. Guides with first-hand knowledge of local terrain and of fruiting patterns were nonexistent because these areas had not yet been traveled by humans, and the local inhabitants' knowledge of forest and game habits appeared to come largely from forest exploitation. This meant turning away from inhabited regions.

The third survey procedure made use of a characteristic behavioral trait of spider monkeys. These primates, particularly the males and relatively isolated adult females, will frequently respond to a human imitation of one of a series of loud calls the animals make at irregular intervals throughout the day. The researchers divided these sounds into three overlapping categories: wails, whoops, and screams. Although not as impressive as the sustained roars made by howler monkeys, these sounds do carry over a considerable distance—about one-half mile—and in the depths of a gloomy forest their abruptness is, if not awe inspiring, at least attention getting.

The researchers' ability to elicit wails, whoops, or screams provided evidence that spider monkeys were in the area, but the sounds gave few clues about the number of monkeys present. Frequently, however, these auditory responses enabled the field workers

to visually locate the animals shortly afterward. With the exception of the howler monkeys, the spider monkeys were the only primates whose vocalizations could be heard for some distance in these forests. The calls of the squirrel monkey and brown capuchin monkey, for example, are not loud, but these animals actively forage for food in relatively compact groups and they were thus easier to locate. These two species differed from spider monkeys, whose activity cycle, as the field workers were to find out later, is much more likely to consist of spurts of eating followed by a rest period before the animals travel on to another eating location.

This second period of surveying was quite rewarding. The anthropologist and his wife were encountering numbers of monkeys and other animals, and the exhilaration of exploring unmapped and uncharted areas—perhaps where no one had ever ventured—filled them with a spirit of adventure. At times they even became a bit reckless. One evening, the anthropologist began following a wild ground bird through the forest and neglected to take a compass reading. He quickly became lost and, after being charged by a tapir in near-darkness, rapidly gave up hope of getting back to camp that night. His first night alone in the forest with virtually nothing but four cigarettes was an interesting, if not restful, experience. The two young guides for that trip assumed that he had been eaten by an anaconda or a jaguar and in all earnestness informed his wife of the likelihood of his untimely departure. When he appeared at the camp the next morning, they at first suspected that he might be an apparition emerging from the forest depths to lure them to some awful fate, rather than being the person they had been looking for.

Gasoline, shoes, and food were the only material problems, in that order of seriousness. The anthropologist would allow no hunting and no firearms. Throughout their stay, the researchers depended on the rivers and creeks for fish. Shoes wore out at the unexpected rate of one pair every two weeks,

Figure 4 (above). The spider monkey shares its habitat with several other species, including capuchin monkeys *(Cebus apella)*, shown here. One aspect of the foraging habits of *Cebus apella* is somewhat unique—they characteristically seek out and break apart rotting branches in search of insects. Figure 5 (below). All New World monkeys are primarily arboreal, spending little time on the ground. The howler and spider monkeys (left) use their tails as a fifth "limb," which none of the Old World monkeys can do. Not all New World monkeys have prehensile tails. The squirrel monkey (right) can use its tail for balancing and for gathering tactile information but not for grasping.

due in part to the humidity. Much of the researchers' surveying was spent wading, and on one occasion they spent four hours in the water at chest level, walking and swimming and trying to keep their binoculars dry. Gasoline was expensive and often scarce. Much of it had to be flown in and then transported in their boat in either sixteen- or fifty-five-gallon drums. On one excursion, after fulfilling an urge to go just past the next and yet the next river bend, the researchers had to float and paddle downstream for two days. It was a beautiful and informative way to spend a weekend.

OBSERVATIONS IN THE FIELD
The surveying established that spider monkeys could be found almost everywhere along the left bank of the Rio Guayabero between the two rapids and on both sides of the La Cabra tributary, probably as far upstream as it was forested. One of the most exciting encounters, however, occurred near a large oxbow lake called Laguna Tigre, about thirty minutes by motor boat from the maloca of their frequent host Vicente, a Kuripáko Indian.

At Laguna Tigre, the two researchers had been the fascinated recipients of an impressive thirty-minute vocal and visual display of some formidable monkey growling, ear-ringing barking, and a great deal of leaping about and frenzied arm-scratching. It was a team effort. The females initiated and maintained the aggressive display until they were reinforced by five newly arrived, freshly bounding, leaping males, who covered for the disturbed perpetrators and their juvenile followers until they had safely drifted away. The intensity of their hostility was matched by the extent of the researchers' pleasure. This incident helped them decide to choose Laguna Tigre as their study site. They also decided to construct a more permanent camp close by.

Some of the problems the field workers had encountered during the survey period remained with them, in that they still had to locate, count, and classify. Now, however, they also wanted to let the monkeys become accustomed to their presence so that they could follow and observe them for long uninterrupted periods. This turned out to be easier than they had expected, for soon after their house was built, the fruit of several large fig trees nearby ripened. These trees were quite tall—about 125 to 150 feet high—and the two field workers were able to sit quietly under them while several animals were feeding. If the researchers arrived early enough, spider monkeys would enter the canopy above their heads and display only slight signs of disturbance.

The feeding went on for about three weeks as the fruit of several trees within 300 yards of each other matured. Thereafter, the anthropologist and his wife attempted to follow individual monkeys when the animals left the trees in which they had been feeding or resting. In doing so, the researchers evoked negative responses from only some of the animals—probably those in the group that had not originally fed in the trees close to the campsite. Yet within a short time, even most of the complainers allowed the researchers to follow as closely as forty feet beneath them as they traveled, ate, slept, or rested. The researchers eventually found that a noisy rather than a stealthy approach was most effective, and from then on they tried to make a virtue of clumsiness. The monkeys were much less likely to flee when forewarned.

During the day, if the Kleins had been able to follow a group of spider monkeys to their daily-changed sleeping sites, the problem of finding the monkeys the next morning was simplified. If the site was not very close to one of the better trails, however, the researchers had to find their way in the dark and, at the same time, make a new trail that would be conspicuous enough to be picked up before dawn by flashlight. On several occasions, they were unable to retrace their steps of the previous night before sunrise, and one night they were unable to find their

Figure 6. *Cebus apella* foraging. The researchers found that, unlike the spider monkey, *Cebus apella* rarely will use its tail to stretch across gaps between trees, although both species will wrap their tails around a branch and hang down from it to reach fruit that is suspended below.

way back as they kept marching into and out of the same swamp. That night, the researchers eventually just quit trying and slept on the damp forest floor rather than continuing through a maze of aerial roots, deep puddles, and long shadows. The nocturnal mosquitoes picnicked on them all night long.

When the field workers were unable to follow or locate spider monkeys preparing to sleep, they usually located the animals by marching along machete-made trails, which came to parallel the arboreal ones, and by scrutinizing the trees that the monkeys were likely to be feeding on or that they frequently used for daytime resting and socializing. Being able to elicit their calls by imitation still proved to be helpful. On most days, contact was made within two or three hours. The exceptions—days in which eight or twelve hours of searching yielded nothing—were much less frequent toward the end of the study than at the beginning, but they did occur even then. A collective change in the area in which the monkeys ranged and an associated shift of arboreal routes were often the cause.

Bad weather could also be blamed. Rain and flooding made certain trails impassable; rainfall also made it difficult to look upward, particularly with binoculars. Perhaps the most serious impairment of bad weather was the deleterious effect it had upon the ability to hear monkey calls and the sounds of moving vegetation, cues that the researchers had come to rely upon. Continuous heavy rain had the additional effect of depressing the activity level of the spider monkeys.

The daily routine soon settled into a pattern determined primarily by the monkeys themselves. Whenever possible, the researchers tried to get to the monkeys soon after dawn and follow them until dusk, unless the monkeys had led their observers into an unfamiliar area. In that event, the researchers usually turned back an hour or two before darkness, allowing themselves enough time to find their way while marking a new trail. The researchers usually spent between three

and four hours lying under various trees, occasionally changing positions in order to secure a better view as the monkeys fed, groomed, rested, or played.

When the monkeys remained in a single tree or a cluster of trees, the field workers recorded all they could see and hear of their feeding and social behavior, including facial expressions, vocalizations, spatial distances, patterns of interaction, and the results of these behavioral activities. Certain types of frequently occurring acts were recorded and timed in detail when the opportunity arose; for example, the number of ripe as well as unripe fruit eaten in a five-minute period and the frequency with which food was plucked by hand relative to the number of times it was taken directly by mouth. When no social interaction could be observed, the researchers concentrated on other types of problems, including what function the monkey's prehensile tail served. Did the monkeys secure themselves with their tails when resting, did its position vary with the thickness and shape of the tree limb they were on, and could its use be correlated with the force of any wind blowing?

The amount of behavior that could be observed and recorded was more limited when the animals were traveling. It took all of the researchers' energy and attention to keep the animals from moving out of sight, particularly when they were following the usual small party. If the paths of the monkeys being observed crossed with those of other moving monkeys, the researchers had to make a superhuman effort or be very lucky to avoid losing them. When they could not locate the monkeys by calls or in the areas where they had recently been seen, the researchers had to walk the entire area where

monkeys had been encountered in the past month. If this tactic still did not lead the researchers to them, they would sit in a strategic spot with a good vantage point of a major crossroads the spider monkeys often used to get from one area to another. With luck and patience, the researchers would see or hear their subjects again and be able to follow them until the monkeys stopped for the night to sleep.

By now, the field workers had become familiar with individual spider monkeys and had named them after certain physical characteristics (for instance, Heavily-Furred, White-Crest, and Two-Dot), attributed personality traits (Pitiful Juvenile and El Diablo), or status (His Mother). They timed individual and group activity, noting who kept company with whom, when, and what they were doing. They noted every detail possible in order to piece together a relatively complete picture of the life of a spider monkey, unhindered in its natural habitat.

Inevitably, there were some interruptions in the daily routine. Of those attributable to the forest, only the grunting, tooth-gnashing peccaries could be considered serious. On several occasions, the researchers had to take to the trees to avoid meeting large groups head-on. Before they could climb down, the monkeys they had been watching had usually moved away, leaving the treed

field workers far behind. Jaguars were seen or heard several times but cost the researchers only one morning of fretful caution. However, all the forest creatures—even those that bit, stung, interfered with, or occasionally even scared them—proved to be interesting and frequently beautiful subjects.

INITIAL ANALYSIS OF DATA

Because this field work has been completed only recently, the anthropologist is still analyzing the data his investigations have yielded. He is beginning to arrive at answers to his research questions, but it must be emphasized that the data presented here are still quite tentative.

One tentative conclusion relates to the nature of the spider monkey's social group. Defining the basic unit of the spider monkey's social organization was initially one of the most difficult problems, and it was several months before the outlines of a solution started to emerge. In brief, the researchers discovered that there were shifting, temporary associations or alliances that were formed daily or weekly. These smaller, shifting subgroups formed from the large groups of more-or-less permanently compatible animals that came together (within 100 to 200 yards of each other) less than 1 percent of the total observation time—collected at all times of the day and night and totaling about 700 hours. Members of these large, compatible groups (on the order of twenty to twenty-five animals) did not associate peacefully with the members of similar groups of spider monkeys that occasionally used some of the same trees for feeding, resting, and sleeping.

The researchers also found that the spider monkeys they observed were almost exclusively frugivorous. The major food sources of these animals were also sought after by many types of birds as well as by one or more of the other types of monkeys. Nevertheless, the spider monkeys were by far the most dependent upon ripe fruit and perhaps were the most specialized in their ability to obtain it. Their relative advantage was in their uniquely patterned eating and resting habits in combination with a flexible social organization. The spider monkeys were not too concerned with the mature leaves, unripe fruit, insects, and spiders eaten by some of the other species of monkey. Another finding was that spider monkeys are much more likely to eat peacefully in the same tree alongside other types of monkeys than alongside spider monkeys belonging to other groups.

Complete and culminated sexual encounters were rarely seen. All copulations observed took place in relative isolation. The females were approached by males rather than the reverse. Both copulation and birth occurred any time of the year, however, in contrast to at least two other types of monkey species, whose reproductive activities were seasonal.

Another conclusion was that infants were cared for exclusively by their mothers. They clung to their mothers' body until they were more than two months old. After this time, they might move briefly onto the bodies of other spider monkeys that were alongside the mothers or venture independently onto the vegetation a few feet away. This limited degree of independence lasted until they were about six months old. Almost from the moment of birth, the infants were a source of curiosity for most of the other monkeys in the group and were approached, touched, and groomed by animals the mother did not actively avoid. After six months, they began to be carried less frequently and were more likely to be moving around independently but within ten or twenty feet from their mothers. They continued to be carried between difficult tree crossings until they were about one year old and perhaps older. The custom of extending locomotor assistance at difficult tree crossings was occasionally performed even between adults.

Juveniles continued to nurse from their mothers and follow them closely and persistently for approximately two years, although

by that time the juveniles were no longer carried about. Females gave birth once every two years and in some instances only once every three years. Infants began eating solid foods when they were about three months old but were not eating substantial amounts until they were at least six months old. Differences in feeding habits between infants and adults probably continued until the animals were three years old.

Spider monkeys kept in contact with one another through vocal and olfactory signals in combination with the noises and visual stimuli created by their movement through the branches. Olfaction appeared to play a relatively important role in intergroup conflict and sexual behavior, and vocalizations played an important part in all contexts except sexual behavior. Visual and tactile information and soft grunts, pants, and chuckles

Figure 9 (above). This photograph clearly shows the remarkable limb adaptation of the spider monkey. It is one of the few primates that can stretch both tail and forelimbs directly above its head. Figure 10 (below left). The flat, widely spaced nostrils of this spider monkey mark it as a platyrrhine. Figure 11 (below right). One of the important ecological factors influencing the adaptative habits of all arboreal neotropical primates —the monkey-eating harpy eagle.

played a somewhat more important role in communicating and coordinating the activities between intimately associated individuals, such as mother and infant.

Over the course of a year, individual spider monkeys moved about in the arboreal canopy in an area of a little more than one square mile without ever coming to the ground. On any given day, individuals might travel as much as one mile or as little as 200 or 300 yards. Weather had some effect on their ranging habits, in that bad weather reduced some activities, including the amount of time spent moving about.

The amount of food available affected group movement and choice of arboreal trails. But the spider monkey home range was large and usually included similar vegetational areas in several parts of it, so extreme changes in range could not be attributed to this factor alone. Nevertheless, food sources were extremely important insofar as they affected the seasonal ranging patterns of bordering groups of spider monkeys and subsequent social conflicts.

Males and females tended to move about in different manners. The males were more likely to approach other groups of spider monkeys and threaten them visually and vocally. They were also more likely to follow isolated females or small groups of females belonging to other groups and were more likely to travel between separated subgroups of the females associated with their own groups on a more permanent basis. It should be stressed that the differences between females and males in ranging habits were quantitative rather than qualitative. Nonpregnant, nonlactating females were more like the males and more likely to follow or be followed by them than were pregnant females or the females caring for infants or young juveniles.

Until this study, reports on the use of the prehensile tail have suffered from a one-sided view based on observations of animals in captivity and very brief observations in the wild, usually as a concomitant of collect-

ing expeditions. In the normal course of activities in their natural habitat, spider monkeys do not use their tails to probe into
small fissures or to reach for or carry objects except when playing or in some unusual circumstances. Pet monkeys and zoo
monkeys, on the other hand, almost always
do so and learn this skill as a consequence of
being enclosed in a cage, restrained with
harnesses or collars, or faced with a large
pile of food in a single spot with many hands
grabbing for the food at the same time.

In the course of aggressive displays in the
natural habitat, the tail as well as the other
limbs may be used to shake branches or to
make bodily contact with a fighting ally. Occasionally a branch may break off during
these bursts of activity and then may be
grabbed by the tail and brandished in saber
or lasso fashion, but this uncommon event
was observed only a few times during this
project. The tails of the spider monkeys were
most frequently used in two contexts: feeding and locomotion. The prehensile tails of
Cebus apella and howler monkeys are used
for similar general purposes but with important differences in specific details. For example, *Cebus apella* monkeys use their tails for
feeding in two ways: they hang down from
their tails to reach fruit suspended below
and they secure themselves to a relatively
thick branch while stretching their bodies
out and over a much thinner branch. Unlike
the spider and howler monkeys, however,
Cebus apella monkeys rarely use their tails
to stretch across gaps between trees. On the
other hand, although both the howler and
spider monkeys used their tails for feeding
purposes in the manner described above for
the *Cebus apella*, the howler rarely used its
tail in combination with one of its forelimbs
in a suspended hanging-feeding posture as
did the spider monkey. Moreover, the howl-
ers were never seen to use their tails in the
regular and precisely coordinated manner in
which spider monkeys do in *brachiation*—a
form of movement performed with body
axes at right angles to the ground and the

body suspended beneath rather than being
held above the branches. This form of locomotion is normally performed only by some
of the tailless apes and the New World spider monkeys.

For long rests during the day, a spider
monkey usually selected a fork in the tree or
a thick major branch, and its exact location
within the tree depended on the time of day,
the type of weather, and the animal's current
social partner. Most often, a monkey took a
sitting position in which the tail was
wrapped around the animal's body rather
than a tree branch. In sunny and clear
weather, however, a monkey often rested in
a prone position, with hind limbs hanging
loosely and arms typically crossed in front of
or underneath the head. In this case, the
monkey's tail could take a variety of positions and was often shifted about; the tail
was stretched out behind the body, resting
upon rather than grasping the same branch
supporting it. When sunning, a monkey was
occasionally seen to stretch out on its back,
and once again the tail's position varied in
an unsystematic way. When the animal was
at rest in a sitting position on supports of six
inches to more than six feet in circumfer-
ence, the force of a blowing wind did not
necessarily mean the tail would invariably be
wrapped around supporting vegetation rather than the body.

When rest periods were very short, when
social activities were imminent or relatively
vigorous, or just before a spider monkey was
about to depart, the tail was used in a different fashion. In these contexts, it was obviously a locomotory intention, which reinforces the view that the main functions of a
prehensile tail are related to locomotion and
feeding rather than anchoring or manipulation. Perhaps these incorrect assumptions
are a reflection of the tense or unnatural
conditions under which spider monkeys had
been observed in the past, to anthropomor-
phisms attributable to a common human
fear of heights and unsteady supports, and to
an emphasis upon human tool use.

Case Study: In the Remote Village

6

Ethnographers, the anthropologists who observe first-hand the life ways of people, rarely describe their deeply personal experiences in gathering data in the field. Even when such personal aspects of field work have been basic to the success of their ventures, ethnographers tacitly avoid mentioning them in their reports of their work. In fact, the inexperienced ethnographer must often depend on passing remarks of his predecessors or on scant references to these matters in ethnographic prefaces. And yet, when the amateur turns professional, he, too, refrains from communicating his own problems of morale and rapport and his compromises between the ideal and the practical, for he may consider them to be reflections of weakness or incompetence. More respectable aspects of field experience—formal research procedures, health hazards, transportation facilities, necessary equipment—are often considered sufficient to satisfy the curious reader.

In the following case study, anthropologist Gerald Berreman analyzes his field research from a specific point of view. His analysis, which is delineated in the monograph *Behind Many Masks*, is an attempt to present the selected aspects that constitute the *human experience* of field work, and some of the implications of its being a human experience. It relates what happened, what the anthropologist did and why, and with what evident effect. As in all field work, the options open to him were often beyond his control and therefore the results were often unanticipated.

OBSERVERS AND THE OBSERVED

Upon reaching the field, every ethnographer must immediately account for himself among the people he intends to study. Only after he has identified himself and made his objectives known can he proceed in his efforts to understand and interpret their way of life. Both tasks involve the control and evaluation of impressions the ethnographer and his subjects convey to one another—impressions derived from observations and inferences about what people do and say both publicly and privately.

This particular research took place in the peasant village of Sirkanda, a close-knit and highly stratified society located in the lower Himalayas of northern India. Its inhabitants, like those of the entire lower Himalayan area from Kashmir through Nepal, are called Paharis, which means "of the mountains." At the time of the anthropologist's field work, the village was small, consisting of only 384

Figure 2 (below). General location of the village called Sirkanda, in the foothills of the Himalayas. Figure 3 (right). One of the land-owning agriculturalists of Sirkanda, a member of one of the high castes. Members of the low castes are primarily agricultural laborers and artisans, as typified by this musician (below right).

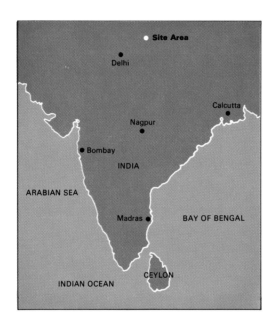

individuals. Situated as it was among rugged mountains, it was accessible only by foot and was nine miles from the nearest road or bus service.

The reluctance of Sirkanda villagers to accept outsiders was proverbial. Forestry officers who were required to make their rounds in the area claimed that a man is forced to carry his own food, water, and bedroll because he cannot get these necessities from the villagers. One teacher in the vicinity was forced to leave after a three-month stint because he and his proposed school were totally boycotted. Another teacher, himself a Pahari from a village only fifty miles away, confided that no one had talked with him or even inquired about what he was doing in the village after four months of residence. Community development and establishment of credit cooperatives, the two governmental programs operating in the area, had met with failure because of their sponsor's inability to establish rapport with the people.

The only way to avoid a negative reception from the Sirkanda villagers is to identify oneself as a member of a familiar group through kinship ties, caste ties, or community affiliation. Because the first two are ascribed characteristics, the only possibility a stranger has of being accepted is to establish residence and, through social interaction, to attain the status of a community dweller—a slow process, at best.

The reasons for the Paharis' reticence are easy to comprehend. Their relationships with outsiders had been confined primarily to contacts with policemen and tax collectors, who were hated and feared not only because of their unpopular duties but also because they demanded bribes and threatened to make trouble for the villagers if their demands were not met. Spheres of governmental responsibility had been greatly extended since the time India gained independence and the number of governmental officials had increased correspondingly. Any stranger might be a government agent and therefore annoying and potentially dangerous. The unjust exploitation by government agents was only one source of the Paharis' reticence, however. The villagers themselves carried on several illegal activities that could have been grounds for punishment or extortion. National forest lands and products were often appropriated illegally, taxable property was reported incorrectly, liquor was manufactured and sold illegally, women were sold, and guns were not licensed. These and other real and imagined infractions were regarded as likely reasons for a stranger's curiosity and were enough to discourage his presence in the area.

Non-Paharis consider the Paharis to be ritually, spiritually, and morally inferior. They are thought to be naïve hill people who practice witchcraft and evil magic. The Paharis, as one might expect, avoid associating with those who stereotype them in this manner. They are suspicious of outside traders who might attempt to take advantage of them, lawyers who might drag them into court, Brahmins from the outside who might discredit the orthodoxy of their beliefs, Christians who might try to impose their alien beliefs, and all potential women abductors or thieves. Any stranger might have ulterior motives, whether he be allied with the government or not.

Paharis are confident that an individual is no threat to them only when they know who he is and where he fits into their own social system. He is then subject to local controls, and if he violates or betrays a trust he can be held responsible. That such access to this society and interaction with its suspicious members is difficult for an outsider is an understatement.

This closed society is rigidly stratified into a number of hereditary, ranked, endogamous groups or castes consisting of two large elements: the high or twice-born castes and the low or untouchable castes. The high castes, Rajputs and Brahmins, are land-owning agriculturalists who account for 90 percent of the population. They are superior economically, in that they possess most of the land and animals, whereas the other castes are dependent upon them for their livelihood. The high castes monopolize political power both traditionally and through official means of control. They are regarded as twice-born, and therefore ritually clean; all other castes are regarded as untouchable. In Sirkanda, as in most villages, Rajputs outnumber Brahmins and thus are dominant locally, but ritually and socially there is little distinction between them, and economically there is generally none.

Members of the low castes are, for the most part, artisans. Not only are they dependent upon the high castes for their livelihood but they are subject to their will in almost every way. Their relationship to the high castes ideally is one of respect and obedience, and this behavior is supposedly accepted paternalistically by the high castes. In practice, however, there is considerable tension in the relationship between the two groups. Within both castes, there are also nonhierarchical divisions that are based on kinship ties and informal factions. The com-

munity is thus divided within itself, and acceptance by one part of the community does not ensure acceptance by the entire community and may in fact preclude it.

HELLO: I AM YOUR ETHNOGRAPHER

It was this community that the anthropologist and his interpreter-assistant entered, unannounced, in September 1957. The interpreter-assistant accompanying the anthropologist was a young Brahmin, named Sharma, who had previously returned from a comparable research project carried out in another village. They brought a note of introduction from a non-Pahari wholesaler of a neighboring market town who for some time had been buying the surplus agricultural produce of the villagers. The note asked that the villagers treat the strangers as "our people" and extend proper hospitality to them. As it turned out, the wholesaler was not well regarded in the village, and it was in spite of his intercession rather than because of it that the ethnographers were able to reside in the village for a year. Moreover, the note was addressed to a high-caste man who proved to be one of the most disliked people in the village—the recent victor in a nine-year court battle brought against him by virtually the entire village. That this individual refused to welcome the anthropologist may well have been a fortuitous—albeit circuitous—move toward gaining the trust of the community.

The first three months of their stay in Sirkanda were almost wholly devoted to keeping house and attempting to establish rapport with the villagers—under totally frustrating circumstances. As revealed by later reports, the villagers first assumed that the new arrivals were missionaries, who were known in the area only by reputation. When the researchers failed to intercede in religious matters or to express amazement at local rituals, this suspiciousness gradually subsided. The anthropologist had purposefully avoided religion as a subject of conversation and had used Hindu rather than nonreligious greetings to avoid being identified as a missionary. He relied on agriculture for a polite and hopefully safe topic of conversation, but even agriculture was not necessarily a neutral subject to the villagers. The anthropologist was alternately suspected of being a government agent dispatched to reassess the land for tax purposes or to investigate the extent of land use in unauthorized areas.

As these fears were dissipated, others arose. Even the genealogical inquiries made by the anthropologist were one source of suspicion, for the villagers thought they might be preliminary to a military draft. There were constant hints about the schemes of foreign spies—a little-understood but greatly feared sort of villain. Almost four months passed before such overt suspicion substantially disappeared. Nevertheless, although some people had been convinced of the innocence of the anthropologist's motives fairly early, others remained dubious for the duration of his stay.

IF NOT ACCEPTANCE, TOLERANCE?

One incident some four months after the arrival of the field workers at Sirkanda proved to be decisive in quelling overt opposition to their village activities. The anthropologist and his assistant had succeeded in engaging the local Brahmin priest, previously a reluctant informer, in an amiable conversation. In the privacy of his own threshing platform, supposedly free from intrusion by his powerful Rajput caste fellows (who outnumbered his people thirty-to-one in the village), he agreed to discuss his family tree. He was no doubt encouraged by the anthropologist's growing rapport with the villagers and by an affinity with Sharma, the Brahmin interpreter. In the midst of the discussion, however, one of the most prominent and hostile of the Rajputs appeared— probably intentionally—and joined the group. Although the Brahmin immediately became self-conscious and untalkative, it was too late to conceal the subject of the discussion. The Rajput interrupted to ask why the

Figure 4. Because of Sirkanda's relative inaccessibility, ordinary village life has for the most part remained untouched by outside cultural influences. Below, a Pahari woman keeps house in the traditional manner.

Brahmin was telling the researchers such things and aggressively demanded to know what conceivable use the information could be to an American scholar. His implication was that the researchers had ulterior motives, and a satisfactory response was evidently demanded. Because the interview was obviously ended, and because a small crowd of onlookers had gathered, the anthropologist took the opportunity, for the first time, to explain his project fully. He gave his audience the following explanation.

Prior to 1947, India had been a nation of little consequence to the rest of the world. When the United States or any other country wanted to negotiate matters that concerned India, it dealt with British spokesmen. Indians were of little importance internationally because they were a subject people and they, in turn, had no need to know about the United States. After a long struggle, India achieved independence and became a nation of proud people who managed their own affairs and participated in international affairs, as in the United Nations, on equal footing with Great Britain and the United States. For the first time, Indians were their own spokesmen.

At this point, it became essential that Indians and Americans get to know one another, and India and the United States began to exchange hundreds of students. These American students, including the anthropologist, worked at mastering the Indian languages and wanted to learn about Indian social customs and behavior in order to understand them *fairly*—just as Indian students were similarly studying customs and behavior in the United States. He noted that Indian and American scholars had studied Indian cities and villages of the plains, but until then the Paharis had been neglected—even though they were the inhabitants of some of the richest, most beautiful, and historically and religiously most important parts of India. He emphasized that Paharis would take on increasing importance in the development of India and that if they were to accept such responsibility and also benefit from it, it was imperative that they become better understood by their fellow countrymen and the rest of the world. His research was explained as a small attempt to contribute to this understanding.

This well-devised speech did not bring the anthropologist instant acceptance as one of

Figure 5 (left). In the agriculturally based society of Sirkanda, most farm labor is still done by hand. Winnowing grain and weeding grain are two necessary but time-consuming activities. Figure 6 (right). The anthropologist's interpreter is shown distributing photographs, which proved to be one means of establishing rapport with the villagers.

the villagers, but the hostile Rajput challenger responded by extending an invitation to the researchers to visit his house at any time to discuss matters of interest to them. He even offered to supply the American with Pahari artifacts to take back with him to the United States. Although it might make a better story to ignore the real ending to this episode, the fact remains that he never did volunteer information beyond his appraisal of the weather, and the Brahmin—apparently shattered by the experiehce—was never again as informative as he had promised to be.

Nevertheless, the incident had one favorable result because of the context in which it took place. It occurred late enough in his stay so that the anthropologist and his interpreter were known by many people. No longer able to attribute their presence to a specific motive, the villagers were ready to believe a convincing case. They realized that the statement was put forth with genuine emotion and they recognized it as an appeal for their confidence and support in a task that they understood to be difficult and that the anthropologist obviously considered important. The anthropologist's explanation was a response to a challenge by a high-caste villager and he had accepted it gracefully.

Perhaps most importantly, the statement had placed the villagers in a position of accepting what was said or denying their own pride in themselves as people and as citizens. The speech was presented as a counteraction to Pahari feelings of inferiority relative to the non-Paharis, feelings that in large measure account for their general hostility. The challenging Rajput, an individual with an acute need for public recognition of his importance, gained some prominence by opposing the researcher's work and evidently gained more by evincing from him an explanation and then magnanimously accepting it.

The anthropologist remained an alien and was never able to feel that his presence in the village was genuinely desired, but after this incident he was treated with increasing tolerance. He was established as a resident of Sirkanda, and no one tried to make him leave. When strangers from other villages asked Sirkanda villagers about his identity, they were answered succinctly with the response, "He lives here."

Another gratifying incident occurred at an annual regional fair some eight months after the project had begun. The anthropologist was photographing a group of brightly dressed young women of various villages, with their consent, when a Brahmin man came up and demanded that they refuse to be photographed. An elderly and respected Rajput woman of Sirkanda who had observed the incident was obviously annoyed by the intervention, and she stepped to the middle of the group and asked that her photograph be taken as well. The anthropologist did so and his photography was in demand from then on. Whereas previously he had been limited to photographing scenery and posing children, he was now permitted to take photographs of ritual events as well as people of all castes and both sexes. Taking and distributing photographs eventually became a valuable means of establishing rapport.

The anthropologist employed other means of promoting good will. Because single men in the village were considered a general threat to womanhood—given Pahari morality—the wives and children of the anthropologist and his interpreter visited the village in an attempt to diminish fears over the anthropologist's intentions. Villagers were received at the ethnographer's home in Dehra Dun, the large town where the researchers' families normally resided. One of the most successful ways of attracting villagers to his village home was a battery radio, the first to operate in the area. Not only did it attract a regular audience, it became a local attraction for visiting friends and relatives.

To villagers' constant queries about why this particular area and village had been chosen for research, the anthropologist answered in terms of its relative accessibility as a hill region, the hospitality of Sirkanda people, the reputation Sirkanda had for being a "good village," and his own positive impression of it based on his acquaintance with several other similar villages. But the most satisfactory explanation was that his presence was largely attributable to fate. The villagers believe that every man has a predestined course in life, and it was simply the anthropologist's fate to visit Sirkanda. When the anthropologist gave an American coin to one villager, the recipient commented that of all American coins only one was destined to remain in Sirkanda and that was it—and similarly, that the anthropologist had come as a consequence of fate.

COMMUNICATION THROUGH RAPPORT
Once the villagers realized that the researchers intended to remain in Sirkanda and to associate with them, they subjected all of the researchers' claims regarding motive and status to investigation. Sharma's claim to Brahmin status was verified. Villagers inspected his home on their trips to town and they inquired about his family and their origins. His behavior was closely observed. Only when all the claims that could be checked proved accurate were the villagers apparently encouraged to believe the claims that could not be verified.

That their motives were no longer suspect did not mean that the researchers could learn what they wanted to know about the village. The villagers knew generally what the researchers wanted to know or what impressions they would like to have received. The newcomers were granted information not shared with other strangers but it was certainly less than what was shared among the villagers themselves. As was discovered later, the researchers were often given information considered appropriate for the ears of a plains Brahmin, as Sharma was. Facts were suppressed, and if they were discovered it was in spite of efforts to conceal them. Conversation with alienated individuals of low esteem often proved to be one source of otherwise unobtainable knowledge. For the most part, however, the informants were high-caste villagers who were intent on impressing the visitors with their near conformity to the standards of behavior of high-caste people from the plains. Most low-caste people were reticent before the visitors because one of the pair was a Brahmin and hence was associated with the high-caste villagers.

In the first three months of establishing rapport and generating trust, the anthropologist held countless discussions on the subject of the weather or something else suitably uninspiring. Although much useful ethnographic knowledge was obtained in the process, more accurate information was often acquired by observation rather than by verbal inquiry.

As his rapport with the villagers improved, the anthropologist found household tasks too time-consuming for optimal research. Unable

Figure 7. Above, the anthropologist's daughter with children of the village. Until his presence in the village was accepted, the people permitted the ethnographer to focus his camera only on suitably neutral subjects of children and scenery.

to find help in the village, he selected, as a third member of the group, a seventeen-year-old boy who was of low-caste plains origin but had lived in a neighboring hill region and was conversant with Pahari ways and language. Although the boy had little direct effect on relations with the adult villagers, his informal contacts with some of the younger villagers proved to be a research asset.

At this time of apparent promise for productive research, Sharma became ill and was unable to return to work in the village for some time. The anthropologist confided later to his colleagues that this news dropped his morale to its lowest point in the fifteen months of his field work—none of which he described as exhilarating. But more than one reason was responsible for this decline in morale. Being away from his family much of the time, the anthropologist was also anxious about the health of his eighteen-month-old child. And there was the strain of maintaining a household in town and doing research in an isolated village, as well as the continuously frustrating relations with petty officials who had the authority to cause numerous difficulties and delays. There was the lack of social contact beyond his family, employees, and the villagers with whom he worked, coupled with the impression that he was merely tolerated by those with whom he was living and working. Under such circumstances, research tends to become the driving principle and its progress assumes the greatest proportions in one's overall perspective. To lose Sharma, whose presence was deemed crucial to the success of the project, was understandably disheartening.

To wait for Sharma's recovery would have meant forgoing the best months for research, because his illness came at the onset of the winter slack season when people would have time to sit and talk for the first time since the anthropologist had arrived. Two months later, the spring harvest and planting season would begin and potential informants would be too occupied or too tired to engage in lengthy conversations. Because the anthropologist was dependent upon help with the language, he resolved to find a substitute who could work until Sharma recovered. Qualified individuals were scarce, and he employed the first prospect who appeared, despite some definite reservations. His new assistant differed from Sharma in three significant respects: age, religion, and experience. He was a middle-aged Muslim and a retired school teacher who had no familiarity with anthropological research, facts that proved to have advantages as well as disadvantages.

The new man was more easily guided in his work and interacted more directly with the villagers than did Sharma because he recognized his inexperience, accepted sugges-

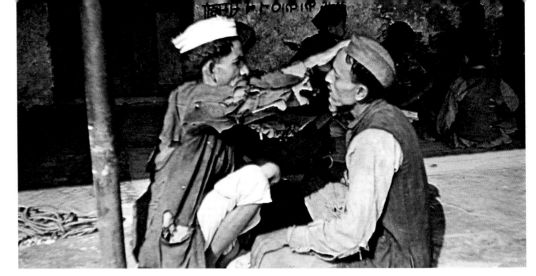

Figure 8. In time, the researcher gained the confidence and trust of many of the villagers when his sincerity became apparent to them, and he was given greater freedom in gathering accurate ethnographic data on the people and their life ways.

tions readily, and simply wanted to help the anthropologist communicate with the villagers rather than demonstrate his own efficiency as an interpreter. His age permitted him to receive a certain amount of respect. Because he was a Muslim, he was able to establish immediate rapport with the low castes, although not with the high castes. Most importantly, perhaps, he felt no involvement with the data. Whereas Sharma had been anxious to avoid presenting an unfavorable view of Hinduism to an American in this unorthodox Hindu village, his replacement was objective. Whereas Sharma had his own Brahmin status to maintain, the Muslim had no such status or obligation.

Because it was anticipated that Sharma would return to work after a few weeks, the anthropologist utilized his assistant in ways that capitalized on his advantages and minimized his deficiencies. He resolved to get as much general ethnographic data from the low castes as was possible and counted on Sharma's return for his original endeavor to procure information from the high castes. When it was apparent that Sharma could not return to the village, they were already beginning to get good ethnographic material with the prospect of much more to come. Moreover, not only was the new interpreter establishing excellent rapport with the low castes, he was also gaining confidence among some high-caste people.

The implications that the differences in status between the two assistants had held for the research were unanticipated. The villagers had determined that Sharma neither ate meat nor drank liquor, and as a result the anthropologist was hardly aware that the villagers ever did. When the villagers discovered that the new interpreter indulged in both and that the anthropologist could be induced to do so, it was brought to the anthropologist's attention for the first time that frequent meat and liquor gatherings, often of an intercaste nature, were held. When it became known that locally distilled liquor was occasionally served at the anthropologist's house, he was more often included in such informal parties, from which outsiders usually were rigidly excluded.

The Muslim's age removed from him the suspicion that Sharma had had to cope with regarding possible interest in local women. And his association with the anthropologist dispelled any lingering suspicions of missionary intent or government affiliation. But his most important characteristic was his religion, for as a Muslim he was, like the anthropologist, a ritually "polluted" individual, particularly because he was suspect of having eaten meat. Both he and the anthropologist were, for the most part, untouchables, although they commanded respect for their presumed wealth and knowledge.

These characteristics resulted in unusually good rapport with low-caste people, who were in many respects the most willing informants simply because they felt they had little status to protect in the eyes of outsiders. Rapport with high castes diminished little, apparently because it had been firmly established in advance via the Brahmin assistant, Sharma. Circumstances thus conspired to maximize research results by allying the ethnographer first with high-caste informants, then with low-caste informants. Each group provided essential information. Although neither group provided a well-rounded view of Pahari life, together they did provide such a view.

It is well known that no ethnography can be complete and objective. This case study emphasizes the fact that one universal source of bias is the social identity of the ethnographer relative to the population he studies. Some people will be his friends and informants—others will not. He must guard against systematic bias imposed by his identification with certain social strata, factions, or interest groups to the exclusion of others. The chance switch from a virtually "high-status" assistant to one virtually "impure" made this fact clear to the ethnographer in this instance to the lasting benefit of his ethnographic account.

Case Study: In a Complex Society

7 One way to learn what anthropologists do in complex societies is to consider the experience of ethnographers working in an American city. Here we shall deal with the experience of two anthropologists, Charles and Betty Lou Valentine. At this writing, they have been living for over a year within a predominantly Afro-American community in a large city of the northern United States. These ethnographers are husband and wife. The wife is Afro-American herself, and her husband is of Euro-American background. A two-year-old son completes their family and their field team.

FORMULATING THE RESEARCH PROBLEM
Two orientations guide the research being done by this family team. One is traditional anthropological interest in cultural differences and cultural change, and the other is contemporary concern about relations between social classes and ethnic groups. The immediate relevance of these scientific and human problems has commanded much attention, and the initial response has been a flurry of ideas about race, poverty, and ways

of life. The work described here is designed to test how sound and useful some of these emergent concepts are.

One widely accepted idea is that a "culture of poverty" exists. This phrase was coined by social scientists, popularized by political writers, and simplified and applied by government agencies and social service institutions. This concept is derived from the long-established theory that each social class has its own life style, plus the popular idea that people in the lowest strata are kept poor by their own behavior. And partly through the politically conditioned focus of antipoverty efforts in ghetto communities, belief in a poor man's culture that perpetuates poverty has been popularly associated with Afro-Americans. Despite some disclaimers from Oscar Lewis, the inventor of the phrase, the "culture of poverty" is now the conventional concept used in dealing with the Afro-American ghettos.

The two anthropologists represented here have long been skeptical of this intellectual notion and its practical applications. More than a decade of training, research, and

Figure 2. People flocking to the cities in search of adequate subsistence are forced to concentrate in overcrowded, substandard slum areas. Rapid urbanization is a major problem throughout the world, including Mexico (above), Brazil and Wales (middle), and Nationalist China. The Valentines are studying this process of change and its manifestations in social classes and ethnic groups in a large American city.

teaching in anthropology helped convince them that the issues had been decided prematurely. Living within or near black ghettos in several American cities, participating in the minority advancement movements of the 1950s and 1960s, and reading contemporary Afro-American literature from Ralph Ellison to Eldridge Cleaver reinforced their doubts, and the works often cited as proving that a poverty culture exists were unconvincing. Out of this background came a published critique of the poverty culture idea, entitled *Culture and Poverty: Critique and Counterproposals*, and a program for the research needed to test this and kindred notions.

Thorough ethnographic studies are required to discover and define scientifically any subcultures that may be peculiar to the poor or to ethnic segments of the poor. The two ethnographers thus formulated the research problem in terms of hypotheses that could be tested by ethnographic field work, hypotheses that include a series of specific propositions and alternatives representing patterns often ascribed to poverty culture— nonparticipation in conventional institutions, lack of commitment to middle-class values, disorganized and unstable families, and so on. The aim of the proposed field research was to gather data that would permit a reasoned choice between each hypothesis and its alternative or suggest a synthesis of opposing propositions.

The anthropologists chose to carry out their empirical testing in an Afro-American community because this ethnic group is most often viewed as following an extreme form of the poverty culture. They knew that the ethnographic approach of cultural anthropology had hardly been tested in such a setting; even recent studies employing so-called participant observation lack a crucial element of ethnography, in that the researchers did not live with the people they were studying. In the process of deciding where to do the work, it became apparent to them that they

might find not a culture of poverty but one or more ethnic subcultures derived from the unique Afro-American historic experience. This made it necessary to clarify the relationships between social strata such as the poor, ethnic groupings such as Afro-Americans, and the distinctive culture patterns possibly associated with either class or ethnic dimensions. The researchers concluded that class and ethnic differentiation are equally fundamental dimensions for cultural studies among poor people. Unlike poverty culture concepts, however, existing notions of Afro-American culture did not seem sufficiently well developed to permit formal hypotheses to be made prior to actual field work. This difficulty was later overcome to some extent when the research data led to hypotheses about ethnic cultural differentiation.

The lengthy process used to develop this research design is not typical. It is unusual to write a book setting forth rationale and methods for a research project before the work is done. Researchers rarely link their proposed work explicitly with value questions or political problems—these ethnographers specified that they were motivated not only by the scholar's scientific interest but also by the citizen's concern about the present crisis in American society. In their opinion, when anthropologists do express political values, most take established liberal positions. The two represented here make no secret of their convictions that massive redistributions of power and wealth are needed, that radical minority advancement movements are legitimate means to these ends, and that social scientists including anthropologists should contribute to raising the general level of political awareness. They intended that the scientific work be clearly related to policy issues and political problems from the beginning. They have encountered criticism from other anthropologists who seem to believe that this approach may compromise the scientific respectability of

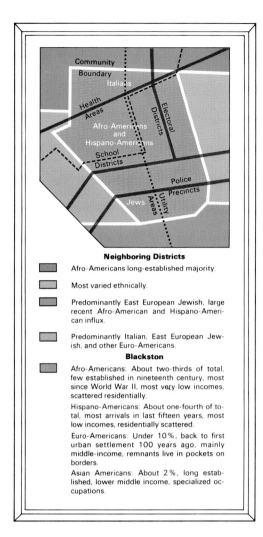

Figure 3. The community of Blackston, its neighboring districts, and externally imposed boundaries. Originally a Dutch and British farming village dating from the eighteenth century, Blackston was predominantly Jewish until after World War II and the influx of Afro-Americans, who now make up two-thirds of the total population of the area.

Neighboring Districts

Afro-Americans long-established majority.

Most varied ethnically.

Predominantly East European Jewish, large recent Afro-American and Hispano-American influx.

Predominantly Italian, East European Jewish, and other Euro-Americans.

Blackston

Afro-Americans: About two-thirds of total, few established in nineteenth century, most since World War II, most very low incomes, scattered residentially.

Hispano-Americans: About one-fourth of total, most arrivals in last fifteen years, most low incomes, residentially scattered.

Euro-Americans: Under 10%, back to first urban settlement 100 years ago, mainly middle-income, remnants live in pockets on borders.

Asian Americans: About 2%, long established, lower middle income, specialized occupations.

their work or perhaps alienate the sources of their research funds. These two researchers see no conflict between their outlook and objective scientific research. They do not profess to be "value-free social scientists"; they do not believe that any such creature exists. They do believe that sponsors and readers of a scientist's work are entitled to know his position on relevant value questions.

Many of their professional colleagues did look with disfavor on the project. Some felt it would be impossible for a white man or an interracial couple to live and work in a ghetto during this period of rising intergroup conflict; still others took the position that such work could not be objective. One prominent anthropologist proposed that Asian scientists be brought in to do the work because they would be less involved in controversial issues, and a famous senior colleague declared the project unworkable because objective research would be demeaning to the poor. Moreover, they were unable to secure conventional funding until after they had initiated the project on their own. Early in 1969,

however, they received a one-year grant from the National Institute of Mental Health (PHS research grant MH 16866–01).

The researchers had studied census data and other information on several potentially appropriate metropolitan areas and had tentatively chosen for their research site the community they call "Blackston" (see Figure 3). Two preliminary visits to Blackston enabled them to make local contacts and record impressions from walking through more than 150 of the 200 blocks in the community. This informal survey revealed a thoroughly deteriorated, poverty-stricken urban area, some sense of community among its largely Afro-American inhabitants, and interesting signs of cultural dynamism—including organized pressures for social change. They found not far away a health institution interested in knowing more about Blackston. This institution was willing to perform certain administrative functions and even to provide supplementary financial support once the ethnographers had been assured of basic funding for the work. On a third visit to Blackston they completed arrangements with this institution, and in July 1968 they rented a tenement apartment in a very poor block with a heavily Afro-American population.

PARTICIPATION IN COMMUNITY LIFE
From the first day in Blackston, these ethnographers have tried to study the community from within by experiencing directly the conditions and activities of life here. This began simply with the problem of being a new family on the block, asking for directions and information needed to establish a new household, and getting acquainted with new neighbors. Their son has been a great rapport builder, making human contacts with a toddler's ease and charming people all over Blackston. The fact that the leading member of the team is neither Afro-American nor Latin American did not hinder his acceptance in the community. Initially many

Table 1. Participation by Ethnographers in Community Life

Type of Activity	On the Block	In the Neighbor-hood	In the Community
Ritual kinship (becoming godparents)	x		
Preparation and interhousehold exchange of food	x		
Membership in the block association	x		
Providing art and recreational material for children	x		
Taking children on recreational trips	x		
Undergoing burglarization of own residence	x		
Neighborhood retailing (clothing, cosmetics, kitchenware)	x	x	
Volunteer work in public elementary school	x	x	
Active membership in neighborhood parent association	x	x	
Participation in community council local elections, activities	x	x	
Exchanging babysitting and informal child care services	x	x	
Informally exchanging goods and credit	x	x	
Celebrating life crises (christenings, weddings, funerals)	x	x	
Informal neighborhood entertainment and visits	x	x	
Accompanying people through relations with the welfare system	x	x	
Accompanying people through other services (legal aid, clinics)	x	x	
Accompanying individuals, families through hospitalization	x	x	x
Accompanying individuals, families through arrest, court, jail	x	x	x
Attending church services, religious rituals	x	x	x
Sharing celebrations of local and national holidays	x	x	x
Initiation into kin and associated networks	x	x	x
Attending demonstrations, public political events	x	x	x
Undergoing harassment by police	x	x	x
Sharing relations with local landlords, merchants, utilities companies	x	x	x
Providing auto transportation for individuals and groups	x	x	x
Social drinking, gambling, and miscellaneous leisure associations	x	x	x
Exchanging miscellaneous minor services	x	x	x
Explaining the project and making selected results available	x	x	x
Membership in credit union and consumer corporation		x	x
Occasional hospitality for temporarily homeless individuals		x	x
Participating in internal operations of community council			x
Participating in internal operations of a local school board			x
Participant observation of community-wide council elections			x
Acting as volunteer consultants to the community council			x
Acting as volunteer consultants to other community organizations			x

Source: Charles Valentine (1970).

people suspected that he was a bill collector or a government spy. There are militants here who distrust all whites on principle and believe that social scientists are categorically exploitative. With few exceptions these suspicions, hostilities, and accompanying stereotypes rapidly melted away.

The researchers have been careful to let the residents know they are anthropologists and what their purposes are, explaining all this whenever necessary. Acceptance has come not from explanations, however, but from people observing them as individuals and ethnographers. Blackstonians generally have found the anthropologists' role understandable and their activities consistent and predictable—seldom troublesome, and sometimes useful. They have found the anthropologists ready to function actively in as many community contexts as possible and ready to take part each day in the ongoing group

activities and individual affairs that make up the life of the community. Local social patterns were learned by living them rather than by any other approach. Some of the anthropologists' activities are summarized in Table 1. The one major community role that the researchers decline consistently is that of leaders or initiators, for this role would compromise their scientific purposes by making them more influencers than observers.

In an oppressed community, individual and group survival often depends on observing closely and judging shrewdly those with whom one interacts. This is a major reason why categorical prejudgments quickly gave way to realism in Blackstonians' reactions to anthropologists in their midst. Without always being aware of it, the ethnographers passed many large and small tests of performance to gain acceptance. Soon after they arrived, neighbors observed that toward the

Figure 4. Tensions between residents of Blackston and the police sometimes take the form of street altercations. Here, Afro-American and Hispano-American welfare mothers demand children's benefits. Figure 5 (right). Origins of Blackston ethnic groups.

end of the month the anthropologists' larder was occasionally as empty as theirs. They invited the anthropologists into the distributional networks that circulate occasional neighborhood windfalls of goods, and the anthropologists in turn contributed to this flow when they could. In situations of local public indignation—for instance, when there were mass protests against external authorities—the community knew that they observed the demonstrations from within the protesting ranks and received considerable harassment from the police as a result. Yet it was also known that they listened attentively and respectfully to community people who opposed the protests. When the anthropologists began to write about Blackston, local leaders and citizens of varied outlooks concluded that they were "telling it like it is" and thus performing a service for the community without compromising their independent integrity as scientists.

At first the ethnographers were observant participators, confining themselves mainly to watching and listening, but they can now make many more-or-less direct inquiries. Many people know them well enough to be comfortable with a sort of informal running interview. This rapport enables the researchers to explain much that they see and to learn much about what cannot be observed, such as past events. No one has yet turned them away in their systematic gathering of genealogical information, which involves probing intimate details of family history and which will eventually include full genealogies volunteered by many hundreds of individuals. Residents offer them their experiences and often their whole life stories in different ways. Some choose unstructured narrative and discussion, others prefer to speak directly into a tape recorder, and still others respond best to informal question-and-answer sessions. The researchers are frequently invited and seldom denied permission to record a great variety of events on film, on tape, or with written notes.

It has proved useful to rely on volunteered information, either in the form of social behavior freely enacted in the researchers' presence or spontaneous verbal testimony. Information becomes available simply by "hanging out" with people, being present when significant events occur, and making oneself available to the many individuals who like to talk. Every human encounter becomes grist for the ethnographer's mill, and most such encounters are within the normal processes of community life. Moving beyond this passive absorption of data is a necessary but delicate operation. Generally it turns out that probing questions are counterproductive unless clear, spontaneous signs from the people have already shown that they are open and ready for direct inquiries. Pushing questions on people can often arouse suspicions, hostilities, or plain discomfort that sharply reduce the flow of meaningful information. Ethnographic inquiry requires a delicate balance of getting as much information as possible from participatory observation, being alert to clues and leads to be stored away for later encounters, continually judging and rejudging individual and group sensitivities, and learning how to

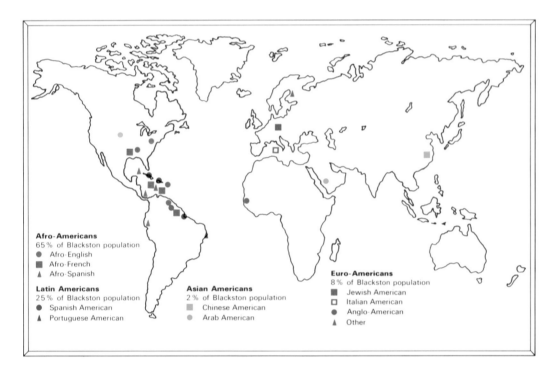

Afro-Americans
65% of Blackston population
- ● Afro-English
- ■ Afro-French
- ▲ Afro-Spanish

Latin Americans
25% of Blackston population
- ● Spanish American
- ▲ Portuguese American

Asian Americans
2% of Blackston population
- ■ Chinese American
- ● Arab American

Euro-Americans
8% of Blackston population
- ■ Jewish American
- □ Italian American
- ● Anglo-American
- ▲ Other

respect local canons of personal or collective privacy, while at the same time gaining access to important circles and networks. By continuously trying to live up to these rules, these ethnographers have found very few doors closed to them in Blackston.

These approaches were originally developed for work in the small, self-contained village or tribal communities traditionally studied by anthropologists. In Blackston, the same approaches are being applied in a community having more than 100,000 members of about a dozen major ethnic categories (Figure 5) with many subdivisions. In addition, many of the significant institutions in the community—schools, hospitals, police, courts, welfare, politics, commerce—are controlled by power centers outside Blackston. The scale of the community means that intensive methods must be applied to carefully selected ethnic segments, residential areas, institutional settings, and structural levels within the community to provide sample data representative of the whole, rather than attempting direct coverage of the entire community. The internal diversification means that the ethnographers must be prepared to recognize and define from six to fourteen different Afro-American subcultures, each interrelated with other subcultures of diverse origins. There is also a variety of class levels associated with differences in income, occupation, education, and the like. Not everyone living in Blackston is equally poor by any means. Although the majority of citizens are poor indeed, the community has one "middle-income" housing project within its

boundaries, and on its border stands a semi-luxury, private apartment complex occupied by many Afro-Americans.

The phenomenon of externally controlled institutions presents a special problem for community-based ethnographers. They need to gain entry to these institutional complexes to observe their workings from within, insofar as these workings affect the people of the community. After arduous work, the anthropologists in Blackston are just beginning to achieve some success in this regard by following their community friends into certain institutional settings such as clinics and a community council, and even by partial access formally granted for the explicit purpose of examining institutional processes such as those found in hospitals. All this requires enormous effort to overcome bureaucratic routine and resistance by noncommunity professionals. One outcome of all these problems of scale and complexity is that it takes much longer to comprehend the cultural life of a community such as Blackston than it does a small or relatively simple social unit. The ethnographers began by thinking that a year or two would be sufficient for their study; now four or five years of residence seem ideal.

There are many other ways in which anthropologists studying complex societies commonly deal with these same problems. One solution is to restrict research to small-scale phenomena such as kinship networks, leaving the larger institutional frameworks to other social sciences, as explicitly recommended by Max Gluckman and Fred Eggan in 1966. Another is to study a miniature social universe. In 1967, for example, Elliot Liebow reported on his work with a single associational network of black streetcorner men in Washington, Ulf Hannerz in 1969 wrote of his work within one residential block of the same city, and R. Lincoln Keiser in 1969 wrote of his studies of one Chicago fighting club, the Vice Lords.

Some anthropologists have tried to deal with larger populations by fielding bigger teams of research workers and combining or alternating formal, standardized questionnaire techniques with participant observation. This was done, for instance, by Alvin Wolfe and his associates in their study of St. Louis poor whites. Some go so far as to abandon observation altogether and rely entirely on questionnaire surveys, as in Norman Johnson and Peggy Sanday's work with the heterogeneous poor of Pittsburgh. The latter type of study, in particular, is considered by the two anthropologists in Blackston to be of little value in itself and only remotely relevant to the ethnographic study of culture. In their view, large impersonal research teams and questionnaire methods produce a spurious precision while sacrificing a great deal. Such approaches lose the intimate knowledge and direct experience made possible by participatory integration into the community, which is feasible only for a small, close-knit research group. On the other hand, microcosmic studies and partial ethnographies are too limited in scope to represent subcultures adequately. The Blackston ethnographers are attempting to stretch the resources of a family team to accomplish a full multicultural urban community study. Only prolonged residence in the field will tell how successful this attempt may be.

ANALYZING THE DATA
Discovering the social order of a community from within requires that information be analyzed and reanalyzed as it is accumulated during field work. Social and cultural patterns often are neither obvious nor easily verified. The anthropologist's understanding grows gradually through successive approximations and trial formulations worked out and revised, improved, or discarded as new evidence comes in. This continuous process goes on at many different levels and in relation to many aspects of the community being studied. Only a few such facets of the present tentative findings in Blackston can be mentioned here.

An arresting aspect of Blackston is its ethnic diversity. A casual visitor or even an uninvolved resident might see it as simply a Negro and Latin enclave, a black and Puerto Rican community in the terminology of local organizations. Some of the actual diversity of origins, language patterns, social histories, and cultural traditions represented here may be seen in Figure 5. In one year, the anthropologists have become acquainted with individuals and families belonging to at least nine culturally distinct Afro-American subgroups. These range from people born and reared in the northern urban United States to Afro-English speakers from the British West Indies, others whose native tongue is the Creolized English known as *Takitaki* spoken in Surinam, people from the A-B-C Islands (Aruba, Curaçao, and Bonaire) who speak a Creole Spanish called *Papiamento*, and native speakers of Haitian Creole French. Another four or five categories of Afro-Americans, including Louisiana Creoles and a small recent influx from West Africa, have been described to the ethnographers but have not yet been observed first-hand.

The anthropologists have had direct experience with seven additional national or cultural subgroupings apart from Afro-Americans. These include a large minority of Puerto Ricans, Jews of eastern European extraction (the dominant element in Blackston until perhaps fifteen years ago), Italian-Americans (still dominant in one peripheral section), Arabs, and Chinese. Other groups said to live in Blackston but not yet directly

Figure 6. Research has showed that Blackston is a culturally heterogeneous community. Here, friendship between black and Puerto Rican reaches across racial and ethnic lines.

known to the anthropologists include Portuguese speakers from Brazil and Spanish speakers from various parts of Central America and South America. The anthropologists' main interest in these people of European and Asian derivation is to compare them and study their relations with the community groups having African roots. With respect to the various Afro-American groupings, their interest is more direct and intensive. The anthropologists are working to determine how distinct the life styles of these groups are, what subcultural patterns they have in common, and whether a unified Afro-American or black culture is being synthesized under the shared conditions of white domination.

This part of the work is designed to test a series of hypotheses derived from the Blackston data and stimulated by the recent works of such authors as Hannerz, Bennett Berger, Robert Blauner, and William Stew-

art. One of these hypotheses is that each of the Afro-American groups is bicultural, meaning that its members grow up simultaneously learning two subcultures. The first is the special life style developed by the group through its own history from the African past and its exposure to various Euro-American social orders; and the second subculture encompasses the dominant patterns of mainstream American culture that are diffused throughout the United States and, to a lesser degree, the hemisphere and the world. The ethnographers look for evidence on whether and how each group differs from the others and from mainstream America. A range of differences emerges in such diverse cultural traits as dialect, music, food preferences, dress, adornment, political allegiance, and supernatural ideology.

Certainly many, probably most, and possibly all these subgroups are socially distinctive in ways varying from local ethnic social

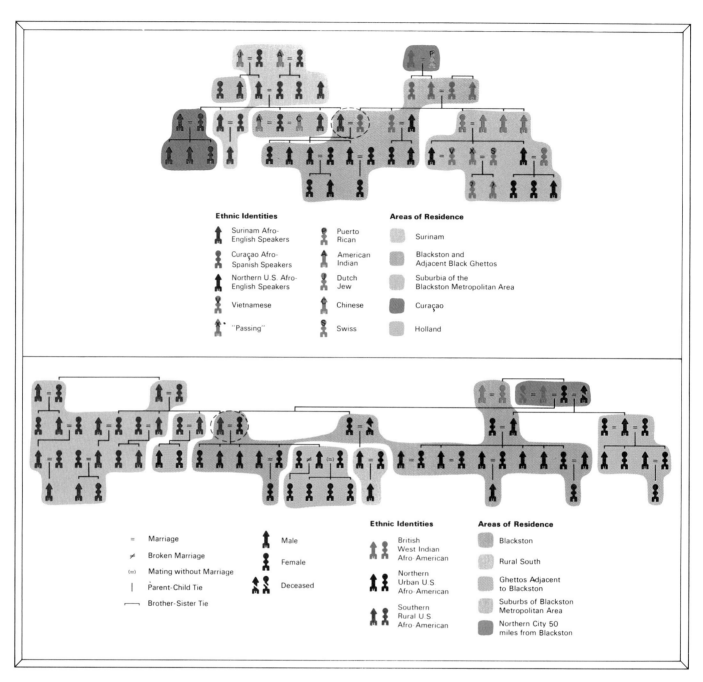

Ethnic Identities

Surinam Afro-
English Speakers

Curaçao Afro-
Spanish Speakers

Northern U.S. Afro-
English Speakers

Vietnamese

"Passing"

Puerto
Rican

American
Indian

Dutch
Jew

Chinese

Swiss

Areas of Residence

Surinam

Blackston and
Adjacent Black Ghettos

Suburbia of the
Blackston Metropolitan Area

Curaçao

Holland

= Marriage

≠ Broken Marriage

(=) Mating without Marriage

| Parent-Child Tie

⌐ Brother-Sister Tie

Male

Female

Deceased

Ethnic Identities

British
West Indian
Afro-American

Northern
Urban U.S.
Afro-American

Southern
Rural U.S.
Afro-American

Areas of Residence

Blackston

Rural South

Ghettos Adjacent
to Blackston

Suburbs of Blackston
Metropolitan Area

Northern City 50
miles from Blackston

clubs to current names for each ethnic category. The two anthropologists want to determine whether or not the contrasts among Afro-American subgroups are declining as black-white antagonisms develop and lead to increased growth of either black cultural nationalism or a revolutionary culture of protest, resistance, and Afro-American group self-assertion. Despite all the many expressions of subgroup parochialism, it is also true that Afro-Americans of many disparate backgrounds do work together effectively on community-wide problems such as education and health care. Thus far, the evidence is running heavily toward supporting all these

hypothetical suggestions on ethnic unity and diversity. Nevertheless, definite conclusions are not in order until much more evidence is gathered and the processes of time at least begin to work themselves out.

Some insight into these questions is already available through the interrelations among kinship or family relatedness, place of residence, and perceived or felt ethnic identity. Figure 7 illustrates the significant kin relations of only two Afro-American married couples who are long-standing residents of Blackston. Nevertheless, they typify structural features and social processes that appear to be widespread in the community.

Figure 7 (left). Kinship, residence, and ethnic groups in Blackston. Above, kin networks linked by a Surinam-Curaçao marriage; below, by a North-South marriage. Both of these marriages are indicated by dashed lines. Figure 8 (below right). Three generations live in this tenement, which is not heated in winter.

Contrary to recent studies in other ethnically diverse poverty areas, they exemplify the fact that within Blackston there is little residential segregation except with respect to the older minorities dominant in earlier years, the Italians and Jews. These two figures also portray the fact that a broad network of social contacts is maintained in spite of segregation and isolation from the wider society, which is also a real fact of life in Blackston.

Significant ethnic diversity can be seen to persist through the generations, resisting standardized influences from the wider society. Relatives living in suburbs not far from Blackston illustrate emerging extremes. The suburban sector depicted in Figure 7 includes a family that is trying to escape the whole ethnic dilemma by disappearing into white America. The one suburban domestic unit in Figure 7 is self-consciously black nationalist in the cultural sense, an allegiance conveyed by wearing Afro hair styles and dashikis, although the members of this household have very few positive relations with their kinsmen in the ghetto of Blackston. Also, immigration is continuing from some of the more exotic Afro-American areas, including Caribbean and Latin countries, and even some new sources of immigrants are apparently being established such as areas of Africa itself.

Nevertheless, the dominant trend at this point appears to be away from interests or allegiances that are narrowly parochial and toward some manifestation of Afro-American unification. In Figure 7 this development is illustrated by the increasing proportions of each succeeding generation that identify themselves as urban Afro-Americans, or perhaps simply as black people. A recent local event mirrored this kaleidoscope of ethnic diversity and unity. At a community celebration of African-American Day, 1969, the master of ceremonies made a special point of welcoming speakers of French and Spanish as well as Afro-English, whereas speechmak-

ers ranging from famous militants to anti-poverty functionaries emphasized and reemphasized the national and international unity of black people, indeed of all nonwhites. In general, the anthropologists are finding that *the most significant cultural similarities and differences of Blackston are associated with ethnic identity or racial status and not with class lines that would indicate a "culture of poverty."*

Another community facet—a favorite topic of those who generalize about the poor and about Negroes—is family life. A sample of Blackston findings in this area is presented in Figure 9. This information is derived from one very poor block inhabited by a higher proportion (77 percent) of Afro-Americans of various extractions than the community as a whole, but also including the homes of Spanish Caribbean, Arab, and European immigrants. From a total of sixty-two dwelling units, the anthropologists eliminate twelve lone individuals, mainly Puerto Ri-

Figure 9. Household structures in Blackston.
Shown are the major family types in a sample of
fifty dwelling units. Figure 10 (right). Such warm
father-child ties belie popular stereotypes of black
family life.

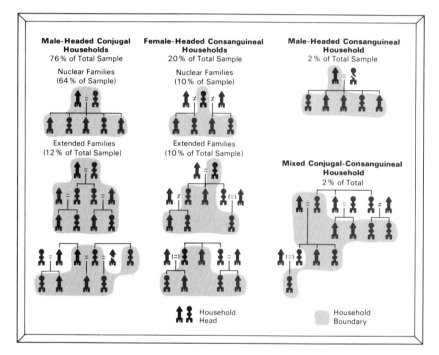

Male-Headed Conjugal Households
76% of Total Sample

Nuclear Families
(64% of Sample)

Extended Families
(12% of Total Sample)

Female-Headed Consanguineal Households
20% of Total Sample

Nuclear Families
(10% of Sample)

Extended Families
(10% of Total Sample)

Male-Headed Consanguineal Household
2% of Total Sample

Mixed Conjugal-Consanguineal Household
2% of Total

Household Head

Household Boundary

perhaps more variety of household organization than might be expected in a typical middle-class community, yet the anthropologists find little that has the quality of degraded or pathological instability so often invoked in the literature on the poor. Even in the husbandless and wifeless households, lines of authority remain reasonably clear, roles appropriate to the sexes and various age levels are communicated, and models for individual identification are found within the family or outside it, either among relatives or elsewhere. The data provide still less support for the popular notion that the Negro family is unstable. In the block that is represented by Figure 9, the multiracial total shows 76 percent of all families living as conventional male-headed households, but when the same calculation is made for Afro-American families alone the proportion rises to 83 percent. The proportion of married women is also higher for this particular ethnic group than for the polyglot block as a whole: among adult Afro-American females 80 percent are married, which leaves only 20 percent in the several categories of women who are single, widowed, divorced, or separated. Thus, the Afro-Americans appear to be closer than other groups to mainstream marital and family conventions. At present, the anthropologists have reason to believe that this sample is reasonably typical of Blackston as a whole. Again, however, it must be stipulated that this belief requires much further work before it can be fully substantiated.

Another favorite generalization of the "culture of poverty" school of thought is that, among poor people enmeshed in this alleged subculture, there is little or no social structure beyond the level of the family. Here again Blackston seems to refuse stubbornly to live up to the generalization and instead presents a complex of organizations. This community is full of local institutions, ranging from dozens of different churches through social clubs organized along ethnic

cans, so that Figure 9 presents information on fifty family households. The label *conjugal household* refers to domestic units in which the marital tie between husband and wife (father and mother) is the principal link holding the household together; that is, the conventional ideal basis for the family in American culture as a whole. As the charts show, more than three-quarters of the sample households are of this type. The minority (less than 25 percent) of families termed *consanguineal households* are those in which marriage is unimportant and blood ties are primary. These are structured differently because of the absence of spouses but are no less organized. The particular constellations of relatives shown in the diagrams illustrate real families, but of course they do not represent all the detailed variations that actually exist.

There is little in this picture to support the widespread idea that family life among the poor is chaotic and disorganized. There is

and other lines to a multiplicity of political organizations. Only a few of the major organizations competing for community-wide constituencies, as illustrated in Figure 11, can be discussed here.

The Blackston Community Council (BCC) is the only one of these organizations that originated locally, and it has a longer history than the others. With more than 100 affiliated groups within the community, BCC presently functions as the conduit for antipoverty funds from the federal Office of Economic Opportunity. As Figure 11 shows, BCC is sufficiently decentralized and democratic to be responsive to local citizen pressure. Yet at the same time it is dominated by external power centers and money sources extending from the metropolitan city hall to the government in Washington. One result of this interaction of forces is that BCC promotes and oversees various enterprises that are more-or-less ethnically exclusive, generally along a cleavage line between Afro-Americans and Hispano-Americans. At the same time, however, BCC is heavily committed to the cause of black and Puerto Rican unity in service of the community-wide interests of the poor.

The Model Cities Agency (MCA), not yet two years old, commands considerable leadership participation from Blackston because of the relatively great resources reportedly at its disposal. Despite the formation of committees to represent the local populace in decisions by MCA, the agency appears to function more as a massive assertion of city and federal power within the local community. The citizenry so far seems to have no real decisionmaking role and little reliable information on what is actually being decided. With this reassertion of metropolitan power centers backed by the federal government, rivalry between BCC and MCA is complex but often explicit and rancorous, reflecting both local factionalism and interagency conflict as far away as Washington. Among the semipublic accusations leveled at MCA is

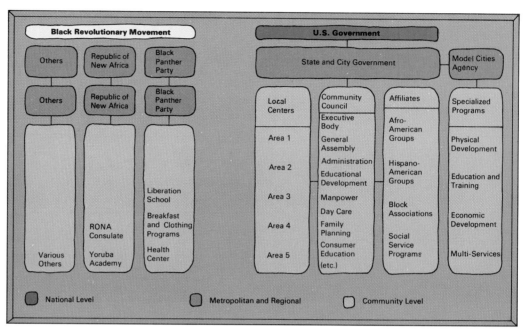

Black Revolutionary Movement				U.S. Government			
Others	Republic of New Africa	Black Panther Party		State and City Government			Model Cities Agency
Others	Republic of New Africa	Black Panther Party		Local Centers	Community Council	Affiliates	Specialized Programs
		Liberation School		Area 1	Executive Body	Afro-American Groups	
					General Assembly		Physical Development
				Area 2	Administration	Hispano-American Groups	
		Breakfast and Clothing Programs		Area 3	Educational Development		Education and Training
	RONA Consulate				Manpower	Block Associations	
				Area 4	Day Care		Economic Development
		Health Center			Family Planning	Social Service Programs	
Various Others	Yoruba Academy			Area 5	Consumer Education (etc.)		Multi-Services

■ National Level   ◉ Metropolitan and Regional   ▢ Community Level

that it is a patronage preserve for West Indians. Mutual influences between this agency and initiatives for local self-determination are further complicated by the fact that MCA's sphere of operations extends over two neighboring poverty districts that differ considerably from Blackston in ethnic composition, class structure, and other respects (see Figure 3, districts A and B).

Figure 11 also presents some of the nationalist and revolutionary organizations that maintain local Blackston operations within broader or nationwide structures. The Black Panther Party (BPP) presents itself as a community self-defense organization, although it is also providing social services that parallel or supplement those of the "establishment." The Republic of New Africa (RONA) sets as its goal no less than the creation of an independent, sovereign Afro-American nation with all the distinctive social, political, and cultural institutions that this formulation implies. The inherent opposition between these organizations and others in the community is symbolized by the appearance of BPP spokesmen at BCC public meetings to denounce the reigning leadership as Uncle Toms. Nevertheless, the BCC, the Panthers, RONA, and other local groups (but not MCA) have also worked in common causes against forces outside the community during such crises as a struggle for control of certain local public institutions. Despite considerable adverse publicity and outside opposition, the BPP has a great fund of good will in the community. RONA, on the other hand, is much less well known among the ordinary citizenry. Neither the Panthers nor RONA is associated locally with any suspi-

cion of domination by any single black ethnic group, beyond the assertion that both make in presenting themselves to the public as standing for black Americans as part of a world-wide revolutionary force. The central position of the Blackston Community Council in local affairs is illustrated by the fact that the African-American Day, 1969, ceremonies mentioned earlier were clearly controlled by BCC—Model Cities, the BPP, and RONA were neither represented on the program nor mentioned by any speaker on the platform. Whatever else may be said about this culturally and politically dynamic community, it is clear that Blackston will not fit into any stereotype of poor communities lacking organization beyond the family.

The organizations just discussed either depend on community involvement or at least recognize the existence of Blackston as a community. Other larger institutions that are more powerful and often more vital to the present life of the people do not even recognize Blackston's existence. This is symbolized in Figure 3, which shows that the territorial boundaries generally recognized by residents and largely observed officially by the Blackston Community Council are completely disregarded by major sources of outside power. Men in distant offices have fragmented the community into as many mutually inconsistent crazy quilts as the institutions they represent, dismembering Blackston and annexing the fragments to neighboring communities, some of which are only less gerrymandered than this one. All this creates a jumbled bureaucratic tangle that ordinary citizens can hardly penetrate, much less deal with effectively. More impor-

Figure 11. Selected organizations operating in Blackston at the national, metropolitan and regional, and community levels. Figure 12 (right). Degrees of local participation in major institutions of the wider society.

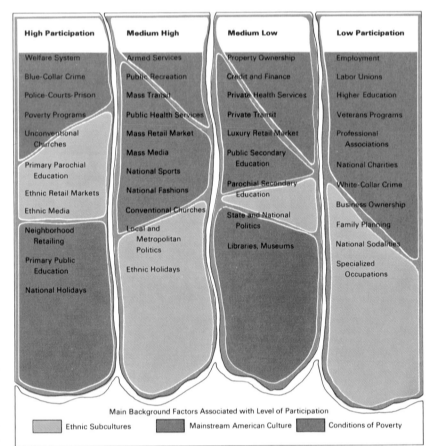

High Participation	Medium High	Medium Low	Low Participation
Welfare System	Armed Services	Property Ownership	Employment
Blue-Collar Crime	Public Recreation	Credit and Finance	Labor Unions
Police-Courts-Prison	Mass Transit	Private Health Services	Higher Education
Poverty Programs	Public Health Services	Private Transit	Veterans Programs
Unconventional Churches	Mass Retail Market	Luxury Retail Market	Professional Associations
Primary Parochial Education	Mass Media	Public Secondary Education	National Charities
Ethnic Retail Markets	National Sports	Parochial Secondary Education	White-Collar Crime
Ethnic Media	National Fashions	State and National Politics	Business Ownership
Neighborhood Retailing	Conventional Churches	Libraries, Museums	Family Planning
Primary Public Education	Local and Metropolitan Politics		National Sodalities
National Holidays	Ethnic Holidays		Specialized Occupations

Main Background Factors Associated with Level of Participation

☐ Ethnic Subcultures   ■ Mainstream American Culture   ■ Conditions of Poverty

tantly, it automatically splinters any attempt by the community as a whole or by community representatives to exert pressure on external agencies in favor of local interests. The anthropologists have observed many instances in which large and small community initiatives are stifled by the bureaucratic evasion that easily is substituted for the open exercise of power in such a structure.

Under conditions such as these, established by the metropolitan and national social structure, a major point commonly made about the poor must be reevaluated. This is the generalization that those who live by a "culture of poverty" fail to participate in major institutions of the wider society. Blackstonians' experiences with larger institutions are distinctive in some respects, but the anthropologists have found no evidence that this distinctiveness derives from any special subculture of the poor man. They believe that the patterns of local institutional participation are influenced by three main factors, indicated in Figure 12. As this chart makes clear, the majority of participation patterns are conditioned by the stark fact of people being poor. When occupations are limited and income is minimal for whatever reasons, people turn to the other available sources of sustenance: welfare, crime, poverty programs, and the peculiarly exploitative forms of credit and ownership open to the poor. At the same time, mainstream values of American culture are fully understood and receive such general allegiance that they are the main motivation for many highly popular activities. These range from home-based retailing of mass-consumption items to public education and cultural institutions open to the public, commercial offerings of the mass communication media, commercialized holidays, sports, and fashions. Ethnic subcultural identification plays a decisive role in the selection of ethnically tailored allegiances ranging from cultural and political group membership through religious affiliation to consumption patterns such as spe-

cialized food products, items for personal adornment, and the available media for artistic expression and enjoyment. Search as they will, the anthropologists have yet to find anything in all this dictated by a "culture of poverty."

Other intercultural relationships can also be seen from Figure 12. Certain institutional areas most influenced by ethnic subcultures are least conditioned by mainstream culture and vice versa. In other words, there is coexistence rather than competition or conflict between different cultural patterns in such spheres as commerce, communications media, holidays, and voluntary associations. The conclusion is emerging that some ethnic patterns survive and are perpetuated in the bicultural condition described earlier, partly because in these aspects of existence, people are allowed to follow two ways of life simultaneously rather than being forced to make a choice.

At the same time, there are three major areas of culture in which there is significant overlap between mainstream and ethnic patterns—religion, politics, and education—and here the anthropologists find intercultural accommodations of a different order. In some groups, ethnic traditions influence people toward participation in major institutions of the larger society, such as the alle-

giance of many Euro-Latins and Latin Americans to the Roman Catholic Church. More often, however, followers of ethnic subcultures are associated with religious bodies that are unconventional or exotic by dominant or mainstream standards. Among Blackston Afro-Americans, these include such traditional segregated denominations as the African Methodist Episcopal Church, various fundamentalist and Pentecostal store-front congregations, as well as the Nation of Islam ("Black Muslims"), the Moorish Science Temple, and the black Jews, some of whom trace their lineage through the West Indies to the Fallashas of Ethiopia and assert their ability to speak both Amharic and Hebraic.

Educational preferences often go hand in hand with religious affiliations because some of these faiths have their own parochial schools. Participation in dominant political processes is heavily influenced by subgroup membership through mechanisms ranging from the older, ethnically structured political machines to more recent forms of bloc voting and patronage promises. Thus, in the spheres of religion, education, and politics, the poles of biculturation do often present people with institutional choices. Yet the out-come is not generally the institutional non-participation suggested by descriptions of poverty culture. For Afro-Americans in particular, the pattern appears to be one of rather high participation in more-or-less ethnically distinct versions of mainstream institutions.

WRITING AND PUBLISHING
Prior to the present research, the anthropologists represented here accepted the traditional assumption that field work time should be devoted only to collecting information, recording it systematically, and composing preliminary analyses for their own use. Now, however, many considerations motivate them to write for publication while still gathering data. One of their first writing efforts was a field report, composed after only four months in the community and presented at the annual meeting of the American Anthropological Association. A typical Blackston citizen asked to read this paper and then made broad and intelligent comments on it, some of which were incorporated into a later version for publication. Subsequently, a number of publications were suggested in part by requests from Blackstonians as well as from institutions interested in Blackston. It has become apparent that even among local people not directly interested in the publications as such, most individuals emphasize the writing component in their understanding of the role of anthropologists. The two researchers have gradually come to feel that part of their function as participants in this community is to write about life here.

Some local people refer to this part of the researchers' work as "giving a voice" to Blackston. The anthropologists have taken care to emphasize the distinction between a "voice" that speaks with intellectual independence and insists on its own scientific integrity as compared with a "mouthpiece" that merely delivers the opinions of others or conveys images of others as they may

Figure 13 (left). By living and working in Blackston, the Valentines hope to bring about public recognition of the conditions faced by the poor in American society and to correct public and scholarly misconceptions about the behavior of the poor and its bases. Figure 14. Their research efforts point to a rich ethnic diversity and unity among the people here, a fact that will have important bearing on emergent concepts of race, poverty, and ways of life.

wish to appear. Community people have accepted this position, especially after reading the publications, deciding for themselves that they are objective and commenting that they describe "the bad as well as the good." The anthropologists do not believe that it is humanly possible for an ethnographer to be totally nonpartisan with respect to any people he studies intensively. Nor do they believe anyone can be genuinely neutral on the great social issues surrounding poverty and minority communities. Living in communities like Blackston has made them appreciate the old civil rights saying that there are no innocent bystanders and Cleaver's more recent epigram—that when you are not part of the solution, you are part of the problem. Carrying out research in such a community has also shown them that use of objective scientific methods and respect for factual evidence as a final determinant need not be inconsistent with these sympathies.

Writing during field work does create a conflict, however, in that it takes time away from the basic information-gathering work of research. This consideration inevitably adds to the length of time required for completing the research project, already a difficult problem in itself. On the other hand, the flood of diverse data that one experiences through intensive participation in a dynamic community within a complex society must be controlled to produce ordered results. One of the best ways to maintain intellectual control over this experience is by periodically ordering the material, relating it to theoretical ideas in systematic ways, and then communicating the resulting understandings to different audiences. This also gives researchers the important advantage of commentary and reactions from professional colleagues and other outsiders, as well as community members, against which their work may be evaluated as it develops. Altogether, the many aspects and outcomes of writing have further enriched the absorbing experience of living and working in Blackston.

THE EVOLUTION OF MAN III

Methods in Physical Anthropology

8 The intellect of an Einstein can encompass the universe and the mind of an idiot cannot comprehend his shoelaces, but the intellectual capacity of most people lies within a remarkably narrow range between these two extremes. In theory, every page of every novel could be written to equal the rhetoric in the best passages of, say, Leo Tolstoy's *War and Peace* or they could be so pointless or boring as to be unbearable, but the overwhelming majority of novels—and movies and plays and television programs, for that matter—lie somewhere between the best and the exceedingly inane.

Furthermore, just as the range of intellectual capacity is circumscribed, so too is physical ability. In the 1950s, for example, Roger Bannister broke the four-minute mile and, although several other runners quickly broke through the previously impassable barrier, the best have continued to stay within a few seconds of Bannister's time. In golf, where the measure of performance is equally precise, the leading professionals have been averaging scores in the high sixties ever since records were first kept. And in other sports too—in tennis or football or baseball—an occasional star may stand out but no superman has appeared, blessed with some favorable mutant genes that enable him to totally overwhelm the opposition.

In everyday living, different levels of human performance are dictated primarily by culture. People tend to behave and perform according to the standards set by their society, and to advance beyond those standards calls for a kind of intrinsic motivation and ability that few people possess. Nevertheless, the similarities in human performance, like the similarities between the physical appearance of parents and children, are closely related to biological—and especially genetic—composition. It is the genetic composition that dictates the physical structure of man, which is the principal concern of physical anthropology.

INDIVIDUAL VARIATION IN MAN

Every individual in the world is unique. No one has ever been born or ever will be born who is exactly like anyone else, dead or alive.

Figure 2. Expected progeny ratios for various matings that involve the gene controlling taste sensitivity to PTC. Shown to the right are the expected outcomes of a mating of double heterozygotes for two independent genes. (After Murray and Hirsch, in *Changing Perspectives in Mental Illness*. New York: Holt, Rinehart and Winston, 1969).

With the world population now over 3 billion and with the millions of humans that have died in the past, tremendous variation has already been expressed. Yet all this variation —together with what can be expected in the future—is but a fraction of the potential available in any given generation.

Every human begins life as a single cell weighing about one twenty-millionth of an ounce. This tiny bit of matter contains an individual's entire complement of *genes* and *chromosomes*, which are the basic units of inheritance. Encoded in the genes and chromosomes is a set of instructions that directs the development of a single cell into an adult consisting of trillions of cells, each containing an exact replica of the original genes and chromosomes.

Each human cell contains forty-six chromosomes and perhaps 100,000 genes. The chromosomes are threadlike bodies that occur in structurally similar (homologous) pairs in the cell nucleus, and in man there are twenty-three such pairs. The genes are located at specific positions on the chromosomes. Each gene has two or more alternative forms, called *alleles*, which represent differences in the chemical effects of the gene. Genes always work in pairs, in that two alleles of a particular gene (or two copies of the same allele) are located at corresponding positions or loci on the two homologues of a chromosome pair. The combination of alleles present at a particular locus determines the effect of that locus on the functioning of the cell.

Heredity and DNA

Chromosomes consist of three chemical substances: proteins, deoxyribonucleic acid (DNA), and ribonucleic acid (RNA). It is believed that DNA is the fundamental material of the genes. DNA is a highly stable substance but at the same time is capable of self-duplication; thus, it has the properties needed to control the development of the individual and the transmission of heredi-tary instructions from parent to offspring. The DNA molecule is composed of deoxyribose (a simple sugar), phosphate, and four kinds of nucleotide bases (adenine, guanine, thymine, and cytosine), linked together in extended chains. According to the Watson-Crick model, the chemical components of DNA are arranged in two long strands twined about each other in the form of a double helix. It is now known that the hereditary instructions carried by a gene are *coded* in the arrangement of adenine, guanine, thymine, and cytosine along the strands of the DNA molecule or molecules of which the gene is a part.

Genes exert their effects by regulating cellular processes that are involved in the growth and development of the organism and in the direct control of body functions. The most immediate effect of the genes is upon the synthesis of proteins in the ribosomes, which are tiny bodies in the cytoplasm, or outer portion of the cell. Chromosomal DNA never leaves the cell nucleus; it is thought that a special type of RNA, called *messenger* RNA, somehow takes on the code sequence of DNA and carries this information to the ribosomes, enabling them to fabricate a particular protein molecule. Depending on the types of proteins synthesized, a human may develop, say, either a normal or abnormal metabolism.

Genes are transmitted from parent to offspring by way of *gametes*, or sex cells that are produced in the testes and the ovaries. Gametes are formed by the splitting of somatic cells, a process known as *meiosis*. The essential result of meiosis is that each pair of chromosomes in a cell separates, and one member of each pair is drawn into each gamete, or daughter cell. Thus, human gametes contain twenty-three unpaired and nonhomologous chromosomes. Reproduction occurs when a female gamete (ovum) is fertilized by a male gamete (sperm) to form a single-celled *zygote*. In the zygote, two sets of unpaired chromosomes are combined to

Parents	Gametes			Expected Progeny Ratio	
				Genotypes	Phenotypes
TT × TT		T	T	all TT	All tasters
	T	TT	TT		
	T	TT	TT		
TT × Tt		T	t	1/2 TT:1/2 Tt	All tasters
	T	TT	Tt		
	T	TT	Tt		
TT × tt		t	t	all Tt	All tasters
	T	Tt	Tt		
	T	Tt	Tt		
Tt × Tt		T	t	1/4 TT:1/2 Tt: 1/4 tt	3/4 taster: 1/4 nontaster
	T	TT	Tt		
	t	Tt	tt		
Tt × tt		t	t	1/2 Tt:1/2 tt	1/2 taster: 1/2 nontaster
	T	Tt	Tt		
	t	tt	tt		
tt × tt		t	t	all tt	All nontasters
	t	tt	tt		
	t	tt	tt		

TtAa × TtAa	TA	Ta	tA	ta
TA	TTAA	TTAa	TtAA	TtAa
Ta	TTAa	TTaa	TtAa	Ttaa
tA	TtAA	TtAa	ttAA	ttAa
ta	TtAa	Ttaa	ttAa	ttaa

Expected Distribution of Genotypes
and Phenotypes, Assuming Dominance at Both Loci:

Pigmented Tasters		Albino Tasters		Pigmented Nontasters		Albino Nontasters
9 { 1 TTAA / 2 TTAa / 2 TtAA / 4 TtAa	:	3 { 1 TTaa / 2 Ttaa	:	3 { 1 ttAA / 2 ttAa	:	1 ttaa

form one set of paired chromosomes, one member of each pair being of maternal origin and one of paternal origin. In this way, each parent contributes 50 percent of his own hereditary instructions to each offspring.

Hidden Genetic Variability

No individual possesses all the traits that his genetic structure makes possible. The combination of genes creates what is known as the *genotype*—the genetic material that exists in the cell. But all this genetic or hereditary material will not be manifest in the individual. His actual structure is referred to as his *phenotype*, those characteristics that show up physically and can be measured.

Because the zygote receives a paired set of chromosomes—each parent contributing one member of each pair—it also receives a pair of alleles at each chromosomal locus. If homologues of a chromosome pair carry the same allele at a particular locus, the individual is said to be *homozygous* for that gene. If different alleles are received at a particular locus, the individual is said to be *heterozygous* for that gene.

A simplified example will make clear how this works. For the sake of illustration, let us assume that the ability to taste phenylthiocarbamide (PTC) is controlled by a single gene with two alleles, T and t, even though it is now known that this ability is determined by several genes. In this simplified example for heterozygotes of genotype Tt, the compound has a bitter taste in solution, whereas to homozygotes of genotype tt, it is tasteless. The fact that heterozygotes are phenotypically indistinguishable from TT homozygotes indicates that the activity of the T allele masks that of t, preventing the latter from expressing itself in heterozygous combination. Masking alleles are said to be *dominant* over the alleles whose effects they cover, whereas masked alleles are said to be *recessive*. For some genes, neither of two alleles is dominant, so that the heterozygote shows a

form of the trait that is approximately intermediate between the homozygous forms.

The fact that a gene can be present without expressing itself has important evolutionary implications, for natural selection and evolutionary forces act only on the phenotype, or on the traits that are manifest. A good deal of variation in the genes thus lies hidden and immune from selection. But the maintenance of genetic variability gives any species the potential to respond to future environmental demands.

In the above simplified example it has been noted that the two homologues of a chromosome pair segregate to different gametes during meiosis. Thus, an individual who is heterozygous for the taster gene (Tt) can produce two types of gametes with respect to that gene: gametes carrying the T allele and gametes carrying the t allele. A mating between two such heterozygotes (Tt × Tt) can produce offspring of three different genotypes—TT, Tt, and tt in the expected ratio 1:2:1—inasmuch as each parent will produce both types of gametes in equal numbers and these will combine randomly in the formation of zygotes. The expected ratio of tasters to nontasters among the offspring is 3:1. Notice that three-fourths of the offspring are expected to be phenotypically similar to their parents, whereas the remaining one-fourth (the homozygous recessive nontasters) are expected to differ from both parents. The expected ratios of genotypes and phenotypes among the offspring of other types of matings can be calculated by entering the types of gametes produced by male and female parents along separate axes of a 2×2 matrix and representing genotypes of the offspring by cells of the matrix. The expected outcomes of several types of matings are shown in Figure 2.

Laws of Inheritance

Observations of this sort on pea plants were the basis of Gregor Mendel's first law of inheritance, the *law of segregation*. Mendel

Interphase

Somatic Cell

Early Prophase I

Late Prophase I

Metaphase I

Early Anaphase

Telophase

Late Anaphase

Interphase

Figure 3 (far left). Each cell of the human body normally contains forty-six chromosomes, with twenty-three chromosomes from one parent paired with twenty-three from the other. The gametes (the sperm and ovum, or the sex cells) that combine in reproduction, however, must each have only half that number so that when they do combine they together will total forty-six chromosomes. The reduction in number takes place during *meiosis.* In this process each sex cell goes through two cycles of division, which gives rise to four gametes that each have twenty-three chromosomes. The illustration to the far left shows this remarkable sequence of events.

Only four chromosomes are shown in this illustration so that the sequence may be followed clearly. In advance of meiosis each chromosome duplicates itself, so that each goes through Division I as a pair of identical strands (called chromatids). These chromatids are still held closely together. Between Divisions I and II, the cells are in an interphase during which the chromosomes are scattered or unraveled throughout the nucleus, carrying out the living functions of the cell. In the prophase of Division I, the chromosomes contract and thicken. The centrioles begin to move toward the poles of the nucleus from which astral fibrils radiate, attaching themselves to each chromosome (remember that each is a *pair* of identical chromatids during this entire first cycle of division). In metaphase of Division I (lower far left), the chromosomes are grouped in the equatorial plane, each opposite its homologous chromosome. In this illustration the original four chromosomes have lined up as two pairs of chromosomes. Because each chromosome initially consisted of two chromatids, these pairs are really tetrads of four chromatids. In anaphase, one chromosome from each pair is drawn toward the centrioles. The telophase completes the division of the original sex cell into two cells, each having twenty-three chromosomes (or forty-six chromatids).

In Division II of the meiotic process, the two identical chromatids of each original chromosome are now separated. The two cells formed by the first division now become four cells, each having twenty-three chromosomes. These cells, which now consist of single chromatids, are the gametes. In fertilization, a male gamete and a female gamete will combine to form the zygote—the cell that is the beginning of human life.

Figure 4 (immediate left). This illustration shows the process of *mitosis,* which characterizes cell division in all cells except the gamete-producing sex cells. In mitosis, the forty-six chromosomes first replicate themselves so that each becomes a pair of identical chromatids. In cell division the chromatids are separated, with each becoming a chromosome. This division yields two cells with the normal forty-six chromosomes in each.

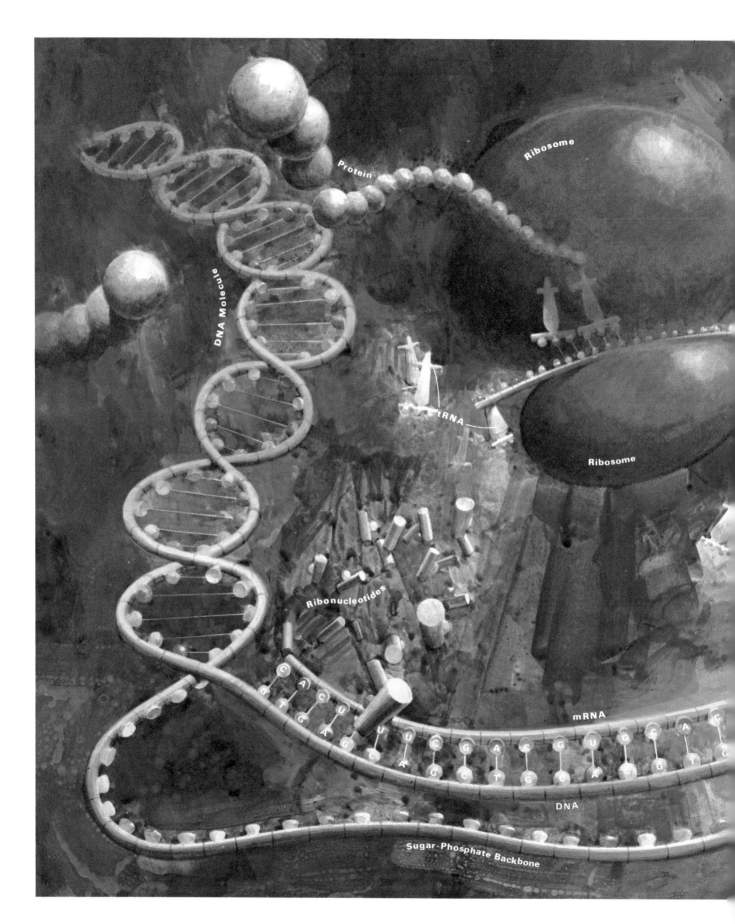

Protein

Ribosome

DNA Molecule

Ribosome

tRNA

Ribonucleotides

mRNA

C
A
G C
T G U
A C
U G U C G A C G U G G C A C
A G C T G G A U G T G

DNA

Sugar-Phosphate Backbone

Figure 5. DNA, the substance of which genes are made, is the repository of genetic information.

For man as well as for all other living organisms, the differences between genes can be attributed to differences in the sequence of nucleotides in the DNA molecule. All hereditary messages—including mutations—are represented by this sequence.

DNA is a long molecule consisting of two strands of nucleotides wound about each other into a double helix. Each strand is composed of alternating sugar (deoxyribose) and phosphate groups. Attached to each sugar is a base of which there are four types in DNA: adenine (A), cytosine (C), guanine (G), or thymine (T). How these bases appear sequentially along the sugar-phosphate backbone defines the genetic information that is expressed during protein synthesis. As indicated in the illustration, weak chemical bonds (hydrogen bonds) are formed between pairs of bases, and they hold together the two strands of DNA. Notice that A pairs only with T, and G only with C.

The expression of genetic information first requires partial unwinding of the DNA double helix, which exposes the bases. Small molecules called ribonucleotides are then strung together by an enzyme to form RNA, another long chain molecule that is very similar to the DNA molecule. RNA also contains a sugar-phosphate backbone with bases attached to each sugar group but the sugar is slightly different and another base, uracil (U), is employed instead of thymine even though it pairs exactly as thymine. Because of the rules of base pairing, the two strands of DNA are *complementary* to one another. When the information is "transcribed" from DNA to RNA, only one of the DNA strands is "read." The RNA molecule is complementary to this strand of DNA. It is called messenger RNA (mRNA) because it carries information (the sequence of bases) from the DNA to the ribosomes, the sites at which protein is synthesized.

Proteins are also long chain molecules. They contain twenty different types of subunits, which are called the amino acids. The sequence of bases in an mRNA molecule codes for the sequence of amino acids in a protein. This *translation* from the nucleic acid code into the protein code, carried out at the ribosomes, is done with the aid of transfer RNA (tRNA) molecules. One part of the tRNA molecule recognizes simultaneously three bases in the sequence of bases in mRNA; another part of the tRNA specifically recognizes the amino acid that is coded by these three bases. Thus tRNA actually does the translation, and the ribosome is more like a factory in which the translation is carried out. The ribosome moves along the mRNA chain, "reading" three bases at a time. For each of these triplets, a tRNA molecule carries an amino acid into the ribosome and attaches it to the end of a growing protein molecule. Finally, a special set of three bases tells the ribosome to stop linking amino acids and to release the completed protein molecule.

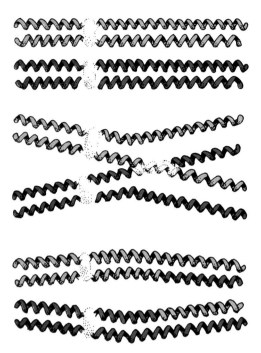

Figure 6. Chromosomal cross-over. This phenomenon occurs during meiosis, when the chromosomes are longitudinally entwined. Segments of each chromosome sometimes get tangled and they break away, with the segments attaching randomly to the broken ends. Cross-over can occur anywhere along the length of the chromosome. This means that the genes from the female chromatid can become part of the male chromatid, or vice versa, which in turn means there is a possibility for genotypic diversity.

postulated that each phenotypic trait of his pea plants was governed by a separate pair of "elements" that somehow divided and then recombined when a plant produced offspring. Geneticists now know that these elements are the allelic forms of genes and that meiotic cell division is the basis of their segregation.

Mendel's second law of inheritance, the *law of independent assortment*, describes the simultaneous inheritance of two or more traits. During meiosis, the segregation of homologous chromosomes to gametes occurs independently for each pair of chromosomes, so that all combinations consisting of one homologue from each chromosome pair are equally possible in the gametes. Thus, alleles located on separate chromosome pairs also segregate independently to gametes, and traits related to them combine independently in the offspring.

For example, an individual who is heterozygous for each of two genes located on different pairs of chromosomes (for example, TtAa) will produce four types of gametes with respect to the two genes, namely TA, Ta, tA, and ta. A mating between two double heterozygotes (represented by a 4×4 matrix) will produce offspring of nine different genotypes, as shown in Figure 2. If T and t are the alleles of the taster gene, and A and a are the alleles of the gene that produces albinism in man (AA and Aa individuals have normal pigmentation, and aas are albinos), the expected distribution of phenotypes is a 9:3:3:1 ratio of pigmented tasters, albino tasters, pigmented nontasters, and albino

nontasters. Note that seven-sixteenths, or nearly half, of the offspring are expected to be phenotypically different from both parents.

The phenomenon of independent assortment of chromosomes ensures genetic variability among members of a species, because it maximizes the number of genetically different gametes that can be produced by species members. A species with two pairs of chromosomes, Aa and Bb, will produce gametes containing four different combinations of homologues—AB, Ab, aB, and ab—whereas only two different types of gametes would be possible if the assortment of one chromosome pair was dependent on the other. A species with three pairs of chromosomes (Aa, Bb, and Cc) will produce eight types of gametes: ABC, ABc, AbC, Abc, aBC, aBc, abC, and abc, whereas four pairs of chromosomes will produce sixteen types of gametes.

In general, n pairs of chromosomes will produce 2^n kinds of gametes. Man, with twenty-three pairs of chromosomes, produces $2^{23} = 8,388,608$ types of gametes, with each type carrying a different set of homologues. Thus, when a set of parents has two offspring (other than identical twins), the probability that the second will have the same genotype as the first is $(\frac{1}{2}^{23})^2$, or less than one chance in 70 trillion. The probability that unrelated individuals will have the same genotype is effectively zero.

Actually, the possibilities for genetic variation are even greater than is suggested by the above examples. Instead of maintaining their integrity from generation to generation, as these examples might imply, chromosomes occasionally break, exchange parts, and then recombine during the course of meiosis—a process known as *crossing over*. This process permits the genes on a chromosome to segregate independently and thus increases immensely the potentialities for genotypic diversity. A second basis for increased variability is the fact that several alleles may exist for a given chromosomal locus rather than only two, as was assumed for the sake of simplicity in the previous discussion.

It thus becomes clear why individual differences are found in human populations. The hereditary mechanisms of segregation, independent assortment, and crossing over ensure that each human being is biologically unique from the moment of conception.

VARIATION AMONG POPULATIONS

When studying how the human species has evolved over time, the physical anthropologist is less interested in individual genotypes than in the *gene pool* of the entire species, the total collection of genes available to man. But when he studies races, he narrows his concern to genetic variations among various groups. Under natural conditions, two species are unable to interbreed or, if they do, may produce sterile offspring. Man, however, has remained one species. All human groups actually or potentially interbreed, adding variety through separation and recombination.

Population Genetics

The term *Mendelian population* refers to a community of interbreeding individuals that is reproductively isolated from other individuals of the same species. Thus, blacks in Rhodesia and whites in Rhodesia are two separate Mendelian populations, or isolated breeding units. Theodosius Dobzhansky has emphasized that a Mendelian population possesses a corporate genotype—its genetic structure—which, although clearly a function of the genetic composition of its individual members, nevertheless obeys its own laws of functioning, distinct from those that govern the genetics of individuals. These laws of genetic structure are the subject matter of *population genetics*, which studies relations between the distribution of genes and the distribution of individual differences in trait expressions in Mendelian populations. Of

particular importance are mechanisms responsible for change in gene distributions, because these underlie the process of Darwinian evolution in natural populations and provide a theoretical framework for analysis of the genetic correlates of individual differences in experimental populations.

Calculating Gene Frequency

The central concept of population genetics is that of the gene pool. If it is assumed that matings among members of a population occur on a purely random basis, then the formation of a zygote represents the random combination of two samples of alleles from the gene pool. Thus, if alleles A and a of a gene have relative frequencies p and q in the gene pool ($p + q = 1$), the proportions of AA, Aa, and aa genotypes in the population will be p^2, $2pq$, and q^2 respectively—the binomial expansion of $(p + q)^2$. Below are examples for calculating actual gene frequency.

In a population where $p = q$ ($p =$ frequency of A and $q =$ frequency of a),

AA	Aa	aa	Total Number of Genes
25	50	25	200

$$p = 25 \times 2 + 50 = \frac{100}{200} = 0.5$$
$$= \sqrt[2]{p} = \sqrt{0.25} = 0.5$$
$$q = 1 - p = 0.5$$

In a population where $p \neq q$,

AA	Aa	aa
16	48	36

$$p = 16 \times 2 + 48 = \frac{80}{200} = 0.4$$
$$= \sqrt[2]{p} = \sqrt{0.16} = 0.4$$
$$q = 1 - p = 0.6$$

As long as matings occur at random among these genotypes, the relative frequencies of both alleles and genotypes will remain constant in succeeding generations of the popu-

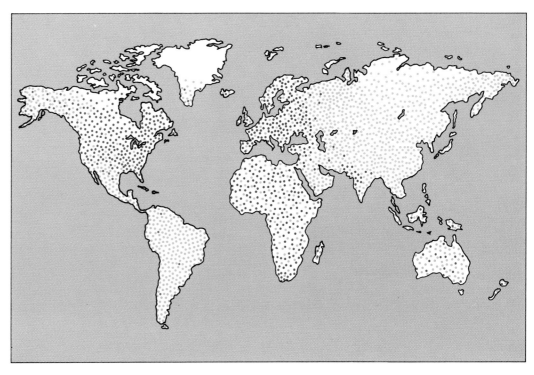

lation. This principle, known as the *Hardy-Weinberg law*, is a fundamental concept of population genetics because it specifies a baseline against which the effects of change-producing mechanisms can be evaluated.

Human races, then, are Mendelian populations that differ in the relative frequencies of various alleles in their gene pools. The fact that races are genetically different implies that behavioral differences might exist between them, just as morphological and physiological differences and differences in the behavior of races and strains in nonhuman species exist. However, in any discussion of race differences it is important to remember that populations, not individuals, are being described. The principles of genetic transmission ensure wide diversity *within* races; thus, particular individuals in one race may be phenotypically more similar to members of another race than to members of their own group. Also, it is quite possible that racial groups could obtain exactly the same average score on a particular trait while still differing in the degree of trait variability or the shape of the frequency distribution of trait scores.

Classifying Human Variation

The most clear-cut differences between human populations are those that are due to frequency differences for single gene traits. The blood groups are such traits. They have a simple mode of inheritance, are not affected by the environment, and do not change during the lifetime of the individual.

Although blood groups are not "racial markers," there are significant differences in their frequencies between some human populations that are indigenous to different geographic areas. For example, western European people are characteristically low in the frequency of the B gene of the ABO system and high in the Rh negative gene of the Rhesus system, whereas Oriental populations are high in the B gene and the Rh negative is in very low frequency or absent altogether. Because there are now a large number of known blood groups, any population can be typed and characterized on the basis of genes at many loci. As to why these differences exist, to date the answer is not clear. It can be hypothesized that now or at some period in the past, natural selection and genetic drift acted to establish these differences between populations. For example, the "sickle cell" trait, which is discussed in the chapter "Modern Man," is now known to have become established at a high frequency in some populations due to the action of natural selection.

Complex human traits such as personality, intelligence, and susceptibility to disease may have a heritable, polygenic basis. But such traits are strongly influenced by the environment (both cultural and physical) and their measurement is difficult, so there is presently no valid way to compare populations for these traits. It is likely that human groups that have been subjected to a given environmental stress for hundreds of generations have developed some appropriate bio-

Figure 7. Blood type distribution by the ABO system. (Red signifies A; green, B; blue, O.) Figure 8. To describe differences below the species level and levels of human groupings based on population differences in gene frequencies, human taxonomists identify *geographic races* (separated by major geographic barriers), *local races* (major breeding populations having partial social and geographic barriers to gene flow), and *microraces* (genetic differentiation in a larger population because of sheer density and the limitation that large numbers imposes on the geographic mobility of gene flow). (After Stanley Garn, *Human Races*. Springfield, Illinois: Charles C Thomas, Publisher, 1965.)

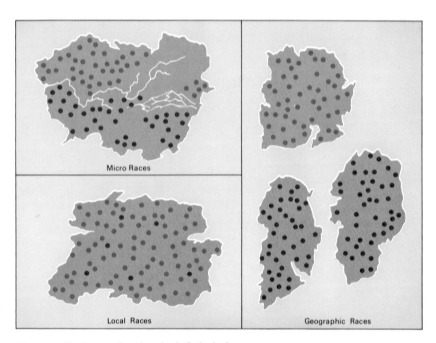

Micro Races

Local Races

Geographic Races

logical responses. Whether these are genetically based and therefore heritable or whether they develop during the growth and maturation period is generally not known. For example, from the anthropological point of view it seems highly unlikely that intelligence would vary in degree between existing populations. No culture is known that has a "simple" language. Different cultures elaborate different areas of their activity. Americans, for example, recognize their existence in vast technological complexity; the Australian aborigine, on the other hand, is immersed in a multidimensional kinship and religious morass that even anthropologists have yet to comprehend fully. Certainly the major feature of *Homo sapiens* is his big brain, and whether he is living in so-called civilized or primitive conditions does not alter that fact. It is not necessary to assume that the tribal forest dwellers of western Europe of a few thousand years ago, who are the genetic ancestors of today's Europeans and today's Americans of European background, were less intelligent than their descendants.

Years ago, when anthropologists were still thinking in terms of human types, there was a great deal of argument and disagreement about whether or not mankind was split into different races, each possessing its own characteristic genetic make-up and capacities. The concept of populations as groups with differences in gene frequencies shows that the typological concept of race usually led to futile discussion about the number of human racial types (three? five? more than five?) based on traits which, in most cases, can only be assessed subjectively. The term *type* was used to define a group of people (usually too large to work with) with certain qualitatively similar traits—even though the genetic basis of such traits is still unknown. In contrast, the more modern concept of populations deals with particular small groups of people and a whole spectrum of characteristics, primarily those about which

the genetic determination is definitely known and about which gene frequencies can be calculated.

Changes in Gene Frequency

In his study of man's physical structure, the anthropologist is particularly interested in how differences in gene frequencies have come about and how they are maintained over the generations, inasmuch as evolution is a change in gene frequency, not in genotypes or phenotypes. Such calculations are shown below.

In one specific population at time 1:

AA	Aa	aa	Total Number of Genes	Total Number of Genotypes
25	50	25	200	100

Frequency of gene A = 0.5 or 50%
Frequency of gene a = 0.5 or 50%
Frequency of genotype AA = 25%
Aa = 50%
aa = 25%

In the same population at time 2 (perhaps a generation later):

AA	Aa	aa	Total Number of Genes	Total Number of Genotypes
36	28	36	200	100

Frequency of gene A = 0.5 or 50%
Frequency of gene a = 0.5 or 50%
Frequency of genotype AA = 36%
Aa = 28%
aa = 36%

The population at time 2 is not in equilibrium, and by definition it is one of the ways in which evolution occurs. There are, in fact, four evolutionary forces that have been

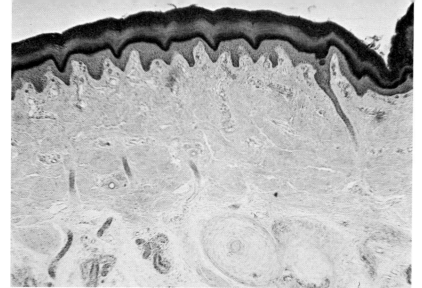

Figure 9. Photomicrograph showing the melanin granules and sweat glands in a human finger.
Figure 10 (below). The concentration of melanin in the skin of these Trobriand Islanders is the result of physiological adaptation over thousands of generations to the tropical environment.

identified as being responsible for bringing about changes in genetic frequency: mutation, natural selection, gene flow, and genetic drift.

MUTATION

Gene mutation, a point change in the DNA code, is the most fundamental evolutionary force acting on genetic frequency. The *mutation rate*, or the rate of this alteration in the basic chemistry of the gene, is evidently the same in all populations, and whether or not a new gene remains in the population after it has first appeared depends on the action of other evolutionary forces.

A mutation is an event that occurs mechanically, regardless of possible function or use-

fulness. If, however, the mutation provides an adaptive advantage to the population and becomes integrated into the gene pool, it may survive. Ultimately the retention of mutations at many loci will result in *speciation* —the origin of a new species. This process is most apt to occur in a subpopulation that exists in a slightly different environmental niche than the rest of the species. Being under somewhat different stresses, some mutants may survive in the gene pool of this subpopulation, whereas they might not in the species as a whole. If this process is accompanied by a period of genetic isolation during which the mutations accumulate, genetic incompatibility leading to reproductive isolation from the original species may result. At that point, speciation is complete. The appearances of new species seen in the fossil record are thus due to the origin of really new genetic material and not just new genetic combinations. It is safe to assume that the difference between modern man and the other primate species must be attributable to genetic differences in *kind*, not just in degree, and that mutations ultimately were responsible for those changes in kind. Apes, for example, have different genes than man, not just different frequencies of the same genes; the actual chemical structure of the hereditary material is different.

NATURAL SELECTION

Genetic similarity between two individuals is often attributed to descent from a common ancestor. On the other hand, when two populations are similar in gene frequencies, the same explanation cannot be used because such similarity in populations may come about for reasons other than shared ancestry.

The Process of Adaptation

Populations can be similar because they have inhabited similar environments and, being exposed to similar environmental stresses, have responded genetically in similar fashions. This kind of response, called parallel

Figure 11. This Amahuaca family of the remote Peruvian Andes draws from a gene pool that has probably remained relatively isolated over the generations, a fact that may stem from cultural conflict. The Amahuaca historically have sought the isolation of the forest and the protection it provides against clashes with stronger cultures, and they prefer living as small, mobile communities that are difficult to locate.

development within a population, comes about through differences in the frequencies with which individuals having particular traits are produced within that population. The assumption is that genes promoting survival over the generations will eventually replace genes that do not. If the capacity to reproduce viable offspring is itself determined genetically, then the absence of progeny signals the demise of the culprit genes. The "fit" individuals, in the strict genetic sense of that term, are those who produce the greatest number of children, and the phrase "the survival of the fittest" means that individuals best suited genetically to their environment will, on the average, and over the generations, leave the greatest number of children.

There can be no evolution unless some individuals of the population reproduce themselves more than others, a condition that can come about only when some individuals experience low fertility during the reproductive period or are unable to live through it. The agent of natural selection is the environmental variable that is hostile to a phenotype. In some cases, the genetic basis is known—for example, a diabetic in a sugar-rich environment. In this example, if the agent acts strongly enough, diabetics will produce fewer children than nondiabetics do, thus decreasing the diabetic genes in the population. It can then be said that the population has responded to its environmental stress through adaptation.

The ability to respond to stress lies in the existence of a tremendous assortment of different genes stored by the population, and this assortment is available to every generation to meet the challenges of changing environments. If the selection pressure is so great that only those individuals with certain genes reproduce all viable offspring in the next generation, the population will be highly adapted to that particular environment—but it will also have lost all or most of its genetic flexibility and will be suscep-

tible to extinction should environmental changes occur.

Natural selection, then, is any environmental force that promotes reproduction of certain members of the population who carry certain genes—at the expense of all the other members. In other words, natural selection favors those genes that place their possessors at a reproductive advantage and tends to eliminate those genes that place the individual at an initial or long-term disadvantage. Something as simple as the amount of melanin present in the skin may fit this example when higher melanin concentrations inhibit natural production of vitamin D by irradiation and so brings about vitamin D deficiency rickets—and subsequent pelvic disproportions that may interfere with pregnancy and a normal delivery.

Population Survival

There is little doubt that many of the characteristics used to identify groups of people, or races, have come about through the force of natural selection. A population whose members have shared the same gene pool for many generations and are all descendants of a common ancestry more than likely has occupied the same geographic area and has thus responded to the same environment for a long period of time. Because the environment has changed over the generations, it can be assumed that natural selection has been at work, retaining some mutations, eliminating others, and changing gene frequencies. The gene pool today is a product of past events, and thus populations that share a gene pool have a common evolutionary history. Many of the genes now in the pool of each particular population were established through natural selection many generations ago. In fact, it has been noted that modern

Figure 12. Fishermen near Wagenia, Leopoldville. Unlike other animals, man's response to the environment is culturally mediated, which allows him to remain an animal capable of even specializing in generalized responsiveness.

man is still a Pleistocene creature in that most of his evolution occurred during that long period of time that began millions of years ago.

Yet some of the greatest forces altering the environment—agriculture, for instance, or the industrial revolution—have taken place since the close of the Pleistocene some 10,000 years ago, which is not at all long enough for equally large changes to have occurred in the gene pool. Genetic change is a slow and conservative process. It is also a strikingly inefficient one. Whether or not an individual has what it takes to survive and reproduce is determined only *after* he has come into being as a fertilized egg. Natural selection, the most important force of evolution, cannot act until it has something to act on, which in all cases is the unborn or born individual. It is difficult to visualize the Ford Motor Company inspecting a car only after it has reached the end of the assembly line and then, finding some fault, junking the entire car. The company would soon be out of business unless it could come up with a system of producing so many cars that, even if a good percentage were rejected, there would still be a sufficient number left to compete with General Motors. Obviously such a system is unworkable for Detroit, but nature does operate that way. The processes of mutation and recombination produce tremendous variation, which is then culled by natural selection.

At one time it was theorized that Nature in her wisdom and economy would produce only viable genes by improving the hereditary material during the lifetime of an individual. This view, first expressed in the early 1800s by Jean Baptiste de Lamarck, was based on the idea that acquired characteristics and not just inherited ones could be passed down from one generation to another. The Lamarckian view was disproved when it was found that populations actually adapt in a much more costly manner. Genetic mistakes in an individual are not corrected so that they will not be carried into the next generation; instead, carriers of these mistakes simply have a lower probability of reproducing than those without them, so that the next generation will have a higher proportion of individuals without the genetic defects, the generation following that an even higher proportion, and so on. The aspect of population survival that depends on genetic adaptation can only come about through differential reproduction of genetically different individuals, usually over the course of a number of generations.

In terms of whole populations, then, the establishment of a new allele requires the elimination of an existing allele, which is called the cost of evolution. Because genes can only leave a gene pool through the death of a carrier of an allele, a certain number of deaths (prenatal or postnatal) are needed to eliminate the allele and establish its replacement. Should this replacement process become too rapid, however, the cost will be the extinction of the species. For example, if survival depended on having alleles for immunity to the effects of radiation and if very few members in a population had such immunity, a great increase in atmospheric radiation might impose excessive demands on those few members to save the species. In such a case, as in all cases of extinction, the species would be unable to meet the challenge of the environmental stress. Thus, genetic survival depends on at least two factors: enough variation to accommodate new demands and a degree of demand that is not excessive.

GENE FLOW
The physical make-up of a population can also be influenced by gene flow, which occurs when genes move from one population to another. Carriers of these genes may arrive in great numbers, inundating the gene pool, or the rate of genetic movement may be slow but persistent. It is unlikely that any human population ever remains genetically isolated

over many generations. For example, the Australian aborigines were separated geographically from the rest of mankind for perhaps hundreds of generations, yet when contact was established with outsiders, viable offspring were produced from matings with the invaders.

Man does not respond to the gross environment, which may vary tremendously from one place to another, but rather to his environmental mediator, called *culture*. Culture does the gross adapting and thus allows the gene pool to remain generalized. In other words, man can do with social organization, communication, and technology what other mammals do with genetic material: his adaptation is one of carrying his effective environment around with him. At one and the same time he alters that environment and then responds genetically to the change, and in that sense he determines his own evolution either purposefully or fortuitously. It is the environmental mediator, culture, that is responsible for the unity of the species. Culture is both an environment and, because man constantly tinkers with it and changes it, an adaptation. Because of this feedback system, culture constitutes both man's ecological niche *and* his primary mechanism for dealing with the environment.

All noncultural ways of responding to the environment—such as a special modified physiology to deal with temperature extremes—are secondary to cultural adaptation. None of the biological adaptations alone could provide viability in all the environments now occupied by man. Thus, it should be no surprise that race crossing, or *miscegenation*, does not produce dire biological consequences. The differences in all human environments are simply not great enough to bring about significant genetic differences between any two populations. Although the magnitude of certain phenotypic differences (such as skin color, facial features, hair shape) and some cultural differences (such as degree of technological sophistication) is striking, it is not as remarkable as the basic similarities that exist among the world's most disparate people. Biological as well as cultural differences turn out to be matters of degree, or variations on common themes. Basic biological and sociocultural requirements for all men are the same; it is their elaboration on these requirements that varies. All men have the same basic nutritional needs, and whether they overeat or barely subsist does not change that fact. Similarly, all men must communicate, and whether they do so in Swahili or English does not change that fact. In these cultural ways and in many others the species has unity. The reliance on culture is the hallmark of man, the world's most widely distributed mammal.

GENETIC DRIFT

Unless mutation, selection, and gene flow are operating on a population, the gene frequencies can be expected to remain unchanged generation after generation, at least in large populations. In small populations the situation is quite different: here the frequency change can have nothing to do with the selective advantages or disadvantages a gene provides for its owner. "Good" as well as "bad" genes are subject to a process—the fourth evolutionary process—called genetic drift, which is not influenced by the fitness value of any gene.

Genetic drift is most effective in small populations. It can be illustrated by taking a population of 50 individuals (or 100 genes at any locus). If 10 individuals have a given allele, the gene frequency is 10 percent. But in a large population—of perhaps 10,000 individuals—a gene frequency of 10 percent means that it is found in 1,000 individuals. It makes little difference in the large population if some of the 1,000 individuals who have the gene do not reproduce, or if entirely by chance in any one generation the allele of one gene is passed on more frequently than would be expected. There will still be many

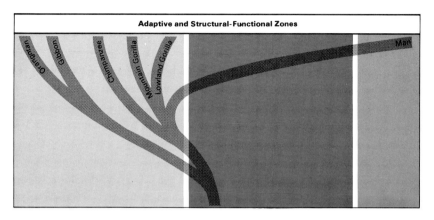

Adaptive and Structural-Functional Zones

Orangutan · Gibbon · Chimpanzee · Mountain Gorilla · Lowland Gorilla · Man

Figure 13. (below left). Evolution is adaptation through time. This diagram shows the primates in terms of their divergence into distinct adaptive zones. Although the chart does not show the time dimension or specific evolutionary lines, it probably is similar to the actual evolutionary pattern. Figure 14 (upper left). Divergent evolution is a process by which subspecies become increasingly dissimilar, eventually emerging as separate species. Figure 15 (right). Man among the primates.

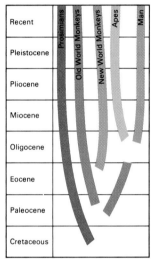

individuals remaining who have the gene, and it can be expected that a sampling error in one generation in one direction will be balanced in the other direction in future generations. In a small population with only 10 individuals having the alleles, however, the balance may never be regained. In this case, sampling error means that the frequency of a given gene in the parent generation will not be the same in the offspring generation due to chance alone. Sometimes by chance alone it will be greater, sometimes less. As long as the given genes do not get completely lost or become completely established at the expense of their alleles, the frequency will simply oscillate.

When anthropologists view population size with reference to genetic drift, they refer to *effective size* of the population, or roughly that percentage of the total number of individuals who are actually carrying out reproduction. In any given human group, there are likely to be many people either too young or too old to be involved in reproduction; moreover, all those who are of the right biological and cultural age may not be reproducing. For example, it has been estimated that about 60 percent of the population in the United States will reproduce the entire next generation.

VARIATION BETWEEN SPECIES

The content of every population and every gene pool is subject to change through time. The maximum population—that is, the whole species—contains by definition a greater continuity than any of its subpopulations or races. Thus, a discussion of population variation over relatively long periods of time is in reality a discussion of the human species.

Gene flow between species does not occur, and the species can therefore be considered a *gene-tight unit*. The importance of this preclusion cannot be overestimated. If genes could flow back and forth across lines of species, the ensuing melting pot of forms would make differentiation and thus adapta-

tion impossible. Fortunately this intermingling does not exist. It is not only scientists who marvel at the remarkable adaptation of different kinds of animals to their environments. Historically this observation has led to theories of special creation and to Lamarckianism, but today the process of speciation is understood as the result of the operation of two of the four evolutionary forces. Gene flow is not a factor because the rare hybrids that occur in mammals are never the originators of new species, nor is it probable that the action of genetic drift has ever been a major factor in species formation. Thus, mutation, the process that produces new genetic material, and above all natural selection may be considered the major forces responsible for speciation.

Chronospecies and Anagenesis

A species over time has four courses open to it. First, it may stay as it is, not undergoing any genetic change. Second, it may become extinct. Third, it may evolve into another species by gradually undergoing enough genetic change, so that *if* a remote ancestor ever met his lineal descendant the ensuing genetic incompatibility characteristic of species differences would prevent them from breeding—a situation described as a chronospecies difference. This meeting of a remote ancestor is hypothetical, but when the fossil record indicates that substantial morphological changes occur in a line of descent, it can be assumed that the animals are as distinct genetically as they are morphologically and that the process of speciation has occurred gradually over time. This process has been called anagenesis by taxonomists.

Cladogenesis

The fourth direction in which a new species can move is through cladogenesis. Here a subpopulation of a new species strikes out into a new environment and adapts to the new conditions it finds there. After formation of an isolation barrier between it and its

Order	Suborder	Series	Superfamily (ea)	Family (ae)	Living Representative Forms
Primates	Prosimii		Tupaioidea		Tree Shrew (?) Tupaia
			Lemuroidea	Lemuridae	Lemur
				Indridae	Indri
				Lorisidae	Loris
					Galago
			Tarsioidea	Tarsiidae	Tarsier
	Anthropoidea	Platyrrhine	Ceboidea	Callithricidae	Marmoset
				Cebidae	Cebus Monkey
					Spider Monkey
					Howler Monkey
		Catarrhine	Cercopithecoidea	Cercopithecidae	Macaque
					Baboon
					Colobus
					Langur
			Hominoidea	Hylobatidae	Gibbon
				Pongidae	Orangutan
					Chimpanzee
					Gorilla
				Hominidae	*Homo sapiens* (Man)

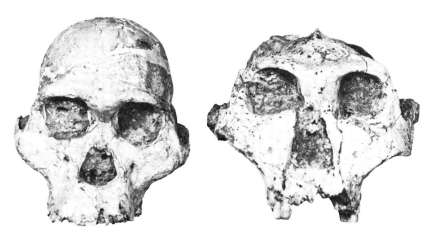

Figure 16. *Australopithecus* and *Paranthropus* skulls from South Africa. Where the various australopithecine forms fit into the human evolutionary scheme is a subject of controversy among anthropologists. The morphological variation in Pleistocene times is often interpreted as evidence of the existence of more than one manlike species.

originating population—a barrier that prevents all further gene flow—the two populations become genetically diverse and become what is termed *biospecies*. Cladogenesis, or divergent evolution, is probably the most important pattern in the history of the primates, as Figure 14 illustrates.

The prosimians were the earliest primates, and divergence took place in the form of a monkey and an ape-man line, with the ape-man split possibly occurring about 30 million years ago or *before* the great apes had evolved into their modern form. It is thus clear that some groups of living primates are older than others. What Figure 14 does not show is that the *rate* of evolution in the various branches of the primate lineage has not been the same. The prosimians not only are older but also have remained much the same as their original form. In contrast, man's divergence is much more recent, yet he has changed drastically from his early ancestors. The "tree" in Figure 15 underscores the enormity of man's divergence from the apes, despite the fact that the time involved is less than half of the total time for all of primate evolution. It should be kept in mind that these qualifications are related to Figure 16, which is an abbreviated classification of the living primates.

The Evolutionary Pattern

It would be a mistake to conceive of the Order Primates as an internal and consistent progression from less human to human, although old museum displays are very apt to give this impression. Apes are not imperfect or incomplete men, just as monkeys are not striving to become apelike. Along these lines, it is also important to remember that what diverges and evolves is a *species*—that is, the maximum population. Species are distinct from one another genetically, morphologically, and behaviorally. They also occupy different and exclusive niches in the environment that they exploit by a method that is unique in each case. Many species of animals often share the same general environment, but close examination shows that each is extracting its existence from different sources and by different means. Chimpanzees, as a case in point, are not slow-witted, uncivilized rogues but, like any other viable species, are full-fledged members of a population adapted to a particular environmental niche.

The fact that some living species of primates are more representative of an original primate stock than another has led occasionally to incautious speculation on the nature of man's ancestors. Monkey and apelike forms may have evolved earlier than the hominids, but monkeys and apes are not necessarily "ancestors" of hominids. The evolutionary pattern has been cladogenic, not anagenic. Species formation by divergence signals the beginning of a totally new pattern, not just the remodeling or elaboration of a previous one. In seeking explanations for the origin of human characteristics, anthropologists find it difficult to strike a balance between emphasizing that part of human evolution common to all higher primates and that part occurring after the divergence of the hominid line.

How many hominids have there been? Have there ever been hominid biospecies or does the whole evolution of man entail no divergences, only anagenesis? Because man today is the only hominid species and because the fossil record is not abundant, it is tempting to consider all fossil men since the beginning of the Pleistocene as representative of one species changing over time. Yet there is increasing evidence—particularly the recent australopithecine finds—that at the base of the Pleistocene and possibly into the mid-Pleistocene the morphological variation in what presumably are hominids is great enough to imply the existence of two or more species. In the case of higher primates, the species problem can be resolved through identification of the ecological niche and way of life of the various fossil groups. Biospe-

Table 1. How the Physical Anthropologist Studies Human Differences at the Individual, Populational, and Species Levels

Methods	Foci of Research	Definition
Morphology	Somatometry	Measurement of human physical characteristics
	Somatotyping	Characterization, classification of body form
	Photography	
	Radiography	Study of joint movement, locomotion, through use of x-ray motion pictures
	Dermatoglyphics	Study of patterns of ridges on hands, feet
	Anatomy	
	Growth	
Skeletal Studies	Osteology	Study of bones in the human skeletal system
	Paleopathology	Study of abnormalities and diseases in bony and tissue remains
	Paleodemography	Study of the numerical relationships of the people in populations no longer existing
	Radiography	
	Reconstruction of individual	
Physiology (Unknown heredity)	Serology	Study of properties, actions, of blood serum
	Metabolism	
	Nonserological physiology	
	Senses	
	Work capacity	
	Blood grouping of bony remains	
	Growth	
Genetics	Dermatoglyphics	
	Twin and family studies	
	Serology	
	Genes and mutations	
	Chromosomes	
	Population genetics	
Behavior	Ethology	Study of animal behavior
	Ecology	Study of relations of organisms and the environment, and relations with other organisms
	Kinesics	

Source: H. Helmuth (1971).

cies differences are attributable to these factors as well as to morphological features, and the realization of this fact has changed the nature of research on fossil man and the way the fossil man story is told.

THE STUDY OF HUMAN DIFFERENCES

There is probably nothing a physical anthropologist does that is not also done by professionals in other scientific disciplines. What distinguishes physical anthropology is not its methodology so much as its specialization in *human* evolution. Unlike the botanist or zoologist, the physical anthropologist is by necessity concerned with *paleontology* because "being human" evidently begins at some time early in the Pleistocene. He is also concerned with *neontology*, a term G. G. Simpson coined to label all those aspects of the study of evolution that do not involve the fossil record. These are aspects of "ongoing evolution" that involve research on the living populations of man. Like his colleagues in archaeology and cultural anthropology, the physical anthropologist studies the evidence and processes of human variation, past and

present.

Thus, beyond his basic concern with evolution the anthropologist stands apart from all other "man specialists"—the physicians, the historians, the sociologists—because of his conviction that culture, in the anthropological sense of that word, is an operational variable in all human evolutionary processes.

In a broader sense, any study of human biology that is carried out in the framework of the modern theory of evolution and that recognizes human sociocultural behavior as a relevant variable can be considered a study in physical anthropology, or "human biology," or "social biology." The techniques and methods used in research based on these criteria help to explain human differences at the individual, populational, and species level (Table 1).

Somatology

There is a long history of attempts to classify individual members of a population with respect to their overall morphological appearance. The study of gross anatomy, with its techniques of dissection and its place in medicine, is distinct from the characterization and classification of human body form, or somatology.

Because of their interest in human anatomy and their training in anthropometry or techniques for taking measurements of the body, however, physical anthropologists occasionally have contributed to the literature on somatology. Today there is very little activity in this area, but the hope lingers that a trained observer of human variation in the body can make predictions about associated human behavior and such characteristics as susceptibility to disease. Although these endeavors have had more than their share of a lunatic fringe—from phrenology to Chinese body divination—some intriguing correlations between body shape and behavior have been found by such early workers as W. H. Sheldon. Yet the biological and cultural mechanisms that led to these correlations remain largely unexplained.

Body Composition Studies

The study of body composition is a relatively new area of research usually carried out by physiologists, and correlation with behavior is not a primary concern. Moreover, research in body composition does not seek to classify the exterior morphology of the body but rather to characterize individuals in terms of their body components—that is, in relative proportions of muscle, fat, and bone.

Twin Studies and Growth Studies

Genetically, identical twins have exactly the same composition and are thus important in studies that attempt to differentiate genetic from environmental effects. Adequate numbers of twins have usually been found in large-scale research on normal human growth and development. Because anthropometry was the primary technique in such studies, in that twins were measured and compared in terms of body proportion, physical anthropologists originally became involved in them. Today there is less satisfac-

tion in describing and in determining normal standards and more in analyzing the causes and evolutionary significance of individual variation in growth and development within and between populations.

Cytogenetics

For many years the normal chromosome number in man was assumed to be forty-eight rather than what is now known to be the actual number, forty-six. The earlier chromosome count was corrected in 1956 following the development of new and improved techniques in cytogenetics—the direct microscopic study of chromosomes. The improved methods of tissue culture that made this discovery possible have also been responsible for increased accuracy in the identification of individual chromosomes and for subsequent investigation of relations between chromosome anomalies and certain human behavioral pathologies.

Serology

Since 1950, the study of gene frequency differences between populations and between generations has been a major research activity in physical anthropology. In a given blood sample, many factors can be identified that are the expressions of single genes. The anthropologist can draw blood samples from people who share a gene pool, send the samples to a typology laboratory, and then calculate gene frequencies—a process referred to as serology. Populations can be compared on the basis of allelic differences at many loci. Genetic "distances" can be calculated by statistical means so that populations can be arranged numerically on the basis of their genetic similarity. These arrangements may be used to answer questions about the relationship between populations and to measure the action of the forces of evolution on the population. For example, the trait called "sickle cell" is frequent in some populations that are subject to endemic malaria, but it is rare or absent in others. It is now known

Figure 17. Antrycide in the cattle complexes of the Sudan, an example of cultural ingenuity serving the survival of modern populations. This compound is used for protozoan infections in cattle, and the protective covering of the antrycide bottles have become fashionable as human adornments ever since inoculation programs were begun in the area.

that possession of the trait provides protection against the effects of malaria, and a high frequency of the trait can be considered adaptive in exposed populations. The selective significance of most other *polymorphisms* (the presence of more than one allele for a given locus in a given population) for natural selection is still unknown, but it is possible that at least some of these do provide selective advantages.

Anthropometrics and Biometrics

Before the concept of population genetics had emerged, the tools of the physical anthropologist were the anthropometer, the sliding caliper, and the steel tape. With them he set out to measure the world's people so that they could be compared and described by the statistical methods of the biometricians. Today he knows that the outside dimensions of the body are determined by *polygenes*, whose expression is greatly affected by such environmental variables as nutrition, exercise, and disease. The outcome of these extensive measurements has been the systemizing of the range of variation that exists within modern human races.

Polygenic Inheritance

Generally, single gene traits are those that can be classified into a few sharply defined qualitative categories, whereas polygenic traits show continuous variation on quantitative dimensions. The genes in a polygenic system may be located on the same or on different chromosomes. Each gene in the system is assumed to behave as a discrete unit and to obey the usual rules of transmission (for example, segregation, independent assortment, and crossing over). However, the contribution of each gene to variation of the trait is small and cumulative rather than all-or-none.

The action of a polygenic system is analogous to the simultaneous tossing of a large number of coins, where the alleles of each gene (assuming only two per gene) represent heads or tails, and the expression of the polygenic trait is determined by the number of heads. The result is continuous variation among members of a population. To complete this analogy, we could represent environmental conditions as the independent tossing of a second set of coins, such that heads and tails represent facilitative and inhibitory environmental effects; the total number of heads in both tosses determines trait expression. It is clear that the range of variation of the trait will be increased by environmental differences among members of a population.

Still, as in the case of single gene traits, genetic distances between populations can be calculated by using these metric variables. In a number of cases where both serological and anthropometric findings were available, the genetic distances that were calculated separately for both single-gene and polygenic traits agreed with one another. Although metric variables are affected by environment and are thus not as "pure" genetically as are factors in the blood, they do lend themselves nicely to all the operations of modern statistics dealing with continuous variation and are helpful in differentiating and describing populations.

Adaptability Studies

Human adaptability studies represent a relatively new approach to population differences. Using techniques derived largely from physiology as well as from social anthropology, demography, and population genetics, the human adaptability investigator studies all the biological characteristics of a population that are caused by such environmental stresses as altitude, temperature, and nutrition. It is not yet clear to what extent these normal stresses have acted as genetic selection agencies and to what extent both genetic flexibility and culture have been responsible for the survival of modern populations. Fundamental research still must be done, but it can be assumed that such population variations as those found in skin color, body hair, and blood polymorphisms are the products of a selection that acted in the past and that many of these traits are no longer relevant to fitness. At the same time, it has been established that human evolution has not stopped and that gene frequencies are changing. Even if there has been a relaxation in natural selection, differential fertility may be greater today than in the past, although sociocultural factors rather than natural ones may be the cause. Technology changes the physical environment, and economic and political changes alter the demographic situation. In other words, man continues to promote or influence his own evolution by willingly or unwillingly altering the environment to which he must adapt.

Osteology

If the physical anthropologist had a time machine he would enter the rock shelter of Paleolithic man or an abandoned Indian pueblo in the American Southwest to study the living, original occupants. Unfortunately, all that he usually has are some bones. These bones—whether mineralized and therefore fossilized or just dried and preserved—must serve as samples of vanished populations. The physical anthropologist working in an archaeological setting is limited more than when he is investigating a living population. By metric methods and through his training in anatomy—particularly in osteology, the study of bone—he can assign an age and a sex to individual skeletons, and from what he knows of modern populations living under similar technological and environmental conditions he can often determine whether skeletons of these individuals are truly representative forms of the population to which they belonged. It is common, for example, for remains of mature forms to appear more

frequently than those of children in an archaeological site.

The physical anthropologist can also precisely measure the bones, describe the variations existing in his sample, and compare his sample to other samples by the same biometric statistical techniques used for living populations in order to determine whether relationships indicated by archaeological material also manifest themselves in skeletal similarities.

Paleodemography

The physical anthropologist is interested as well in the factors involved in the evolutionary processes affecting prehistoric populations, and he depends extensively on the archaeologist for information about factors that the bones cannot provide. He will, for example, want to know about population density, food sources, indications of contact with outsiders, warfare, drought, and social practices affecting longevity, health, and fertility.

Early man is represented by ancient skeletal remains, usually fragments that seldom come from more than one individual. All that the physical anthropologist can really do with these scant remains is make comparisons with other hominid fossils, particularly those estimated to be of equal antiquity. The paleontological and taxonomic problems surrounding a fossil that has been recovered are enormous, to say the least. But when finds become as plentiful as they now are for the australopithecines and Neanderthalers, once again there is some hope that questions about human evolution can be answered.

Paleopathology

A group of paleontologists, some of them trained as medical doctors, are engaged in study of abnormalities found in fossil material. From their studies has come knowledge of the effects of healing practices, diet, and disease on the dentition and on the bones of early man. For example, one ancient practice

that has been studied by paleopathologists is *trephining*, a method used to open up the human skull. This operation is still used in extreme cases of tumors or of skull damage, but until recently the chances of survival were not great. The pre-Inca Indians of Peru performed this operation with obsidian flakes for surgical knives and saws using no better pain killer than the leaves of narcotic plants—and indications are that nearly half the patients survived. Other studies in paleopathology point to a tentative relationship between the heavy carbohydrate diet of the prehistoric New World Indians and the high incidence of caries present in the fossilized dentition.

Morphology

Individual fossils present difficulties to the taxonomist because it is not possible to judge precisely how representative the deceased individual was of his population. Perhaps he was an extreme variant—a freak—perhaps that is why he, rather than his normal brother, was preserved in the fossil record. Consider the massive, long skull of an Irish male and compare it to the slight, small-jawed skull of a female Australian aborigine. Will the future human paleontologist recognize these two individuals as members of the same species? Perhaps variation within the same species was even greater in the past than it is today, which makes the

question of whether a particular fossil represents a man or an ape even more difficult. Nor is it necessarily true that a comparison of the fossil in question to a modern man or to a modern ape will provide an answer. Perhaps an opinion can be formed about its relative apelike or manlike characteristics, but where it lies in the ancestral "tree" of modern man and modern apes cannot be decided on the basis of the remains alone. Evidence must also come from ethology (the study of animal behavior) and ecology (the study of environmental relationships).

Studies of Primate Behavior

Anthropological observation of the behavior of nonhuman primate species in their natural habitat has influenced the concept of the origin and evolution of man, yet it is still difficult to relate the social organization and behavior of living nonhuman primates to primates in the fossil record. On the one hand, the field studies of primates have certainly made anthropologists aware of the great differences that exist between living primate species, but they have also given indications of some basic primate behavioral characteristics. Perhaps the greatest effect of these studies has been to focus attention on the importance of behavior as an adaptation and on the fact that the evolution of an animal can be understood only in terms of its position in a total ecological framework.

Primate Social Behavior

9 Man, as Aristotle observed, is a social animal. All human societies and almost all of human culture depend on the fact that people like to live in groups and are in fact incapable of living otherwise. Even a person who is not particularly gregarious is likely to become dissatisfied with his own company after a few hours, which explains why hermits are generally regarded as such remarkable creatures. Despite this social cohesiveness, however, people are far less sociable than either monkeys or apes. Very few of these creatures ever choose to be alone for more than a few minutes, and most spend their entire lifetime within a few feet of at least one of their kind. Far more than humans, the majority of monkeys and apes could not long survive except as members of a tightly knit social group.

WHY STUDY THE PRIMATES?

In its pure sense, anthropology is the study of man—a subject, one might suppose, that would effectively preclude the study of any other species. Nevertheless, physical anthropologists value the study of the nonhuman primates as well because of the light it throws on the story of human evolution. By examining the locomotor movements of monkeys and apes, it is possible to contemplate with greater clarity how changes in the foot, the leg, and the pelvis enabled the early hominids to walk erect on two legs and thus free their hands for manipulating tools and weapons. Similarly, by comparing the brains of monkeys and apes with those of humans, it is possible to suggest how the growth in particular areas of the brain enabled the hominids to improve their capacity for language, memory, and forethought in their transformation into the species known as *Homo sapiens*.

But such comparisons can be extended beyond interesting physical relationships to the intriguing aspects of the evolution of human culture. During the past few years, anthropologists have learned that nonhuman primates in their natural habitat possess certain social characteristics that are curiously reminiscent of human behavior. In every species, the young must be socialized in a way appropriate to the survival

Figure 2. Over 200 million years ago, terrestrial upheavals created cool moist zones that may have triggered the biological evolution leading to mammalian life forms and, as a later radiation, the primates. Elevated metabolism, one adaptation, ensured mammalian survival through the climatic cooling that brought to a close the Age of Reptiles. It was only 70 million years ago that features unique to primates began to evolve — including forward-directed ultimately stereoscopic vision and long, mobile, flat-nailed fingers useful for manipulating things. (Here, a male macaque appreciates the dexterity of his cohort as he grooms his coat.) Figure 3 (right). As essential to primate survival as biological evolution is their behavioral adaptation. Baboons, as terrestrial primates, face numerous predators in their search for food and find relative safety in numbers. Moreover, the prolonged dependency of their offspring means social order must exist to ensure the young will get the sustenance and training needed to survive. Baboons carry behavioral adaptation one step further in their symbiotic relationship with animals grazing on the savannas — although they sometimes mix survival and symbiosis by eating a gazelle or two.

in the protection of infants and pregnant females. And, by extension, the first hominids developed behavioral responses to meet the changes in environment—the effect of which is echoed in human behavior today. Group solidarity so firm that one member will risk its life to protect others, battles among males for a position of dominance in a group, inheritance of status, even baby-sitting or differential social experience for juvenile males and females—all are characteristic of some species of monkeys. Although it must always remain speculative, the study of nonhuman primates may offer insights into the reconstructive study of the behavior of the nonextant hominid forms as well.

PRIMATE BEHAVIOR PATTERNS

The importance of social life to monkeys and apes can be perceived by examining the way of life of baboons—the large, heavily built monkeys that inhabit much of Africa from the desert areas of the north to the Cape at the south. They live in groups ranging from ten to several hundred members, and almost every aspect of their life is conditioned by their membership in the group.

The Savanna Baboons

Like all monkeys, except for the South American owl monkey, baboons are diurnal. Most sleep in the trees at night in order to avoid predators, and they do not climb down to begin feeding on edible plants and roots until daylight. The group consists of full-grown males and females, juvenile males and females three to seven years old, and the infants still dependent on their mothers. Each animal except for nursing infants gathers its own food, but most remain within a few feet of one another while they are feeding. When the first meal of the day is over, the group moves slowly but steadily until about midday and then stops to rest. The adults sleep or laze in the shade; the infants stay nearby, and the juvenile male monkeys

of that species. Every social group of all species has its own home range, and every group uses some means of preserving peace among its members to reduce the possibility of disruptive conflict. The study of primate behavior offers insights into the question of which human attributes are inherited, which are learned, and which are shaped by both genetic and cultural factors.

When the prehominid primates first descended from the trees, they probably were subject to attack by ground-dwelling predators, and, unlike other primates, they gradually acquired such protective features as long canine teeth. Perhaps it was this same threat that led to the development of such forms of behavior as group solidarity to aid

frolic around the periphery of the group. By late afternoon, the baboons are ready for their second big meal of the day, and they eat steadily for about two hours. By the time they have finished eating, evening is beginning to fall, and the group slowly makes its way to one of its regular sleeping places in the trees.

Throughout this entire period the group stays together. When the group is on the march, a young adult male may move several hundred yards away from the others, but most baboons remain within sight and sound of one another when they are walking, feeding, playing, and sleeping.

Savanna baboons are one of the most cohesive species of monkeys and apes. A chimpanzee, if suddenly alarmed, might run off without warning other members of its group. The langur monkeys of southern Asia might, if alarmed, race for the safety of the trees without a thought for their fellow monkeys. A baboon would never do this. When in danger or when passing through an area where predators can be hidden from view, the young adult males and juveniles move out in front. Behind them come the adult males, followed by the females with their infants, and juvenile males bring up the rear. Loyalty to the group can come before individual safety, and the extreme cohesiveness and group loyalty of baboons can serve as a starting point for understanding the basis of why monkeys and apes behave as they do. But first it is necessary to make some distinctions in the behavior of monkeys and apes, which are different kinds of animals.

Comparisons With Other Species
There are four apes—the chimpanzee and gorilla of Africa and the orangutan and gibbon of Southeast Asia. It is difficult to generalize about the social behavior of these apes, because behavior in each case is very different and has not yet been explored sufficiently. Gibbons live in small groups consisting of the male, the female, and their offspring. Each group occupies a particular home range, and once an infant is old enough to survive on its own, it is driven away from the family group. Individual orangutans often seem to live in complete isolation, although single males and females have been seen close together. The orangutan has been hunted heavily and only a few thousand remain, and it is difficult to describe the survivors because they have not yet been studied in much detail. Chimpanzees inhabit dense forest areas and seem to live in several types of groups. One group might contain mothers and infants, a second might contain individual adults without offspring, and a third, mated pairs. Gorilla groups are always small, rarely including more than a dozen or so animals led by one dominant male.

A distinction must also be made between the majority of monkey species that live almost exclusively in the trees and the few species that spend most of their time on the ground. The langur of India and the vervet of Africa spend almost all of the day on the ground, but these monkeys always remain in the vicinity of trees and the safety the trees provide. Most monkeys, including the great variety of South American species, are tree-dwelling animals. In contrast, the African baboon and several Asian macaques are willing and able to move out completely into open country. More is known about the social life of baboons and macaques because these monkeys do spend more of their time out in the open and thus have been easier for anthropologists to study.

ENVIRONMENTAL ADAPTATIONS
The behavior as well as the physical make-up of different species is conditioned by the kind of habitat they occupy. Originally, all monkeys including the ancestors of baboons and macaques—and the ancestors of today's ground-dwelling gorillas and chimpanzees—were probably arboreal. Although it is un-

Figure 4. The four living apes — the orangutan, chimpanzee (below left), gorilla, and gibbon (below right). It is difficult to generalize about the social behavior of these apes because each has adapted differently to its environment. The difficulty is compounded by the lack of sufficient research data on the subject.

likely that we will ever know why some species left the trees, it seems reasonable to assume that their venture to the ground was related to the search of food.

In any event, at some point in time these ancestral monkeys left the trees, and in leaving the branches they risked attack from the ancestors of modern lions, leopards, and cheetahs—and from hyenas and jackals. This danger probably helped bring about the adaptations that differentiate the baboon and macaque from the monkeys that remained in the trees. Most tree-dwelling monkeys such as the colobus of Africa or the langur of southern Asia are exceedingly timid and are quick to hide or to flee at the first sign of danger. They are lithe, slender, and remarkably agile. A colobus or langur monkey can run with ease along slender branches and can race down the length of a 100-foot tree in a few seconds. Such agility gives them great advantages in obtaining food and also enables them to escape from such predators as the monkey-eating eagle. Given their agility, arboreal monkeys can evade a carnivore or a snake, and by staying away from the tops of the trees they can avoid most attacks by predatory birds.

To arboreal monkeys, a sturdy, powerful body would be of little value and would, in fact, be a severe disadvantage because it would make them less agile. It is a different matter for baboons or macaques, for they spend most of their waking hours on the ground. As they moved away from the trees in search of food, the danger of attack from powerful predators increased, and the ancestors of male baboons and macaques developed formidable cheek teeth, and long canine teeth for defensive display. Compared with short-snouted colobines, these animals have teeth housed in long muzzles. Because they use their teeth for chewing, they also need powerful chewing muscles.

Baboons also acquired another form of defense: they learned to cooperate in order to fight or intimidate predators. This cooper-

Figure 5. Irven DeVore studying baboons in Nairobi Park. Despite the intriguing humanlike attributes of baboons, comparisons of their social behavior with that of man should not be pushed too far. They can also be dangerous animals when aroused, and only an experienced primatologist would carry on an investigation at this close range. Figure 6. The distribution of living nonhuman primates throughout the world.

ation lies at the root of the intense cohesiveness of their social life and affects almost all aspects of their behavior. Female baboons are more aggressive than female langurs or colobus monkeys, but they are far less aggressive than the males of their kind. Female baboons do not have long canines and their bodies are only about half the size of the males. It is the male baboons that protect the group, especially the females and the infants.

Cooperative behavior explains the group's order of defense, as was mentioned earlier. In the same manner, if one baboon group happens to encounter another, the dominant males of both groups will come forward in a body. This behavior is in sharp contrast to gorilla behavior. The gorilla is so large that it can afford to ignore the predators it encounters, which, except for an occasional leopard, are unlikely to challenge it. And if one gorilla group encounters another gorilla group, only the two leaders will come forward and will attempt to frighten each other away by beating their chests and otherwise displaying their aggressiveness and strength.

It is because they must always be prepared to deal with sudden danger that individual baboons never move far from the group. At the same time, every individual is constantly on the alert. When they are feeding, and apparently secure and at rest, every member of the group will look up every few seconds to determine whether danger is approaching. Baboons further guarantee their security through a symbiotic relationship with animals such as gazelles, whose senses of hearing and smell are superior to their own. Baboons and gazelles may stay together all day. If a baboon sees a predator approaching, it will give a bark that warns the

ungulates as well as the other baboons. Similarly, if the gazelles hear or smell an approaching predator, their warning will serve to alert the baboons. The relationship between the different species is so close that gazelles may continue feeding while male baboons advance and drive the predator away.

There are variations in the behavior patterns of baboons and macaques, even between different variations of the same species, that can often be traced to adaptations in special environmental conditions. The hamadryas baboon can serve as an illustration of how social behavior is adapted to the environment. Most baboons live in areas where there is usually adequate food and plenty of trees, so that fairly large groups can eat together and also find safe sleeping places that are far enough away from other groups. The hamadryas baboons are scattered throughout Ethiopia and Arabia. Many live in areas such as the highlands of eastern Ethiopia, where both food and sleeping sites are in short supply, and during the day the scarcity of food tends to make the hamadryas baboons split into small groups of one male and several females. But there are few safe sleeping sites available, and at night many of these individual groups are likely to come together to sleep in the few places, such as rocky promontories, where predators cannot reach them. Even among the several hundred animals that may come together to sleep, the smaller groups remain cohesive, with the members staying as closely together as they do when foraging for food.

INSIDE THE HOME RANGE

Hamadryas baboons, like all monkeys and apes, are intensely cautious in their habits, another trait that arises from the need for security. Their cautious nature is revealed vividly in the way a group of monkeys remains within its home range. The arboreal colobus monkey stays within a vertical zone

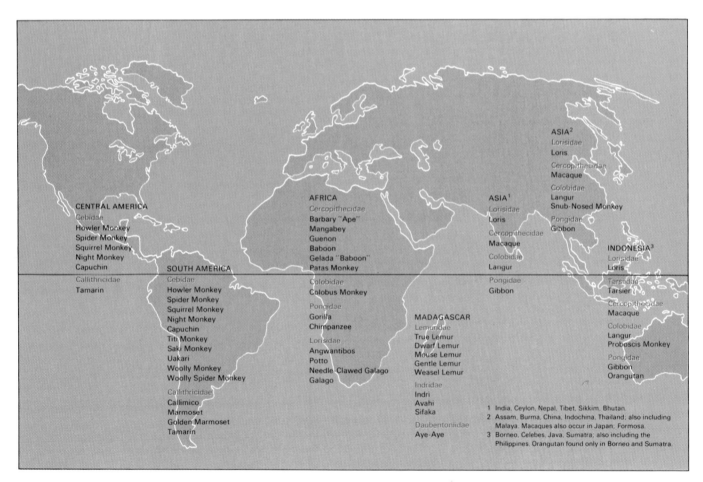

Figure 6. General distribution of living nonhuman primates. Primates are listed not in taxonomic order but as they approximately occur from north to south in each of the major geographic regions indicated. The family as well as the common name for each genus is given. (Source: Clyde Hill, 1971.)

CENTRAL AMERICA
Cebidae
Howler Monkey
Spider Monkey
Squirrel Monkey
Night Monkey
Capuchin
Callithricidae
Tamarin

SOUTH AMERICA
Cebidae
Howler Monkey
Spider Monkey
Squirrel Monkey
Night Monkey
Capuchin
Titi Monkey
Saki Monkey
Uakari
Woolly Monkey
Woolly Spider Monkey
Callithricidae
Callimico
Marmoset
Golden Marmoset
Tamarin

AFRICA
Cercopithecidae
Barbary "Ape"
Mangabey
Guenon
Baboon
Gelada "Baboon"
Patas Monkey
Colobidae
Colobus Monkey
Pongidae
Gorilla
Chimpanzee
Lorisidae
Angwantibos
Potto
Needle-Clawed Galago
Galago

MADAGASCAR
Lemuridae
True Lemur
Dwarf Lemur
Mouse Lemur
Gentle Lemur
Weasel Lemur
Indridae
Indri
Avahi
Sifaka
Daubentoniidae
Aye-Aye

ASIA[1]
Lorisidae
Loris
Cercopithecidae
Macaque
Colobidae
Langur
Pongidae
Gibbon

ASIA[2]
Lorisidae
Loris
Cercopithecidae
Macaque
Colobidae
Langur
Snub-Nosed Monkey
Pongidae
Gibbon

INDONESIA[3]
Lorisidae
Loris
Tarsidae
Tarsier
Cercopithecidae
Macaque
Colobidae
Langur
Proboscis Monkey
Pongidae
Gibbon
Orangutan

1 India, Ceylon, Nepal, Tibet, Sikkim, Bhutan.
2 Assam, Burma, China, Indochina, Thailand; also including Malaya. Macaques also occur in Japan, Formosa.
3 Borneo, Celebes, Java, Sumatra; also including the Philippines. Orangutan found only in Borneo and Sumatra.

that stretches from ten to thirty feet above the ground. Arboreal howler monkeys of South America stay near the canopy of the trees and rarely travel over a range exceeding one square mile. The more terrestrial monkeys are, the more they extend their range. The common langur of India roams about in one to three square miles, and baboons may travel over an area ranging from ten to fifteen square miles.

On an average day, a group of baboons may walk from three to five miles, but they always follow the same tracks as they journey between their feeding areas, their water-holes, and their sleeping sites. When they approach the limits of their home range, they become increasingly timid and cautious, and they never wander beyond the boundaries. The group feels safest and most relaxed in the heart of its home range, where it is intimately acquainted with the best feeding places and the safest sleeping sites. As the infants grow up, they observe the paths their elders follow on their daily journeys. They also observe the caution with which the elders approach the boundaries of the home range, set perhaps by a stream, a line of trees, a steeply rising bank. Beyond these boundaries lies unknown and therefore dangerous ground, and when the infant baboons grow to adulthood they follow the same paths. Thus, from generation to generation the same territorial experience is passed down.

Socially inherited experience keeps each group inside its home range. This experience is reinforced by a system of warning signals. As soon as they awaken, the adult males of a howler group set up a roar that lasts as long as one-half hour. This roar is repeated when the group moves from one feeding area to another. Langurs whoop to let other langur groups know where they are, whereas the spider monkeys of South America give a special warning bark. Vocal signaling is particularly adaptive to arboreal life, where dense foliage might conceal one group from another.

DOMINANCE AND LEADERSHIP

The suspiciousness and bellicosity of the macaque indicate still another important distinction between tree-dwelling monkeys and the baboons and macaques. The ground-dwelling macaques and baboons possess the kind of aggressiveness necessary in animals that defend themselves by fighting rather than by hiding or running away. With their long canines, both macaques and baboons are quite capable of killing. In fact, given their aggressiveness and their powerful dentition, the members of a group might kill themselves off unless some system existed to preserve the peace. In the case of baboons and macaques, a hierarchy has been established within the group. The hierarchy, in which every monkey knows its place, also serves another purpose. Any group requires leadership, and a group of baboons is no exception. Some member or members of the group must decide when the group will begin to move, which path it will follow, which sleeping sites it will occupy, and what action it will take when threatened by predators. Because baboons must be ready to act

Figure 7 (left). Two Old World monkeys—above, the African vervet and below, the Asian macaque. An important characteristic of most primates, including these species, is their dominance hierarchies, where each member of a group has an established position in relation to all other members. Figure 8. The male baboon threat. This posture is employed to intimidate disruptive members of the baboon group as well as predators.

rapidly in case of danger, the group needs strong, decisive leadership. In large groups, this leadership is provided by a number of dominant males that command the unquestioning obedience of all the other members.

Aspects of Subordination

It is easy for even uninformed observers to recognize a dominant male baboon or macaque. His hair is sleek and well groomed. His walk is calm and assured, and he moves apparently without taking any notice of the subordinate monkeys that scatter at his approach. The position of a dominant baboon or macaque normally is unchallenged. If a tangerine or some other desirable food is tossed between a dominant and a subordinate male macaque, the dominant macaque will take it. Even if the dominant male does not want it and leaves it untouched, the subordinate monkey will rarely approach the food, for even an approach of this nature would be regarded by the dominant monkey as a challenge to his superiority and would be met instantly by an attack. Normally, however, the subordinate monkey knows he would be defeated if a battle took place and avoids giving the dominant monkey any reason to attack.

It is their unquestioned superiority that enables the dominant monkeys to preserve the peace. Whenever a squabble breaks out, a dominant male monkey often may not even have to move to put an end to the quarrel. His first reaction will be to stare at the offenders. The stare is a threat: it is long and steady and normally is enough to make the offending monkeys cease their squabbling and even run away from one another. If the stare does not produce any effect, the dominant monkey will pull back the skin on top of his scalp, draw back his ears, and open his eyes wide. These movements are preparations for a fight—they protect the ears from possible bites and allow the monkey to see with maximum clarity—but they have also become ritualized as a threat. If

the facial threat does not impose order, the dominant male tenses his body and perhaps grunts, takes a few steps forward, and slaps the ground threateningly. And if all these threats are not enough to stop the squabble, the dominant baboon will run at the offenders, who invariably scamper for safety. When the dominant monkey has caught the offender, he may pin the monkey to the ground to show his superiority. Or he may mount the subordinate monkey, as a male mounts a female in copulation, as a symbol of dominance. In extreme cases, the dominant monkey may bite the annoying subordinate, but this bite is merely a disciplinary measure and rarely draws blood.

Ways of Assuming Leadership

The drive to become dominant is part of the aggressive nature of a macaque or baboon. From their earliest years, baboon and macaque infants play with their peers, and in this infant play the more powerful and aggressive monkeys assert their superiority. When they become juvenile, the males gradually extend their dominance over the females of the group, and when they are fully grown the more aggressive may attempt to challenge the weaker members of the dominant group. These challenges, if resisted, can lead to serious fighting in which the defeated monkey may be badly injured and in some cases driven from the group.

Leadership among baboon groups is particularly interesting because it is exercised by a number of ruling males—in a large group there may be a half dozen of them—who usually support each other against challenge from an aggressive young male. The monkeys that constitute the ruling group are arranged in hierarchical order, and their relative positions in that order are clearly understood. An aggressive young baboon is likely to challenge the weakest, and he may very well be strong enough to win. But the change that his winning would bring about in the hierarchy is disturbing and constitutes a challenge to the whole ruling group. Thus, the first, second, or third dominant monkey may come to assist the one with lowest status.

As in some human societies, strength and aggressiveness are important qualities in winning a position of dominance. But *inheritance* also plays its part, and the male offspring of a dominant female macaque will undoubtedly have a greater chance of becoming one of the ruling group.

Although the hierarchical structure is not as clearly marked among female macaques as it is among the males, they, too, have a hierarchy. Each infant macaque takes on the social status of its mother. A dominant female may, for example, intervene in fights among infants to protect her offspring. In this and other ways the experience of her infant will thus be one of dominance. It will come to take on the rank order of its mother, just as the infant of a subordinate female will take on her rank order.

Advantages of Being Dominant

Dominance and leadership impose their responsibilities. It is the dominant baboons that must advance to challenge predators and so risk their lives. In return, they enjoy the benefits and deference given to the leaders. Grooming is one example. One monkey grooms another by picking through its hair to clean out the dirt and the parasites. At one level, grooming is a cleaning mechanism and it is highly effective; it keeps the hair of a monkey or ape clean and free of ticks and other insects. But baboons and macaques have adapted grooming to reinforce the social harmony of the group. When a male baboon is being groomed, usually by a female, he sits or reclines in serene contentment. Because being groomed is enjoyable, the dominant males are groomed far more often than the subordinate males, and this explains why the hair of the dominant male always appears sleek and well kept.

The dominant males also have access to the most comfortable sleeping sites and they enjoy the first turn at the waterholes. Another important advantage enjoyed by the dominant males is that they also have first choice of the females when the females are in their period of receptivity.

GROWING UP TO BE MONKEYS

Of all the functions served by primate social life, the most important one is that it provides a safe and secure environment in which infants of the group can grow up and experience what they need to know to survive. Many prosimians—and one primitive, small South American monkey, the marmoset—usually bear their young in pairs. Monkeys and apes normally bear only a single offspring, probably as a result of the primate adaptation to life in the trees. The mother of a young infant is obliged to keep up with the group and she can manage it only if she is able to move all four of her limbs freely. The infant must be able to cling to the mother without any assistance from her, and it does so by firmly grasping her hair. Some infant monkeys cling to their mother's back as soon as they are born, but the infants of most monkeys, and all apes, cling to the front of their mother, although

Figure 9. All mammals develop slowly and need the continued care of an adult female. The female of nonmammalian species generally gives birth to many offspring but few ever live to reach adulthood. Although mammalian females such as this baboon have relatively few offspring, most of their infants do reach maturity and will have experienced a close mother-child relationship. Figure 10 (below). As in human societies, grooming among baboons is not only a means of keeping clean but also a way of reinforcing harmony among members of the group.

some shift to a more convenient position on her back when they are a few months old. In either position, the mother is able to carry one infant quite easily, whereas carrying more than one would be difficult. If she were to bear more than one infant at a time, either the additional infants would have to be left to die or the mother would be unable to keep up with the group.

A newborn infant is carefully protected at all times. Even when its mother is not present, there is always some other female or male nearby to watch over it. However, the ground-dwelling baboon and macaque males pay particularly close attention to their offspring, which also shows how almost every aspect of primate social life reflects the interests of survival.

For about ten months after it is born, an infant langur monkey has almost no contact with the adult males of the group, and a female has very little contact with them until she is three or four years old. Both male and female baboon infants, on the other hand, receive great attention and affection from the adult males. An infant baboon can approach the most dominant members of the group and can even disturb them at rest—something no other member of the group except an equally dominant male would dare to do—without being chastised. Indeed, adult baboons are so fond of infants that a dominant male will occasionally approach a subordinate female who is holding a newly born baboon and request the pleasure of playing with the infant.

The difference in behavior between langurs and baboons reflects the survival defenses of the two species. More closely attached to the arboreal habitat, a langur is much less dependent on the rest of the group for its safety. If danger threatens, a mother langur will seize her infant and carry it up to the safety of the trees, but the male langurs will race to safety without paying any attention to the infants. Consequently, there is no particular reason why an adult

Figure 11. The success of primate social organization rests on several behavioral factors that work to assure group harmony. Infant baboons have the effect of calming even the most aggressive males and in fact serve as one factor that helps bind the group together. Despite the tolerance and affection that males show the infants, however, they tolerate little once the young reach about two years of age, and thereafter the relationship takes on overtones of dominance and submission.

male langur should display much interest in the infants. In contrast, the adult male baboons have a principal responsibility for protecting the infants. It is the adult males who approach predators to keep them away from the group. If the mother of a very young infant is injured and cannot keep up with the group, a male baboon may drop back and walk beside her in order to provide protection. In both cases, the male may be called on to risk his life in order to protect the infant, and he is more likely to do this if he feels strong affection for it. This affection is reflected in the intimate attachment that binds male baboons to the infants from the time of their birth.

Still, it is the females who pay the closest attention to the infants, and the degree of their attachment can be seen in the privileged position that the mother of a newly born infant enjoys. A female baboon may occupy a low position in the hierarchy, but once she gives birth she becomes a center of attention. The other females gather around her to inspect the infant, and their desire to hold it is so strong that they will wait in line for a turn to do so. The mother will allow other females to hold the infant, but she keeps a jealous eye on them, and at the first sign of distress she will seize her infant even if it is being held by a female far superior to her in the group hierarchy.

All the females are intensely protective toward a newborn infant. If an infant gives a cry of distress—perhaps when injured by the vigorous play of a careless juvenile—the nearest female will race to its aid. The females' strong protective instincts are stimulated by the infant's movements and cries and also by its hair color. A langur infant, for example, is distinguishable during the first three to five months following birth by a dark coat that provides a sharp contrast to its pink face, hands, and feet. This distinctive coloring is clearly an adaptation that helps guarantee attention and protection. Once the infant's coat becomes lighter, the females of the group become less protective and are likely to ignore cries that, to the human listener, sound exactly like the cries of distress it made shortly after it was born. Presumably, the langurs can distinguish between the distress cries of a very young infant (which will bring them racing over to help) and the distress cries of a slightly older infant (which they will ignore).

The mother, however, remains continually protective, and for several months her infant is never far from her side. It learns much of what it needs to know by copying her behavior. When the mother forages for food, the infant forages also, selecting the same kinds of plants and leaves. The mother makes no effort to feed her infant, for it must learn to pick food for itself, and she will occasionally lean over and snatch some particularly tasty morsel from its grasp. But she watches it constantly, and if the infant picks up some unfamiliar plant or leaf, the mother will take it away and keep on doing so until the infant learns that this is something it must not eat.

For more than a year—about fifteen months in the case of a langur—the infant remains the prime object of its mother's attention. This period comes to an end when the infant is weaned. Weaning is a painful process, punctuated by cries of intense distress from the infant as it tries and fails to reach its mother's milk. The struggle may continue for several months and is a great strain on infant and mother alike, but it marks the end of the true infant period. For a while, the young langur continues to follow its mother around and may continue to ride on her. But a few months after the weaning is over, the mother gives birth again. From then on, the infant, now approaching the juvenile stage, must make its own way.

The Importance of Monkey Play

Despite its attempts to remain close to its mother, an infant langur—or baboon or ma-

Figure 12. Young savanna baboons cavorting. Play is another behavioral adaptation for survival, providing practice in swiftness and coordination and the opportunity to mingle with others of the group. Figure 13 (right). A Japanese snow monkey. Unique in their adaptation to an extreme environment—which has led even to bathing in hot springs as a way of surviving the winter cold—these monkeys are nearing extinction as their food supply dwindles.

need to race down the trunk of a tree in a few seconds. The period of play, and the practice that play provides, gives monkeys the kind of agility and facility of movement that later may save their lives.

Both male and female monkeys expend a great deal of energy in play. But once they become juveniles, their group behavior begins to change in a way that echoes the segregation of the sexes among human children. The female juveniles stay close to the center of the group, near the adults. They spend most of their time with the adult females and their infants, acting as baby-sitters when the mothers move away. By playing the role of mother, they gain the kind of experience that will help them when they in turn become mothers. As the female juveniles move closer to the center of the group, the male juveniles move away. They spend almost all their free time playing. When their play becomes more vigorous and more mobile, they move out toward the periphery of the group, where their noise and antics will not disturb the elders.

caque—starts to venture away from her and play with other infants as soon as it can walk. Most monkeys in their natural habitat give birth at those seasons of the year when the food supply is richest. Thus, in a group of any size there will be several infants in the same age group. When the infants are still comparatively unsure of themselves, the mothers watch them at play, intervening if the playing becomes too rough and stopping it with a threat or, if necessary, a light slap. As the infants grow older, the maternal surveillance becomes more relaxed, and in this respect it is similar to human behavior. The young monkeys move farther away from the adults to play on their own, and their play becomes more vigorous.

Play is intensely important to all young monkeys, especially in their juvenile period. They are tremendously active and continually run, climb, wrestle, and play such games as follow-the-leader. Their play is more than a way of "letting off steam." Play is another adaptation for survival. Throughout its life, a monkey must be ready to move quickly to avoid danger. When attacked by a monkey-eating eagle, for example, it may

The Importance of Peer Groups
Through their play, the young male monkeys form the close associations that will help bind the group together when they become adults. In their competition and play fighting, they establish the order of dominance that they will carry into adult life. But play and the consequent mingling with peers also serve a more fundamental role: it is the contact with its peers that makes a monkey a truly social animal, capable of functioning effectively as a member of the group. This, at any rate, is the conclusion implied by a series of experiments carried out by Harry Harlow of the University of Wisconsin.

Harlow raised several groups of macaque monkeys from birth without giving them any opportunity to play with their peers. Some were raised in total isolation and others were raised in sight of other infants but without any physical contact with them.

All these infants developed into extremely disturbed animals. Some sat dumbly in their cages, staring blankly. Others rocked and swayed compulsively, hour after hour, sucking at their thumbs and fingers and pinching at their skin. And some actually chewed and tore at their bodies in terror when approached by humans. When Harlow brought these young macaques into contact with one another, they were unable to effectively join together. They could not establish friendly relationships. They fought with each other and they were unable to copulate.

Harlow then tried another experiment. He raised several more infant macaques, keeping each animal alone in its own cage but allowing it to play with the others for twenty minutes a day. This period of play, although brief, produced astonishing results. After a short period of uncertainty, the infants played together with confidence and vigor. In less than a year, the males and females began to take on their normal roles, the males displaying dominance and the females submission. And all behaved in a way that indicated they would be able to copulate.

These experiments confirmed what field observations of monkeys would suggest: that mingling with their peers is essential for proper monkey development. If they did not live in groups, most monkeys would be physically unable to survive. They would not be able to learn what they need to know, such as what food to eat or where to go for water. They would be in more danger of being attacked and killed by predators. And the need for company—an adaptation necessary for physical survival—appears to have produced a further result. Social contact with its fellows is essential if a monkey or an ape is to achieve a fully integrated "personality." A monkey or ape raised in isolation and living by itself is no more a monkey or ape in the fullest sense than a human raised in isolation and living by himself would be fully a man.

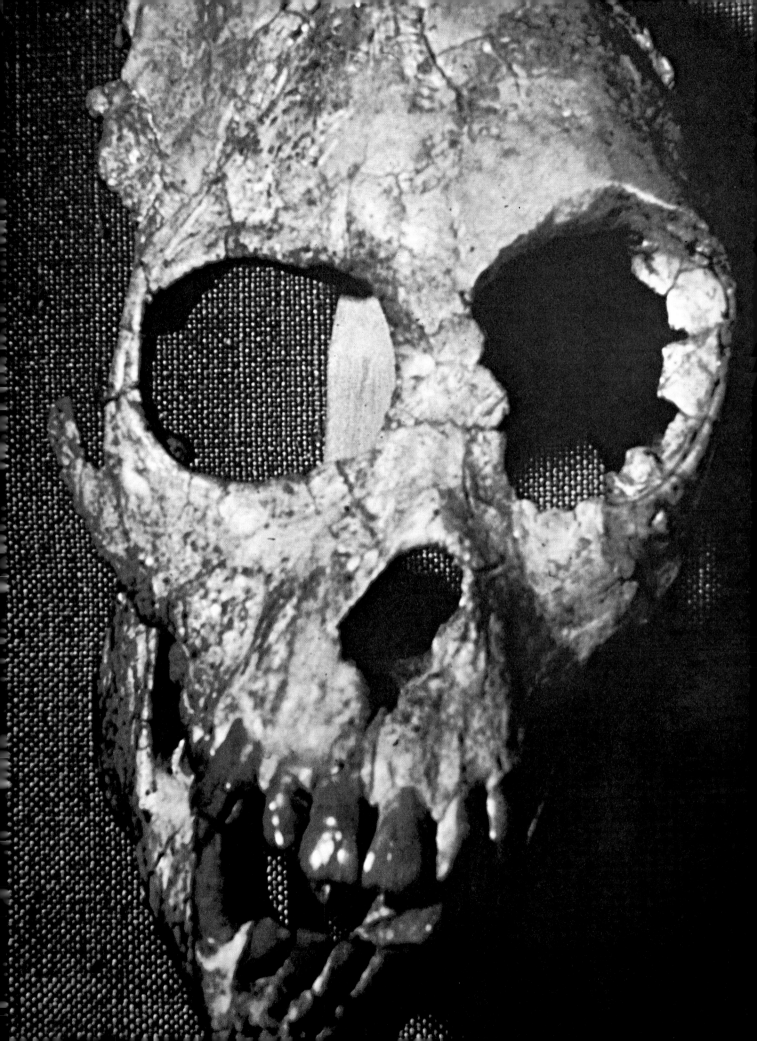

Prehuman Primates

10

The close relationship of man to other primates has been recognized intuitively for centuries, and well over a hundred years have elapsed since Charles Darwin first proposed a mechanism to explain this relationship. But it is only during the last decade or so that anthropologists have begun to acquire a broad perspective of the entire span of primate, including human, evolution. Man is typically a plains dweller but in this characteristic he is radically unlike most other primates, and it is to the forests that we must look for evidence of the beginnings of primates and of man.

THE ARBOREAL ADAPTATION

One of the most important distinguishing features of modern primates is the possession of a grasping hand, acquired through the opposition of the thumbs to the other digits. In some primates—for instance, the loris—the thumb is set at 180 degrees to the other digits. However, the earliest primates of which anthropologists have knowledge probably lacked the ability to grasp, relying instead on claws that could be dug into the bark of trees during climbing, in much the same manner as squirrels do. But by the beginning of the Eocene, some 60 million years ago, most primates had lost their claws and had acquired grasping fingers terminating in flat nails, which provided support for their sensitive tactile finger pads.

As yet, there is no definite evidence of what the very earliest primates were like, but it is reasonable to speculate that they broadly resembled the modern tree shrew. In fact, these small animals were at one time considered to be the most primitive living primates, but the weight of evidence now accumulating indicates that they do not belong to our own order. Nevertheless, although the tree shrew has a snout too long, a nose too large and moist, and eyes too far to the side of its head for it ever to be mistaken for a monkey, or even a lemur, it is still the best living approximation of the small proto-primate from which all primates, including man, probably descended.

THE PROSIMIANS

More than 70 million years ago, the prosimians (pre-monkeys) began diverging from primitive insectivores. After about 10 million years of evolution, they had acquired brains that were relatively large for the size of their bodies and had also come to possess refinements in dentition and in locomotion. Their digits had lengthened and the thumb and big toe had become mobile enough to

Figure 2 (left). The grasping adaptation — the basis of the manual dexterity of the higher primates. Figure 3 (right). The flow of primate evolution. Although much is still unknown about the timing and the relations of events in this evolutionary sequence, it is possible to suggest some likely correlations on the basis of the known fossil evidence. Figure 4 (below right). An abbreviated chart of mammalian and primate adaptations in correlation with the geologic record.

spread apart into a grasp. This grasp gave them the ability to move out onto the ends of both horizontal and vertical branches and thus enlarged the area in which they might feed and provided them with a more secure refuge from enemies. The primitive prosimian grasp formed the basis of the manual dexterity of the higher primates. Today, the prosimian's skill in handling food and other objects is well beyond that of any lower arboreal animal, and no prosimian has to depend on the two-handed grasp that is seen in the classic posture of a squirrel holding a nut.

Like monkeys, some prosimians move on all fours along the tops of branches, and some are slow, four-handed climbers. Others move in long leaps, using their back feet to propel them. This latter mode of locomotion, termed "vertical clinging and leaping," is dominated by the hind limbs, which are greatly elongated in comparison with the forelimbs. Vertical clingers and leapers such as the African galagos prefer vertical supports for resting positions, and they leap from one tree to another by propelling themselves with their powerful legs—often for distances of as much as twenty feet. Because such prosimians have such strong and elongated hind limbs, most of them must use a bipedal hop or a sort of bent-kneed walk to move about on the ground.

Although prosimians are undoubtedly primates, they retain traits that mark them as primitive forms. Some have rather advanced behavior patterns related to group cohesiveness, but they delimit their territories by using scent marking to a much greater extent than do the higher primates. This is a device used by many relatively generalized mammals. Some prosimians—the lemurs, for example—have long, projecting snouts with moist muzzles. For these animals, the sense of smell is very important in obtaining information. Compared to monkeys, apes, and men, the eyes of some primitive prosimians are too far to the sides of their

heads for them to achieve complete stereoscopic vision. In addition, only the tarsiers among prosimians have their eyes protected by partly formed bony eye sockets, which are always present and completely developed in higher primates.

Moreover, the prosimians are relatively short-lived in comparison to higher primates, which presumably limits the extent of behavioral complexity they can achieve. Yet for more than 40 million years, prosimians dominated the trees. They spread across several continents and diversified as they went. By Oligocene times (30 million years ago), however, it appears they were challenged by better-equipped animals of prosimian origin—the earliest monkeys—and, unable to compete successfully with the challenge, they have since become restricted severely in habitat. One group of prosimians still survives in certain areas on the mainland of Asia and in Africa. They have adapted to the pressure of competition from other primates by living nocturnally, feeding and moving about at night when most monkeys are asleep. The Asian loris and the African pottos have specialized further by having acquired through evolution a cryptic, slow-moving pattern of locomotion that serves to obscure them from predator and prey alike. They hunt lizards, insects, and birds by stealth, a habit not seen among higher primates. Most continental prosimians have also increased their ability to survive by living singly or in very small family groups, thereby improving their chances of being unobserved and unmolested.

Until relatively recent times, prosimians have flourished on the island of Madagascar (Malagasy Republic), which they probably reached before the higher primates came into existence. On this island sanctuary, the lemurs have had perhaps 45 million years to diversify without much interference from other mammals. Forms evolved that resemble a variety of higher primates. These included large terrestrial forms, now extinct

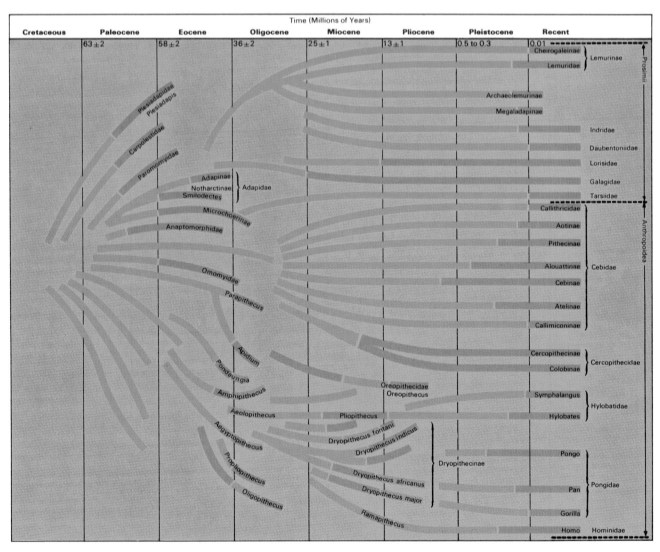

Time	Era	Period	Epoch	Abbreviated Evolutionary Record
0.01	Cenozoic	Quaternary	Recent	Temperate climate; modern man established throughout the world. Decline of game herds; rise of domestication and proliferation of man.
3 ± 1			Pleistocene	Massive glaciation; evidence for upright walking and tool use for hominids. Increase in brain size; signs of social organization related to hunting the great animal herds.
13 ± 1		Tertiary	Pliocene	Terrestrial uplift; gradual cooling of climate. Increase in size and numbers of mammals.
25 ± 1			Miocene	Mild, wet climate. Rain forests and grasslands. Wide distribution of primitive apes throughout Old World. Probable time of appearance of man's apelike ancestor.
36 ± 2			Oligocene	Oldest known remains of anthropoids, presumably including the basal ancestor of the dryopithecine apes.
58 ± 2			Eocene	Extensive forests. World-wide distribution of primate forms. Appearance of grasping, flat-nailed fingers for most primates. Increased brain size, refined dentition and locomotion.
63 ± 2			Paleocene	Beginning of climatic cooling. Prosimian divergence from primitive insectivores. Signs of arboreal adaptation.
120	Mesozoic	Cretaceous		Disappearance of large, dominant reptiles; appearance of modern insects and flowering plants.
180		Jurassic		Continued reptilian domination.
200		Triassic		Volcanic activity. Temperate climate and swamplands encourage reptilian radiation into land zones, oceans, and air. The Age of Reptiles; inconspicuous development of small, true, placental mammals, including forbears of primates.
285	Paleozoic	Permian		Major terrestrial uplift creates dry zones where reptiles thrive. Cool, moist zones giving rise to mammal-like reptiles; e.g., Therapsids, with elevated body temperature and metabolism, limb and dentition changes, separation of breathing and eating passages. Evidence for glaciation.
350		Carboniferous		Appearance of moist, swampy lowlands; rise of amphibians. Later geologic uplift produces dry climate. Some amphibians adapt to terrestrial life as primitive reptiles. Appearance of five-digited amphibian foot.
400		Devonian		Widespread terrestrial uplifting and desiccation, forcing adaptation; e.g., Crossopterygians develop muscular lobes at the bases of fins to help push them from puddle to puddle in drying streams. Lung, nostril development.
450		Silurian		Appearance of Ostracoderm, a fresh-water fish. Probable ancestor of all vertebrates.
500		Ordovician		Hints of primitive fishes.
600		Cambrian		Appearance of marine invertebrate forms.
1,500	Proterozoic			Appearance of bacteria, algae, fungi, Primitive multicelled organisms.
5,000	Archeozoic			Formation of earth's crust, earliest known life. Single-celled organisms.

(Millions of Years)

Figure 5. An *Adapis* skull from the Late Eocene, found at Quercy, France, and a *Plesiadapis* skull from the Late Paleocene found at Mont-de-Berru, near Cernay-Les-Reims, France. Figure 6 (right). What the prosimian *Plesiadapis* may have looked like. It was from such arboreally adapted, placental mammals that the later primates were to evolve.

(at the hands of man), as well as a number of arboreal species. They have also developed fairly complex social groupings and even types of vocal communication found elsewhere only among monkeys and apes.

THE TRANSITION TO PRIMATES

Although most texts discussing primate origins touch on the question of basal transition from or origins within the insectivores, there appears to be almost no actual fossil material that convincingly documents such a transition. The lengthy debate on primate origins appears to have its roots in hypothetical considerations. From what is known of the evolution of tetrapods in general and of Cretaceous and subsequent placental mammals in particular, it is likely that the forerunners of primates were small terrestrial animals. This assumption is plausible because it is unlikely that the forebears of the primates that existed some 75 to 100 million years ago could already have been arboreal. The period was too early in the history of placental mammals, very few of which have ever become accomplished arborealists in any case. The fossil record tells next to nothing about the locomotor adaptations of earliest placentals in question, but insectivore and primate fossil evidence from the period between 75 and 60 million years ago does give clear indications of arboreal adaptations in the limb bones of these later animals. The teeth of many archaic prosimians appear to have been suited to the husking of seeds and fruits—activities usually carried on in the trees, not on the ground. This dental adaptation is significant when viewed in light of the fact that much of the history of primate evolution is essentially a history of the degree to which various species have adapted to life in the trees.

PALEOCENE AND EOCENE PROSIMIANS

The best-preserved prosimian remains from the Paleocene (65 to 50 million years ago) belong to species of the genus *Plesiadapis*,

and these species are also the most widespread and perhaps the most abundant in fossil sites of any early member of this order. *Plesiadapis* possessed distinctive front teeth: each of the upper central incisors had three or four projecting cusps that gave it a glovelike appearance. It has been proposed that *Plesiadapis* teeth were used to chew seeds and fruit, a suggestion that implies this animal fed principally in the trees.

A *Plesiadapis* skull found in France shows that the characteristic primate bony eye sockets had not yet appeared. Moreover, the flaring cheek bones and elongated face of this specimen give it a marked resemblance to archaic mammals in general rather than to more highly evolved Eocene primates such as *Adapis* and *Notharctus*, both of which exhibit far greater development of brain size and frontality of the eyes.

Although *Plesiadapis* was about the size of a squirrel, with its thick limb bones it was much more heavily built. *Plesiadapis* was arboreal but it probably was not as agile in the trees as were later primates. Skeletal remains recovered in Paleocene deposits in the western United States and in France indicate that it may have moved about in much the same manner as the modern gray squirrel, but more clumsily; its forelimbs were adapted to function in a manner similar to those of vertical clingers and leapers. In fact, the *Plesiadapis* mode of locomotion may have been a stage preadaptive to the vertical clinging and leaping mode that is common to nearly all Eocene prosimians. Perhaps, like some kinds of tree shrews, certain *Plesiadapis* species were semiterrestrial, occasionally using their large, compressed claws to scramble up the bark of trees as the modern South American marmosets do.

Whatever its ecological niche may have been, *Plesiadapis* lived throughout a remarkably broad geographic range. It shares with two other extinct prosimian forms and man the distinction of being one of only four

genera of primates to inhabit both the Old World and the New World. The number of finds and the geographic range of *Plesiadapis* would seem to indicate adaptive success. *Plesiadapis* and its close relatives became extinct after surviving from about 60 million years to perhaps 40 million years ago.

The fossil remains of ancient primates or possible primates are seldom as complete or as wide in occurrence as those of *Plesiadapis*. It is only when the Eocene Epoch is studied that the record begins to be revealing. *Tetonius*, the oldest primate of "modern aspect" for which a skull is preserved, lived about 55 million years ago, during the Early Eocene, but it already exhibited many features similar to those of later prosimians and was a remarkably advanced Eocene mammal. Its braincase was large in relation to the size of its face and snout, and it had large eye sockets. Moreover, it exhibited signs of a more erect posture than was typical of early mammals. Forward-directed eyes, which provided full stereoscopic vision, and elongated hind limbs of closely related forms strongly suggest that *Tetonius* moved about by vertical clinging and leaping. Altogether, the evidence provided by *Tetonius* and by the flora and fauna associated with it indicates that by the early Eocene, small, agile, arboreal primates were already engaged in successful diurnal insect feeding in the warm rain forests.

During the Middle Eocene in France, guano-filled caves and fissures were built up to form the celebrated Quercy phosphorite deposits, and here abundant small skulls and skeletons are preserved. Skulls of *Necrolemur*, *Adapis magnus*, and *Adapis parisiensis* are among the numerous informative fossil remains recovered from these deposits. Most of the specimens are relatively uncrushed, and they provide an unparalleled sample of comparatively well-preserved Eocene primates.

All the Quercy phosphorite prosimians appear to have been diurnal, presumably occupying an ecological niche in Eocene times somewhat similar to that occupied in the tropical forests today by monkeys. *Necrolemur* and related forms are almost certainly close to the direct ancestor of modern tarsiers. The teeth of the *Necrolemur* relative, *Pseudoloris*, are extraordinarily similar to those of living *Tarsius*, indicating that the feeding mechanism of these creatures has changed little in the past 45 million years and possibly suggesting a direct ancestor-descendant relationship. The two species of *Adapis* and forms allied to them are the most probable forerunners of the modern lemurs. The forelimbs and hind limbs of *Adapis* appear to have been more nearly equal in length than those of most other primitive fossil prosimians. Thus, *Adapis* may have already been adapted to quadrupedalism of the sort seen in some of today's lemurs and in most Old World monkeys.

MONKEYS AND APES: THE ANTHROPOIDS
The higher primates, or Anthropoidea, are classified into three main groups: New World monkeys, Old World monkeys, and

Figure 7. Along with the grasping adaptation and increased visual acuity, it has been suggested that brachiation — the arm-swinging/suspending mode of moving about — was prerequisite to the emergence of the higher primates. Humans and the modern great apes have similarities in the chest, shoulder, and arm structure that have been cited as indications of a brachiating adaptation that directed their forbears toward a habitual vertical position.

trol over refined hand movements, and more sophisticated social interactions including complex systems of vocal communication are all characteristics typical of this group of basically herbivorous tree-living animals —the higher primates—that were becoming more successful through acquisition of social systems demanding greater and greater capacities for learned behavior. When anthropologists speak of specific higher primate adaptations, it is difficult and not particularly useful to separate cause from effect, yet it is probably fair to say that the social demands were of central importance in shaping primate evolution.

The average higher primate brain is several times the average size of the brain of a living prosimian. The increase in size is attributable to an increase in the cortical areas concerned with vision (occipital lobes), with vocalization and hearing (temporal and parietal lobes), and with associations between these areas of primary memory storage (the so-called association areas). Higher primates perceive their world in a manner unique among animals, principally through their remarkable three-dimensional color vision in combination with a fine sense of touch and a large capacity for tactile discrimination and manipulation of objects. This sensory setup provides the basis for a feedback system that enables the primate to perceive and deal with its environment by structuring it in terms of distinct components and patterns. In addition to expanded cortical areas, an expansion that also involved rearrangements and "improvements" on the cellular level, the nervous systems of higher primates are characterized by an expanded cerebellum. This latter increase in size provides the increased sensory-motor control over fine movements, particularly of the hand, and by additional, more direct and efficient central-peripheral connections in the form of the lemniscal system of neurons.

There is also a trend among higher primates toward longer lifespans, presumably a

apes and man. The nonhuman primates of this suborder are often popularly referred to as anthropoids or less commonly (and incorrectly) as simians.

Anthropoid Adaptations
A principal distinction between monkeys and prosimians lies in a shift in the relative importance of the senses. The world of the trees is a visual world. The ability to judge distances is of obvious importance in allowing a primate to move rapidly and efficiently through an unpredictable three-dimensional world. Success in the trees is also contingent upon the ability to perceive variations in movement and color that indicate the presence of food or threat. At the same time, the sense of smell is of greatly reduced value: in the arboreal habitat, where aspects of the surrounding environment must be located in three dimensions and at a distance, smell is not a reliable indicator. As they became adapted arboreally, monkeys appear to have lost much of their sense of smell, and partly for this reason their snouts became shorter. They lost the moist muzzle of the prosimian and the proportion of the brain devoted to smell became relatively smaller.

It is important to view the characteristics used to distinguish higher primates from lower primates as a mutually reinforcing, interrelated set of adaptations. Thus, increased visual acuity, improved motor con-

Figure 8. Adaptive differences between Old World monkeys (catarrhines) and New World monkeys (platyrrhines). Catarrhines are marked by narrow, closely spaced nostrils, whereas the platyrrhine nostrils are flat and widely spaced. The dentition of New World monkeys is more primitive in that they have three instead of two premolars.

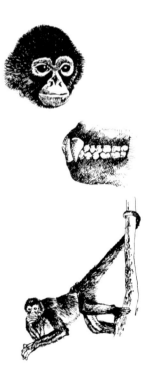

result of the increased time required for socializing the primate infant as the social system becomes more complex. And once socialized, the animal comes to have an individual value for the survival of the group, which provides an additional selective pressure for longer life.

Locomotor Adaptations

Like some prosimians, Old World monkeys today can be classified as arboreal quadrupeds, although in comparatively recent times baboons, macaques, and patas monkeys have come to live almost exclusively on the ground. Cercopithecid monkeys are fairly uniform in the conformation of their shoulders, rib cages, limbs, and other postcranial features. They seem to represent a specialized adaptive form that diverged from the main line of primate evolution. Quadrupedalism is a very efficient mode of arboreal locomotion but is limited in that only branches of a thickness capable of maintaining the entire weight of the animal can be used as supports.

Clearly, an animal that is able to distribute its weight between two or more branches at a time and still reach out to grab for food can move about in a wider zone in the arboreal canopy, thus exploiting food sources unavailable to strictly arboreal quadrupeds such as the cercopithecids. Certain primate groups have evolved to the degree that they have this ability. Some South American monkeys such as the spider monkey move through the trees by suspending their weight beneath the branches they grasp with their forelimbs, and they are able to stand on one branch while holding onto another, thus distributing their weight between the two branches. Some New World monkeys, including the spider monkeys, even have a special prehensile tail that allows them to hang onto yet another branch and distribute their weight even further. However, it is in the apes that the arm-swinging/suspending mode of locomotion

has been most developed. The orangutan, for example, can be described as a four-handed (quadrumanous) hanger-swinger. This ape has long arms and legs and is capable of suspending itself beneath supports by either or both sets of limbs. The orangutan, although bulky, can reach the outermost portion of the smallest branches by hanging from three of its limbs and feeding with the fourth. The most agile arm swinger (brachiator) of all is the gibbon. With its enormously elongated arms, this remarkably agile creature can swing thirteen feet or more from one branch to another—in effect, leaping with its arms. The gibbon is the only true brachiator. It should be pointed out, however, that brachiation as seen in the gibbon is not an efficient way of moving for long distances and may account for the fact that these apes live in small family groups and have small, fixed territories.

Dental, Auditory, and Cranial Adaptation

Other major physical distinctions serve to differentiate monkeys from one another and all monkeys from apes. New World monkeys have a more primitive dental arrangement (or formula) than Old World monkeys in that they have three instead of two premolars. The Old World monkeys and apes possess a bony tube for the auditory canal between the middle and the external ear. The Paleocene/Eocene prosimian *Plesiadapis* and the tarsiers also possess such a tube. The primitive ape *Aegyptopithecus* does not, however, which indicates that this feature has been acquired independently in several groups of primates.

It was once believed that the ancestors of all apes and men had proceeded progressively through stages of development, first resembling lemurs, then tarsiers, and then monkeys, finally achieving some primitive apelike level. The fossil evidence provides no support for this theory: As far back as Old World and New World monkeys can be traced, both possessed distinguishable den-

Figure 9. Comparison of *Parapithecus* from the Fayum (lower mandible) with a modern talapoin monkey. The four front teeth of the *Parapithecus* specimen were found separately from the cheek tooth row but are of the proper size and shape to be assigned to this primate. Figure 10 (below). An *Aegyptopithecus* skull from the Oligocene of Egypt, perhaps 28-30 million years old. The cranium is articulated with a mandible that has been pieced together from several specimens. The skull combines primitive features (e.g., the large premaxillary bone) with advanced features (e.g., the bony closure behind the eye that forms an eye socket).

tal and cranial characteristics. It is likely that the higher primates arose not from anything that resembled the more primitive forms existing today but from less-specialized forms. The ancestors of apes may have resembled New World monkeys postcranially. And the ancestors of Old World monkeys are very poorly known.

THE FOSSIL ANTHROPOIDS

The oldest remains of anthropoids are fossils from the Oligocene Epoch. Prosimian remains are rare from that time onward, and it can be surmised that the prosimians were replaced by more advanced forms. Six indisputable genera of primates have in fact been recovered from the rich Oligocene deposits of the Fayum badlands near Cairo in the Near East, and these fossils can be used to trace aspects of the transition from prosimian to identifiably anthropoid (monkey or apelike) characteristics. This transition is best observed in features of the skulls and jaws of the specimens. The Fayum primate skulls together with skull fragments that have been found exhibit the closed and protected eye sockets that are typical of higher primates, and the dentition is more generalized than that of many prosimians.

Many specimens of Fayum primates *Apidium* and *Parapithecus* have been recovered recently by Yale University expeditions. In mandibular, cranial, dental, and postcranial anatomy, *Apidium* and *Parapithecus* bear unmistakable resemblances to modern Old World monkeys and should probably be regarded as the earliest members of this group. *Parapithecus* has the square, four-cusped, partly cross-ridged molars typical of Old World monkeys; *Apidium* also has generally monkeylike molars but has accessory cusps similar to the teeth of the problematic Late Miocene fossil primate *Oreopithecus*.

Oligopithecus is clearly distinctive, although it is known only from a single find in the Fayum. It is the smallest, oldest, and structurally the most primitive of the African Oligocene primates, with a dentition that places it not among the later Fayum monkeys but probably in or near the ancestry of the Fayum apes. *Aeolopithecus* and *Propliopithecus* were small Fayum primates that were similar in size, but they differed considerably in their dental mechanisms. Both had somewhat unusual dental features, and both were primitive apes, perhaps related to the extinct lesser apes *Limnopithecus* and *Pliopithecus* and to the smallest of modern apes, the gibbon and the siamang.

The Fayum ape *Aegyptopithecus* is known from several fossils, including a nearly complete skull found in 1967. It closely resembles the 20-million-year-old *Dryopithecus* species originally called *Proconsul africanus* that was found in Miocene deposits in East Africa. This similarity makes *Aegyptopithecus* an excellent candidate for being the basal ancestor of the dryopithecine apes that subsequently spread throughout Eurasia and presumably included the stock from which the first hominids evolved.

With the exception of these fruitful discoveries in the Fayum, the finds of early anthropoid remains have been less than satisfactory. Two poorly known fossil primates —*Amphipithecus* and *Pondaungia* from the Late Eocene in Burma—may represent archaic apes, but each is known only from an individual find. The fragments indicate resemblances of a sort to the earliest African apes known from the Fayum and the two fossil primates may well be earlier representatives of the same adaptive radiation, but the evidence is far too limited for such a claim to be a strong one.

The earliest monkey skull found in South America is of the type known as *Dolichocebus* and dates from the Late Oligocene; the oldest known South American monkey, *Branisella*, dates from the Early Oligocene, but it is only an upper jaw fragment. Other skull and jaw fragments, described under the genus *Homunculus*, have been uncovered in Argentina and Patagonia. These early

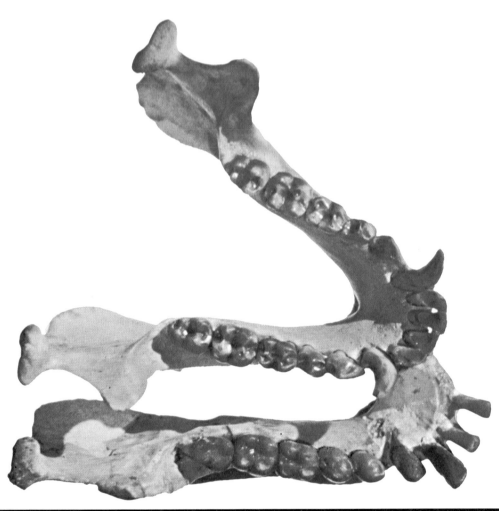

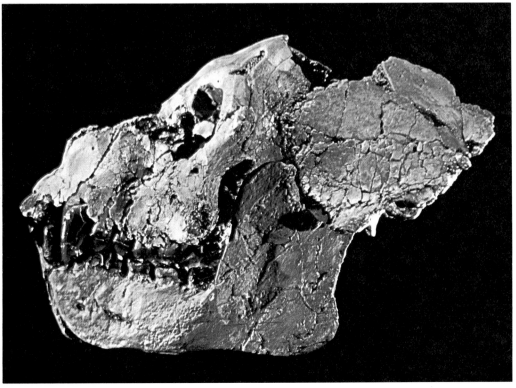

Figure 11. What man's apelike ancestor may have looked like. This reconstruction is based on the dryopithecine evidence recovered throughout the Old World. Figure 12 (right). Excavating the rich fossil beds of the Fayum badlands in Egypt. This 1967 Yale expedition was directed by Elwyn L. Simons, shown on the far right.

monkeys are reasonably advanced ceboids, but they appear to represent side branches not related to subsequent forms. A few other South American fossil monkeys are known and as a group are of interest because they indicate that monkeys presumably reached South America by rafting or island hopping during or before Early Oligocene times some 33 to 35 million years ago (North and South America were not then connected by a land bridge).

Not much is known about Miocene monkeys, but there is enough information about some lesser apes to provide useful insights. Fossils resembling gibbons recovered in East Africa and in Europe have been designated *Limnopithecus* and *Pliopithecus*, respectively, although they may even be the same genus. The fact that there have been no signs of them in Miocene sites in Asia suggests that gibbons achieved their present range of distribution in Southeast Asia only in more recent times. This view must be considered nothing more than speculation, however, until additional fossil hunting in pre-Pleistocene deposits has been carried out in areas where gibbons now thrive. In any event, these two Miocene anthropoids possessed dentitions and facial conformations as well as general similarities in size and bone structure that imply special affinities to the modern gibbon and siamang. If they were direct ancestors of the gibbons, *Limnopithecus* and *Pliopithecus* probably did not fully possess the sophisticated locomotor-feeding adaptation of their descendants, although they were presumably as efficient at arm swinging as are some of the New World monkeys.

LINKS WITH THE HOMINIDS
Dryopithecus
During the Miocene and Pliocene epochs, primitive apes of the genus *Dryopithecus* were widely distributed throughout the Old World. Several of their physical characteristics as well as the date of their occurrence

led to the claim that they were ancestral to the hominids. Although man is almost certainly descended from some early dryopithecine, it is clear that no known species can definitely be given the status of man's undisputed apelike ancestor.

Dryopithecus africanus, fossils of which have been found in Middle Miocene deposits in Kenya, probably existed about 18 million years ago. Because a number of good fossils have been recovered, it is best known of the dryopithecines. It was a small creature, about the size of a modern female baboon, and was delicately built. Its dentition resembles that of both the earlier *Aegyptopithecus* of the Fayum and modern chimpanzees. Its skeletal remains indicate that it was an agile, arboreal quadruped that may have already undergone some terrestrial adaptations. *Dryopithecus major* from the Middle Miocene of Uganda and Kenya was also primitive, but it shows many resemblances to the modern gorilla. It was as big as the female of this modern great ape species, and the skeletal remains that have been found suggest that *Dryopithecus major* was probably more terrestrially adapted than was *Dryopithecus africanus*.

There is only one candidate for the possible ancestor of the orangutan, last of the remaining great apes to be mentioned. This is *Dryopithecus sivalensis* of the Late Miocene and Early Pliocene periods in India. Unfortunately, the details of cusp structure between this fossil ape and the orangutan are dissimilar, so judgment about the evolutionary link in question must remain extremely tentative.

Oreopithecus
Well known from excellent fossils found in the Late Miocene and Early Pliocene swamp deposits in Italy, *Oreopithecus* is one of the most puzzling primates ever discovered. Strong claims have been made for its candidacy as a direct ancestor of man because it exhibits a number of features closely asso-

ciated with hominids. It had a humanlike skull, an extremely flat face, and small canines and incisors. But the joints of its hips, shoulders, forelimbs, and hind limbs were constructed not for stability but rather for mobility. Nor was it bipedal; it is possible that it moved and lived somewhat as the orangutan does now. The close similarities between certain human and *Oreopithecus* characteristics therefore seem to be the result of parallel evolution rather than of an ancestor-descendant relationship that would link this extinct primate directly to man. *Oreopithecus* may have been a descendant of *Apidium* from the Oligocene, but it is not a likely forerunner of man. Nevertheless, parallels between *Oreopithecus* and hominids remain intriguing, and further research on this primate may throw more light on the kind of adaptations that eventually produced man.

Gigantopithecus

Gigantopithecus is another fossil primate for which hominid affinities have been claimed. Until recently, the origins of this enigmatic form were unknown, but in 1968 a Yale-Punjab University expedition working in Middle Pliocene deposits in India discovered a lower jaw that was made the type of the species *Gigantopithecus bilaspurensis* that is ancestral to the long-known *Gigantopithecus blacki*, which lived in China in the Early or Middle Pleistocene. *Gigantopithecus blacki* was the largest primate that ever lived. These huge apes foraged for grasses, seeds, and other vegetable food in the open country. *Dryopithecus indicus* of India, which lived about 12 million years ago, shows marked resemblances to *Gigantopithecus bilaspurensis*, suggesting that it or one of its close relatives gave rise to these giant primates during the Late Miocene or Early Pliocene. As in the case of *Oreopithecus*, resemblances of *Gigantopithecus* to man are the result of parallel evolution rather than direct ancestry. *Gigantopithecus*

and the earliest human ancestors became adapted to similar habitats and probably acquired similar dietary preferences.

Ramapithecus

This genus was originally named from an upper jaw that was found in the vicinity of Haritalyangar in India, about 200 miles north of New Delhi. The beds yielding this find have not been geochemically dated, but the associated fauna from these sites suggests an age somewhere between about 12 and 8 million years. Since *Ramapithecus* was named, evidence has been growing to support the claim originally made by G. E. Lewis in 1934 that it is the earliest known hominid. Over a dozen specimens of *Ramapithecus* have now been found. Studies done at Yale University by Elwyn Simons and others confirm that of all the fossil primates older than 5 million years, only species of this genus presently qualify as functional hominids. A *Ramapithecus* find in Late Miocene deposits near Fort Ternan, Kenya, is the oldest known, correctly dated hominid. It was mistakenly considered by its discoverer to be a new form and was designated *Kenyapithecus wickeri*. Actually it should be spoken of as *Ramapithecus*, cf. *punjabicus*. Since the early 1960s, several additional specimens have been identified in collec-

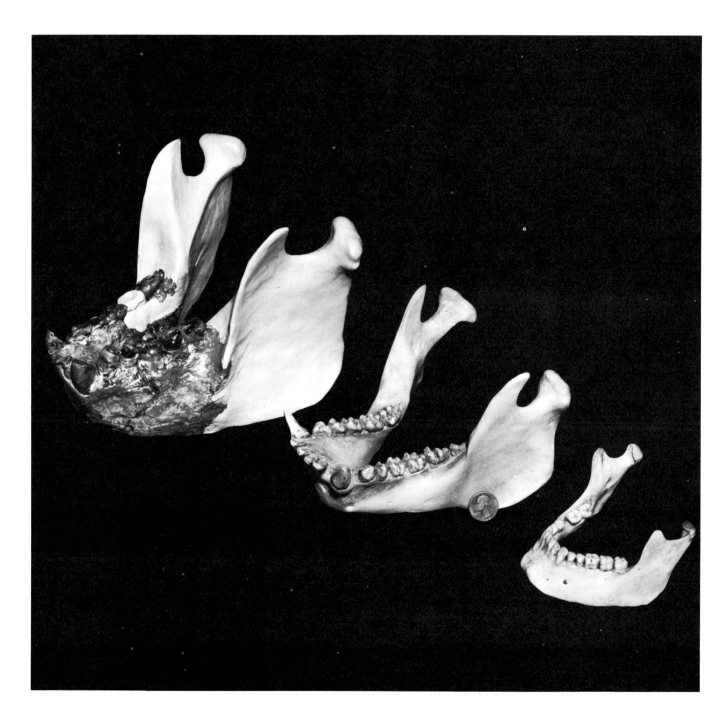

Figure 13 (left). Comparison of a male *Gigantopithecus* jaw from China with that of a male mountain gorilla and modern man. Figure 14. Part of the left upper jaw of a *Ramapithecus* specimen discovered at Fort Ternan, Kenya, in 1960. The site has been dated to 14 million years. As can be seen here, *Ramapithecus* is characterized by widely spaced molar cusps, flat molar crowns, small canines, and packed-together teeth.

tions. There are now at least four lower jaws with teeth, three upper jaw fragments, and some of the anterior teeth. When taken together, all these specimens suggest that in dentition and facial structure, *Ramapithecus* was more diminutive than *Australopithecus;* the jawbones are not more delicate, only smaller. Some of the mandibles are unusually thick compared to those of apes of the same absolute size—for instance, those of the female pigmy chimpanzee. In *Ramapithecus,* as in *Australopithecus,* canines are small and small-rooted. Incisors are relatively small and small-rooted and are also more vertically emplaced than is typical of apes of similar size. The molars are flat, round, of similar size, and strongly emplanted in thick jaws. The ascending part of the lower jaw as well as the point where the cheekbones join the face are both shifted forward relative to the molar teeth, which has the effect of increasing the mechanical efficiency of the chewing muscles in grinding. These and related features strongly suggest that *Ramapithecus* is in or near the ancestry of *Australopithecus,* and later, men.

ADAPTIVE TRENDS TOWARD MAN

From the paleontological point of view, the most important indicators of the distinct appearance of the hominid basic adaptation —that to ground feeding and foraging in open country—are seen in the powerful hominid dental mechanism, characterized by robust jaws, reduced canines, vertically emplaced incisors, and closely packed, flattened, and broadened cheek teeth. There are many differences between this early hominid tooth and mandibular conformation and the dental mechanisms of any fossil ape or living ape, and it is probable that the manner of feeding and the type of food ingested by the earliest hominids such as *Ramapithecus* and *Australopithecus* differed in kind from that of the apes, even though it is not entirely clear what the actual foodstuffs were. There is a high degree of probability that

these foodstuffs were found on the ground and were generally small, tough morsels such as seeds (which the grinding cheek teeth are well adapted to handle). The earliest hominids probably foraged out into the open country to an ever-increasing extent and evolved increasingly complex social groups. The danger of attack by predators in open country might have been met by stone throwing, screaming, and a return to the trees or to cliffs at night.

Their possession of a distinctive sort of tooth structure and masticatory muscular system makes it possible to include species of *Ramapithecus,* *Australopithecus,* and *Homo* in one family, Hominidae, and to exclude fossil apes, which characteristically have different tooth and jaw proportions that indicate different feeding adaptations. What is perhaps even more important is the recent inference that the delayed molar eruption typical of the genus *Homo* also occurred in *Australopithecus* and probably in *Ramapithecus* as well—as inferred from highly differential degrees of wear on successive molars. Inasmuch as the full eruption of the wisdom teeth of great apes and man approximately correlates with full skeletal maturity, delayed eruption of the twelve-year molars and wisdom teeth probably indicates that, like modern man, *Australopithecus* species had a period of infant dependency much longer than that of the apes, with the consequent advantages for socialization and cultural transmission. The three most worn mandibular specimens of *Ramapithecus* also show a high differential of decreasing wear toward the back on the molars. It may well be that a lengthy period of infant dependency has characterized hominids throughout most of their long history. Because there is no evidence from the Pliocene or earlier regarding the emergence of bipedalism and tool use among hominids, at present the definitions of Hominidae that depend on the presence of these characteristics are unsatisfactory.

Presapient Hominids

11

In November 1887 a young Dutch army physician, Eugene Dubois, sailed for Padang in Sumatra, determined to discover the "missing link" in the chain of human evolution. Earlier, in 1856, a heated controversy had raged over the identification of a large skull that had been found near the German town of Düsseldorf. With its great bony ridges over the eye sockets and its thick cranial bones, it was certainly not the skull of a man—at least any kind of man in existence—but neither was it the skull of any known animal. As Dubois grew up, the controversy somewhat waned, but he continued to ponder the meaning of the skull and eventually decided that it must have belonged to a primitive man, perched somewhere on a ladder that led up from the apes. But if there were one such skull, there were surely others, even more archaic, going back to that obscure and intriguing ancestor who, somewhere in the remote past, had formed the link between man and the apes.

Dubois reasoned that man must have come into existence in the tropics—either in Africa, where the gorilla and chimpanzee still live, or in the Indo-Malayan region, home of the orangutan. Dubois' reasoning was excellent and he did indeed find the remains of the earliest member of the genus *Homo* ever to be unearthed, but he was misguided in his search for a missing link. First, the missing link theory was based on the assumption that man had developed from an animal very similar to modern apes and that the missing link would therefore be half ape, half man. But modern man did not descend from modern apes. What did happen is that some 30 million years ago the apelike animals that were to evolve into men diverged from their ancestral line and set out along one evolutionary course while the animals that were to evolve into modern apes proceeded along another.

The other main flaw in the missing link theory is the implication that the characteristics distinguishing man from apes are primarily physical. It is true that considerable physical differences do exist between them. Man has different kinds of teeth, adapted for eating different kinds of food, especially meat. Unlike the apes, man's feet, leg mus-

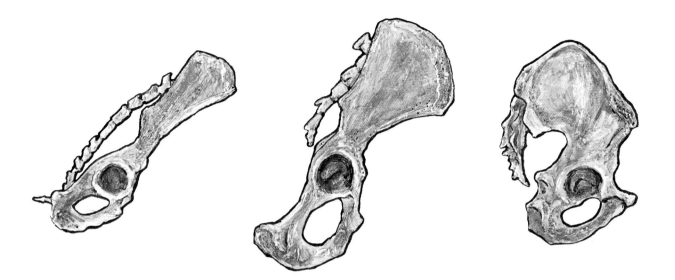

cles, and pelvis are adapted for bipedal (upright) walking and running. Moreover, man's skull is shaped differently and set on reduced neck muscles that permit the skull to rest on a vertical neck rather than on the nearly horizontal neck that is characteristic of apes. But the most important difference between man and apes—and all other animals, for that matter—is that man alone possesses *culture* and can use the inventions of his mind to adapt to different conditions. If a bird is to acquire an improved method of flight, it can do so only if changes happen to occur in its genes. Man has invented airplanes. When the polar bear evolved into an animal that could live in the arctic cold, it did so only because the forces of evolution provided it with such protective physical equipment as thick fur. Man is capable of living in cold climates because he has invented clothing and shelters and forms of power that produce heat. Alfred Kroeber gave to such forms of human adaptation the name *superorganic* (beyond the physical), and it is man's superorganic behavior and characteristics that really distinguish him from any other animal.

In the course of human evolution, then, the most decisive changes have occurred not in human anatomy or physiology but in what man thinks and does and how he relates to his environment—that is, in his behavior and ecology. And the really significant differences between man and apes seem to have stemmed from one principal source: man's capacity for conceptual thought. It is possible to perceive the faint beginnings of cultural activity in nonhuman animals and in them the roots from which human culture may have sprung. But man's well-developed capacity for conceptual thought is so far beyond that of any other known organism that it makes him qualitatively different, and as his technology continues to improve, he is becoming increasingly free from the otherwise universal genetic mechanisms of biological evolution.

THE EARLIEST HOMINIDS

The earliest manlike creatures sufficiently distinct from apes to be given a special name are usually considered *hominids*. The first identified hominid remains were discovered less than fifty years ago when a juvenile skull of the genus *Australopithecus* was found in a lime mine near Taung, South Africa. Its dentition indicated that it was comparable to a modern child six years old. In 1924, it came more-or-less accidentally into the care of Raymond Dart of the University of Witwatersrand in Johannesburg. Dart decided that it had belonged to a manlike ape, evolving in the direction of man, and he named it *Australopithecus africanus*. His view was not accepted; the consensus was that the skull was merely that of a fossil ape. But Robert Broom, a Scottish medical practitioner who spent most of his life in South Africa, became convinced that Dart was right. In 1936, in a lime mine at Sterkfontein near Johannesburg, he found some fragmentary materials of adult specimens that were similar to the Taung child, and in 1938 at nearby Kromdraai he uncovered a different type of hominid, which he named *Paranthropus robustus*.

These early finds whetted scientific appetites, but not until after World War II did the chief period of early hominid discovery begin. Broom died early in 1951, but the research that he and John Robinson started in 1946 had, by 1953, yielded almost 300 speci-

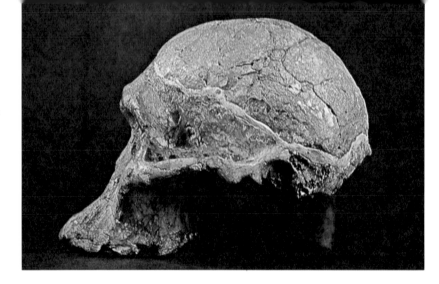

Figure 2 (left). Pelvic comparison of monkey, gorilla, and modern man. Just as bone structure can illustrate the stance of these creatures, so also can fossil remains provide an idea of the posture and locomotion of the early hominids. Figure 3. The most complete *Australopithecus* skull found thus far at Sterkfontein. Figure 4 (lower right). The well-developed lumbar curvature of *Australopithecus*, sure evidence of erect posture.

mens of *Australopithecus* and *Paranthropus* from three sites in South Africa. Meanwhile, specimens were being gathered from two other South African sites, and students of human evolution had, for the most part, been converted to the view that the australopithecines really were early hominids.

In 1959, another period of hominid discovery began when Louis and Mary Leakey found a fine *Paranthropus* skull at Olduvai Gorge in Tanzania and followed it up with further discoveries of early hominid material. Of the scores of fragments that have now been found at Olduvai, about 90 percent consist of material relating to the head—isolated teeth, bits of jaws, crushed pieces of skulls, and a few almost complete skulls. But there are also pieces of pelvis, scraps of femur bone, lumbar vertebrae, ribs, thigh bones, pieces of foot and ankle bones, shoulder blades, and upper-arm bones. Although some differences of opinion persist, it seems clear that all these fragments come from either *Australopithecus* or *Paranthropus*, and from them it is possible to get a fairly complete picture of what our earliest hominid ancestors must have looked like.

Australopithecus: Closer to Man

The *Australopithecus* female probably weighed between forty and sixty pounds and was about three and one-half feet tall. She had a slender build, except for rather wide hips and a bulging abdomen. The males were probably not much taller than the females but were probably more heavily built. *Australopithecus'* posture was more manlike than apelike. He had the relatively long legs of modern man, not the short ones of the ape, and his knees could be fully extended so that he could easily straighten his legs instead of having to keep them at least a little bent at the knee, as apes must do. His foot was compact, arched, and not very mobile, and it had a well-developed big toe that was held close to his other toes. His foot differed considerably from the rather mobile flat

foot of the African great apes, in which the big toe is more like a thumb than a human big toe. There was another major difference between *Australopithecus* and modern apes. Apes do not have *lumbar lordosis*, that strong curvature in the lumbar region of the spine that gives man a hollow in the small of the back and enables him to keep his trunk erect over his pelvis while he maintains his pelvis in a position suitable for striding. But *Australopithecus*, like modern man, possessed a well-developed *lumbar lordosis*, and his chest cage, too, was shaped like that of modern man.

Australopithecus carried his head much as modern man does. His face was not as vertical as that of modern man but it protruded less than the face of an ape. His canine teeth were small and manlike, not large and apelike, and his incisor teeth were placed vertically as in modern man instead of leaning outward and forward as in apes. His nose had almost no bridge, so that his nasal region must have been rather flat and apelike. But he possessed a well-developed forehead that definitely was not apelike, and his brow ridges were not at all prominent. In spite of a moderately prominent jowl and flat nose, *Australopithecus'* face must have looked much more like that of a man than that of an ape. But his brain was still in the ape size range, with an average volume of about 450 cubic centimeters compared to averages of 400 for chimpanzees, 500 for gorillas, and 1,450 cubic centimeters for modern man.

Paranthropus: Closer to Apes

Paranthropus was more like an ape than was *Australopithecus*. He was much larger —a male *Paranthropus* weighed between 150 and 200 pounds and was about four and one-half to five feet tall. He had a bulging abdomen and probably a more thickly set trunk than *Australopithecus*. His lower limbs were not as short as those of apes but they were proportionately shorter than the legs of *Australopithecus* and modern man,

Figure 5 (left). One of the best *Paranthropus* skulls from Swartkrans. Figure 6 (lower left). *Paranthropus* and *Australopithecus* skulls, illustrating the former's greater robustness and lack of forehead. Figure 7 (right). Life as it may have been for *Australopithecus*. Just as the modern chimpanzee has been known to throw rocks at an intruder, so perhaps did this early hominid learn to throw crude missiles to ward off a predator and — in some sequence of experiences that would have profound implications for the evolution of his kind — to grasp the significance of turning them against prey.

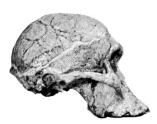

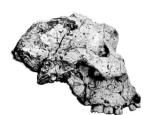

and his foot, too, was probably a compromise between the flexible, rather handlike foot of the apes and the almost completely manlike foot of *Australopithecus*. *Paranthropus* evidently held his head like *Australopithecus*, and his neck muscles were developed and arranged in a similar manner. But his braincase was low and he had no forehead. His frontal bone hardly rose above the level of his brow ridges, and he had a short, low, vertical bony crest running most of the way from his brow ridges to the uppermost point of his neck muscles. His face was closer to being vertical than that of *Australopithecus*, and his big chewing (masticatory) muscles made his face look even more massive. His brain was about the same size as that of *Australopithecus*.

Perhaps the most significant difference between *Australopithecus* and *Paranthropus* was in the lower limbs. In apes, the bones and muscles are so arranged that the limb is pulled back slowly but with great power. In modern man, they are arranged so that the limb can be moved less powerfully but more rapidly, and much longer strides can be taken. The ape limb is better suited to climbing, whereas the human limb is much better adapted for erect walking with relatively little effort. *Paranthropus*' lower limbs were not as short as an ape's, but they were shorter than modern man's, and their mechanism provided much more power. *Australopithecus*, in contrast, possessed the mechanisms that enable man to move quickly over long distances.

In sum, there were definite physical differences between the two early hominids, and all point to the same conclusion: *Paranthropus* was closer to the apes than *Australopithecus*, who was closer to man.

EARLY HOMINID LIFE PATTERNS
Every animal's anatomy, physiology, ecological adaptation, and behavior are closely integrated and interdependent, adding up to a total biology that allows it to function as

effectively as circumstances make possible. It is because these characteristics are so closely integrated that a great deal can be learned about the ecology and behavior of an animal by studying its anatomy. For example, the anatomy and entire way of life of a modern wild horse is influenced by the fact that it is specialized as a plains grazer. Similarly, the anatomy and way of life of a lion is influenced by the fact that it is a large carnivore. Even the most cursory examination of the teeth of a horse and those of a lion demonstrate that the diet and behavior of these two animals differ considerably. A lion has jagged, bladelike cheek teeth, long sharp canine teeth, and medium-size gripping incisors. A horse has no canines, its incisors are large for cropping, and the cheek teeth have very large, flat chewing surfaces with complicated low ridges of enamel over them. The teeth of the lion function primarily to pierce, grip, and slice; the teeth of the horse serve to grip as well as to crush and grind.

But teeth often serve other functions. The teeth of a lion, for instance, also help form a ready-made weapons system. Although the teeth of a horse are used in fighting, they do not provide a fully effective basis for defense, and the horse must defend itself primarily by outrunning its enemies.

Diet and Dentition
From the teeth alone, a great deal is known about the ecology and behavior of *Paranthropus* and *Australopithecus*. In *Australopithecus*, the teeth and associated aspects of the masticatory apparatus closely resemble those of modern men, and there is no reason to suppose that his dietary habits and behavior were very different. Presumably *Australopithecus* was an omnivore who lived as a hunter and gatherer.

The masticatory apparatus of *Paranthropus* was quite different. He possessed small front teeth suitable for gripping, piercing, and tearing and large flat-surfaced cheek

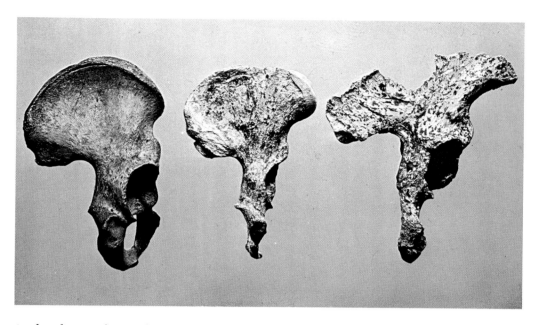

teeth whose primary function must have been crushing and grinding. He also possessed massive chewing muscles. Evidently he used his teeth for crushing and grinding, and he therefore must have been much more of a herbivore than *Australopithecus*. He probably did not eat food with a tough outer covering, such as bamboo stalks, but concentrated instead on berries and fruit, shoots and leaves, and bulbs and nuts. Moreover, the geologic evidence indicates that *Paranthropus* usually lived in much wetter climates than did *Australopithecus*. The anatomically more apelike *Paranthropus* was evidently also more apelike from an ecological point of view. The wetter regions he lived in were probably open woodland, whereas the anatomically more manlike *Australopithecus* was a hunter and gatherer of the dry plains. Because the ancestors of the hominids were probably apes of one sort or another and because all higher primates other than man appear to be essentially herbivorous, it is probable that the transition from ape to man meant a change from herbivores to omnivores. Judging from their teeth, *Australopithecus* made the transition, but *Paranthropus* did not.

Posture and Locomotion

Fossil remains can also tell a great deal about the posture and locomotion of the early hominids. *Australopithecus*, it seems, could walk and stride as we do; he was about as effective an erect biped as modern man and would have had as much difficulty as we experience in moving on all fours. But his efficiency at moving erect indicates that he was also efficient at the sort of body movements needed to throw objects or otherwise manipulate them. *Paranthropus* must have been much less efficient as a biped. Neither his feet nor his leg muscles were as effectively adapted to bipedal movement, and these limitations, together with his herbivorous behavior and preference for wetter environments, suggest that *Paranthropus* still spent some of his time in the trees.

The Use of Tools

In 1949, Dart began to publish a series of papers suggesting that *Australopithecus* could use tools. He first based his arguments on the evidence of depressed fractures in the skulls of animals that *Australopithecus* may have killed, and later he produced further evidence in the shape of bones that, he claimed, *Australopithecus* had used as tools.

At first, few people accepted Dart's views, but during the late 1950s stone objects were found near the caves where *Australopithecus* had lived. These objects were made of a kind of rock that does not occur naturally in the immediate vicinity of the site. A year or two later, several hundred stone objects were discovered in the Sterkfontein site that were significant for two reasons: the objects were made of rock that was not indigenous to the immediate vicinity, and several had been flaked so many times that they were noticeably modified from their natural condition. It was obvious they had been carried from the places where they were found and had been shaped deliberately by their users. With these tools was a surprisingly beautiful implement that had been formed from a piece of long bone, the broken portions of which had been polished to glossy smoothness. This implement alone

Figure 8 (left). Hipbone comparison for modern man, *Australopithecus,* and *Paranthropus.* Figure 9 (lower left). Artist's view of *Paranthropus (cf. Zinjanthropus),* whose dentition suggests he was not a meat eater and, by implication, not the Pliocene-Pleistocene maker of tools. Figure 10 (right). From Richard Leakey's East Rudolf expedition, supported by the National Geographic Society, a rock flake dated at 2,600,000 years (±260,000) that may be one of the oldest known tools. The rich beds in East Rudolf have yielded both *Australopithecus* and *Paranthropus* remains.

provided excellent support for Dart's view that even at the australopithecine stage hominids were using bone as well as stone objects as tools and weapons. His arguments were further strengthened by the discovery of large numbers of stone artifacts and at least one fine example in bone at Olduvai. Collectively, this evidence indicates that stone artifacts were systematically made and used by the early hominids, and it is quite likely that even earlier hominids had been using bones, stones, sticks, and other objects, either unmodified or only slightly modified from their natural state, as tools.

One of the earliest stone-working traditions or "industries" known to have existed is represented by artifacts found in the oldest part of Bed I at Olduvai, and it is some 2 million years old. The identity of the tool makers is unclear. But in all the relevant sites in which stone tools have been found, both *Australopithecus* and *Paranthropus* were almost certainly present or nearby. There are no sites that allow a positive identification of who the tool maker was or that demonstrate with reasonable certainty that the tools were made by both *Australopithecus* and *Paranthropus,* but it is possible to distinguish between the two by logical argument. All the evidence indicates that the two hominid lines existed at the same time. Although *Paranthropus* remained stable in his major features for millions of years, *Australopithecus* was undergoing a steady change, starting from a state already more manlike than *Paranthropus* and proceeding to become even more so. At the same time, stone tools were undergoing a progressive change from crude to more refined forms, and it therefore seems reasonable to associate the developing and more manlike lineage—*Australopithecus*—with the developing sequence of artifacts.

Some may be tempted to suggest other reasons for doubting that *Paranthropus,* a wet-woodland herbivore, was a systematic tool maker. He may well have been a rudi-

mentary user of tools, much like the chimpanzee. But if he had been an accomplished tool user, he presumably would have already embarked upon the course of adaptation by cultural means. The two hominid lineages apparently coexisted over long periods of time, and if both had been developing in the same manner by becoming dependent on culture, they surely would have come into direct conflict, with one being killed off or displaced. It is therefore reasonable to speculate that, at best, *Paranthropus* used tools no more effectively than the chimpanzee does today. If so, then *Australopithecus* was the only early hominid stone tool maker. But not all local populations of australopithecines made and used tools, and it is likely that only a few effectively made the transition to tool use and then went on to displace or destroy other local populations of australopithecines that had not achieved an equal degree of cultural evolution.

Ecological Adaptations

Although both *Australopithecus* and *Paranthropus* are classified as early hominids, they must have been very different animals. *Paranthropus* followed a way of life that was basically that of an ape. He lived in wet woodlands, apparently spending a good deal of time in the trees for feeding purposes as well as for protection. It is likely that he also slept in the trees. He was a herbivore living where relatively soft plant food was abundant, so there was little if any need for tool using, hence no selection in favor of it. Moreover, there was no pressure for him to develop the more elaborate behavioral repertoire of a hunting primate; in other words, to know the habits of the animals it hunts and to develop a complex of skills related to predation and eating meat.

The Pleistocene was a period of increasing aridity in Africa. One effect of this aridity was the reduction of forest regions and the increase of woodlands and eventually of grass savannas. *Paranthropus* apparently re-

Figure 11. *Paranthropus, Australopithecus,* and modern ape jaws, showing the contrast between the compact tooth row and small canines of the hominids with that of the ape. Figure 12 (right). Choukoutien, where *Sinanthropus pekinensis* was found along with evidence that cannibalism had been practiced. Man as well as animals apparently had been dismembered, with his bones fractured and the base of his skull broken away, presumably for access to the marrow and to the brain. Figure 12. Lungkushan (Dragon Bone Hill), where *Homo erectus* specimens were found. Figure 13 (far right). The most complete *Homo erectus* skull found in Bed II of Olduvai Gorge.

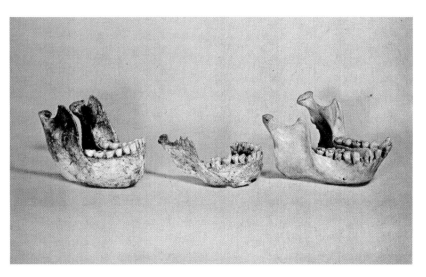

presents an adaptation to woodland conditions of a forest ape large enough to be free from much harassment by predators. The most obvious change that occurred during this process of adaptation was the acquisition of the basic features needed for the erect posture that was evidently *Paranthropus'* normal mode of movement on the ground.

Australopithecus adapted differently, becoming instead a plains-dwelling predacious omnivore. Such a creature, given the physical limitations it had, could not have followed this way of life without tools, and it is not difficult to see how the necessary complex of characteristics could have come into existence. One way to account for this development may also explain the relationship between the two hominids. This notion is that *Australopithecus* may well be a descendant of *Paranthropus,* and it is possible to trace the probable course of such a development.

Consider how the changes in environment might have affected *Paranthropus.* As the climate became more arid, his woodland habitat would in most cases have changed to savannas, thereby reducing the amount of plants he could eat. When his normal food supply dwindled in the dry season during the earlier climatic stages of desiccation, *Paranthropus* may well have supplemented his diet with animal protein in the form of insects, rodents, hares, and other small animals; indeed, field observations and experience with captive animals have demonstrated that primates readily take to animal protein. As desiccation progressed and the dry season became longer and more intense, this use of animal protein would have become increasingly important. Under such changing conditions, there would have been great pressure for selection to favor improved intelligence and the making of tools.

A lithe body and agile movement would also have been favored, and this new pattern of selection would readily explain the improved level of bipedality of *Australopithecus* as well as his more manlike teeth and skull. Consequently, the transition of a woodland *Paranthropus* into a plains-dwelling *Australopithecus* seems to present no difficulties. The sequence moves from forest ape to woodland herbivore (*Paranthropus*) to plains hunter and gatherer (*Australopithecus*), and the progression appears to be quite logical. It need not have occurred in all local populations. In areas where the changes in environment were negligible, the stimulus for evolutionary progress would have been absent and *Paranthropus* would have continued with his established way of life—an assumption consistent with the known fact that *Paranthropus* did continue to exist for some millions of years after *Australopithecus* had emerged. But even while the two were living side by side, *Australopithecus* was developing his cultural facility along with his dietary changes, all under the general pressures of natural selection.

It seems reasonable to conclude that an intermediate stage existed between the ape form and that of true man. In the ecological and behavioral sense, the members of this

intermediate stage were more apelike than manlike, but anatomical characteristics were present that allow them to be placed easily in the hominid categories. One final distinction must be made, however. When judged on morphological features alone, *Paranthropus* ranks as a hominid. On the other hand, if judgment is based on the presence of a capacity for superorganic adaptation, then *Paranthropus* apparently was not a man. But *Australopithecus* was.

LATER PRESAPIENT HOMINIDS

It is a curious fact that the later presapient hominids, now generally grouped together as *Homo erectus*, are not as well known as the earlier hominid forms. When Dubois set out in 1887, he did not succeed in finding the "missing link," but he did find the first example of presapient man. At Wadjak in Java, he discovered a human skull that has since come to be known as Java man. The skull was much less primitive looking than his notions about the missing link he was searching for, however, and Dubois did not report his find until many years later. In November 1890, he found a fragment of a jaw with one broken tooth attached to it at Kedung Brubus on the Solo River. Nearly a year later he was back at this Javanese site, where he soon found an isolated molar and then an entire skull cap that had prominent brow ridges, a very low forehead, and thick

bone in the braincase. He returned again in 1892 and found a complete femur remarkably like that of modern man. Because this femur evidently belonged with the skull cap, Dubois concluded that he was dealing with an early man who possessed a fairly modern type of body but a relatively primitive skull, and he named it *Pithecanthropus erectus* (erect ape-man) in 1894. As was to happen many years later with Dart and his *Australopithecus* theories, Dubois' colleagues did not believe that the find was significant until years later. Ironically, by the time his interpretation of the fossils finally did become widely accepted, Dubois himself no longer held faith in what he had once advocated. He had come to believe that *Pithecanthropus erectus* was a giant gibbon.

Distribution of *Homo Erectus*

In the 1920s Otto Zdansky, an Austrian working with a Swedish party, reported on two manlike teeth found years earlier on Dragon Bone Hill near the village of Choukoutien near Peking, China. The teeth were of immediate interest to Davidson Black, a Canadian anatomist at Peking Union Medical College. Black had been looking for fossil men and was convinced that the two teeth from Choukoutien belonged to a very ancient form. In 1927, he obtained support from the Rockefeller Foundation to begin excavation of the site, and the work con-

Figure 14. Sites marking the known distribution of *Australopithecus* and *Homo erectus*. Figure 15 (right). *Australopithecus, Homo erectus* (pithecanthropine), and Cro-Magnon skulls. This comparison shows the consistent trend toward increased cranial capacity.

tinued until war conditions put an end to it in 1941. After Black's death, Franz Weidenreich, a German anatomist, took charge of the investigations. Altogether, remains of about forty representatives of this so-called Pekin man were found. Most of the specimens consisted of teeth or pieces of skull, but a number of reasonably complete braincases were found although very little of the faces were recovered. Together they amounted to the largest local sample of *Homo erectus* yet discovered.

In 1941, conditions in Japanese-occupied China were so unsettled that the investigators decided to send the specimens to the United States for safekeeping until after the war. The packaged material arrived on the China coast en route to the United States on the day Pearl Harbor was attacked. The people in charge of the fossils were taken prisoners and the fossils disappeared. The fossils have never been seen again, despite extensive searches. Weidenreich fortunately had described the material in minute detail, and his volumes of descriptions and some very fine casts made of the material are now all that remain of what was once the finest collection of *Homo erectus* specimens.

Meanwhile, during the late 1930s, more excavations were being made in Java under the guidance of the German paleontologist G. H. R. von Koenigswald, who taught the local villagers to collect fossils, which he then purchased from them. From 1936 to the early 1940s, when hostilities ended the Java research and Koenigswald was taken prisoner of war, he unearthed several pieces of skull and jawbone, several teeth, and two incomplete skull caps of Java man, all of about the same age as the material found at Kedung Brubus by Dubois.

In 1907, Otto Schoetensack had found the single specimen in Europe thought to be of the same species as Java man. Schoetensack's Heidelberg man consists of a single, well-preserved and robust lower jaw dating back probably to the Lower Pleistocene, or approximately the same age as the older Java specimens. Since World War II, the distribution of *Homo erectus* has been further expanded by discoveries that involve specimens comparatively small in number but that have been recovered at widely scattered sites in South Africa, Algeria, Morocco, and at Olduvai Gorge in East Africa. The oldest specimens seem to date back to the late Lower Pleistocene or early Middle Pleistocene, going back roughly 1 million years. The most recent specimens date back to the Middle Pleistocene—possibly 200,000 years ago—and the evidence seems to indicate that during this period, *Homo erectus* was distributed throughout the Old World.

Morphological Characteristics
Homo erectus stands between *Australopithecus* and modern man. As far as the trunk and lower limbs are concerned, only a moderate increase in size and a few minor refinements to improve mechanical efficiency were necessary to bridge the gap from *Homo erectus* to modern man. Above the neck, however, the differences between *Australopithecus* and *Homo erectus* and between *Homo erectus* and modern man are greater. The average skull of the South African australopithecines measures about 450 cubic centimeters; of *Homo erectus*, about 1,000 cubic centimeters; and of modern man, about 1,450 cubic centimeters. The skull capacity increased progressively, then, as *Australopithecus* gave way to *Homo erectus*, and *Homo erectus* to modern man, and other consistent trends also developed. The teeth became smaller, the face shortened and became more vertical, the nasal region became more protuberant, and the braincase expanded. The head of *Homo erectus* was more rugged and less refined than that of modern man, having a low forehead,

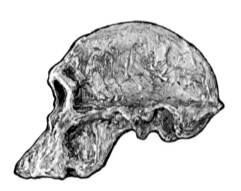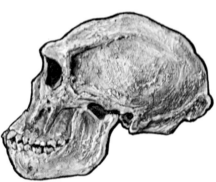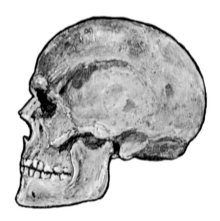

heavy brow ridges, and a broad and low-bridged nose. But the differences are not enough to put *Homo erectus* in a separate species. Even his brain size is within the range of modern man, although it is well below the average. It seems likely that in structure, functioning, and body size, *Homo erectus* was quite similar to modern man.

Culture and Life Habits

There is enough evidence—detailed in the chapter "Paleolithic Culture"—to indicate that *Homo erectus* was a true man. Stone tools were already being made at a time when no being more advanced than *Australopithecus* was known, at least a full million years before recognizable *Homo erectus* had emerged. In Bed II at Olduvai Gorge, most of the early *Homo erectus* finds are associated with developed Oldowan artifacts, and in the uppermost levels, from which the full-fledged *Homo erectus* skull came, the African Acheulean or hand ax culture is represented even though no artifacts actually were found with the latter skull. Developed Oldowan or early Acheulean artifacts were present in the Sterkfontein Valley a little before the time of the Swartkrans *Homo erectus* specimens. At Choukoutien a stone tool industry, as well as bone tools and shell objects, was associated with the remains. At least some stone tools were associated with the later *Homo erectus* finds in Java, although artifacts are surprisingly scarce in the early hominid levels and plentiful later. Artifacts were common in the levels yielding the Casablanca hominid material, as they were in the case of the Ternifine specimens. The Sterkfontein and Olduvai bone implements demonstrate clearly that long before the time of Pekin man (400,000 years ago), bone was being used for working hides.

Moreover, there is clear evidence that hearths were present in the Choukoutien deposits, leaving no doubt that Peking man was well acquainted with the use of fire. It was presumably used for heat, light, and perhaps protection. Great numbers of animal bones were found in the caves, of which about three-quarters belonged to deer, indicating that it was the preferred prey. The relatively large number of braincases without faces and with the bases missing that appear in sites containing *Homo erectus* and early *Homo sapiens* in China and Java has led some scholars to believe that man there was given to cannibalism. Although this interpretation may be correct, other plausible explanations do exist.

All this evidence suggests that by the time he had reached the stage of Pekin man, *Homo erectus* was skilled in the ways of man. The fact that he had spread to almost all corners of the Old World indicates that he was well adapted and was effectively holding his own against all comers and against an appreciable range of climatic and environmental conditions. He must surely have had reasonably effective means of communication, although there are no means of judging what sort of language he employed. Being as scattered as he was, some diversification probably had already occurred in the nature and level of cultural development. The evidence suggests that he was culturally somewhat backward in Java but not in China, although the fact that most of the Javanese material dates further back in time may account for the difference. *Homo erectus* was probably a progressive hunter and gatherer whose potential and whose achievements as man are not to be ignored. It is probably incorrect to think of him as being primitive and bestial; indeed, it may well be incorrect to think of him as being a different species from *Homo sapiens*. In him the full foundation for modern man was undoubtedly complete, with only minor physical refinements remaining to be added to it. The greatest difference between the *Homo erectus* stage and *Homo sapiens* is almost certainly the extent to which cultural potential was being realized.

Homo Sapiens

12

In a zoological sense, modern man is species *sapiens* of genus *Homo*—but when did *Homo sapiens* first appear? This question has stimulated the interest of layman and professional scholar alike ever since the idea of biological evolution started to gain respectability with the work of Charles Darwin a century ago. Although many have pondered the question "When?" a smaller but growing number has added to it the question "Why?" The two questions are not entirely unrelated.

Unfortunately, evidence for the early development of man has always been scanty, at best. Throughout most of his existence, man tended to live in small bands in areas that did not favor the preservation of his physical remains. The few fossilized forms that have been discovered represent only a few individuals preserved under special conditions, and their remains provide only a fleeting glimpse into the world of our ancestors. Perhaps if anthropologists could establish the specific circumstances controlling the course of human evolution—indeed, the record of climatic change as well as behavioral response in terms of stone tools is far more complete than the evidence for human form itself—they would be in a better position to concentrate on and search for those direct relics of human forms that can confirm the suspicions about the timing of the events in human evolution. Knowledge of the selective forces that have been important in controlling human form can help clarify both the sequence and the timing of the modifications in shape that constitute the course of human evolution, and for this reason attention should be focused on the evolutionary process.

WHAT IS MAN?

Homo sapiens is translated literally as "man, the wise." But what exactly is man? The physical anthropologist is not totally concerned with the question, for most of the answers will come from the philosopher and the social scientist interested in studying the peculiarly human aspects of human behavior. On the other hand, he cannot completely ignore the question, even in some of its larger aspects. Anatomists and physical anthropologists occasionally have tried to define man in physical terms only, regarding their subject merely as a shape to be distinguished from other shapes. Although this approach has its value, it does have certain drawbacks, for equal value may be placed on all variations in form. In the past, anatomists established the status of certain fossil

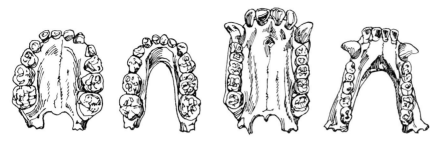

Figure 2. *Australopithecus* and chimpanzee dentition. Chimpanzees subsist on vegetation but they, like baboons, sometimes eat small animals. Jane van Lawick-Goodall has described how two chimpanzees teamed together to kill a colobus monkey — and how the meat was shared with other members of the group, who quickly gathered about with hands outstretched for a morsel. Although we may never know the answer, it is nevertheless intriguing to wonder how closely such behavior reflects the beginnings of hunting organization among the early hominids.

specimens by comparing them, trait by trait, with modern men and then with anthropoid apes, finally adding up the resemblances and differences and letting the totals determine the outcome. Comparisons of this sort ignored the fact that some traits are of much greater diagnostic significance than others.

Consider canine teeth, for instance. For at least 2 million years humans made a better living not by biting things but by manipulating tools, whether in food gathering or in self-defense. Human canine teeth have thus served a function that is indistinguishable from that of incisors and, as might be expected, human canines do resemble human incisors considerably. This means that if we were asked to assess the possible status of a creature with three-inch-long canine teeth, we could state immediately that it was not human, regardless of its other characteristics. Diagnosis must be made on the basis of those features that are particularly related to the *humanity* of the creature under consideration, and this in turn requires a concept of humanity that is more than an unedited list of morphological traits.

The evolutionary success of the human line has been assured, at least in the past, by a particular set of behavioral characteristics that constitute man's capacity for culture. Without culture he is completely helpless. Hand-held tools are important in and of themselves, but they represent only one part of an entire behavioral realm, much of which is verbal. In any prehistoric assemblage, verbal instructions on the manufacture and use of the tools are implied, among other things, but the important point is that the tools signify the existence of a cultural behavioral milieu. It is this point that must be kept in mind in attempting to understand the basic nature of human adaptation.

What is edible and what is not? Which animals are dangerous and under what circumstances? Which animals can men hunt and by what means? Where can one get water when the familiar source is dry? Instinct does not provide man with the answers to these and other questions, yet the answers are of vital importance. As individual men discovered important pieces of information, either by accident or by trial and error, these facts entered into the traditions of the group to which the discoveries belonged. Verbal transmission to other members of the group made it unnecessary for vital bits of information to be learned anew, by accident or by trial and error, each time their use could be of benefit.

The importance of language to human survival has been recognized for centuries. When fossils differing in form from modern *Homo sapiens* began to be discovered in the latter half of the nineteenth century, investigators wondered about whether the beings they represented had the capacity for articulate speech. Some anatomists claimed that the shape of the tongue muscle attachments on the jaw could provide the answer; others claimed that the shape of certain regions of the brain, as indicated by the interior of the skull, were diagnostic. Today these claims are discounted. The shape of the mouth, the tongue, the jaw, the throat, or whatever has little relation to the capacity for speech. The spectrum of sounds produced by even a dog or a cat or a cow seems to be of sufficient variety to be used as the basis for an articulate language, but the mental dimension simply does not exist.

Unfortunately, the crude shape of the skull cannot provide the details of mental dimensions. In fact, even modern neuroanatomy based on the microscopic study of fresh tissues with all sorts of sophisticated equipment has so far revealed disappointingly little about the details of brain function. There is hope at the neurophysiological and biochemical levels, but this research is far removed from examination of the crude shape of the skull.

Still, the feats of information storage and retrieval that separate men so markedly from other animals should have some discernible effect on the brain and this should be visible in its skeletal housing, the skull. This in fact is the case. In proportion to the size of the human animal, the braincase is remarkably large. Some creatures—whales, for instance—have larger brains than man, but a whale is enormous and needs a large switchboard simply for controlling its enormous network of muscular and circulatory machinery. Relative to body size, a whale brain is proportionately smaller than a human brain. A good idea of the sheer relative size of the human brain can be gained by comparing man with his nearest relative, the chimpanzee: body bulk is about the same, but the human brain is three times as large.

The size of the brain, being triple that of the most intelligent nonhuman animal, should be a fairly good criterion for establishing the identity of *Homo sapiens*. Among the various living groups there are some differences in brain size, but these appear to be reflections of average differences in body bulk. For instance, large sizes are recorded among the larger people of the world, such as the Eskimo, the Siberians, and the northwest Europeans; smaller sizes occur among the slender people of the tropics in Asia, India, Africa, and South America. The modern brain, housed in a skull averaging 1,450 cubic centimeters, is a relatively recent achievement—recent, at least, on the evolutionary time scale. Direct evidence for prehistoric men with fully modern cranial capacities dates back only 100,000 years, and even at that the record is extremely sketchy and precise dating is difficult.

TRANSITION FROM *HOMO ERECTUS*

What evidence anthropologists have suggests that half a million years ago, the brains of those who then represented humanity were distinctly smaller on the average than is the case today. This characteristic, along with certain other features, has led most authorities to classify these early men as specifically distinct from modern man. In fact, the first men who described these early fossils placed them in a separate genus as well, calling them *Pithecanthropus erectus*. The species is still regarded as valid, but now most authorities feel that there is no reason to regard them as generically distinct, and the proper technical designation is now *Homo erectus*. For ease of reference, however, they are often called "pithecanthropines," a nontechnical form of the earlier designation.

On the average, pithecanthropine brain size 500,000 years ago was 1,000 cubic centimeters, or about two-thirds that of the modern average. There is considerable overlap, however, and many modern individuals, including some highly distinguished ones, have brains as small as or smaller than the pithecanthropine average. (None, however, is as small as the smallest pithecanthropine.) With this overlap, the line between *Homo erectus* and *Homo sapiens* is blurred to the extent that no absolute distinction can be established. When anthropologists finally have found fossils to fill those gaps in the geologic record between pithecanthropines and modern forms, there is every reason to expect that they will document a gradual evolutionary change characterized principally by a slow, continuous increase in brain size.

At present, there are a few tantalizing scraps from the period between the full-scale pithecanthropines and undisputably modern man, but these scraps have created almost more confusion than clarification. Much of this confusion is wrapped up in the history of scientific traditions. The milieu in which many early studies of fossil man were pursued was opposed strongly to the interpretations of Darwinian evolution. With human fossils being as rare as they are, the discoveries of the nineteenth and early twentieth centuries still play a major role in documenting the course of man's prehistoric development. Inevitably, the accounts of

Figure 3. Evidence suggests that *Homo erectus* had adapted biologically to the hunting of large animals. The ability to move over long distances in the pursuit of game is debatable for the australopithecines, who may have been much less efficient at walking upright.

today rely heavily upon the descriptions of a generation gone by and frequently reflect a surprising although covert amount of anti-evolutionary thinking.

One of the signs of this lingering opposition to a frank scheme of human evolution is the stress that many writers have placed on the supposedly "modern" features of the various fragments between the clearly *Homo erectus* and clearly *Homo sapiens* populations. At a time when the possibility of human evolution was viewed with alarm, there was a feeling that if "modern" form could be proven to have existed at the same time as or earlier than the pithecanthropines, or any other archaic human form, then it would be obvious that modern man had existed all along. Thus, there would be no need to invoke an evolutionary relationship. Vestiges of this viewpoint still exist in the continuing attempts to portray as modern various fossils that shall be considered shortly.

ADAPTATIONS TOWARD *HOMO SAPIENS*
The evidence for certain aspects of prehistoric behavior has been far more abundant than the actual remains of prehistoric people themselves. Although thousands of artifacts have been recovered, they represent a highly biased sample—biased in terms of preservability—of the activities of their makers. This factor must be kept in mind in any speculation about the life way of the times represented. One thing that is quite clear is that the pithecanthropines were hunting large game animals and that their immediate ancestors probably did not—at least there is no evidence that they did and several hints that they did not. Hunting, even of the crude variety practiced by *Homo erectus*, suggests a whole complex of biological adaptation—much of which is only inferential. Some investigators have taken the attitude that it is useless to discuss these issues because most of it is speculative and will always be so. Although the speculative

nature of the discussions cannot be denied, they can still be considered of some value, for without some concern of this sort, anthropologists would be entirely at a loss to understand some of the crucial differences between ape and man and how they came about.

In a recent and highly speculative book, *The Naked Ape*, Desmond Morris presents some suggestive information on human physiology. The author notes that in a series of traits, *Homo sapiens* differs from virtually all other primates and that in these traits he resembles hunting carnivores. The dietary adaptation of all primates except *Homo sapiens* involves the continual ingestion of small quantities of plant food, and with this prolonged nibbling goes continual and rather indiscriminatory defecation. This perpetual fouling of the environment is associated with the fact that nonhuman primates, at least the terrestrial ones, tend to sleep in a different place each night. Man, on the other hand, limits his eating to shorter periods, occasionally going for substantial lengths of time—perhaps days—between meals. The time between defecations is also prolonged, relatively regular, and under far better voluntary control than is true for any other primate, as anyone who ever attempted to housebreak a monkey can testify. Food sharing and a reused home base where infants remain and to which adults regularly return are also traits that are unique to man among the primates and that man shares with carnivores.

The argument is not that *Homo sapiens* is phylogenetically related to carnivores, but rather that these traits are the evolutionary consequences of a long history as a hunting animal. Speculative though it may be, it is fair to suggest that these characteristics of *Homo sapiens* developed along with the hunting adaptation first seen among his pithecanthropine ancestors. There are further consequences for human form that can be guessed at from the existence of a hunting component in subsistence activities. Among the few remaining hunting and gathering human populations, the simplest method of big game hunting, albeit a most laborious one, is simply trotting after the animal for two, three, or four days or more until the animal drops from exhaustion. Admittedly, this technique is confined to young men in excellent physical condition, but the evidence indicates that, in the remote past, people rarely survived beyond early middle age.

This simple if tedious hunting technique is based on several behavioral, physical, and physiological traits that humans possess. The ability to function effectively for relatively long periods between meals contrasts with the typical herbivore, which must spend a good portion of each day looking for nourishment. If a herbivore can be kept from grazing for several days and kept on the move, it can be tracked down and speared or clubbed to death by a man who is, under normal conditions, far slower of foot. Certainly the frequently pictured scenes of early men sprinting across the plains and running down quadrupeds in a contest of speed is ludicrous, at best. Although the human locomotor apparatus is definitely not designed for speed, it is well adapted to long-distance locomotion with minimum energy expenditure. *Homo erectus* leg bones suggest that the locomotor adaptation of pithecanthropines was identical to that of *Homo sapiens*. The immediate australopithecine ancestors of the pithecanthropines, in contrast, were erect-walking bipeds but of a much less efficient sort. Sherwood Washburn has suggested that the australopithecines had not yet developed the long-distance locomotor adaptation that probably appeared with *Homo erectus* and that can, by inference, be associated with the development of large game hunting as a subsistence technique.

One of the physiological features that further assists man in this type of endeavor is his ability to dissipate metabolically generated heat by sweating. All animals perspire, but man alone among those of less-than-elephantine size has a hairless skin richly endowed with sweat glands. The evidence of his tools indicates that man was essentially a tropic creature when hunting became a part of his subsistence activity. Geographically, man remained a creature of the tropics or of warm, temperate climates until after he had evolved from *Homo erectus* to *Homo sapiens*, and, physiologically, man is still a thoroughly tropical mammal. Moreover, like almost all other primates and quite unlike the carnivores, man is thoroughly diurnal and relatively night blind. Right up to the twentieth century, man has been the only predator capable of successful hunting activities in the heat of the tropical noonday sun. Speculative though it may be, it seems reasonable to suggest that coincident with their long-distance locomotor adaptation, the pithecanthropines lost the hairy coating that characterizes virtually all other primates and almost all other mammals.

With the normal mammalian hairy coat having been eliminated by natural selection, the pithecanthropines can be envisioned as hairless and sweaty hunters and gatherers, exposed to the tropical sun without the benefit of protective clothing. Certainly the tools they made did not include any that today can be associated with the preparation of skins for clothing, and for the most part, the climate in the areas where they flourished would not have required clothing as a condition for survival. This leads to one last inference concerning the appearance of the immediate ancestors of *Homo sapiens:* their skin color.

Normal mammalian skin divested of its coating of fur is susceptible to damage from the ultraviolet component of tropical sunlight, and prolonged exposure can lead to the development of skin cancer. The adaptive response to this danger is the skin pig-

Figure 4. That man's biology is the product of adaptation is shown by this New Guinean. Adaptation to a tropical environment presumably led to the protective pigmentation that he shares with African peoples.

ment melanin. Except for albinos, all normal people have granules of melanin in their skin, but among those whose immediate ancestors were inhabitants of the tropics for some thousands of generations, the concentration of melanin produces dark skin color. This serves as a shield that blocks the penetration of ultraviolet radiation. In modern times, the reduction in pigmentation characterizing some populations is almost certainly related to the length of time that the ancestors of the pithecanthropines actually lived in an area where the problem of ultraviolet-produced skin damage was a reduced or insignificant factor in human survival. In the Middle Pleistocene, the immediate pithecanthropine ancestors of all modern *Homo sapiens* were probably hairless, sweaty, and dark-skinned.

The hunting way of life produced two other visible effects on human form, one that stabilized relatively early and another that continued until the development of *Homo sapiens*. There is skeletal evidence for both of these effects, but the specific association with hunting is again just educated guesswork. Hunting provided an enormous change in diet, and it would be surprising if the effects of this were not visible in the evolution of the jaws and teeth. The size of the pithecanthropine dentition, particularly the molars, is markedly reduced in comparison with that of the preceding australopithecines.

Meat, to be digestible, requires far less chewing than uncooked plant foods, and the relaxation in the selective forces maintaining the huge australopithecine molars was probably followed by a reduction in tooth size. Although cooking would further increase the digestibility of the new foodstuffs, it is not certain that the pithecanthropines cooked their food even though there is some evidence for their use of fire. It is clear that after the pithecanthropine tooth evolved to a certain size, the dentition remained largely unchanged for a long period of time. In fact, there is little significant difference between pithecanthropine teeth and the teeth of early members of *Homo sapiens* or even the teeth of the long-isolated Australian aborigines, which suggests that the selective forces relating to dentition—those of diet and food preparation techniques—must be comparable among existing primitive hunters and gatherers, early *Homo sapiens*, and still earlier *Homo erectus*.

The second discernible effect of the hunting way of life is an increase in brain size. *Homo erectus* had twice the brain of the preceding australopithecines, and the brain of *Homo sapiens* is three times as large. It can be suggested that the advantage of increased brain size in a hunting animal is such that an increase will be selected for, at least up to a point. Where the hunting animal is not equipped with a predatory dentition, with powerful claws, or with great speed on foot, intelligence will be even more important. The available evidence indicates that brain size increased slowly until the *Homo sapiens* level was reached, whereupon the increase stopped.

Zoologists have occasionally considered it puzzling that something of such adaptive significance as intelligence should cease to be selected for, particularly after its value had been clearly indicated by several million years of steady increase. The anthropologist finds this less difficult to understand. Because the main key to the success of the human line has been culture, it is not surprising that the cessation of brain size increase coincides with the first archaeological evidence for a significant level of cultural

Figure 5 (below left). Neanderthal skull from La Ferrassie, France, and the double burial from the Grimaldi caves near Monaco. Both these discoveries were used as evidence for supposed morphological variation in the Late Pleistocene. Figure 6 (right). Neanderthal bear hunt. Whether he used them for meat or raw materials, we know that the Neanderthaler hunted large cave bears for the skulls and bones that are often found in special arrangements, suggesting some kind of cult activity associated with these awesome creatures.

complexity. By the time *Homo sapiens* appeared, roughly 100,000 years ago, even the least intelligent members of a given human group could probably understand and benefit from the transmitted wisdom of previous generations as well as from the discoveries of the exceptional group members. At this point, culture ensured that the duller members of a population would have just as good a chance to reach maturity and reproduce as would the brighter members. Increase in brain size ceased at this point.

THE MOUSTERIAN TRADITION

By the end of the Last Interglacial, a cultural tradition existed that archaeologists have called Mousterian, after the French village of Le Moustier, where evidence for it was first found. The Mousterian culture is known chiefly from stone tools found in western Europe, in central and eastern Europe, including southern Russia all the way to Uzbekistan, and all around the Mediterranean basin, including North Africa and the Middle East. Typical Mousterian stone tools include knives, scrapers for skin preparation, and points that could have been used as spear tips. Regular and reused hearths as well as some indications of hut construction have also been found, and there is every sign that the makers were hunters of greater efficiency than the preceding pithecanthropine populations. Not only did the Mousterian culture represent an apparent improvement in hunting techniques, it also represented a first partial solution to the climatic limitations otherwise imposed on the geographic range of a physiologically tropical mammal. The manufacture of shelter, the occupation of caves, the making of clothing, and the deliberate control of fire were all part of the Mousterian tradition, and all contributed to the ability of man to survive in a climate normally too cold for him. The development of the Mousterian, coinciding with the onset of the last glaciation, allowed man to remain in an area ranging from western Europe

through southern Russia and the Middle East in spite of the cooling climate. The advantage of remaining there was in the apparent abundance of game in the ice-free lowland areas.

Several skeletal remains of Mousterian men have been preserved. The earliest of these is clearly a form of *Homo sapiens*, and it suggests that our species was recognizably established by the beginning of the Mousterian. Between the pithecanthropines (about 300,000 to almost 1 million years ago) and the beginning of *Homo sapiens* (about 100,000 years ago), there is a gap of 200,000 years. There are several pieces of fossilized human bone representing this gap, and much has been written and claimed concerning them. Unfortunately, the evidence is incomplete and inconclusive, but some mention of it should be made nevertheless.

Three of the most famous and most controversial fossil specimens are Swanscombe, Steinheim, and Fontechevade, each of which has been offered as proof that fully modern man existed long before the onset of the last glaciation. In each case, however, there are serious problems that reduce the diagnostic value. The famous Swanscombe skull, pieces of which were found in a gravel pit in southeast England in 1935, 1936, and 1955, includes only the back end of a skull. Without the front, it is impossible to guess what the forehead and face looked like, and brain size can only be a rough estimate. A recent and sophisticated statistical analysis by the British anthropologists B. G. Campbell and J. S. Weiner shows conclusively that it was not of modern form, although the problem of whether it could be distinguished from the Neanderthal subspecies of *Homo sapiens* was not considered.

The Steinheim skull, discovered in western Germany in 1933, is not much better. The base is crushed and warped, and the preserved portions of the facial skeleton include only the rear teeth. The skull clearly is small for a modern man, and the brow ridge is

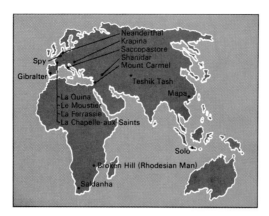

Figure 7. Sites of Neanderthal remains, including the allegedly more modern types, such as those discovered at Mount Carmel and at Krapina. Figure 8 (right). Upper arch, lower arch, and profile view of Neanderthal dentition. These teeth are unmistakably modern — if somewhat robust — and show little crowding.

enormous. It would be difficult to use this to demonstrate the existence of modern man, and it is not certain just which species, *Homo erectus* or *Homo sapiens*, it belongs to. The Fontechevade specimens from southwest France include the skull cap of one individual—less face, brow, back, and bottom—and a fragment from over the left eye of another. Neither piece is complete enough to be used to prove or disprove anything.

At the time when *Homo sapiens* definitely existed—as evidenced by Mousterian cultural traditions just before the onset of the last glaciation—he appears in a form that has been called "Neanderthal man." Neanderthal is a valley in western Germany that, over a century ago, produced the first recognized specimen and has given its name to a whole stage in human evolution. For years, the Neanderthalers were regarded as specifically distinct from modern man. Emphasizing the differences, many early studies portrayed them with apelike imagery and concluded that they were so different from modern man that they must have been an aberrant side line that became extinct without giving rise to any descendants. On reassessment, however, it is clear that Neanderthalers differed from modern man chiefly in their greater average muscularity and robustness, and in the larger teeth, jaws, and related facial architecture. Brain size has not changed since that time, and there is virtually no evidence that brain structure was different from that of modern man. Although traditionalists object, most authorities now regard the Neanderthalers as *Homo sapiens neanderthalensis*, for it is becoming increasingly difficult to deny them status as the direct ancestors of *Homo sapiens sapiens*, that doubly sagacious creature who threatens either to blow up the world or destroy it as a habitable place by his own unchecked fecundity.

Somewhere between 45,000 and 35,000 years ago, the Neanderthal face and teeth underwent a reduction that transformed human appearance into what is traditionally called "primitive modern" form. The evidence is actually quite incomplete, and there is reason to suspect that the change was a gradual one and that it is still going on. Certainly the faces, jaws, and teeth of the first "moderns" are substantially larger on the average than those of twentieth-century Europeans, and during the last 30,000 years there has been a clear trend for dental and facial reduction that has, if anything, been accelerating in recent millenniums.

If the transformation of Neanderthalers into modern form was accomplished largely by the reduction of the jaws and teeth, it is legitimate to ask what caused this change. The archaeological record shows that earlier changes were the direct result of changes in life ways, as indicated by the tools men left behind. The Mousterian tool-making tradition, first associated with *Homo sapiens* of Neanderthal form, was developed to help ensure survival in a climate otherwise too cold for man. Generalizing further, human survival in areas severely affected by the last glaciation depended upon manipulation of the environment to a substantially greater degree than had been done before. This increase in manipulative activities is reflected in the increase in number and variety of special tools that were being manufactured. The tool kit of the Mousterian represents a diversification that is a quantum jump when compared with the tools of the Lower Paleolithic.

In addition to the evidence from the tools, the increased amount of manipulative activity can also be seen in the form and the degree of wear of Neanderthal front teeth. Neanderthal incisors are as big as or bigger than front teeth at any other stage in human evolution. Despite their large size, by early middle age they were worn to such an extent that only stumps of the roots are left. This amount of wear and the rounded form of the teeth indicate that they were being used for a good deal more than just eating. It is hardly speculative to suggest that they were being used as a general all-purpose tool— vise, pliers, clamp, snippers, and so on. At first, the value of large, healthy front teeth may have led to their increase under the pressures of natural selection, but as stone tools were developed for an increasing variety of purposes, the survival value of large and powerful front teeth was reduced proportionately.

The development of a manipulative technology, then, reduced the intensity of those selective forces that maintained large faces and teeth. As time went on, chance mutations occurred that affected the face and teeth. With the reduction in the forces of selection, however, the mutations remained in the population gene pool. Most such mutations result in a reduction of the structure whose development they control, and the continuing reduction of the human face and dentition has been the consequence.

This reduction is a perfectly standard evolutionary phenomenon, but it is interesting to note that it has not proceeded to the same extent in all of the various populations of modern *Homo sapiens*. This dissimilarity can be traced to the fact that the technological innovations altering the forces of selection occurred at different times in different parts of the world. At first, the relevant technology was specifically developed to cope with an increasingly inhospitable climate. For the first time in the 2,500,000-year record of human cultural activities, significant differences appeared in different portions of the Old World. Prior to the Mousterian, the archaeological record reveals a way of life that was substantially the same from place to place at any given time. It would appear that the major forces of selection also must have been substantially the same, and the appearance of pre-Mousterian people could be expected to have been much the same throughout the inhabited world at any given time.

This similarity changed with the Mousterian. For the first time, selective forces

influencing human form differed substantially in the various parts of the Old World. The technology that led to facial reduction was first developed in an area extending from western Europe through the Middle East. With the reduction in the size of large and powerful teeth taking place tens of thousands of years earlier in this area, it is interesting that the modern populations of these areas include exactly those people in whom facial reduction has proceeded to its greatest extent. Generalizing from this particular instance, one could argue that differentiation of human populations—which many choose to label "racial" variation—does not predate the differentiation in cultural adaptation. In this view, then, human "races" are no more than 100,000 years old.

If it can be argued that populations with the longest history of elaborated technology now show the greatest amount of facial reduction, it should be possible to turn the argument around. Those living human groups possessing the largest (in other words, the least reduced) jaws and teeth should be those where technology has remained at a primitive level for the longest period of time. Significantly, modern Australian aborigines possess the most formidable dentition of the living people of the world and also maintain the least elaborated technology. The relationship can be shown in other populations as well.

Aside from facial size and form, the other aspect in which modern human populations are most visibly distinguishable is skin color. The pithecanthropine predecessors of all modern men were probably heavily pigmented, and the appearance of what is euphemistically called "white" skin color is evidently a more recent development. This characteristic, too, undoubtedly had its genesis as a result of Mousterian technology. One of the cultural attributes that allowed Mousterian people to survive under glacial conditions was clothing. The use of skins for clothing helped a physiologically tropical

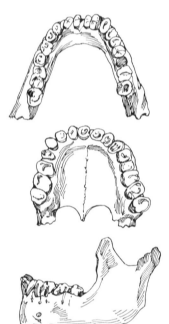

Figure 9. Men of the Upper Paleolithic. Although their life was simple by our standards, these people developed a good missile system, used tailored clothing, and had a deep knowledge of animal behavior and anatomy, as implied by the tangible remains of their culture. Yet they were modern in the fullest sense of the word, for all these characteristics require the same skill and intelligence that are found in modern life and indeed are the basis of it.

mammal survive the rigors of glacial cold, and it can be suggested that it further meant a significant reduction in the human epidermis. Not only did clothing allow men to live in latitudes where ultraviolet intensity was greatly reduced, it also interposed a barrier between the human skin and the lowered intensity of incoming radiation, so that skin pigment was of far less importance to human survival.

Just as face size reduced once the forces of selection relaxed, so also was the need for pigmentation reduced. With melanin less important to human survival, mutations affecting the development of epidermal melanin could accumulate in the gene pools of early Neanderthal populations. Because most mutations interfere with the development of the structures whose existence they influence, reduction is the probable fate of any structure that is no longer of importance for survival. It is probably more than coincidental that the maximum amount of depigmentation among the living people of the world today occurs in exactly those areas where the archaeological record shows that animal skins were first being prepared systematically for what must have been clothing.

Modern populations of *Homo sapiens* differ from one another in traits other than face form and skin color, and some of these traits have been tied to variation in the nature of selective forces in different parts of the world. Most of these, however, can only be understood through the biologist's studies on living populations.

THE UPPER PALEOLITHIC

Somewhere between 30,000 and 40,000 years ago, refinements in Mousterian-derived cultures that had adapted to the cold climates proceeded to such an extent that the subsequent cultural traditions are at least as distinct from the Mousterian as the latter is from the preceding Lower Paleolithic. These outgrowths of the Mousterian are called Upper Paleolithic and last from about 35,000

years ago until the end of the Pleistocene, some 10,000 years ago. When they first appear, they are associated with men of "modern" form—the famous Cro-Magnon skull from southwestern France is a frequently cited example—although their form on the average is substantially more rugged than that of the average man of twentieth-century Europe, and some practically fit in the Neanderthal range of variation. Nevertheless, it has been traditional to include these Upper Paleolithic men in the same subspecies as all more recent men—the *Homo sapiens sapiens*.

The variety of special tools for special purposes in the Upper Paleolithic is far greater than in the preceding Mousterian, suggesting an increase in the ability to cope with adverse climatic conditions. Not surprisingly, the evidence shows that there was a marked population increase in the Upper Paleolithic, not only in the same areas inhabited by their Neanderthal ancestors but in other areas as well. The increased cultural efficiency allowed Upper Paleolithic *Homo sapiens* to spread north and east, occupying new territory previously uninhabited by man. Population expanded into the north temperate and subarctic areas running from European Russia all the way across the Old World to Siberia. Nor did it stop there. What is now the Bering Strait was then simply a "land bridge" between Siberia and Alaska. Although this land bridge had the climate of an arctic steppe, this was no barrier in view of the Upper Paleolithic cultural adaptation. As a consequence, human populations expanded into the previously uninhabited New World as the ancestors of the aboriginal American Indians.

By the end of the Pleistocene, some 10,000 years ago, *Homo sapiens sapiens* was established in all parts of the world, and here he continues to exist. The stage was set for the enormous expansion of sheer human numbers, triggered by the food-producing revolution and now threatening the livability of much of the world.

Modern Man

13

Modern man is the end point, yet not the end, of perhaps 5 million years of evolution. During this time, his genetic material has been constantly subject to the forces of selection and there has been a turnover of genes, a constant renewing, as old environmental conditions have given way to new. Even today, new directions of selection appear and many old directions have slackened or have been eliminated entirely. Modern man is also the end point of dozens of directions of local selection. Each local population has faced its own unique selective pressures, with populations on one continent experiencing diseases and privations not experienced by populations on others. Modern man, therefore, is more properly modern *men*, a network of populations marked by genetic differences as well as genetic similarities.

Man has modern advantages. With potentially better nutrition, control of diseases, and fewer accidents he may live twice as long as either ancient man or modern men still following ancient ways. He matures earlier, lives longer, and has an assured daily diet, a refuge from cold, and protection from heat—and he lives to see his children grow to maturity and have children of their own.

Yet modern man is not all modern, for in every population there are ancient genes that were once advantageous but may be disadvantageous in the existing scheme of things. Nor is modern living all good. An assured supply of calories, plentiful animal fat, and less exercise together conspire to bring about disorders of fat metabolism that kill or debilitate. Moreover, chemical and biochemical hazards have appeared that were previously nonexistent—the blood transfusions and drugs that have unexpected side reactions, for example, and smogs and environmental pollutions of all kinds. Removed from his original geographic context, modern man may face other biochemical problems. Western Europeans experience painful headaches and nausea in the "Chinese restaurant syndrome," owing to their intolerance to monosodium glutamate. Chinese and other Orientals, in turn, may have lactase deficiency and therefore an intolerance to milk. One man's meat may truly be another man's

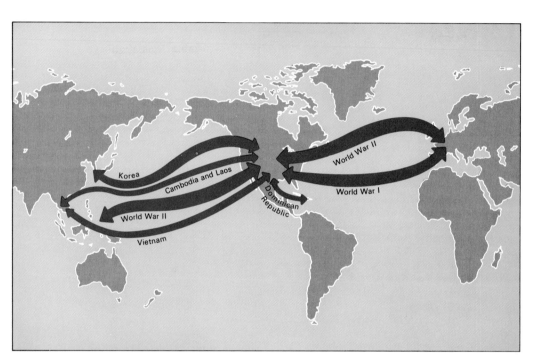

poison: a favorite dish on one continent may be more than indigestible on another.

Old or ancient genes may prove to be a liability in new or newer environments, for they belong to a human form that has found its adaptive niche, ecologically speaking. When faced with new situations, new demands, new ways of living, and changes in the life situation, old adaptations are no longer adaptive, and old genotypic combinations are no longer optimal for survival. In the modern world of surplus and famine and of changing selective agents, both the common heritage of all mankind and the separate heritages of different populations prove disadvantageous in numerous respects.

OLD GENES IN NEW CONTAINERS
The gene pool of modern man taken as a species is the sum of the gene pools of his component populations. The total human gene pool generally consists of genes thousands to hundreds of thousands of years old. This condition is true for the component populations of mankind as well, but here there are differences in gene frequencies and differences over time, with changes occurring in number, identity, and size. New populations have repeatedly formed from old, bringing about new gene pools and new genetic combinations, with the result that man today represents ancient genes in changing relative numbers, in new combinations, and —with changes in physical size and combinations of features—new containers as well.

New populations also form when contiguous populations meet and mate or when immigrants are introduced into a neighboring country, or when explorers explore by day and mate by night, or when military troops introduce new genes half a continent away. New genetic combinations are one inevitable result of such situations and in some cases temporarily represent reduced evolutionary fitness or even a new evolutionary mode. With the breaking up of a breeding isolate, gene flow takes new paths and old genetic combinations are lost. Rare recessive

Figure 2 (left). War produces disruptions in the normal structure of breeding populations, introducing large intrusions of genetically displaced persons in armies and refugee populations.
Figure 3. All major cultural institutions affect or restrict gene flow. Religions, for instance, often prohibit marriage to nonbelievers, thus setting up new genetic boundaries that may cut across preexisting ones. An extreme although numerically minor effect of religion may be the exclusion of the priesthood from marriage.

genes are thus redistributed and growth-limiting recessive combinations become less likely. With a loss of inbreeding, genes are redistributed and certain effects of inbreeding are then lost. To some slight degree the recent increase in human stature may be attributable to this redistribution effect.

The containers themselves change and face different life experiences. In the United States, malarial selection is practically non-existent, so that the advantages of the sickle-cell heterozygote, described below, are no longer advantageous. In still other cases, genes that may be beneficial or adaptive to hungry people may be useless or harmful when the people are no longer hungry. The geneticist J. V. Neel, among others, views the gene for simple insulin-deficiency diabetes as a "thrifty" gene, useful in the past but now no longer so. The gene for hypercholesterolemia appears to be advantageous to the young or to young adults consuming little fat and exercising much. But it is disadvantageous in a high-fat, low-exercise way of life. With the breaking down of breeding isolates or with simple admixture, man finds himself becoming taller and fatter, earlier to mature and longer to live, and no longer experiencing old causes of death but dying of different diseases.

THE HUMAN GAME OF NUMBERS

The enormous changes in the size of various populations are a recent and temporary phenomenon brought about by hundreds of historical accidents and hundreds of technological advances. By accident of geography and isolation, some groups today are no more numerous than they were 20,000 years ago, yet with the overall expansion of human population they now represent a scant proportion of modern man. Still other groups, scarcely visible in the late Pleistocene world and at that time numerically insignificant, have undergone later and disproportionate population expansion. The population of Europe has expanded 10,000 times, whereas the native inhabitants of the Kalahari or the aborigines of Australia have barely increased their numbers. Numbers in some parts of the Middle East are not so different from Mohammed's time and the North American Indians are now no more numerous than they were in Tecumseh's day. Yet the people of Ireland celebrate Saint Patrick's Day in a thousand cities around the world and the last Tasmanian died in 1913.

Some men have expanded their numbers merely by acquiring new foods or because of advances in food technology. Consider the potato and its effects on numbers in Russia, Poland, northern Germany, and Ireland. Consider maize, or Indian corn, and the numerical expansion it encouraged in the highlands of Central America to the land of the Incas —and its effects on population development in Africa now. Consider, finally, the sheep that brought a wave of civilization across Europe, followed in turn by the swineherds spreading from the Balkans to Brittany.

The size of human populations has been further revolutionized by major advances in public health, ranging from the advent of the aqueduct and pure water, a Roman achievement, to the flush toilet and the indoor bathroom. It is difficult to comprehend that only half a century ago malaria, typhus, typhoid, diphtheria, scarlet fever, and tuberculosis were recurrent risks faced by men, women, and children in even the most advanced countries. Today, immunizations have reduced the toll of smallpox in Europe and the Americas from thousands to one or two cases a year, and controls have reduced world deaths from malaria from millions in 1880 to perhaps 27,000 in 1969.

Nor has man's accidental or deliberate tinkering stopped with food supplies or innovations in medicine. Turning now to his own potentials, he muses over such biological possibilities as *cloning*, or the mass-production of genetically identical individuals. Indeed, Robert Sinsheimer indicates cloning will be possible with humans within the next ten to twenty years; it has already been done with chickens and rats. Individual human lives

Figure 4 (left). New Guinean body build generally shows a very high degree of muscular development that Western man could match only through a select group of athletes. The stark muscle definition is the result of the near absence of subcutaneous fat, probably the adaptive result of a low-fat diet and the requirements of good heat dissipation. The muscle apparatus is maintained at high tonus in readiness for strenuous work. Figure 5 (right). The world presents a spectrum from the well-fed to the starving, each aware of the other's affluence and suffering. The shape of the future is generated by this polarity.

may be prolonged even more through organ transplants and organ regeneration, and genetic intervention to correct defects before birth may reduce the number of children born with structural or functional defects.

The relative sizes of populations have also been subject to accidental occurrences. Such "accidents" include who got the hoe first and then the iron-pointed plow, who first developed technologies sufficient to expand into the colder zones, and who began to associate cleanliness with godliness and so increased in numbers. Similarly, who got the pill first and who will accept population control as an alternative to death and starvation are also in a sense accidental.

So it is that human populations today—and thus the proportion of different genes in the species as a whole—do not exactly reflect the benefits of natural selection or some special form of genetic fitness. Instead, they represent a host of historical advances and accidents and not necessarily evolutionary virtues possessed by the genes themselves. Although gene frequencies at the population level respond to selective pressure, although the bulk of genes in *Homo sapiens* are those that have made him what he is, the actual proportion of some genes in modern man has been influenced by the game of numbers, with the winners riding high on chance.

THE COMMON HERITAGE

Modern man evolved as a tropical, omnivorous hunter and gatherer having endurance and a predator's reactions, designed to last approximately thirty-five years. His tropical adaptation is known not only from the climates in which man originally existed but also from the temperature ranges that man now can endure comfortably without clothing. His endurance limits can be verified by calculating human protein requirements, which are approximately one gram per kilogram of body weight, and by determining human walking and running speeds on the basis of the distances that can be covered in a six- or eight-hour day. His predatory nature can be proved on the basis of his responses to alarm and to stress, and his original life-span from the age at which both loss of muscle and loss of bone ordinarily begin.

Modern man rarely lives in the tropics, although in retirement he goes to California and Florida and Arizona or to southern France and Majorca and Malta. But he does tend to re-create the tropics in his home, in school, in places of work, and within the clothing he wears in all but the warmest weather. Having left the tropics, for the most part, he still keeps the tropics at a price—which includes the tremendous cost of fuels and of environmental pollution that comes from the by-products of heating.

Modern man is still able to walk and run at considerable speed, easily six miles an hour. He responds to alarm by an outpouring of adrenaline and its derivatives and by an increased secretion of steroid hormones of gonadal and adrenal origin. Yet in contemporary society he walks less and less, to the degree that a mile a day is now called "exercise," and at the same time he diminishes his accustomed energy expenditure by a thousand or more calories a day. His stresses now are both continuing and recurrent, springing in part from his work situation and in part from his general living habits. Exercising less, more than adequately fed, and with fewer outlets for discharging stress, modern man is subject to the penalties of having ancient response mechanisms and adaptations. So hypertensive heart disease and atherosclerosis are the new products of his ancient heritage.

Generally speaking, modern man avoids famine through more efficient food production and distribution of the resources of a continent rather than a local area. He assures himself of a constant and rather large supply of animal fats and additional hardened vegetable fats and oils. With an over-supply of calories, with a high-fat diet, he also assures himself of atherosclerosis.

But not all modern men are in the midst of a nutritional surplus. In the course of the

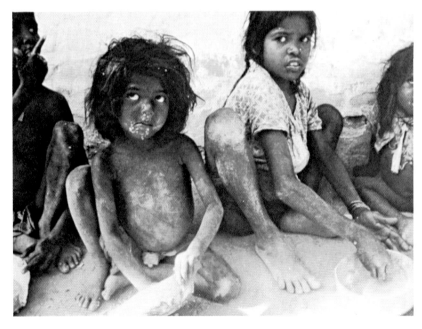

transition from hunting and gathering to food producing, new forms of famine are liable to appear. Two-thirds of the people of the world—or 2 billion people—now have a caloric deficit and at least half have a deficit of quality protein. Where men have concentrated excessively on rice in some areas and corn in others, protein-calorie malnutrition looms as an ever-increasing problem. Man is not the child of a frugivorous ancestor nor is he yet a herbivore: he needs his quality protein, with lysine and arginine and histidine, with the sulfur-containing amino acids —cystine and methionine. One of the growing problems in some parts of the world is a form of starvation called "kwashiorkor," a disease due to deficiency of quality protein in the diet that often occurs when infants are weaned and put on a diet exclusively of one cereal, such as rice or corn, that has limiting amino acids. Kwashiorkor unfortunately is common in many underdeveloped areas in parts of the world where rice or corn are extensively and preferentially fed to infants and young children. In fact, it is

estimated that millions of children die from protein-calorie malnutrition every year and that whole populations in Central America, Africa, and Asia are stunted not only because of inadequate animal protein intake but because folk beliefs restrict the child's diet and prevent him from being given "adult" foods that would remedy the missing amino acids.

Modern man inherits the ancient human inability to synthesize vitamin C. He must consume fruits and shoots and kraut or he develops scurvy. He must have sources of vitamin A and, in most areas of the temperate and frigid world, of vitamin D. Deficiencies of A, C, D, and the B vitamins are supposedly met by new sources of food produced as part of man's cultural adaptations, but culture is not always sufficient. Such deficiencies should be rare in a genuine omnivore, but modern conditions have limited man's use of food sources to the point where cultural means must be used to make up for the cultural deficiencies—by protein-supplemented noodles in the Orient, by Inca-parina in Central America, and by vitamin supplementation of breakfast foods in the United States.

Half the world's population has conquered the problem of hunger but has yet to conquer the problems caused by ingesting too many calories and expending too few. In view of the numbers of people still dying each year of starvation, it may seem ironic that many people still ruin their health and shorten their life expectancy by eating too much. Yet the problem of overconsumption is exceedingly grave, and it stems from the fact that men have not adapted physically to many of the conditions created by modern technology. Long periods of time, certainly tens of thousands of years, may be required for basic genetic changes to take place, but civilizations based on industry and technology have come into existence so quickly that the genetic changes needed to adapt man to these new conditions simply have not had time to occur.

Essentially, the human body is still adapted to ways of life that require a considerable expenditure of physical energy. Simply to survive, hunters and gatherers and even the early agriculturalists and pastoralists were obliged to exercise a great deal. But in a society such as that of the United States, much of the population requires very little exercise in order to survive. In such societies, the use of high nitrogen and phosphorus fertilizers, insect controls, highly selected and hybrid seeds, and improved techniques of animal husbandry all permit far more food to be produced by far fewer individuals. In some parts of the world, one in four or five individuals are still involved in food production; but in the United States, approximately one in twenty are actual food producers and a larger proportion of people are actually involved in transporting, packaging, processing and selling the food than in producing it. Americans now pay more for the convenience than for the growing to the people who squeeze the oranges and freeze the juice, instantize the potatoes, and cook the cocoa.

In so doing, the energy expenditure of the average adult has decreased tremendously. In fact, the energy output per person has

Figure 6. Combines in Nebraska and hand labor in the Philippines (Figure 7). In the United States perhaps one in twenty people are involved in food production in comparison to the one in four producing food in other countries.

plummeted while adult caloric intakes have probably increased 500 to as many as 5,000 calories per day in some age categories. There are fewer farmers—and other laborers—who use human rather than mechanical energy. And adult energy expenditures have been further reduced by the widespread use of the automobile as a means of transportation. People sit on the way to work, sit at work, and sit on the way back. Exercise is now relegated to play—although the work is going out of exercise, too, with bicycles that go nowhere and belts that jiggle and television broadcasts of athletic teams that allow a few to expend energy while millions watch. For Americans today, energy requirements are lower and energy expenditures lower still, with the difference stored as fat.

Unfortunately, the human body is not adapted to this kind of existence. The result is that modern man eats better and copiously, grows faster, matures earlier, then dies from overeating. Meanwhile, the other half of the world's population must confront famine and protein deficiency, having exceeded their food supply and, in particular, the supply of quality protein and useful fats.

By common heritage, all modern men share climatic and nutritional determinants. Even though genetic adaptations to both have occurred on a local level to a limited degree, modern man is still largely limited by his common ancient heritage. At no point is this more obvious than in nutrition, where human needs lead to protein calorie malnutrition at one nutritional extreme and to atherosclerotic heart disease at the other. Even if man lasts longer than his old accustomed time by virtue of good nutrition, he still begins his decline at the regular and traditional age.

THE SEPARATE, UNEQUAL HERITAGES

All modern men enjoy some abilities and face some disabilities simply because of their common heritage. The Eskimo, still tropical creatures under their traditional parkas and mukluks, can and do live happily

in San Francisco. Civilization, with its altered food composition, food texture, and changed oral flora, brings dental cavities to all, and the orthodontist expensively aligns teeth that in past generations were self-aligning. Better food and better care notably extend life and then nip it in the bloom. In less than a generation, Yemenite Jews in Israel have begun to exhibit coronary artery disease at a rate that Ashkenazic Jews had seemingly worked 2,000 years to develop.

Still, many disabilities or abilities are not common human property but may be race-specific, group-specific, or limited to a single but extended kinship. Apparent abilities include such diverse phenomena as cold tolerance, heat tolerance, and altitude adaptation. Apparent disabilities include Rh incompatibility, which is, or rather was, practically a European specialty. Rh incompatibility refers to the incompatibility between a fetus of one Rh type and the mother of another Rh type and the production of antibodies resulting in red cell destruction in the fetus. Until transfusion techniques had been perfected, the probability of fetal loss or death of the newborn was common.

Today, as a result of American involvement in Japan, Korea, Vietnam, and Thailand, the once-limited Rh negative gene has been introduced into populations that formerly lacked it. Now Rh incompatibility and Rh babies will constitute a medical problem in those countries as well. Prior to World War II, however, classic Rh incompatibility

Figure 8 (below). Incompatibility in the ABO blood group system. Interest in blood groups began in the 1900s, when it was discovered that a "clumping" reaction sometimes occurred when the blood from one person was mixed with the blood from another. Figure 9 (right). When blood samples from a sufferer of severe anemia are placed in a low-oxygen environment, the red blood cells twist into the angular shapes that earned them the name "sickle" cells.

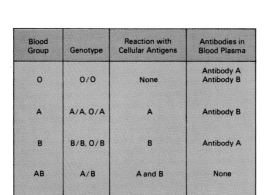

Blood Group	Genotype	Reaction with Cellular Antigens	Antibodies in Blood Plasma
O	O/O	None	Antibody A Antibody B
A	A/A, O/A	A	Antibody B
B	B/B, O/B	B	Antibody A
AB	A/B	A and B	None

was, for all practical purposes, limited to people of European ancestry: the Rh negative gene (r) was found only in 15 or 20 percent of European individuals.

Sickle-cell anemia, for another example, was and is primarily a disability of people originating in some parts of Africa. It is a genetically determined disease, due to the presence of the abnormal hemoglobin S, and it is lethal or nearly so in the homozygous state—as in some of the offspring of two parents who are both genetic "carriers." The homozygotes for the sickle-cell trait rarely survive and, if they do, they rarely reproduce. Yet the genetic carrier, the heterozygote for hemoglobin S, is actually at an advantage in the presence of some kinds of malaria. The malarial parasites do not reproduce as well in the blood cells of individuals who have the sickle-cell trait, and such individuals may have a better chance of surviving than individuals without it. Here is a genetically determined *disease*, if we take the homozygote or the person with a double dose of sickle-cell genes, yet it is also a genetically determined *protection* against malaria in the form of the heterozygote effect.

The discovery of the molecular basis of sickle-cell disease and the abnormal hemoglobin S is one of the human triumphs of our time—shared by the chemist Linus Pauling and the human geneticist J. V. Neel. And Anthony Allison deserves much of the credit for establishing the link between malarial selection and the sickle-cell gene. The sickle-cell story is a complicated one, extending beyond Africa to the Middle East and to the discovery of other abnormal hemoglobins. The sickle-cell model helped to explain the condition called Mediterranean anemia, similarly caused by an abnormal hemoglobin and similarly showing its relationship to malaria.

Deficiency of the red-cell enzyme glucose-6 phosphate dehydrogenase (G6PPD) exists in two forms, an African form (B) and a Mediterranean form (A). The enzyme deficiencies differ yet also resemble each other. Affected individuals may develop hemolytic anemia when exposed to certain antimalarials, to some more common drugs, or even to the *fava* bean that has long been cultivated in the Middle East. The deficient gene seems to be another adaptation to malaria, and it is a further illustration of a disability that is also an ability. But it primarily represents a further example of a modern disability of part of mankind that arises from separate heritage. The Eskimo do not have G6PPD, nor do northern and central Europeans, Australian aborigines, or American Indians. But the gene is common in Africa, in the Middle East, and in parts of the Far East—all malarial areas. In parts of Iran, it is actually the more common gene.

People in the United States have been reared on a quart of milk a day. Milk is regarded as good, and in fact it is an excellent source of calcium and an inexpensive source of animal protein, one-third as expensive as steak. But many people in the Orient cannot make use of a quart of milk a day. Because they suffer *lactase deficiency*, they can tolerate little more than a half pint—if that. People with lactase deficiency (deficiency of the digestive enzyme lactase) cannot use the milk sugar *lactose*. Why and how this deficiency arose is not known, nor is it known how Europeans came to possess the gene for higher lactase levels. Whether the gene was originally present in all populations but lost in some or absent in early man but gained in Europe can only be guessed at.

Figure 10. The quality as well as the available amount of water and land resources decreases as modern man increases in number and intensifies his exploitation and consumption. Today environmental exploitation is no longer confined within the boundaries of any given area, for modern societies depend on resources extracted from all over the world.

Lactase deficiency, however, is one more example of a human disability shared not by all mankind, but by part of it.

Modern man has also adapted physiologically to heat and cold. He has adapted to extreme cold through elevated blood flow and increased metabolic activity and to moderate cold through reduced peripheral blood flow. Dark skin, abundant in melanin granules, is an advantage when sun tolerance is considered but is a disadvantage in terms of biosynthesis of vitamin D in climates where there is less sunlight.

In sum, all men share some abilities and some disabilities that are part of their common, ancient heritage, and as they face the modern world, different groups of mankind have some different abilities and different inabilities by virtue of their separate genetic heritages.

ENVIRONMENTAL COST OF LIVING

The most important resources to man are the land and the food that grows on it. The more men there are, the less land per individual there is for raising food. To make matters worse, the prime land in most parts of the world is that immediately surrounding urban centers; probably because many cities grew out of agricultural cradles. Moreover, for every new individual added to the population, two-tenths of an acre is taken from agricultural land for urban needs. How much land does a civilization require? Kenneth Watt estimates that if a population were to eat only cereal grains, it would take about one-quarter of an acre per individual to feed that population; and if a population were to eat only meat, it would take an entire acre. As urban populations overrun prime farmland, they will come to experience real shortages of foods.

Or consider water pollution. Waste products from industrial plants, sewage treatment facilities, and the run-off from acreage sprayed with insecticides have made the water in many areas undrinkable and the survival of aquatic plants and animals prob-

lematical. So acute is this problem that, in the near future, it is altogether possible that entire areas of sea life will exist no longer. Even the oceans, once considered vast enough to absorb all of man's effluence, are now in danger of eventual pollution comparable to that found in rivers and lakes. Already many aquatic species are endangered by discharges into the sea. And how the ecological balance of the seas might be restored once it is disrupted no one has yet been able to say.

In addition to the association of air pollution with such modern afflictions as lung cancer and emphysema, it appears that man's pollution of the atmosphere may also be affecting the weather. In California, cities are getting hotter, primarily because of the laying down of expanses of asphalt paving combined with the elimination of trees and evaporative surfaces. But in rural areas, there are indications of a trend toward a global chilling that meteorologists are attrib-

Figure 11. The catastrophic effects of a major volcanic eruption, including atmospheric chilling, are readily apparent to populations that live through the aftermath. In comparison, the environmental exploitation and pollution that has paralleled population increase (Figure 12) has been a slow process, and only now is the cumulative effect being recognized as a like catastrophe of man's own making.

uting to the continuing increase in atmospheric pollution. This consequence is particularly worrisome in light of the magnitude of the effects produced by major volcanic eruptions. Krakatoa, Asamaya, and Skaptar Jökull each put enough fine ash into the upper atmosphere to chill the world for at least five years following the eruptions. The 1815 explosion of Mount Tambora in the Dutch East Indies put about five cubic miles of fine ash into the upper atmosphere, and the following year was one of the coldest in history. It was the summer of 1816 in North America, in fact, that was referred to as "the summer that never was."

In effect, pollution is doing what these volcanoes did, but cumulatively. Depending on how high fine particles from air pollution ascend and how dense they become, atmospheric dirt eventually can deflect as much as 20 percent of the incoming solar radiation back into space. Such a deflection can produce major effects on the weather. It may well be that man and his perpetual global pollution will lead him back to an Ice Age of his own making.

THE PAST IN THE FUTURE OF MAN
Modern man is an improbable mixture of old evolutionary adaptations in new evolutionary situations. Migration has carried old genes to new places, and out-marriage, the dissolution of old barriers to gene flow, and the mixture between local races and between geographic races have worked to introduce old genes in new containers and in new genetic combinations.

Judged by his limbs, his length, and his endurance, modern man is still basically a predator. But nine-tenths of the world population are active predators no longer. Indeed, one-fourth of the population is now more sedentary than not. Modern man, in consequence of modern agricultural technology, is less and less a food producer; fewer people are engaged in food production yet in some parts of the world there is now more food for more to eat. Man has successfully low-

ered the human death rate but has not done much to lower the birth rate, and human population as a consequence will *double* in about thirty-five years. Unfortunately, population growth is still exceeding man's ability to produce and distribute the right kinds and the right amounts of food. More men now go hungry than all the men who existed in 1875.

Against the old record of thirty-five years of life—man's average for 2 million years —the human lifespan in the West has doubled or more than doubled. As a result, man now dies of disabilities once rare, in many cases of metabolic adaptations lethal in later life but actually useful in younger years. In fact, man now outlives much of his genetic potential and continues for decades more, where past evolutionary adaptation cannot protect him.

Modern man matures earlier sexually, yet maintains his reproductive capacity longer. He is taller and fatter, both results of more and better food. Although more sedentary, he paradoxically now consumes fewer calories as an adult. He is heir to disorders of dentition such as dental caries and malocclusions, the causes of which are still imperfectly known. Although psychoses are probably not any more common today, disorders of fat metabolism are prevalent, and these serve to kill him.

Because of medical technology, once-lethal enzymatic deficiencies need be lethal no longer. Insulin can be obtained by injection, and by careful dietary control many disordered pathways of amino-acid metabolism can be bypassed. Growth hormone can be administered to counteract its genetically determined deficiency. Genes no longer eliminated by natural selection can therefore pile up in the population, resulting in a far more significant loading of mutant genes today than fallout from nuclear explosions has so far produced.

Man inevitably upsets the balance of nature once he exceeds one man per square mile, or two, or ten. Man pollutes the land and the air and the water to the point where he may soon have difficulty breathing, or drinking, or even living. Collected in cities, he affects the rainfall and the temperature. Living cheek-by-jowl, man next to man, he spreads his diseases faster and, with modern transportation, farther as well.

In the past, human evolution has kept pace with change, slowly providing adaptations to heat and cold, to altitude, to malaria, and to other diseases. But evolution requires time. Bacteria can adapt to antibiotics and insects can adapt to chlorinated hydrocarbons quickly, but the rate of change in modern times is such that human generations are not short enough for genetic adaptation.

So the important generalization about modern man is that his past has caught up with him and that time has caught up with him. Designed for thirty-five years, he is underengineered for living seventy years or more. Designed to eat and run, he is not adapted to more eating and less running. In the modern world, old local adaptations may be adaptations no longer because the ecology can change or because the gene pools can move, or both. In the modern world, rapid cultural advances must now substitute for slower evolutionary changes. Man is still ahead, as he numbers into the billions. There is still some world space to expand into, still-untapped sources of fuels, still-unused sources of water. But man is approaching the limits of the world he knows, as he has come to know it.

THE ARCHAEOLOGICAL RECORD IV

Methods in Archaeology

14

In the late 1960s, a United States senator declared, in support of greater defense expenditures, that if a nuclear war broke out he wanted to be sure that the survivors would be Americans. With luck, the particular event the senator contemplated will never take place, but even if world-wide nuclear war or any other cataclysmic event is avoided, American civilization will eventually come to an end. The idea may be unimaginable to some and intolerable to others, but the lesson of history is that all civilizations and life styles inevitably cease to exist and that, barring the extinction of man, people who perform the functions of archaeologists will probably one day be trying to explain American culture on the basis of an examination of its remains.

Consider the archaeologist who will be the first to uncover the rubble of a middle-class suburban American home. Fake eyelashes, an antique Chinese incense burner, an aluminum TV dinner tray, a small plastic doll with movable arms (all potential signs of religious rites); a football helmet (symbol surely of some warrior tribe?); a child's bow and arrow (they do fit in neatly with the helmet); a bronze plaque commemorating the 1970 Olympics . . . you can see the archaeologist's dilemma.

The archaeologist of the future will probably soon explain the true function of such vestiges of American society, for he will more than likely uncover enough enduring forms of writing—such as the words on the plaque—that can be translated to serve as a guide. The archaeologist today is not so fortunate. In general, he concentrates on *prehistory*, the extremely long span of man's existence that began about 5 million years ago and ended around 6000 B.C., and for this timespan there are no written records and therefore no history in the usual scholarly sense.

THE SCOPE OF ARCHAEOLOGY

Archaeology impinges on so many other subjects that it can best be considered as a set of complex techniques for learning about man's past from the tangible remains of his activities and from the surviving effects of those activities. Archaeological findings are used by anthropologists, classicists, historians, and artists alike. Historians, however, have had less need for the techniques of archaeology, for they most often have been concerned with chronicling the documented, specific events of the recent past. To many contemporary archaeologists, recording the historical sequences of events is but a preliminary step to their main work; it is taken because it provides a time-space framework for the organization of their data. They are more interested in using archaeological findings to test particular anthropological hypotheses, many of which relate to processes of culture change and to the ways men relate to their environment, both subjects of great concern in general anthropological research.

THE SPACE-TIME FRAMEWORK

It is not possible to dig up an idea or an emotion. Archaeologists necessarily work with artifacts. On the basis of what they find they are able to develop remarkably complex pictures of past civilizations, but the first and essential step is to identify distinctive kinds of artifacts and to establish their distribution in time and space. If the location of each known find of a type of weapon or a household utensil or a form of architecture is plotted on a map, the results provide clear clues to the extent of the area once occupied by a group of people sharing some aspects of the culture. Because the diffusion of any artifact type may have been a slow process, however, the map may reflect a spread that took place over several centuries.

A culture develops and reaches through time as well as across space, and although archaeologists are interested in doing far more than simply working out historical sequences of events, they do attempt to organize their material in chronological sequence. A variety of dating techniques can be applied to particular levels in complex sites that were built over long periods or to whole sites that were built in a short period, and through these techniques a chronological se-

quence of artifact types and clustering of types can be worked out. The most effective method is usually to first develop the chronology of one small area after another and finally to match up these sequences to determine the relative chronology. A more general chronology can then be constructed for a larger area, and once this is done, it becomes possible for the archaeologist confronted with a newly found specimen or site to say with assurance that it belongs, for example, to the 8000 B.C. time period and is associated with the Natufian culture.

The next task is to categorize the different periods and cultures, and many laymen or beginners in archaeology find themselves confused by the seemingly endless array of names that have been devised by archaeologists to identify various kinds of artifacts and segments of a chronology or culture. Still, names are essential for identification, and inasmuch as all the different sequences must be differentiated from one another, an enormous collection of names inevitably becomes part of the archaeologist's investigative apparatus. In the United States the normal method of naming is to select some local geographic name and apply it to some time period or phase, such as the names White Mound, Red Mesa, Windgate, and Bonito to differentiate phases in New Mexico. In the Old World, numbered and lettered sequences have more commonly been used, such as Early Iron Age 1A, 1B, 1C, 2A, 2B, and so on. The latter may seem easier to remember at first, but it is less adaptable. It is difficult, for example, to insert a newly defined phase or period between 1B and 1C.

And such newly defined phases are constantly being introduced. As soon as he has constructed a satisfactory space-time framework for a region, the archaeologist can use it as a frame of reference for approaching other problems, such as the response of a people to changing food supplies, or the gradual refinement of an art style, or the relation of social organization to architec-

Figure 2. Le Moustier, a site in southern France where Neanderthal forms were first found in association with a flint tool assemblage, thus reinforcing the growing belief that these "apelike" creatures had the capacity for conceptual thought and were likely hominids.

ture. But all such frameworks and frames of reference are tentative. Sooner or later it generally becomes necessary for the archaeologist to revise, correct, and refine his basic schemes of distribution and chronology as new information becomes available or as flaws appear in his original structure.

CULTURE THEORY AND ARCHAEOLOGY

Although much of their time is spent in identifying and describing cultures of the past in terms of their unique characteristics and their unique occurrence in space and time, archaeologists are also increasingly interested in culture change and the process by which culture A of one time period becomes culture B of a later period. How, for example, will a future scholar explain how the Puritans of the 1600s in New England became Playboy Club members, demonstrators, hippies, art collectors, and sports fans of the 1900s? These are ongoing processes, and analysis of the forms they took in the past helps elucidate the forces at work in the rapidly changing contemporary world.

Factors of Evolution and Diffusion

One of the processes of culture change, recognized as early as the eighteenth century, is evolutionism. Christian Thomsen in 1836 devised a simple scheme of developmental stages as a way to arrange archaeological museum specimens. His three-age system is based on the correct deduction that man first used stone tools, then eventually learned the use of bronze and finally of iron. Other early evolutionary schemes, most notably Lewis Henry Morgan's view of all mankind progressing through a single sequence of seven universal stages, were relatively inflexible and were contradicted by archaeological fact and ethnographic example. In the 1950s, Julian Steward proposed the idea of multilinear evolutionism, suggesting that evolutionary processes had varied from one area to another and that the search for regularities—or laws of social and cultural

change—should be limited to situations for which positive, empirical evidence could be found.

Another process that affects the complex story of culture change is diffusion. Much of the progression of mankind has been marked by the invention of completely new ideas, such as the use of the wheel, of irrigation ditches, of gunpowder and armed cavalry, and of steam power and atomic energy. But how many times is the same invention reinvented? Does it occur just once and then diffuse throughout wide areas? Or are the same or similar inventions frequently invented anew in different places by different people at different times? The archaeological record provides abundant documentation of the diffusion of certain cultural traits from one group to another. It has demonstrated, for instance, that farming spread from its beginnings in the Near East along the shores of the Mediterranean and up the Danube Valley into northern Europe, reaching Great Britain some 4,000 years later. There is increasing evidence that farming was invented independently in the New World, with plants entirely different from those domesticated in the Old World. But there is not enough evidence to demonstrate whether or not other complex innovations, such as iron smelting and the concept of a single supreme deity, were made once or many times.

Defining Culture Areas

At one time archaeologists and ethnologists commonly grouped together the cultures of the world's preindustrial societies within each continent, classifying those cultures that resembled one another into a culture area. This concept was frequently used to group together groups that shared such similar economic pursuits as farming, hunting, and fishing as a consequence of their dependency on similar natural resources. As more information became available, it was found that variations within each culture area were greater than had been realized at first,

Figure 3. One of the *kula* boats used in the ceremonial exchange network of the Trobriand Islands. With his functional analysis of the *kula* ring, Bronislaw Malinowski provided the archaeologist with a conceptual tool for reconstructing many aspects of cultures of the past. Figure 4 (right). Kachina corn dance, seldom observed by outsiders. This dance profoundly expressed the ecological relationships on which the Hopi life way is grounded.

and boundaries were impossible to define precisely. Culture area terms eventually proved to be useful only for the most preliminary descriptions, and both ethnologists and archaeologists have since adopted smaller, more precise units of classification.

Culture Patterns and Functionalism

Even when dealing with a relatively small and compact group, archaeologists face a problem, for the cultural traits of any group are not random but are clustered in a coherent and integrated pattern. The idea of cultural patterning was popularized by Ruth Benedict, and the idea that an entire culture can be conveniently characterized by a single term paralleled the archaeological practice of picking one single important feature—for instance, the Early Farmers Period or the City Builders Period—to identify an entire prehistoric cultural complex. This pattern or single-feature approach oversimplifies the situation, however, and distorts it by concentrating attention on only one of several tendencies in a culture.

Nevertheless, in attempts to describe cultures that are now extinct—as most are—it is important to realize that certain traits are frequently found associated with others and that the elements of a culture tend to fit into an integrated whole. It is this holistic view that permits an archaeologist to make reasonable inferences about many facets of culture for which he cannot recover direct evidence.

Equally important in this respect is the concept of functionalism, in which culture is viewed as composed of parts, with each one making some kind of contribution to many other parts and to the whole. For example, in his famous study of the ritual exchange of valuables among Melanesian islanders, Bronislaw Malinowski, a leading functionalist, found that he had to pay careful attention to canoe building and sailing practices, to songs and chants, and to the important economic exchanges that accompanied the ritual exchanges. No segment of a culture can, in fact, be understood without some reference to many other segments. Functionalism, like the concept of culture patterns, provides the archaeologist with a sound basis for hypothesizing about many aspects of a culture when tangible evidence is lacking.

Adaptation and Interaction

Anthropology in the last decade has relied heavily on *ecology*, the study of the interaction and interdependence of all organic and inorganic components of a particular system —the plants, animals, soil, and climate of a forest, for example. Archaeologists are finding it useful to view prehistoric man in terms of the adaptations that were made to his environment as well as the potentialities the environment offered him. It must be recognized, however, that any group makes use of only certain parts of the environment —selected on the basis of its technology, social systems, and value orientations—and that at the same time certain aspects of the environment may strongly influence the life ways of a group. For instance, the helium, oil, gas, and uranium of northern Arizona were of no importance in the lives of the Indian hunters and farmers who occupied the area for thousands of years, but they are of great importance to the present-day white occupants of the region and to the Indians on whose reservations mining leases are made. On the other hand, these miners are not much affected by the yearly variations in rainfall, whereas changes in precipitation greatly affected the lives of the Indians of the past.

The manner in which man has used his culture to adapt to the environment and achieve a degree of ecological balance may

also be evaluated in terms of the *microenvironment*, the ecological niches for which specific cultural patterns are developed. The early inhabitants of northern Arizona, for example, did not adapt in a general way to the environment, but instead each group made use of certain portions of it, such as the mountains, meadows, and high forested mesas, or the arroyos and stream bottoms. For each ecological niche with its particular potentialities, men developed a suitable assortment of exploitative techniques. Yet certain limitations were imposed that no degree of adaptation could overcome. Agriculture, for instance, was possible only where there was sufficient moisture and soil and a long enough growing season, and only after domestic plants had diffused northward from Mexico, along with the techniques for using them. Moreover, prehistoric population density for the region as a whole never exceeded ten or fifteen people per sixty square miles, far too few to encourage the growth of urban centers and the concomitant elaboration of society that occurred prehistorically far to the south in Mexico.

The concept of *cultural ecology* has been particularly useful in providing a theoretical framework with which archaeologists can advance from the accumulation of data to the generalization of or the testing of hypotheses. As described by Steward, cultural ecology is concerned with the *interaction* between technology and the particular social arrangements and organizations by which people of a given culture exploit their environment. In fact, many of the social changes that occur through time can be traced to new adaptations required by changing technology and productive arrangements. From this point of view, archaeologists can perceive some degree of consistency and continuity in the varieties of technological detail they record and in the sequences into which they place their data.

Although no conceptual tool provides a means for answering all questions, studies of ecological adaptation and interaction are proving to be an important means of understanding more clearly the many varied patterns of life that developed in prehistoric times and of discerning some of the reasons for their changes through time.

THE ARCHAEOLOGIST IN THE FIELD
Archaeological field work falls into two general categories. The first of these is the survey, followed by the second, the more detailed archaeological excavation.

Techniques of Surveying
Before the archaeologist can make his studies of vanished societies, he has to find evidence of them, insofar as evidence is observable from the land's surface. He may come across ruined walls or visible traces of architectural structures, but he more often deals with less conspicuous remains such as a few chips of flint that have been unearthed in a newly plowed field, which might indicate that someone made a stone tool there, or perhaps a faint depression running across a desert, which might signify the presence of an ancient irrigation canal. Survey workers must have keen observation, experience, and good judgment if they are to avoid being misled by a frost-shattered boulder that looks like the remains of flint chipping or an old jeep track that resembles an ancient canal.

The information found in a field survey must be recorded in terms of maps, photographs, detailed notes of all pertinent observations, and frequently samples of the cultural material found in each site for fu-

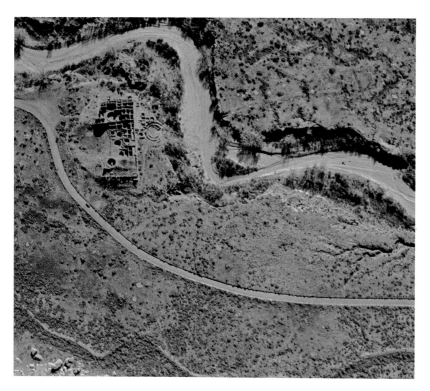

ture study and comparison. The main purpose of a survey may be to find a site or sites for excavation, but usually it can also help to determine the distribution of particular kinds of sites or the evidence assignable to certain time periods. Most importantly, it can reveal a great deal about the kinds of locations chosen by man in the past for his camps, villages, or farmlands, and it is therefore essential to the ecological framework of archaeological study.

Aerial photography is a technique being used increasingly by archaeologists. With it, they can discover a number of traces of earlier cultures that are simply not visible from the ground, such as slight mounds that show up in slanting light or changes in the color of crops, which may indicate ancient disturbances of the land. Some recent infrared aerial images of an area in north central Arizona disclosed parallel ridges that proved to be prehistoric agricultural sites. *Magnetic surveying* of archaeological sites is another recent development that has led to the disclosure of iron objects; fired structures such as kilns, furnaces, and ovens; pits and ditches filled with refuse; and occasionally walls, foundations, roads, and tombs.

Techniques of Excavation

The second major part of archaeological field work—the excavation—is a painstaking, complex, and time-consuming task devoted primarily to carefully securing as much information as possible about man's past ac-

tivities. In the nineteenth century, excavations were usually undertaken to secure specimens for museums, and even today they are often undertaken for this aesthetic but unscientific purpose. More frequently, however, an excavation is a search for information, and specimens—the tangible objects that can be brought back to a museum or laboratory—are only one means to that end.

Just as important as the specimen is the context in which it is found. It makes a great deal of difference whether a bronze dagger lies at the bottom of an abandoned well or beside a carefully buried skeleton or among the ribs of a skeleton jumbled beneath a burned and fallen house. The archaeologist must record not only the exact location of objects found and the details of their association with other objects but also the countless details he has observed while digging, even though no specimens are involved. For example, a thin layer of windblown sand on the floor of a room, beneath the debris of collapsed walls and roof, provides evidence that the door stood open for some time after it was abandoned, whereas the presence of ashes and burned roof timbers directly above the floor, together with everyday tools and utensils, shows that the room burned when it was being occupied and was not abandoned.

The archaeologist knows that excavating a site inevitably destroys it. The process is analogous to the somewhat improbable predicament of entering a library of rare books, for which no other copies exist, and having to read them even though you know the mere turning of the pages will result in their destruction. Under such circumstances, the conscientious scholar would, as he read, make his notes as accurate and comprehensive as possible, and this is what the archaeologist must do.

Immediately before the actual excavation, the archaeologist must draw a scale map of the site. He then makes the first excavation at a point removed from the immediate site

Figure 5 (left). Infrared aerial photograph of Pueblo del Arroyo in Chaco Canyon, New Mexico. The fine lines on the opposite side of the stream bed are field and water systems. Figure 6. Solvieux, an open-air settlement of the classic Paleolithic period, is being excavated under the direction of James Sackett. This site is a day's walk from the rock shelters at Les Eyzies. The photographs show some of the artifacts that were found at various levels, along with numerous cobblestones. Analysis of the horizontal grid patterns suggests that these cobblestones were probably the foundations of early dwellings.

but in an area that is likely to contain some cultural remains. This site is called a *control pit*, and it serves to verify the nature of soils and deposits in an undisturbed state. Once excavation of the actual site is under way, the archaeologist continues to dig until he reaches a level without any cultural remains or until the pattern of finds becomes repetitive. The skillful archaeologist stops digging when he has a record complete enough to substantiate cultural reconstruction, and this is one of the differences that distinguishes him from the collector, who digs as long as he finds specimens.

The excavation of a small camp of hunters and gatherers may require a few days of labor, whereas that of a large, complex site of agriculturalists may require years of steady work. The archaeologist's task is a painstaking one. Some of the most delicate jobs in excavation, for example, involve the discovery of forms of structures that have long since decayed away, and it is commonplace for the archaeologist to obtain detailed information about perished material by gently scraping away the various strata, repeatedly sweeping away covering dirt, and noting all changes in color and composition of the soil. Careful shaving of the soil under Bronze Age mounds in the Netherlands, for example, has exposed as a faint stain the shadowy outlines of skeletons of men whose bodies had been disintegrated by the acid sand. In another instance, the excavator of the Sutton Hoo ship remains in England had to shave away sand that had filled the vessel until he came to rusted nails and began to detect a slight change in the texture of the sand that indicated where the timbers had been.

The ability of the archaeologist to accurately depict the life ways of an earlier culture can be illustrated by the archaeological reconstruction of a Paleo-Indian bison hunt in 6500 B.C. From a pile of bones and scattered projectiles unearthed in a dry gulch in Colorado, archaeologists were able

Figure 7. A Plains Indian bison hunt depicted by Charles Russell. Careful archaeological analysis provided the basis for one detailed description of a bison hunt that took place in 6500 B.C., long before the appearance of the horse, let alone written accounts or artistic record of it.

to determine the month the hunt took place, the direction the wind was blowing, the direction of the hunters' drive, the Indians' organization in butchering, and the approximate number of hunters involved.

The remains of 200 buffalo were found in three distinct layers with thirteen untouched skeletons at the bottom, partly butchered animals in the middle, and single bones at the top. The archaeologists realized that they had discovered a trap into which the bison had been stampeded: the intact carcasses at the bottom had been trampled by the animals that had been stampeded on top of them. Because none of these skeletons faced north, northeast, or northwest, it was deduced that the animals had been running in a southward direction because the hunters would have approached them downwind in order to prevent their scent from being detected (learned by analogy with later bison hunters), the wind must have been blowing from the south. The distribution of projectiles indicated that a flanking party of hunters had been positioned at the east end of the site.

The way the bones were piled revealed the butchering procedure. As the meat was removed from a carcass, the bones were discarded in separate piles. Those at the bottom were generally forelegs, then pelvises, then spinal units, indicating the Indians' preference of cuts. Skulls were usually located at the top of the pile. The position of the skeletons even revealed the steps used to strip each carcass: they were arranged so that they could be rolled onto their bellies and the skin stripped from the back. The date of the kill was fixed at late May or early June because of the presence of the skeletons of calves judged to be but a few days old.

By calculating how much each individual could eat, how much meat could be preserved, and the number of pounds the average individual could carry away from the site, archaeologists further hypothesized that the meat would have fed about 150

people for the three weeks it might have lasted without serious spoilage, and that a much smaller group could neither have eaten it on the spot nor dried and carried away all of it on their backs. It was determined that 100 people could have performed the necessary 210 man-hours of work in half a day.

Underwater Archaeology

Underwater archaeology has only recently come to be recognized as a legitimate branch of the field, and what was once considered the adventurer's haphazard search for sunken treasure has now become the systematic approach of archaeological investigation. The knowledge gained from underwater sites is by no means limited to ship construction and trading routes, for ancient cargoes are cultures in miniature, containing artifacts ranging from simple tools to elaborate sculpture. It is estimated that from 10,000 to 100,000 ancient vessels lie on the floor of the heavily trafficked Mediterranean alone, and presumably each could offer information to the archaeologist. In addition, many coastal regions of the world have been inundated over time by rising sea levels, and some have sunk during earthquakes and volcanic eruptions. In still other places, artifacts have been deliberately placed under water as offerings to gods. Recent excavations of cenotes (natural water wells) in Yucatán, for example, have turned up relics that provide valuable information about Mayan religious practices and artistic achievements.

Considerable experimentation with devices and instruments is now taking place in attempts to discover how to thoroughly excavate an underwater site in as short a time as possible. Television cameras and a stereophotogrammetric (three-dimensional) mapping system are being used in surveying, and a metal detector has been devised that pinpoints objects beneath the sand. In addition, a plexiglass dome is being used by divers who wish to communicate under water, and

Figure 8. Archaeology is also moving into underwater realms as well and is taking its precision techniques with it. This excavation of a Greek merchant ship, which was sunk off the coast of Cyprus around 4 B.C., is being directed by Michael Katzev. The grid frame that is essential to archaeological analysis is in this case constructed of plastic irrigation pipe.

a two-man submarine has been in use for some time. The future of underwater archaeology will depend increasingly on the development of sophisticated techniques. Probably the most important equipment for the future will be the underwater dwellings now being developed for prolonged submergences. New techniques may indeed make the archaeologist at home under water, but it is difficult to imagine that precision instruments will diminish the need for the care with which the archaeologist handles the fragile and fragmentary remains of cultural man. Underwater archaeological excavation is the same painstaking task as is carried out on land.

ARCHAEOLOGICAL ANALYSIS

The analysis of archaeological information generally proceeds from a first stage of organizing the data in a number of systematic ways to a second stage in which selected parts of the data are examined according to the issues suggested by specific integrative concepts.

Spatial Organization

The first stage of archaeological analysis includes many elaborate procedures for efficiently categorizing large amounts of information. During excavation, records are kept of the locations of all objects and traces of human activity. When these finds are plotted on maps, plans, and cross-sections of the sites, an organized record emerges that can reveal not only village layout but the special activities carried on in certain houses and courtyards or the time relationship between successive camps and hearths.

If a site has been occupied for a long period and shows changes from one level to another, it is convenient to use the term "component" to refer to a single culturally homogeneous level of the site. The word "locality" is used to describe larger units, which can range from a single site and its surroundings to a considerable area including many sites; in practice a locality implies some degree of cultural unity. The concepts of area, region, and, in the Old World, zone are also used to refer to larger spatial units and provide convenient means for grouping sites that are thought to have some relationship to each other or for specifying a geographic unit for archaeological investigation.

Chronological Organization

Archaeological data must be placed into time sequences, and the means of determining the age of archaeological sites, levels within sites, and single artifacts are constantly increasing in number. Archaeology has drawn successfully on many natural sciences for aid in chronology, including geology, botany, physics, and chemistry. Dating techniques are intended to provide either relative dates (A is older or more recent than B, but the antiquity of neither is known) or absolute dates (the age of A is given in years, usually with a margin of error; for example, 2000 B.C. ±200).

Stratigraphy. Unless subsequently disturbed, older material underlies younger, a concept borrowed from geology. Strata are the index to the chronology of a site. The archaeologist works to reconstruct the chronology by peeling off the layers (or strata) that represent subsequent stages of culture—in reverse chronological order. But the task of sorting the layers and formulating a sequence is not necessarily straightforward. Often the strata have been disturbed by movements of the earth's crust, erosion of the surface, excavations of earlier inhabitants themselves, or the work of burrowing animals. Barring total destruction of the layers, analysis will show definite changes between the base and the top level of a site representing a series of

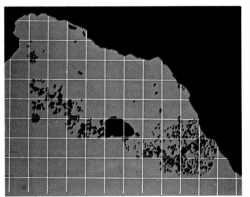 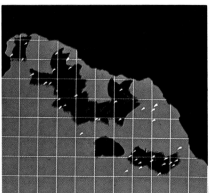 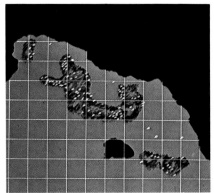

occupations. If four distinct cultures inhabited one general locale over hundreds of years and moved about considerably, different sites would have somewhat different stratigraphies. However, by numbering each stage and comparing which levels of occupation are consistently above or below others, a relative chronological framework can be established. The methods of stratigraphy have formed the basis of much of the chronology of modern archaeology.

Seriation. The popularity of a particular style or type of artifact tends to increase from its initial introduction (whether borrowed or invented), reach a maximum, and eventually decline. While the frequency of one kind of artifact is increasing, however, the frequency of another will be decreasing, so that half a dozen items will appear in different frequencies in successive periods of time. For example, at one time in the United States all houses were lit by candles. Later, the use of candles declined as oil lamps came into wide use. Later still, oil lamps declined in use as gas lamps succeeded them. Eventually electric lights began to be used, at first in a few homes and finally in most dwellings. If the percentages of each kind of lighting in use in a town were known for each decade, it would be possible to approximately determine the decade of occupation of another nearby settlement that had been abandoned. The mere presence of oil lamps would have suggested a general time period. Because they were used for so many decades, however, the relative proportion of all types of lighting would have been more revealing. Similarly, styles of prehistoric pottery, once their relative frequencies are known, can be used by seriation to "date" additional sites. This method was called "sequence dating" by its originator, Flinders Petrie, about 1900; recently it has been revived and is referred to as seriation.

Geologic Dating. Artifacts or deposits often occur within or are associated with geologic deposits, which in turn may be dated. *Varves* are the thin deposits in calm glacial lakes that show by color and texture the material laid down in successive summers and winters and thus provide a seasonal record year by year. Variations in the thickness and texture of individual varves also reveal climatic fluctuations. Although no single lake is large enough to contain a sequence of varves covering the entire retreat of one of the Ice Ages, a full chronology can be established by locating and piecing together a number of overlapping segments. Study of varves has made possible fairly accurate dating in a few areas for the last few thousand years, but these are primarily areas with few or no archaeological remains. Changing sea levels leave beaches and other kinds of shorelines and may provide a means of placing archaeological sites in a time sequence.

Palynology. Pollen is often preserved well in naturally accumulating deposits such as bogs or in artificial accumulations such as the trash in an occupied cave, or in the refuse dump of a village. Through time, the percentage of the various plants contributing the pollen alters, due to climatic and other environmental changes, and such changes are reflected in the changing percentages of different kinds of pollen. The palynologist takes the grains of each species represented in a sample and counts them and plots them on a graph. He can compare pollen graphs from different sites with one another and thus establish a regional framework. An artifact found with a pollen sample can be positioned in this sequence. The results of palynology permit dating of objects that are not susceptible to closer dating, but vegetation phases do not in themselves offer a refined chronology.

Dendrochronology. In a few parts of the world, tree rings of certain species show variations in width from year to year that reflect widespread climatic fluctuations. By matching many fragments of wood or charcoal from prehistoric sites and extending the tree-ring sequence back from the present with borings

Figure 9 (left). A few charts recording Henry de Lumley's excavation of Lazaret on the French Riviera give us a glimpse of human life 130,000 years ago. The first shows a rough semicircle of rocks enclosing an area along the cave wall, with all stone tools falling within it — clearly a shelter had been built there. The next chart shows a pattern of seashells even though they probably do not represent a food source — but such shells often are attached to seaweed that is washed ashore during storms. The final chart shows animal claws (all that would remain of furs) concentrated only with the shells, a clear indication the seaweed was used as a mattress and covered with furs from the animals early man hunted. In a range of prehistory where little is known of man, archaeology has shown where and how he lived, what he ate, and even what he slept on. Figure 10 (below). Pottery decoration from the Chavín period (1000-200 B.C.), the first of three horizons in Andean prehistory. The archaeologist also traces changing patterns in pottery in search of clues about the directions in which past cultures moved over time.

of living trees, master sequences for particular areas have been constructed that permit a sample of unknown age to be matched against it, giving an absolute date in years before the present. The ring pattern of the sample is moved along the master chart until it corresponds to a particular section of the chart. In order to obtain an absolute date in years it is necessary to have a sequence of overlapping rings extending from the date of the object to the present, but a long series of rings not linked to an absolute date can provide relative dating for wood from sites within that particular period.

Radiocarbon Dating. All living organisms absorb carbon from the atmosphere from the time they are born until the time they die. Atomic scientists, particularly Willard Libby, determined that a radioactive isotope, carbon 14, is formed by cosmic rays in the upper atmosphere and that this form of carbon is also absorbed by life forms. The amount of carbon 14 is nearly constant in the atmosphere and in life forms, so the amount present in any plant or animal at the time of its death is a known quantity. Radioactive carbon has a half-life of about 5,770 years. In other words, the intensity of radioactivity being emitted after 5,770 years have passed is one-half the intensity of that emitted at the time the organism died. At the end of another half-life period, the remaining intensity will again have diminished by half, and so on.

At the famous ceremonial center of San Lorenzo on the tropical coast of Veracruz, Mexico, excavations have shown that the Olmec civilization, with its enormous and elaborate stone sculptures, is not only the artistic and cultural ancestor of the other Mesoamerican civilizations but predates them—as shown by carbon 14 dates on samples of charcoal collected by Michael Coe of Yale University in 1966 and 1967. The sculptures were related to construction that in turn could be assigned places in the sequence of ceramic styles. Potsherds of dis-

tinctive styles occurred in hearths, and the charcoal from the hearths could be dated in the radiocarbon laboratory of Yale University. Although estimates had placed San Lorenzo as late as the early centuries of the Christian era, ten dated samples fell between 1300 B.C. and 800 B.C., a consistent enough grouping of a significant number of dates to firmly fix the time of the beginning of the Olmec culture.

Other radioactive dating techniques are being developed, including potassium-argon dating of certain kinds of volcanic rock. This technique is rarely useful for archaeological sites, although a few extremely old sites have been dated by it. Similarly, measurement of the thermoluminescence of radium and uranium contained in pottery is a

Figure 11. Distribution of a culture trait, reflecting the rise and fall of the Huari empire in Peru (A.D. 600-800). In the first phase, traditional religious motifs in Tiahuanaco pottery are traded to coastal areas in the Ica and Nazca valleys and a second center of production is established at Chakiparnpka. In the second phase, four production centers of the Tiahuanaco pottery style distribute wares throughout the Mantaro, Callejon de Huaylas, and the Central and South coasts. In the third phase, the Huari empire spreads north past Cajamarca and south to the Ocoña Valley. Within the empire a new pottery style, emerging at Pachacamac, spreads along the coast between the Chicama and Nazca valleys. After A.D. 800, the empire disintegrates and regional pottery traditions are quickly established. (After Edward Launing, *Peru Before the Incas.* Englewood Cliffs, N.J.: Prentice-Hall, 1961.)

technique that has proved to have too many difficulties to produce satisfactory archaeological dates thus far.

Typological Organization

Although no two artifacts made by preindustrial man are precisely alike, any archaeologist who attempted to make a complete and detailed description of each individual item would be burdened needlessly, as would his readers. Instead, he may group together similar objects and give a general description of their characteristics and variation. Generally, the groups are called *types* and the decision of how to divide a large number of specimens into types requires careful thought and close study of the material. *Functional types* are often used when it is possible to identify certain objects as knives, others as arrowheads, and so on. But usually these identifications are difficult, inasmuch as the users of the objects are gone and the function of the item can only be inferred from analogy with surviving customs. The same chipped stone tool may serve as a spear point, a knife, an awl for leather working, and a scraper, and to name a type by a single functional term is usually misleading and often no more than guesswork. Simple descriptive terms are devised instead and include such classifications as chipped stone uniface or biface (chipped on one or two surfaces), which are then modified by names and numbers. The array of types becomes enormous, but it is essential for analysis to have names, just as it is in the naming of biological species, and to provide clear, detailed definitions for each type.

Even a simple object generally has several characteristics that contribute to its form. An arrowhead, for example, has length, width, thickness, a degree of concavity or convexity of its edges, and a form of the base (notched, tapered, flared). For this reason it is also possible to record characteristics of each specimen and determine statistically which of these most frequently occur together—preferably with the use of a computer when many characteristics and hundreds or thousands of specimens are involved.

A typology represents the perspective of the archaeologist (or the computer) and not necessarily that of the makers of the artifact. It is not important that a category is arbitrary, however, as long as it provides a usable mechanism for ordering and comparing artifacts from various sites. Neither spatial determinations nor seriation would have much significance without the use of typology. The new trend in archaeology is more concerned with cultural process than schemes for descriptive content, but computer analysis of types has contributed to recent studies. William Longacre studied an Arizona site occupied about A.D. 1200 and determined from the distribution of 175 design elements on potsherds (delineated by a computer) that the occupants were probably divided into two local matrilineal groups, each with its own ceremonial structure. Using computer factor analysis on forty classes of tools found in seventy-seven assemblages from three different sites in the Near East, Lewis Binford was able to calculate that there were five distinct tool clusters, and with this information he could attempt to answer questions about the regularity of the behavior of the occupants or whether any occupational level corresponded to any single human activity.

Integration of Data

The second stage of archaeological analysis consists of extracting from the organized data certain parts that can be examined in terms of what are sometimes called *integrating concepts*. Several of these are shared with the rest of anthropology and include cultural ecology and cultural processes. Still others are unique to archaeology.

The concept of an archaeological *horizon* is a set of traits that links various cultures over a broad area in a brief time. Given a

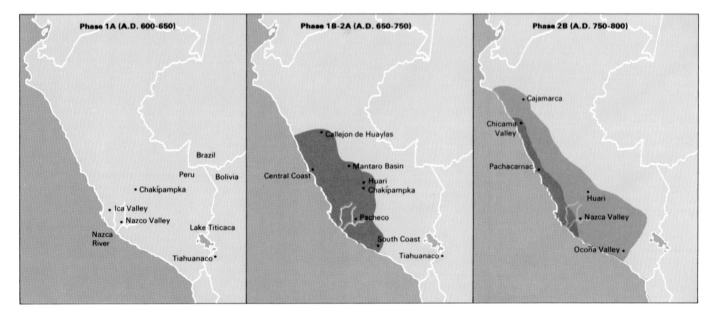

Phase 1A (A.D. 600-650) · Phase 1B-2A (A.D. 650-750) · Phase 2B (A.D. 750-800)

time-space graph where the horizontal axis represents a number of adjacent geographic regions and the vertical axis represents successive chronological periods, a horizon would be mapped with a shallow slope indicating the rapid spread of a trait. The Chavín art style of Peru serves as an illustration. The style is found throughout a large area, but it seems to have endured for a relatively short time. The archaeologist reasons from this timespan distribution that the spread was accelerated by some kind of pressure and is ultimately able to conclude that the Chavín horizon represents a kind of religious cult spread. "Horizon" is a useful concept for relating to each other a number of local sequences, and horizon markers are generally used to define particular horizons. These markers are distinctive traits or artifact types that diffused rapidly and thus mark a point of simultaneity in each local sequence in which they occur.

Tradition is a temporal concept referring to a cultural trait or cluster of traits persisting through time that permits otherwise quite different cultural assemblages to be considered related to each other in a sequential manner. A tradition plotted on a time-space graph would have a steep slope. The pottery motifs of the American Southwest, which are limited to a relatively small area but persisted with little variation for over a thousand years, are an example.

Successive major time units within a region or area are often called *periods*, and the definition of a period both in chronological terms and as to cultural content is the major, although intermediate, goal of much archaeological research. Periods in adjacent and related areas may be grouped into *stages*, generally on a continental basis, and each is usually characterized by a single dominating pattern of economic activity and social organization.

Inference and Analogy

Because the archaeologist observes only the material residues of extinct cultures—and spatial and associational details concerning them as they are being excavated—it is impossible to understand the human behavior that accounted for these material remains without comparison of information from ongoing cultures with those no longer in existence. Inference is a means of reasoning from available, although usually limited, data in order to add other data or ideas. Analogy, in archaeology, means reasoning that if an object is used in a certain way by a living or known group then it possibly or probably was used in a similar way by the people responsible for the archaeological remains. Both of these kinds of reasoning have expanded the meaning of prehistoric data, but each has led scholars astray in specific instances, either by limiting their analytical approach to the inductive method of inference (reasoning from known particulars to previously unknown generalizations) or by providing attractive but wholly wrong analogies. In addition, ethnographic data on living or recent groups are frequently lacking in precisely the details the archaeologist needs. It is essential that the archaeologist fully understand the culture of the people with whom he is comparing his prehistoric material, and when he does, he finds the literature of ethnology and social anthropology an indispensable source of ideas enabling him to make fuller use of his data.

Paleolithic Culture

15

The Paleolithic Age, or Old Stone Age, was the first and by far the longest epoch of human history. It began more than 2 million years ago, with the appearance of man's oldest recognizable artifacts, and it ended only with the emergence of certain new kinds of society that accompanied the establishment of modern world climates around 9000 B.C. Throughout this span of time, man was completely dependent on wild sources of food that he could forage by hunting and gathering. His only source of motive power was human muscle, and his technology was restricted largely to raw materials that could be cut, pierced, smashed, and broken.

At first glance all this seems utterly remote from modern life. Why, then, are anthropologists concerned about the Paleolithic? One good reason is the staggering fact that probably more than half the men who ever walked the earth, and surely the majority of human societies that ever existed, departed well before the Old Stone Age had run its course. Another is the complementary fact that modern man is the product of a long evolution, that his present form and actions are the result of a succession of more primitive biologies and behaviors that carry him back through the Paleolithic to ancestors who, were they alive today, would most likely be put in the zoo. Man is as much a product of evolution as is a horse or a dog, and an accurate explanation of why he is what he is today must be founded on knowledge of what he was in the past. To ignore the Paleolithic is to ignore the bulk of man's history and the source of his nature.

Physical anthropologists are a long way from understanding the specific route taken or the forces at work in man's biological history. The cultural side of early man's development, which interlocked with the biological, remains equally obscure. The difficulty is that, like most prehistorians, archaeologists of the Paleolithic must first attend to the enormous task of documenting the stratigraphic and typological composition of their archaeological record, and they have thus far had little time to ponder the cultural significance of the artifact assemblages they dig up.

In attempting to reconstruct and interpret early man's life, they must also contend with two problems that are unique to this era of human history. First, for most of the Paleolithic, men were biologically distinct from men today and presumably had different behavioral capabilities and limitations. The other problem, in part related to the first, is

Cenozoic		
Quaternary	Recent	
	Pleistocene	
Tertiary	Pliocene	
	Miocene	
	Oligocene	
	Paleocene	
	Eocene	

Pleistocene				
Stages	Periods	Climate Cool	Warm	
Upper	Würm Glacial			9,000 B.C.
				75,000
	Third Interglacial			100,000
Middle	Riss Glacial			200,000
	Second Interglacial			300,000
Lower	Mindel Glacial			600,000
	First Interglacial			800,000
Basal	Pre-Mindel Glacial Advances and Retreats			1,000,000
				4,000,000

Figure 2 (left). Correlating Pleistocene environments and the archaeological record in the Old World. Figure 3. Aside from a more-or-less unmodified hammerstone, the most elementary form of core tool is a chopper — simply a nodule from which a few flakes have been detached to form a rough, somewhat straight cutting edge. But core tools may be sophisticated instruments made by extensive shaping retouch. Most important here are hand axes — flat, pointed tools with a continuous cutting edge. Because both upper and lower faces are normally retouched, as shown below, they are often called bifaces.

that the majority of Old Stone Age societies were based on cultural forms not paralleled in the societies that exist today and that can be studied by social and cultural anthropologists. Even the most imaginative archaeologists have therefore hesitated to compose rich narrative accounts of Paleolithic culture history, let alone attempt to explain why things happened in the manner they supposedly did. There are no guidebooks for touring the Old Stone Age, and even road maps like the one that follows must devote as much space to pointing out the questions raised by the data as to tracing the answers they provide.

THE PLEISTOCENE SETTING

A proper introduction to the Paleolithic calls for at least passing acquaintance with the nature of early man's world and of the artifacts he left behind. All Paleolithic sites are found in deposits of what geologists call the Pleistocene Epoch, the second-to-last period of the Cenozoic, or Age of Mammals. This epoch began 4 million years ago and ended simultaneously with the Paleolithic in 9000 B.C. Its deposits are crucial to archaeologists because their stratigraphy provides the framework for dating and correlating sites, as was observed in the chapter "Methods in

Archaeology." Equally important, it is by analyzing Pleistocene soils, animal bones, and plant remains that archaeologists are able to reconstruct the successive environments that provided the raw materials of early man's existence and channeled the development of his cultural evolution.

The Environmental Stage

The coming of the Pleistocene represented the birth of the modern world, for it established the kinds of landscape, animals, and weather that exist today. It began with the appearance of new forms of mammals, easily recognizable as the ancestors of modern types of cattle, horses, elephants, and many others. Their appearance and progressive evolution toward contemporary species was but one aspect of the world-wide environmental changes that were triggered by changes in climate.

In the first half of the Pleistocene, a process of cooling that had begun much earlier in the Cenozoic started to accelerate, and the tropical, temperate, and arctic zones gradually assumed the marked climatic differences known today. World temperatures then began to fluctuate midway through the Pleistocene in concert with changes in precipitation. In semitropical areas such as Africa, these fluctuations resulted in a succession of cooler-wetter (*pluvial*) periods and warmer-drier (*interpluvial*) periods, each of which caused major adjustments in the life forms and geographic boundaries of forest, grassland, and desert. In higher latitudes, such as temperate Europe, the effect was even more marked. There, cool and wet climates resulted in the formation of so-called *glacial* periods, when vast ice fields descended from the north and from mountain chains, such as the Pyrenees and the Alps, to encircle areas in which conditions could be so rigorous that subarctic tundra and steppes often prevailed. But during the *interglacial* periods, much of temperate Europe was covered by heavy forests, and tempera-

tures were often higher than they are today. Europe's climatic alterations became so dramatic in later Pleistocene times that rivers inhabited by hippos during an interglacial period might be occupied by Greenland seals in glacial periods.

The successive Pleistocene environments of the Old World may be grouped into the stages in Figure 2. This approach provides the basic framework for correlating both geologic and archaeological phenomena over time. The ancient deposits are not as well understood as the recent ones, however, and each stage is progressively shorter than the preceding one. In fact, the Basal stage encompasses more than 75 percent of the entire Pleistocene and continues through the era when important glacial and pluvial activity had already begun. But only during the three succeeding stages is climatic history sufficiently clear to provide a basis for subdividing the stages into alternating cool-wet and warm-dry periods that might have some validity for the Old World as a whole.

These periods are usually named after six phases of alternating glacial advance and retreat in the Alps, where the fluctuations of Pleistocene climate were first defined by ge-

ologists, starting with the so-called First Interglacial that opened the Early Pleistocene stage. Thus, anthropologists may speak of "Riss" times in Kenya in referring to that relatively cool and wet period in East Africa that presumably corresponds to the Riss glacial period of Europe. But such correlations should not be taken too seriously, for although various dating techniques have brought considerable precision to chronology in recent years, only the most general relations between geologic deposits in different parts of the Old World may be viewed with any confidence. The scheme in Figure 2 is therefore a convenient framework for discussion rather than an accurate timetable of Pleistocene events.

Artifacts of Paleolithic Man

In turning from the environment to the artifacts of early man, it should be stressed that stone was not the only raw material on which his technology could be based. It is likely that shell, bone, and a variety of highly perishable organic substances such as wood, leaves, sinew, and hides were also used extensively. But stone tools are enduring and are the richest and sometimes the

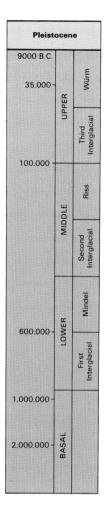 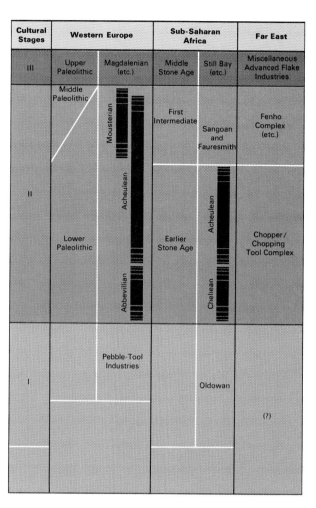

Figure 4. Tool traditions that prevailed during the Paleolithic. All these traditions incorporate unretouched raw flakes that served as cutting, scraping, and piercing tools as well as miscellaneous retouched flakes that cannot easily be assigned to any standardized typological category. But any of the later, mature chipping technologies produced several classes of retouched flakes that fall into clear types. Like the core tools, most of these flake tools bear names that imply specific functions, but we presently can only guess at the real uses to which many of them were put. Some undoubtedly had multiple functions, whereas others may have served different purposes among different groups of men.

sole artifacts found in archaeological sites, and they inevitably provide the starting point from which all classification and interpretation of Paleolithic cultures begin. Indeed, the Paleolithic was traditionally defined as the age of chipped or "knapped" stone implements, in opposition to the Neolithic, in which stone grinding and polishing were common.

Paleolithic man had the ability to knap tools out of the most unpromising raw materials, but he preferred to work fine-grained homogeneous rocks, such as flint, that break in a fairly predictable and controllable manner. The primary technique entailed striking off one or more sizable flakes from a nodule or *core* of rock. If these flakes are removed so that the nodule is shaped into an implement, as was shown in Figure 3, the result is known as a *core tool*. If the removals themselves serve as implements, they are called *flake tools*. Rocks such as flint are easily broken into a variety of shapes with extremely sharp cutting edges, and primary chipping alone yields a broad array of cores and flakes that can serve quite well as tools. To obtain a tool kit of relatively standard-

ized implements, however, it is usually necessary to employ a secondary chipping phase, which involves *retouch*, or the removal of a series of smaller chips or spalls from the raw flakes and cores so that implements take predetermined shapes.

By tracing successive phases in the evolution of stone tool technology and geographic differences, prehistorians are able to identify the major blocks or *traditions* of cultural development that make up the Paleolithic. Exactly how these traditions should be defined, dated, and subdivided into their component tool industries and cultural periods is one of the most complex and controversial topics in archaeology, but an elementary review of Paleolithic culture history requires only the general classification depicted in Figure 4. Here, these major traditions are identified, correlated with the Pleistocene time scale, and grouped into three broad developmental stages of Paleolithic culture.

The first stage, which covers about three-fourths of known culture history, saw the emergence of systematic, albeit extremely crude and generalized, chipped stone technology. This technology matured in the second stage, when man equipped himself with an array of fairly standardized tools, many adapted to specific tasks. In the third and final stage of the Paleolithic, specialization and refinement of chipped stone tools were carried almost to the limits of the art. Although these stages are highly schematic divisions imposed somewhat arbitrarily on the development of stone tool technology, they may well represent fundamental steps in the evolution of human nature and society.

STAGE I: PEBBLE TOOL CULTURES

The oldest chipped stone artifacts now recognized as tools are ancient, even though they date from an era long after the Pleistocene itself had begun. They belong to what archaeologists call the *Oldowan tradition*, named after Olduvai Gorge in northern Tanzania. The extraordinarily rich lower beds of

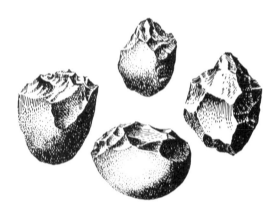

Figure 5 (left). The most common tool in Oldowan assemblages are crude choppers, made by removing flakes along one side of a pebble to form an irregular cutting edge. Figure 6 (below). The living floors at Olduvai Gorge in Tanzania are exceptionally rich in fossil remains. A carefully excavated portion of lower Bed II shows an elephant rib, bones and teeth of various animals, and a typical Oldowan stone tool.

Olduvai have yielded to their excavator, Louis Leakey, the world's finest collection of Basal and Lower Pleistocene hominid fossils. Some fossils appear as isolated finds, but many occur on occupational surfaces or "living floors" of ancient campsites that were rapidly sealed in and protected from erosion as the deposits built up. It is the concentration of stone implements, animal bones, and other debris on these floors that defines the Oldowan tradition, for which some or all of the associated hominids may have been responsible. The range of deposits throughout Bed I and the lower part of Bed II in which these campsites are found can probably be equated with the period from 2 million to 600,000 years ago (assigned to Stage I).

The Oldowan Assemblage

The tools that make up a typical Oldowan assemblage are extremely crude. Many consist of no more than natural chunks of rock whose edges show signs of battering, which suggests that they may have been used for such tasks as crushing bones, fracturing other rocks, and serving as missiles. The most characteristic intentionally chipped tool is a chopper, usually a fist-size nodule on which a single jagged cutting edge has been bashed. Equally crude but more extensively chipped core tools are also present, including picks and more elaborate forms of choppers. Because their core tools were often derived from naturally smooth rocks, the Oldowan and similar Stage I industries are often referred to as *pebble tool* cultures. There are flakes of all shapes and sizes scattered over the surfaces of the campsites at Olduvai, many with nicked and broken edges, indicating that they also served as tools. Although some of their denticulated edges may suggest intentional retouch of a crude sort, it is difficult to see anything like a standardized typology of preconceived tool forms. An occasional fragment of bone found with the stone tools may bear signs of having been used without further modification

as a prying, scraping, or piercing instrument. Because they are extremely crude, it is difficult to distinguish legitimate Oldowan tools from the naturally fractured rocks that can appear in any river or hill slope gravels. Consequently, judgment must be suspended on several sites in Africa and Europe for which pebble cultures have been claimed. Nevertheless, there are several localities besides Olduvai where pebble tools are found together with bones of butchered animals or, in special instances, where natural fracturing agencies can be discounted. These finds indicate that Oldowan tool makers lived throughout much of the grassland area of East and South Africa at about the time they occupied Olduvai Gorge.

About 1 million years ago, when the Early Pleistocene succeeded the Basal Pleistocene, tool industries similar to the Oldowan began to develop around the shores of the Mediterranean in such sites as Ain Hanech in Algeria and the cave of Vallonet in southeastern France. All pebble tool assemblages are so crude and simple as to look much the same, and it is difficult to say whether these sites represent a northern expansion of Oldowan culture or an independent development. It is also debatable just how far pebble tool cultures extended beyond Africa during Stage I. Despite increasingly frequent claims for pebble industries in temperate Europe and the Far East on this time level, there is no firm evidence that these regions were occupied by tool makers earlier than 600,000 years ago.

Clearly, several mysteries surround the origins and spread of tool making in the Lower Paleolithic. For one thing, a period 2 million years ago may not be as remote as it might seem, for paleoanthropologists are becoming increasingly convinced that proto-men first appeared at least 10 million years ago and that tools were an important factor in bringing about their divergence from the apes. But where are these earlier tools? It is difficult to imagine a more primitive industry than the Oldowan, and many archaeologists believe it represents the very beginning of chipped stone technology. Perhaps pebble tool assemblages will never be found in deposits even 1 or 2 million years older than the earliest campsites at Olduvai.

It is possible that our remote ancestors *used* naturally fractured stone tools for an immense span of time before they learned to chip them deliberately. Perhaps other, more perishable raw materials such as wood or bone were used for tools long before stone itself became very important. In attempting to prove the existence of a so-called osteo-dontokeratic (bone-tooth-horn) culture at the South African australopithecine site of Makapansgat, for example, Raymond Dart has convincingly shown that a great variety of "ready-made" tools can be obtained from animal carcasses.

Another series of questions is raised by the distribution in time and space of the Stage I pebble industries. Did tool making, or at least chipped stone technology, really begin in sub-Saharan Africa, or are there

Olduvai Gorges waiting to be discovered in Europe and Asia? Even if it does turn out that pebble tool assemblages developed later in areas beyond the Sahara, it will not necessarily follow that their gradual spread must be equated with the original migration of men themselves from an African cradle. Perhaps it was merely that the idea of stone chipping first caught on in Africa and later diffused to, or perhaps was independently invented in, other regions where hominids themselves had long been established.

Equally tantalizing problems crop up when the archaeologist attempts to assess the meaning of pebble tools for the general pattern of man's cultural evolution. Most present speculation focuses not on interpreting the archaeological assemblages themselves but rather on the more basic issue of who produced them, for during this time period, East and South Africa were inhabited by a bewildering biological array of early hominids. The question of who actually made the tools and who did not is important to the understanding of these early hominids and to the broader problem of how biology and behavior are interrelated in man's evolution. For this discussion, however, perhaps the only crucial biological fact to keep in mind is that, assuming the early tool maker is represented among the presently known fossils, he was a man basically like contemporary men but whose brain need not have been much larger than that of a modern chimpanzee or gorilla.

Hints of Temporary Campsites

The only rich source of information now available about life during Stage I comes from the living floors at Olduvai Gorge, which seem to represent temporary encampments around the margins of lakes or swamps in a grassland area that abounded with animal life, not unlike the savanna of modern East Africa. Although these sites lack all evidence of fire and many other features that appear in later Paleolithic

Figure 7. The appearance of hand axes in the Lower Paleolithic signals a new stage of cultural development. A whole category of tools from the Middle Pleistocene drew its name from St. Acheul in France, where hand axes such as the one depicted below were discovered.

sites, there are many indications of structured activities. Particularly intriguing is the large number of *manuports*, unmodified rocks that were deliberately carried into the sites but whose functions are unknown, although it is possible they served sometimes as foundations for windbreaks.

The scatterings of animal bones and stone tools that appear in all the campsites are considerably more informative. Evidence about food, and the tools used to obtain and process food, is immensely important because it tells the archaeologist about the capabilities of prehistoric man and the economic conditions that shaped his cultures. Although the occupants of Olduvai presumably ate large amounts of bulbs and roots, it is significant that they were sufficiently like modern man to have eaten more meat than any other known primate. But early man was not yet a formidable hunter. Most of the animal remains represent "slow game," such as rodents, reptiles, and birds—the type of quarry that can be caught by hand and dispatched with a rock. There are also young forms and even an occasional mature specimen of one of the herbivores, such as antelopes and horses. The remains of all the large full-grown animals are scarce and sporadic, however, suggesting that they were simply what man had been able to scavenge from carcasses after the carnivores had finished with them. Although he had the tools to butcher these carcasses, perhaps man still lacked the technology, skills, and organization to exploit systematically the abundant supply of big game around him.

The first and tentative returns of archaeology therefore indicate that man at this time had not made much of an impact on the world. It is tempting to view him as a minor part of the landscape, less numerous than any other African higher primate and constantly on the move from one ephemeral campsite to the next in search of food. Yet the evidence at Olduvai suggests the presence there of a most extraordinary animal,

already committed to the potentially explosive course of an omnivore who exploits the world by the intelligent use of technology.

But did the inhabitants of Olduvai possess other behavioral characteristics that might suggest similarity to modern man? Did they talk? Was their group life already organized in a manner that foreshadowed human society? No one really knows, and if answers are to be found they will require much greater knowledge of the nature of Stage I archaeological sites, the behavioral needs and limitations dictated by early man's biology, and the social and economic life of nonhuman primates.

STAGE II: EARLY HUNTERS
Commencing with deposits in the higher portions of Bed II, made approximately 600,000 years ago, stone tool assemblages at Olduvai Gorge begin to take on a new character. The typical pebble tools and utilitarian flakes of the Oldowan still appear as an integral part of almost every archaeological assemblage until the end of the Paleolithic, but they are now accompanied by a new tool form, the *hand ax*. Early hand axes were very crude, and indeed they evolved as more elaborate forms of double-edged choppers. However, their appearance is a convenient

signal to mark the beginning of a new epoch in human history that was to produce a type of man and culture vastly different from anything the world had known before.

Archaeological sites representing the period just after 600,000 years ago became considerably more frequent and more rich, and stone tools first begin to appear over broad areas of Europe and Asia. Simultaneously, stone technology in this period started to undergo a relatively rapid evolution, although the rate of change was infinitely slow by present-day standards. Within 100,000 or 200,000 years, perhaps beginning early in the Middle Pleistocene, men had become highly skilled stone artisans and had invented almost all the basic elements of chipped stone technology that were to be exploited during the remainder of the Paleolithic. These elements include the development of special techniques for detaching flakes of predetermined size and shape from carefully prepared cores, a variety of different kinds of shaping retouch, and the standardized types of tools that are illustrated in Figures 7 and 8. As a result of this evolution, Stage II tool assemblages became sufficiently elaborate and diversified over space and time that it is possible to distinguish several different traditions that presumably reflect distinct lines of cultural, and perhaps biological, development.

Assemblages in Africa and Europe

Throughout most of Stage II, Africa and Europe were dominated by a great tradition in which hand axes were the most characteristic form. Emerging from pebble tool industries through a transitional Lower Pleistocene phase of crude hand axes (known as the Abbevillian in Europe and the Chellean in Africa), this tradition reached maturity in the Middle Pleistocene with often elegant hand axes and a full complement of fairly standardized flake tools in a development known in both continents as the Acheulean. Despite numerous differences in the style

and frequencies of tool forms (bifacial cleavers, for example, were much more common in Africa), the Acheulean traditions of Europe and Africa were sufficiently alike to indicate that they probably had a common origin and continued to share ideas throughout their long periods of florescence.

Historically much more puzzling are a series of European assemblages that lack hand axes and may represent one or more distinct cultural traditions. They begin with a remarkable site in Hungary called Verteszöllös, dating from the Mindel glacial period long after hand axes first appeared elsewhere in Europe. This site yields what must be considered no more than an evolved Oldowan-like pebble tool industry. A few fairly standardized flake tool categories are present, but the core tools consist almost exclusively of various kinds of choppers, albeit considerably more carefully and thoroughly refined "evolved Clactonian" industries continued to appear right to the end of the Acheulean development.

Assemblages in the Far East

The Stage II picture becomes more complicated when attention is shifted toward the Orient. Acheulean industries continue eastward from the Mediterranean all the way to

Figure 8 (left). Tools of the Abbevillian tradition (called Chellean in Africa). These crude bifacially worked implements are the forerunners of the more developed Acheulean hand axes. Figure 9 (right). Overall view of 1963 excavations at Torralba, an Acheulean site in Spain that contains stone hand axes resembling those made by *Homo erectus* in Africa.

peninsular India, but in southwestern Asia and China there is a quite distinctive assemblage referred to as the chopper/chopping tool complex.

Each subregion of this vast and largely unexplored area possesses its own local version of the complex, such as the Anyathian of Burma, the Patjitanian of Java, and the Choukoutienian of China, but all appear to reflect the same overall development. It seems to begin with a Lower Pleistocene industry of crude pebble tools and flakes that are quite similar to the Oldowan. Slowly, standardized tool types begin to appear, fashioned by intentional retouch, but these represent little more than somewhat refined versions of the forms in the original tool kit. This development continues at least through the Middle Pleistocene, with little real evidence of any obvious contact with the more sophisticated traditions of the West. As a result, most archaeologists seem to believe that, regardless of whether the original pebble tool cultures of Asia derived from the West, Asia's technological history throughout most of Stage II may well represent one or more cultural traditions that evolved independently.

Architecture and the Use of Fire
Knowledge of most of the developments outlined above is restricted by the fact that archaeological evidence for these times actually comes primarily from geological deposits such as river gravels, into which artifacts were washed after the original sites had been destroyed by erosion. Fortunately, information is now becoming available from a handful of undisturbed sites, throwing considerable light on the nature of man's culture as it emerged in Stage II. The Late Mindel site of Verteszöllös is of particular interest. Although its occupants possessed no more than an evolved pebble tool industry, they were systematically hunting animals in quantity and cooking the meat with fire. The same is true of a more-or-less con-

current early Acheulean site on the French Riviera, called Terre Amata. It contains temporary encampments of crude huts with fireplaces and the remains of a variety of animals, including boars, oxen, and even elephants. The huts seem to have been rebuilt and occupied every summer over a period of several years.

There is also fairly substantial architecture at the Second Interglacial site of Latamne in Syria, where Acheulean people constructed some kind of foundation of stone rubble. The only occupation site known in the Far East at this time is a cave occupied by chopper/chopping tool people at Choukoutien near Peking. Again there is evidence of fire and a great variety of butchered animals, including such quantities of deer as to suggest that venison made up perhaps two-thirds of Pekin man's diet. However, the most dramatic expression of man's economy during the Second Interglacial comes from the Acheulean site of Torralba in central Spain, where there are butchered carcasses of great numbers of elephants, apparently bogged down and slaughtered as they passed through the region on their seasonal migrations.

These sites indicate that men entered the Middle Pleistocene under conditions greatly different from those in which their Stage I ancestors had lived. For one thing, they were beginning to insulate themselves from some of the more direct pressures of the environment by means of housing and the control of fire. Aside from providing warmth and de-

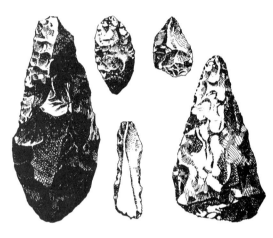

Figure 10 (below). An Acheulean core tool assembly. These tools are far more symmetrical and refined than the robust tools of the Abbevillian tradition. By Acheulean times, flakes were being retouched into standard tool types such as knives and scrapers. Figure 11 (right). The increasing refinements in Acheulean stone tools, proof of the growing knowledge and skill of prehistoric man, reflect as well his growing intelligence and capacity for culture. Here, an artist interprets the social order that may well have been brought into being by the thought, learning, and cooperation entailed in successful hunting.

fense against predatory beasts, fire could have served such technological ends as driving game, cutting timber, and hardening the cutting edges of wooden tools. Moreover, it undoubtedly contributed to the adaptive efficiency of man's omnivorous diet, in that cooking meat not only increased the number of edible plants but also enabled meat to be digested much faster. The meat itself was of paramount importance, for the sites strongly suggest that it was now obtained in substantial amounts. It could have played a primary role in the great dispersal of cultures that took place early in Stage II, for a meat eater can more easily find nourishment in a variety of different environments than can a vegetarian, who is more likely to be adapted to the specific plant life of a given region.

In any case, systematic hunting must have greatly increased the number of men and their chances of survival by making available a food source that was plentiful, concentrated, and portable and could be rapidly converted into energy.

Signs of Increasing Intelligence
Men now hunted several animals as large as or larger than the hunters themselves. Although big game hunting was efficient in terms of the amount of meat it yielded for

the energy expended, it presumably called for something beyond the capabilities of an Oldowan tool maker. No doubt part of the solution came with the development of such hunting weapons as the stabbing spear; and a wooden spear has actually been found preserved in a Second Interglacial deposit. But success in hunting was primarily a matter of knowledge and skill, which raises the question of *intelligence.*

It hardly seems accidental that men's brains had grown considerably by this time, often so much as to overlap the lower range of modern brain size. And certainly the stone tools themselves suggest the operation of a new kind of intellect. Unlike Oldowan tools, which vary little in shape from natural rocks and flakes, stone implements by the Middle Pleistocene were often fashioned in *preconceived* types that bear little relation to natural forms and often exhibit stylistic elaboration. Stamping a mental template on rock is a form of symbolic behavior, and it implies the existence of a type of man whose actions were governed by purposeful thought and a rich memory: a man, in other words, who could conceive of a hunting technique that equated his own capabilities and tools to the behavior of the animal to be hunted, who could learn and practice the skills it required, and who could pursue his quarry with a singlemindedness of purpose over a territory whose details were fixed in his memory.

Beginnings of Social Order?
What might be inferred about the state of man's culture at this time? Most anthropologists would perhaps agree that the thought, learning, and cooperation entailed in successful hunting requires spoken language. They might also be willing to speculate that, even if it provided only a small fraction of man's diet, hunting promoted the development of a recognizably human form of society. A division of labor might have emerged, for example, because only males

would have had the time necessary to learn hunting skills and the freedom to range from home for any length of time. Females are more likely to have specialized in plant gathering nearer the campsite, where they would have been aided by the children they had to tend.

This division of labor, the consequent sharing of food by males and females, and perhaps the requirements of raising children may in combination have encouraged the sexes to form permanent liaisons in domestic units, foreshadowing the human family. The emergence of family life and of the sexual tabus that protected it would in turn have benefited the group economically by reducing sexual competition among men and thus allowing them to cooperate in ventures such as hunting with a minimum of friction. Moreover, if the sexual tabus were sufficiently strong to outlaw all mating except by "married" couples, young people would have been forced to seek mates in neighboring groups. The resulting exchange of young males and females between groups would also have produced great economic benefits by establishing the social relations upon which neighboring bands could cooperate in times of need or, perhaps as indicated at Torralba, when an especially rich food source was available for exploitation.

Even if this argument is reasonably correct, the formation of human society was a gradual process that could have taken hundreds of thousands of years to complete. Archaeology suggests that bands of twenty-five to fifty people may have existed early in Stage II, and indeed the seasonal occupation of the same hut foundations at Terre Amata hints that they might have been fairly permanent. However, the density of human populations was still very low, perhaps averaging only one person to every twenty or even forty or more square miles.

An enormous length of time could have passed before man was successful enough economically to live in groups that were

Figure 12 (below left). One of the ironies of early French antievolutionary thinking: more sites containing the remains of early man and his artifacts are found in this country than anywhere else. Figure 13 (below). Mousterian tools are found from western Europe through the Middle East and beyond the Caucasus, and they reflect the culmination of stone tool technology developed in Acheulean times. Although local variations persisted, all the cultures used scrapers, knives, and points of similar manufacture. Scrapers may have been used to prepare animal hides for clothing, which would provide protection from the subarctic climate in which these people lived.

sufficiently large or stable for a human type of social organization to form. Social evolution simultaneously depended upon and stimulated what must have been very gradual processes in biological evolution. The division of labor, for example, would not have become marked until women were tied down by children who needed the long period of infant dependency required for the growth of a large brain. At the same time, the emergence of permanently mated pairs and some kind of family life would have to be reinforced by the development of year-around sexuality among females, a strictly human phenomenon among the primates. And quite possibly, biological changes in addition to the development of a large brain may have been necessary before men would be capable of letting ideology and social pressure dictate their sex life.

Expansion of Human Settlements

It is likely that such transformations in man and his culture were completed by the beginning of the Late Pleistocene. The archaeological record seems to become markedly richer at this time, particularly in the closing phases of Stage II dating from the first half of the Würm glacial period. The more recent sites undoubtedly have had a better chance to escape destruction by the erosive forces of Pleistocene climates, but the richer

sites reflect as well the progressive economic success that stemmed from the development of man's technology and social organization in the Middle Pleistocene. This success, and perhaps population pressures that resulted from it, are implied by the expansion of human settlement at this time into many previously unoccupied areas, including Central Asia, Siberia, and no doubt expanses of territory in the Far East.

Although they contain all the basic core tools that were established by the beginning of the Middle Pleistocene, the traditions that appear at the end of Stage II are characterized by relatively sophisticated flake implements. In the well-known Mousterian or Middle Paleolithic of Europe and western Asia, for example, François Bordes has demonstrated the existence of four distinct tool industries. Their specific affinities to earlier Stage II industries remain unclear, particularly because an evolved Acheulean tradition continued in the same area and only one of the industries of the Mousterian itself had hand axes. Many archaeologists believe that the variability of Mousterian assemblages expresses no more than different activities of a single advanced Acheulean society. One type of industry, for example, may represent a more-or-less permanent home base, whereas another may reflect the existence of a male hunting camp or perhaps a station where females and children processed plant materials. If this assumption proves to be true, the Mousterian should provide an excellent basis for studying the relationship between social, technological, and economic patterns in the archaeological record.

The Mousterian is also of interest because relatively rich vestiges of it were protected and preserved in rock shelters and cave deposits, in contrast to the scarce remains of the more exposed open-air sites in which Stage II cultures are normally found. Particularly fascinating are burials of Neanderthalers sprinkled with red ochre and placed in stone-lined cists with tools and

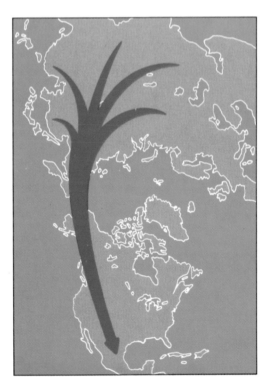

Figure 14 (right). The land bridge between Siberia and Alaska, now submerged, almost certainly was used early in the Würm period by advanced hunters who moved into the New World along the major migration route indicated.

animal bones, a practice implying belief in an afterlife. There are indications also of some kind of religious cult that involved killing bears and carefully arranging their skulls and long bones in unoccupied caves. Such customs seem to foreshadow what was to come in the final stage of Paleolithic life.

STAGE III: ADVANCED HUNTERS

In the last 25,000 years of the Pleistocene, almost all the inhabitable portions of the earth came to be occupied by men, except for certain isolated spots such as Madagascar and the Pacific islands of Oceania. Movements in the western portions of the Old World can be traced in some detail, but too little is known about the Far East to provide a clear picture. Siberia, Japan, and the Philippines could have been occupied late in Stage II, and New Guinea and Australia certainly before the end of the Pleistocene—but exactly when and how is not known. Furthermore, it is not clear to what extent the final Paleolithic cultures of Asia developed in isolation from those of the West, and this ignorance is particularly unfortunate because it obscures the developments that led to the peopling of the New World, a process that may well have been taking place at this time.

The New World Hunters

There is little question that all New World aborigines were of Asian origin and that they entered North America by means of a land bridge between Siberia and Alaska, left exposed by low sea levels during glacial times. It is unlikely that their movements began in the Riss glacial period, because the most ancient New World skeletons are of unquestionably modern types of men and because well-documented artifacts have been dated no earlier in the Americas than the Late Pleistocene.

The first migrants probably crossed the land bridge fairly early in the Würm period when Alaska was no more than the eastern

portion of the great Siberian steppe. Just about the time that Stage III began in the Old World, they were able to pass through a corridor that appeared in the vast Canadian ice sheet and infiltrate the great hunting areas of the New World. Archaeological evidence unfortunately does not become substantial until almost the end of the Würm period, by which time a seemingly original New World "Paleo-Indian" tradition had already evolved. This tradition is characterized by distinctive types of bifacially retouched leaf-shaped points, which are best known from several butchering stations of the mammoth hunters in the American Southwest. Some archaeologists argue that there were much cruder stone industries paralleling the Paleo-Indian tradition that represented more generalized foraging activities in areas where big game hunting could not have been productive. This supposition is quite likely, in view of the great variety of environments to be found in the New World, but it is not until post-Pleistocene times that the evidence becomes sufficiently abundant to define distinct regional traditions.

The Old World Hunters

It is difficult to generalize about the Old World cultures in Stage III times. Men everywhere were now accomplished stone knappers, and each region exhibited its own distinctive blend of traditional themes and new stylistic variations of flake tools. These new traditions pose interesting problems of

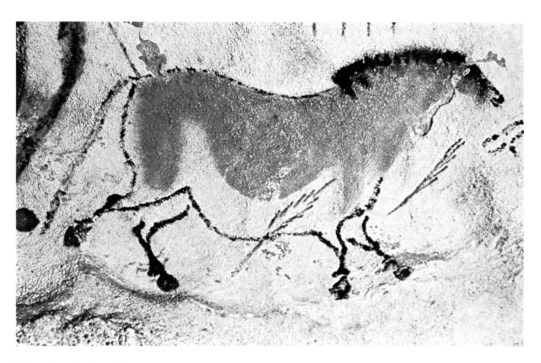

historic relationship and of the nature of man's economic adaptation to varying environmental conditions—problems that archaeologists are only now beginning to understand.

In any case, it appears that there was a series of highly successful cultures that differed in few significant ways from hunting and gathering societies known in historic times. They may have lacked certain technological advantages such as good watercraft, domestic hunting dogs, and the kind of metal tools that contemporary foragers borrow from their more civilized neighbors, but these deficiencies were amply compensated for by the fact that men in Stage III were free to exploit the world's richest environments rather than contenting themselves with the marginal habitats to which their modern counterparts are restricted.

The most striking example of the level a hunting and gathering economy may attain under favorable natural conditions is the Upper Paleolithic complex, which dominated Europe, the Mediterranean basin, and much of western Asia throughout Stage III. Technologically, Upper Paleolithic cultures are identified by extremely refined stone assemblages whose most characteristic tools are made on narrow and elongated flakes called *blades*. Blades and the more diagnostic blade tools such as end scrapers, points, and burins actually appeared in small numbers in the early Acheulean, but they only became dominant in the Upper Paleolithic, where they underwent so much elaboration that almost 100 typological categories are often needed just to describe their basic variability in a single assemblage.

The origin of the Upper Paleolithic is obscure and may well have involved parallel evolutionary developments in several regional Mousterian groups. Equally puzzling are its subsequent regional expressions, whose successive cultural traditions indicate that diffusion and migration must have been frequent and relatively easy in much of the Upper Paleolithic domain. Fortunately, ignorance of the developing network of historic relations that underlies the Upper Paleolithic world does not prevent archaeologists from gaining some knowledge of the way of life it represents.

THE UPPER PALEOLITHIC ACHIEVEMENT

Almost everywhere it is found, the Upper Paleolithic constitutes a quantum jump over Stage II cultures, in terms of the size and

Figure 15 (left). Cave painting of the Magdelanian tradition of the Upper Paleolithic. It has been suggested that this is a form of functional art, related more to survival through hunting and procreation than to aesthetics, even though we may well consider it beautiful by our standards. Figure 16. Tools from the Upper Paleolithic. Above, five of these stone tools are burins, used as chisels for working or engraving wood, bone, and ivory, and the remaining three are scrapers; middle, bone awls, a bone eye needle, and a barbed harpoon head. Below, an incised antler.

number of sites and the elaboration of the artifacts they contain. This achievement is especially marked in the ice-free zone that extended from France to the South Russian Plain during the Würm glacial period. Although this zone was most often a rigorous tundra or steppe, such as is found only in the arctic today, its more southerly and sunnier position allowed it to support a considerably more luxuriant plant life, which in turn sustained vast herds of bison, reindeer, and horses. There were even larger animals, such as woolly elephants and rhinos, a great variety of birds, and abundant river resources that included seasonal runs of salmon.

The success with which Upper Paleolithic men exploited this game is reflected in the enormous garbage deposits they have left, such as the ravine filled with 100 mammoth carcasses alongside the hunting settlement of Dolni Vestonice in Czechoslovakia, or the mound of literally thousands of horses that were stampeded over a cliff at Solutré in central France. It is also attested to by the sheer intensity of their occupation. Along the bases of many cliffs in the famous Périgord region of southwestern France, individual settlements apparently extended over several neighboring rock shelters for distances of hundreds of yards and sometimes involved permanent habitation. Moreover, both in France and throughout central and eastern Europe, where rock shelters are scarce, there were open-air villages that often extended over several acres.

Archaeologists are finding it difficult to account for this apparent florescence in man's economic success, which by the end of the Würm period may have involved a tenfold increase in population over Mousterian times. Environment alone was not the cause, inasmuch as the food resources of mid-latitude Europe were fundamentally no richer than they had been earlier in the Würm period at the end of Stage II. Nor can they find an explanation in the fact that men

identical to modern man appeared more-or-less simultaneously with the beginning of the Upper Paleolithic, for anthropologists are becoming increasingly convinced that the earlier Mousterian Neanderthalers, whose brains were fully as large as that of modern man, represent nothing less than a somewhat extreme racial variant of modern man.

Moreover, a biological argument for the Upper Paleolithic achievement cannot explain why the types of men who presumably occupied other regions of the world in Stage III and who were as physically advanced as the Neanderthalers did not achieve comparable success. The so-called Middle Stone Age cultures at this time in Africa, for example, seem to represent no more than the entrenchment of life ways that had been established during the First Intermediate period and did not entail marked increases in either population size or cultural elaboration.

It is tempting to attribute the economic success of the Upper Paleolithic in mid-latitude Europe to innovations in culture, many of them perhaps relatively minor but whose cumulative effect was to carry man over a new threshold of exploitative efficiency. Certainly the Upper Paleolithic possessed several technological features that have yet to be found in earlier stages. One was a relatively sophisticated missile system that incorporated the throwing board for propelling

spears, and another, at least by the end of the Pleistocene, was the bow and arrow. The range of projectile heads was simultaneously broadened by the introduction of bone points and, ultimately, the barbed harpoon. New bone tools also included a variety of fishing gear such as the gorge, a primitive form of fishhook, and the stabbing leister with flexible prongs. At the same time, life under what must have been severe climatic conditions was made easier by the invention of tailored skin clothing, sewn with bone needles, and improved forms of architecture that included cobblestone pavements for insulating structures from muddy and frozen ground.

The manner in which Upper Paleolithic men employed their technology was probably greatly improved by changes in social organization. Ten or twenty men in an organized work party would have exploited a salmon run or a migrating herd of reindeer much more effectively than the same number acting individually or in small parties. Perhaps Upper Paleolithic society incorporated new rules of behavior and new kinds of groups established along kinship lines, such as lineages or clans, that allowed sizable communities to form and provided a social basis for organizing large, cooperative task forces. These suprafamily kin groups could have provided the structure by which communities broke up and regrouped in response to seasonal variations in the kinds and distributions of natural resources that were available. Although the existence of these more complicated features of social organization cannot yet be demonstrated, they are implied by the great variations in size and distribution of settlements that existed within a single culture period in many regions of Upper Paleolithic Europe.

Archaeologists have also speculated that some sort of tribal structure might in turn have coordinated several local communities into broader economic and social networks. Particularly for the closing and richest phases of the Upper Paleolithic in western Europe, it is tempting to visualize complex tribal systems directed by a centralized authority who coordinated local specialized economic tasks, the redistribution of foodstuffs, and even technological manufactures among several communities. It is certainly premature to claim that Upper Paleolithic men had anywhere attained the level of a chiefdom or a semiformal political state, but there are a number of historically documented societies that had such organization and whose archaeological remains are less impressive than those of the Upper Paleolithic.

Unfortunately, archaeologists have been too easily seduced away from these basic questions of economic and social life by the extraordinary rich evidences of ideology and aesthetics that are to be found in Upper Paleolithic sites. Personal ornaments, elaborate burials, and even what appear to be tally sticks involved in some kind of lunar calendar are common throughout mid-latitude Europe. Equally fascinating is the variety of art, which becomes increasingly abundant and elaborate as the Upper Paleolithic evolves. Much of it comes directly from the occupation levels of settlements, in the form of enigmatic "Venus" figurines of grotesquely endowed females and of plaques and even tools of bone and ivory intricately carved with naturalistic depictions of game, plants, and an occasional human being.

These latter themes also dominate the most extraordinary aspect of Paleolithic art, the engraving and painting of walls in unoccupied caves. This art depicts the major quarry of the hunt, frequently pregnant and often "killed" by spears, accompanied by curious geometric designs and an occasional crude sketch of a man that contrasts strikingly with the realism and grandeur with which the animals themselves are rendered. Aside from the probability that such cave art most likely entails hunting magic, archaeologists disagree over its meaning. But

almost invariably, it makes a deep impression on many modern observers, who often instinctively sense in it the operation of an intellect and psychology much the same as their own.

THE DECLINE OF PALEOLITHIC MAN

The Upper Paleolithic appears to have had an inherent tendency toward continual expansion and evolution. It is interesting to speculate on what levels of population size and cultural complexity it ultimately might have achieved had it been allowed to develop unchecked. But this was not to be. About 9000 B.C. the world entered a new interglacial period known to geologists as the Recent Epoch, whose moderate climate persists to the present day. As the great animal herds of the steppe and tundra were replaced by the inferior bulk of forest game, the economic base of Upper Paleolithic man was destroyed. His Mesolithic descendants continued the hunting and gathering life for a few thousand years, but their cultures were often but a pale reflection of what had gone before. The dislocation was less marked elsewhere in the world, particularly in the more tropical areas where the transition from Paleolithic to Mesolithic times did not entail such dramatic environmental change. But, except for marginal areas of tropical forest, desert, and arctic waste, the foraging life disappeared after a short interval and was replaced by expansion of the farming and herding culture, and the civilizations that so quickly developed from it.

The abrupt and perhaps unlikely cultural changes that have taken place since 9000 B.C. have revolutionized society and technology several times over and have increased the world's population by almost a millionfold. But it remains to be seen whether the quality of human life has really improved and whether the new directions that have been taken during this last fraction of 1 percent of our history will, in the end, prove beneficial to man.

Beginnings of Domestication

16 Shortly after the close of the Pleistocene, around 9000 B.C., human groups in several different parts of the world underwent a cultural revolution whose effects were as great and far reaching as those of any other event in man's history. The archaeological stage representing the emergence of this life way was first called the Neolithic, or New Stone Age. As the name implied, this epoch witnessed many changes in stone tool technology. And the people at this new level of cultural development in fact made great contributions in several areas of technology, ranging from pottery and the use of metals to many of the structural elements that are to be found in architecture today. Nevertheless, these and many other material advances that accompanied them were only secondary expressions of a much more important and fundamental change in human life, for this new level represents not only a period of elaboration but a basic reorientation of the direction of cultural evolution and man's place in nature.

The key was the shift in subsistence economies. Paleolithic man lived by hunting wild animals and gathering wild plants, an economy that could produce remarkable achievements in areas where food resources were especially abundant. Even under the best conditions, however, hunting and gathering imposes severe restrictions upon man's numbers and his opportunities for cultural development. As long as he is dependent upon wild food, man remains merely one of several competing species locked in an elaborate network of ecological checks and balances. Around 9000 B.C., man broke out. He accomplished this by domesticating plants and animals, which meant that he took on the role of determining which varieties should reproduce and flourish at the expense of others. And domestication resulted in farming and herding, which form the basis of what anthropologists call a food-producing economy. In gaining this control over his food supply, man ultimately found that he could produce food with almost the same degree of freedom that he could produce other necessities of life, such as tools.

The effects of food production were far reaching. Tied to their crops and herds, men usually found it necessary to settle down in more-or-less permanent villages and towns.

Figure 2. It was with the rise of village life that such developments as pottery emerged in Southwest Asia, the Far East, and the New World. Figure 3 (right). Some of the distinctive archaeological sites associated with the evolving food producing way of life in Southwest Asia.

Just as the shift in economics required new tools and skills, so group life in permanent settlements required new forms of social and political organization and, no doubt, new ethical and religious principles as well. At the same time, village life fostered the development of many new arts and crafts, which in turn promoted the formation of trading networks for distributing both raw materials and finished products.

The change in man's condition as a level of food production became truly effective was quantitative as well as qualitative. Food production eventually led to an increase in human numbers that was similar to—and indeed the ultimate cause of—the population explosion of modern times. This was in large part due to a relaxation of natural restrictions upon human breeding that came about once man had relatively assured supplies of food during even the leanest months of the year. But it probably reflected as well the loss of such practices as infanticide and the abandonment of the aged, which must have been common in Paleolithic times when food was often scarce and men had to cover great distances to find it. When people settle down in villages and make their living by farming and tending animals, however, old people and children also can make economic contributions.

Food production proved to be so successful that within a few millenniums of its appearance—in all the separate regions of the world where it did independently appear—the new life way had spread to almost every region of the earth where domesticated plants and animals could survive. It is for this reason that hunters and gatherers today are found almost exclusively in marginal areas such as arctic wastes, deserts, and the depths of tropical forests. In addition to providing a means of existence for the overwhelming majority of men born since the close of the Pleistocene, food production was a necessary prerequisite for the still higher forms of culture known as civilization, which ultimately expanded the village-farming level to that of literacy and urbanism in many parts of the world.

No civilization has been or ever could be developed by hunters and gatherers. All the key features of civilization—social classes, specialists, political states, writing systems, and great engineering projects—ultimately must be viewed as cultural responses to the needs created by dense human populations. And, given the limited wild food resources available to men in even the most favorable natural environments, really large groups cannot develop or be maintained without food-producing economies. Thus, although the early village farmer no doubt considered himself merely to be making a living, we view him as the pioneer who built the bridge leading from savagery to life as we know it today. Without the Paleolithic we could not have been men, but without the achievement of food production we could not have been civilized.

EARLY CENTERS OF FOOD PRODUCTION

Most early food-producing societies shared several material traits in common although perhaps not at the very beginning. Pottery, for instance, usually appeared soon after food production was established. Milling equipment for converting plant materials into edible form and tools such as axes, which were made by pecking and grinding stone, were also part of early food-producing inventories although in some cases these items as well as pottery appear before there is evidence for produced food. But their specific form and content varied widely. The differing forms of these traits seem to group into distinct geographic centers, each undoubtedly being responses to the manipulation required by the set of plant and animal domesticates of their particular region. Thus, we see them as distinct forms of technology, craft products, and cultural life. Archaeological knowledge of many of these centers is poor indeed, and their identification is complicated by the fact that the complexes of plant and animal

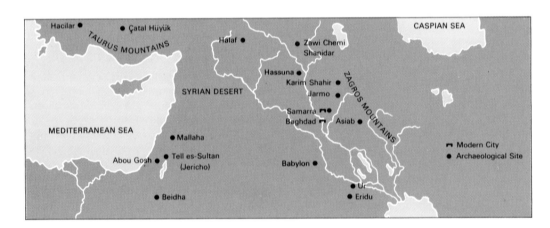

domesticates (or of the plants alone, in one or two cases) that define them often spread far from their original homeland and mixed with one another. The diet of a modern American or European in fact heavily samples all of them. But it would appear that at the very least, three distinct centers of food production were native to the Eastern hemisphere and two to the Western and that many additional secondary centers may also have been involved.

Old World Centers

One of the most important and by far the best-known center in the Old World was that of Southwest Asia, which emerged in the lands surrounding Mesopotamia some time before 7000 B.C. Its primary domesticated plants were the cereal grains wheat and barley, which were supplemented by such legumes as peas and lentils. The domesticated animals were sheep, goat, pig, cattle, and dog. Together these domesticates provided the economic base for the village-farming level that spread throughout the Near East, North Africa, Europe, and in Asia itself as far east as India. And with the later addition of some new domesticates (the horse and the camel, for example), they subsequently nourished man's most ancient civilizations in Mesopotamia and Egypt, as well as all of the societies following that make up

the high tradition of Western civilization. A second center of food production apparently emerged later among cultures in the Yellow River Valley of northern China. Although it presently shares domesticates with the Southwest Asia complex—and there are differing opinions over whether it may even have been generated by influence from the west—its principal food crop was a regional grain known as millet, and it included several additional nonwestern elements such as hemp and silkworms. Somewhere to the south emerged an even more important and totally Asian complex of food production whose origins are obscure to archaeology. This complex had rice as the major plant food and such domesticated animals as the chicken, zebu cattle, and the water buffalo. Rice agriculture continues to support some of the world's densest populations and traditionally has been associated with civilizations across southern Asia from the Pacific Ocean to eastern India. Also lost in obscurity, but perhaps inspired by the preceding center, is a complex made up of such root crops as taro and yams and of such fruits as bananas, breadfruit, and coconuts. Quite recently, reports of new work in Thailand have suggested the appearance of domesticated legumes and root crops, with radiocarbon determinations of 11,700 years ago. Aside from playing a major role

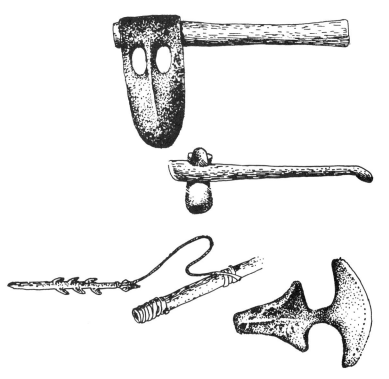

in Southeast Asian diets, this complex formed the basis of food production throughout the Pacific islands. Finally, at least one center must be postulated for Africa south of the Sahara to account for a regional complex of several plants such as sorghum and native forms of millet, rice, and yams. The genesis of their domestication is still unknown. Some experts think it may have been stimulated by the spread of Southwest Asian knowledge of farming and herding up the Nile Valley and across the Sahara, but the matter has not yet been decided.

Centers in the New World
The New World possessed an exceptionally large number of plants capable of cultivation but extremely few domesticable animals. Even as late as the European conquest the Americas as a whole possessed only the dog, the llama, the alpaca, and a few household animals including the guinea pig and turkey. The excellent condition in which organic remains are preserved in dry cave sites in central Mexico has allowed archaeologists to trace the beginnings of a Mesoamerican plant complex seemingly as ancient as that of southwest Asia. Gourds, beans, and squash appeared first, followed by the extremely important plant Americans know as corn (maize). Maize agriculture came to dominate food-producing economies throughout the New World save for those in the deepest tropical forest areas. A second and perhaps independent center of domesti-

cation emerged in the Andean coastal strip of South America some time after 3000 B.C. This complex included gourds, squash, and several variations of beans, strongly supplemented around 1800 B.C. by the introduction of maize and other domesticates from Mesoamerica. Despite the lack of archaeological evidence, it may also be necessary to postulate a separate center to account for the origin of South American jungle root crops, such as manioc.

APPROACHING THE EVIDENCE
Clearly, questions about the origins of food-producing cultures greatly outnumber the available answers. Some scientists even claim that the present evidence is misleading because it implies that grains such as wheat and maize were the earliest cultivated plants. They argue that root crops would have been much easier to domesticate and logically must have come earlier. It is a crucial point, inasmuch as the evidence from Southwest Asia and Mesoamerica would be explained in different terms if these early cultivators were in fact already familiar with the idea of domestication itself.

Another factor affecting interpretation is that the evolution of food production and its associated cultural traits did not conform to a single universal pattern throughout the world. For example, sedentary village communities appear to have accompanied or even preceded domestication in Southwest Asia, but it may have taken at least 5,000 years for communities to have coalesced in Mesoamerica following the cultivation of maize. The lack of a single developmental pattern means that archaeologists must be extremely wary of postulating the presence or absence of food production on the basis of artifacts and settlement types alone, or, conversely, of attempting to reconstruct the nature of a prehistoric culture solely from a knowledge of its subsistence economy.

Moreover, archaeologists still know too little to gauge precisely the extent to which developments in the different centers were

Figure 4 (left). Many of the tools used by the Upper Paleolithic cave dwellers were carried over into the Natufian inventories of Southwest Asia. Evidence of axes (above) and harpoons and celts (below) indicates a continuing reliance on a hunting-fishing way of life, but there is evidence that the early Natufians may have been harvesting wild grains as well. "Sickles" have been found that have a sheen that may have resulted from the cutting of wild grains. Figure 5 (below). This sickle from the later Fayum Merimbde assemblage of Lower Egypt contains an obsidian blade. Obsidian, with its hard, sharp cutting edge, was sought after during the period of incipient domestication and apparently was a key element in a trade network radiating outward from Turkey.

interrelated. Were the varieties of plants and animals that were held in common by Southwest Asia and northern China domesticated independently in the two centers, or were they carried from one to the other? Even where the domesticates involved in a given center appear to have descended from wild plants and animals native to the region, the idea of domesticating them in the first place could have been borrowed from the outside. Similar questions are involved in attempting to explain the many kinds of tools and crafts that recur in all or almost all of the different centers. Were traits such as ground stone axes and pottery invented in only one of them and did they then spread to the rest, or were they independently invented several times as almost inevitable technological responses to new living conditions created by incipient food production?

It is apparent that archaeologists interested in the origins of food production must contend with enormous gaps in the evidence and many basic uncertainties in their interpretations. In fact, it is quite impossible at the present time to write even a general review of the topic that would give a reasonably balanced account of all of the potential centers of domestication. Delving further into the specific questions raised by each of them in turn would be of interest only to archaeologists themselves or to incorrigible trivia experts. For this reason, the remainder of this chapter concentrates on the one center that is best known archaeologically and in which the nature of the problems and evidence entailed in this field of archaeology are consequently most visible. This is Southwest Asia, where excavations during the past twenty-five years have revealed the most comprehensive and perhaps the most fascinating archaeological evidence for the origins of a food-producing way of life.

DOMESTICATION IN SOUTHWEST ASIA

The evolution of domesticated plants and animals cannot be treated separately from the development of the total complex of archaeological traits that together make up the village-farming community way of life. By 7000 B.C., when the Southwest Asian domesticates are clearly present in the archaeological record, they had already been fully integrated within a distinctive regional complex. The particular sites in which they are found consist of villages of fairly substantial houses, among which appear hearths, ovens, and subsurface storage pits or "silos." Many of the stone and bone tools invented in the Paleolithic continued to be manufactured but were now supplemented by a variety of new forms. An interesting addition to the chipped stone tool kit were "sickle blades," rectangular flint flakes whose edges bear a peculiar sheen that seems to have resulted from reaping grasses and grains. The technique of pecking and grinding stone, the traditional hallmark of what has been referred to as "Neolithic" technology of Europe, was used to make several new forms such as *celts*, which were most likely used as axes or hoes, or both. The same techniques were used to make milling equipment—mortars, pestles, and querns. The earliest positive evidence for their use consists of traces of ground pigment, but they were presumably used to crush wild seeds and nuts and later to grind cereal flour from which a variety of foodstuffs, including bread, gruels and porridges, and beer, could be made. Containers for these and other foods are represented by stone bowls and, ultimately, pottery. Finally, a variety of personal ornaments of bone and stone appear along with human and animal figurines that may have had ritual significance.

Focus on the Artifacts

How did this food-producing way of life get started, and what was the nature of its subsequent development and spread? Interestingly enough, this question did not begin to be considered seriously until the late 1940s. Traditional archaeologists working in Southwest Asia were interested primarily

in ancient urban civilizations of the regions and knew of the "Neolithic" only in terms of its later phases. These often appeared in the same sites where the traces of the still later cultural levels they called the "Bronze Age" and "Iron Age" cities could be found. Often even these relatively evolved phases of the early village-farming settlements were seen only in piecemeal fashion at the bottom of deep test trenches that had been excavated through the successive building levels of the great cities themselves. Moreover, archaeologists were strongly inclined toward the humanities and often bothered with the prehistoric levels only out of curiosity. The fully prehistoric levels seldom contained the spectacular beautiful artifacts that these archaeologists had to ship home for display in museums in Europe and America in order to assure continuing financial support. Thus, the early village farming level in Southeast Asia was largely known only in the developed form it had achieved by about 5500 B.C. or just prior to the birth of civilization, which came about 3500 B.C.

To the extent they could speculate at all from the limited kinds of artifacts that had been saved, archaeologists therefore tended to guess that the beginnings of food production were a relatively recent development, evolving suddenly from a regional "Mesolithic" culture of post-Pleistocene hunters and gatherers. Given the abrupt-

ness with which it emerged, the appearance of food production was viewed as an almost inspired cultural reaction to a sudden and drastic shift in Near Eastern climate that threatened the wild food resources that man had depended upon.

This picture has changed dramatically in the last quarter of a century. The appearance of village farming is now viewed not as a sudden event but as an extended process, one whose origins are as far removed in time from the birth of civilization as the latter is distant from ourselves. Moreover, the beginning of food production is now seen not as an abrupt shift in man's economic behavior but rather as a gradual and most likely quite unconscious outgrowth of hunting and gathering practices. This new perspective has come about as a result of digging in different areas and studying kinds of data that differ from those of interest to the traditional archaeologists. It should be no surprise that this development stems from the introduction of an anthropological point of view into Southwest Asian prehistoric research.

Humanistic archaeology became severely restricted in the aftermath of World War II, when the private fortunes upon which it depended began to dry up under taxation and when most Near Eastern governments simultaneously began to limit exportation of antiquities. The anthropologically oriented archaeologist, on the other hand, suddenly found himself in a highly favorable position.

Figure 6 (far left). From Jarmo in Iraqi Kurdistan, a clay figurine of a pig. This artifact is considered to be about 9,000 years old. Figure 7 (left). A high Zagros valley in Iranian Kurdistan, typifying the natural habitat zone of potential domesticates in the Near East. Figure 8. Mills and grinders from Southwest Asia.

He was welcomed by the regional governments because his interest in artifacts was not one of shipping them home but rather of studying them for clues about the prehistoric cultures. At the same time, the new breed of archaeologist he represented was more likely to obtain support from the many research foundations that emerged after the war, particularly because he was delighted to conduct his research jointly with natural scientists.

Focus on the Cultural Whole

The interest in natural science reflects a shift in emphasis to a new kind of data. The humanist might tend to value pottery, architecture, or ground stone tools for their own sake, but the anthropologist views them as material expressions of a greater cultural whole. And in this perspective, it becomes clear that, especially as regards the beginnings of food production, we must first concentrate on reclaiming understanding of the domesticated plants and animals and the environments that nourished them, both before and after their domestication. Certainly neither farming villages nor their inventory of artifacts would have developed at all without food production.

It seemed logical to this new breed of archaeologists and to their colleagues in paleontology and paleobotany that the animals and plants upon which cultivation and husbandry evolved could only have been domesticated in areas where their wild prototypes were available. Preliminary investigations suggested that, contrary to what had traditionally been assumed, Southwest Asia had not undergone a very profound climatic or environmental change since before the Pleistocene came to an end, about 9000 B.C. If such was actually the case, it would follow that the present natural distribution of the remaining wild relatives of the domesticates should be the same now as it was when domestication took place. The remaining potential domesticates (wild cattle, for example, are now extinct) are still to be found in the higher foothills and the mountain valleys that border the Tigris-Euphrates basin. Mesopotamian civilization proper subsequently appeared in the lower alluvial plain of these rivers, but domestication took place along its hill flanks. Although very recent evidence suggests that this natural habitat zone for the potential domesticates was in fact somewhat broader than was first conceived, the general notion still appears valid.

Archaeologists have thus turned their attention to three principal regions of the hilly flanks, within which it was believed the nuclear area of plant and animal domestication in Southwest Asia was most likely to be found. These regions are the uplands on either side of the Zagros range on the Iraq-Iran border, the southern slopes of the Taurus Mountains extending from northern Iraq along the southern coast of Turkey, and the western slopes of the Lebanon-Amanus chain, which stretches southward behind the Levant coast of Syria, Lebanon, and Palestine.

This research has been rewarded in the past two decades by the discovery of an almost unbroken succession of prehistoric settlements that allows archaeologists to trace the culture history of Southwest Asia from late Paleolithic times right down to the birth of civilization. Although the evidence is still sparse and ambiguous for the earlier phases of this development and is not yet available from every conceivably pertinent subregion, it does seem to provide at least a skeletal view of the evolution of the village-farming community type of culture. It is tempting to see the

Table 1. Southwest Asian Levels of Domestication From 11,000 B.C. to 4750 B.C.

Level	Timespan*	Representative Sites	Potential Domesticates and Domesticates
Developed village farming	6000–4750 B.C.	Çatal Hüyük Halaf Samarra Amouq A-B Hassuna	Wheat, barley, peas, lentils, vetches; sheep, goat, pig, dog, cattle
Primary village farming	7250–6000 B.C.	Suberde (Hunting) Basal Hacilar Ramad Palestinian "PPNB" Jarmo Cayönü Ali Kosh	Wheat, barley, lentils; sheep, goat, pig, dog; still much collected food, nuts, snails, clams; some hunting still
Incipient domestication	9000–7250 B.C.	Mureybit Ganj Dareh Developed Natufian Tell es-Sultan "PPNA" Karim Shahir Zawi Chemi Shanidar Mallaha Cave Natufian	Prototypes of the domestic grains; incipient herding? *cf.* wild food sources as below; mollusks in some cases
Final Paleolithic	11,000–9000 B.C.	Known only from caves so far Kebaran Zarzian	Wild sheep, goat, ox, pig, onager, gazelle, deer, etc.; nuts, seeds; evidence for softer vegetable foods not yet recovered

* Approximate dates (±250 years) based on carbon 14 dating.
Source: After Robert Braidwood, *Prehistoric Men* (Glenview, Ill.: Scott, Foresman), 1967.

evidence falling into a series of major eras or levels, which suggests a logical succession of stages in this evolution and which even hints about the causes that produced it.

The remainder of the chapter summarizes these levels, to each of which is tentatively assigned a name suggesting its role in the evolution of food production (see Table 1). The dates for these levels are based on the radioactive carbon dating technique, but they must be considered only approximations made to the nearest quarter of a millennium (250 years). Even though the levels represent what seems to be a reasonable view at this moment, the reader should be warned that few fields of science change with such swiftness as does this aspect of archaeology. It may well be that by the time he reads these words, their author will himself be holding somewhat different opinions.

FINAL PALEOLITHIC LEVEL

The Paleolithic of the Near East proceeded through the same general succession of cultural stages that is found in Europe. Late in the Pleistocene, however, the stone tool in-

Figure 9. Aerial view of Çayönü, an open-air settlement on the flanks of the Taurus Mountains in southern Turkey. This site is representative of the primary village farming level of cultural development.

dustries found here began to take on an increasingly distinctive regional appearance. Much of this distinctiveness may have been stylistic, but economic factors as well were involved. Before the end of the Pleistocene, climates in the Near East seem to have assumed much the same character they have today, which means that local hunters and gatherers did not enjoy the tremendous resources of big game that allowed their European counterparts to develop the rich and complex Paleolithic culture described in the preceding chapter. At the same time, however, it meant that the Near Easterners in at least certain areas must have been exploiting a range of plants and animals that included the wild prototypes of these domesticates.

Of interest here are the traces of two contemporary and similar cultures occupying areas that definitely seem to have been part of the natural habitat zone of the potential domesticates. These are the Kebaran of Palestine and the Zarzian of the Zagros flanks, which may have begun around 13,000 B.C. and continued to the end of the Pleistocene at 9000 B.C. In addition to all the basic Upper Paleolithic stone implements, the Kebaran and Zarzian inventories included large numbers of *microliths*, small geometrically shaped segments of blades that probably served as points or barbs for projectile weapons. Hunting no doubt played an important role in the economy of these cultures, and it has been suggested that 90 percent of their meat diet consisted of wild sheep, goat, ox, pig, onager, gazelle, and deer. Of singular interest, however, are several examples of grinding stones or mortars, which could have served to make edible such hard-surfaced foods as nuts and seeds. These are the earliest known prototypes of later milling equipment, and they represent a technological adaptation toward plant foods that is almost totally absent in Europe at this time.

There is nothing to indicate that Zarzian and Kebaran people were in the process of domesticating plants and animals, and there is no reason to believe that they were even consciously focusing upon those species that could be domesticated. The use of microlith-tipped hunting weapons and grinding equipment was indeed well suited for exploiting them. Yet these same tools appeared simultaneously at many points around the eastern Mediterranean from Greece to Egypt, much of which certainly was outside the natural habitat zone of the potential domesticates. Nevertheless, it is still tempting to see a form of hunting and gathering at this time that would have involved day-to-day contact with the prototypes of the domesticates in areas where they were available, such as Palestine and the Zagros flanks. Even some amount of experimentation and manipulation could have been involved. It seems logical that, given the limited natural wealth of the environment, men might have been assured of more to eat by attempts to exploit all the possible food sources in a fairly restricted territory than by ranging over broad areas in search of just a few. It is unfortunate that almost all of the data for the Zarzian and Kebaran comes from cave sites rather than open-air settlements, which would tell much about the extent to which human occupations were localized at this time.

INCIPIENT DOMESTICATION LEVEL

Above final Paleolithic deposits along the eastern shores of the Mediterranean, from southwestern Turkey to Cairo, are found the scattered remains of a post-Pleistocene culture that is marked by considerable advancement over what went before. It appears in its most distinctive form as the *Natufian* inventory of Palestine. Although long known from several caves, the Natufian

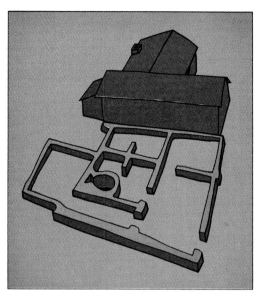

Figure 10 (left). Architectural configuration of the stone-walled dwellings that were built during the Developed Natufian cultural level. These dwellings contained bell-shaped storage pits, suggesting these foraging people may have been storing surplus harvests of wild grains.

is now beginning to appear in open-air sites exhibiting many features that foreshadow classic inventories of early Near Eastern farmers. The most interesting open site is Mallaha, adjacent to Lake Huleh in north Israel. In part of a site covering at least half an acre are the remains of circular houses with stone foundations, often paved with flagstones and having built hearths and boulder mortars, or milling stones. To the microliths of the previous (Kebaran) phase were now added blades with the characteristic sheen of sickle flints. Bone artifacts such as fishhooks and harpoons continued in the older forms, but they now included handles for flint blades that bear sculptured decoration. Stone bowls and some of the mortars also carry geometric designs in relief, and there are even some simple attempts at sculpture in the round. In the living areas at Mallaha are found both single and multiple burials of Natufians, who—like all occupants of the Near East ever since—look essentially like modern Mediterraneans.

Some time around 8000 B.C. the type of culture represented at Mallaha evolved into what is known as the *Developed Natufian*. The most publicized remains of this later phase are represented by the "Proto-Neolithic" and "Pre-Pottery Neolithic A" (PPNA) levels at Tell es-Sultan, or Jericho, in the valley of the Dead Sea. The site is a multilayered mound of some seven and a half acres in area adjacent to a magnificent spring. In the earliest (or Proto-Neolithic) level at Tell es-Sultan, houses seem to have been simple huts. But these were replaced in the next level by more substantial circular structures of hand-made, sun-dried bricks. Much more remarkable on this level are traces of what

appear to have been a large circular stone tower and walls. Aside from its size, architecture, and seeming permanency, the site also presents the interesting feature of chipped stone tools of obsidian, or volcanic glass. The nearest source of obsidian was in Turkey, and the inhabitants of Tell es-Sultan could only have obtained it by trade.

A similar if less spectacular form of the same general level is found east of the Euphrates on the flanks of the Zagros mountains, which in the final Paleolithic was occupied by the Zarzian people. Remains of this culture in 9000 B.C., roughly contemporary with Mallaha, have been found at the sites of Karim Shahir, Zawi Chemi Shanidar, and Asiab. Here, simple, round, and probably semisubterranean houses are characteristic, and the chipped flint industries contain little if any obsidian, and sickle sheen is rare. However, the ground stone tools include milling stones, mortars, celts, and personal ornaments such as beads, bracelets, and pendants. Zawi Chemi has yielded some well-made bone tools, including flint blade handles whereas simple clay figurines appear both at Karim Shahir and Asiab.

Two newly excavated sites in the general area exhibit greater complexity and more likely fall on the same time level as the Developed Natufian. One is Ganj Dareh, a small conical mound in the Persian flank of the Zagros near Kermanshah. Excavations here reveal a basal meter of deposit without structure, followed by a succession of levels with multiroomed houses made of *touf* (loaded sun-dried mud) and unfired handmade bricks. Although milling stones and mortars are common, the finer items in ground stone are rare, and there are no celts present. Obsidian tools are also absent, and even sickle blades are rare. Nevertheless, a more progressive note is apparent from the recovery of animal and human figurines, including at least one fine impressionistic sculpture of a female. The second of these more recent sites is Mureybit, a mound stretching out over seven and one-half acres

Figure 11 (left). The "Venus" of Munhata. Figure 12 (below right). Plastered and painted skulls from the "Pre-Pottery Neolithic B" level of cultural development. These skulls reflect an obvious concern with the dead, but the ritualistic significance of this practice is as yet unknown.

on the east bank of the middle Euphrates in semiarid Syria. The lower levels of Mureybit contain the remains of rough stone and clay circular walls and pavements that often have fragments of milling stones or mortars incorporated into them. Circular subfloor pits and, finally, multiroomed rectilinear houses appear at the higher levels. The inventory includes flint tools generally in the tradition of the Developed Natufian industry. Obsidian occurs but is rare, and there is a variety of heavier ground stone bowls, mortars, and querns.

During this era, then, nearly the entire complex of material traits that archaeologists have thought to be typical of the earliest farming villages of Southwest Asia emerged. Many traits remained in an unrefined state and all do not appear at any single site, yet the complex was already established with its fairly large and seemingly permanent villages of substantial architecture, reaping tools in the form of sickle flints and milling equipment for making flour, and ground stone tools such as bowls and celts. Even less-utilitarian elements such as personal ornaments, and figurines had made their appearance. Obsidian, which provides a sharper cutting edge than does flint, was beginning to be imported for cutting tools.

In light of these traits, many archaeologists have concluded that food production as well must have been present. But the primary evidence of the plant and animal remains themselves does not support this conclusion. Although the natural scientists are not in complete agreement, their general opinion is that neither the bones nor the seeds found at any of these sites definitely exhibit any of the physical signs of domestication. Even at Mureybit, which presumably

falls rather late in the era, the seeds represent wild forms of wheat and barley and wild legumes such as lentils and vetches. The animal record tells the same story. Although there are major gaps in the record, when their remains *are* found the goats, sheep, pigs, and cattle seem to be as undomesticated as the deer and gazelles that accompany them. The large numbers of sickle blades and milling implements do suggest that men were devoting special attention to reaping the wild grains that were present, and the plant remains from Mureybit indicate they included the prototypes of some domesticate grains. It is also known that lush stands of wild wheat were also to be found in the areas of Palestine occupied by the Natufians. Moreover, there is some interesting evidence from Zawi Chemi that men were already exercising some control over animals: although the sheep bones do not yet show the morphological traits of domestication, a statistical analysis of the age at which the animals were killed at this site strongly suggests that they were being herded. It is for such reasons that this group of sites is considered to represent the incipient level of domestication.

PRIMARY VILLAGE-FARMING LEVEL

By at least the beginning of 7000 B.C., the evidence for food production becomes firm. Some sites at this time still seem to have been occupied by hunters and gatherers, and wild food resources continued to play an important role in the more numerous sites where farming and herding were practiced. In many cases, the plant and animal remains indicate that the transition from wild forms to domesticated forms had by no means been completed. Yet change, to the prehistorian's relative way of thinking, seems to have been rapid, and by the end of the millennium or even around 6250 B.C. a fairly intense food-producing economy had become established over broad areas of Southwest Asia. It was accompanied by a trading network for distributing obsidian,

Figure 13. Below right, a horn core of a goat from Jarmo, about 8,700 years old, showing the slight twist in one typical of early domestic goats in this area. Wild goats then and now have the horn core curved plane only, much like the blade of a scimitar; in most modern domestic goats, the horn and enclosed horn core are twisted much more. To the left (above), the jaw of the modern wild pig from Iraq and, below it, a partial jaw of an early domestic pig from Jarmo showing the difference between their three lower molars. Below left, four upper molars of prehistoric pigs offer a comparison between the wild state and the prehistoric domestic state. The largest is of a wild pig from the earlier levels at Jarmo; the one next to it is from a higher level. The next is the same tooth from a later period at Amuq A, a prehistoric site and level in the Hatay of south central Turkey. The last is the third upper molar of a domestic pig from Banahilk in northern Iraq, about 7,000 years old. Figure 14 (right). Charles Reed at Sarab, in the low-lying hills of the Zagros range. The animal bone fragments he has recovered are being sorted for identification.

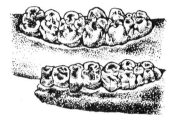

the earliest experiments with copper, and, at the end, the appearance of pottery.

At least ten sites in this time range cluster along the Syro-Palestinian coastline and its hinterland. The so-called "Pre-Pottery Neolithic B" (PPNB) at Tell es-Sultan is a good illustration of the local cultural elaboration that accompanied the beginnings of food production. The houses are, as a rule, multiroomed rectilinear structures with plastered walls and floors, in which are found numerous hearths, ovens, and subsurface storage pits. A stone wall seems to have surrounded at least part of the settlement at this time. Aside from a considerable elaboration in technology and crafts, the "PPNB" phase is said to have indications of cult activity. Special buildings appeared that have been interpreted to be sanctuaries, along with the striking practice of plastering over and painting human skulls that had been removed, minus their lower jaws, from normal burials. This latter aspect of ritual was elaborated upon near the end of the millennium at the site of Ramad, near Damascus. Here, headless human torsos were modeled in clay, apparently to serve as a base for the plastered skulls. What seems to be the evidence of the earliest pottery in the Levant coast also appears at this site.

Ramad also furnishes important evidence for domesticated plants—including barley, three varieties of wheat, and lentils. Probably earlier, as at Beidha in Jordan, domesticated wheat and the goat appeared, but the barley was still wild at the time of the "PPNB" phase at Tell es-Sultan. But for Tell es-Sultan itself, the evidence is scanty, and the important new site of Munhata in its "PPNB" levels has no primary trace of food production. The sites of Bouqras and Kowm in middle Syria indicate food production had extended to the Levant hinterland by the end of the era. Both present a somewhat rustic aspect, and their inhabitants may have continued to subsist largely upon wild foodstuffs. But even they were sufficiently in touch with general developments to have been included in the obsidian trade from Turkey.

Again, about ten sites may be assigned to this era in the hilly flanks of the Zagros range. Jarmo, lying east of Kirkuk in Iraqi Kurdistan, has been the most publicized of these because its excavation was the pioneer exposure for this time range in the entire Near East. Nevertheless, subsequent work at other sites, including Ali Kosh, Guran, and Sarab, has greatly broadened the knowledge of this period in the Zagros. As in Palestine, there is now a general shift to rectilinear multiroomed houses, the appearance of significant amounts of obsidian, and considerable elaboration in such areas as ground stone, bone, and modeled clay figurines. Fortunately, plant and animal remains are well preserved in this region and furnish considerable evidence for food production. One variety of both wheat and barley appeared early in a domesticated condition, and there is evidence for first the herding of sheep and goat and then their full domestication. By the end of the era the range of crops had broadened considerably, and sheep, goat, pig, and possibly the dog have all been identified in domesticated forms. In the last quarter of the seventh millennium, even pottery made its appearance.

It is around 7250 B.C. that relevant archaeological materials occur in any abundance outside the Levant and Zagros area of Southwest Asia. In the Taurus flanks on the headwaters of the Tigris, far to the north of classic southern Mesopotamia, these first appear at the site of Cayönü in what is now southern Turkey. Cayönü was a food-producing village roughly contemporary with Jarmo and the "PPNB" of Palestine, and its

artifacts show some similarities to those of both the Levant and the Zagros region. Obsidian was plentiful, and native copper was already being hammered into simple pin and reamerlike forms.

It is not yet clear how far northward the primary village-farming way of life extended at this time. There is certainly no good evidence for its existence in the Caucasus. However, what seems to have been an advanced Jarmo-like culture with pottery appeared near the end of this era or shortly thereafter as far to the northeast as Turkmanistan.

Toward the west, evidence for food production also begins to emerge for the 7000 B.C. level in the Anatolian peninsula, although the picture is by no means clear. For example, the "hunters" village of Suberde in the Taurus slopes near Konya exhibits nearly the full range of Neolithic material equipment, but the only food remains consist of great quantities of wild animal bones. Nevertheless, a generally similar artifact inventory found somewhat farther to the west in the lower, or *aceramic*, deposits at the mound of Hacilar is apparently accompanied by seeds of domesticated wheat and barley. In any case, it seems likely that further excavation will bring evidence of widespread early food production in Anatolia, inasmuch as the Southwest Asian complex of domesticates was soon to become established in the site of Argissa in the plain of Thessaly in Greece. Artifacts similar to those from Argissa also appear at the Franchithi cave in eastern Peloponnese and in a deep test pit at Knossos in Crete. By 6000 B.C., an even more developed inventory with pottery existed at the village site of Nea Nicomedia in Macedonia.

Thus, by the end of the seventh millennium, food production had become established in Southwest Asia and was already spreading out toward Europe and Soviet Central Asia. But what of Egypt and southern Mesopotamia, the two areas in which the earliest civilizations were to arise? There is no evidence of a food-producing economy in southern Mesopotamia until after 6000 B.C. and in Egypt until perhaps even a millennium later. It would appear that both of these areas then as now were outside the natural habitat zone of the potential domesticates and had to await the development of strains of domesticated plants and animals that could tolerate the relatively hot and rainless environment characteristic of both locations.

DEVELOPED VILLAGE-FARMING LEVEL

By the beginning of 6000 B.C., food production was established upon a broad spectrum of fully domesticated plants and animals. The size and density of sites suggest that foodstuffs were sufficiently abundant on a year-around basis to be effecting the marked increase in human numbers. Population pressure and the resulting need to find ever more farmland and grazing lands were probably factors in the rapid geographic expansion of the new way of life that characterizes this time period. Many farming villages began to appear in the Caucasus, Turkmanistan, and far east on the Iranian plateau, where they may already have been leap-frog-

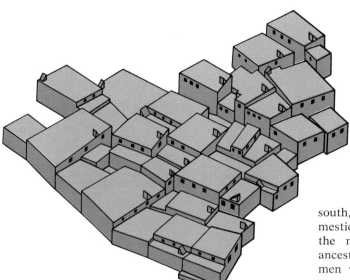

ging one another in the direction of northwest India. To the west, food producers were expanding simultaneously through the Balkans into temperate Europe and westward across the Mediterranean—two streams in the diffusion of food production that well before 4000 B.C. met in England—more than 1,500 miles away from Southwest Asia.

In the heartland of Southwest Asia itself, there is now the relatively well-developed inventory of the village and town sites that, until twenty-five years ago, in effect constituted nearly all that was known about early food-producing culture in the Near East. The region was divided into several different provinces, each of which possessed its own distinctive types of pottery, architecture, and craft products. Most had domesticated cattle, and copper working became somewhat more common; some archaeologists have thus referred to this period as the "Calcolithic," or "Copper Age."

The degree of cultural elaboration could sometimes reach impressive levels. Perhaps the most spectacular site is Çatal Hüyük, a large mound in south central Anatolia, where materials are exceptionally well-preserved. A number of multiroomed houses have been exposed, some of which include rooms with wall paintings and mud-plaster sculpture, which the excavator interprets as shrines. More even assessment of the pace of cultural development and change can be observed in the evidence from other areas—as in northern Iraq and northeastern Syria, where there was a succession of inventories known as the Hassunan, Samarran, and Halafian. Each of these appears to be more substantial than its predecessors in this subregion, and the Samarran inventory penetrates well to the

south, near Baghdad. But perhaps the domesticates already had been moved beyond the natural habitat zone of their wild ancestors. Certainly by Samarran times, men were approaching the margin of the enormously fertile lands of southern Mesopotamia itself.

THE QUESTIONS REMAINING

The sequence of eras revealed by archaeology in the last twenty-five years suggests a gradual and cumulative process of evolution that seems reasonable in terms of current anthropological thinking about culture dynamics. But there are many question marks in the evidence. The natural scientists are not in complete agreement either about how to specify the nature of Southwest Asian environments at certain key places and time periods or about how to identify the earliest signs of domestication in plant and animal remains. Even more important, there are enormous gaps in the archaeological record for many areas, which may be obscuring important aspects of the picture.

Although there is so far only the tentative new evidence from Thailand to suggest that Southwest Asia did not have the first food-producing economy in the Old World, it is very possible that other evidence may also be found. As for Southwest Asia itself, further excavation may demonstrate, for example, that farming and herding were under way earlier in Anatolia than in the Zagros and Syro-Palestinian areas or in the more semiarid steppes, as Mureybit and Kowm hint. Good archaeological coverage of the entire region is necessary in any case, because there is no reason why all the important innovations would have had to take place in the same spot. As the trade in Turkish obsidian indicates, prehistoric men in Southwest Asia shared a common sphere of diffusion in which ideas originating in one locality might easily and quickly spread to others.

But while the outlines of what happened are beginning to emerge, the "how" and

Figure 15 (left). Architectural style of the developed village farming level, as exemplified by Çatal Hüyük. Shown is Level VIB. The rooms designated with *s* are considered shrines and contained cult statues. (After Jas. Mellaart, *Earliest Civilizations of the Near East*. New York: McGraw-Hill, 1965.) Figure 16. Why did man become more experimental during this period of human history? The change in behavior that led him toward manipulation of his environment is a puzzle whose solution is still being sought in archaeology.

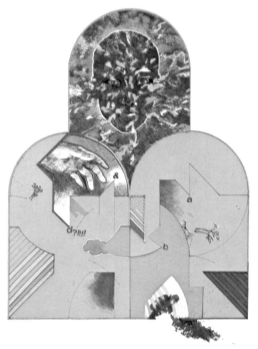

"why" are still elusive. Perhaps the most important clue provided by the evidence is that the complex of material traits that has traditionally defined a village-farming level bears a different historic connection to domestication than might be supposed. Archaeologists have often assumed that at least most of these traits could only have developed following the advent of food production. Now, quite the opposite seems to have been the case.

The basic tools and equipment that are associated with effective agriculture in typical village sites in Southwest Asia were actually first developed by hunters and gatherers. Perhaps some may have been developed during the "incipient" level, but much of the human manipulation of plants and animals during this level still cannot be specified. As we have seen, food collecting in the late Pleistocene apparently involved a trend toward exploiting the broadest possible range of food resources in increasingly localized situations. In any case, intensified by the beginning of the incipient domestication level, food collecting seems to have been successful enough to assure fairly permanent settlement and to promote the development of new material items especially adapted to regional foodstuffs, such as the prototypes of the cultivated grains.

But what in turn led men of this era to begin domesticating plants and animals? One factor involved was certainly the nature of the proto-domesticates themselves and the manner in which they reacted to human manipulation. It is no doubt significant, for example, that all of the earliest animals that were herded are capable of being tamed in the wild state and capable of reproducing freely in captivity. Ecology undoubtedly was another important factor. Many theories of domestication suggest that there must have been subtle shifts in man-land relations during the incipient domestication era that were brought about by environmental change. This shifting is entirely feasible, for

it is known that minor changes certainly did occur in Near Eastern climates and environments, even though claims for really dramatic change since well before the end of the Pleistocene are few and, at best, relative. However, there must have been an additional factor in the equation. Man has lived among potentially domesticable plants and animals from the very beginning and has exploited them through a vast range of environmental changes. Yet domestication itself appeared only within the last percent of human history. Perhaps an additional element was involved that somehow concerned a change in man's behavior.

Men are inherently experimental and manipulative, and experimenting with the raw materials of nature has no doubt been the source of the change that underlies cultural evolution. But it would seem that experiments must have taken on a somewhat new character in this era to have entailed such procedures as storing seedcorn—often through periods of want—and later sowing it at the appropriate time. Even if this were the case, one can only guess as to why men became more experimental or what made their cultures particularly receptive to it. It will undoubtedly require the efforts of archaeologists working in other food-production centers of the world and much help from anthropologists and the natural sciences before even the problem itself is fully defined.

The Rise of Civilization

17

There is an educational children's game called *Get Civilized*, played on a board with spaces running along the edge. The first space is marked "Uncivilized" and the last space "Civilization." There is a deck from which each player draws one card per turn. Every card has a value, measured in the number of moves it allows him to make. The winner is the first player to reach civilization with enough of the requisite cards. A typical game may proceed in the following manner:

The first player draws a card that says, "Settle fertile valley (two spaces)." The next player gets a card saying, "Intensive cultivation and animal domestication supports increasing population (three spaces)." A player gets a card marked "Religious and political hierarchies established (four spaces)." Another picks "Adopt economic specialization and diversification (three spaces)." The next card says "Population becomes stratified (two spaces)." One player gets the coveted "Develop metallurgy (five spaces)." One draws the prized "Experience urban growth (five spaces)." Another is lucky and picks "Writing developed (five spaces)."

The game is really going now. Markers are moving toward the goal, hands are becoming filled with valuable cards, and it seems certain that someone is going to be the first to get civilized. But on the board itself certain spaces give instructions. A player can land on one marked "Famine and disease decimate population (back four spaces)." The message on another is "Barbarian invasion (back two spaces)."

The game is won by the player who reaches civilization and whose hand contains enough of the high-value cards listed in the winning space, and in no two games does the winning hand have to be the same. The components of civilization vary from game to game, in a sense reflecting the variation that characterizes the rise of civilizations in the past. And in analyzing the remains of the earliest civilizations, scholars have learned to appreciate how difficult and complex are the ways that getting there have been.

CHARACTERISTICS OF CIVILIZATION

Before anthropology had emerged as a separate discipline, Assyriologists, Egyptologists, and Sinologists were investigating the art, literature, and history of the earliest civilizations of the Old World, but most of the material these scholars had to work with was recovered by field workers trained in the techniques of classical archaeology. As a consequence, they were concerned primarily

Figure 2. Features of Sumerian civilization as it may have looked in 3000 B.C. Although such early centers of civilization were small by modern standards — they seldom had populations over 50,000 — they represent a quantum jump over the village organization of the early agriculturalists. Figure 3 (right). Iranian bronze stags. By 3000 B.C. copper and tin were being alloyed into this harder material, a technological development that contributed to dependence on foreign trade for the two metals.

with the artifacts themselves, rather than with what such artifacts told them about the origins of these civilizations. It has been maintained that an anthropologically oriented archaeology, devoted mainly to prehistory, might help to shed light on these early societies. With the revival of interest in evolutionary theory and more attention being paid by social anthropologists to the structure of complex, nonindustrial societies, many anthropologists are becoming convinced that they can contribute to an understanding of the social and political organization of ancient civilizations. Recent studies have led to a growing appreciation of the diversity of these ancient societies and of the complexities involved in any attempt to explain their development.

The impact of these ideas is reflected in recent theories about the origin of civilizations. In the past, the advent of civilization was often attributed to a single primary cause—such as the richness of midlatitude river environments; postglacial desiccation that forced the people of these regions to make more efficient use of the remaining fertile areas; or the development of irrigation, which Karl Wittfogel has argued gave rise to "oriental despotism." Another argument has been that once civilizations had begun, all those located in river valleys tended to develop in a parallel fashion. Today explanations along these lines are generally viewed as oversimplifications. Anthropologists now recognize that many factors are involved and that the relative importance of any single factor may vary from one cultural situation to another. There is a growing awareness of the variation among civilizations—not only in detail but in their fundamental structure—especially in the early stages of development.

Few anthropologists now try to define civilization in terms of the presence of one or more specific features, such as writing or urbanism. Important as many specific factors may have been in the development of

particular civilizations, the basic distinction between so-called civilized and primitive societies lies in *social organization.* According to Robert Adams, the principal characteristics of civilized societies are social stratification, the development of political and religious hierarchies administering territorially organized states, and a complex division of labor with full-time craftsmen, servants, soldiers, and officials. A principal feature of early civilizations and of many later ones was a large peasantry whose agricultural surplus supported a relatively small elite and their retainers. As Marshall Sahlins points out, what differentiates civilization from the tribal organization is a sovereign government, separated structurally from the underlying population and set above them. The state is thus an extension from kin-based to territorially based power. The trouble is that this critical transition is remarkably difficult to extract from archaeological evidence alone, in the absence of records.

CIVILIZATIONS OF THE OLD WORLD

The development of civilization in the Near East must be approached in terms of the broader spectrum of cultural adjustments that apparently were initiated around 10,000 B.C., at the end of the last glacial period. The large migratory game that had inhabited this area declined rapidly, and many groups of people who had formerly hunted these animals began to settle down and exploit the permanent food resources that were available locally. There was a considerable increase in population in rich environments such as those where fish, small game, or wild grains were abundant. This adaptive process apparently encouraged experimentation with the natural environment, and food gathering in some areas became transformed into food production.

As was discussed in the preceding chapter, villages began to appear throughout the well-watered upland regions from the Balkans eastward to the Iranian plateau and in the hill country along the eastern Mediterranean littoral. The economy of these villages was based on domestication of sheep, goats, pigs, and cattle and on cultivation of wheat, barley, and less important crops. As they became increasingly sedentary, these people acquired possessions on a scale that had not been possible before, and a newly created demand for goods stimulated craft specialization. After 6000 B.C., pottery making and metallurgy developed and spread throughout this region. A growing demand for scarce and exotic materials led to the expansion of trade, which also helped to spread new ideas. Increasing wealth brought with it growing inequalities in the distribution of goods and power.

Although the hill regions of the Near East were dotted with small farming villages, by 7000 B.C. more spectacular developments were occurring in a few places, as evidenced earlier in the discussion of Tell es-Sultan and Çatal Hüyük. Yet both of these settlements eventually ceased to exist, and very little similar development is noted in the same regions for more than another millennium. Spectacular as these societies may have been, they apparently were too isolated and too few in number either to resist the challenges of their more barbarous neighbors or to move toward more advanced stages of civilization. By building on the experience of all the upland societies, however, other groups were to achieve a new level of cultural development elsewhere.

THE MESOPOTAMIAN ACHIEVEMENT

The area that was to become the heartland of the world's first civilization apparently did not figure in these earlier developments. The swampy, lower valley of the Tigris and Euphrates rivers was rich in fish, game, and date palms but lacked the wild plants and animals that formed the core of the farming economy in the Near East. It also lacked stone and metal, which in later times had to be obtained in trade or as tribute from the

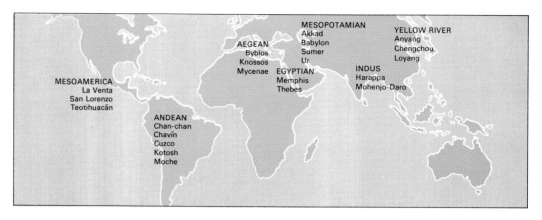

adjacent highlands. But the valley did provide ideal conditions in which farming could develop and flourish, once domesticated plants and animals had been introduced from the highlands. The flood plains were richer and more extensive than any agricultural land in the hill regions and could support a far larger and more densely settled population. The indigenous plants and animals diversified the economy, and adjoining the fertile plains were grazing lands where herdsmen could pasture their flocks. The whole region was tied together by a river system that facilitated the movement of produce from one area to another. These conditions encouraged the development of a complex and highly diversified subsistence pattern, a pattern fundamentally different from that which prevailed in the highlands.

The earliest agricultural settlements in the Tigris-Euphrates Valley date before 5000 B.C.; excavations at Eridu have revealed small rectangular houses and shrines from this period. It has been suggested that at least some elementary form of irrigation was already being practiced, which indicates the adaptation of techniques of highland domestication to a radically different environment.

In the period between these earliest agricultural settlements and the dawn of recorded history, life in the Tigris-Euphrates Valley changed greatly. There is a strong continuity in these changes, however, which suggests that whatever new people may have entered the region, they adapted to the general pattern of life that was evolving there.

One of the most important changes was a dramatic increase in population, resulting from and helping to encourage the development of more intensive patterns of land use. One facet of this development was a growing reliance on irrigation. As arable land became increasingly scarce it became more valuable, and as wealth increased there was probably growing concern about land owner-

ship and property rights in general. At least there is some evidence of this from the archaeological discovery of stamps and cylinder seals that were used as a means of marking private property and indicating ownership. The growing complexity of society led to a further deterioration of the egalitarian relationships of the earlier settlements.

Concurrently, there was a spectacular development in craft specialization. Some new inventions, such as the *potter's wheel*, may have been a response to an increasing population that represented a ready market for inexpensive, mass-produced goods. Many tools were made of copper, which was handier to import than stone, and by 3000 B.C. copper and tin were being alloyed into bronze, which was considerably harder. A consequence of this development was a growing dependence on foreign trade, not only for luxuries but also for necessities. Increasing specialization and economic interdependence appear to have been major factors in encouraging adjacent towns and villages to unite to form larger integrated economic and political units, a process called *synoecism*. These economic factors, together with a growing rivalry over access to limited resources, may have led to the development of walled cities. Much of the population of these cities was not divorced from agriculture but instead engaged in full-time or part-time labor on fields within or adjacent to the city.

In early dynastic times (3000–2400 B.C.), southern Mesopotamia was divided into fifteen to twenty city-states, each with a walled city as its capital. These cities were located along what were then the courses of the Tigris and Euphrates rivers, occasionally within sight of one another and without natural boundaries between them. Although these ancient cities were small by modern standards—few if any had a population over 50,000—they required patterns of behavior that were far removed from those of the early agricultural villages. The economy was now far too complex to be managed solely on the basis of individual exchange and barter, and the invention of coinage to facilitate retail transactions was still more than 2,000 years into the future. The complexities were simplified somewhat by the various temple communities that had grown up in each city. Each temple owned farm land and also employed craft specialists, thus serving as the center of a redistributive network embracing numerous dependents. Although the farmers who worked the temple lands received only a fraction of the crops they produced, the temple storehouses supplied them with tools, clothing, and other necessities. The temple functioned in many respects as an expanded and more complex version of the self-sufficient household of earlier times.

Each temple was staffed by professional priests who also administered temple business. The earliest known tablets inscribed with writing—dating to around 3200 B.C.— are accounts that appear to be associated with the management of such large corporations. The pictographs on these tablets form the basis of the Sumerian *cuneiform* script, and it seems clear that the speakers of this language (which has not yet been proved to be related to any other known language) were now quite influential in the development of Mesopotamian civilization. Semitic-speaking people were also present, however, especially in the north, and in later times it was their language (Akkadian and later Old Babylonian) that was predominant in written texts. Administrative concern also may have stimulated the Mesopotamian interest in mathematics and in astronomy for calendrical purposes. We still use their sexagesimal system for clocks and for dividing a circle.

Each city had a patron god or goddess, whose temple was built atop a high brick *ziggurat*, or temple platform. This ziggurat and its associated temples, granaries, maga-

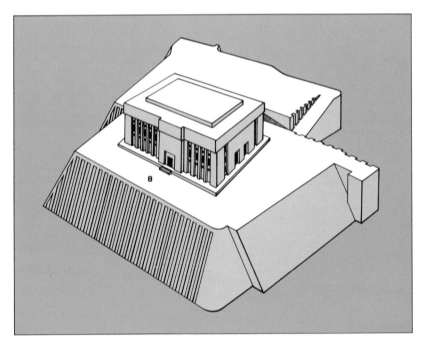

zines, and workshops dominated the center of the city. The temples were monumental brick structures ornamented with elaborate projections and recesses, and the production of stone and metal objects used by the temple dwellers required many highly skilled specialists.

As evidenced by the imposing walls of their cities, defense was a major concern of these tiny states, and by early dynastic times, war leaders had become kings whose palaces rivaled the temples in size and architectural splendor. The primary function of these kings apparently was to maintain the cities' defenses and to raise and equip armies. As competition between cities became more intensive in the early dynastic period, the power of these kings tended to increase. The graves of the rulers of Ur about this time have yielded not only the remains of carts, chariots, and a rich array of utensils but also the bodies of many sacrificed retainers—including numerous ladies of the

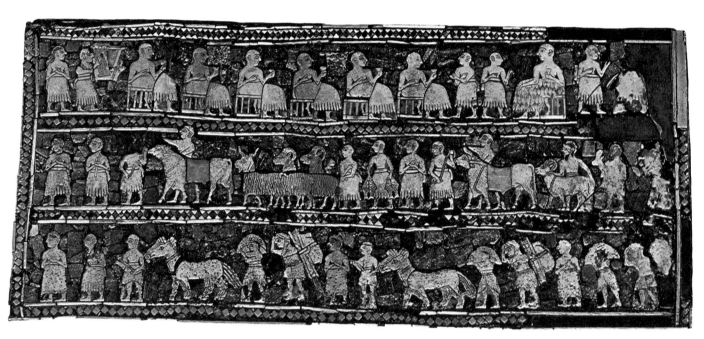

court whose heads and necks were adorned with jewelry made from gold, silver, and semiprecious stones. As in other Old World civilizations, however, human sacrifice was practiced for only a brief period in Mesopotamia before it died out or was suppressed. In any event, the needs of the army and the court further stimulated occupational specialization in the supplying of both luxury goods and armaments. As a result class structure became increasingly hierarchized.

Although wars were frequently fought over irrigation rights or the ownership of fields, these factors were not the only pressures for waging war, or even its most important cause. To the victorious ruler, war was a source of wealth in the form of booty and tribute, and by controlling the distribution of this wealth, rulers could enhance their power and prestige among their own people. Whereas an ordinary city was often poor and susceptible to invading armies, a victorious one was inevitably prosperous. Leo Oppenheim stated that real prosperity characterized a Mesopotamian city only

when it had in its midst the palace of a victorious king. The sanctuaries and palaces of such cities were adorned lavishly, and the population grew as traders, craftsmen, and retainers flocked to the city to serve its ruler.

Despite the warfare, the Mesopotamians no more questioned the principle of the city-state than did the classical Greeks. Tribute was imposed on defeated cities, but no attempt was made to interfere with their local forms of government. This pattern was broken, however, with the rise of the state of Akkad near present-day Baghdad, around 2300 B.C. When the Akkadians conquered the rest of Mesopotamia, they replaced the local rulers with their own governors, thus welding the conquered territories into a short-lived but prototypic *territorial state*. This pattern provided the basis for the later Babylonian, Assyrian, and Persian empires, whose monarchs successively conquered larger areas of the Near East and ruled an ever greater diversity of people. In each case the underlying motives were the same: these

Figure 7 (left). The Royal Standard of Ur. Figure 8 (right). Funerary papyrus of Princess Entiu-ny from the tomb of Queen Meryet-Amun at Deir el Bahri, Thebes. Entiu-ny is plowing and reaping stands of wheat, activities the early Egyptians associated with the afterlife.

empires desired to control as many people and as much wealth as possible and to include within their frontiers all the raw materials needed for their survival. Rivalries within the ruling royal families played no small part in undermining the stability and power of successive dynasties.

THE NILE VALLEY OF EGYPT

It is not surprising that the second great civilization in the Near East developed in the Nile Valley of Egypt. Here was another vast flood plain capable of supporting a dense agricultural population. Moreover, in Egypt the annual flood waters drained back into the river instead of lying on the fields and thus carried off the salt that posed such serious problems for Mesopotamian soil. According to Herodotus, the soil of Egypt was the richest and easiest to work in the world, and Egypt remained a reliable breadbasket for its neighbors.

Egypt's disadvantage in early times was that it lay farther from the major centers of plant and animal domestication in the Near East than did Mesopotamia, which may have held back its development of a food-producing economy in comparison with southwestern Asia. Unfortunately, the evidence for the beginnings of such an economy seems to be buried under layers of silt that have been deposited since that time in the Nile Valley. The presence of domestic goats in Cyrenaica by 6000 B.C. and possible hints of an incipient stage of plant domestication in Nubia even earlier suggest that much remains to be learned about the beginning of food production in this region.

Beginning around 4000 B.C., there is evidence of pastoral and village life throughout Egypt. During the predynastic period, which lasted until about 3000 B.C., there were considerable cultural differences between northern and southern Egypt, although in late predynastic times these differences lessened as increasing numbers of traits from the south diffused to the north. As in Mesopota-

mia, there is evidence of a growing population and increasing occupational specialization. The latter is manifested by improving skills in metallurgy and, in particular, in working hard stone to make vases, mace heads, and a variety of ornamental objects. The greater attention to luxury as manifest in some graves provides evidence of increasing social differentiation.

Despite these general similarities to events in Mesopotamia, the manner in which civilization developed in Egypt differed radically from its eastern neighbor. By 3000 B.C., rulers from southern Egypt had conquered the entire region and united it under a single government. In later times this event was conceived of as the unification of two kingdoms that had already developed in northern and southern Egypt. Throughout Egyptian history, kingship was in fact viewed as a dual monarchy over these two regions. Nevertheless, most scholars now doubt the existence of these two predynastic kingdoms and regard the unification as a piecemeal conquest of a series of embryonic states and regions. At the time of unification there were large villages in all parts of Egypt, but there is no evidence of walled cities or ceremonial centers with monumental architecture, such as had already existed in Mesopotamia for several centuries. The king of Egypt, however, controlled the real and potential resources of a large number of peasant villages.

The question remains: how and why did the political unification of Egypt take place when it did? There is evidence of cultural contact between Egypt and Mesopotamia both before and at the time the country was unified. Mesopotamian art motifs and cylinder seals were introduced into Egypt, and it is possible that paneled brick architecture and the basic ideas behind Egyptian hieroglyphic writing are of Mesopotamian origin as well. But there is no evidence to support the theory that Egypt was united by foreign invaders, as many early scholars imagined.

It is far more probable that some of the proficiency of Mesopotamian civilization was seized upon and adapted to Egyptian needs by an indigenous population ripe for change. Whatever effect foreign influences may have had at this time, Egypt did not become a copy of Mesopotamian civilization. In both art styles and political structure Egypt was to prove radically different.

Throughout the Egyptian early dynastic period (3000–2700 B.C.) that followed unification, the art and architecture of Egypt developed rapidly, and basic styles were evolved that were to endure for over three millenniums. At first the kings and important members of the nobility were buried in large mud-brick tombs, and in at least some instances their artisans and retainers were slain and buried with them. Around 2700 B.C., King Zoser had built for himself a huge mortuary complex surrounded by a high stone wall over a mile in length, with a six-tiered stone pyramid over 200 feet high at its center. This building marks the first attempt by an Egyptian ruler to erect a large stone structure, a monumental architectural endeavor that had no contemporary counterpart anywhere in the world.

Later kings began to construct true pyramids, the largest of which was that of King Khufu, built only about a century later. This pyramid is over 480 feet high and contains more than 2 million blocks of limestone, some weighing as much as fifteen tons. Various interior chambers were lined with blocks of granite brought down the Nile River from the southern borders of the kingdom. These pyramids and their attendant temples, erected during one reign after another, were a formidable achievement for a civilization that as yet had no wheeled vehicles and had copper tools but no bronze ones. Building on a similar scale would have been unthinkable in Mesopotamia, for no ruler commanded sufficient wealth or manpower to undertake such tasks.

The same period that saw the development of Egyptian architecture also witnessed the florescence of monumental sculpture and bas-relief decoration, developments foreshadowed on the ceremonial palettes and mace heads that were being carved by royal artisans prior to and at the time of unification. In the reign of Zoser, life-size statues were carved out of limestone and later out of harder rock, such as diorite, which had to be obtained from the western desert. The sculptured reliefs in the tombs of officials of the Old Kingdom (2700–2180 B.C.) mark a high point in Egypt's artistic creativity.

A significant feature of this art is that it developed under the aegis of a royal court that controlled the entire economy and labor force of Egypt. All foreign trade was carried out by royal officials, and all the most skillful artisans and craftsmen were attached to royal workshops. Elaborate furniture, jewelry, and tombs were constructed at state expense and bestowed by the king as rewards upon relatives and officials who had served him well. This centralized control of the economy did not favor the growth of cities similar to those in Mesopotamia. Agglomerations of craftsmen and specialists came together only under the direction of the government to work on royal projects or

Figure 9 (left). Reconstruction of Saqqara, tomb of Zoser. Figure 10 (below). The courtyard at Luxor. To the Egyptians the focus of interest was the dead, and their reality was not the life that follows birth but that which follows death. Yet beneath the facade of the awesome monuments that they erected in celebration of the afterlife, we may catch glimpses of a lighter side of their nature — a finely wrought senet gameboard and game pieces from the XVIII Dynasty.

in centers where the royal court stayed part of the year. This centralization is reflected in the artistic poverty of provincial centers in Egypt at this time, and in the slowness with which metal tools replaced stone ones at the village level.

At the pinnacle of Egyptian government was a king, who was not merely the "tenant" or high priest of the gods, as the Mesopotamian kings were, but who was himself regarded as a god incarnate. The king ruled Egypt by means of a skilled bureaucracy, and officials were frequently moved from one part of the country to another to prevent them from developing strong regional ties. Records were kept on papyrus scrolls rather than on clay tablets as in Mesopotamia. The Egyptians used a solar calendar, which is the basis of our own, and a decimal system of counting, as we do today. Like other officials, the priests were royal appointees and the temples in which they served were royal gifts to the gods. In the Old Kingdom, these temples tended to be small, especially in comparison with the royal tomb complexes.

With the decline of the Old Kingdom around 2200 B.C., Egypt witnessed a weakening of royal power and the slow growth of a regionally based "feudal" aristocracy. Much of the later history of ancient Egypt is a struggle between centralizing and regionalizing tendencies. With growing contact between Egypt and the Near East and the eventual annexation of Egypt by the Assyrian and Persian empires, the structure of Egyptian society began to approximate more closely that of its neighbors.

THE EASTERN MEDITERRANEAN

In both Mesopotamia and Egypt, the traditions of civilized life took firm root. In spite of periodic dynastic instability and occasional invasions by less civilized people, the patterns of literacy, religion, and government that had evolved in these regions did not perish. Instead, the newcomers adopted

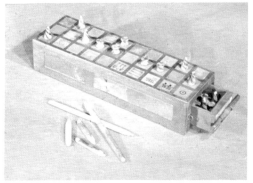

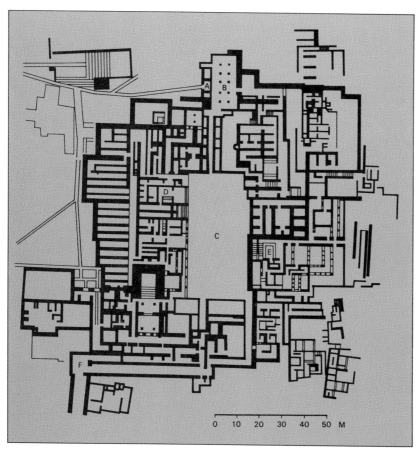

Figure 11. Architectural plan of the palace of Knossos, Crete. Points of reference are (A) the north entrance, (B) hall of pillars, (C) central court, (D) throne room, (E) grand staircase, and (F) the southwest entrance. Figure 12 (right). The evolution of the alphabet from northern Semitic to modern capitals. (After *The Alphabet: A Key to the History of Mankind.* Copyright © 1968 by David Diringer. By permission of the publishers, Funk & Wagnalls, New York.) Figure 13 (far right). A stater of Aegina, earliest silver coin from 700 B.C., and a stater of Mesopotamia, dated at 550-470 B.C.

noan palaces were being built in Crete; later the closely related Mycenaean culture began to develop on the Greek mainland. In both areas palaces appear to have played a crucial role in the conduct of foreign trade and there was little tendency toward the development of cities. Like the Levant or Greece in historic times, Mycenaean Greece was divided into many small states that often were isolated from one another by mountainous terrain.

Significantly, the eastern Mediterranean areas that lay outside the heartland of the earliest civilizations gave birth to three inventions that were essential to the later development of Western civilization. The first was an efficient technique for forging iron, which apparently was invented in Asia Minor and first became common in the eastern Mediterranean around 1200 B.C. Copper, hitherto the most common metal, was manufactured from ores that were found in only a few places, and trade in this relatively rare metal as well as in tin had long been a state monopoly. Iron ore, on the other hand, could be secured locally in many places, and for the first time it was possible to manufacture metal tools at the village level. The impact of this discovery on agriculture and industry both within and beyond the borders of the civilized world was tremendous.

The second invention was the alphabet. The alphabet was first widely used in the Levant about 1100 B.C. and was adopted in Greece about 300 years later. With the diffusion of this simplified script, writing was no longer the prerogative of specially trained scribes but became potentially available to all classes. It revolutionized small business and affected the whole sphere of communications. The third invention, that of coinage, was made in the Kingdom of Lydia in Asia Minor about 700 B.C. The eventual production of small change made for a far more flexible economy and diminished drastically the economic importance of institutions such as temples and palaces. These three

them. This pattern contrasts rather sharply with the later beginning and less continuous development of civilization in some adjacent regions.

In the Levant, urban life began to develop by 3000 B.C. Although the cities of this region superficially resembled those of Mesopotamia, the major factor promoting their growth appears to have been trade, which was usually under the control of a local king. These cities profited from their location by becoming major centers of the caravan trade and for the manufacture of goods for export to surrounding regions. High standards were achieved in metallurgy, and the textiles that were produced came to surpass in quality those of Egypt and Mesopotamia. Perhaps because of the nature of its economy, the Levant remained a region of small competing states whose material culture was eclectically influenced by those of their powerful neighbors and rarely assumed a consistent character of its own.

Trade, both internal and with the Near East, also appears to have been an important factor in the development of civilization in the Aegean area. The agricultural societies there became more complex after 2500 B.C., perhaps as a result of the development of metallurgy. By 2000 B.C., the first Mi-

North-Semitic	Early Phoenician	K 9 1 △ ⅃ Y	⊢ ᒿ	↓ ∤ ⟨ ⅄ ⊃ ⊃	⊅ W +
	Early Hebrew (cursive)	K 9 7 9 ⅃ ⅄	⊟ ᒣ	⅄ ⅃ ⅄ ⅄ ⊘ ⊃ Y ⅃ W X
	Moabite	K 9 7 △ ⅄ Y	⊢ ⅃	Y ⟨ ⅄ ⅃ ⊘ 1 ⅁ ⅃ W X
	Phoenician	X 9 7 ⅄ ⅃ ⅄	H Z	Y ⅃ ⅄ ⅃ ⊘ ⅃ ⅁ ⅃ W ✝
Greek	Early	A ⅄ 1 △ ⅂ ⅃	B ⟨	∤ ⅃ ⅄ ⅄ ⊘ ⅃ ⅄ ⅃ ⟨ ⟨ X
	Eastern	A B ⟨ △ ⅀	B I	K ⅃ ∧ N O ⅁ Г ⅁ P ⟨ T Y	X
	Western	△ ℭ ⅃ △ ⅀	I	K ⟨ M ∧ O ⅁ Г ⅁ R ⟨ T Y	X +
	Classical	A B Γ Δ E	H I	K ∧ M N Ø Π P Σ T Y	X
Etruscan	Early	A B 7 ⅃ ⅃ ⅃	⊟ I	X ✓ ⅄ ⅃ O ⅃ P ⟨ ⅃ ⅃ Y
	Classical	A ⟩ ⅃ ⅃	B I	X ✓ ⅄ ⅄ ⅃ Q ⅄ ⅃ ✝ V
Latin	Early	A ⅃ ⅃ ⅃	B I	⅃ ⅄ ∧ O Г ⅄ V
	Early Monumental	∧ B ⟨ D ⟨ ⅀	H I	K V M ∧ O Г Q R ⅄ T V	X
	Classical	A B C D E F G H I J K L M N O P Q R S T U V W X Y Z
Modern Caps	Gothic	𝔄 𝔅 ℭ 𝔇 𝔈 𝔉 𝔊 𝔥 𝔍 𝔍 𝔎 𝔏 𝔐 𝔑 𝔒 𝔓 𝔔 𝔕 𝔖 𝔗 𝔘 𝔙 𝔚 𝔛 𝔜 𝔷
	Italic	A B C D E F G H I J K L M N O P Q R S T U V W X Y Z
	Roman	A B C D E F G H I J K L M N O P Q R S T U V W X Y Z

inventions combined to transform Greek society and ultimately those of the Mediterranean and the entire Near East.

THE INDUS VALLEY

Although village agriculture had been established in the Turkish and Iranian highlands from early times, the population of this area was more sparse and mobile than that of Mesopotamia, and civilization there developed more slowly and exhibited greater regional variation than it did in the great river valleys.

Farther east in the Indus Valley, however, farming villages had begun to evolve a civilization by 2500 B.C. Unfortunately, all too little is yet known about this development. It appears to have been encouraged by the diffusion of ideas from Mesopotamia, yet the basic differences between the Mesopotamian and Indus civilizations demonstrate that the latter, like Egypt, was essentially the product of an indigenous pattern of growth and development.

The Indus civilization is best known from its two largest cities, Harappa and Mohenjo-daro. These cities consisted of baked-brick dwellings, laid out in a distinctive and orderly grid pattern more than three miles in circuit. Broad streets separated large, oblong blocks of houses. Each city was dominated by a fortified citadel containing granaries, ritual tanks, and various public

buildings, and the city drainage system was the most elaborate in the ancient Orient. At its peak, the Indus civilization reached as far south as Gujarat, thus covering a greater area than either the Mesopotamian or the Egyptian civilizations.

Despite its size, the Indus civilization died out before 2000 B.C. Its decline has tentatively been attributed to tectonic changes in the Indus Valley, which destroyed the economy of the region, as well as to the invasion of Indo-European (Sanskrit-speaking) people from the northwest. The very size of the Indus civilization suggests that no single cause is likely to account for its decline. Classical Indian civilization was not born in the Ganges and Jumna valleys until after 1000 B.C. Soon afterward, however, city life began to flourish there. Rice was one of the crops grown in this area. The three inventions of iron, coinage, and the alphabet gradually penetrated this civilization from the west in Persian and Hellenistic times.

YELLOW RIVER VALLEY OF CHINA

The origins of Chinese civilization have been traced to the middle portion of the Yellow River Valley. Although it developed later than did the first civilizations in the West, Chinese civilization has enjoyed a unique cultural continuity. Some of the traits that went into building Chinese civilization no doubt diffused there from the west, but the

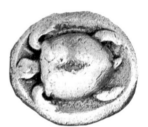

Figure 14 (left). An unglazed pottery bowl and a pottery jar from the Yangshao culture, dated about 2000 B.C. Figure 15 (below). A ceremonial bronze vessel of the *Kuang* type from the Shang Dynasty, dated at 1200-1100 B.C. The outside is evenly patinated in shades of gray-green with flecks of cuprite; inside, some azurite is still found with areas of the original metal. Figure 16 (right). Outline of dynastic rule and political division in China from legendary times to the present.

general configuration of Chinese culture is clearly the result of developments that took place within China.

It now seems possible that the first steps in the development of a food producing economy in East Asia may have been taken in southern China and Southeast Asia, beginning as early as 9000 B.C. The earliest known agricultural settlements in the Yellow River Valley belong to the Yang-shao, or Painted Pottery, culture that seems to have flourished prior to 2000 B.C. The Yang-shao people lived in small, unfortified villages. Their chief crop was millet, but wheat and perhaps rice were also grown. They had domesticated pigs, cattle, sheep, dogs, and chickens. Clothing was made from hemp and silk. The Yang-shao culture evolved into the more widely distributed Lungshan, or Black Pottery, culture. By this time large settlements were defended from behind earth walls. The Lungshan culture developed into the earliest Chinese civilization, the Shang, which flourished in northern China between about 1500 and 1027 B.C.

By this time, Chinese craftsmen were producing many highly sophisticated products.

Jade carving was well developed, but the real glory of Shang was its bronze ceremonial vessels decorated with stylized animal patterns. Large numbers of animal bones that were used for divination have been found decorated with the earliest known form of the Chinese ideographic script.

Shang society, as in the other civilizations, was divided into classes. At the late Shang capital near Anyang, traces of large wooden palaces built on low earth mounds have been discovered. Human beings appear to have been killed and buried in rites associated with the erection or functioning of these buildings. Likewise, humans as well as animals were sacrificed and buried in great, cruciform royal pit tombs outside the city. There is literary evidence of a complex royal ancestor cult by this time.

It is not clear as yet whether the Shang kings ruled over a united country, as did the Pharaohs of Egypt, or whether Shang culture, like that of Mesopotamia, consisted of a number of city-states or small territorial states. According to traditional Chinese history, the Shang dynasty was overthrown in 1027 B.C. by the Chou, a more primitive people to the west; the Chou kings may have been the rulers of just another city-state. For a time they seem to have compelled a large number of political units to acknowledge their sovereignty, but eventually, as Chinese civilization expanded to the south, the power of the Chou rulers dwindled and a number of newly important states began to compete for power. Their rivalry encouraged increasing technical and military efficiency, and it does not seem to be an accident that China's principal philosophers, including Confucius and Lao-tzu, appeared during this time of social crisis. Among the Chinese inventions of the Chou period was the discovery of a method for casting iron, knowledge of which did not reach the West until almost 2,000 years later.

In 221 B.C., the ruler of the state of Chin in western China conquered the entire coun-

Timespan	Historic Events in the East
2000-1500 B.C.	**Hsia Dynasty.** Known from legends. Potter's wheel, extensive domestication.
1500-1000 B.C.	**Shang Dynasty.** Loose political organization in Yellow River Valley. Irrigation works, granaries, palaces. Stylized picture writing. Bronze art. Wheeled chariots.
1000-221 B.C.	**Chou Dynasty.** Eclipse recorded; first firm date in Chinese history. **Book of History.** Iron plows and swords. Rise of feudalism. Confucious. Lao Tan (Taoism). The Period of Warring States.
221-206 B.C.	**Ch'in Dynasty.** China becomes centralized empire under Shih Huang-ti. Standardized custom duties, weights and measures, and writing. Great Wall of China built.
206 B.C.-A.D.220	**Han Dynasty.** Exploration; Silk Route to the West. Confucianism becomes state religion. Buddhism imported. Paper invented. Astronomic instruments improved.
A.D. 220-618	**Six Kingdoms.** Taosim emerges. Coal and tea used. Map of China developed. Water mill invented. Four centuries without stable government.
A.D. 618-907	**T'ang Dynasty.** Buddhist pilgrimages. Grand Canal built. Gunpowder invented.
A.D. 907-1126	**Five Dynasties.** Chang-an observatory draws astronomers from all over Asia.
A.D. 1126-1280	**Sung Dynasty.** Ships for ocean travel. Paper money. Mathematics. Music flourishes. Judaism imported.
A.D. 1280-1368	**Yüan Dynasty.** Islam, Christianity, Lamaism imported. Abacus invented. Distillation of liquor.
A.D. 1368-1644	**Ming Dynasty.** Critical scholarship, dictionaries, libraries. Maize, sweet potatoes, peanuts introduced from West. Colored porcelain.
A.D. 1644-1912	**Ch'ing Dynasty.** European influences. Opium smoking. Literary inquisition. Protestantism, Western education imported. Steamships, railroads. Period of rebellion.
A.D. 1912-1949	**Republic of China.** Japanese invasion, World War I. Mass education. Aviation. Archaeologic excavations.
A.D. 1949-Present	**Communist China, Nationalist China.** Political division.

try and welded the old states together under a single centralized administration. In becoming the first emperor, he established a social and political order that was to survive, with some modification, into modern times.

CIVILIZATIONS OF THE NEW WORLD

From the time of their initial discovery by the sixteenth-century Spanish conquistadors, the New World civilizations have intrigued Western man. Impressed by parallelisms with Old World cultures, some of the Spaniards thought that these high cultures were the creation of already-civilized people from the Old World, particularly the Ten Lost Tribes of Israel. Later scholars reached the conclusion that these cultures were *autochthonous*, or indigenous to the area, and that the "Indians" who had evolved these cultures had migrated as fairly primitive hunters from Asia many centuries before the conquest of the New World.

Although the consensus is that the American Indians did indeed migrate from Siberia into the New World, there is little agreement on whether the civilizations of Mesoamerica (part of Mexico and neighboring Central America) and the Andes were completely independent developments from those of the Old World. Even more curious, there is no firm evidence for the initial peopling of the Western Hemisphere despite decades of careful archaeological research. In North America, a number of camps and kill sites used by early hunters armed with the kind of spearpoint called "Clovis" can be dated to the final glacial advance about 12,500 years ago. The lithic industries of these people were relatively advanced and have no clear Asiatic counterparts, so it is reasonable to suppose that even more ancient and primitive cultural remains are yet to be found. Several have been claimed for North America, but so far the most convincing pre-Clovis industries have been located in South America. At the present state of knowledge,

a conservative guess would be that the Mongoloid ancestors of the American Indian first crossed the Bering Strait, perhaps by a land bridge created by a lower sea level, more than 15,000 years ago.

The nonmaterial culture brought in by these first Americans can never be recovered. It would be a mistake, however, to assume that it was simple, for even studies of modern hunting and gathering tribes such as the native Australians show that the mental capacity for culture of "primitive" people can often be complex. It should also be remembered that there have probably been innumerable cases of migration from Siberia and into Alaska, and back the other way. In fact, the Eskimo on both sides of the Bering Strait maintained a considerable trade and general contact with each other until the 1930s. Thus, there was no real barrier to Asiatic people and ideas until quite recently, and it may well be that some of the resemblances between native American conceptual systems and those of Asia can be explained in this manner.

The strongest evidence for the basic independence of the New World civilizations is that they were developed on an agricultural base almost totally alien to that of the Old World. The Mesoamerican people relied on a complex of domestic food plants, which included principally maize, the common bean, and several kinds of squashes. The Andean people to the south added to these several important root crops, particularly the white or "Irish" potato, along with a high-altitude cereal known as *quinoa*. These, and a host of minor domesticates including tomatoes, peanuts, and chili peppers, were not known in the Eastern Hemisphere before the time of Columbus, nor were any of the great plant foods of the Old World found in the New World prior to A.D. 1492. The only plant species cultivated in both hemispheres—the bottle gourd—probably originated in Africa and was carried to South America by ocean currents. An intermediate case is the sweet

Figure 17 (below left). Hieroglyphics from Mesoamerica—delicately carved and highly conventionalized abstractions and symbols that have been classified somewhere between ideographic and phonetic. Because they are stylized and complicated with religious symbolism, however, these hieroglyphics have been difficult to translate. Figure 18. Machu Picchu, the enigmatic ruins of an elaborate city high on a remote and nearly inaccessible plateau in the Peruvian Andes, about fifty miles northwest of the ancient Inca capital of Cuzco.

potato, which seems to have been taken out into the Pacific by American Indian voyagers, but this case is unique.

If the American Indian civilizations evolved independently, it should be recognized that they evolved in different ways. Archaeologists are agreed that there were only two regions—Mesoamerica and the Andean area—that could be called "civilized." Mesoamerica includes much of central and all of southern Mexico, Guatemala, British Honduras, and parts of Honduras and El Salvador. The Andean area comprises Peru, southern Ecuador, western Bolivia, and northernmost Chile. These two nuclear regions are separated by the Intermediate area, basically the isthmian part of the Western Hemisphere and highland Colombia, within which few cultural developments could ever be called civilized.

Although Mesoamerica and the Andean area used quite similar agricultural bases, there were some striking differences between the two before A.D. 1492. The Mesoamericans, particularly the Maya, had evolved an elaborate ceremonial calendar based on a ritual cycle of 260 days permutating with a 365-day "vague year" to produce a supercycle of fifty-two years. In their folding-screen books, fashioned either of deerskin or figbark paper, they recorded not only ritual matters relating to these cycles but also complex calculations having to do with the heavenly bodies, such as the planet Venus. The Maya, in fact, were adept at predicting eclipses, which is a highly developed skill. They also enjoyed literacy, for they had developed several different writing systems, of which the Maya was the most complete (it has only been partially deciphered).

The Andean people, in contrast, were not interested in elaborate calendars and astronomy and they were illiterate. The only form of making records, found among the late Inca, is the *quipu*, an involved method of keeping accounts with knots based upon decimal numeration (the Mesoamericans used vigesimal numeration, counting by twenties instead of tens). Although the intellectual level was not as developed, the Andeans perfected technology far beyond the achievements of the Mesoamericans. In the construction of stone buildings, and above all in great engineering feats such as long-distance roads, suspension bridges, and great canals and dams, the Andeans were master craftsmen. Metallurgy has deep roots in the Andean area, and the people there developed a metal technology equivalent to or even surpassing that of the "Bronze Age" in the Old World. From the Andeans, the people of Mexico learned the art of metal working at a relatively late date.

A significant number of other traits found in one area but not in the other suggests that the two evolved fairly independently of each other. Mesoamerica is characterized by such features as complex markets, frequent human sacrifices, a rubber-ball game with ritual overtones, and an elaborate religious pantheon of gods that combined the features of animals and men. The people of the Andean area domesticated the llama and guinea pig and used coca as a narcotic; they also had a simple pantheon and placed heavy emphasis on shrines and oracles.

Although they show clear dissimilarities, Mesoamerica and the Andean area did evolve in ways that exhibit a striking chronological parallelism. By about 5000 B.C., a very primitive form of agriculture had begun, based on a few crops that later were to have great importance. Pottery began to be made about 2000 B.C. but by 1800 B.C. was widespread. Indisputably civilized temple centers had taken form by 1000 B.C. and possibly a little earlier. This would suggest some degree of contact at critical times.

MESOAMERICA

In Mesoamerica, the first known civilization is Olmec. The context in which it must be viewed is that of the Formative period, lasting from about 1500 B.C. to A.D. 300. There

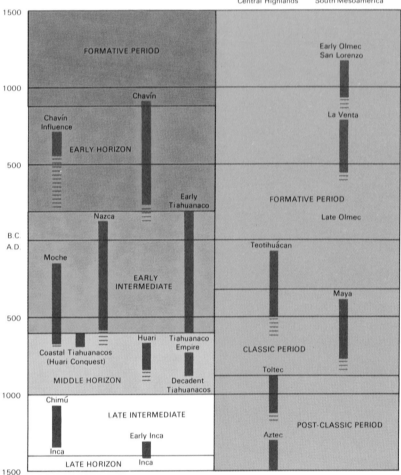

were earlier, more simple people who had used pottery and who had preceded the great civilizations of the Classic period (A.D. 300–900) and who in a way set the stage for them. These formative cultures were thought of as the New World equivalent of the Neolithic, in a setting of peasant villages with all the arts of sedentary life—ceramics, figurines, loom textiles, and agriculture—but with no real social stratification, little religious development, and only the rudiments of the so-called higher arts. Although the Olmec civilization of Mexico's southern Gulf Coast had been known for some time, it was generally held to be Classic in date, on the same level as the far greater Maya civilization and surely not ancestral to it.

Recent excavation and radiocarbon analysis have proved, however, that the Olmec civilization first arose shortly after 1200 B.C., in sites such as San Lorenzo, a great man-made plateau lying in the drainage of the Coatzacoalcos River in Veracruz. The Olmec appear on the scene as master carvers, creating enormous sculptures of basalt that celebrate gods and men. Their best-known productions are the Colossal Heads, magnificent portraits of helmeted rulers on an immense scale. The heads average eighteen tons in weight, and other monuments weigh up to thirty or forty tons. Considering that these stones had to be brought in to Olmec sites from their source many miles away, the engineering feat is indeed impressive.

A series of Olmec temple centers, presumably all of them relatively "empty" capitals staffed by the rulers, priests, and their entourages, succeeded San Lorenzo after its destruction around 900 B.C. Of these, La Venta, a kind of remote citadel on an island surrounded by swampland, is the most notable. La Venta, like all known Olmec sites, is laid out in a north-south linear plan and has many mounds built entirely of earth and clay. La Venta's principal mound is a 100-foot-high construction that has recently been

shown to be shaped deliberately like a volcano, a concept that has no equivalent elsewhere in the New World. Along the north-south centerline have been found magnificent caches of finely carved jade and serpentine figurines, testifying to the wealth and craftsmanship of the ancient Olmec.

La Venta itself seems to have been destroyed around 400 B.C. Long before this time, Olmec influence and perhaps the Olmec themselves had spread widely in highland Mesoamerica and as far south as El Salvador. By 30 B.C., late Olmec (or Olmecoid) people of the Gulf Coast had perfected writing and the calendar from that area come the oldest dated inscriptions, in a calendrical system called the Long Count, which was once thought to have been a Maya invention.

It was at this time, shortly before the Christian era, that the Maya civilization was crystallizing in the lowlands of Yucatán and northern Guatemala, which were characterized by dense tropical forests. By A.D. 300, it had been perfected. Like the Olmec, from

Figure 21 (left). Excavations at Palenque, a site of the Classic period in Mesoamerica that has been called the Athens of the Maya. Until recently lost to the encroachment of the rain forest, Palenque attests to the architectural genius of its builders and the power at the disposal of the centralized theocratic state that controlled the populace. One of the puzzles concerning the Classic period is that many of these monumental ceremonial centers were abandoned between A.D. 850 and 900 for reasons as yet unknown. Figure 22 (right). The remains of Cajamarquilla of the Andean area, another reminder of the power of the theocracy in the New World.

whom they may have been descended, the Classic Maya built what have been called ceremonial centers, great conglomerations of temples, so-called palaces, ball courts, and plazas that show no sign of urban planning or of very dense populations. Tikal, for instance, the greatest of all Maya sites, probably had a population of no more than 10,000 within an area of sixteen square miles.

The Maya are noted for their towering pyramid-temples built of limestone and stucco, for their wonderfully sophisticated relief sculpture and painting, and for the refinements they made in their writing and calendar. They were undoubtedly the greatest of the New World people in intellectual achievement, but they had surprisingly little influence over other groups.

If influence is what counts, then surely the Teotihuacán civilization of the Mexican highlands was far more important than the Maya. By the time of Christ, a remarkable center had been established on the northeastern side of the Valley of Mexico, in which modern Mexico City is located. From its foundation, Teotihuacán apparently was always a true city, laid out on a regular grid pattern and divided into four quarters by two cross-cutting avenues. For six centuries until its destruction about A.D. 600, it dominated most of Mesoamerica, apparently holding even the Maya highlands and possibly the lowlands within its sway. It has been suggested that irrigation agriculture was the basis for Teotihuacán power, but for this suggestion there is remarkably little evidence. For that matter, it may have been control of the reclaimed *chinampa*, or "floating garden" region, in the southern part of the Valley of Mexico that fed the Teotihuacán armies.

The Classic period was a sort of Golden Age for Mesoamerica, and a number of local cultures flourished. Around A.D. 900, however, the Classic Maya culture fell into ruins, and a number of other regional cultures seem to have collapsed by that time. In their place

came a hardy but civilized Mexican people
called the Toltec, who probably were as militaristic and imperial-minded as the Teotihua-
canos. The latest of all to appear were the
Aztec, who, according to their own traditions, were originally a barbaric people of
northwestern Mexico. By A.D. 1200 they had
settled in the Valley of Mexico, and by the
time the Spaniards observed them in A.D.
1519, they had become the greatest and most
powerful of all the Mesoamericans.

THE ANDEAN AREA

The same pattern of alternating periods of
integration and regionalism can also be seen
in the Andean area. Here the moments of integration, called *horizons*, are probably representative of widespread political empires
such as that of the Inca, which is the third
and the latest horizon. It must be kept in
mind, however, that the Andes is a very
different landscape from that of Mesoamerica. The latter can usually be divided into a
moderately high and semidry highland region and the wet, tropical lowlands. The
Andean area encompasses a contrast between the very high, wet, and cold highlands

and the coastal desert that fronts the cold
Pacific waters, rich in marine foods. Cutting
down from the highlands to the coast are
numerous little valleys that offer the possibility of good agriculture if irrigation techniques are used.

Civilization has some surprisingly deep
roots in the Andean area. If temples and
ceremonial centers are some criteria for defining the point at which civilization appears, these have been shown to have appeared at the beginning of 2000 B.C. For
instance, the Chuquitanta site on the central
Peruvian coast is preceramic, yet it already
has a complex of stone-and-mortar buildings
centering on a temple. Such a precocious
development may probably be attributed to
the antiquity of sedentary life along the
coast, where flood-water cultivation supplemented by fishing and mollusk collecting
had been established for millenniums before
that.

Even more surprising is the site of Kotosh
in the central highlands, where an extraordinary masonry temple complex, embellished
with clay reliefs of humans with crossed
arms, is definitely preceramic and therefore

Figure 23. An example of Peruvian textile, which has been called the finest hand weaving the world has known. Figure 24 (left). The ruins of Cuzco, a center of Peruvian civilization in A.D. 1500. The organization needed to build such monuments was possible because almost every aspect of life was rigidly controlled by the state, which even moved "surplus" men and women to less populated areas during expansion programs. As compensation for being told where to live, what to grow, and what to do, the state provided free food to districts whose annual crops were inadequate — food gathered from districts that had exceeded their established quota.

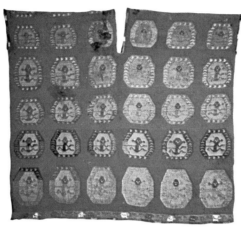

older than 1500 B.C. The next rebuilding of Kotosh is associated with an early kind of pottery that can only have been introduced from the Montaña, the tropical forests of the Upper Amazon drainage lying to the east.

The Montaña element present in the great Chavín civilization that succeeds these early proto-civilizations has long been recognized, but the Kotosh evidence gives it further weight. Chavín is the first of the three horizons that integrate Andean prehistory. Estimated to begin about 1000 B.C. and to endure until 200 B.C., it is the exact temporal and developmental equivalent of Olmec, and some have suggested Olmec influence upon it. The type site is Chavín de Huantar, a peculiar stone-masonry complex of temples and courtyards. The temples contain long subterranean galleries that must have been the focal point for the cult practiced at the center. Chavín art, expressed in stone reliefs, pottery, textiles, and other objects, is awe-inspiring, with its horrific pantheon of transformed man-animals. As in Olmec art, the jaguar is the beast worshiped, but there are also condors or eagles and several Montaña animals besides the jaguar, such as the cayman.

Chavín or Chavín-like art was found over much of the Andes in the 1000 B.C. period, and its influence was probably the stimulus for many local developments. In the succeeding Early Intermediate period (200 B.C.– A.D. 500), regionalism again set in, but certain important cultural advances were registered. In particular, canal irrigation made its appearance in the coastal valleys. The consequences soon became clear, with the increase not only in village and town size but also in the building of fortifications to defend the irrigation systems from attack. Some of the coastal civilizations are indeed impressive, perhaps the greatest and most attractive being the Moche, found across several valleys of northern Peru. Moche pottery is highly descriptive, with many scenes of daily life and religion. Weaving, fishing,

Figure 25. A portion of the *Codex Mendoza,* an early and minutely detailed ethnography of the beliefs and customs of the Aztec compiled eight years after their capital was destroyed by the Spaniards. Fra Bernadino de Sahagun, a Catholic missionary, trained young members of the Aztec nobility as researchers for his ambitious project and went about gathering hieroglyphic paintings supplemented with descriptions in the native Aztec tongue — written in Spanish script.

seal hunting, and even sexual activities are shown in a lively and anecdotal style. Cities, as opposed to the ceremonial centers, surely appeared by this time, as did public works on a grand scale. Some of the adobe-brick towns and pyramids of the coast are impressive.

As the Toltec seem to have finished off what remained of the declining civilizations of the Mesoamerican Classic period, so did a group of people originating at Huari in the southern highlands obliterate the Early Intermediate cultures of Peru, apparently around A.D. 500. The identification of this horizon is based on a beautiful and somewhat abstract art style derived from the great city of Tiahuanaco, which flourished for many centuries on the Bolivian side of Lake Tiahuanaco. Just as suddenly as it appeared, however, Huari influence disappeared all over the Andean area to be replaced by a resurgence of local traditions. One of these, the Chimú civilization of the north Peruvian coast, was responsible for what was probably the largest city of South America: Chan-chan, an enormous urban complex with huge walled compounds. At its height, Chan-chan may have sheltered more than 100,000 people, its inhabitants drawn from all the neighboring valleys that were thereby depopulated.

The Chimú and their capital were made captive by an upstart highland people, the Inca, who made their own capital at Cuzco in the south highlands of Peru. By A.D. 1450, this tough, warrior tribe—so similar in many respects to the Aztec in Mexico—had taken all of the Andean area proper and had overrun most of Ecuador, northern Chile, and northwest Argentina. At its height, the Inca empire extended more than 2,300 miles along the backbone of South America and included millions of people within its iron grip. The extraordinary Inca bureaucracy, organized on the decimal system, was described in some detail by the admiring Spaniards who destroyed it. Like all the Andean

people, the Inca were great craftsmen and technologists. Many of their works still remain in the form of roads and bridges, giving testimony to the statement that they were without question among the world's greatest stone masons. The still-standing walls of Cuzco, which have defied repeated earthquakes, and the fantastic battlements of the Sacsahuaman fort bear testimony to their prowess in this art.

Returning to the question of the autochthony of the New World civilizations, there recently have been some strong arguments for trans-Pacific contact. Many resemblances have been pointed out—for instance, between the art and architecture of the Maya and that of Southeast Asia. Suggestions have been made that Chavín art was diffused from "Bronze Age" China, and in the last several years a case has been made that fishermen from "Neolithic" Japan transmitted such arts of settled life as pottery to the inhabitants of coastal Ecuador.

Most of these studies do not hold up on close examination, however. In most cases, the chronology and locality of the proposed contacts have not been closely controlled. What has been lacking is a methodology that will allow one to say that long-range contact has or has not taken place, within a framework of probability. One such analysis made with a sound methodology has been able to show conclusively that the art of making bark paper and bark cloth—and books—had been diffused to Mesoamerica from some center in eastern Indonesia by 1500 B.C. This opens up the possibility that the contact involved more than paper making. Perhaps the heddle loom, a complex machine, came to the New World natives at the same time —perhaps there were even more intangible items, for there are intriguing resemblances between Mesoamerican religious systems and those of China and Southeast Asia. The careful study of such possible diffusions should open up a new chapter in New World prehistory.

Primitive Societies

18

Suppose you are on an airliner that is forced down in some remote, uncharted region—an inaccessible mountain plateau, an uncharted island, an unexplored tropical forest, or the vast arctic tundra. All on board survive the crash landing, but you now find yourselves isolated in an environment characterized by extremely harsh conditions and you realize that your most urgent task is to assure your own survival. Certainly you could not hope to instantly re-create the niceties of the civilization from which you came, simply because you would not have the resources or facilities to do so. You would have to settle for far less. In fact, the manner in which you adapt to the limitations of your new circumstances may well approximate the manner in which primitive societies have come to terms with their environments.

As in primitive societies, your way of life would be simple and basic. It would be organized with fundamental needs in mind —food, shelter, and protection from predators and from your own fears of the unknown. You would find yourselves tied closely to the environment and to each other. Roles and relationships eventually would be accepted and commonly understood. Sex, ability, and age would replace civilization's more subtle distinctions of relative social importance. And you would quickly learn to appreciate the plight and accomplishments of the remaining primitive societies in the contemporary world.

Primitive people struggle for survival in the world's most remote and difficult environments. Their social and economic organizations as well as their technologies are responses to the meager resources they have at their disposal. And as civilization comes to more and more of these remote regions, primitive societies take on new characteristics or simply cease to exist. The few truly primitive societies that are found today represent a rapidly vanishing way of life.

DIVERSITY OF PRIMITIVE SOCIETIES

All primitive societies are alike in that they are close to their environment, controlling and altering it less than modern industrial societies. Although primitive societies differ markedly from one another, the diversification that exists stems partly from the fact that each has been forced to adapt to a specific and often unique set of environmental conditions. In recent times, most of these societies have felt the impact of advancing civilizations, and the character of their cultures has changed under the pressure. The few truly primitive societies that still exist are usually found only in out-of-the-way places in the arctic, in the deserts, in the deep tropical forests of Africa, Southeast Asia, and South America, and in a few remote mountain regions. Their range of habitat is therefore more extreme and polarized than it was before the modern epoch of exploration, colonization, and imperialism.

Primitive cultures also show differentiation because a culture tends to reach equilibrium at some point in its adaptation to a particular environment. A given technology will function not only to exploit an environment but also to define population size and density and several aspects of sociopolitical structure as well as a host of more specific cultural traits, as the chapter "Cultural Ecology" indicates. For instance, a hunting-gathering-fishing technology tends to restrict the size of the foraging group and creates a migratory tendency, and together these two factors limit the degree of complexity that social structure and cultural institutions can achieve. Even the culturally related societies of the American Indian Shoshonean speakers ranged from the small, simple foraging band of a few related families of Nevada "Diggers" to the city-state of the Aztecs in Mexico, numbering in the thousands.

Some aspects of culture are not directly related to technological adaptations, although they may serve an important purpose. All societies have codes of etiquette, belief in the supernatural, origin myths, games, music, ornamentation and art, and birth, marriage, and death ceremonies, and this universality suggests that these aspects of society serve important social and psychological needs. But the specific content of art, or music, or whatever else forms the culture is usually unpredictable as well as unexplainable and gives the flavor of historic uniqueness.

But the evolutionary process that was so important in creating the diversity of primitive culture is now being reversed. The power of modern industrial nations has so dominated this planet that primitive societies are disappearing or becoming adapted to the dominant cultures. There was tremendous demographic change as war, slavery, forced migration, and, above all, unfamiliar diseases nearly annihilated the natives of North America, South America, tropical Africa, Australia, and Oceania. Henry Dobyns calculated in 1966 that there was a 95 percent reduction of the American Indian population within 100 years after contact with Europeans. In consequence of culture contact, the survivors usually built up their societies on a new basis, one that would be unfamiliar to their ancestors. Because of this factor, anthropologists keep primitive cultures distinguished from those that have undergone acculturation.

PRIMITIVE CULTURE AREAS

Most major books and monographs describing primitive culture have been written within the last 100 years. Anthropologists usually write about primitive cultures in the "ethnographic present" tense, which is the "present" that the sources describe, no matter how long ago or how recently the books were written. For this reason, it is often difficult to define cultures from sources that describe primitive societies now vanished or in different degrees of breakdown. But for research purposes, an attempt must be made at generalization, and anthropologists have agreed that contiguous societies that share a broad ecological zone are likely to share important cultural characteristics—both for reasons of similar adaptations to the shared environmental zone as well as a shared diffusional continuum. Such generalized zones are called *culture areas* and are depicted in Figure 2 for the primitive culture areas of the world.

North American Zone

The culture area concept began with the classification of North American Indian material culture for museum exhibits and it is still in use. As Alfred Kroeber and Robert

	PRIMITIVE CULTURE AREAS OF THE WORLD			
Culture Area	Ecological Zone	Examples of Culture Types	Primary Subsistence Activities	Social Organization
NORTH AMERICA	Arctic	Eskimo	Hunting and fishing	Family and band organization
	Northern Forest	Athapaskans and Algonkians	Hunting and fishing	Band organization
	Northwest Coast	Northwest Coast Indians	Dependence on sea food; some hunting	Class structure: nobles, commoners, slaves; unilineal descent groups.
	Great Plains	Plains Indians	Dependence on bison	Large-band organization; military associations.
	Basin-Plateau	Shoshonean Indians	Hunting and gathering (mainly the latter)	Scattered migratory band groups.
	Southwest	Pueblo Indians	Sedentary agricultural	Village as basic political unit.
	Eastern Woodlands	Iroquois League	Hoe cultivation and hunting	Village; tribal organization; egalitarian society.
	Southeast	Creek, Natchez	Intensive cultivation of maize, corn, pumpkin, etc.	Hierarchical societies; village organization with confederation of tribes as maximum political unit.
LATIN AMERICA	Highlands	Aztec; Inca	Intensive cultivation of maize, potatoes, gourds.	Hierarchical state organization; large empires.
	Tropical Forest	Brazilian Indians	Hoe agriculture and hunting	Kinship-based social organization; village units.
	Marginals	Araucanians; Tierra del Fuegians	Hunting and fishing with intensive hoe agriculture.	Band organization, kinship based.
OCEANIA	Micronesia	Truk, Palau, the Carolines, etc.	Coconut, pandanus, breadfruit, and taro; fishing; domesticated pigs.	Administrative unit under chiefs; growth through conquest.
	Polynesia	Tahiti, Samoa	Fishing; cultivation of taro, breadfruit, coconuts, bananas, yams, sugar cane.	Stratified societies; conquest led to large political units.
	Malaysia	Malaya, Java, Bali	Dry rice; domestication of water buffalo, cattle, sheep, goats, chickens, pigs.	Small villages that move when lands are exhausted.
	Melanesia	New Guinea, Admiralty Islands	Cultivation of taro, yams and sago; domesticated pigs; fishing and hunting.	Kin-based social organization; politically independent villages.
	Australia	Australians	Hunting and gathering.	Band organization.
ASIA	Asian Steppes	Mongols	Horse milk, sheep, goats, camels.	Large-band organization.
	Siberia	Chukchee	Hunting; fishing on coast; reindeer domestication. In interior.	Band organization.
	Chinese	China	Millet and wheat farming in North; wet rice in south.	Traditional bureaucratic administration with divine sovereign.
	Hindu	India	Farming of wheat, barley, legumes	Caste organization; relatively strong village autonomy.
	Moslem	Arabs, Afghani	Wheat and barley agriculture; goat and sheep domestication	Pleasant village and pastoralists; empires.
AFRICA	Mediterranean Littoral	Moroccan peasants	Wheat and barley agriculture; goat and sheep domestication	Peasant villages; organization into large states.
	Saharan	Berbers	Camel and horse pastoralism; oasis cereal cultivation.	Class stratification with pastoralists dominating peasants.
	West Africa	Hausa; Tallensi	Intensive cultivation of yams, bananas, sorghum, millet, maize, manioc.	Village and state organization.
	East/South Africa	Swazi; Nyoro	Cattle herding, cultivation.	Villages and kingdoms; kinship based social organization.
	Bushmen	Bushmen	Hunting and gathering.	Band organization.

Spencer pointed out, the North American cultures seem to fall into distinctive geographic zones that share many traits, especially in material culture. In broadest terms, the North American culture areas may be classified as Arctic, Northern Forest, Northwest Coast, Great Plains, Basin-Plateau, Southwest, Eastern Woodlands, and Southeast.

The arctic Eskimo are one of the most distinctive culture types and one of the best known. Their material culture is ingenious in its adaptation to the rigors of the arctic winter. Dog teams and sleds, snow goggles to prevent snow blindness, tailored animal-skin clothing, permanent stone and earth dwellings and temporary snow igloos, the kayak, carved ivory and bone implements, and harpoons with detachable barbs are among the more distinctive culture traits of the Eskimo. Their environment is notable for its sea mammals, fish, and caribou herds.

South of the arctic archipelago, the tundra gives way to shrubs and scrub trees and finally to the tremendous forest zone of Canada. Here the most northerly of the American Indians, the Athapaskan speakers and the Algonkian speakers, have developed a hunting-fishing adaptation that is different from that of the Eskimo in some important respects. The Eskimo have lived rather permanently through the long winter by ice hunting and fishing, but they have hunted the migrating caribou in summer. The forest Indians, on the other hand, migrated throughout the year after the caribou herds. Their most sedentary camps were made during summer months, when they congregated at good fishing lakes. In modern times, however, the Indians have specialized in trapping for the fur market.

The Northwest Coast area is heavily forested, and its inlets and streams abound with fish and sea mammals. The Indians here are still foragers, but the wealth of the sea—particularly spawning salmon—and the food storage techniques of smoking, drying, and packing fish have permitted their vil-

lages to become as large and permanent as those of successful primitive agriculturalists. Of the material culture traits, the carving of cedar is the most distinctive. The multiple-family houses and the large seagoing canoes are constructed of cedar planks, but totem poles and other cultural objects are given more delicate treatment. Sociopolitically, the Northwest Coast Indians are the only existing hunters and gatherers with a hierarchical or chiefdom form of organiza-

tion—that is, with hereditary leadership, ranks, and degrees of prestige. All other groups of this type are distinctively egalitarian.

Obtaining food in the Basin-Plateau area was limited primarily to acorn gathering in California, piñon nut gathering in upland sections of the Nevada-Utah-California basin, and salmon fishing in a few favored spots in the northern plateau zone. The people, mostly Shoshonean speakers, existed as widely scattered migratory groups of hunters and gatherers until some groups acquired horses from the Southwest and others obtained guns from the Northwest fur traders. The resulting imbalance in mobility and weaponry enabled these groups to muster large bands of buffalo hunters and raid their less fortunate neighbors, who then scattered into the desert areas. These latter Indians were known collectively to the invading whites as "Diggers" and the others were variously recognized as Utes, Shoshoni, and Snakes.

The Indians of the Southwest culture area were not nearly as homogeneous as those of the Basin-Plateau region. Offense-defense tactics helped to polarize the various Indians, and, as a result, some became sedentary, intensive agriculturalists who lived in fortresslike pueblos. Others, such as the Navajo-Apache, became seminomadic, predatory raiders who practiced agriculture and herding or were fisherman-agriculturalists in the lower Colorado flood plains. Still others, such as the Paiute and some Indians of northern Arizona, became scattered hunters and gatherers.

Of all the Indians of the Southwest, the Navajo and the Pueblo are the best known. Even today they exist as large population segments—about 90,000 Navajo are scattered throughout northern Arizona and parts of New Mexico, Colorado, and Utah. They herd sheep, grow maize, beans, and squash, and make pots, wool blanket-rugs, and silver ornaments for the market. The Pueblo Indians are usually classified into eastern and west-ern cultures. The eastern, Keresan-speaking Indians live in small, close-knit communities along the Rio Grande in central New Mexico. The western culture, of which the Zuñi and Hopi are best-known examples, is found in Arizona. Although several language families are found among the Pueblo, their culture is relatively homogeneous and distinctive.

The Great Plains provides the best justification for the culture area approach to general classification. The climate and topography are much the same throughout this region, and the prime resource—great herds of bison—resulted in simplification of the culturally adaptive responses. As horsemanship diffused throughout the Plains, buffalo hunting became quite productive and dominated the material culture. Many tribes, originally of diverse cultures, moved into the Plains and adopted the prevailing way of life —a culture featuring horsemanship, skin tipi, travois, pemmican, sinew-backed bow, feather headdress, sun dance, and other traits made so familiar to us by the motion picture industry.

The Eastern Woodland culture area—a temperate forest region—extends from the northern limit of a horticulture complex of maize, beans, and squash to the Mason-Dixon line. The basic difference between the Eastern Woodland and the Southeast is in population density and the complexity of sociopolitical organization. The Eastern area is made up of small egalitarian tribal societies, whereas the hierarchical Southeast is composed of larger towns. It is possible that a longer growing season, in combination with the sizable rivers and estuaries, made the larger towns of certain southeastern areas possible. But perhaps more important was the political innovation of permanent leadership similar to the chiefdoms of the Northwest Coast region.

Latin American Zone

The Mesoamerican culture area encompasses the chiefdoms and states—often referred to as empires—of the highlands of Central

Figure 6. The Manus of the Admiralty Islands in Melanesia are a seafaring people who live by fishing and trading. They act as "middle-men" among the peoples of the interior and the small fringe islands who are linked together in interdependence by their specialized production of certain crops or crafts. Intensive acculturation has taken place since the 1880s under European administration and through the effects of two world wars. Many have moved through education to new occupations, and others pursue the traditional subsistence patterns even though they use some imported techniques.

Mexico and Guatemala and the lowlands of Yucatán and adjacent regions. The best-known cultures are those of the Aztecs of the Valley of Mexico and the numerous Maya states in Guatemala and Yucatán.

Somewhat similar to the Maya were the numerous chiefdoms and states making up the circum-Caribbean culture area. Most of these groups bore the brunt of the early Spanish explorations. In areas where they were not exterminated or scattered as refugees into the interior, the societies quickly became simplified and deculturated.

The Andean cultures resembled the highland empires of Mexico and Guatemala. Irrigation created a truly intensive form of agriculture resulting in considerable population density and large communities. The political system, one of hereditary leadership and rank, enabled the classical empire to extend its power over huge areas and disparate provincial societies. Art, architecture, and various crafts were highly specialized and of very high quality.

The Tropical Forest area, a tremendous lowland of many rivers and dense forests, extends from the eastern slope of the Andean and Colombian cordillera across the continent to the Atlantic. There are some highlands in the interior of Brazil, however, where a few enclaves of Marginal area cultures—probably refugees—live. Generally the Tropical Forest tribe is strongly egalitarian and warlike, although it is simple in sociopolitical organization. Food sources are maize, beans, squash, and manioc, along with fish, turtles, and birds. The tribes of this culture area depend heavily on the river systems for transportation. Perhaps their most unusual trait is the great use of herbal drugs in healing, hallucinating, spear and arrow poisoning, and fish poisoning.

The Marginal area is a residual category. The people here are essentially hunters and gatherers who do not correspond to the previous culture types. The largest contiguous area is from northern Uruguay, through Argentina to the Strait of Magellan, including the adjacent Chilean archipelago. But there are also nomadic hunters in the Brazilian highland, the Gran Chaco and Matto Grosso, and, at the time of the Spanish conquest, in a few of the Caribbean islands. Methods of obtaining food range from fishing and shellfish gathering in the coastal area to hunting large game in the inland regions.

Oceania Zone

Oceania may be subdivided into the culture areas of Micronesia, Polynesia, Malaysia, Melanesia, and Australia—areas that are, to a considerable extent, racial and linguistic subdivisions as well. Micronesian and Polynesian people are very similar in physical traits and they both speak the Malayo-Polynesian language. There are some cultural differences between the people living on the larger, so-called high islands and those living on the low coral atolls. The main distinction is created by the type of food available, inasmuch as high islanders rely on many root and fruit crops, and the low islanders such as the Micronesians depend much more on fishing and the coconut palm. Political

Figure 7. The Ainu are the native inhabitants of Hokkaido, the northernmost island of the Japanese Archipelago. The couple shown here are in ceremonial costume, and the woman displays the facial tatooing outlawed more than sixty years ago by the Japanese government. Under such assimilative pressures, Ainu is a rapidly disappearing culture. In the lower photograph, Ainu observe an annual festival held on Lake Akan to honor the spirit of *marimo,* a rare algae.

organization is more advanced and complex in the populous high islands, but all of the islands have one form or another of hereditary leadership. The potentiality for further development of this type of structure is evident in the rise of large-scale kingdoms in Hawaii, Tahiti, and Tonga subsequent to the acquisition of European weapons.

The Malaysian area is a complicated hodgepodge of diverse migrants from continental Asia. A few Pygmy groups who now live in scattered regions are considered to be the oldest inhabitants, but the majority of the culture is a mixture of early Chinese and Hindu traits, with a later overlay of Muslim and modern European influences.

In Melanesia, an important cultural florescence exists in the large island of New Guinea, and the many large and small associated islands have evolved a basically similar mode of minimally hierarchial organization in which leadership is primarily achieved and its scope is limited to the village. Larger integrations of people are built on this politically atomistic base through the maintenance of trade and exchange.

The Australian culture area is an entire continent of hunters and gatherers. The interior of Australia is an extremely arid desert, and the remnants of aborigines who live there are thinly scattered and migratory. These people have aroused anthropological interest, especially with regard to their rich and complex social, ceremonial, and mythological life.

Asian Zone

Because of the millenniums of dominance by classical empires of the Chinese, Hindus, and Moslems and the rise and fall of still other minor empires in the southeast regions, Asia is difficult to classify into areas of primitive culture. For this reason, it seems better to use these terms as classificatory devices with the understanding that they refer to the primitive aborigines enclaved within, and adapted to, these complex civilizations. The inner Asian steppe region and Siberia, however, seem better classified in terms of geographic culture areas.

The Chinese area—China, Korea, Japan, and Tibet—contains only a few such groups having few remnants of their aboriginal culture. The Ainu of Japan are the best known, but even they are noticed more for their rather distinctive physical characteristics than for their culture.

The Hindu area—India, Burma, Thailand, and Cambodia—represents a civilizational overlay that becomes less pervasive in a few remote mountain regions. But even the most remote Montagnards are no longer very primitive because these people have now acquired agricultural methods and other traits from their more technologically developed neighbors.

The Moslem area is characterized by the overlay of Islamic custom. The cultures of some of the nomadic camel breeders and horsemen, such as the well-known Bedouin Arabs, resemble primitive cultures in terms of custom and hierarchical organization. However, these same people are close to their original Islamic homeland in Arabia and they maintain the early pastoral aspects of Moslem religion and law in a more pure form than the more urbanized, richer areas.

In Southeast Asia, both Chinese and Hindu influences have been felt in mountain areas, where enclaves of primitives-turned-peasant may still be found. The most primitive and also the most studied are the Semang, Pygmy "Negritos" who practice only hunting and gathering.

The inner Asian steppe was once a region dominated by chiefdoms of militaristic horsemen. These people rarely practiced agriculture, but instead they traded and plundered for grains and metal implements. The Turkic and Mongol "hordes" were the classic specialists in this mobile blend of pastoralism, successful warfare, and predation.

Siberia contained many primitive tribal people before the Russian expansion. The pastoralists of the inner Asian steppe gradu-

ally gave way to a simpler life style as the bitter, cold winters of the Siberian forest and tundra became longer. Although pastoralism persisted—with domesticated reindeer taking the place of the horse—hunting and fishing became the predominant means of subsistence. Reindeer were used primarily for transportation. Because reindeer were neither as numerous nor as strong as horses, however, they never functioned importantly in military tactics. The well-described Chukchi of Siberia have been classified into two groups, one specialized as reindeer herders and the other as coastal fisherman. Although they are believed to have arrived in North America from Siberia by way of the Bering Strait, there are no Eskimo in Siberia today.

African Zone
There are more types of primitive societies in Africa than any other area, and geographic regions are easily classified. The

Mediterranean littoral contains no primitive societies, although there are small peasant villages, such as those of the Berbers in the Atlas Mountains of Morocco. The Saharan area is largely Islamic in culture. The inhabitants are primitive only to the extent that migratory herding of sheep, goats, camels, and a few horses may force them to live occasionally in small groups with few permanent possessions.

In the West African area the people intensively cultivate yams, bananas, sorghum, millet, maize, and manioc. Cattle herding is rare, and only a few fowl and pets are domesticated. Large city-states and kingdoms emerged along the Guinea coast as early as the thirteenth century, but the inlanders retained their forms of village organization. Agriculture based mainly on grain, predominates in East and South Africa but cattle herding is also important, and in some societies it is the prized form of activity. In the northwestern part of East Africa there are societies with a caste-like system, with dominant herders ruling subordinate cultivators. These are, in general, well-developed centralized kingdoms. Also found in East Africa are mainly pastoral societies based on lineages and age grade organizations.

Following the tremendous displacement caused by the slave trade, large militant kingdoms such as those of the Zulu arose in the southeast. The unsuccessful and less powerful tribes were scattered to remote areas of East Africa and remain there to this day as hunters and gatherers. This warfare and vast migration generally created a shock wave from north to south, and one of the major consequences was the dispersion of settled peoples as well as the Bushmen, hunters and gatherers who before had been found over a third of Africa.

The Bushmen are still migratory hunter-gatherers but are now limited to the vast and inhospitable Kalahari Desert and Okavango Swamp. They are forced to migrate constantly because of the scarcity of food.

They use simple spears and clubs to hunt small game; bow and poisoned arrow are used against occasional larger animals. Big game is not easily brought down, however, because the poison is weak, and more often than not the wounded animal must be followed relentlessly until it drops from exhaustion. Living as they do, the Bushmen do not require a complex social organization. They instead live as small bands of relatives, with loose ties of relationship with other bands. They construct temporary shelters during their migrations or, in a more permanent camp, dome-shaped brush huts. A significant part of their life in the desert is spent in search of water, for the amount of it will determine the available animal life and will consequently limit the number of people that the environment is capable of supporting.

ASPECTS OF PRIMITIVE SOCIETY

The term "primitive" has been used as an antonym to "civilized"—but what is civilization? The most obvious difference between civilized and primitive society is that of scale. Modern civilizations such as India, China, and the United States each contain, organize, and govern a population of at least 100 million. Primitive societies at most number in the hundreds, or in very few cases, thousands.

Division of Labor

Related to the sheer size and density of society is the complexity of its institutions. Civilizations have certain formalized organizations and institutions that have no counterpart in primitive societies. Although both primitive and civilized societies have some small-scale organizations, such as family households, interrelations among households, clubs, and special-purpose groups, all of these are close, *interpersonal* systems of social relationship. Civilized societies have formal, specialized organizations of technicians, merchants, scholars, and engineers; at most, primitive societies have only individual specialists—shamans, carpenters, and musicians—who are usually available only on a part-time basis. The division of labor in primitive society is based primarily on familistic principles of age and sex: some tasks are considered appropriate for adults and others for the aged or the young, and there is a rigid dichotomy of male-female labor.

There are also some important differences in the division of labor from one primitive society to another. The smallest societies—the hunters and gatherers and the rudimentary horticulturalists—are egalitarian and unspecialized except for the family age-sex distinctions and the part-time curing shaman. The hierarchical societies, or the chiefdoms, often have a specialized group of craftsmen—carpenters, brewers, dancers, and musicians—and a ruling bureaucracy, which is usually an organization of priests. Again it is a matter of scale. These aspects of specializations are ordinarily performed by a few individuals who are subsidized directly by the chief.

Egalitarian Forms and Hierarchical Forms

Because of the economic specialization in civilized societies, people are divided socially —rich or poor, powerful or weak, high or low prestige and status, and so on. But in primitive society, there is division into egalitarian and hierarchical types. The egalitarian society is furthest removed from civilized society in that it has no stratification of class—not even rank ordering—other than the family sex-age distinctions. The buffalo-hunting Indians of the North American Great Plains are examples of egalitarian tribes. The primitive hierarchical society does have a full-scale differentiation into ranked kinship statuses, but this system also differs from the socioeconomic class system of civilized society. The primitive hierarchy is based on heredity. The more closely one is related to the chief, the higher his status will be—and this kind of differentiation is based on rank or prestige, not on economic standing. Moreover, this differentiation is es-sentially primitive in the sense that primitive society is *familistic* in its social distinction. In contrast, socioeconomic classes in civilized society are not composed of relatives, nor is status based on analogies to kinship. The interrelated noble lineage found in some of the European aristocracy is an obvious parallel that can be drawn between rank in a civilized society and in a primitive one, for both are hereditary, familistic, and based on primogeniture. But even here there is a distinction, for in primitive hierarchy, heredity and kinship are the principles operating in the whole society—there is no lower class of peasants or workers, no middle class, and no class of technicians.

ECONOMY AND POLITY

The absence of socioeconomic classes in primitive society is related to the absence of private property. Individuals do own clothing, amulets, weapons, hunting dogs, horses, and so on, but these material goods are intensively private, to the degree that they may be given a legal term, *personalty*. This term calls attention to the individuation of it. But it is not private *property* in the Western economic sense of business or capital.

Examples of Personalty

A Plains Indian takes intense pride in his buffalo-hunting horse, and when he dies his favorite horse will be killed to accompany him on his spirit journey. Inasmuch as the horse is highly valued in the way the Indian acquires food, it would seem to be a good example of private property. But there are many instances of such personalty that are as "private" but that are in fact simply aspects of the division of labor. A hunter must have his own horse because he has to train it to respond exactly and precisely to his own signals. Another rider might confuse and "spoil" the animal, as any modern cowboy knows could happen to his favorite cutting horse. Similarly, a spear is normally made by a person for his own use to fit his own special abilities and needs. Neither the horse nor the spear could be monopolized, or used in an exploitative situation, to promote the "owner's" gain over another individual. In fact, if one hunter has a superior weapon, the extra game he acquires with it is simply *given* away—not sold for profit. Nor are there middlemen who move goods between producer and consumer at a profit to themselves.

Reciprocal Exchanges

The exchange of goods in primitive society is done in two ways, neither of which resembles commercial exchanges. The most widespread, day-to-day exchange activity is *direct reciprocity*—the giving of goods, services, and mutual aid on the basis of friendship, trust, obligations, and family relationships. In American society, friends and relatives exchange gifts on special occasions such as birthdays and holidays. This is an example of reciprocity, but it is sporadic and occasional and does not characterize the predominant American economic system of exchange. In primitive society, reciprocity is not only a matter of gift giving and mutual aid in a family but also a characteristic of the society's wider economy and even of exchange between different societies. The rules of reciprocity may be casual and unspecific about the return gift, as in the way brothers or lifelong friends might help one another without mention of a return favor. The rules may also be careful and specific, as when two strangers exchange needed goods or when the utility or desirability of the goods themselves rather than sentiments of love or generosity dominate. But this is still not a commercial exchange that yields a profit: it is still phrased and acted out as a social act, as an exchange of *gifts*.

Indirect reciprocity is another way of exchanging goods, and it can be illustrated by the game drive where different individuals collaborate in performing different tasks. Suppose a number of Nevada Indians meet to have a rabbit drive, in which the first task is to herd the animals into a box canyon. Old

people might be stationed at the flanks to frighten the rabbit deeper into the canyon by waving their arms and yelling. Young boys might be stationed at strategic points where quickness and alertness are required. Eventually everyone is involved in clubbing the rabbits when they have been herded into the confined area, but some experienced men might be able to kill more rabbits than others and therefore might be given more room to move about.

Although the Nevada Indians have an egalitarian society, in the case of the rabbit drive someone has to make decisions—who is to be stationed where, when to begin—and for this endeavor a so-called rabbit boss is appointed. Following the drive, the boss has another important function. All individuals will have participated in the drive in different ways, so the rabbits must be divided among them on some basis of need, such as family size, rather than on the basis of who killed the most. This indirect form of reciprocity is called *redistribution*, perhaps best stated in the phrase "*From* each according to his ability, *to* each according to his need," familiar in other contexts.

To some degree, all primitive societies use these two forms of reciprocity, with goods distributed according to the amount of collaborative effort involved in production. Egalitarian hunting and gathering and small-scale horticultural societies usually engage in direct reciprocal exchanges, with redistribution practiced only occasionally. But in hierarchical societies, redistribution is normal, highly structured, and an expected and usual activity of chiefs and subchiefs. These societies practice direct reciprocity between neighbors and families, as do most societies; still, the hierarchical chiefdoms require that the *extra* production of family specialization be given to the chiefs, who later redistribute these extra goods to the people who need them, usually on a ceremonial or festive occasion. The effect of this redistribution is to stimulate specialized production, with families tending to produce

Figure 10. The "big man" of Melanesia gains prestige by amassing goods and then distributing them in calculated generosity. The more wives he takes, for instance, the more gardeners he has; the larger the gardens, the more food can be produced to feed more pigs — pigs that can be used as payment of bridewealth for some young man in order to obligate him to further the big man's influence. Success in hunting and, in the past, in warfare also contributed to the renown of the big man and provided more food to distribute, as in the pig feast shown being prepared in the illustrations.

more of whatever they can produce best, or more easily, in order to receive more of the things they need but do not produce themselves.

Polity and Leadership

Perhaps less evident is the way redistribution helps to develop and increase the strength and size of the chiefdom. Not only does greater specialization lead to more effective production, it also strengthens the structure of the hierarchy itself. And the longer this structure lasts, the more indispensable it becomes, for the economy comes to depend on the polity—the structural hierarchy. Redistribution also strengthens the apparent personal power and charisma of the chief, "from whom all bounties flow." In time, the apparent greatness of the chief becomes an attribute of a true office that does not depend on personal abilities. This is the source of *authority*, which resides in the strength of the hierarchical structure itself, not in the person of the chief.

The very character of leadership as well as related matters of social control is an important issue that may be understood by noting the differences between egalitarian tribal society and those of chiefdoms. Egalitarian primitive societies do not have the formal legal and governmental structures that are found in complex societies. Although they have the same problems of decision making for concerted action and of settling quarrels between persons and groups, they have no formal and standardized means to solve them. They have problems of governing, but no governmental organization. The issue carries over to the basic question of controlling deviant behavior: primitive society has customary norms and family sanctions but has neither formal laws nor standard public punishments.

Primitive egalitarian and hierarchical societies differ from each other in the matter of leadership. The leader in an egalitarian society is a person of influence who achieves status according to his ability. He may thus be a leader in only one kind of endeavor, such as a game drive, whereas someone else may lead a different endeavor, such as a complicated ceremony or dance. In contrast, the chief of the hierarchical society is permanently established for all forms of authoritative leadership. Even when he does not actually lead any particular activity, he is the one who delegates authority to do so to someone else. The permanence of his post is ascribed by heredity and his role is inherent in his post. It is in fact the important part and very definition of the authoritative hierarchy that structures the society.

Still another advantage of centralized chiefdoms over decentralized egalitarian tribes is the ability to wage sustained and organized war. The egalitarian "tribe" does not have a cultural boundary that corresponds to its political or economic limits or to its ability to command concerted action, as in war. Usually a tribe consists of a series of local groups or segments who resemble one another culturally and linguistically more than they do some other groups in the vicinity. The similarity is often ascribed to common origin and therefore a generic kinship. Marriages among the segments tend to link the groups together in close contact with one another.

Pan-tribal *sodalities* (nonresidential common-purpose groups) usually include clans. The clan lineages (formed by real or imagined descent ties among dispersed local units or lineages) create, along with other cross-cutting sodalities, the main binding political tie. The total collectivity, the tribe, is therefore not a firm entity. An individual member of a clan can get help from a distant clan member, but members of two different clans might be antagonistic or help each other only when a common enemy is threatening. There seems to be a kind of principle of complementary opposition, as expressed by the old Arab proverb: "Me against my brother; me and my brother against our cousins; me, my brother, my cousins against our nonrelatives; me, my

Figure 11. When food is abundant, Bushmen participate in all-night celebrations that, in this society without a formal priesthood, take on magical and medical functions. During the dance, some men reach a deep trancelike state which they believe enables them to draw out the evil that inflicts a person and makes him fall ill.

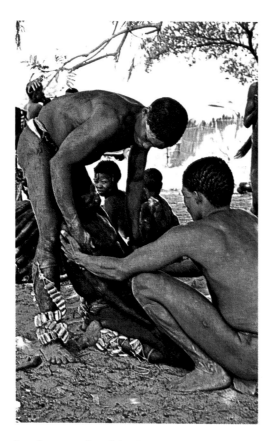

brother, cousins, friends against our enemies in the village; all of these and the whole village against the next village, . . ." and so on. In any event, different portions of a tribe, which is itself a cultural continuum, may fight or unite with one another. A chiefdom is much more of a unity more of the time. The chief's authority pyramid defines the society and holds it together.

One notable instance of this waxing and waning of the political entity occurred in New England during the early florescence of the American colonies. The Iroquoian confederacy formed not long after the arrival of Europeans and the beginning of the great dislocations of tribes. By 1649, the Iroquois mustered about a thousand warriors—an absolutely unprecedented army for primitive tribal societies, which normally make only hit-and-run raids. This army so destroyed the enemy Huron and later the Chippewa that even the modest communities of these two Indian tribes were fragmented into discrete family units to better practice a sort of hide-and-seek defense. Concurrently, the Iroquois began to form the central authority that is the core of the hierarchical society.

IDEOLOGY

Ideology encompasses the intellectual patterns of a society. Clearly, any individual in any culture may think differently from his fellowmen; ideology refers only to the characteristic forms of knowledge that a culture makes available to all its members. Ideology functions to explain the unknown. Whereas complex society depends on scientific explanation about the "why" of things, primitive society is pervasively supernaturalistic. Primitive man makes little use of naturalistic generalizations about the world, despite the fact that he may have a great deal of first-hand experience with the plants and animals in his environment. For instance, the Eskimo have always been considered the most technically ingenious of all primitive people. The hemispherical igloo, with its tunnel entrance and movable snow block door, can be adjusted to accommodate the precise amount of cold air that will be easily warmed by a seal oil lamp and that will rise and escape through a variable aperture in the ceiling. Vilhjalmur Stefansson, who spent many years among the Eskimo, was intrigued to discover that despite their experience with building igloos, they could not be persuaded to accept a general statement about it—not even the statement "heated air rises." The Eskimo consider that the general behavior of things is determined by gods and spirits, not by causal law.

In some societies, religious supernaturalism pervades as an explanatory device. In the minds of some peoples, all things in nature—wind, water, even sticks and stones—have spirits that "move" them, spirits that can thus be used to explain the properties and behavior of these things. Spirits are the fountainhead of creation: some are creator-gods and culture heroes who made human beings, as well as nature, and even gave them their habits, customs, and rules of behavior. In this respect such a society is essentially nonhistoric: the creators of it made everything and set it in motion, and it has merely maintained equilibrium ever since.

Many primitive societies are also totemistic, believing that the creation of their own group is interwoven with the creation of ancestral spirits that are different plant or animal forms, or *totems*. Much of the ritual as well as the ideology of these religions is related to totemism. The hierarchical chiefdoms, with their focus on genealogy, have understandably exaggerated one particular form of spirits—their ancestors—and have attempted to trace ancestry to the very founders of their whole societies. Much of their ritual and ceremony revolves around this genealogical interest and serves to reinforce the structure of this kind of society. Polynesian chiefs, for instance, claimed the ability to name their ancestors through fifty generations.

The function of religious practitioners differs in the two kinds of primitive societies. The shaman in egalitarian society is primarily a "medicine man" who can control spirits and divine the future; in chiefdoms a full-scale hierarchy of priests often exists as well as the shaman. Chiefdoms are normally theocratic, in that priests are usually an important part of the ruling group.

In recent times, the defeats, migrations, and general depressions endured by primitive people in many parts of the world have fostered the same kind of religiopolitical movements that led to Christianity in the Near East. For example, the zealous Ghost Dance religion arose in the late 1800s among western American Indians, who prophesied a return to the old ways and the return of the dead, who would bring the new millennium. The Handsome Lake religion of the eastern Iroquois and Chief Tecumseh's rebellion of midwestern Indians were essentially similar movements. The Cargo cults of Melanesia are messiah-based, supernatural movements to restore the "old ways" and to regain the good will of ancestors who are being "lured" into giving cargo to the white foreigners, cargo originally intended for the native Melanesians. But these messianic, nativistic, millennial movements are not primitive religions; they are instances of supernatural power occurring in the absence of real power, and they are being used for modern political and psychological purposes.

The functions of such movements change. Once Christianity had evolved from a rebellious cult into a church that was established as part of the Roman state, it changed its character, becoming instead a conservative political force, a keeper of the status quo. The Ghost Dance religion lost its momentum, but today the revival of some of its songs, dances, and ritual uses of peyote seems to serve an ethnic purpose—to provide an American *Indian* religion that "you practice because you are an Indian." It is not, however, a *tribal* religion. It is pan-Indian in its aims: Indian tribes that once fought one another now face a common destiny, and all hold a relatively common view of it—mostly despairing. The role of this nativistic supernaturalism, now institutionalized as the Native American Church, is to serve new social, political, and psychological needs for all the American Indians.

The changed character and functions of religion in modern society are so radical in comparison to primitive religion that it really should be given another name. In addition to the messianic origins of many modern religions there is an institutional separation from everyday individual behavior. True primitive supernaturalism is pervasive; it is inextricably woven into all ordinary behavior, not just into the minds of men on Sunday morning at a special place.

Peasant Societies

19

If you were to write of the anonymous man in history, it is likely that you would describe a peasant. Peasant societies have existed for at least 6,000 years, since they first emerged in the lowlands of ancient Mesopotamia. Along with merchants, peasants paid the taxes that maintained church and state through much of human history and provided the manpower for battles that served the glory of gods and monarchs as well. In the ancient civilizations of India and China, Greece and Rome, Mexico and Peru, they were the most numerous kind of citizen. From the Middle Ages to the nineteenth century they were the "average" Europeans. And even today, a very large number of the people of Latin America, the Middle East, North Africa, the Far East, and South Asia are peasants still.

Perhaps the most influential process of this century has been the change and ferment that has occurred as agrarian societies have struggled to industrialize and peasants have fought for a share of the benefits of twentieth-century technology. And yet, despite the fact that they represent one of the major forms that society has taken—indeed, they number in the millions—peasants today retain much of the anonymity that characterized them in the past. It is ironic that they historically have been overlooked, for as J. Chambers indicated, you would assume they would be studied if for no other reason than because there are so many of them.

The problem was that early anthropologists concentrated almost entirely on primitive cultures in remote regions of the earth, partly because anthropology developed as a science at a time when the establishment of colonies and the growth of empires were bringing Westerners into direct contact with the non-Western world. Many anthropologists came to believe that all human societies fell into either one of two categories: small-scale, kinship-based societies with relatively undeveloped technologies and simple economies, or high civilizations marked by occupational specialization, advanced technologies, and scientific knowledge.

These sharply distinguished models of society were and continue to be useful for the study of certain cultures and certain kinds of problems. But as anthropologists learned more about the life ways of settled agricul-

turalists in such areas as India and Latin America, they found that these two models had limited value. Gradually they came to realize that they were working in societies that could be viewed more usefully as members of a third structural type: traditional agrarian societies, where the whole society consists of partly urban and partly peasant segments.

THE NATURE OF PEASANT SOCIETY

Peasant societies were first defined as a type by Alfred Kroeber, who suggested that peasants are rural groups who live near market towns and form a segment of a larger population that also has urban centers or even metropolitan capitals. Peasants are not isolated, as are tribal groups, and they lack the tribe's political autonomy and self-sufficiency even though they do retain much of the same identity with and attachment to the land.

George Foster expanded on Kroeber's suggestion when he described peasant society as a "half-society"—one that is part of a larger unit (generally a nation) in both a horizontal and a vertical sense. The peasant part of this larger unit is related in a symbiotic way to the more complex part, which

is composed of the upper classes of the preindustrial center. Peasant groups and urban groups are therefore not disparate concepts. Instead, both are integral constituents of a particular type of sociocultural unit to which the preindustrial city is central. In fact, the existence of the peasant society depends on the presence of this type of urban unit, as Figure 3 indicates.

In 1956, in his *Peasant Society and Culture*, Robert Redfield further explored the relationship between the peasantry and the elite. He pointed out that in trying to understand the peasant way of life, the anthropologist must integrate his research with the traditional humanities, inasmuch as studies of history, literature, art, religion, and philosophy are all necessary for comprehending the culture of the elite. In particular, he felt that the study of peasant cultures must follow two important guidelines that are not relevant to the study of an isolated primitive band or tribe.

First, a peasant culture cannot exist without communication with the local urban community. Because intellectual and often religious and moral life in the peasant village is not self-contained, the anthropologist must know about the influence of the re-

Figure 2 (left). Dreams for a better life have at times united peasants, but the effectiveness of their coalition has often been short-lived where leadership from without was not provided. "With or Without Reason," from the *Disasters of War* by Francisco Goya. Figure 3 (below). The symbiotic relationship between the peasant and the elite, illustrating the lines of communication that bind the two together.

mote teachers, priests, and philosophers whose thinking affects and may be affected by the peasantry. Second, the study of a peasant village (the *little tradition* of the "unreflective many") invites study of the long history of its interaction with local centers of civilization (the *great tradition* of the "reflective few"). In these agrarian societies, differing cultural forms exist at different social levels. But there is a continual communication of ideas and borrowing of traits from the elite to the peasants, and vice versa, with complex modifications being made by the receiving segment so that the new items can be incorporated into its ongoing sociocultural system. Traits cannot be looked at in isolation but rather must be seen in their historic and social context. Certain basic values are expressed in differing forms, so that anthropologists may speak of the civilization as a whole and of the total society held together on the basis of at least a minimal degree of consensus.

Eric Wolf places greater emphasis on the existence of the state as the crucial factor in defining and characterizing peasant society. According to Wolf, the birth of the state was paralleled by the birth of a peasantry that occupied a social stratum separate from that of the holders of power. Peasant customs and institutions are, in part, a response to the forms of economic and political control exercised by the elite. Thus, administrative forms, modes of tax collection, and types of land tenure all influence the little tradition by asserting the limits within which the peasant must work, marry, market, and worship. In a feudal barony, for instance, or in a village controlled by conquerors, a group of peasants may be treated as a single entity in the legal system, so that each peasant is responsible for the deeds of all, and a failure by one individual to adhere to the strict order is punished by sanctions against all.

In this situation, peasants develop closed forms of social organization. The village be-

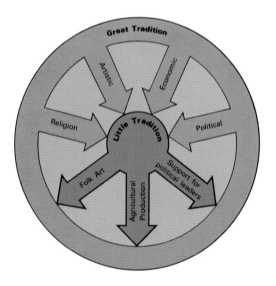

comes a tight corporation demanding the unquestioning loyalty of its members, and distrust and fear of the hostile outside world may be expressed in conflict or in rituals of opposition against other villages. Here, the elite sees the peasant as conservative, truculent, and xenophobic. In cases where the structure of the wider society allows for social and geographic mobility of peasants, the local peasant community is less likely to close its doors to outsiders. However, community relations may be characterized by distrust and competition, and the peasants may find it impossible to mobilize themselves effectively for cooperative endeavors.

ECONOMIC AND SOCIAL ORGANIZATION
Both peasants and farmers are found in high civilizations, and both are agriculturalists. In the anthropological usage, however, the terms have different meanings. *Peasants* live in societies that contain preindustrial urban centers, whereas *farmers* live in societies in which industrial production forms an important part of the national economy and where cities are industrial as well as com-

Figure 4 (below). An example of labor intensive agriculture. Over the centuries, an ingenious system of agricultural terraces has been painstakingly carved out of the steep Philippine hillsides. Figure 5 (right). "The Harvesters" by Bruegel. Romanticization of the peasants was one of the idylls of the upper classes. At the same time it reflected a nostalgia for the assumed closer unity of man and nature.

mercial centers. Peasants farm in order to support the members of their families; farmers farm for profit in a money market; and both relate in characteristic ways to the market system. The peasant's needs are defined by his culture, and he produces cash crops for the market largely because he is unable to meet his needs within the social unit to which he belongs. The money he receives is then used to buy goods and services necessary for his subsistence and the maintenance of his social status, rather than for the enlargement of his operations.

The farmer, in contrast, regards agriculture as a business operation. He sells crops not only to provide goods and services for the maintenance of his farm but also to liquidate his debts and to expand his business. The aim of the peasant is subsistence; the aim of the farmer is reinvestment.

Peasant Economy

The peasant's economic organization is firmly grounded in his local community. His daily decisions are made with reference to the traditional technology and scientific knowledge he shares with other villagers, a knowledge acquired through centuries of trial and error and reinforced by the sanctity of custom. His economic choices are directly related to the natural resources of land, water, weather, and sun, for he is tied closely to an ecological system that gives him very limited control over the natural world. His is a risky operation. Too much rain or too little, a strong wind, a late thaw or an early frost, an invasion of insects—any number of unpredictable events may mean failure. His conservatism and his resistance to new techniques derive from his fear that any change in procedure is likely to increase the risks of an already precarious enterprise. This conservatism, however, is relative to unchanging conditions in the overall society of which the peasantry is a component. Where development exposes peasants to innovations where there *is* clear demonstration of possible advantages, the risks involved in change are often accepted.

Peasant agriculture is *labor intensive* rather than *capital intensive*. In most cases the peasant's capital consists only of the land available to him for cultivation and pasture and as a source of raw materials (wood, fiber, or clay, for example); of his animals (sources of power); and of his "physical plant" (house, animal shelters, and tools). It can be made to yield a profit only by intensive use and intensive labor; there is nothing available to be set aside for speculation. However, additional workers beyond the members of the nuclear family are needed for certain tasks and at certain crucial times of the year, and characteristic forms of *labor exchange* can be found in many areas of the peasant world.

One of them is the *cooperative work party* in which relatives and neighbors participate in such activities as harvesting, mowing, and house building. Individuals who participate do so with the knowledge that they will later receive similar services in return. Participa-

tion is further rewarded in the drinking, feasting, and dancing that may be a part of the event. Looking at such an activity strictly in terms of economic goals, it can be seen that an individual may be acquiring inefficient labor at high cost, and indeed an important element in the modernizing of agriculture has been the substitution of wage labor for cooperative work. Still, inefficient as they may be, these cooperative activities also contribute to village integration and provide experience for the participants that lends added meaning to membership of the community.

In some regions, peasants form voluntary associations for a multitude of purposes. This *associational principle* played an ex-

tremely important role in the social organization of traditional societies in the Far East and in a few other areas, such as Scandinavia. Irrigation societies, money lending clubs, religious associations, leagues for the operation of grinding mills and communal saws—all have been institutions that peasants have organized to achieve particular goals.

The Dyadic Contract Model

In many areas of the world, peasant society is characterized by the lack rather than the presence of corporate structures. The members of a peasant community are instead bound to one another within the framework of what Foster, in his study of the Mexican

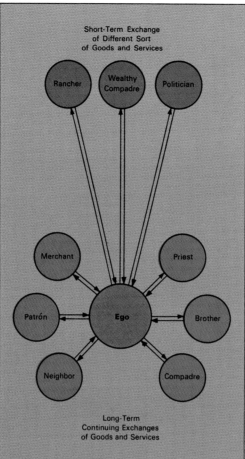

Short-Term Exchange
of Different Sort
of Goods and Services

Rancher

Wealthy
Compadre

Politician

Merchant

Priest

Patrón

Ego

Brother

Neighbor

Compadre

Long-Term
Continuing Exchanges
of Goods and Services

Figure 6. Dyadic (two-person) relationships may be horizontal, as between two peasants exchanging goods in the marketplace, or vertical, as in the relationship between a peasant and a moneylender. The more complicated vertical polyadic relationships, as when peasants work on plantations or in factories, involve an exchange of favors and good will that is exasperating to managers, who must avoid favoritism among the workers. An alternative is the horizontal polyad, where peasants join together to form voluntary associations.

peasant village of Tzintzuntzan, described as the *dyadic contract* (Figure 6). This contract is a social relationship formed between individuals for their mutual benefit. The relationship is structured to help integrate the society and provide social ties, but it is flexible enough to accommodate personal preferences and adapt to changing circumstances. In fact, this kind of informal structure, which binds together individuals rather than groups, forms the network for all important ties in the society, and each individual theoretically is tied by bonds of mutual obligations and expectations to many other people.

Because no individual could possibly fulfill all the roles that all possible ties would impose on him, he concentrates on establishing bonds with only a few other people. In practice, he establishes significant working relationships with certain individuals who in turn establish relationships with individuals *they* have selected. Each individual becomes the center of a private network that does not overlap with other networks. If A has a contractual relationship with B, he is in no way bound to B's partner C. Although he may well have another, separate contractual relationship with C, the three do not recog-

nize group bonds or group obligations. One way of looking at this is to view their relations with one another as a number of two-way streets: at the end of each street is one partner, completely separate from all others. In Tzintzuntzan society, an individual forms ties with persons of similar social and economic rank inside or outside the community, with people of greater power and influence, and also with supernatural beings such as Christ, the Virgin Mary, and the saints.

These relationships between partners are maintained and expressed through continuing exchanges of goods and services. The exchanges are *reciprocal*, and contributions and receipts are balanced out over a period of time, but the system can only continue to operate if an exact balance is *not* achieved. If goods and services are returned immediately, the relationship comes to an end. Peasants maintain these bonds by offering and receiving trays of fruit, bowls of cooked food, serenades, help at harvest, loans of money, services at funerals, and baptismal gowns for godchildren. Moreover, the goods and services are always welcomed without effusive thanks, inasmuch as peasants believe that such effusions would pay off the debt immediately in words and thereby negate the gift.

KINSHIP SYSTEMS

In peasant societies, the primary social unit —the family—is also the basic unit of economic production, and the roles of individuals as family members determine the part they are to play as producers and consumers. Ceremonies and rituals further reinforce the tight cohesion. The status and honor of each affects the fate of all, and, as a consequence, more control is probably exerted over the behavior of family members than city dwellers in the United States would find bearable. However, the invasion of modern technology even into backward areas of the world has tended to weaken the traditional rigidity of peasant family life. Today when the opportunity presents itself, young peasant boys may choose to be independent of the head of the household and may move to the city to seek employment.

In any case, peasant society is not characterized by the overwhelming importance of kinship that dominates the social organization of tribal societies. Among peasants, kinship provides only one means of social order and integration. It is true that in some peasant societies lineage organizations perform important economic and social functions, as in some areas of the Balkans and in traditional China, where the family property was owned and managed by the lineage as a corporation. But in most of the peasant world, the kinship principle is primarily expressed in family and marriage. In these societies, wider ties are usually formed on the basis of the dyadic contract or by an artificial or fictive form of kinship.

The Fictive *Compadrazgo* Bond

The fictive kinship bond can be seen most clearly in the *compadrazgo* system of Latin America, in which people who are not related by ties of blood voluntarily adopt a form of relationship connected with a religious ceremony. The *compadrazgo* system can exist in a variety of situations—ranging from marriage to the blessing of buildings to the crowning of fiesta queens—but it occurs primarily within the context of Catholic baptism. The basic element is the godparent relationship, the tie that is established in baptism between godparent and godchild. But more importantly, the rite creates a bond between the sponsors (that is, the godparents) and the parents, or, as they can also be viewed, between the two sets of co-parents or *compadres*.

Thereafter these two sets of parents will address each other formally and with the term *compadres*. They are expected to be respectful and helpful to each other and to come to each other's aid when called upon. Sometimes this fictive kinship relationship between *compadres* is used to bind the members of two families who belong to the same social and economic status. Sometimes it is used to establish a new formal relationship between one family of lower status and another of higher status, a relationship between patrons and clients.

The *compadre* device allows for great flexibility, inasmuch as the parents of a child about to be baptized can select the *compadre* with whom they are forming the new relationship. They can reinforce existing ties by selecting relatives or friends as *compadres*, or, by selecting strangers, they can extend their relationships to a wider sphere. The *compadrazgo* system is popular and widespread. Similar forms of fictive kinship can be found around the Mediterranean and in parts of India, Nepal, Tibet, and the Balkans, where it is a major device for smoothing the relations between Moslems and Christians.

The Egalitarian Village

So far as external appearance and material possessions are concerned, social life within a peasant village is normally *egalitarian*. Some individual families may be more powerful and enjoy greater prestige than others; they occupy different positions in the local hierarchical system. But, generally speaking, in outward behavior and in patterns of consumption, they must appear to remain equals, for conspicuous consumption arouses envy. Instead of acting as a spur to competition and individual achievement, it creates hostility, and sanctions have been developed to prevent it. A person who is visibly wealthier than his fellows is regarded as having snatched more than his fair share of the limited good things in life. He will be subject to malicious gossip; he may be ostracized; in some societies accusations of witchcraft may be leveled against him.

Other social mechanisms are also used regularly to siphon off excess wealth that might be acquired. A person who accumu-

lates more possessions than the average may be required to spend the excess on feasts or elaborate ceremonies. His ability to provide feasts or ceremonies contributes to his own personal prestige, and the dividing of excess food among the other members of the community has the added advantage of strengthening social cohesion instead of allowing it to be weakened by envy and resentment.

POLITICAL AND LEGAL INSTITUTIONS

In all societies peasants must deal with the officials, landlords, and merchants who are part of the local society and whose wealth, power, and prestige inevitably influence the lives of the peasants. The peasant's aim may be to bolster his economic position, to gain access to more land, or to obtain political protection or political favors from the powerful, and to do so he attempts to establish and maintain relations with those who can help him. The relationship between the peasant (the *client*) and the rich or powerful man whose help he desires (the *patron*) is mutual and individual, and it constitutes a form of dyadic contract. It benefits the client by providing him with services, and it benefits the patron by increasing his status in the society, for a man's political and economic power depends largely on his having followers, an advantage that he must pay for by providing financial support or political favors.

The patron-client relationship, which is to the advantage of both parties, has for thousands of years been more characteristic of village politics than any form of official government administration. At the same time, the relationship is not a simple one. A peasant may be afraid to approach a rich landowner, or the landowner may not wish to take up his time mingling with the peasantry. The solution is to rely on *middlemen*, or cultural brokers, to mediate between the client and his patron. This role is often played by members of the local gentry, by

middle-class residents in the community, or by members of the village community whose careers have brought them into closer contact with urban life.

These brokers also transmit, interpret, and introduce elements of the great tradition to the peasants. They may introduce some new fashion in clothing, some new household utensil, perhaps some improvement in agricultural methods. By doing so, they form a channel of communication between the two major sectors of the society and may be an important source of innovation for the peasant community as a whole.

Mediation not only is a necessary part of the relationship between the elite and the peasants but also plays an extremely important role in the interrelationships among the peasants themselves. In some societies peasants only trust or feel at ease with members of their own families. When obliged to deal with members of other family groups—to arrange marriages, perhaps, or to seek introductions to the clerk who records land transfers—the peasant is likely to employ the services of a go-between.

The go-between is particularly important in making marriage arrangements. Very often his task is to find a prospective bride for a young man who has reached the marrying age. The man and his family do not want to directly approach the potential bride's family for fear of being rebuffed. The approach is made by the go-between, who can test out the reactions of the bride's family without formally involving the prospective bridegroom and therefore sparing him and his family any possible humiliation. This diplomatic role, in many respects comparable to that of ambassadors, is so important that very often the go-between remains a friend of the bride and bridegroom for life and may even be the first person to whom they turn for advice and assistance.

The middleman can be equally important in what in Western society would be legal matters. One peasant may quarrel with another over, say, the right to farm a certain piece of land. He is reluctant to invoke formal legal processes and turns instead to a middleman to mediate the dispute. In this way the dispute can be settled diplomatically, without involving the peasant in the risk of paying the kind of penalty that might be enforced by a formal court of law.

In business matters the peasant is likely to feel insecure when dealing with the outside world, so, grown accustomed to relying on personal relationships and mediation, he is likely to use the same mechanism for his business affairs. He may set up a patron-client relationship with the person who buys his produce, or he may establish a middleman relationship or incorporate a merchant from the town in his fictive kinship system. As with the *compadrazgo* system, as well as the patron-client arrangement with his landlord, this kind of personalization provides benefits both for those who buy and for those who sell.

CULTURE FLOW AND COUNTERFLOW

When examining the relationship between the peasantry and the elite, it is natural to concentrate on the flow of goods and the flow of power. But the flow and counterflow between the culture of the great tradition and that of the little tradition are also important. Each group adapts any trait it borrows, so that it fits into the already existing

culture and serves the ends of the borrowers —which may be quite different from those of the givers. During the Middle Ages the divine and queenly figure of the Virgin Mary was transformed by peasants into the weeping and humble Mother; or the motifs on fine porcelain might be adapted to the simple brush and paint work of folk pottery making. Alternatively, some culture traits move the other way, as when some traditional folk song is adapted as the theme of a symphony, or when the Forest of Arden is included in formal dramas played self-consciously by aristocrats before a court audience.

In this exchange between peasant and elite, the advantage almost always lies with the latter, for the culture of the elite carries with it the prestige of the elite. The peasant is unequal to the task of emulation primarily because he lacks the resources to be able to copy faithfully. However great the natural talent of a peasant, he lacks the opportunity to develop the refined and eclectic techniques of the trained artist and artisan who often produce exclusively for the wealthy patron. And his efforts are further limited by his peers, who resent the efforts of a fellow peasant to rise above his station. Peasants are in more than one way fated to stay behind the times.

THE PAIN OF MODERNIZATION

Peasants do not live in seclusion, and one of the main themes of modern history has been the merging of traditional peasant societies into contemporary states. Indeed, one of the most important fields of current research in anthropology has been the study of the effect of modernization on the peasantry. In today's world, peasant societies are anachronisms and their eventual disappearance is inevitable.

Poverty and Revolution

From the peasant's point of view, the process of modernization has both advantages and disadvantages. Most peasant societies are wracked by poverty, oppression, disease, and relentless labor, and the peasants themselves tend to be eager for a different kind of life when they are made aware of its existence. In societies all over the world they have shown an increasing receptiveness to the benefits of modern technology. Yet the process is far from painless. Very frequently it is forced on the peasants by the rich and the powerful, who are anxious to make use of the land that for hundreds or thousands of years has provided the peasant with his livelihood. In England during the Tudor period and again in the eighteenth century, thousands of peasants were forced from the small plots they traditionally had worked when the rich landowners enclosed plots to facilitate extensive cultivation and the raising of sheep.

Today, by using new machinery, rich individuals or corporations can often farm land far more economically than the peasant, and the peasant is more likely than ever before to be forced off the land, just as millions of black workers were forced off cotton plantations in the southern United States by the invention of the automatic cotton picker. The history of communist countries has perhaps been even more instructive. In the first stages of communism the land might be promised to the peasants who farm it, but in practice such promises have rapidly been followed by forced collectivization in which small-scale peasant farmers are forced to work in huge collectives for very low wages. In Soviet Russia, peasants fared even worse when they resisted the process of collectivization.

How do the peasants themselves react to the threats that confront them? In the past, when peasants were dissatisfied, they often tried to by-pass local or regional authorities and communicate directly with the leader of the central government. Characteristically they saw the monarch as the "Good Father" who would set things right if only he knew

Figure 10. Political prisoners being deported to Siberia. In times of turmoil, the goals of peasants are usually utopian, but the outcomes have often been increased suffering and oppression, at least temporarily.

about the abuses they were suffering. Their demands were that the traditional order be reinstated, that traditional rights and privileges be returned. Even when peasants rose to the cause, took up hoes and flails as weapons, and marched into conflict, their intention was to restore what they saw as the normal or traditional order of things. The peasants looked backward to a view of a mythical golden age as their model of a utopia. Thus, in the past, peasant social movements have been one of two kinds. The first was the violent *Jacquerie*, a paroxysm of uncontrolled fury in which peasants destroyed and burned but that rarely if ever produced effective organization or action. The second was the millenarian or utopian movement, in which the peasants, led by a charismatic leader, awaited the New Kingdom, expecting it to come suddenly in the form of mass conversion, of a total change of heart in all men, so that the oppressors and the oppressed would finally be at peace together.

Still, peasants traditionally have been individualists. It was always difficult to organize them for community action; it was more difficult to organize them for revolution. During the early stages of the French Revolution the aristocrats, made fearful by scattered peasant uprisings, surrendered many of their traditional privileges, and the new revolutionary government continued the process of reform by giving most of the peasants possession of the land they had farmed. Once the peasants had become proprietors, their natural conservatism was so strongly reinforced that, when revolution broke out in Paris in 1848, they refused to join in. Their refusal convinced Karl Marx that peasants were basically reactionary and at best were a force that had to be neutralized by the revolutionary urban worker.

Much subsequent political experience has served to justify his belief. It was the factory workers and the disillusioned soldiers and sailors who provided the bulk of support for the Communist Revolution in 1917. Yet, in this century, peasants have also demonstrated that they are no longer willing to suffer passively or to be content with sending occasional humble delegations to ask favors of a king or president. In the squatter settlements of Peru, for instance, the residents have effectively organized themselves for community action, and pressure groups have been able to demand, and sometimes obtain, consideration from officials. Moreover, peasants have participated energetically in several revolutions. The leadership may have come from other groups in the society, but numbers of peasants in Mexico, China, Yugoslavia, and North Vietnam were active revolutionaries.

Trends Toward Urbanization

Perhaps the greatest change in peasant life and the greatest threat to traditional peasant society has come not from any form of political or direct economic action but as a result of the gradual and inevitable process of modernization and urbanization. One of the most striking and important consequences has been a world-wide movement of

Figure 11. The Colombian slum of Cartegena. When peasants migrate to urban centers, they become members of the proletariat and are forced to live in the substandard fringes of the cities. Figure 12 (right). An anachronism of the shift from country to city, where old ways thread through urban sectors in Turkey.

people from the country to the city. In some cases, peasants have left the countryside in order to meet the ever-growing demands for cash to buy goods and for taxes. In some cases, they have been driven from the country because their land was expropriated or because they were replaced by machines that could do the work more cheaply. But often peasants have moved to the cities voluntarily, seeking employment where wages are reputed to be higher and where they can hope to get hold of the material items made available by twentieth-century technology. Year after year, the call of the city attracts ever-increasing numbers of unskilled peasants. Many find the economic and social adjustment difficult or even impossible. Never achieving any degree of economic security, they form a depressed urban proletariat. And this problem has been greatly intensified by the explosive growth of population, most particularly in the undeveloped countries, that has left both cities and rural areas teeming with far more people than they can support.

Nevertheless, very large numbers of peasants have enjoyed happier fates in the cities. They have been able to find work, stabilize their life, adjust to urban cultural habits, and educate their children to take their places easily in the cities. As part of their adaptation to city life, these peasant emigrants from the country are obliged to adopt wholly new modes of existence. As a peasant member of the rural community, his place in the society was ascribed to him at birth and he had little chance to escape from it; in the city his status is the product of his achievement.

Family relations change, too, especially for women. In peasant societies the women rarely work for wages. They do their work, and very often it is hard physical labor, as the wife and mother of the household. It was in the cities that women were first offered paid employment, and the independence they acquired by earning their own wages has given them a far greater independence from their parents or, if married, from their husbands.

Even the membership of a household changes when a peasant moves to the city. In the country, people often lived in extended family households; parents or occasionally other relatives, no longer able to live by themselves, moved in with their child's family as a matter of course. Life in the city has almost destroyed this tradition, for most urban apartments and suburban houses are designed for nuclear families.

One of the first aims of peasant families who moved to the cities has been to acquire the material comforts made available by modern industry, and the desire for such goods has also diffused back into rural areas. A study of the Indian village Champiret near the city Hyderabad has shown that the villagers have acquired a taste for mass-produced clothing, shoes, sun-glasses, and razor blades and for motion pictures and modern medical care. But it is when the peasants actually move to cities to live that the change in their tastes and behavior is most marked. Daniel Lerner's study of six countries in the Middle East has shown that urban dwellers are more ambitious than villagers, more secular in their interests, eager to change their status, and more interested in political affairs above the local level. They are also less loyal to their traditional religions, to their families, and to their local communities.

In the industrially undeveloped countries of the world, a shift is taking place from peasant to farmer or agricultural laborer, from agricultural predominance to industry, from country to city. But it has not gone to completion. In countless villages, the outlines of peasant values and behavior patterns are still visible. Tradition may still be evident but nowhere is it intact, undisturbed by the massive forces of change. These forces emerge largely from domination by the more advanced industrial powers and from newly independent nations experimenting with political autonomy, social reorganization, attempts at rapid economic development through agricultural reform and industrialization, and, finally, the inexorable effects of population increase and urbanization. The result will have to be seen in the future as it unfolds.

Some imagine that the whole world will be transformed eventually into a kind of Los Angeles, and that inevitably the culture of the future will be like that of the United States. This may be true in part, but there is much room to doubt it. The process of industrialization for at present undeveloped countries is taking place under conditions very different from that of the earlier industrialization of Europe and the United States. There may be some advantages in "backwardness," inasmuch as countries uncommitted to obsolete industrial institutions and practices have the possibility of starting with the latest technology and going on from there. Nevertheless, they must industrialize in *competition* with the already advanced countries, which are themselves not standing still but industrializing the very process of research and development. They must compete while struggling, as yet ineffectively, with the growing burden of the population explosion. It is also unlikely that industrialization will necessarily mean total

Westernization. Japan is an important industrial power, but the social organization of its factories and businesses is Japanese in many respects, not Western.

In short, the ancient patterns of peasant life have been violently disrupted. The larger society in which peasants once had their place has been transformed to a dimension that is almost unrecognizable from what it was before. An alternative life mode—the urban, industrial, and agricultural complex —has received the "ex-peasant" in some parts of the world, but this newer mode, still evolving rapidly, has not yet proven its universal availability to the mass of peasants to whom the past no longer offers refuge.

Complex Societies

20

Edward Burnett Tylor, writing in 1871, perceived that ethnographic understanding is valuable to the "promoters of what is sound and reformers of what is faulty" in modern society. When cultured men worked to promote a doctrine of development, they would be continuing the progressive work of past ages—continuing it all the more vigorously because of their increased knowledge of the world. And "where barbaric hordes groped blindly," cultured men could move onward with clear perspective. Tylor thought that it was a harsh, even painful, task of ethnography to expose the crude aspects of culture that have, with the passing of time, been transformed into harmful superstition and to mark these aspects for destruction for the good of mankind. Because the "science of culture" aids progress and concurrently removes hindrances to it, Tylor considered it to be essentially a reformer's science.

The tradition has continued. In 1911, Franz Boas wrote *Anthropology and Modern Life*, in which he showed the importance of an anthropological understanding of human behavior for contemporary problems. And in modern times, this general point of view is represented by the controversy over the concept of a "culture of poverty." It is this awareness of the human condition that lies at the root of anthropological inquiry—that provides the motivation to alleviate the real and critical problems that unfold with time and change.

ANTHROPOLOGY AND SOCIAL ACTION

No other science regularly studied primitive peoples until long after anthropology had been established, and thus there has been no problem about the relation between anthropology and other disciplines. When anthropology examines modern society, however, it runs into conflict with numerous specialized and highly developed fields of scholarship already at work. What distinguishes the anthropological approach from those of sociology, political science, and social psychology? Both in theory and in method it is distinct.

The focus of anthropology is on culture, and this means that it begins with the supposition that all facets of behavior are interrelated. The anthropologist is interested in demonstrating the relation between all aspects of life, from the modes of economic production to the character of belief, the structure of the family, or the sexual practices of the community. This holistic point of view is a major differential of the anthropological approach. The anthropologist also

recognizes that man's behavior operates not merely in the external world of natural events, but within the context of his perceptions of these events. He is therefore concerned with the meanings of actions to the actors and the symbol system in which social behavior takes place.

These theoretical differences make for important methodological differences. The anthropologist focuses on a community or another definable sector of the society and seeks an understanding of the whole range of relevant behavior, obtaining information by such means as he can. Important to him are the techniques of participant observation and the use of informants, for he must come to understand the subjective meaning of social actions as well as their objective expression.

The anthropologist also studies modern societies from a broad comparative point of view. When one's study is limited to a few related societies at generally the same level of complexity, it is difficult to determine what in the situation is common to all men —what is a part of human nature—and what is determined culturally. Even the historian does not have as broad a base of comparison as does the anthropologist. These comparisons enable the anthropologist to avoid the pitfalls of a false human-nature approach and to discredit older biological and racial explanations of human difference. Thus, modern societies become to the anthropologists further examples of cultural and social forms, giving additional information on the possibilities and limitations of culture. At the same time, the comparative base makes it possible for him to separate those elements in man's behavior that are predetermined genetically from those elements that are a product of cultural tradition or social necessity.

THE STUDY OF THE COMMUNITY

The most important empirical research dealing with contemporary society is the study of the village, town, or local community. The study of American community life was initiated under Franklin Giddings as an investigation into the evolution of rural communities early in this century. Such studies came to be the special province of rural sociology. They were generally unsophisticated surveys, but some—for example, Lowry Nelson's study of Mormon communities—display an anthropological sophistication. Urban studies developed by the Chicago school, such as Harvey Zorbaugh's *Gold Coast and Slum*, are also forerunners of an anthropology of modern life, but Robert and Helen Lynd's investigation of "Middletown" —the very name conjures up the notion of the normative for American culture—had wide impact, both public and academic, because it succeeded in presenting a cultural view of ordinary modern middle-class tribalism in America. Although the Lynds were sociologists, the foreword to *Middletown* was written by Clark Wissler, an eminent anthropologist.

The Middletown study was carried out with anthropological and sociological field techniques. For over a year, the study team lived and worked in Middletown, relying heavily on participant observation to get as much knowledge of community activities as possible. They also consulted documentary material—newspapers, diaries, and minutes of organization meetings—and compiled statistics and developed a series of questionnaires to be used in interviews with people of various statuses in the community. They eventually put together a composite picture of the Middletown of 1890 in order to compare it with the Middletown of 1925 and to show how the latter was an outgrowth of the former. This time-depth approach provided an excellent means of assessing the effects of such cultural elements as the automobile, motion pictures, and radio on social relations.

Their research showed that the most important single thing in the life of Middletown was money. For the majority of men daily activities were concerned with acquir-

Figure 2 (left). The Amish of Pennsylvania are one people who have managed to maintain a separate identity as a subculture within American society. Figure 3 (below). Civic pride is manifest in the parades, fairs, and festivals that still take place in most American communities.

ing it, and jobs were valued for monetary gain rather than for any intrinsic satisfaction. Education was universally valued—not for the knowledge gained, but for its perceived efficacy as a way of enhancing earning power. The researchers found that the automobile and motion pictures were revolutionizing leisure patterns and were unraveling closely woven family ties. Tensions within the community were not faced, but ignored. These were the tensions inherent in conflicts between parents and children, in seasonal unemployment among the working class, in the incomplete understanding of problems facing the community, and in the lack of ability of institutions such as churches to fill the needs of identification and close personal contact of large numbers of people. People thus developed a set of patterned responses that regulated their behavior in ways that obviated the need to face problems. One aspect of this behavior was the attitude that the world cannot be perfect and what exists is as good as one can hope for. There was also a civic boosting (especially by the business class) that included ferocious pride of the high school basketball team, emphasis on the opportunities open for business expansion in Middletown, jovial camaraderie rather than substantial discussion of problems in businessmen's clubs, suppression of news deemed to be unfavorable to the town, and denigration of those who expressed concern about community problems (the "knockers"). Finally, the researchers found that patriotism (national boosting) had combined with intolerance of the minority groups and social action groups such as the IWW, and that there was tacit acceptance if not support of the Ku Klux Klan.

Middletown proved to be the first and most successful of a long line of anthropological studies of the American community. The most elaborate and extended of these were initiated by W. Lloyd Warner, who turned from field work among the Australian aborigines to field work in Massachu-

setts and, subsequently, to towns throughout the United States. His Yankee City study involved not only detailed interviews with a sample of the city's population but also analyses of its institutions. Several volumes have been published under the general title "The Yankee City Series." The first presented the general social framework: a sixfold class structure based on identification, social interaction, and social attributes. Other volumes were concerned with particular aspects of social life—for example, the factory and ethnic relations. Among works on American community life for which Warner was directly responsible were the analyses of a Southern city, of an urban black community, and of a Midwestern town. Warner summarized and generalized his class approach in *Social Class in America*, in which he defined social classes and the measures he developed for their determination. To Warner, social class is not economic class but refers instead to recognizable levels in a social hierarchy based on self-identification, divergent life styles, and particularly differential prestige.

Other anthropologists turned to an examination of the American community. Carl Withers focused on the life-cycle patterns as they varied according to social status groups in an Ozark rural community he called

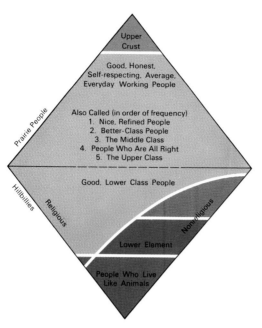

Upper
Crust

Good, Honest,
Self-respecting, Average,
Everyday Working People

Also Called (in order of frequency)
1. Nice, Refined People
2. Better-Class People
3. The Middle Class
4. People Who Are All Right
5. The Upper Class

Prairie People

Hillbillies

Religious

Nonreligious

Good, Lower Class People

Lower Element

People Who Live
Like Animals

Figure 4. Plainville social classes . . . as viewed by the good, honest, self-respecting, average everyday working people. When the good lowerclass people were asked what they thought, however, they classified the preceding group as "rich people who think they're better" but placed themselves above "lawbreakers and crooks" and "people who live like animals." The "lower element" in their turn called the good lowerclass people "all the church hypocrites who try to keep people from making a living and having a good time." All groups kept prairie people and hillbillies on the fringes. (After James West, *Plainville, U.S.A.* New York: Columbia University Press, 1945.)

Plainville, U.S.A.; Hortense Powdermaker directed her attention chiefly to the mode of life of different status groups in a Southern Negro community and to the distinction between the reality of that society and the image the white people had of it; Walter Goldschmidt demonstrated the social cleavage between farm labor and the "nuclear group" in a California town and analyzed the effect of industrialized agriculture on community life. Studies investigating rural life were initiated at the University of North Carolina, and from this program emerged an analysis of plantation life and of black society. Still other researchers analyzed the values and attitudes of people in an upper New York State town and the discontinuity between the public image and reality in community life. Governmental studies of rural community life were made by the Bureau of Agricultural Economics, and the Japanese Relocation Authority studied World War II internment camps.

The central theme in most of these community studies was the existence of a system of social differentiation—the separation of "classes" based on economic condition, length of residence, social prestige, political power, life style, or some combination of these. However, whereas Warner found six social classes in Yankee City, other students found diverse numbers ranging from two to seven, and Withers showed that people of different social standing see the "class structure" of Plainville quite differently. One might conclude that each community defines its own class system. But Goldschmidt has pointed out that although there are great differentials in social status related to income, occupation, and life style and that people at different levels in the social hier-

archy have different attitudes, values, and orientations to society, the important dynamic in American society is status mobility and status anxiety rather than fixity and class identification.

The description of social class (or the dynamics of status) is common to American community studies, but the more significant contribution of these studies has been to provide a rich ethnography of modern social life, not only in its formal aspects but in an informal and intensely personal manner. They err in their frequent tacit assumptions that the community represents the nation in microcosm, for modern America is a network of social communication in which the towns are merely at the terminals. But they give the necessary matrix in which American life—as analyzed by other social scientists—can be understood.

It was such considerations that led Arthur Vidich, Joseph Bensman, and Maurice Stein to state that the perpetuation of the community study relates to the fact that it has not totally absorbed the major techniques of the more "advanced" social sciences. Community studies have always worked to show the interrelationships among the various segments of community life. Consequently, the total picture has been neither neglected nor shattered into unrelated segments. Most community researchers are unwilling to forsake direct observation and direct reporting of the community life, and for this reason it is still possible to obtain coherent images of the community and social life that are unattainable by other methodologies.

In spite of the grandiose elaboration of research methodologies and abstract theories, the authors continue, it appears that the ear and the eye are still important instruments for gathering data, and that the brain is not always an inefficient mechanism for analyzing them. Because these instruments are still effective, sociologists of all methodological persuasions as well as laymen have come to rely on the community study as a source for their overall images of society. They use these studies for building their substantive theories of society, and they use them as reference points in doing other research and for their commentaries on the society at large.

PEASANTS IN THE MODERN WORLD

Anthropologists have also studied modern peasant communities in diverse regions of the world. Few had examined village life among farmers of literate, politically oriented societies until Robert Redfield studied Tepoztlan, Mexico. Redfield's close association with the Chicago sociologists and the then-important dichotomy between rural and urban in sociological theory must have influenced this choice. Village studies claimed increasing attention of anthropologists as well as sociologists, so that representative studies are now available for most countries where peasant farming is practiced. These studies generally concentrate on single local communities, carrying into the study of peasant life the methods and assumptions of tribal ethnography—reliance on informants rather than questionnaires or other instruments, the implicit assumption of cultural homogeneity, and the focus on customary usages rather than on behavioral diversity. They also tend to treat communities as isolates, focusing on the internal structure of community life rather than interrelationships with the broader society and assuming that the village is a microcosm of the whole. Redfield conceptualized the distinction between the little tradition (the peasant or local community) and the great tradition (the national or intellectualized level) and saw the interdependence between them. There have been no consistent efforts either to define the general characteristics of peasantry or to show the essential uniformities and diversities of peasant communities as they exist within a single country or culture area.

Nevertheless, like the study of the American community, the ethnography of peasant life has provided insights into the everyday

life of the people it describes. Anthropologists are now much better able to understand the behavior of the people of India, for instance, than when they had to rely on the formal accounts and histories of the caste system and the teachings of Indian scholars. They learn the role of caste and caste relationships in the daily life of the people; they see social mobility within castes and learn that whole castes can alter their status through time. The fixity inherent in the formal accounts gives way to the fluidity and dynamism that characterize real life in the villages.

THE STUDY OF INSTITUTIONS

The natural community of primitive people is spatially based, and the anthropologists examined the physically delimited town or village first. But communities in modern life are diverse, and most Americans live significant sectors of their lives within a community of fellow workers. For this reason, anthropologists have also contributed to the study of formal institutions.

Industrial Anthropology

The classic studies made at the Hawthorne plant of Western Electric under the aegis of Elton Mayo are an early example of research in industrial institutions. The essence of this work was to demonstrate that the status system and the structuring of social relationships were essential ingredients in

Figure 6. The funeral of Jawaharlal Nehru, a leader of India. In every society there is a complex of ritual modes for dealing with the fact of death, and even though his death was his own, society dictated the religious form of Nehru's funeral despite his wishes to the contrary.

work satisfactions and factory output. This initial source was the starting point for a body of literature analyzing various work situations and institutions, including the motion picture industry and the restaurant industry. Charles Harding has summarized the anthropological study of industrial enterprises, pointing out that the factory—or an entire industry—is a social system, that it operates on the assumption of communication among its component elements, that this involves not only the formal system but also the informal, and that the latter is a major consideration in the daily operations of the work routine.

Medical Anthropology

Another example of institutional ethnology is William Caudill's study of a psychiatric hospital, in which he analyzes the day-to-day personal relations of doctors, ward personnel, and patients, treating the hospital as a small society whose functions affect the behavior of its personnel in many subtle ways outside the awareness of the participants themselves. Caudill discovered that there is a hierarchical structure in the hospital, that direct communication between levels is faulty, that actions by persons are symbolic (communicative) expressions, that these actions or events are disregarded or

misunderstood, and that an anthropological investigation can interpret these events and lead to a restructuring of action beneficial to the institution and hence to the patients. Although the hospital may be viewed as a community, it is not sealed off from the society around it, and events in the homes of patients affect those in the hospital and vice versa. Moreover, the patterning of events in the hospital setting reflects generic American culture patterns, as a comparison with behavior in Japanese hospitals confirms.

Educational Anthropology

American schools have been subjected to anthropological investigation. Early studies emphasized the role of social class, pointing out that the teachers have largely been of upwardly mobile lower-middle-class origin, strongly attached to the values of thrift, industry, cleanliness, competitiveness, and the virtues of success. This setting gives the advantage to middle-class children and reinforces these values in the society at large. They appear not only in the formal structuring of class work and grades but also in the informal extracurricular activities and the interpersonal relations among the pupils. Jules Henry has shown the transmission of values and attitudes in the latent content of classroom discourse and their relationship to the domestic problems of the children: the reinforcement of materialistic over intellectual and moralistic values, the inculcation of attitudes of hostility and competitiveness in classroom recitation, and the continuity between the classroom events and problems in out-of-school relationships.

Behavioral Anthropology

Another means of contributing to the understanding of modern life through anthropological methods of research has been the more detailed examination of some particular facets of behavior of institutions, not as corporations but as patterned modes of action. Essentially anthropological in its approach, for instance, is David Sudnow's

Passing On: The Social Organization of Dying, which deals with the subjective side of the phenomenon of death among those habituated to and closely associated with it.

Sudnow's study is an analysis of the handling of dead bodies in hospitals, of the treatment of dying patients, of how family members are informed of a death, and of the effects of the occurrence of death on the social organization of the hospital.

A key concept is that of "social death," which is the point at which the behaviors and procedures appropriate to a dead person begin (for example, wrapping in a winding-sheet, mourning, funeral arrangements). Social death may begin before, during, or after biological death. For example, one doctor told a woman that her husband had little chance to pull through, whereupon she ceased visiting the hospital. The husband did improve, however, and after being released from the hospital returned home to find that his wife had disposed of his clothing and personal belongings, had made funeral arrangements, and was keeping company with another man. He left his home and began drinking, suffered a massive heart attack, and died.

The social organization is affected in a number of ways by the fact that death occurs. In the context of the hospital, dead bodies are considered "unclean," and hospital employees with high status have little to do with them except as required by the technology of their work. Tasks involving gross handling of the body, such as cleaning it and wrapping it in the winding-sheet, are carried out by attendants and orderlies, who are lower on the hospital status scale. Doctors, for instance, leave the room immediately after pronouncing a patient dead, and all the work of preparing the corpse and transporting it to the morgue must be done by other personnel. In performing autopsies, doctors touch the body only to the extent necessary to carry out their procedures, leaving any turning or other gross handling for the morgue attendant. Even some of the more unpleasant parts of the autopsy itself, such as sawing open the skull and removing the brain, are left to the attendant. This attendant always removes his bloody gown, which is "ritually unclean" and indicative of the closeness of his work with the dead, and dresses in clean clothing before going to the hospital cafeteria, thus distancing himself symbolically from his work. Young doctors, on the other hand, wear their bloody smocks to the cafeteria as a status symbol to show the closeness of their work to life preservation. Thus, the same object—a bloody smock—can have highly positive or highly negative value, depending on the context in which it occurs and the status of the person with whom it is associated.

Other studies, more in keeping with a major anthropological interest, have focused on kinship and kin relationships in modern society. The pioneer work in this area was initiated by Raymond Firth in 1956. Such studies have demonstrated the continuing importance of the network of kin ties in modern life, a point that contradicts assumptions long held by sociologists that instrumental social ties of work, politics, and neighborhood override and all but destroy the saliency of kindred. Moreover, they show that effective kinship systems are not adequately comprehended when seen merely through American legal and formal institutions as expressed in naming and in inheritance rules. In fact, Firth and J. Djamour assert that the structure of personal relationships in London's "South Borough" is matricentered in action and in sentiment. Studies of American kinship have also demonstrated the continuing importance of this most ancient of human institutions. In 1968, David Schneider analyzed the kinship system in the United States and found that, despite the flexibility of the American pattern of kinship and the variety of specific forms of kin terms, there are nevertheless certain basic consistencies. Chief among them is that the notion of "relative" has two valences. In its broader meaning, it includes

Figure 7 (left). The annual historical pageant at the Nikko shrine in Japan. The movable shrine in which the spirit is confined is derived from Chinese culture at an earlier period of syncretism. Western influence is also in evidence in this illustration. Japanese orientation to change combines ready acceptance of elements from other cultures with a strong sense of continuity of their own tradition. Figure 8 (right). The influence of Western technology is apparent even in this Bakuba village in the Belgian Congo.

all persons demonstrably related by blood and all those related through marriage; in the narrower sense, "real kin" or those related by blood are distinguished from "in-laws." This distinction he believes reflects a basic dichotomy in the symbolic meaning of kinship, for the former are seen by Americans to be a product of man in nature, fundamentally biological in character, whereas the latter are a product of social institutions, a matter of law and customs and not of nature. Such a division of relatives is not a universal occurrence in human societies of the world.

NATIONAL CHARACTERISTICS

Another approach to the anthropological study of modern life is the study of *national character*, the generalized delineation of the world view, the ethos, and the patterns of behavior characteristic of a culture or a social group. Historians and men of letters have often depicted the character of a people or an epoch—for example, Jacob Burckhardt on the Italian Renaissance, Edith Hamilton on classical Greece, and Alexis de Tocqueville on America. Anthropology has contributed to this literature and has sought to formulate both method and rationale for it. The anthropological investigation of national cultures was initiated during World War II to facilitate military decisions through better understanding of enemy cultures, and it has continued into the present period of hostilities.

Anthropological studies of national character may deal with any population sharing a culture—a nation, a region, or an ethnic group, such as eastern European Jews. In essence, this genre endeavors to relate the institutions characteristic of the society to the psychological characteristics of the individuals who make up that society. As practiced by anthropologists, it was influenced by Freudian thought, particularly that portion of Freudian theory that relates the formulation of adult personality to infantile experience. The theoretical basis was set forth in 1953 by Margaret Mead, who stated that national character investigations attempt to trace the way in which a given cultural behavior is represented in the intrapsychic structure of the individuals in the culture. These studies combine cultural theory and psychological theory—mainly learning theory, Gestalt psychology, Freudian psychology, and child development studies—into a new psychocultural theory in order to explain "how human beings embody the culture, learn it, and live it."

The first full-length anthropological national character study was Mead's *And Keep Your Powder Dry*, in which she related parental anxiety for status striving not only to the democracy of American institutions and the monetary basis of American social position, but to the fact that major sectors of the nation are second- and third-generation descendants of immigrants, anxious to deny their peasant origins and become a part of the mainstream of American life.

The most widely read and influential work of this kind is Ruth Benedict's *The Chrysanthemum and the Sword*, which endeavored to show the unity and consistency of Japanese culture and its continuity with the past. Although the book has been criticized for its overgeneralization and for its many specific errors, it affected American occupation policy during World War II and contributed indirectly to the reconstruction of that nation. It remains the best exemplar of the study of national character. The Columbia University research project in contemporary cultures gathered scholars from different disciplines to "study culture at a distance," that is, to investigate societies to which scholars did not have direct access. This involved not only the interviewing of immigrants, refugees, and prisoners of war but also the detailed analysis of current literature, humor, motion pictures, and other expressions of the current popular culture.

National character studies have been much criticized for their lack of methodological rigor and for their involvement with *psy-*

chodynamic theory. The study of national character cannot explain the origin of diverse forms of behavior. But it can discuss them in an ethnographic sense and discuss the internal dynamics of how generic cultural practices engender in infants certain attributes of character that are an essential part of the culture, even though the people themselves are not aware of them. The culturally established common modes of handling children, the nature of cultural rewards and punishments, and the affect patterns between parents and children are seen as the mediating—not the causative—forces in transmitting and preserving the national character.

ACCULTURATION STUDIES

With the massive technological change of the postwar world, the isolation and independence of tribal people are rapidly disap-

pearing, bringing forth the state of affairs that was anticipated by Franz Boas at the beginning of the century. The opportunity to investigate a culture unaffected by Western technology is available only to a privileged few. Yet the subtle and pervasive force of culture is such that the past retains its hold on people despite their being thrust into the middle of the industrial world. The processes by which tribal people adapt to the modern world is an important area of anthropological investigation.

Detailed studies of the process of adaptation of native cultures forcefully brought the phenomenon of acculturation to the attention of anthropology and led to the Social Science Research Council's request of a committee of anthropologists to examine the problems. Ultimately this committee published a memorandum outlining the appropriate area of investigation. Acculturation

Figure 9. A gathering of Buganda chiefs. Despite years of contact with outside cultural influences, including a period of colonial rule by the British, the traditional political structure of the Buganda has been preserved in broad outline. Figure 10 (right). All segments of a complex society form complementary images of one another and are profoundly influenced by their participation in the whole of that society.

was defined as comprehending those phenomena that ensue when groups of individuals having different cultures undergo continuous first-hand contact, with subsequent changes in the original cultural pattern of either or both groups.

Acculturation studies have come to constitute a large body of literature, but little systematic generalization on these data has been made. The fact is, very little generalization can be sustained. The most important of the recognized regularities in acculturation situations are the quick assimilation of certain kinds of material goods, the undermining of native systems of authority and social values, the recurrent tendency to develop millenarian or nativistic religious cults, and the greater resistance to change of religious beliefs and psychological sets or attitudes. But the most apparent generalization regarding the entry of tribal people into modern society is that no generalization is universally applicable. Some people, notably the Masai in Africa and most Pueblos in the American Southwest, show a high retention of native culture despite long and continuous contact with the West, whereas other people—for example, the Maori of New Zealand—readily adopt Western patterns of behavior.

Whether or not anthropologists may ultimately be able to generalize about the *process* of acculturation, they can state now that the past culture of a people influences present behavior in diverse and subtle ways, however much the people have accepted the external features of modern life. To take but a single example, Lloyd Fallers and his associates examined both the history and the current cultural practices in the ancient Kingdom of Buganda, which forms the nucleus of the modern Uganda nation. They show how the old patterns of authority, both in the household of the peasant and in the arena of politics, continue very much as they were when J. H. Speke first visited them in 1859. These cultural and social forces were a dominant feature of the negotiations when

Uganda was seeking its independence from British overrule in 1961 and 1962, and formed the basis for patterning national affairs afterward.

Nevertheless, change did take place in Buganda during the sixty years of the British Protectorate. For example, new groups of "modern" specialists emerged, taking places as civil servants in the government of the Buganda king, as teachers and ministers, and to a lesser extent as doctors and lawyers. In the economic sphere, there was an increasing dependence on cash crops, although most peasants remained subsistence farmers, and a fairly large force of wage laborers grew up in and around the capital although most of these people also cultivated small plots of land to provide themselves with at least part of their food. Before the Protectorate was established, the local village chiefs were the landowners, but in 1900 a reapportionment of land took place that allowed the more prosperous people to buy land. Today, the majority of people are tenants on landowners' property. The village chief is only one of several landowners—if indeed he owns land at all—and lacks much of his previous authority. On the national level, the king is now a constitutional monarch rather than a despotic ruler, and "modern" political parties and factions are beginning to emerge that represent the interests of and are led by educated specialists and professional people.

These changes have taken place without a breakdown in the traditional organization of Buganda society, although strains have been evident at certain points, as in the case of the decreasing authority of the village chief. There are several reasons why the traditional social structure was able to absorb the changes without being destroyed. First, the British ruled Buganda indirectly, through the king and his traditional governmental apparatus. The Buganda tended to think of themselves as a sovereign people in partnership with the British. Second, the traditional social structure maintained a relatively high degree of mobility. Peasants, for instance, were not tied to the land; if they did not like their chief they could move. This meant that the village chief had to be responsive to the needs and views of his people if he wanted to maintain his status and that the most successful chiefs—those who attracted many followers and were able to keep them happy—tended to move up in the political system. Moreover, the possibility of upward mobility in the political system for men of ability led to the victory within the government of progressive elements who wanted to make the most of the relationship with the British. Thus, the traditional structure remained flexible enough to adjust to contact with Western society. And third, the level of investment of European capital in Buganda, which is several hundred miles inland, was low compared to that in states along the coast of Africa, and there was not much incentive for people to abandon the traditional modes of subsistence agriculture and the social organization adapted to them in order to participate in a cash economy.

Such forces of cultural tradition, particularly the underlying presuppositions and attitudes laid down by the culture, must be

taken into consideration whenever any social planning is undertaken involving peoples of minority status or tribal groups within a modern nation.

UNITS OF COMPLEX SOCIETIES

The involvement with complex societies, with the relation between tribal groups and the modern nations throughout the world, raises the question of the proper unit of study. When a Margaret Mead generalizes about the culture of the United States, she usually has in mind middle-class white America; when a Ruth Benedict generalizes about Japan, she does not worry about the remnants of the ancient Ainu or, for that matter, the pariah Eta communities of the cities. Yet increasingly anthropologists are dealing with social systems that they call nations, which encompass a range of cultural and institutional diversity. Although it is appropriate for some purposes to obscure these differences, a full record of events must take them into account. Furthermore, the behavior of a dominant group may reflect the existence of a subordinate one—the patterns of white culture in the American Deep South in ante-bellum days is one example. Indeed, continuing into the present, this behavior can readily be shown to be dependent upon the existence of a large substratum of enslaved or impoverished and hence dependent labor force. We can no more understand the "aristocracy" of the South without taking into account the black population than we could consider black culture without recognizing the controls exerted by the white culture.

This internal diversity has been taken cognizance of in a variety of ways: by treating *ethnic groups* as separate cultures, by recog-

Figure 11. The king and queen of Tonga, a group of islands in the South Pacific. For the newly emerging states, a variety of symbols of the nation's unity and continuity are employed. Here, the models of Polynesian monarchy are fused with their surviving European counterparts.

nizing the existence of *subcultures*, or by the analytic framework of the *plural society*. Which unit will be utilized will depend partly on the particular situation and perhaps to a greater extent on the theoretical presuppositions of the investigator and the nature of his work. An American Indian tribe in Wisconsin and the self-conscious Italian group in Boston that was described by Herbert Gans may conveniently be thought of as ethnic enclaves, especially when the problems under investigation focus on their internal relationships rather than on their relationships to what Redfield, in another context, called the great tradition. When dealing with the interrelationships among groups and such matters as difficulty in communication raised by culturally diverse symbols, it is useful to think of separate subcultures.

The idea of plural society entered anthropological thought through a concern with the integration of culturally diverse groups into newly formulated modern nations. It was first expressed by J. S. Furnivall in his analysis of Netherlands India, where he found different cultural groups living side by side but retaining their individual identities within the colonial society. A plural society is defined as a political unit in which different groups have different systems of basic institutions. Any effort to deal with a modern nation, especially a "new nation," must take cognizance of this situation, for neither the institutions nor the attitudes of their populations are uniform. The continued existence of tribal loyalties, which is largely ceremonial in such old nations as England (although not merely ceremonial with respect to the Irish), is a dominant element in the politics of emerging nations. The war in Nigeria was a most dramatic exemplar of this universal circumstance.

The problem is not easily resolved within the framework of anthropological theory or by existing methods. The central concept of the field, *culture*, has enjoyed a wide variety of meanings, but certainly the element most essential to it is the idea of a shared system of symbolic meaning. In homogeneous societies, the meaning of events and of individual acts is consistent among normal adults. In older complex societies, there may be a symbiotic relationship among groups within the community of a kind that relevant meanings of one group are understood by others in situations where they interact. In others, there may be what one might call a dialectic variation, with shifts of meaning and emphasis, so that they may be referred to as subcultures. But in the new nations, for which the concept of plural society was developed, the commonality of the political unit was enforced either by the colonial power or by the newly formed elite, and the nation is a society only by force—or by courtesy.

Until a common bond of symbolic meanings has been forged and given institutional reinforcement, it is not reasonable to speak of such entities in terms of a commonality of culture. The leaders of many new nations have sensed this, for there have been con-

Figure 12. A great deal of controversy now
centers on the role of the father in families
deprived of adequate economic opportunities. The
questions seems to be: Is there a cultural
response to poverty that has its own inertia, or are
the behavioral characteristics of the urban poor
purely situational, lasting only as long as the
situation itself? Culture versus situation may be a
false dichotomy, however, for culture is a set of
adaptations to environmental conditions that are
themselves shaped by culture.

sistent efforts to give symbolic expression to the unity. Such modern names as Ghana and Mali, evoking ancient kingdoms of West Africa, are expressions of this intent. Until the relevance of such symbols is accepted by the rank and file of the nations, until the populace develops loyalties to the larger entity that are at least as persuasive as its loyalties to the subdivision, the nation will remain a synthetic entity held together by physical or economic force and will not be actually amenable to anthropological analysis but rather to that of political science or law.

URBAN ANTHROPOLOGY

Although the study of complex society has always been a part of anthropological consideration, the interest in the attendant problems waxes and wanes. Before World War I, when immigration and racial problems were important, Boas and others concerned themselves with the American scene. During the postwar period this interest slackened until it was revived by the problems of the Depression, which led to the study of the American community. .After World War II, anthropologists were increasingly concerned with matters relating to the "Third World," the uncommitted new nations, and their problems with local tribalism. With the reawakened concern in the United States over problems of ethnic minorities, urban deterioration, and popular discontent, there has been an increased interest among anthropologists in the study of the American scene. This new development is referred to as urban anthropology.

The descriptive and analytic literature in this field remains sparse. Gans' work on the Italian enclave and Elliott Liebow's study of single black males in a Washington neighborhood in 1967 are perhaps the best general descriptive works in recent years of aspects of urban life drawn in anthropological perspective. Through his studies in black family life, Liebow became acquainted with a group of men who "hung out" on a street corner, and this acquaintance led to friend-

ship and intimate knowledge of their lives. *Tally's Corner* is an attempt to present the view from the street corner to illuminate the forces that defeat men in the urban ghetto.

The key set of relationships for these men seems to revolve around economics. Because of a combination of racial discrimination, lack of educational opportunity, and other factors, the men are unable to earn enough money to support a family, and they know it. Only low-paying service jobs are available to them—running elevators, doing janitorial work—and only the physically able can handle the unskilled and semiskilled construction jobs, which are higher-paying but seasonal. They are all dead-end jobs, in either case. There is no hope that through hard work these men can or ever will be able to support a family, and they have no incentive either to work steadily or to stay with their families. Doing either means constant confrontation with their inability to be adequate providers. There is thus a strong tendency for both jobs and relations with women to be temporary. Liebow is, in effect, arguing that there is no distinctive culture of poverty. These men hold the same set of values as the overall society, including values on love, marriage, and family ties, but in the face of their inability to approach fulfillments of these values they flee to the street corner, where they can associate with other "failed" comrades and build up a set of relations that mask their deep-seated sense of failure.

One other set of works, however, bears on matters of public policy. This has been the work of Oscar Lewis, who has given us detailed descriptions, drawn from tape recordings of the informants' own statements, of life in ghetto areas of Mexico, Puerto Rico, and the United States. These best-selling works, which began with *Five Families*, attained greatest popularity with *La Vida*, the personal account of the Rios family, whose members reside in the slums of San Juan, Puerto Rico, and in New York. One of the characteristics of Puerto Rican migration to

New York is that it is not permanent. People can move back and forth between the island and the mainland for very little money, and often do so. Lewis presents both typical days and autobiographical material, focusing primarily on the women of the family. This emphasis on the female is an outcome of the fact that Lewis is studying families and households, and men are not permanent members in them. One woman will typically form unions with several men and will receive adequate support from none of them. If her "husband" is not an adequate provider, or if she is temporarily on her own, she will have to work in order to feed, clothe, and house herself and her children. Fernanda, who lives in a slum in San Juan, has had six husbands and has worked for most of her life as a house maid, a laundress, and a prostitute. When she was unable or unwilling to support and care for her children she sent them off to live with various relatives or ex-husbands.

In addition to the frequent shifts of residence and family membership, which are dislocating to a child, the children were frequently treated brutally. Fernanda and family elders would beat them with pots and pans, attempt to cut them with broken bottles, or burn them as punishment for various real or imagined infractions of family discipline. These acts were a tradition handed down from their own parents and grandparents to teach proper behavior and moral standards. One result of this upbringing is that children tend to leave home early and have highly ambivalent feelings about their parents. Soledad, Fernanda's eldest daughter, who lives in New York, feels that no one has ever loved her and that she must rely on no one except herself. She left home at fifteen to live with her stepfather's cousin. She has had six husbands and three children and has "adopted" one other child. She is twenty-five years old.

Lewis says that the behavior exhibited by these people may be shocking to the middle-class American, but that given the condi-

Figure 13. The nuclear family as we know it is not an irreducible unit. Where economic insecurity weakens the ability of males to maintain a stable family, the burden of nurturence and constancy is often capably borne by the mother.

tions in which these people must live it is surprising that they are able to cope with their problems as well as they have.

The controversy over these studies does not involve the quality or importance of Lewis' research or his methods. The use of edited tapes to record the responses to lengthy interviews of the members of a family, which gives a personal insight into the history of that family and the dynamics of the interpersonal relationships of its members, is universally recognized as a major contribution to humanistic understanding, as well as being a methodological innovation of the first order. The issue Lewis raises is in the theoretical implications he draws from these data, particularly in his concept of the "culture of poverty." This Lewis has defined as a specific model of a subculture of Western society with its own structure and rationale, a way of life passed along family lines from one generation to another. The culture of poverty not only is related to deprivation or disorganization (which might signify the absence of something) but is a culture that, in the traditional anthropological sense, provides individuals with a design for living, with an existing set of solutions to human problems, and thus serves an important adaptive function. This life way transcends national boundaries as well as regional and rural-urban boundaries within nations. Wherever the culture of poverty appears, Lewis argues, the people within it show marked similarity in family structure, interpersonal relations, spending habits, and value systems and in their orientation in time.

This concept has entered the arena of politics and social policy. The idea lies behind the analysis and proposals set forth in a 1965 government publication generally referred to as the Moynihan report. Implicit in the concept of a culture of poverty is the idea that slum dwellers develop a culture of their own and that the problem of the poor is therefore not essentially one of a condition derived from the social system but that it is,

like the culture of a primitive tribe, merely the continuation of patterns of behavior laid down in childhood.

The issue has been joined by Charles Valentine in his book *Culture and Poverty* and debated in the journal *Current Anthropology*. As indicated in the chapter "Case Study: In a Complex Society," which represents the other aspect of this controversy, Valentine argues, first, that the substantive basis for delineating and establishing the concept of a culture of poverty has not been made by Lewis and, second, that it obscures the nature of needed social reform, for it implicitly places the blame for the conditions of the poor upon the poor themselves rather than on the conditions that create poverty. The first point is clearly the case, and, as Valentine says, much of the material in Lewis' voluminous record belies his own conceptual model.

Yet the failure to prove, or even to demonstrate, the existence of a culture of poverty does not undermine the potential validity of such a view. If there are certain underlying features that characterize poor people in Western society—and that what an older literature might call pauperization occurs in the circumstances of child rearing—then the second objection is not entirely correct. Any culture is the product of the ecological conditions in which it exists, and certainly the impoverished sectors of modern society operate in the ecological context of a dominant society. Thus, reform, when properly conceived, rests on altering those ecological relationships—that is, changing the institutional setting within which the slum culture develops. Treated in this way, the culture of poverty concept helps us to understand that the removal of slum conditions will not automatically and immediately alter the patterned behavior to which the living generations have been adapted any more than the introduction of Western technologies automatically eliminates underlying cultural proclivities among tribal peoples. A recognition of cultural consistency in slum and ghetto

Figure 14. The Ashanti Golden Stool, sacred symbol of nationhood, became the focus of violent uprising against British rule until an anthropologist pointed out to the British administration its importance to these African people. Figure 15 (right). Cultural understanding implies acceptance of major cultural differences. The contrary has been the rule in much of human history, where men took their differences as banners in wars of cultural dominance. The Crusades of Europe perhaps epitomize this struggle for dominance.

can serve as an excuse for failing to eradicate the conditions of poverty but it need not do so. On the other hand, it makes for the recognition that institutional reforms are not in themselves adequate to effect the cultural changes that middle-class America would like to see among its underprivileged sector.

Perhaps the importance of this controversy lies outside the issue itself. Tylor visualized anthropology as "a reformer's science," believing that an understanding of culture enabled man to change the habits and behavior in keeping with the dictates of modern knowledge. The intervening century has not borne out Tylor's view, for anthropologists have not been drawn heavily into policy matters, in comparison with such sister disciplines as economics, political science, and sociology. When reform has been instituted, it has been through a changed intellectual attitude—through writing—rather than through action, politics, or public controversy. The anthropologist's concern with urban life, and particularly the debate over the cultural force of slum life, may serve to bring anthropological understandings into the realm of public decision making. If it succeeds in doing so, if it brings the cultural viewpoint into policy-making decisions, it will have had an importance beyond the controversy engendered by the culture of poverty concept.

APPLYING CULTURAL UNDERSTANDING

Every discipline has a potential application to daily life. In anthropology this potential was recognized by Tylor and is currently expressed as *applied anthropology*. The Society for Applied Anthropology was formed in 1941 and publishes the journal *Human Organization*. It recognizes that changes in the human situation, either as a result of "natural" causes or deliberate efforts, are potentially disruptive to the fabric of social life and that an understanding of the cultural context and ideological meaning of behavior is a necessary precondition for the minimization of such disruption.

Agents of social change have long demonstrated an intuitive awareness of this need. George Foster, in his *Traditional Cultures and the Impact of Technological Change*, mentions that Pope Gregory in the sixth century advised the abbot Mellitius to utilize the heathen places of worship in England and adapt them to the purposes of Christianity in order to take advantage of local cultural patterns rather than confront them. Peter Duignan pointed out that the Jesuits doing missionary work in Africa in the sixteenth and seventeenth centuries also applied a knowledge of local culture in the furtherance of their efforts to change religious belief.

In recent years, the recognition that the changes brought to native cultures by Western domination led governmental officials to turn to anthropologists for advice and help on both sides of the Atlantic. In Britain, the importance of an understanding of native customs was expressed dramatically when the anthropologist R. S. Rattray brought peace to Ashantiland by virtue of his understanding of what the Golden Stool actually meant as a sacred symbol of nationhood. It became a part of policy in most European

metropolitan countries to seek an understanding of native cultures in the formulation of administrative policies, and John Collier, the Commissioner of Indian Affairs during the Roosevelt administration, sought similar aid in the United States with respect to the indigenous Americans. Applied anthropology was not limited to the administration of native people, however, but was also directed at the analysis of institutions of American society. The studies of behavior of workers in factories and other business establishments, of schools, and of hospitals had as one aim the application of cultural understanding for the improvement of organization, production, and work satisfaction.

Applied anthropology, then, may be defined as the effort to understand the total social and psychological relationships in-

Figure 16. The building of modern apartments to house low-income families such as these high-rise dwellings in Egypt may disrupt patterns of kinship, coresidence, and community. Figure 17 (right). The contrasts involved in rapid economic development are illustrated here, as a sheepherder inspects an office building under construction in Shiraz, Iran.

volved in a given institutional form, and to take cognizance of these when endeavoring to change existing patterns of behavior for economic or administrative purposes. Anthropologists have learned that no element of culture stands alone and isolated from attitudes, sentiments, and the meaning of social relationships. Thus, any alteration in one aspect of behavior brings in its wake a host of potentially disruptive consequences. When the native perceives these consequences, even though the agents of change do not, he will be resistant to innovations for what appear to be irrational motives. When he does not perceive these consequences, they nevertheless will be disruptive and may do greater harm than the benefit that was intended.

This process may be illustrated with the case of steel axes introduced by missionaries into the native Australian tribe called Yir Yoront, people of a "Paleolithic" culture who fully appreciated the efficacy of steel. But the stone axes were a deep and integral part of the social and ritual life of the Yir Yoront. Although they were used by women and children, they were the possession of older men, the only ones who knew how to make the handles and haft the stone heads and who had the right to trade for these heads with the people to the south who supplied them with the stone. The stone axes therefore related to male-elder authority roles, to trade relationships, to totemic beliefs and ceremonies, to self-definition of males, and to a host of other considerations of a subtle kind. By the quixotic introduction of steel axes readily made available to everyone on a chance basis, all these meanings were undermined so that the very fabric of social life was torn apart by what was intended to have been a gracious act of the donors.

The record is replete with instances in which "better" techniques are rejected because they run counter to established patterns. High-yield hybrid corn is rejected here and there because it does not form good tortillas or it does not taste right. In some places hospitals are rejected because only the most severe cases are taken in and it is observed that the patients "always die." Elsewhere hospitals are rejected because hospital programs do not permit native customary usages to be continued or because they isolate the patient from the companionship of friends.

These conditions can be overcome by taking cognizance of the important cultural elements. Hospitalization was accepted in rural

Greece, where informality, unrestricted visiting, and even picnicking with relatives in the hospital room is permitted and where, according to Ernestine Friedl, the treatment of illness in the hospital shows a marked similarity to treatment at home.

In Ecuador, hospitalization of expectant mothers was hampered by several cultural factors but nevertheless was increasingly followed despite this fact because the people had observed the differential mortality rate among the children born in hospitals from those delivered in the home. They had to give up two cherished beliefs—that they must remain indoors for a period of forty days (five was the hospital limit) and that the placenta must be buried under the hearth. But the hospital did permit those cherished beliefs that did not interfere with hospital routine, such as a tabu against bathing or cutting the fingernails.

Ideally, before initiating a change, a study of the factors entering into consideration should be made, and such studies frequently offer surprising insights. Isabelle Kelly reports that before a housing program was initiated in El Cuijo, near Torreón, Mexico, a survey was conducted to determine practical ideals in housing as viewed by the prospective beneficiaries of the program. One of the many relevant findings was that water taps were preferred in the patio rather than inside the house. Why? Because water taps, in a country of inadequate technical know-how, inevitably leak and a leaky tap indoors can create damage and discomfort, whereas an outside tap serves to water the plants.

These examples demonstrate the basic thesis of applied anthropology—that each element in a culture has many ramifications and that even a beneficial innovation may have far-reaching and deleterious consequences for the people, leading to either rejection or disruption. The applied anthropologist does not object to change per se but believes that effective change must be made only after taking all consequences into account, so that it is introduced in a way that minimizes the disruptive effect inherent in the innovation. In order to make changes, it is therefore essential that as complete a knowledge of the cultural context as possible be examined prior to its initiation. Beyond this, the applied anthropologist can formulate no generalizations.

Each culture is unique. What in one area may be contrary to local custom will be readily acceptable in another; some cultures and some situations are highly resistant to change, and others are readily adaptive. But a human society engaged in humanitarian programs for the betterment of mankind must take into account the values, the beliefs, and the meanings of the people themselves. The first step in this direction is to appreciate the force of culture in giving meaning to the lives of its participants. The second is to recognize that an individual's own culture, however desirable and "natural" it may be for him, is but one of many and is not the aim of all people. When these steps have been taken, it then follows that a program of "betterment" must parallel the value orientations of those whose lives are to be improved. This is the essential lesson of all anthropology.

Methods in Cultural Anthropology

21

Culture is the one fundamental concept that underlies the anthropological approach to the study of mankind. From their definition of culture, anthropologists derive the scope of their study and its principal methods.

Culture is all that an individual learns to do as a member of his society through the knowledge, the skills, the mutual expectations, and the common understandings that he shares with others of his group and that his children learn. What every individual can learn and does learn is what distinguishes the human species from the rest of the animal world. Only man has sophisticated language, uses symbols, and makes specialized tools. Among the world's creatures, only man can transmit to his children great quantities of information and accumulated experience. There are obvious biological resemblances between mankind and other species, especially between man and ape, but the study of evolution shows that man's possession of culture has also been an important force in human biological evolution. When men first developed language and other rudiments of culture, their whole species embarked on a course of continual development, both physical and social, that has never ceased.

Human culture, the general characteristic of the species, is enacted in a great variety of particular cultures, the special ways of life that different groups of people follow. A particular culture, in distinction to "culture" in general, is made up of certain ways of acting, thinking, feeling, and communicating that are used by the people of a group and that distinguish them from other groups. Those who share in a culture use the same language, honor the same values, acknowledge similar ideas, and maintain similar social institutions.

Culture is what all men have in common; their respective *cultures* differ, however, and one culture can be vastly unlike another. It is therefore the central task of cultural anthropology to study how all men are alike and also how their groups and separate cultures differ. All people must learn to *cope* with certain basic problems. Some are imposed by biology, such as the problems of

birth, growth, and death; others arise from social relations, such as those of cooperation and conflict. Each group has produced its own set of answers through the process of adaptation. The cultural anthropologist examines the processes of cultural change to learn in what ways all men follow the same modes of cultural adaptation and in what ways they use different processes of adaptation.

This definition of generic human culture and of distinctive, separate cultures also outlines the scope of anthropological studies. The cultural anthropologist studies all of human social behavior from the beginning of man's development to the great issues of the present time. All cultures are taken into account, including those carried on by remote tribal societies as well as by complex civilized nations. The anthropologist examines every type of social behavior, rational and seemingly irrational, intended and unplanned. He takes note of all aspects of a culture—the technical means of dealing with the natural environment, the patterns of relating to other people, the special experiences of religion and art. He considers inter-

connections among the various aspects of a culture, such as the relations between religion and society or between family and economy. The cultural anthropologist gives careful attention to daily life as well as to high achievement, to the ordinary villager as well as to the elite leader.

From this scope of study and definition of culture, five of the basic methods and concepts of cultural anthropology follow. The cultural anthropologist practices cultural relativism; he takes a holistic view of the subjects he studies; he characteristically gathers his data in field work; he makes comparative analyses among the world's cultures and societies; and his theoretical work usually develops from his own close observations of actual behavior.

CULTURAL RELATIVISM

Every modern anthropologist agrees that in order to understand the behavior of a group of people, he must first refer their behavior to the standards and values held by the people themselves. If the values of his own culture differ from those of the group being studied, he will not see the behavior in ques-

Figure 2 (left). Diego Rivera and other artists of Mexico have attempted to interpret the Mexican cultural tradition in their work. Members of all cultures form complex conceptions of their own way of life, particularly when they see this life in contrast to that of other societies. Their cultural self-image is a blend of subjectivity and objectivity, under pressures of ethnocentrism, revindication, and national self-affirmation. From self-portrayal to the extreme assertion of a national myth brings us to Figure 3 — the mass rally at Nuremburg.

tion in one of its most important contexts— the context of how that behavior meets *their* needs and interests.

This anthropological perspective has to do with *understanding*, an intellectual exercise, not with *judging*, a moral exercise. To take one of the most extreme examples with which history has presented us, if for whatever reason the anthropologist is to understand why the Nazis behaved as they did during World War II, he must view their behavior in the context of Nazi goals, values, beliefs, and standards. Such cultural relativism does not imply any approving judgment of what happened, but rather that the approach is more likely to show why it happened in the first place. In his study of other cultures, the anthropologist may strongly desire to assert universal moral standards, as all religious and other kinds of ethical systems do, such as the idea that the killing of innocent people is always wrong. But to fully understand the behavior of this or any other group, he must first exercise the intellectual detachment inherent in cultural relativism.

The insistence that the behavior of a group be seen relative to the group's culture does not mean that this is the *only* way to look at that behavior, however. When the anthropologist wants to compare the activities in different cultures in order to gain an understanding of human behavior in general, he may find it useful to look at the results the behavior produces instead of, or in addition to, what it means to the people themselves. For example, a number of East African groups knock out the incisor teeth of their young men when they reach puberty. In some groups, this is taken as a test of the youth's bravery; in others as a cosmetic operation; and in still others as a way of ensuring that the boys will not be vicious when they are adults. Apart from the meanings that teeth removal has in each culture, the anthropologist can look at the social consequences of the operation even if the various groups are themselves quite una-

ware of them. Thus, he can try to find out whether the boys in all the different groups come to feel a greater unity with one another after having gone through the dentistry together, or whether their identity as men is reinforced by this practice, from which girls are excluded.

The anthropologist can practice cultural relativism without excluding other perspectives, especially because the nonrelative perspectives give him understandings that relativism cannot. Even in studying a single group, it is often useful to look at the behavior of that group in a cross-cultural way in order to better assess, say, the economic and human costs of following the practices found in that group as compared to the practices that achieve similar ends in other societies. When he studies a group holistically, much of the anthropologist's time will be spent looking at the behavior he finds in it in terms of its own culture, but a holistic view does not preclude *also* taking a nonrelative perspective.

THE HOLISTIC VIEW
In taking a holistic view, the cultural anthropologist is free to examine any kind of human behavior that is relevant to the problem he is investigating, for he does not feel constrained to work only on particular subjects. He may look into economic behavior, religious ceremonies, technical procedures, or whatever fields of action may shed light on the problems and people he is studying. An anthropologist who studies economic development in an Indian village, for instance, finds that he must consider the importance of marriage ceremonies and the methods of settling disputes as well as the adoption of improved agricultural techniques. Or a cultural anthropologist who traces the growth of an ancient civilization includes in his studies the settlement patterns of the people as well as their pottery styles, their trade routes as well as their subsistence economy. A single book cannot fully show all of the culture of even a small and simple society,

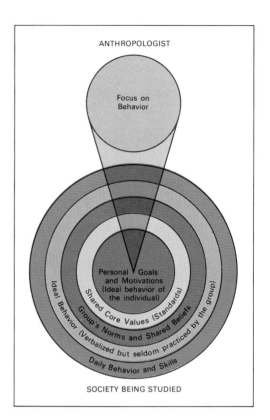

ANTHROPOLOGIST

Focus on Behavior

Personal Goals and Motivations (Ideal behavior of the individual)

Shared Core Values (Standards)

Group's Norms and Shared Beliefs

Ideal Behavior (Verbalized but seldom practiced by the group)

Daily Behavior and Skills

SOCIETY BEING STUDIED

but the combined efforts of cultural anthropologists have by now sketched the main facets of many cultures and have depicted the salient characteristics of human culture.

IMPORTANCE OF FIELD WORK

Field work is a central feature of anthropological method. The cultural anthropologist typically records his scientific evidence by direct observation. He also searches out whatever data are relevant to his research, whether these data be census records, travelers' accounts, agricultural statistics, or laboratory findings. But he relies primarily on anthropological reports of real behavior made from direct observation. The cultural anthropologist who studies the ways of living people goes to live among them and learns about their culture and society through watching what goes on, talking with the people, participating in some of their activities. His is an observational rather than an experimental method; the data are recorded in the context of social reality rather than from the more controllable situation of the laboratory. Each culture is, in a sense, an experiment set up in the course of human development, and the anthropologist derives his theoretical propositions from studying the results of these natural experiments.

An important consequence of conducting field study is that the cultural anthropologist learns the inside view of a culture. He discovers how the people he studies see their world—what things are important to them and the rewards and goals they actually seek. This inner perspective is usually quite different from the outer face of a people as seen by an observer from a different culture. Thus, anthropological analyses can take into account internal forces within a society as well as influences from the outside.

In doing field work, the anthropologist looks for the patterns of behavior that are meaningful to the people rather than at bits of their behavior that may be convenient

units for measurement. He describes the regular sequences of their behavior, noting the explicit patterns the people are well aware of as well as the implicit patterns they are not aware of. He distinguishes what people say they ideally ought to do from what they say they really do and from what observations reveal that they actually do. He studies how patterns of action are altered in different contexts or by individuals of various status positions. Cultural anthropologists like to have statistical data, for their primary interest is in learning about the regularities, discontinuities, and interrelations in the behavior of a group of people. The anthropologist is likely to use questionnaires and other devices for gathering statistical information only after he knows a good deal about the culture and the people he is studying, so that he has some idea of what is worth measuring rather than what items of behavior can conveniently be measured.

COMPARATIVE ANALYSIS

The method of making comparative analyses comes into every stage of an anthropologist's work. Consider a field worker who is studying social organization in a village in India. He begins by finding out how the villagers sort themselves into different groups—in India, these are primarily caste groups. One of his first tasks of comparison is to see how these caste groups differ and how they are alike. Once the field worker

Figure 5 (left). The anthropologist begins with the observation of behavior and proceeds by analysis and inference to the inner patterns underlying behavior. Figure 6 (right). Anthropologist Ted Schwartz employs a projective test to learn about patterns of perception and cognition through the responses given by Manus people to ambiguous stimuli — in this instance, the Rorschach inkblots.

understands the similarities as well as the differences among the caste groups in one village and their systematic relations with each other, he can proceed to compare that village with other villages in the vicinity. From this comparison, he can begin to classify types of villages and typical processes of village relations.

When such studies are made in the principal regions of India, the anthropologist can compare social organization in all regions and can then outline the social features that are shared by most of the people of India. Caste stratification is one such feature, and this, in turn, can be compared with social stratification in other parts of the world, as in Japan, Africa, and the United States. From this broad comparison, the anthropologist can go on to consider social stratification as a general attribute of human society.

The comparative method is used to illumine cultural change over long reaches of time as well as within a single period. For example, cultural anthropologists have been interested in finding out whether civilizations have necessarily developed out of similar conditions of ecology and technology. They have compared the several early civilizations in these respects and have thereby added to our understanding of the grand processes of human development. Such development is further clarified by comparative studies that are being made of contemporary societies, especially of those that are shifting from older, traditional ways to those of a modern, industrialized nation-state. Again, our understanding of human society and culture is enlarged when we can see the similarities among the new nations and the similar problems their people face and at the same time grasp the important differences among them.

THEORETICAL CONCEPTS

Another of the characteristic methods used by the cultural anthropologist is his way of building theoretical concepts. He is inclined to formulate new concepts on the basis of

what he sees and hears among the people he is studying. The cultural anthropologist, like all other scholars and scientists, is guided by the accumulated ideas of his discipline and of science in general. It is on this basis that he selects certain parts of the real world for observation, asks certain kinds of questions, and generates and tests concepts. But the cultural anthropologist is less likely than are other social scientists to begin with a rigid model or with a guiding hypothesis and to focus his research on testing one model or a particular proposition. He is more likely to construct his concepts from the ground up than from the abstract hypothesis down.

In the same way, the field experience of a cultural anthropologist commonly influences his selection of theoretical problems to study. The circumstances and the dilemmas of the people among whom he works often stimulate the concepts he develops. The cultural anthropologist does not usually observe people in order to test a particular theoretical idea. He instead marshals and develops whatever ideas he can muster in order to understand people. If he finds no concepts adequate to explain the processes of behavior that he has observed, he conceives of and tests a new concept. In this procedure, he has the advantage of sharing with the subjects of his study the qualities and feelings that are common to mankind. Robert Redfield once wrote that before one can discover what it is that a Zuñi Indian is ashamed of, one must first know what it is to be ashamed.

ANTHROPOLOGY AND HUMANISM

The cultural anthropologist uses the procedures of scientific inquiry in the meticulous collection of data, the formulation of hypotheses from the data, and the systematic testing of hypotheses by many observers. But there is also an important humanistic component in the anthropologist's approach to the study of man, partly because his studies encompass art and religion, including the aesthetic and religious life of the ordinary person as well as the creative productivity of the most sophisticated and talented members of a society. The humanistic element in anthropological writing also arises from the anthropologist's typical relation to the subjects he studies. He tries to understand them as individuals and as people. He experiences some part of the life he describes, and that experience usually is reflected in his writing and teaching so that they involve humanistic insights as well as scientific objectivity.

An anthropologist who has lived among the people whose culture he analyzes is likely to be aware of the strains and conflicts they feel and of the rewards and pleasures for which they strive. That awareness is usually reflected in his account of their culture and society. He generally tries to take a balanced attitude of both compassion and reserve, of attachment and detachment, of involvement and objectivity. If he is too closely involved with the people he studies, his report may be biased by their biases, yet if he tries to be too rigidly aloof and objective he may overlook the realities of the society.

Although the cultural anthropologist takes every way of life as suitable for study and the leading values of every group of mankind as worthy of serious consideration, he does not necessarily discard the values of his own culture. He is generally able to view them in broad perspective and thus may not be as likely as are others to be roused by parochial pressures of the moment. He does not necessarily spurn his own culture because he gives respectful consideration to others, nor is he necessarily indifferent to the values of his culture. Thus, anthropologists are generally as zealous in their support of scientific and academic values as are other scholars and scientists.

The anthropologist's method of getting the inside view of a culture leads him to appreciate the importance of the position of the observer in the study of man. He gets different views from people of different status; he learns that their appraisal of his own status can influence their responses. He finds that the same person may alter his views at different times in different circumstances. In some degree, this is also true for the observer as well as for those who are observed. Yet the anthropologist also learns that there are constant elements of objective reality that he can discern within the shifting perspectives and among the varying reports.

The cultural anthropologist changes the angle of his own vision as he proceeds from one level of description and analyses to another. In one stage of his work, for example, an anthropologist may take the village as the main social entity, and at another stage he sees the village as part of a larger social order. He depicts village life as a stable, ongoing system to bring out one dimension of its existence and then analyzes the same behavior as part of a stream of historical change. He tries to reconcile the differing perspectives so that he can derive conclusions about changes over time that will hold true across time.

LIMITS ON CULTURAL PERSPECTIVES

As with all scientific and scholarly methods, there are drawbacks as well as benefits. The holistic approach avoids arbitrary, disciplinary limitations to investigation but also makes it difficult to present a clear framework and firm boundaries for inquiry as the research worker moves from one field to another. The cultural anthropologist's emphasis on pattern rather than on detailed, measured specification is likely to be more fruitful in the initial, exploratory stages of a research problem than in the later stages in which hypotheses are tested. Cultural an-

thropologists have not often given full details on the number and kinds of observations they have made, under what circumstances, and with what people. They have been inclined to sketch the contours and modalities of behavior with perhaps too little concern about deviant and variant behavior.

Anthropological field research, as it usually has been conducted, has also entailed certain deficiencies. The anthropological observer has mainly followed a natural history procedure in which he has mapped the social and cultural terrain and has followed the flow of events in a society. He has indeed started with certain research plans and ideas, but he has always held himself ready to try out new ideas, to encounter new events, to record new situations as they come up in his field work. This fine freedom and intellectual agility, however, have occasionally led to more description than analysis. A field worker may be tempted to turn out disparate blocks of information rather than to construct a coherent account of a way of life. He may well fail to recognize underlying forces because they do not appear as such in a descriptive mapping of a culture.

Moreover, an anthropologist who tries to learn about various aspects of a culture during a stay of a year or two necessarily produces a less-than-complete account of any one facet. His accounts of the people's music or their agricultural economy cannot be as detailed as those of a musicologist or agronomist who devotes a similar period of field research to pursuing a single topic. This problem is now being improved through repeated field trips to the same society, by restudies carried out by other observers,

and by team research. Nevertheless, unlike most other social scientists, a cultural anthropologist is more likely to be a jack-of-all-trades than the master of a single subject.

The method of cultural comparison requires that the accounts on which the comparisons are based should follow similar standards of observation and classification. It is often difficult to judge from the available literature whether two accounts of presumably comparable behavior are really comparable. Some comparisons that have been made on the basis of existing reports have indeed led to significant findings, but when anthropologists want to push beyond these findings to more exact results, they often find that the available data are not precise enough for further analysis.

The development of concepts from micro-observation through successive levels of abstraction often presents difficulties. There is some temptation to vault directly from the immediate case to a high level of generalization. Because anthropologists take the broadest view of the human universe, they have been called the astronomers of the social sciences. But they also go to far-off places to collect their data at first hand, and in that sense they take it on themselves to be the astronauts of the social sciences as well.

Anthropologists have been mindful of these shortcomings and have worked steadily at trying to improve their methods. They firmly believe that any deficiencies in scientific precision that come from studying behavior in the context of real experience rather than in the controlled environment of a laboratory are more than compensated for by the greater relevance of field observations to significant problems. The results of laboratory experiments are useful—indeed essential—to explain some aspects of human behavior, but laboratory methods have their severe limitations. In the same way, statistical data are essential for some types of analysis but not for others. An apocryphal story that illustrates this point concerns the social scientist who asked a carefully selected sample of individuals in his city about the game of baseball. One of the findings in his research was that the number of strikes to make an out—according to the average of the replies—was 2.35.

Each of the social sciences is both the master and the captive of its prevailing methodology; cultural anthropology, too, is constrained as well as advanced by its chief methods. The use of these methods has contributed important results that have not been produced by other disciplines. In his contributions to our knowledge of man, the cultural anthropologist finds the justification for his methods.

STUDIES OF SOCIETY AND CULTURE

One basic result of the use of anthropological concepts and methods is that something is now known about almost all of the societies and cultures that mankind now maintains. For many of these, our knowledge is not yet detailed and intensive. There are large, populous societies for which only limited data have been compiled. Yet the main dimensions of human culture are known. *Universals* of culture have been noted—the incest tabu is one example—and the range of cultural variation is recognized. Incest tabus in one society may be applied to only a few relationships, as is true in Western societies, whereas in other societies an individual may have hundreds of people who, for purposes of marriage, are "tabu" to him. A cultural universal of another kind is body decoration. All people have forms of expression that they consider to be beautiful and that the observer can understand as art. Yet what is selected as a proper vehicle for aesthetic enjoyment among one group—elaborate skin tattooing, for example—will be unknown to or disdained by another group.

Anthropological study is broadly of two kinds. One kind of study emphasizes the cultural dimensions and looks at behavior from the viewpoint of shared norms, values, the customary means for doing things, and how all this is transmitted from generation to generation, changed over time, and affected by contact with groups having different cultures. This emphasis is usually carried out in practice by studying behavior over time or, as it is called, "diachronically."

The other kind of study looks at basically the same data, but in this case the focus is on social relationships, the effects these have on one another, their properties as systems, and the connections that exist among various subsystems of interpersonal relations. The first emphasis raises questions about how people acquire, maintain, and change their patterns of life and how whole cultures and societies are shifted, adapted, and evolved. The second looks at issues concerning the determinants and consequences of the roles people take, the effect of the existence of various kinds of groups, the ways in which individuals and groups interact with each other, and the consequences of the types of relationships that are present for the group as a whole.

Social Anthropology

Studies emphasizing social relationships and systems of interpersonal and intergroup ties and cleavages are usually labeled social anthropology. A. R. Radcliffe-Brown was the modern founder of this school of thought, although it has been more prominent in Great Britain than in the United States. This school has stressed the ways in which particular types of relationships have contributed to the continuation of the total social system. Their interest in showing how social—as opposed to psychological or biological—requirements are met has led them to refer to themselves as "structural functionalists."

Figure 8. Bodily decoration is a cultural trait that occurs in all societies of the world. A sampling of the universal urge to beautify the body: meticulous painting in New Guinea, tattooing in America, and scarification in Africa, a beautification process that is as painful as it looks.

Figure 9 (below). A synchronic study portrays the workings of a culture at a given point in time; a diachronic study shows the processes of stability and change over time. Figure 10 (right). The relations between supernatural beliefs and social order are apparent among the Huichol of Mexico, who hunt the hallucinogen peyote. Following the hunt, each pilgrim withdraws to allow the peyote he has eaten to take effect. Visions are culturally influenced but only the mara'akame, the leader of the Huichol, expects to see Tatewari, the principal deity and First Shaman who in ancient times led his people into peyote country. The feathered arrows in this pilgrim's hat are symbolic deer horns representing Kauyumarie, the deer-person who assists the shaman and is a type of culture hero.

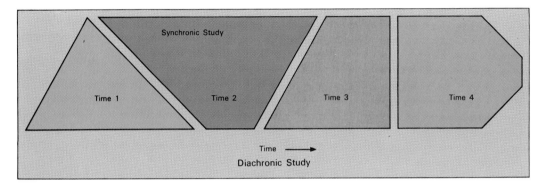

Synchronic Study

Time 1   Time 2   Time 3   Time 4

Time ——➔
Diachronic Study

That is, they approach human behavior from the viewpoint of the contribution particular kinds of interpersonal and intergroup relations make to the maintenance of the total social structure.

This approach has led, for example, to studies of the relations between supernatural beliefs and the maintenance of the existing social relationships. Thus, one study has argued that in some societies at least, accusations of witchcraft and sorcery occur within relationships that are not clearly defined, and these accusations serve to channel the tensions that arise from the vague limits on the expectations and responsibilities characteristic of these relationships. By channeling the tensions, the accusations limit them and prevent them from spilling over into the wider network of social ties that make up the total society. In this way the existence of behavior based on supernatural beliefs is understood from the perspective of the function it performs for the social structure.

Many other studies have been done by social anthropologists showing the contributions of various kinds of practices and patterns of social relations to the maintenance of either the society as a whole or particular parts of it. In all these studies, there is an emphasis on existing relationships—between individuals or between groups—and how they support one another and the whole system. Social anthropology looks at the same sorts of phenomena that cultural an-

thropology does, but it stresses the forms of association among people above all else. This emphasis leads to different kinds of problems for investigation than those that come from a focusing of attention on meanings, values, and the practices resulting from them. Both social and cultural anthropology are moving into new areas, and both are developing new concepts and techniques. Social anthropology worked out its basic approach on relatively small-scale and stable societies; it has recently expanded its interest to complex and rapidly changing societies with all the theoretical and practical issues these raise for understanding the relationships between patterns of association in such different aspects of life as politics, religion, economics, and kinship. At the same time cultural anthropology has also been opening new avenues for advancing our understanding of human life.

Cultural Ecology
One avenue for such development is that of cultural ecology, in which the system of a particular culture and society is studied in relation to the larger systems—both man-made and natural—of which it is a part. One viewpoint that can be taken in this form of analysis is presented in the chapter entitled "Cultural Ecology."

Linguistics and Value Studies
Another approach is based on the methods of linguistic analysis. Linguistic anthropolo-

gists have formulated the categories of classification that are inherent in a language. In like manner, the categories of thought that are inherent in a whole culture are being studied. Related to this method is the study of values, in which anthropologists try to understand the basic outlook or world view held by a people and the pattern of choices that they regularly make among the available choices that they perceive.

Psychological Anthropology

New methods and concepts are also being developed in psychological anthropology, also known as culture and personality studies. These studies focus on the qualities of personality that are characteristic of individuals in a particular culture or group. The same cultural form—parliamentary democracy, for example—can be used in quite different ways in various societies, depending on differing meanings of an individual's relation to authority and prevalent ideas about personal equality.

Urban Anthropology

The anthropologist who studies a complex modern society, as most social anthropologists now do, often takes over methods and concepts that have been developed by scholars in the other social sciences and in the humanities. The study of the people of India, Japan, or France, for example, requires familiarity with the writings of historians, sociologists, political scientists, economists, and others who have studied these people. To their descriptions and ideas, the anthropologist adds his understandings based on field research and then tries to integrate the several approaches in a broad, comparative way.

Social and Cultural Change

The same integrative efforts are made in the anthropological studies that focus on culture change and growth, on diachronic development rather than on the synchronic relationships. The two kinds of analyses are not

completely separate, but there is a difference in emphasis between the two. Studies of culture growth range from descriptions of shifts over a few years in a small group to the grand view of the whole of human development considered as one course of biological and cultural evolution.

The concept of cultural *diffusion* was one of the first to emerge from anthropological studies of change. When anthropologists began to inquire about how any given culture developed, they soon discovered that very little of it had originated within a single society. There has been a constant taking over of elements of culture by one group from another, even between people who were bitter enemies. The process of diffusion is evident from ancient archaeological remains; today it has been greatly accelerated by modern communications. Yet there are resistances and limitations to diffusion. Determined efforts to encourage diffusion, as in the economic development of the new nations, have not proceeded smoothly. The study of the conditions that favor the transfer of cultural elements and of those that hinder such transfer have become central problems in the study of culture change.

The *rate* of culture change is another phase of this inquiry. There clearly has been a speed-up of the rate of change in certain parts of most cultures, particularly in technology. But people change different parts of their culture at different rates. Although technological change has been cumulative, there is little clear evidence for cumulative, progressive change in such matters as kinship, ritual, and art.

In general, however, man's potential to attain longer life, better health, and greater creature comfort has risen successively as new thresholds of culture have been reached. Thus, the technical developments of the "Neolithic," then the social inventions of civilization, and lately the sociotechnical advances of science have allowed men to extend their cultures in ways that were not possible before each of these innovations

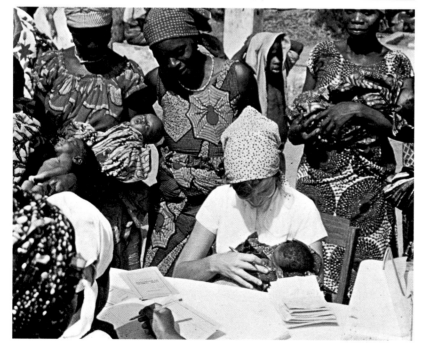

was made. All societies do not cross a cultural threshold at the same time, nor do all exploit its further possibilities in the same way. Yet the attainment of a cultural divide by one people sooner or later enables all mankind to share in its consequences. In that sense, the modern attempts to enhance the economic base of developing nations can be understood as an episode of cultural evolution in which the benefits of the new science and technology are being diffused to most of mankind.

Cultural Evolution

The concept of cultural evolution was a prominent one in the beginnings of cultural anthropology in the nineteenth century. It was presented as a series of cultural stages through which all people had to pass. This notion was soon challenged, especially by those who became aware of cultural diffusion. They realized that it was possible for one group to take over much of the culture of another and that the borrowers did not have to repeat the culture history of those whose ways they took over. The first concepts about cultural evolution were discarded because it became clear that every society had not evolved through identical stages of development; moreover, the combination of cultural features that was postulated for each stage did not hold true when tested against the ethnological evidence.

Anthropologists who took the concept of diffusion as their central interest turned their efforts toward reconstructing the history of particular cultures on the basis of likely paths of diffusion. These studies were, in turn, criticized by a succeeding generation of anthropologists who took their primary task as that of showing the ongoing, functional interrelations within a society rather than reconstructing its cultural history. These "functionalists" are now criticized as being too narrow in the scope of their research and as too dogmatic in their assumption that there must be a close interrelation among all parts of a culture. Yet each of these trends of anthropological analysis concentrated on certain concepts and made positive contributions to the anthropological study of man. In their critiques of their predecessors, the proponents of each trend now appear to have given oversimplified refutations of too simple concepts.

RECENT DEVELOPMENTS

Cultural anthropologists have reached for new methods and concepts as part of the marked growth of anthropological work in the years since World War II. They have done intensive studies of people in complex societies, in cities and villages, in factories and agricultural settlements. They have explored topics such as law and leadership that they previously had not given much attention to, and they have deepened their knowledge of such standard anthropological topics as kinship and ritual.

Cultural anthropologists have also reconsidered some of the basic precepts about their field. Eric Wolf points out that they are placing more emphasis on clearly formulated propositions about human behavior and on systems of propositions and less on romantic portrayals of primitive, small-scale societies. Wolf also notes the increased interest in civilizations and complex societies, an interest that was never absent in anthropology but that was, for a time, second to the interest in small, tribal societies. Another trend is toward emphasis on the constant features of human society and personality, on the limitations to possible change at any given time, and on the imperative requirements for any social organization. This focus is in sharp contrast with an earlier view of human potentiality as quite open and quite unbounded.

These earlier views, mainly of the period between World Wars I and II, advocated that each way of life be judged as being as worthy as any other way of life. This cultural relativism continues to be held as a necessary condition for gathering field data. An anthropologist can hardly make an objective study if his own value judgments and his personal likes and dislikes constantly affect and color his observations. Such suspension of value judgment, however, is not indefinite, and complete moral relativism is not often defended now. Each individual, anthropologists recognize, must take some moral stand in order to function in a real society. Anthropologists generally share a similar ethical position in their views about the importance of the study of anthropology.

It is a truism, perhaps a bit tattered by much repetition but a truism nevertheless, that scientific knowledge of the world of man has lagged behind knowledge of biology and even further behind knowledge of the physical world. And for good reason. Men are complex creatures that do not easily stand still for scientific study in their natural habits and behavior. In the critical effort to increase our understanding of our own kind, anthropology can help provide a broad view in time, place, and circumstance. When we begin our study of man from a time before the human species existed, we are less likely to get bogged down with transient troubles of the moment; when we become informed about peoples of many places, we are less likely to assume our outlook is the only proper and possible one in the world; when we appreciate the life circumstance of a peasant or planner in an impoverished country, we are not so apt to make hasty judgments about his efforts. This broad view contributes to our sense for the long-range working of society, to our awareness of the many linked aspects of culture, to our insight as to the possibilities for development. The anthropologist attempts to translate, in a scientific way, the beliefs and behavior of one people so that they will be intelligible to many. Of course mutual understanding in itself is not enough—two nations may come to understand each other quite well and then dislike each other all the more for that reason. Yet, as a beginning, translations and translators of cultures are much needed in the world today.

Ethnographic Field Work

22

The distinctive thing about the work of the social or cultural anthropologist is that it always involves ethnographic research: the study of the way of life of a people. His humanistic science requires an understanding of the entire and distinctive life way of those he studies rather than merely some of its aspects, but at the same time it requires that he focus his investigation on specific problems, whose answers will increase understanding of human behavior in whatever cultural setting it may occur. These are stringent requisites, ones that perhaps can never be fully met, but most anthropologists believe they are worth striving for.

They view culture as a pattern, with each element in the pattern directly or indirectly linked to other elements and in fact not clearly separable from one another. To understand any aspect of this pattern, it is necessary to have some understanding of what the people being studied actually do and what they say they do, what is actually expected of them and what is encouraged. Most anthropologists believe that in order to investigate specific problems—whether those problems concern the factors that give rise to cult movements, the effects of adapting new cash crops, or whatever—the entire cultural and social milieu must be investigated. Thus, all studies are dual, with one aspect being the intensive concentration on the investigator's special problem and the other leading to an extensive examination of every part of the culture being studied. Nothing people do as members of society is exempt from the anthropologist's ethnographic curiosity, which is based both on his efforts to understand the society as a unique entity and on the necessity to put the data bearing on his particular research problems into their proper setting. Ethnographic research seeks two interlocked goals: to describe in all its uniqueness the culture being studied and to contribute to understanding of human life wherever and whenever it occurs. The second goal can be attained only if the first is also attained, however. To understand what is universal in behavior, it is first necessary to see it in its many local and distinctive forms.

What the ethnographer will look for and what he will emphasize in his analysis depend on what he thinks is important to study, what he believes to be important in the culture of the people he studies, and what his theories are about the nature of human society and culture. Thus, even the most dispassionate descriptive account will be heavily colored by its author's interests, experience, and personality. Recently, a number of anthropologists have turned to organizing and analyzing their ethnographic data according to the way their informants see the world around them rather than according to the categories of the observer. But even these accounts must be analyzed according to scientific assumptions or theories if they are to contribute to a cumulative understanding of why people do what they do. Therefore, ethnographic accounts continue to be descriptions of the ways of life that ethnographers have observed in detail, described as they seem to be organized, with indigenous concepts combined with the analytical concepts of the ethnographer. As in all science, personal bias exists in ethnographic work. But this bias is controlled by producing statements that can be tested against empirical reality by other investigators. This control is not as easy to achieve in anthropology as in, say, astronomy, but it can be done.

GOING INTO THE FIELD

In any research study, there are many practical problems with theoretical and ethical implications. But no two research situations are identical, and the result has been that some ethnographers have given up any attempt to convey their research methods to others. A few generalizations can be made, however. First, prior training in the language and prior reading in the geography, history, and cultures of the proposed study area are important in saving the ethnographer many false starts and much tedious preliminary work in the field. When this preparation has been made, attention must be turned to potential political deterrents, another problem that is increasingly preva-

lent in the world today. Some governments do not admit foreign scholars to study their people, whereas other governments make it difficult for their scholars to study first-hand the people in nations that do not agree with their own ideology. These difficulties aside, there are the many considerations of theory, of the existence of needed supporting studies, and of personal preference—all factors that influence the decision about where the researcher will work. Rarely can the ethnographer himself describe all the factors that went into his choice of a specific site for research. Most often, no doubt, the general location is dictated by ethnographic and theoretical considerations, the specific location by factors of convenience.

The unit of intensive study is necessarily small—usually a single settlement. These units are, among nomads, a band that moves from place to place as a unit; among settled people, a village; in densely populated areas, a neighborhood. Rarely is this unit studied in isolation, for the ethnographer knows almost all such units are related in some way to other, similar units that make up some larger entity such as a tribe, a city, or a nation. But the unit of intensive study is usually assumed to be representative in specific ways of the larger entity. The basic criterion for the ethnographic unit of study is that the group being studied comprise an interacting aggregate of people (a *society*) who share learned and transmitted behavior and ideas (a *culture*) or that it form a separable part of a larger group with these characteristics. It is up to the ethnographer to demonstrate that this criterion is met and to explain how and to what extent his study represents the society and culture in which he is interested.

The duration of ethnographic research undertakings varies considerably, although one or two years is standard for work in the field. It takes at least a year to become familiar with a society and to observe most

of the activities taking place within it, and even this is all too brief a time in which to obtain an understanding of the richness and complexity of behavior the people themselves have spent a lifetime acquiring. Nevertheless, the anthropologist has an important factor in his favor that helps counterbalance the necessary brevity of his field research. This factor is his objectivity and lack of emotional commitment and habituation to the way of life being followed.

The implication is not that the field worker feels superior to the people among whom he lives or that he is aloof from them. On the contrary, a fundamental operating assumption of anthropology is the dignity and worth of every way of life and the need for the anthropologist to establish a relationship of mutual respect and acceptance with his hosts. Even with this objectivity, however, the basic fact remains that the

ethnographer sees what is happening in a perspective that is different from the perspective of the local people. It is this difference, in combination with theoretical orientations, that alerts him to what is important and what is less so and makes it possible for him to obtain information of scientific value in the limited time he can spend in the field. Things can be so commonplace and ordinary that they may not even be noticed by the people who do them, and yet they may be new and startling to the ethnographer. In Western society, for example, how many people are consciously aware that men's shirts and coats button left to right and women's garments always button right to left? An ethnographer from another culture would find the difference striking.

The ethnographer is also more free to look beneath the surface of social life. In every society, there are connections between events and practices, meanings, and the consequences of customary beliefs and activities that are obscure or completely hidden from the view of those whose lives are built around them. But such connections are thrown into bold relief by the anthropologist's perspective as an outsider and by his theoretically guided observations and inquiries. People often "explain" their behavior by saying "everybody does it" or "we have always done this," but the fact that many people follow a pattern or that the pattern is old tells little about why many people follow it or why it has persisted over time. The intellectually detached and theoretically alert anthropologist has opportunities for gaining insight into such issues, opportunities that are not available to the people totally involved in the behavior in question.

PARTICIPANT OBSERVATION

The ethnographer's main technique is called participant observation. In following this approach, he lives among the people he studies and comes to know them in their daily lives through intense and nearly continuous interaction. He learns their language, and through it he learns about their beliefs and their behavior in some of the same ways that any stranger learns to function effectively in a different social group. The ethnographer participates as he observes; he participates *in order* that he may observe. Much of his research is therefore based on subtle inference that he derives from informal situations. He may interview formally for particular kinds of information, or he may use questionnaires, psychological tests, or other standardized and relatively rigorous techniques. But regardless of what other methods he may be following, he is always alert to record the events going on around him and to understand their significance for his particular problems and for his general understanding of the life of the people. In the last analysis, the ethnographer himself is the most important "instrument," and the value of his work depends on his participating broadly in the life of his hosts and sensitively observing what is happening around him.

Participant observation in an unfamiliar culture is never easy, and, as would be expected, the initial stages are the most difficult. The anthropologist must earn the cooperation and confidence of the people he wishes to study—which means he must gain their trust—for it is both ethically unsupportable and practically impossible to compel them to tolerate his presence or answer his questions. In this task, a friendly and a genuine respect for the group's culture is indispensable. The ethnographer benefits from the widespread tendency to allow a respectful and interested outsider the role of neutral observer and to be indulgent of his naïve mistakes and the seeming impertinence of some of his questions. Moreover, the ethnographer's own customs and preferences very often will prove to be of as much interest to those he studies as theirs will be to him. This interest can be a valuable research asset, for the ethnographer's ignorance and curiosity about the ways of his hosts are made more intelligible to them by their own unfamiliarity with and interest in the culture from which the ethnographer comes. By accounting for himself and the ways of his home area, he helps establish the kind of reciprocity upon which all successful social interaction and all successful social research is based.

Another aspect of the reciprocity between an ethnographer and his hosts stems, interestingly enough, from the ethnographic task itself. In every group there are individuals who, when they feel secure and are not suspicious of the investigator, are not only willing to participate in the study but are even actively motivated to do so. Telling what has happened to them during their lives and explaining the meaning of what they have

Figure 3. A linguist interviewing Montagnard tribesmen of Southeast Asia. The linguist often must devise a system for writing languages never previously written down. He systematically elicits and composes a large body of utterances in order to arrive at a set of grammatical rules that can generate an even larger set of correct statements in that language.

done and what the ethnographer has seen is a gratifying experience for many people. In showing his deep and respectful interest in what they do and say, the anthropologist gives his hosts a partial repayment for their hospitality and patience. His scientific and ethical debt to them can be paid only by an accurate and objective public presentation of their way of life and its implications for understanding human behavior in general. His immediate debt while in the field is paid in many ways, not the least of which comes from his genuine and sympathic wish to understand.

Cultures differ, as do ethnographers, and because of this difference the amount of active participation and the amount of detached and interviewing observation employed in ethnographic studies is quite variable. Some anthropologists have participated almost as full-fledged members of the society they study, whereas others have remained apart or aloof—almost as alien observers. That the degree of participation is not always a matter of choice was suggested by E. E. Evans-Pritchard in his 1940 account of his research among two groups in the Sudan. The Azande, with their strong attachment to hierarchy and social differences, would not permit him to live as one of them and insisted he be treated as a superior, but the thoroughly egalitarian Nuer would not permit him to live otherwise than as they did. Most often, however, neither of these extremes occurs and the ethnographer is accepted as a friendly stranger who is accorded a more-or-less special position in the community. On the one hand, he *is* an outsider, as his obvious differences of all kinds and his ignorance of local ways make clear. On the other hand, he is unlike other strangers in that he lives among the people on rather intimate terms for a prolonged period and shows a continuing and respectful interest in their ways. As time goes on, it becomes increasingly clear that the ethnographer's in-

terests and behavior are quite different from those of missionaries, traders, officials, and other outsiders with whom the local people have had experience. The special role he establishes often leads to his being indulged to a far greater degree than if he were merely one curious member of the society attempting to pry into another's affairs.

Although it is true that the alien overlooks much because he is a stranger, it is also true that he learns much that would be overlooked or taken for granted by a person belonging to the society. Moreover, information that might be concealed from a person living in the community might be freely given to a neutral observer who can be trusted not to use the information against the informant or his group. Because he is outside the system, the ethnographer is free of direct involvement in whatever competition and conflicts characterize the system. But even the ethnographer can be subject to the suspicions that people attach to all strangers—is he a spy, perhaps, or a political agent? He cannot avoid such suspicions, but he can counteract them by behaving in ways that reassure his informants of his good intentions. One of the difficulties many an anthropologist faces in the field is getting

Figure 4. Observations of women's activities and interviews with women will often provide a picture of a culture that is quite different from that attained by relying solely on male informants.

his hosts to understand just what it is he is trying to accomplish. If he can succeed in doing this—in getting the people to see that his motives are scientific and humanistic—he will have gone a long way toward allaying suspicion.

Through friendship or through mundane accidents of circumstance—setting up residence in one neighborhood and not another, dealing with the landlord of the house he rents, being known through the kinship affiliations of his cook, doing business with certain merchants—the ethnographer may find himself inadvertently allied with particular factions or interest groups within a community. And it is altogether possible that such real or imagined alliances will preclude his interaction with competing groups in the community, or that they will color the information he receives, the attitudes he hears, and the behaviors he observes. In other words, by his own social position in the community, he may receive a biased impression of what goes on. Ethnographers are aware of this problem, and they usually attempt to work among all segments of the community even though it may not always be possible to do.

How representative the sample of informants is of the entire society is enormously variable. In a relatively peaceful and homogeneous group, the anthropologist can remain on good terms with the whole community through the exercise of some tact and a conscientious effort to divide his attention more or less equally among the various local

groupings. In a group that is deeply divided internally, it may be that the very act of working with the members of one political, religious, or socioeconomic group makes working with the members of the opposing groups very difficult, and great efforts must be made to win and keep the confidence of all parties. The more diverse the segments in a society, the more important it becomes to seek information from representatives of all of them in order to avoid a partial or biased account.

A weakness in many ethnographies is that they are derived largely from male informants. This weakness comes from the fact that most anthropologists are men and find it easier and more acceptable in the local community to work with other men. The difficulty is compounded by the fact that men are dominant in almost all societies and tend to monopolize the investigator's time and attention. Similar biases must be guarded against in societies with wide social differentiation based on age, occupation, wealth, and ancestry. The presence of the anthropologist's wife (or husband) and even his children can provide entry into segments of the society that would otherwise be difficult to deal with. The same is true when the ethnographic team includes students, especially from schools in the country of the group being studied. Additional personnel offer the possibility of additional problems in relations with the hosts, but they also present the possibility of expanded contacts and consequent diminution of the chances of an incomplete view of the culture.

Breadth of social relations does not in itself ensure against incomplete or distorted understandings of the culture in general or the particular problem being investigated. The investigator must be able to learn from his hosts, and, as a first step, he must be able to communicate with them adequately. In most of the societies the anthropologist studies, he must therefore deal with the problems presented by a language very different from those of the European group. One way around this difficulty is to use an interpreter. The use of an interpreter allows the researcher to begin gathering useful information soon after he arrives at the site of his work. But it does interpose an individual between him and the people he studies, and there is probably an irreducible minimum of distortion that enters into even the most skillful translation. When the anthropologist attempts to learn the language himself, he must cope with the difficulties inherent in becoming really fluent in a foreign tongue. Even when it is possible to begin to learn the language before going to the field, many months of daily use are required to gain a real command of it, and awareness of its subtle nuances may take years. Whether the ethnographer has worked through an interpreter or learned the local language—and how thoroughly he has been able to learn it if that is the course he has followed—will make a substantial difference in the kind and amount of information he is able to get as the basis for illuminating his theoretical problems and constructing his overall understanding of the culture of the people.

Increasingly, there is a tendency for ethnographers to believe that their work can be properly assessed only if all such limitations are fully conveyed in their written reports. Beyond command of the language, reproduction of interview schedules, or the other relatively concrete and readily communicated details of research methods, they are beginning to convey the more subtle aspects of their interaction with their informants—their own response to research conditions and the response of informants to the fact of their presence. They are, in effect, viewing ethnography as a process of human interaction in which the ethnographer and the individuals with whom he works, as well as their mutual attitudes, beliefs, and behaviors, are as inseparable in understanding the written accounts that result from field work as are the elements of a culture in understanding the entire culture.

WRITING THE ETHNOGRAPHY

Before the ethnographer can present his collection of data in written form, he must analyze the significance of his findings. His analysis is the process by which he moves from the many observations he has recorded to the generalized statements about what his observations might imply. The analysis actually begins before the first observations are made. The theoretical problems and interests the researcher develops before he enters the field determine, in an important way, the sort of findings that will be made by directing ethnographic attention toward some phenomena and away from others. It is impossible to observe everything, however, so there will always be *selective* observation. In scientific ethnography, this selection is guided by explicit theory. One aspect of all the various theories that are used to channel observation—and that necessarily affect analysis—is the presence of a model of the significant "categories" of social life. Ethnographers use such models as devices for looking at a society. It must be remembered, however, that they are patterns for the *ethnography*, not the patterns of the society being described, although the more adequate the first are, the clearer will be the understanding they give of the second. The distinction, although it is an important one, is often overlooked.

The search for more accurate models deriving from more adequate theories of culture and society is a main task of anthropological research, and the dual goals of modern ethnographic investigation both contribute to this search. The results of each study provide information for the theoretical problem being studied as well as material on the way of life of the people among whom the study was done. And through the

Figure 5. All aspects of a culture are unified in the events that it generates; in turn, culture is abstracted from these events by the people who participate in them. From the Mexican fiesta, for example, the anthropologist may isolate descriptive information it provides into various ethnographic categories, including religion, folklore, and art.

theoretical contributions that are made they help refine the models to be used in further studies. Anthropology, like all learning, is a social enterprise. Results are cumulative, and every study is strengthened by what has been learned in previous studies. The need to look at cultures in particular categories will always be with us, but as more and increasingly revealing research is done, these categories more accurately reflect the ways of life they are used to describe and analyze.

Culture as a Library

Perhaps the simplest and oldest notion of categorizing a culture is the one that is like a traditional classification scheme for library shelving—every book, new or old, regardless of its size, binding, or point of view, is placed on the shelves according to an established and unchanging system of categories. All cultures can be, and customarily have been, described under a set of headings or rubrics that have grown out of nineteenth-century Western concepts about the universal framework of human life. The usual major headings in cultural descriptions based on this framework include consecutive treatments of physical environment; technology, the arts, manufactures, and economics by which the society is related to its environment; kinship, politics, and other aspects of social organization; and finally religion. Additional headings for language, folklore, life cycle, personality, and history are frequently included. Under these major rubrics are many other possible headings selected according to the theoretical views of those who construct the various schemes of categories that are used.

The Human Relations Area Files begun by George Peter Murdock and his associates as a way of indexing descriptions of all cultures show how complicated this scheme of headings may be. The broader labels in this indexing scheme are considered applicable

to all cultures. These labels are based on propositions such as "the family is universal" or "religion is present in every society." These statements may be true, but only at the expense of having very broad definitions. The Nayar of southern India, for example, can be said to have had social units approximating "families" only if even the simple definition of the family is modified to refer to one or more husbands with one or more wives and all their children. If religion is a cultural universal, the category must be defined so that it can encompass societies where the official ideology, or the majority of the population, in fact denies the existence of supernatural beings or power. The definition must, in addition, exclude a view that was common in the past and can still be encountered—especially among recent converts from a tribal religion to one of the world religions—that "pagans" or "heathens" have no religion, that only "true believers" and perhaps "heretics" and "infidels" hold what can be properly called religious beliefs.

The library model also includes pigeonholes for cultural traits that are not universal. Not all societies have pottery, or riddles, or clans, for example, but there are schemes for classifying them when they do occur.

This model is useful for many purposes. It is a convenient filing and indexing device, and it helps suggest certain lines of inquiry and observation for a field worker. However, the usefulness of grouping together the phenomena it puts in a single category is not established beyond doubt, and the theoretical questions it raises may not prove to be the most productive ones. By asserting rigid compartments such as "the family" and "religion," it suggests that there are divisions in nature requiring that attention be focused on religious activity and then, separately, on family life. Although the scheme does not require that family life and religion (or politics and either of the last two) be looked at in isolation from one another, it does suggest that they are in some important sense separate and that they should be studied as discrete aspects of life. This approach carries with it the possibility that the real life way of a society can be distorted, and models of society that do not depend on common-sense divisions of life into the categories just noted may be more productive of understanding.

One alternative to the "library catalogue" approach is to view communities from a completely problem-oriented perspective—for example, tracing all the factors that influence the system of internal trade without primary attention to the categories from which these influences come. Another alternative is to make an attempt to discover the categories the people themselves use and to gather and present the findings according to these rather than any sort of imposed categories. These alternatives have important uses, but so does some form of the universal catalogue such as the one developed by Murdock. Such a system makes it possible to classify and compare information from the most widely different sorts of societies, including those known from only their archaeological remains or from inadequate descriptions by early observers. For the purposes of compiling and examining the entire human record from all societies and all historical periods, some system of universal categories is necessary, but in doing field work it is usually more fruitful to use these categories in conjunction with other and more specialized guides for research.

Culture as a Species

There are also evolutionary and ecological models for cultural patterning. With these models, cultures are classified according to levels of evolutionary complexity in terms of various dimensions—such as technological sophistication and degree of political elaboration—and the ramifications of the ways that cultures adjust to their environments are examined. In many such approaches, an underlying concept is that of adaptation and selection, developed first in evolutionary biology. Cultures treated in this manner are looked at by the anthropologist in a way that is similar to the zoologist's view of animal species. In other words, each culture is taken as a competitive unit in the process of evolution, subject to the forces of adaptation to the environment, mutation, and variation.

In human groups, these adaptive forces are manifest in organizational and technological innovation and invention, and the results of selection are seen in which cultural traits survive and in whether or not the whole culture survives or becomes extinct and whether it comes to dominate or is

Figure 6. Eskimo culture is a highly specialized adaptation to one of the world's most inhospitable regions. Such an environment seemingly presents few natural materials with which the Eskimo can work, but those that are available — including all parts of the animals they hunt — are fully exploited. Here an Eskimo woman chews seal skin to soften it into pliable material for clothing and shoes.

replaced by other cultures. Such models also usually imply a developmental ordering of cultures, from the least developed to the most highly evolved in their adaptations. In the analogy between cultures and animal species in evolutionary process, however, the areas of human life and capacity that do not lend themselves to the analogy must be kept in mind. For example, although animal species cannot transfer their adaptive ability to other species, humans can transfer their adaptive ways to other human groups because there is no genetic limitation on this particular human capacity.

Culture as an Organism

The functionalists may be said to conceive of cultures as organisms. Bronislaw Malinowski emphasized the contributions or uses of the parts of the organism. In his view, the function of cultural "institutions" is the satisfaction of universal, basic human "needs," just as organs—by digesting, circulating, and so on—satisfy the needs of the body. Malinowski saw culture from the perspective of its contribution to individual welfare and survival. A. R. Radcliffe-Brown and his followers also work with an organic analogy, but they see function more as the interrelation of parts for the preservation of the whole, and they look at the contribution that the "organs"—such as kinship systems, religion, and economy—make to the continuation of the total social and cultural system rather than to the meeting of the individual's needs.

Culture as a Work of Art

Another model used for describing cultures is the categorization of each cultural whole as a work of art, or perhaps as an individual personality. The best-known study based on such a model is Ruth Benedict's *Patterns of Culture*, in which her two principal subjects, the Zuñi and Kwakiutl, are respectively labeled "Apollonian" and "Dionysian," terms taken from Nietzsche's writing on Greek tragedy. The Zuñi of New Mexico were characterized by sobriety, moderation, conformist subordination of the individual to society, ritualism, and the avoidance of excess. In contrast, the Kwakiutl of Vancouver Island were typified by competitive rivalry for prestige, and they valued frenzy, emotional excess, and mortification of the flesh—they were in fact somewhat like the megalomaniac paranoid considered abnormal in Western society.

Other anthropologists made similar attempts to identify one central aesthetic characteristic of a given culture under such labels as "ethos," "focus," "dominant drive," "culture patterns," and *"Weltanschauung,"* but most anthropologists now consider these to be serious oversimplifications, often resulting in near-caricatures. Subsequent developments have taken two directions. In one of these, the culture of a society is not assumed to be homogeneous but is viewed instead as differing according to the posi-

Table 1. Postulates Illustrating the Contrast Between Chinese and American Cultures

Characteristics of Chinese Culture	Characteristics of American Culture
The most important duty and the greatest responsibility of an individual are toward his parents; these take precedence over any other interest, including self-interest.	Self-interest is the main concern of an individual; his self-expression, self-development, self-gratification, and independence take precedence over all group interests.
Men and women are not equal; women are inferior.	Men and women are equal; men are not superior.
The people are subordinate to political rulers, who protect and guide them but do not interfere with their traditional way of life; the invariable law operating among all gods, men, and things is reciprocity.	Government exists for the benefit of the individual; all authority, including government, may be examined critically; the government and the symbols of government should be accorded respect; patriotism is a good thing.
China is the world's oldest country and Chinese ways are superior to other ways of life; because human beings are not equal, many Chinese are ignorant and as inferior as many non-Chinese people who do not follow the Chinese ways.	America is the epitome of progress; to be American is to be progressive; all human beings are equal; progress is a good thing and is inevitable.

Source: After Francis Hsu, *The Study of Literate Civilizations* (New York: Holt, Rinehart and Winston), 1969.

tions individuals occupy in a social structure, with further variation arising from the biological differences between individuals as well as from the contingencies of individual life histories. The result of these sources of variation is a range of personality types occurring in certain frequencies that characterize the group.

The other direction of some contemporary studies has been to discover sets of characteristics pervading many aspects of a single culture. When these sets are abstracted by the ethnographer, they provide one means of unifying the different aspects of a culture. The aim of these studies is to find underlying beliefs and understandings about the nature of the world. These basically intellectual elements are referred to by such terms as "themes," "premises," and "postulates," and they are used to define fundamental emotional orientations and values, and broadly sought-after goals and ideals. These

general beliefs, feelings, and goals are formulated by the ethnographer, who traces their influence into such diverse areas of activity as kinship, religion, and economics. Table 1 is one example of a comparison of such postulates.

Although this approach is more flexible than trying to characterize a whole culture by a single tendency, it is difficult to specify how the ethnographer can extract a limited number of such generalized themes or postulates from the mass of more specific evidence he accumulates. The problem is especially apparent for such complex and internally differentiated societies as those of China and the United States, but in even less complex groups it is very difficult to decide what is "fundamental" or "basic" and what is not. There may be as many sets of postulates for a single culture as there are anthropologists studying the culture, and there is no way to choose among them with confi-

Figure 7. Cultures have been viewed as species. The analogy breaks down, however, in that species are irreversibly separate genetically. Cultures, on the other hand, however much they may have become different in isolation, may transmit or exchange the patterns and information of their stored traditions.

dence. It may be that the direction of research developing along the lines of cultural diversity and internal variation may prove more fruitful than the search for underlying postulates.

Other Models

Although other models have been proposed, none of them has been worked out as thoroughly as the preceding. Several have been productively applied to selected aspects of a culture, but they are usually not suggested as models for whole cultures. Each, like the evolutionary and organic models, is based on an analogy with a system having known internal relations among its parts. The type of relations in the system, it is hypothesized, will approximate the kind of relations that are found among the parts of culture being studied. Some of these analogies are carried over from physical or biological systems. In part, this carry-over is true of cybernetic models, which involve notions of feedback controls and homeostasis.

Other models are based on certain formalized parts of culture itself, and the models attempt to extend the relations found in these clearly understood spheres to less-known areas of culture. For example, the notions of rules, strategies, losses, gains, risks, and games of chance, as formalized in game theory, have been applied to human ecology as a kind of man-versus-nature game, as in William Davenport's study of the fishing strategies of Jamaican fishermen. Another such model drawn from culture is the theatrical analogy, with an interest in behavior and interaction looked at as "scenarios," "scenes," "social dramas," and—by a slight excursion through advertising—"image management."

A most important source of models has been language and communications, through their formalizations in linguistics and information theory. These models are providing stimulating suggestions for understanding the structure and process of culture in general, and they have had an important influence on ethnography. In recent years, some anthropologists have tended to organize their materials for presentation in the categories derived from the ways of thinking and organizing found in the society they study rather than in the categories found in anthropological theory. This idea is not new, but it is being applied with new rigor under the headings "ethnoscience" or "formal analysis."

Some of the methods and rationale for this kind of analysis are taken directly from modern linguistics, where each language is analyzed in terms of its own grammar rather than according to some model derived, for example, from Latin or Sanskrit. The ethnographer, following this model of analysis, presents his ethnographic materials in the way members of the society organize those materials, as indicated by the words that informants use in describing their lives. The ethnographer seeks to understand his informants' logic in the organization of their world rather than imposing his own logic upon it.

The anthropologist's own experience and his own preferences cannot be expunged from the ethnographic record, for during his research in the field he makes choices that are interwoven with his personality, his experience, his training, and his preferences. But by clearly distinguishing his interpretations from those of his informants, and by relying heavily on his informants' own logic, he may lessen the impact of his own biases on his written report. In this regard, it is instructive to look into accounts of the same society produced by different ethnographers, especially into accounts produced by ethnographers of different cultural backgrounds. The differences in their reports and interpretations readily illustrate the pervasive influence of the culture, personality, and personal experience of the ethnographer on his

research. Part of the benefit sought from the ethnoscience approach is the ability to produce ethnographies that are relatively free from external bias—including external categories. At the same time, when a culture is described in its own unique terms and according to its own categories, it is difficult to compare it to other, similarly described cultures, for it is difficult to determine which unique category in one culture is comparable to a unique category in another.

ETHNOGRAPHY AND MORALITY

The problem of the morality of the ethnographer's undertaking is now being brought to the attention of the very people he studies, and by their governments. Few people regard knowledge of human society per se as dangerous, but some fear that control will result from such knowledge. It might be suggested, however, that ignorance is not to be confused with freedom. An individual cannot be said to act freely if he is in ignorance of the consequences of his actions—and would-be tyrants have never been deterred from their goals of domination by ignorance of the cultures of those they tyrannize. But many people have questioned the motives of those who study members of alien societies, just as they have questioned those who study ethnic minorities in their own society. The questioning stems from the fact that anthropologists have usually been members of dominant groups, and their findings have not always redounded to the discernible or immediate benefit of those studied. In some cases, their research has been financed directly by agencies whose interests are regarded as inimical to the interests of those studied—for example, by colonial governments.

There is no simple or universal answer to such questioning. Some are guilty of indifference to the welfare of those they studied and a few have acted contrary to their interests; others are unwittingly implicated in these things; and many are no doubt innocent. But it must be remembered that ethnographers are people, and ethnography is a truly human and cultural undertaking. The responsibilities borne by the ethnographer in his work are human responsibilities. Some will bear them honorably, some will not. Some will err. There is no inherent moral "right" to do ethnography, nor is there any inherent moral prohibition. The justifiability of the ethnographer's intrusion into a society is of the same order as that of any intruder. With increasing self-government in the world, the choices are increasingly being made by those studied. Without their cooperation, ethnography has never been possible. Now they are casting a more critical eye on their observers, an act to be applauded rather than lamented. On the whole, ethnographers have maintained a level of responsibility and integrity during their research in various societies, which has made it possible for subsequent ethnographers to be welcome in their continuance of this work. Hopefully, with increasingly stringent demands for justification of their work, ethnographers will continue to be accorded and to deserve this response.

The Psychological Perspective

23

Among the native families of Guyana, getting divorced is easy. If a wife is unhappy with her husband, all she has to do is take her children and return home to live with her mother. Among the Sarakatsani, a pastoral people who live in the Greek mountains, divorce is almost non-existent, and even a wife who loathes living with her husband will stay with him until she dies.

Why the difference? Economics provides one obvious explanation. A mother living in Guyana can usually obtain employment once her children no longer need constant care, and, receiving little or no financial help from her husband, she may prefer complete independence to living with a man she has come to dislike. The Sarakatsani, in contrast, form a rigidly patriarchal society, in which all the family property is owned and controlled by the males. When a woman marries, she goes to live with her husband and his relatives and becomes totally dependent on them. She is expected to be subservient, and the Sarakatsani believe so strongly in their system that even if a woman is beaten regularly by her husband and pleads to be allowed to return home, her own family will refuse to take her back.

There is no question that the difference in family attitudes of the two groups is related to differences in economic structure, which can only be understood by looking at the way the whole societies are structured. However, the two different forms of behavior can also be interpreted from a completely different point of view, by examining the psychology of the people concerned. A further example will help elucidate this point.

Most Americans have a tremendous drive to succeed. One of the ways they express this drive is through their preoccupation with money, not only because they want the goods money can buy but also because they want the prestige Americans accord with wealth. This kind of drive is far from universal; many people, including the easy-going people of the South Pacific, are only slightly concerned with acquiring possessions. But Americans tend to be propelled by an intense drive toward achievement, a psychological inheritance associated with the Jewish and Protestant idea that a man should justify his place on earth by hard work.

From this point of view, the economic behavior of Americans can be explained by their drive to succeed, just as the domestic behavior of the wife who lives in Guyana can be explained by her attachment to independence and that of the Sarakatsani woman by her acceptance of male dominance. All these examples involve individual behavior, which is one of the main concerns of psychological anthropology. But another view of these differences is possible with the psychological approach. The American drive to succeed, the Guyana wife's obvious attachment to independence, or the Sarakatsani woman's acceptance of male dominance may be seen not as an explanation of their individual behavior but as a consequence of the way they are brought up, another principal concern of psychological anthropology.

INDIVIDUAL CHARACTER

The method of trying to comprehend the behavior of societies through the behavior of their individual members became popular largely through the influence of Edward Sapir. In 1936, in the *Journal of Social Psychology*, Sapir pointed out that culture exists only in the minds of individuals and can therefore be understood in terms of ideas, feelings, and actions of the individuals who make up a society. In particular, Sapir urged anthropologists to pay more heed to the question of how children acquire the mental attitudes characteristic of their society, for the acquisition of culture is by no means an entirely passive process. Any child actively interprets, evaluates, and modifies every pattern of behavior he takes over, so that culture becomes something different for every individual. Some Americans are better adjusted than others to the drive for achievement and monetary gain. And people with easy-going and passive temperaments

fit better into a peaceful, uncompetitive society such as that of the Lepchas of the Himalayas, just as aggressive and competitive people fit better into military cultures such as those of fourth-century Sparta or Nazi Germany of the 1930s.

Early Culture-Personality Studies

The psychological approach became known as the study of culture and personality, and several years before Sapir advanced his ideas, Margaret Mead had already begun to practice it in the field. In 1927, when she was only twenty-three years old, she went to American Samoa in the Pacific to observe how adolescence affected Polynesian girls. Mead had come to question what was then the generally accepted view that adolescent unrest was the unavoidable mental state accompanying the physiological changes that occur at puberty. Because people everywhere achieve puberty, investigators had assumed that such unrest was everywhere unavoidable. Mead knew that inner turmoil was widespread among American adolescents, but she doubted that it affected every child. She observed that the overt attitudes through which American adolescents expressed this turmoil—by rebelling against authority, by living in doubt and uncertainty, and by worrying about choosing the right career—were responses to specific pressures of American culture. It therefore occurred to Mead that adolescent unrest might stem not from a person's biology but from his attempts to deal with the difficult problems originating within his culture.

She went to Samoa to test this theory, and there she found that the adolescent Samoan girl differed from her younger, prepubescent sister only because of physiological changes. The inner turmoil characteristic of adolescent American girls simply was not present, and Mead cited two characteristics of Samoan culture that influenced the comparatively easy transition to adulthood. The first was the general casualness that character-

Group	Arapesh	Mundugamor	Tchambuli
LIFE WAY	Men and women gentle, responsive, cooperative, subordinating themselves to needs of the younger and weaker of the group.	Men and women violent, competitive, aggressive, jealous. Ready to recognize and avenge insults. Delight in display, action, and fighting.	Men flighty, unstable, nervous, dependent on female figures. Men in groups are strained, watchful, prone to gossip. Women practical, dependable; do all fishing, provide basis for economy. Women in groups are stable, work well together.
WESTERN EVALUATION	Act in the manner expected of Western women.	Act in the manner expected of stereotype Western male.	Reversal of sex roles expected in the West.

ized Samoan life and was strikingly absent from American society. In Samoa, no one was moved to lay down his life for patriotic or other causes. Disagreements were easily settled. There was little threat of poverty or disaster. Children were not hurried along or punished for being slow. And no one person was overwhelmingly important in the life of a child: although mothers were frequently away from their children, there were always substitute mothers as well as fathers who were available to play the role of parent. Moreover, Samoa was a relatively primitive society and tended to be homogeneous. There were no divergent or highly competitive groups; there was no generation gap, and children were not confronted with irreconcilable philosophies from which they had to choose. So, free of all such pressures, the Samoan girl grew up without feeling any great drive to achieve, without agonizing conflicts of choice, and without the compulsion to satisfy the ideal and often unrealizable standards that afflicts American boys and girls—as well as grown men and women—still struggling unconsciously to meet the standards of their parents.

In the years after her Samoan field work, Mead made several more trips to the South Seas and learned more about how the culture of a particular society molds the psychology of its individual members. In the interior of New Guinea, among the Arapesh, the headhunting Mundugamor, and the Tchambuli, she learned that men and women are not born with traits of temperament that everywhere predispose men to aggressiveness and women to passivity. According to Mead, Arapesh men and women are both passive, Mundugamor men and women are both competitive and aggressive, and Tchambuli women are dominant and the men retiring and especially given to gossip.

Early Culture Patterning Theories
While Margaret Mead was studying the personalities of different people in exotic socie-

ties, Ruth Benedict was developing similar theories based primarily on library research. Her book *Patterns of Culture*, one of the best known of all works of anthropology, was based mainly on the ethnographic writings of anthropologists who had described the southwestern Zuñi Indians, the Indians of the Great Plains, the Kwakiutl Indians of Vancouver Island, and the Dobuans of the South Pacific.

Benedict advanced the theory that a culture is made up of more-or-less consistent patterns of thought and actions evoked by a society's special and characteristic purposes. These purposes shape, or pattern, such cultural traits as religion, the arts, forms of recreation, economic behavior, and the inclination toward passivity or aggressiveness, and they also shape or pattern the personalities of individuals.

To illustrate her theory, Benedict contrasted the Pueblo Indians with the Plains Indians. The Pueblo Indians were a mild-mannered people who never pushed themselves forward and avoided excess. The Plains Indians, on the other hand, were a self-reliant and venturesome people who could bear self-torture without flinching. They were willing, even eager, to reach past the ordinary limits of experience, for example, by fasting to induce visions. Benedict was able to demonstrate even more dramatic cultural patterns in her description of the Dobuans and Kwakiutl. She portrayed the Dobuans as dominated by jealousy, fear, and suspicion, and the Kwakiutl as one of the most achievement-oriented of all primitive societies. The Kwakiutl were status seekers to the extreme. Their potlatches—feasts in which competitors tried to outshine each other by giving away the most gifts—were by Western standards an uninhibited, even megalomaniac, exhibition of self-glorification. But just as the exhilaration of a manic depressive in his manic period is balanced by the gloom of his depression, so was the self-glorification of the Kwakiutl bal-

Figure 3. Margaret Mead in *Sex and Temperament in Three Primitive Societies* (1935) reports a study of the patterning of sex roles in three tribes of the Sepik River area of New Guinea. She found that, although there are obvious and less-obvious organic bases for differences in temperament and behavior between men and women, cultural patterning (the learning of sex roles) is capable of modifying, even reversing, our own sex role expectations.

anced by a fear of defeat so strong that failure and humiliation were likely to provoke him to suicide.

NATIONAL CHARACTER

The kind of approach to the study of personality taken by Mead and Benedict can also be applied to nations. Although it is impossible to study a complex modern culture with the comprehensiveness that anthropology reserves for small tribes, anthropologists can study the nations of the modern world as they are revealed in the psychological make-up of their individual members. Mead was the principal theoretician of modern national character research, and she approached it with the assumption that, in any social system, groups of people will tend to display the same mental characteristics, or the same *psychological regularities*. Even people of different social classes or regions within a nation will think and act in characteristically related ways, much as different regional dialects will express relationships with the same basic language.

For example, contemporary Russian character developed as a compromise between prerevolutionary national personality characteristics and the Bolshevik drive to imbue the Russians with an ideal personality best suited to the needs of the continuing revolution. In some instances, the traditional way of life seemed completely at odds with what the Bolsheviks desired. For instance, Russians traditionally exhibited little capacity to plan, work toward, and carry out a long sequence of steps toward a given objective —but this was precisely the kind of capability that long-term Soviet policies required. Similarly, as Feodor Dostoevsky's novels so vividly describe, disciplined thought and action seemed to be the antithesis of the nature of the Russian character. Soviet life has required the imposition of unremitting discipline, and the degree of modern Russian social and economic success has often been a function of the people's ability to accom-

modate the tensions between traditional national tendencies and imposed national strictures.

The opposition between Soviet ideals and prerevolutionary traits does not mean that Russia does not still exhibit a definite national character. The opposing tendencies are part of diverse regularities. The regularities concern themselves with the same things—in this case, discipline—and apply to the Russian people in general.

As part of her approach to national character, Mead knew that the responses of each person selected for research would be influenced by his social standing, and she therefore conducted her research on the basis of *anthropological sampling*. With this approach, she first established where her subjects fit in a framework representative of the social stratification and then systematically related their responses to one another before making her generalizations about national character.

One of Mead's disciples, Geoffrey Gorer, continued the same form of investigation in his study of the American character, although he concentrated on the child's attitudes toward his parents as the clue to national character and behavior. In his 1964 book *The American People*, he observed that the single most decisive element in the formation of national character among first-generation Americans has been the rejection of the father, who represents the values of an immigrant culture that the children try to escape, and a turning instead to the mother, whose position in the home is unaffected by the immigration from Europe and who therefore retains the authority and respect that the father has lost.

One result, Gorer suggested, has been the remarkable distinction between the kind of morality that Americans follow or claim to follow in their private lives and the absence of morality in their business dealings. In private life, Americans still feel obliged to behave in a way that would earn the respect

of their mothers, whereas in their business lives, a province with which mothers are not associated, they feel no particular inclination to follow any moral code whatever and are therefore free to do whatever might best promise success.

Erik Erikson has recently pointed out that the United States is undergoing a severe identity crisis, brought on by the accelerating pace of technological progress and social change. American youth are caught in the kaleidoscopic shifting of life patterns that characterize contemporary American life. They no longer enjoy the relatively simple situation of the young Americans that Gorer described. They often find it hard to identify the parental ideals they wish to oppose because the adult world itself is in the throes of rapid change. They are left to establish and constantly change for themselves their notions of proper conduct and good conscience. Aware of the bewildering complexity of modern life, some have turned their thoughts toward their own resources, seeking the pleasing simplicities of humanism that places human values above scientific realities or national policy. Others unquestioningly accept the world as they find it—something too powerful and self-sustaining to overcome—and leave the mechanisms of government and industry to work their will. And still others take drugs, celebrating the "now" experience with no concern for a future they cannot control.

THE FORMATION OF PERSONALITY
Most of the early work on personality and cultural patterning has had as one of its most important underlying concepts the idea that unconscious psychic processes are manifest in various patterns of culture.

Culture and Psychic Processes
The investigation of the personality of groups or of individuals through a study of childhood experiences derives from the theories of Sigmund Freud, and these theories

Figure 4 (left). American youth in search of a more satisfying identity. Figure 5. A recurrent theme of culture is that there is no escape from the wheel of identity — that an individual slips from one conformity to its negative counterpart. A recurrent response has been the personal search for some nirvana that will allow an individual to assume a new and genuine state of being.

have influenced psychological anthropology in two principal ways. Freud called attention to the way in which psychophenomena, such as unconscious defenses against anxiety, unconscious motivation, and responses to forbidden material, show up in many more-or-less disguised forms including wit, magic, religion, and other customs. In *The Future of an Illusion*, he suggested that religion expresses man's insecurity in the face of nature and society and is illusory because it is grounded not in an objective assessment of reality but in personal hopes and fears. Longing to be spared the dangers and disappointments with which nature and civilization threaten him, man personifies nature and then peoples the unseen world with beings like himself, albeit more powerful than he is. In such fantasies, he also uses memories dredged up out of the helplessness of his own childhood. When he has created these fantasies, man can feel at ease in the

face of the supernatural and can deal with his desperate anxiety. It is true that psychologically oriented anthropologists rarely analyze the religions of the people they study in precisely these terms, but many have been influenced by Freud's basic idea that culture patterns express or project unconscious psychic processes.

Freud made his second contribution to anthropology through his focus on the gratification or frustration of childhood impulses as the key to personality formation, which then expresses itself in the cultural phenomena the anthropologist tries to understand. According to Freud, the three main avenues of early impulse gratification—the oral, the anal, and the genital—are each associated with a specific bodily zone that, when stimulated, provides pleasure. The norms of any particular society determine how mothers gratify, or fail to gratify, the child's impulses through feeding, toilet training, or controlling genital behavior, and these norms determine the kind of personality the child develops. Inasmuch as the norms vary from one society to another, members of different societies will develop different kinds of personality or different basic character structures founded on the gratification or frustration of childhood impulses. Even if they did not wholly accept this view, many anthropologists began to pay attention to the details of early feeding, weaning, toilet training, sex play, and sexual training in the societies they studied, as well as to other stages in the life cycle on which Freud laid emphasis, such as the Oedipus complex.

Many debates have raged over Freud's concepts, the most notable being the one in which Bronislaw Malinowski questioned the universality of the Oedipus complex. Malinowski took the view that the Oedipus complex as defined by Freud (a sexual attachment of the male child to his mother, accompanied by hatred and jealousy directed toward his father) is peculiar to Europe, where it stems from a combination of

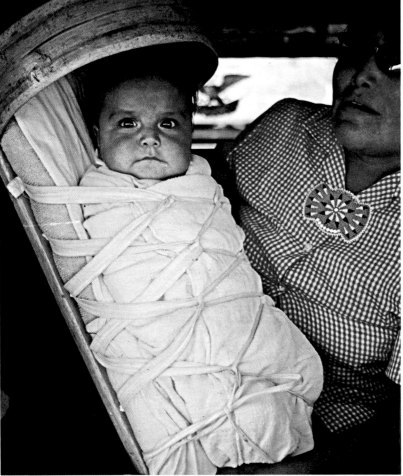

Figure 6. An assumption of basic personality theory is that early experiences provided by the care, training, stimulation, and restraint by parents, siblings and others closest to a child lay foundations for patterns of characteristic response and expectation that later experience can only partly modify. Each culture has a theory of child rearing rationalized in terms of promoting the child's welfare and growth. For example, some see the child as requiring constraint; others believe the child requires maximum body contact with the mother—a difference that may lie behind the use of the sling and cradleboard.

Puritan morality that prohibits sex play in early life and the existence of an overly strict patriarchal father and a timid mother whose fear and awe of the powerful husband are communicated to the child, leading him to identify closely with her. Where the European family does not exist—as in the Trobriand Islands, where Malinowski did his main field work—the classical Oedipus complex does not exist either. Malinowski's contention was challenged by Geza Roheim, a Hungarian psychoanalyst and anthropologist who had done field work in the matrilineal Normanbe Islands not far from the Trobriands and who claimed to have found evidence of the Oedipus complex even among these islanders. The debate has not yet been resolved, although it no longer commands as much attention.

Basic Personality Structure
Freud's theories lead to the conclusion that the behavior of all people in all societies must be understood in the same manner, for he considered his views of personality formation to be universally valid. It is possible to accept this basic position that human personality is affected by the kinds of considerations that Freud stressed, but one should pay far more attention to the variation from one society to another in the actual forms of child rearing than Freud did. This procedure was followed by Abram Kardiner, who showed how certain patterns of behavior in a society, especially in child rearing, help to determine how members of a society adapt to the conditions around them.

Kardiner applied the term basic personality structure to this adaptive process. Here the *ego* is the sum total of an individual's adaptive process, a process that is governed by the manner in which a society's customary modes of thought and behavior prepare an individual for meeting both the demands of the outer world and his internal biological drives. Kardiner characterized the cus-

Figure 7 (right). Primary institutions, following Abram Kardiner, are those concerning the child and most directly affecting behavior toward him; they are therefore formative in personality development. Secondary institutions provide for the maintenance activities of a society. They reflect, express, and require the personalities that primary institutions furnish.

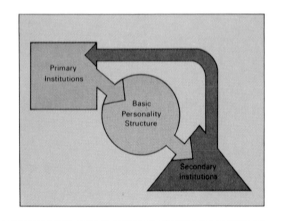

Table 1. Examples of Man's Universal Nonbiological Needs

Psychological Need	Forms It Can Take
Relatedness	Love, submission, wielding power over others
Transcendence	Creativity, destructivity
Rootedness	Nationalism, racism, brotherhood
Identity	Hero worship, style imitations

Source: John Honigmann (1970).

tomary modes of thought and behavior that act on a child early in life as a society's *primary institutions*, which include maternal care, the kind of affection given to children, and disciplines imposed upon the child connected with eating, excretion, and sex in general—that is, all the attitudes of the society, both permissive and restrictive, that affected the child's personality. To study the effects of these primary institutions, Kardiner characterized such adult modes of behavior as those included in magic, ideology, and art as *secondary institutions*, which he saw as society's means for compensating, rationalizing, denying, or vicariously gratifying blocked impulses. He wished to show that the secondary institutions were closely related to the primary institutions, and that in order to understand one, it was necessary to understand the other.

Because all these institutions will be shared by the members of a social system, the people will have had common childhood experiences and common means for expressing the psychic consequences of those experiences, so that the members of the society will come to possess a common, basic personality.

Kardiner's best-known analysis of personality was conducted with materials collected in the southwest Pacific islands of Alor by Cora DuBois. The Alorese employ one of the most traumatic patterns of child rearing in the world: the children are frequently left hungry when the mother is absent and there is no substitute to take her place, and little attention is paid either to their wounds and

sores or to their general distress. The only compensating feature of Alorese childhood is permissive sexuality, including masturbation, that enables the child to develop a modicum of self-assertion.

The Alorese personality that develops out of these conditions is filled with defensive inhibitions and confusions. As a result, the people are incapable of sustained effort. They collapse quickly in the face of danger. They are chronically anxious and suspicious of one another. Their weak egos do not allow them to express aggression directly, although indirectly they do release it in competition for ceremonial objects and prestige. Moreover, their superego—that element in the human personality concerned with moral behavior—is also weak because the child has no inspiring parent who can become his ideal and serve as his model for proper and righteous behavior. The Alorese manage to survive, but only on a thin thread, and their survival, in DuBois' view, must be accounted for largely by the absence of external enemies.

Social Character

Another psychoanalyst, Erich Fromm, also applied ego psychology to the study of social personality. He paid less attention to biological drives, focusing instead on universal, nonbiological needs that he believed are inherent in man (Table 1).

How a society satisfies these needs is determined by its social character, which is the set of motivating conditions shared by most of its members. This social character is an

instrument through which culture or society is maintained. Every society is organized to meet certain objectives—for example, a certain level of production, a system of distribution, and access to resources—and the social character of a society equips its members to function successfully within the social organization.

In short, social character channels energy, relieves members of much of the burden of choice, and ensures that they will want to act as the structure of their society requires them to act. It stabilizes the social system by conditioning the perception, ideas, and values of its members so that they will do willingly what must be done. This stability is not always constant, however, for if the social character has evolved in a way that frustrates the needs of man, a dynamic is created within the individual and his society alike that will force him to search for a new way of life.

Unlike Kardiner, Fromm did not emphasize child rearing, although he recognized that an individual as a child is exposed to the demands of society and that in his parents he has models of what he is expected to become.

THE SOCIALIZATION PROCESS

Today an important distinction is often made between *socialization*, which is the general process by which one generation sets the pattern for the behavior of the next, and *enculturation*, which is the specific manner in which this behavior is transmitted.

Socialization is a learning process that continues from birth to death, although it is most important in the formative years of childhood. It is the process by which people are conditioned to live in a particular society. It can be effected, as it is in Western society, by parents and peers, by teachers, and through books, whose purpose essentially is to maintain the standards that exist. Or socialization can be effected by a powerful elite group, such as the Bolsheviks in

Russia or the Nazis in Germany, who set out to alter drastically certain aspects of national character that they assume to be widespread and that they dislike. Socialization often proceeds less dramatically and imperceptibly alters behavior patterns as cultural and environmental conditions change. What happens at any given time in the socialization process is added to what has already happened, so that each new experience is affected by what the individual has already become.

The most effective method of socialization is to put every child into a situation where he is helpless and dependent and has little alternative but to learn. This is part of the human condition, and every child comes into the world helpless and dependent. In addition, however, a society can prolong dependence beyond what is biologically necessary through schools and other institutions of learning, thereby giving adults additional time to exert their control over the young and bring them to learn more. But socialization is not a wholly passive process for the child or the adult. The act of learning involves actively trying new endeavors and reaching out to new experiences, especially

Figure 9. Schools in New Zealand face the problem of providing an adequate learning program adjusted to the needs of both Maori and European children. The survivors of the Maori wars against European encroachment in the early nineteenth century dwindled from an original population of 100,000 to about 40,000. Largely through the efforts of their own chiefs, however, they have reemerged as an economically self-sufficient minority in the New Zealand nation, proud of their distinct cultural tradition.

those that produce or promise gratification, so that what is being taught is not necessarily exactly the same as what is learned.

Positive and Negative Disciplines

The actual methods of socialization differ widely. It can be assisted by positive disciplines that encourage performance by offering rewards or by negative disciplines that punish unsatisfactory behavior. Middle-class American mothers, for example, favor the negative disciplines of chastisement, ridicule, and the kind of psychological isolation that occurs when they withdraw their warmth from a child in order to show their displeasure, perhaps adding a physical dimension by banishing him to another room. American Indians made a greater use of ridicule, whereas in the Ghotuls—houses where boys and girls live together before marriage among the Muria of central India —discipline is maintained primarily by physical punishments that also involve an element of ridicule, as when a disobedient child is forced to rise from a sitting position twenty or thirty times while holding his ears.

Socialization and Technology

The specific forms that socialization takes will be determined largely by the cultural conditions of the society. In food-gathering societies, every individual is responsible for collecting his own supply of food, and considerable effort is made to encourage independence and self-reliance among members. In pastoral societies, which accumulate larger food surpluses, individuals who are obedient and possess a strong sense of responsibility are favored. This example illustrates the general rule that in any social system, among the personality characteristics most encouraged are those needed to perpetuate the technological systems on which the society is based.

The same tendency can be seen in American society, beginning with earliest child-

hood. In the United States, individuals are encouraged to pay close attention to numbers and other measurements of quantity as symbols of success and achievement, a preoccupation that embraces almost the whole spectrum of American behavior, ranging from pride in the size of incomes or the length of bridges, to an almost obsessional concern with athletic records or the speed at which men can travel to the moon.

The actual learning processes of any child will also reflect the personal situation and interests of the people who exert the most influence on him—his parents. Among American Indians, if either husband or wife is white, a child's learning will be more closely geared to the cultural standards of the surrounding white society than it will be in a home where both parents are Indian. And a study in a northern Canadian town showed that Indian schoolchildren who came from homes that conformed most closely to North American middle-class standards—particularly in having one white or partially white parent—are best prepared to do outstanding school work. The pupils who came from homes less representative of middle-class culture were more often conspicuous for their poor performance.

PSYCHOLOGY AND SOCIAL CHANGE

All these glimpses into social personality or, as it is sometimes called, modal personality might imply that the psychology of a people

Figure 10 (below). An Algonkian Indian from Lake Barriere in Quebec bearing unmistakable signs of acculturation. Figure 11 (right). Anthropologists often use forms of thematic apperception tests — ambiguous drawings about which an individual is asked to tell a story, thus giving responses reflecting his own personality and the culture in which it was formed. Shown are types of pictures from a projective test Pertti Pelto used among the Skolt Lapps of Finland, which demonstrated obvious differences between reindeer herders and men who had turned to wage labor or other nontraditional activities. The stories the herders told expressed socially uninvolved causality (e.g., *this man decides to go out of his herding shack to do some fishing; while he's gone lightning strikes the shack and it burns down*), but the other men expressed concern with socially involved causality (e.g., *some men cutting timber for a new corral engage in a quarrel and while they argue one of them flips a cigarette into the building and it later burns down*).

is static and continues without change. But societies do change, often radically, and a number of psychological anthropologists have been investigating the degree to which changes in social and cultural conditions are reflected in the personalities of the members of a society.

Hallowell and the Algonkians

A. Irving Hallowell, one of the most notable researchers, did his principal work among the Algonkian-speaking Indians of North America, and he discovered that their personality characteristics have changed relatively little despite 300 years of contact with French, British, American, and Canadian explorers, fur traders, missionaries, and government officials.

Hallowell used as a base for his study various seventeenth- and eighteenth-century records that were written by explorers and missionaries and still give a vivid picture of the aboriginal Indians' personality at the time they first encountered Europeans. The

records emphasize the Indians' practical rather than abstract intelligence and their independence, individualism, and stoicism. One French Catholic missionary wrote that these Indians considered it a maxim that each man is free—that he can do whatever he wishes and that it is not sensible to put constraints upon him. Yet the aboriginal Indians were renowned for their stoicism. In the face of provocation they tried to remain amiable, mild, and unaggressive, but the hostility they expressed when drunk on the Europeans' alcohol showed that they were not free from hostile impulses, however strongly they sought to constrain those impulses in personal relationships. Some 300 years later, using *Rorschach inkblot tests,* Hallowell found that his Manitoba Ojibwa Indian subjects revealed essentially the same personality characteristics, and other students, following him with *Thematic Apperception Tests* (TAT) and further Rorschach tests, confirmed his interpretation of contemporary northeastern Algonkians.

Yet the changes they had undergone had not left the psychological make-up of the Indians wholly untouched. Among the more isolated people who have remained unchristianized and speak little English, Hallowell found a particularly introverted personality, one strongly on guard against upsetting emotional experiences. Others who belonged to the same language-speaking groups but who had been more exposed to contact with outsiders were not as great emotional suppressors. Fundamentally, however, they possessed the same psychological complexion as their more isolated neighbors. In northern Wisconsin, researchers visited an even more acculturated community belonging to the Ojibwa group, and they, too, uncovered the same centuries-old basic psychological structure, altered only by a more emotional responsiveness to the outer world.

Changes were particularly evident in the Indians who have been most exposed to contact with white culture and have been af-

fected by it, and these groups gave clear signs of being in psychological difficulty. Apparently their personality was not equipped to meet the conditions thrust upon them by white culture, and their adjustment was suffering in consequence. Yet even the changes that have taken place seem to reflect the Indian aboriginal psychological traits, because the most obvious evidence of their maladjustment, anxiety, and introversion can be seen as exaggerations of the characteristics they displayed 300 years ago.

Spindler and the Menomini

Another anthropologist, George Spindler, also worked with an Algonkian Indian group —the Menomini Indians of Wisconsin—and he showed how the degree of acculturation (which is acceptance of another culture's ways of thinking, evaluating, and doing things) is correlated with changes in personality type.

Spindler believed that the personality of an individual appears to vary with where he stands on the gradient of increasing acculturation. Native-oriented Menomini who have not become subject to white culture are highly introverted and still strive to maintain tight control over their feelings, much like the aboriginal Algonkians whose personality Hallowell reconstructed from the records. The second level on the gradient of increasing acculturation is occupied by a group called the Peyotists—from the Peyote cult that they practice—and they are emotionally more open and less stoical. They also experience more anxiety, tension, self-doubt, and inner conflict than the native-oriented group. The next category contains the transitional men who stand between the Indian and white cultures. They display some of the same stressful characteristics of the Peyotists and have difficulty controlling their hostility, but they are less introspective. The next group on the gradient are the lower-status acculturated men who live with many trappings of Euro-American culture

and are reasonably well adjusted, although not as completely as the elite acculturated, who hold the best jobs and are emotionally the most relaxed and extraverted Indian group on the reservation.

Spindler's findings are particularly important because they demonstrate that culture change does not, from a psychological point of view, become more devastating as it becomes more radical. These conclusions, however, must be seen against the near unanimity among most anthropologists who have considered the psychological aspects of culture change and found that it tends to be psychologically traumatic. Yet Spindler's findings were, in a sense, confirmed by Mead when she reported on her visit to the Manus in 1953. She found that under the influence of military and political activities imposed by the Americans, the Manus had been able to transform their life and exchange one culture for another without experiencing any psychological deformation.

CROSS-CULTURAL STUDIES

One way to search for generalizations about human behavior is to conduct a study of the same subject in several different kinds of cultures. Today anthropologists study as many as fifty or more societies to test their hypotheses, and these large-scale investigations have added to their understanding of cultural phenomena.

Alcoholism and Social Order

Consider, for example, the question of alcoholism, the subject of one of the earliest cross-cultural studies, conducted by Donald Horton among small-scale societies in various parts of the world. He discovered that people drank more heavily when they became more worried about getting enough food to eat and that this tendency was increased when the people were in contact with a more powerful civilization that had brought great changes in their way of life and so deepened their anxieties. Another

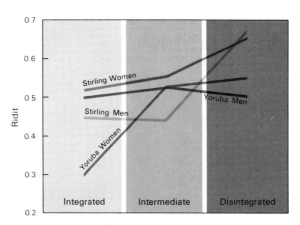

Figure 12 (left). Correlating social disintegration and breakdown in mental health. The Stirling County data represent the entire county; the Yoruba data were obtained from fifteen villages. (Adapted from *Psychiatric Disorder Among the Yoruba* by Alexander Leighton et al. Copyright © by Cornell University. Used by permission of Cornell University Press.) Figure 13 (right). Balinese children are taught grace and skill in dancing through the physical manipulation of their movement as well as through observation and imitation. This learning experience may also be one basis for trance dancing in Bali, in which the dancer's movements are thought to be beyond his own control, manipulated instead by an ego-alien force or spirit.

study has shown that people tend to drink heavily in conditions where the social organization is comparatively informal and unstable, and where individuals tend to submit to few external controls on their behavior.

In societies that still retain a strong patriarchal tradition—such as those of the Middle East, where property is owned communally by the family and the father exercises strict control over his sons—alcoholism is unlikely to be a problem even in groups where alcoholism is not forbidden by their religion. But where family discipline has crumbled and traditional moral values have been abandoned, as among some of the Mexican slum communities described by Oscar Lewis, a high rate of drunkenness is likely to be one of the consequences. Precisely the same situation seems to exist with prostitution. It is rare among societies that retain strong patriarchal principles, but it can become quite commonplace when members of those societies move to cities where the traditional moral rules cease to apply.

Whiting and Child on Discipline

In another well-known cross-cultural study, John Whiting and Irving Child tried to determine the validity of the theory that children who are punished by threats of ostracism, denial of love, or deprivation of rewards grow up with strong feelings of guilt—an assumption confidently made in most psychoanalytic theories. Their study confirmed that the assumption is justified, for it showed that in societies where parents use the technique of withholding love as a means of punishing and disciplining their children, adults are likely to suffer from strong guilt feelings. In societies where parents do not employ such techniques, the researchers found signs of guilt feelings among adults are far less pronounced.

RESEARCH INTO MENTAL ILLNESS

Thirty or forty years ago, it was generally assumed that an association existed between the kinds of psychological sicknesses that characteristically afflict people in different cultures and the main psychological emphasis in those cultures. The Cree-Ojibwa Indians, for example, suffered from what was known as the Wiitiko psychosis, in which the patient became obsessed with cannibalism. This mental disorder, which would be remarkable in normal American society, apparently reflected the importance of cannibalism in Cree-Ojibwa society, and it has also been compared recently to the *pibloktoq*, a similar kind of mental disorder that affects Eskimo women. It seems likely that whereas the Wiitiko psychosis springs from, or is associated with, the strong sense of personal independence that is characteristic of Indian groups, *pibloktoq* is associated with the relatively high level of dependence permitted among the Eskimo. In fact, *pibloktoq* can be interpreted as a hysterical cry for help by people facing a psychological crisis.

During the 1940s, the three disciplines of sociology, anthropology, and psychiatry came close together in attempts to account for personality disorders, largely through the efforts of Alexander Leighton, who was a psychiatrist as well as an anthropologist. Leighton's theory of psychiatric disorder was based on the assumption that all human beings experience certain strivings that may be blocked by cultural conditions and that are especially likely to be blocked in communities in a state of social disintegration. If the strivings are persistently blocked, the individual's general equilibrium can become so disturbed that he ends up in the hospital as a mental patient.

Social Breakdown in Stirling County

Between 1948 and 1950, as part of Leighton's research, field workers visited several small towns and hamlets of Stirling County in Nova Scotia. Having found local informants to show them where to look, they settled down to study a number of communities

that were suffering acutely from poverty and cultural confusion brought on by the mixing together of various racial groups. The field workers then compared these communities with relatively stable groups in the same area, conducting their research mainly through interviews with about 1,000 respondents, which they wrote up and later showed to a group of psychiatrists. The psychiatrists rated each person who had been interviewed on a four-point scale that ranged from almost complete certainty that he had been psychiatrically disturbed to no evidence of psychiatric difficulty.

Their analysis suggested that *57 percent* of the county's population was psychiatrically disturbed and 24 percent had suffered noticeable psychological damage. The significant finding of this study is that the likelihood of people becoming psychologically disturbed increases steadily as a move is made from socially integrated to socially disintegrated communities, a finding that Leighton further confirmed in 1959 with a study of Yoruba personality disorder.

Disintegration of Moral Order

Leighton's conclusions do not suggest that a mingling of different ethnic groups necessar-ily produces psychiatric disorder. It is quite possible for different ethnic groups, even when undergoing considerable cultural change, to form stable and harmonious societies. The damage comes when a community—whether composed of one or several different ethnic groups—undergoes social change so acute that the traditional moral values of the people are destroyed. Floundering helplessly in a situation where they no longer know how they are supposed to live or by what standards, the people stand in severe danger of coming to experience psychological disturbance or possibly even severe mental illness.

It is not the mere fact of change that is responsible for psychological disturbance. The essential fact is the social disintegration of the group and the collapse of accepted moral standards—conditions that can come about even when no dramatic social or cultural changes have taken place. The psychological anthropologist may be concentrating his attention on the individual members of a group, rather than on the group as a whole, but he manages to retain his perspective with the knowledge that what an individual is depends to a very considerable degree on what his society makes him.

Cultural Ecology

24

Hominids have occupied this planet for perhaps 5 million years. During most of this time, they were food foragers, collectors, and hunters interested primarily in staying alive. It is a relatively infinitesimal time since they mastered agriculture some 9,000 years ago and only a few hundred years since the industrial revolution brought their apparent mastery of nature. But it is only within the last few decades that the cost of this mastery has become recognized. Agriculture has led to soil erosion and the spread of pesticides with disastrous as well as beneficial results, and industrialization has brought a concurrent pollution of water and air. The control of nuclear energy, the latest pinnacle in technological achievement, represents a threat to human survival that overshadows its potential benefits. The term "ecology" has entered our everyday vocabulary, unfortunately as a consequence of these harmful but unanticipated effects.

Almost the entire history of the hominids has been one of useful ecological adaptations that have altered but not threatened the environment and its resources, and for this reason man's adaptations to his environ-

ment during the 2,500,000-year span prior to the present can be used as a means of examining creative factors and processes in the evolution of culture.

The explanation of why culture steadily if slowly evolved during these years in a multitude of ways is a question that had generally been evaded. At one time, scientific theories of the development of different cultures were of no interest because theological or orthogenic explanations prevailed. During the present century, the general view has been that explanations of the constitution and character of particular cultures should not be sought because they are too complicated and difficult to prove. Because no two cultures are identical in all particulars, a view known as *cultural relativism*—whereby each total culture is considered unique—has prevailed. Many anthropologists believe that each culture and each sequence of cultural development should be described in its distinguishing details and that a search for the causes of cultural differences and of such similarities as can be found be disavowed.

In fact, many striking cross-cultural similarities have been discovered, some of which seemed related to the way in which man had

Figure 2 (below). Social theories have often differed, not in terms of the determinants they include but in the importance and order of effect they give to these. Economic determinists have focused on technology and the relations of men around the means of production, a view that takes ideology as a derivative superstructure. Other theorists such as Max Weber have asserted the causal importance of ideas and values. Relations within cultures, however, are characteristically intercausal. Figure 3 (right). Pomo basket from the Salinas Valley in California. The restriction of decorative art to basketry reflects their major subsistence activity.

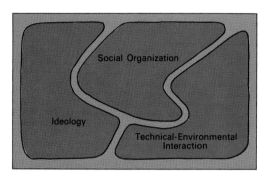

to live in his environment. In the early 1930s, Julian Steward compared primitive hunting and gathering bands and suggested that there were similar adaptations of certain societies to their environments. For many years, however, the concept of cultural ecology was viewed with suspicion because it was difficult to persuade anthropologists that this was not a new way of stating environmental determinism, a long-rejected view that asserted a one-to-one relationship between environment and culture. Cultural ecology gained interest in the following decade and is now widely used. The concept has great value in helping disclose causes of culture change without denying the importance of historic factors.

In this chapter, *culture* signifies all the socially learned and transmitted patterns of behavior. It implies that all human behavior —be it social forms, technological inventions, or music and art styles—is not determined by heredity or race. The history or evolution of culture also leaves no doubt that a totally holistic view of particular cultures—the idea that all aspects of any culture constitute a tightly integrated whole—is untenable. On the contrary, all cultures consist of many aspects that may or may not vary independently so that viewing them entirely as a single piece is not warranted. This can be seen in the finding that the nature of social groups throughout the pre-agricultural history of man represents very close social adaptations to the technological means of utilizing the environment, whereas

art forms have often developed independently according to their own separate determinants. Paleolithic cave art apparently reflects concern with big game hunting and may have been part of magic. Great Basin and California art, which was limited largely to basketry designs, is purely an aesthetic expression. Whether any aspect of culture is modified by other aspects must always be an open, empirical question, and it cannot be assumed that what affects one aspect will affect another in the same way or at all. How complicated this is can be seen in the fact, stressed in this chapter, that quite dissimilar forms and styles may serve the same purpose or function. Thus, containers of skin, bark, basketry, pottery, and even eggshells may be of about equal value in transporting water in desert areas.

The cultural ecologist looks at the structure of social groups and their interactions as they exploit various environments by means of particular technologies. He is interested in the mutual dependency of the sexes, the nature and functions of the nuclear family, the various extensions of such families, and the larger aggregates of families, bands, villages, and still higher levels of social integration such as tribes, states, and empires. He is also concerned with the various institutions in the areas of economics, religion, and art. Through his investigations, it is possible to see that all sorts of social institutions that are quite similar to one another in many respects may be brought about by quite diverse factors.

APPROACHES IN CULTURAL ECOLOGY

Ecology is derived from *eco*, meaning house, habitat, or environment, and today it is defined as adaptations of all features to one another within a given territory. In practice, its most common form has been plant and animal ecology, which examines the interrelatedness of plant and animal species to one another and to all other phenomena within the environment. Inasmuch as all biological species have some degree of inherent adapt-

Figure 4. Melanesia offers examples of differing adaptations in adjacent environmental zones. On New Guinea, for instance, an economic complex includes upland sweet potato cultivators, bushland taro gardeners, and coastal fishing groups. This economic system can be likened to the ecosystem of the animal world, in which each organism is uniquely adaptive while remaining essential to the functioning of the whole. In human societies, ecological complementarity is an inducement to form larger social integrations through political and economic ties.

ability, the total network of interacting features will create optimum circumstances for some species and marginal circumstances for others, as shown in Figure 4. Biological species are thus seen largely in terms of competition and are arranged in zones of successful adaptations, the climax being the optimum area surrounded by marginal zones where other species begin to flourish.

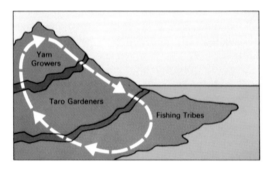

Adaptive Features of Man

The adaptability of life forms is limited by genetic potentials. Species generally are larger and stronger in their optimum environment. Particular characteristics, however, may also become adapted to the environment. Some species change the color of their coats in order to survive by acquiring, for example, a white fur in winter snow areas. Behavior is also adaptable, especially among the higher mammals. Primates are the most adaptable, and they may change their habits and foods to adapt to particular environments.

An ecological approach to man also focuses attention on his adaptations to his total environment. It should be stressed, however, that the common practice of making ecology synonymous with environment is incorrect. Ecology emphasizes adaptations, of which environment is only part; the other part is the adaptability of the species. Unlike all other species, whose adaptation is limited by genetically determined capabilities, man's adaptability includes his seemingly unlimited capacity for culture and cultural variation. The biological or innate factors in human adaptations constitute preconditions rather than specific factors.

During his evolution, man has acquired a physique for bipedal locomotion, specialized hands that can make use of tools, the capacity for speech that permits the social transmission of ideas and other elements of culture, an enormously enlarged cerebral cortex that increases the capacity for memory and rational solutions, and a prolonged period of immaturity that requires parental care. None of these is part of his primate heritage. But his sexuality, with its concomitant potential for complementary activities between male and female, as well as his omnivorous diet are shared with other primates.

The distinctive feature of man's cultural evolution is his great extension of adaptive behavior. Man has met his survival needs by means of tools, implements, weapons, and other technology and by appropriate social arrangements. That many features of human behavior are not rational does not mean that they are instinctive or determined genetically. Some may have endured after losing their usefulness, some may have been inadequate or incorrect solutions, and many are purely stylized features, such as art forms, which have little direct utility.

The entire history or evolution of culture represents a continuum of various transformations of behavior patterns that may be understood precisely because they are, on the whole, reasonable or rational. But many writers who are almost entirely outside the field of anthropology propose genetic explanations of behavior, which opens the door for racism, eugenics, and other views that obscure and distort the cultural factors involved. Certain biologists, such as Herman Muller, see competitive and cooperative behavior in man as abstract qualities that can be managed by selective breeding. Donald Fleming even looks to a "new biology" that, through manipulation of genes, may some day create the kinds of people that master-

minds decree are desirable. Robert Ardrey, a playwright, has endeavored to popularize the notion that mankind along with all other animals is innately territorial and therefore aggressive and warlike in defense of territory. In providing an easy explanation of why existing societies are warlike, such views obscure the fact that hunting and gathering societies are essentially cooperative, and they fail to examine the various kinds of hostilities loosely designated as warfare and to understand the cultural preconditions of aggression. For example, most hostilities in these small-scale societies that arise from homicide can be traced to continuing family feuds, the killing of an unsuccessful medicine man, and other matters pertaining to the individual rather than the group.

Another distinctive characteristic of human societies is that basic goals or values have changed, thereby motivating quite dissimilar patterns of behavior. Prior to about 9,000 years ago, or before agriculture provided security, the goal of virtually all societies was simple biological survival. There were certain localities that yielded enough subsistence to permit considerable security and no doubt social elaborations. For instance, the Paleolithic site at Solutré in France is estimated to contain the bones of 20,000 wild horses, which suggests a very adequate food supply. But this is a fairly late site in the total span of evolution and it is exceptional. The predominant goal of physical survival dictated cooperation among men. Colin Turnbull and others have commented on the absence of aggressive behavior among primitive hunters, and Steward has recorded peaceful relations among the Great Basin Shoshonean societies.

When reliable surpluses were assured after plant domestication, survival became secondary to culturally evolved goals. The new goals concerned control of wealth in ways that afforded political, economic, and religious power and prestige. In recent decades, however, the biological needs of a large portion of mankind have still not been met. Ironically, the predominant ideology in the United States still holds that these needs should be met within the profit system—that food should be destroyed or not produced unless it can be sold for a profit, which points out that the goals dictating ecological adaptations take many peculiar forms.

The Nature of Culture Change

An ecological approach makes several assumptions about the nature of culture change inescapable. First, because environment is external to culture—that is, not part of culture per se—it should not be reasoned that all of culture change must be understood only in terms of what Alfred Kroeber, following Herbert Spencer, called the "superorganic" level or what Leslie White has called the "culturological" level. Both authors argued that "reductionism" below the cultural level to factors of biological or environmental levels is inadmissible. The fact that man must adapt to his environment breaks the circular reasoning that culture comes from culture alone.

Second, the varied cultural-ecological adaptations brought about by the use of particular technologies in different environments pose the question of what *latitude* for variation exists in different aspects of culture. There is no universal answer. For example, the social arrangements required for subsistence in a given society may be comparatively stable, whereas ritual practices, religious beliefs, or art styles may vary because of other factors, including the borrowing of such features from other societies. Culture is not an entity in which change in any feature requires change in all other features.

Third, all human societies have neighbors who constitute part of their total environment. The nature of the interactions between human societies, whether cooperative (in many cases through intermarriage) or hostile, is a factor in each case.

Fourth, after agriculture began to produce surpluses, the effective environment of any

Figure 5 (left). The evolution of weaponry has been accompanied by changes in the nature and function of warfare in human society. Figure 6 (right). The ships plying the Red Sea trading routes are of a design that may be traced back thousands of years to Middle Eastern prehistory.

society was extended enormously beyond its local territory. The evolution of large settlement centers and of states made each society dependent on other societies. Trade and other economic and political institutions eventually extended the functional environment of each social unit to many parts of the world and modified the nature of the adaptive processes. The apartment dweller in New York City today depends on manufactured goods from many distant lands, and the nature of his society is a response to factors very different from those that affected the native Indians of Manhattan. The present technological potentials are such that man has created largely artificial habitats in Antarctica and a completely artificial environment for space travel. The limitations on his adaptability to such an environment are not yet known.

Fifth, that cultural evolution has been stimulated by a steady improvement in technology does not mean that social progress can be measured by the technological inventory, whether it was invented locally or borrowed. Few developing societies have drawn upon the total available technology of the world and each has adapted technology to its local requirements, with somewhat distinctive effects. Moreover, it is being discovered daily that a high degree of technological development does not necessarily mean a rich or happy life. Externally, there is an increasing threat of nuclear extinction; and internally, even the affluent segments of society are torn by conflicting goals and uncertainties while the basic biological needs remain unfulfilled in enormous portions of contemporary populations. These technological side effects make the adaptation of social segments to one another and of nations to one another more complicated than adaptation to the natural environment.

Finally, man's utilization of his environment rarely leaves it unaffected; even in pre-Columbian California, the natural forests were destroyed by fires set deliberately in order to create grasslands for the herbi-

vores that were an important food. During most of his existence, however, the degree of man's exploitation of resources did not greatly damage the land. More recently, overgrazing, deforestation, and careless cultivation methods have seriously impaired the soils, and use of insecticides and herbicides has had deleterious side effects. Traces of DDT are now detectable even in penguins in Antarctica. In the United States, urban growth has preempted huge areas and has dumped sewage and industrial waste into the major rivers and lakes. Little of the landscape would be recognizable today in terms of its appearance even fifty years ago, except for certain mountain ranges—and even these bear the scars of man's presence. It is no wonder that disclosures of what man is doing to the balance of nature is a current theme attracting increasing attention today.

EARLY HOMINID ADAPTATION

The following examples of cultural-ecological adaptations begin with the earliest cases that can be inferred from prehistory or that are known ethnographically and proceed to more complex ones. In all of these cases, the proto-hominids and hominids were oriented toward biological survival. Stylized or culturally derived features had minor importance.

Much of the evidence for the earliest hominids comes from Africa, where the archaeological sites contain proto-hominid remains and simple forms of deliberately worked flints without handles. The sites, however, contain bones of such large mammals as rhinoceros and hippopotamus. These finds

Figure 7. The first Australians probably migrated from Asia before the last glaciation, or before the rising sea level cut off their continent. Adapting superbly as hunter-foragers, they grew in numbers until their population reached an estimated 300,000 in the late 1700s. At that time, disease and European intrusion began to decimate the nomads, and by 1947 only 46,000 remained. Aboriginal progress in gaining a foothold in the larger society has been slow, retarded by damaging and isolating race relations. Incorporation is now accelerating under recent government policies.

might indicate ability to hunt large animals. Although such hunting cannot be categorically denied, evidence of hunting devices such as spears, which were known in the Upper Paleolithic, and the fact that large game that had been crippled were scavenged in later times throw doubt on claims that early hominids were true hunters. The historical tribes of the Chilean archipelago gathered in large numbers to feast on stranded whales. Eating spoiled meat is not inherently repulsive but is a consequence of cultural standards, which vary widely. The mounted Mongols, for example, often placed meat under their saddles to "ripen" it.

Until more evidence is obtained on the extent of hunting large animals by special means, it must be assumed that the earliest hominids were all essentially food foragers like other primates. Their bipedal locomotion, however, enabled them to range over areas thirty or more miles in diameter, and their cultural equipment enabled them to transport foods to a central point and perhaps store them. It cannot be assumed that the nuclear family had evolved, for this presupposes sexual complementarity in subsistence activities that cannot be shown positively to have evolved until the Upper Paleolithic, after which it became basic to all societies. Before this, sexual unions were probably not formalized and the family was most likely *matrifocal* (centered on the mother) because it consisted of a female and her offspring by various males.

Our understanding of the nature of the early hominid family and of larger groups is based largely on speculation. It is known, however, that about 50,000 years ago a technology was evolved that enabled men to adapt to hunting in the glacial climates of the north. They were aided in these adaptations by spears and spear throwers (atlatls); probably by use of drives, pitfalls, deadfalls, and ambushes that may have had much greater antiquity; by a variety of specially shaped stone implements for cutting and scraping; by awls or needles for sewing pro-

tective clothing; by knowledge of how to make fire; almost certainly by means of preserving and storing both vegetable and animal foods; and possibly by using houses as well as caves that served as headquarter settlements but not necessarily as permanent habitation sites. Men now could survive in many kinds of areas. Our knowledge of overall population densities, size, permanence, and composition of social groups, however, is only speculative.

With this subsistence technology, it is reasonable to assume a complementarity developed between the sexes that thereafter formed the basis of the nuclear family. The task of the men was the more arduous one of hunting, which could be performed by lone individuals but was frequently more productive if a number of men helped one another, as in drives. Women became custodians of the camp, protectors of the young (whose period of helplessness was now extended), cooks, carriers of water, and collectors of vegetable foods. The last activity was competitive, and where the number of women was large, each would collect less than if working alone.

Thus, the basic sexual divisions of labor developed and the main components of recent human society were established tens of thousands of years ago. Most of what is known about the nature of larger aggregates of families comes from ethnography; however, ethnographic interpretation can be projected back in time only with extreme caution. Useful ethnographic cases have usually been recorded only within the last 100 years, and, as a further limitation, factors relevant to ecological adaptations have been systematically examined mainly within the last thirty or forty years.

HUNTING AND GATHERING ADAPTATION

In assessing the technologies of hunting and gathering societies, it is necessary to view such technologies as functional devices that can get jobs done rather than as formal or stylized features. In hunting, there are two

main categories: those techniques used for small game and those for large game, although some may be used for either one. Spears seem to have been used for large game, especially the now-extinct species, because these devices were probably more effective owing to their greater weight. They were probably first used without stone tips, but later they had large stone points, as compared with the size of arrowheads, and these were distinguishable by form or style. Other common means of hunting large game, such as deer, antelope, caribou, bison, rhinoceros, and elephant, were drives with fire, often over cliffs or into ambushes. Traps, nets, bolas, blow guns, pitfalls, deadfalls, as well as arrows were used for smaller game.

For collecting and transporting vegetable foods, nets and containers of basketry, skin, and other materials served equally well. Food preservation and storage was less de-

veloped in the tropics because of the heat, moisture, and insects. In the far north, meat was more abundant and could be smoked and mixed with fat. A lone fisherman could use a variety of techniques—nets, hooks, multipronged spears, and arrows—whereas fishing groups more often relied on seine nets, traps, and weirs. In South America alone, more than 200 species of wild plants were used as drugs to stupefy fish in quiet pools. Where watercraft were needed, they were usually dugout and bark canoes and balsa reed rafts, depending on the materials available. Canoes also served for transportation along the coast and over the inland waterways, as in Canada. Dog packing and dog-drawn toboggans or sleds were used to travel over the snow of the far north, and people traveled on snowshoes. People were thus able to maintain some contact with one another over areas much larger than those inhabited by desert groups. In deserts, water

Figure 8 (left). The Australian aborigine probably affected his environment to a significant degree. His practice of setting fire to dry woodland areas to drive out small game may have contributed to the formation of grasslands in the northeastern rain forests, and fire-resistant trees in woodland areas still mark his path today. It is also likely that the large Pleistocene kangaroo became extinct at his hands. Figure 9. Sepik River fishermen still use the multipronged spear developed during the Upper Paleolithic.

was transported in baskets, skins, pots, and even eggshells, thereby extending populations into otherwise uninhabitable areas. House types were extremely variable, for nomadic people could use only locally available materials for temporary shelters. Clothing ranged from loincloths in tropical areas to full fur garments in the north.

Equipped with knowledge of virtually every edible plant and with effective means of exploiting most vegetables and animals, population density varied according to the abundance of resources. It ranged from one person per square mile—and rarely more than this—to one person per 50 to 100 square miles. Within this wide range, however, the size, permanency, and character of social groups depended on cultural factors and the nature of the local environment.

A few areas, such as the Northwest Coast of North America, offered a combination of riverine resources, maritime foods, and animals and plants, as described in the chapter "Primitive Societies." Here, societies could nucleate in large permanent villages. These villages had clans and moieties (descent groups based on a fictive relationship) and ceremonial organizations. Leisure afforded by these resources permitted high achievements in house and canoe construction, wood carving, painting, weaving, and other crafts. It had even made possible hereditary lineages of superior status within the otherwise egalitarian clans, and thus resembled proto-states.

Dogrib, Shoshoni, and Bushmen

Most of the world's hunting, gathering, and fishing societies had a much sparser population than the Northwest Coast, were seasonally nomadic rather than permanently settled, and were divided into groups of fluctuating size. Despite many dissimilar features of environment and technology operating on them, some fundamental similarities in conditions and requirements are associated with the emergence of comparable adaptive processes and social traits in such

groups. For example, the northern Canadian Athapaskan Dogrib, the Great Basin Shoshoni, and the South African Bushmen are three societies that occupied completely dissimilar environments and survived by developing somewhat dissimilar technologies, yet their social groupings were strikingly similar because of the operation of similar adaptive processes.

These three societies had very sparse populations: the Shoshoni about one person per twenty square miles, the Dogrib about half this density, and the Bushmen about one person per eleven square miles. The total populations apparently varied over the years as famines, droughts, and disease struck, but the general patterns of population nucleation and fragmentation and of group composition seem to have remained much the same.

Even today, most hunting and gathering bands characteristically subdivide during portions of the year into units that consist of some four or five families that remain together at all times. These have been called local bands, task forces, or family clusters. A group of this size is necessary to ensure mutual aid and cooperation in certain subsistence chores and in tending children. The Shoshoni, Dogrib, and Bushman family clusters did not depart greatly from this figure. The social composition of these smaller

Figure 10 (above). Bushmen playing ball at a headquarters camp. The uncertainties of their existence have given rise to collective sharing of food, water, and objects, for without cooperation they could not survive the famines and droughts of the Kalahari. Figure 11 (below). The aboriginal California Indians lived in small, local, autonomous groups that seldom exceeded a few hundred people. The abundance of acorns as subsistence permitted them to remain economically self-sufficient, with each such segmentary tribe concerned only with its own activities.

groups was also similar in that children preferred to remain with their parents and bring spouses from elsewhere. An equal number had to marry into other groups according to the group size, proximity, and resources rather than by a fixed rule.

Each family camped separately, but several family camps clustered in a region and foraged and hunted as a unit throughout the year. Bushman headquarter camps were made, often with other clusters, at the few permanent water holes; Shoshoni wintered in a region that had been most productive of pine nuts and that also had water; and the Dogrib gathered at summer fishing sites. During the remainder of the year, the Shoshoni and Bushmen carried water between water holes in search of vegetable foods and game, and the Dogrib traveled in search of game and trapping areas.

Territories exploited by the larger groups were overlapping, and there was no claim of ownership rights. The total areas covered by the Dogrib were much greater than those of the Shoshoni or Bushmen, both of whom were limited by the scarcity of water. The largest so-called "band" of hunters and gatherers was rarely more than 500 persons, but in many cases it was smaller. The large band, however, represented little more than the limits of intermarriage and common dialect. It included areas so large that the family clusters could not possibly have participated and cooperated in common activities with all inhabitants to gain any sense of unity or overall leadership; in fact, among these societies the leader was no more than a competent individual whose influence extended little beyond his kinfolk.

Among the Shoshoni, intermarriages extended from the Death Valley region into southern Idaho, causing a kind of network of local alliances that even cut across language groups, such as Shoshonean and Paiute, but these networks lacked social ties. The fairly clear boundaries of the large Dogrib and Bushman bands were marked by natural barriers.

Although the Dogrib, Shoshoni, and Bushmen were sufficiently similar in their adaptations to be thought of as a cultural type, other hunters and gatherers varied in important ways. The Indians of California had adapted to subsistence on acorns by leaching out the tannic acid found in them and making flour from the purified seeds. The abundance of acorns, supplemented by game and coastal shellfish, permitted an unusually dense population. However, the population was nucleated into many small permanent villages that were largely independent of one another. The fairly ample subsistence al-

Figure 13. Copper engraving of a Plains Indian hunting bison. After contact with white culture and the introduction of the horse, the Indians formed large, mounted hunting groups to encircle the bison and, later, intruding settlers.

lowed the villagers to elaborate certain aspects of their culture, although not as greatly as the Northwest Coast people. Material elaborations included extraordinarily fine basketry on the central coast, crafts of Northwest Coast influence in the northwest, and complex rituals, especially in the initiation ceremonies for young people among the Chumash on the south coast and the Channel Islands.

Plains Indian Adaptation

A very different adaptation is exemplified by the Indians of the Great Plains. The huge herds of bison in this region seemingly were an unlimited source of food, and the sodded grasslands precluded the spread of native farming by means of digging sticks, except in certain river bottoms. Hunting alone has rarely afforded a subsistence basis that yields important surpluses, however, as indicated by the low population density of areas where hunting predominated. The Plains population was not much denser than that of the Great Basin Shoshoni.

The Plains Indians were not well equipped to hunt large and dangerous game until they acquired horses from the Europeans. Drives over cliffs (assisted by dogs and occasionally by burning of the prairie) and the use of spears (later supplanted by the bow and arrow) were used prehistorically. Animals could also be pursued by hunters on snowshoes in deep snow. Such hunting, however, did not deplete the bison herds except west of the Rocky Mountains, where they became extinct about 1830.

The social effects of bison hunting are known from historic times, when the horse had already reached the Plains, and some features of the later adaptations probably existed before then. The bison hunt had become a truly collective enterprise, for it was carried out by a large group of mounted hunters who encircled the animals, killing individual bison with bows and arrows and spears. To ensure success, special societies of men had authority to regulate the activi-

ties of the hunters lest an individual hunter frighten the game away.

The Plains Indians made large encampments during the hunting season, and many tribes of the Plains were structured in intermarrying clans and several kinds of men's and a few women's organizations. The hunting bands broke up into individual family clusters, much like those of other hunters, to gather vegetable foods each spring. The precise composition of these groups before the horse appeared is not known. It is clear, however, that the horse not only expedited hunting but also gave the Indians greater mobility. The regions of exploitation of each group expanded and the territories of the different tribes began to overlap, leading eventually to patterned warfare and to alliances.

The Patrilineal Band

Another type of hunting society, which Steward termed the patrilineal band, arose in widely diverse regions of the world—Tasmania, Tierra del Fuego, southern California (a different group of Shoshoneans than those of the Great Basin), and possibly parts of Australia—as a result of similar ecological adaptations. The early data on Australia and the Bushmen are questionable, but the other societies consisted of thirty to fifty persons who lived together permanently and hunted small herds of nonmigratory game. This masculine task was of such importance that men remained with the group of their birth all their lives. All the men were presumed to be related to one another owing to a myth of common descent, and they brought wives into their own band instead of relocating upon marriage. Such bands were made possible by an adaptation to an environment that supported groups larger than the family clusters that developed else-

where, which were known to be interrelated. With some exceptions, such as the Northwest Coast and Plains Indians, these hunting and gathering societies generally lacked social elaborations. The smallest bands or subsistence groups had so little contact with one another that any further restrictions on marriage through exogamous clans or moieties would so reduce the number of potential spouses that they could not survive. The principal divisions of society were based on sex and age, and men and women had their distinctive roles and activities. In some cases a social elaboration that was present was a man's secret tribal society, which affirmed adulthood as well as the distinctiveness of men.

SURPLUS AND NONSURVIVAL GOALS

After man developed a relatively effective level of agricultural technology, subsistence needs were soon cared for and new kinds of goals in addition to that of simple physical survival emerged and became important. These goals were made possible by the food surpluses that were now potentially available. But the goals took several forms. They were not conceived as purely logical or rational objectives that guided social change, and they were not whimsical, without causes. The potentials led to various kinds of change, each of which had certain preconditions and determinants that were rooted in cultural-ecological adaptations.

During a long period, new social arrangements evolved so gradually that each succeeding generation was unaware that change was occurring. State-structured societies, in which hereditary segments or social classes developed within the former egalitarian societies, appeared without foresight or planning, but they were accepted as essential features of an original creation. It is only during the last few hundred years that change is recognized to be an inherent characteristic of society and technology and that efforts have been made to understand its direction and perhaps find means to control

Figure 14. In many parts of the world the extensive irrigation systems of the early civilizations still exist. Above, a Roman aqueduct in Urbino, Italy; below that, the aqueduct at Morelia, Mexico. The lower photograph shows a village in Spain that actually has been built into the walls of a Roman aqueduct.

it. For example, domesticated plants required a thousand years or more of selective breeding before they figured prominently as subsistence. At first, these plants were grown to supplement the gathering of wild vegetation, which meant that nomadic societies had to return each year to the same place for the harvest. This early farming eventually led to one of two major social arrangements: either every member of society had more time to pursue activities not directly related to survival, or society divided into hereditary groups of food producers who worked full-time to support hereditary classes of rulers, priests, warriors, artisans, and builders.

PRIMARY CLASS-STRUCTURED STATES

The early, primary states or civilizations developed independently of one another in Egypt, Mesopotamia, the Indus Valley, and China in the Old World, and in Mesoamerica and the Andes in the New World.

The agricultural basis in the Old World was wheat, barley, rice, millet, and other plants in different localities, and in the New World it was maize, beans, and squashes together with more than a hundred other locally grown species. But the growing of these crops was not enough to produce the adaptations that led to highly developed states. There were many inhibiting factors, including the difficulty of cultivating soil with nothing more than a wooden digging stick. There were also preconditions of state development.

The primary civilized states developed in large, arid river valleys. Wild vegetation clogged the land immediately adjoining the rivers, but there were no extensive forests that required clearing with metal tools, which did not emerge until the Iron Age (about 1000 B.C. in the Old World). Bronze, invented about 3000 B.C. in the Old World and about 1000 B.C. in the Americas, was so scarce that it was reserved for weapons, for ornaments, and for religious artifacts. Because irrigation was essential to agricul-

ture in many areas other than the flood plains of the rivers, Karl Wittfogel in 1938 postulated that as irrigation works expanded, the communities served by the canals and ditches had to cooperate to get them built. A managerial force developed to oversee this cooperation and grew into a class of rulers who controlled all production and eventually all activities of the state. This is certainly a partial explanation of state evolution in some areas of deeply entrenched rivers, such as those in the central Andes, which could not have been exploited in any other way. It was subsequently found, however, that extensive irrigation works often followed rather than preceded state development.

In 1966 Robert McC. Adams found that during the early stages of state growth in Mesopotamia, the low-lying Tigris and Euphrates rivers could easily be diverted by short, lateral canals. Meanwhile, the importance of irrigation in the Valley of Mexico was questioned. Yet states developed in strikingly similar ways in both areas. Adams proposed that specialization in small territories brought local populations into a dependency relationship with one another through exchange of crops. This exchange became so intense that it required centralized control. This function was carried out in the beginning by the priesthoods of the earlier independent villages. Thus, the first states in Mexico and Mesopotamia, and apparently elsewhere, were *theocratic*.

Political control by priests continued until militarism appeared, apparently stimulated by the desire to increase goods at the expense of neighboring states. But the centers of civilizations remained in the same river valleys for at least 2,000 years.

After flourishing for more than 2,000 years in the centers of primary civilizations, cultivation began to be adapted to other environments in different parts of the world. The new adaptations in the Old World were made possible by the production of iron tools, used for clearing the land and culti-

Figure 15. While Europe was in the throes of the Middle Ages, the people of Mesoamerica were building one of the most elaborate civilizations ever known. Symbolic of this "Golden Age" of Mexico is Teotihuacán, an agriculturally based urban center probably founded about 150 B.C. and eventually dominating a region over a hundred miles in all directions. Complex rituals and organized priesthood characterized this period and are reflected today in the still-standing massive pyramids, gigantic plazas, detailed frescoes, and stone carvings of plumed serpents.

vating it, and by the harnessing of draft animals to pull the plows. The focus of civilization spread to the eastern Mediterranean and then into northern Europe.

PASTORALISTS AND FARMERS

As farming diffused to societies other than the primary civilizations, it created a more dense population—but it did not lead to civilized states. There were various local kinds of adaptations that served as inhibiting factors to this form of state evolution. A few of these societies developed a system of hereditary status and power over land ownership, which suggests an important basis for the original evolution of state-structured societies. Others, however, remained independent, egalitarian communities, although their life was enriched by the possibilities afforded by agriculture.

The Pueblo Adaptation

An outstanding example of an intensive farming society that did not develop a state structure is the Pueblo Indian society of the southwestern United States. Today, the Pueblos grow sufficient crops to provide ample surpluses against famine, they build large multistoried towns of stone walls, they are expert in weaving, pottery, and other manufactures, and they have an extraordinarily complex social and religious organization. Although the villages intermarry and carry on trade with one another, their interdependency has not reached the point that requires any kind of superordinate controls.

Pueblo agriculture can be traced back some 2,000 years. During this time, the various ecological adaptations, together with certain historical factors, entailed the evolution of different kinds of societies. At first, there were many small, independent farming communities scattered over a wide area, but they were closely spaced with reference to one another. Each community presumably consisted of a group of persons related by common descent traced through the women (matrilineality), inasmuch as this is the type of kinship system that has characterized these groups since they first became known to outsiders. During the Great Pueblo period, which began about A.D. 1200, many of these small farm communities had been abandoned, probably because of warfare initiated by raiders who were possibly Athapaskan-speaking people from the far north. The survivors of the small villages found refuge in much larger pueblos, where each matrilineage became the beginning of the contemporary clans that are found today in the western Pueblo towns. The rich ritual and religious cultures of contemporary and historic Pueblos are in large part the result of the mingling of the different beliefs and practices of the small villages when their residents came together to form the larger communities.

The Pueblo adaptations in the arid Southwest precluded state development for several reasons. First, the villages were somewhat precarious, for they had been eliminated from most of the larger area they had occupied during the preceding millennium. Second, the large villages following the great period were too widely separated

to form meaningful alliances. And, third, there was no local specialization that could lead to an interdependency; each village produced the same kind of goods and was self-sufficient.

Proto-States in the Americas

In eastern North America, intensive agriculture had spread throughout the major river valleys, especially that of the Mississippi River and its tributaries. Land was cultivated in the rich river bottoms, where annual floods replenished the soil. Although the adjacent forested lands were ill-suited for intensive cultivation, the dense populations supported by these river bottoms provided the basis for the complex of temple mounds that apparently constituted the integrating center for basically theocratic proto-states. These "mound cultures," however, did not survive into historic times. Society reverted to the hunting and farming carried on by independent tribes, although certain confederacies in the southeastern United States and the League of the Iroquois in the northeast represent vestiges of earlier development. Nevertheless, all these tribes were structured on a kinship basis that united rather large numbers of people into exogamous groups (matrilineal clans), each with a common ancestress traced through the mothers of the members.

The influence of agricultural efficiency on state formation was inhibited by other adaptations. In the tropical forests of South America, dense populations (twenty persons or more per square mile) bordered the major rivers, but each village had access to abundant riverine resources, each could cultivate certain crops on the river margin between floods and other crops just above the flood level, and each could hunt in the forested hinterland. Consequently, there was no need for interdependence. The leisure afforded by this abundance allowed aesthetic development in ceramics and other crafts. Ceramics are among the few artifacts that have been preserved in this hot, humid cli-

mate, but their stylistic elaboration does not indicate a highly developed state society. The modern riverine villages were all independent, and each was structured on egalitarian principles, except for a tendency toward hereditary status differences on the upper Amazon.

The rich salmon fisheries of the Northwest Coast Indians provided the economic basis for a status system of nobles and commoners within clans, and even slaves. This system operated on the basis of competition for prestige through ceremonial gifts, or potlatches. The principal noble or chief of one village sought to prove his superior wealth by potlatching the chief of another village. His fellow villagers and kinsmen willingly contributed their own goods because of the vicarious satisfaction they received. Fishing, combined with farming, also produced proto-states in much of Polynesia.

Egalitarian Adaptations in Africa

In sub-Saharan Africa, farming and pastoralism were combined in different degrees. The so-called "cattle complex" has acquired what Robert Manners calls a mystique, in that the value placed on cattle allegedly explains the whole culture. However, cattle raising is actually a very rational business. During the 1950s, Rada and Neville Dyson-Hudson lived with the Karamojong of Uganda and studied the cultural-ecological adaptations required for cattle raising. This society has a dual economy: farming by

Figure 17 (below). Masai herders collecting blood from the neck of one of their cattle. In East Africa, pastoralism is extensive but is often combined with cultivation associated with the sexual division of labor: cattle keeping left to the men and gardening to the women. The pastoralists and farmers are interdependent economically, bound together in raid or trade relations. Figure 18 (right). These Anharic nomads of Ethiopia prefer the freedom of mobility to the accumulation of wealth practiced by the Danakil, with whom they trade in the village of Bati. Proud of their heritage, the Anharic invoke Owen Lattimore's words, "the pure nomad is a poor nomad."

women near a permanent central settlement and herding by men who move about over the arid savannas with their herds. Droughts, raids, and epidemics are constant threats to the herds, so that surpluses for commercial use of dairy products and beef are impossible. Moreover, the society's marginal position relative to the external world and lack of transportation preclude access to markets. In order to survive, the Karamojong rarely eat meat, except on ceremonial occasions. They subsist mainly on the milk and on blood drawn periodically from the live animals. They have no developed technology for storing foods in this extremely hot country, although butter mixed with urine and boiled may be stored for a short time.

Domesticated plants, cattle, sheep, and goats had spread widely through sub-Saharan Africa. In some portions of East and West Africa, there was sufficient surplus to serve as the foundation for elevating certain clans and lineages to superior status. These have been designated "kingdoms," although, to take one East African tribe as an example, not more than 2 or 3 percent of the Baganda were relieved from the ordinary chores of subsistence and supported by their tribesmen. In other words, privileged lines of close relations developed within otherwise egalitarian clans. The limited portions of sub-Saharan Africa having such kingdoms had the unusual population density of more than thirty persons per square mile. In the less fertile portions of this area, domesticated plants and animals did not constitute a subsistence basis for even proto-states, and despite government efforts relatively few tribes are yet part of a market economy.

The few kingdoms aside, most East African tribes were essentially egalitarian subsistence farmers and cattle raisers, although some were transformed drastically under the impact of colonialism.

The case of the Karamojong presents an interesting contrast to the camel nomads of North Africa, who extend through the Mid-

dle East into central Asia, where the horse took the place of the camel. In this case, the necessary nomadism of cattle breeders brought conflicts over grazing territories, which entailed warfare and raids, for the mounted nomads had far greater mobility than such herders as the Karamojong which increased the opportunity for raiding. Many of these societies tended to become predators. Among the Arabs of North Africa and the Middle East, many centuries of warfare had introduced rules, somewhat like a game, which served to redistribute the camels without entirely depriving any society of them. The camel nomads raided the oasis dwellers for their vegetable produce but usually limited such raids, for they needed to preserve the farmers to ensure a continuing supply of produce. The horse nomads of inner Asia became more extreme predators, raiding in all directions from Asia and sweeping over China. China, however, absorbed them in the end.

THE INDUSTRIALIZED WORLD
The tremendous acceleration of technological progress and scientific discovery during the last few centuries makes it less profitable to think of social development with reference to cultural-ecological adaptations. The natural environment is still with us, although it is modified increasingly by technology. Nevertheless, the exploitation of the environment is no longer limited mainly to the locality where a particular society lives.

Every modern society uses goods that are manufactured from resources extracted throughout the world, from places usually quite distant from the society itself. Moreover, the social components of the modern environment are so diversified and so widespread that adaptation has taken distinctive forms today. For these reasons, an analysis of modern life has traditionally been the topic of different disciplines of the social sciences, such as economics, political science, and sociology.

In the modern world, for example, efficient technology and transportation have made tin from Bolivia and Malaya, uranium from Canada, oil from the Near East, and cattle and sheep products from Australia and New Zealand essential factors in the lives of every American in the United States. Moreover, the social ideals and military intentions of eastern Europe, of China, and in fact of all other nations become considerations that affect national thought, foreign investments, armaments, and all aspects of foreign policy. None of these factors is within the distinctive scope of anthropological studies, although anthropologists are becoming increasingly aware of them.

On the other hand, anthropologists pay increasing attention to subcultural groups, or those groups that are part of the larger society and yet are distinctive in their life ways. These are the various ethnic minorities, racial groups, and recent migrants from alien cultures. Whatever the nature and origin of subcultural groups, however, cultural ecology can throw some light on the nature of their adaptation to the larger environment in which they develop.

Analysis of the ecology of subcultures becomes very complex if attention is focused on a place such as New York City. This city has a concentration of supranational-level institutions, such as corporations of many kinds, mass media, and religious organizations, in virtually all fields. These give character to the totality of the city. As a settlement, New York City is now part of a megalopolis that extends from Washington, D.C., to Boston. The city itself has urban-level government institutions that operate within the framework of the state, and it has neighborhoods. The character of these neighborhoods is determined by their residents' adaptation to the city as well as by their ethnic, racial, and religious backgrounds, their incomes, and their occupations.

Many people connected with the institutions that function in New York have formed communities in suburbs of states surrounding the city. Their subculture is determined partly by income, partly by a stereotype of how they should live, and partly by local factors, such as accessibility to the city or the presence of river and ocean fronts and other features of physical geography. In any urbanization study, such as one of New York City, the adaptive processes are implied but rarely spelled out as ecological processes.

THE DEVELOPING NATIONS

Prior to the industrial revolution, many large areas of the world were occupied by tribal societies, several adaptations of which have already been discussed. Under colonialism, all of these became dependencies of the imperialist nations that introduced economic institutions and extractive processes that rapidly changed the subsistence societies into ones with new kinds of goals, particularly goals dictated by the colonial powers. In more recent years, colonialism has given way to new, independent, and developing nations, which have also been referred to as "underdeveloped" nations. The effect of modernizing influences on these diverse societies is extremely varied, but a few examples of similar but independent internal transformations that occurred when new cultural goals were introduced by external influences can be briefly sketched.

Even prior to the era of colonialism, contacts with the modernized world of Europe had introduced factors that had changed local life before the societies had continuous contact with Europeans. An example of this is the horse, which spread widely in North and South America from the Spanish conquistadors and completely altered native life, in that it gave the Indians greater mobility and consequently greater efficiency in hunting and converted many of them into predators who raided one another and the European settlers.

Another example is the case of the fur trappers of the far north and the rubber tappers of the Amazon. Although both societies began as quite different types of social groups, the effect of the fur trade and the rubber trade respectively was to bring about marked similarities in the local societies. In much of Canada, the bands of predominantly large-game hunters found that a market for furs yielded returns in terms of the manufactured European goods they coveted, so that the family trapping territory developed in place of the band. Each territory was bounded and in parts of Canada was registered with the local provincial government.

In South America, farming tribes such as the Mundurucú (who are described in detail in the chapter "Social and Cultural Change") abandoned their village organization to collect wild rubber along the river banks. Eventually all families moved to their rubber-producing areas along the rivers and such organization as had existed in the bands and villages disappeared in favor of the local family unit. Among both the Canadian and Amazonian tribes, this re-

mained the permanent unit, partly because it produced an exchangeable commodity and partly because such family ownership enabled the people to practice conservation of their resources. The factor that now held the families together was more the trader and his access to the foreign market than the former bands or villages and their local chiefs.

Elsewhere in the world, a widespread form of European exploitation of native people was the establishment of a plantation economy, where local resources permitted. Such an economy has variously been based on the extraction of rubber, tin, and other minerals, and on agricultural produce such as sugar, coffee, cotton, palm nuts, and sisal. Such extraction basically alters the local economy, the values, and the social structure of the native people.

Many plantations initially started with fairly primitive technology and as small family-owned enterprises, but with the improvement of technology the local plantation developed in size until it required such financing as to be corporation-owned. In addition, the workers went through certain transitional stages in their adaptation to the total plantation situations and the larger national societies. At first, they were bound as laborers through various mechanisms and were required to do the work needed on the plantation. Later, they became permanent residents of the plantation towns, moving away from their villages of origin and associating, frequently, with persons of other villages. They became proletarianized wage laborers. A further stage was entered when the workers moved to other jobs, frequently to the now-developing urban centers. Thus processes of urbanization began to appear in all parts of the world.

A complementary development was that the plantations and the European towns associated with them required foods, so that in those areas where truck gardening was possible the native people began to claim individual rights to farm plots, which were

then passed on through inheritance to their own children. An example of this is western Kenya. Here the Kipsigis formerly lived in small clusters, farming and herding cattle on communal land; about a generation ago, however, they took up all the land privately and enclosed it so that others could not drive herds over it.

Probably the most important factor in these processes of modernization is that the people acquired new goals that differed completely from the previous subsistence objectives. They now saw what modernization could give them—especially manufactured goods but also education and other means of improving their wealth and status.

The processes of modernization have taken many forms in different parts of the world. These forms include sharecropping, tenant farming, and even owning where it has been possible to amass capital for investment. Few native people today retain the traditional values that were associated with subsistence farming. Nor do these values remain unaffected by the larger institutions that were mediated to them formerly through colonialism and more recently through their own efforts.

LOOKING TOWARD THE FUTURE

The present mood seems to be one of subdued but pervasive pessimism. Partly, this reflects the many simmering hostilities that may boil over into nuclear conflict and that may well lead to extermination of all mankind. There is also not only discontent among those who remain below the subsistence level but among those who strive in a competitive world for a larger share of industrially produced goods. The pessimistic mood also reflects the omnipresent destruction of the environment. Pollution of water is a problem everywhere, and air is being polluted not only by industrial waste but by noise.

From a world view, however, probably the greatest source of alarm is the destruction of irreplaceable resources. The most meager subsistence needs of much of the population are not being met, despite dramatic improvements in certain crops, and with the foreseeable population growth it is not likely to be met. Meanwhile, industrialization is using up sources of energy and raw materials as if the supplies were unlimited. Utilization of new kinds of energy, such as nuclear energy, obscure the limitations of the environment.

Finally, the industrial societies are changing so rapidly that the younger generation of today finds itself maladjusted to the values of only a few years ago. How long can man continue to readapt to a changing world? Or has the limit already been passed?

Structural-Functional Analysis

25

If you have ever lived for an extended period in a society other than your own, you know the sequence full well. At first, the people and customs are totally foreign and in some ways frightening, but eventually this "culture shock" wears off and you begin to gain a new perspective. What had been indistinguishable in its foreignness gradually comes into focus as a composite of wholly distinct individuals behaving in an almost endless variety of ways. However, after you return to your native society and are asked informally about your experiences, some patterns begin to emerge, if only in the telling. You find yourself uttering generalizations about the behavior of groups and institutions that only a short while ago you had perceived as unique entities.

Social anthropology involves much the same sequence. The social anthropologist, too, must reduce a mass of perceptions about individual behavior to some kind of order; he must make sense out of what might initially appear to be wholly discrete and unconnected behavioral phenomena. In addition to merely "making sense" of his observations, however, he must bring to bear the accumulated wisdom of his discipline. His analysis is often based on two key concepts: structure and function. In the interactions among individuals and groups that represent the behavior of a population, the anthropologist sees certain formal relationships that persist regularly over time— for example, relationships between religious acts and economic acts, between the ways in which his informants refer to their kinsmen, even between themes that typically occur in myths and folktales. Regularities that tend to appear in the *form* of the interactions, rather than in what such interactions mean, are the framework of social structure. Together these regularities make up a social system, and through his observations the anthropologist attempts to perceive the "rules" on which such a system is based, the "rules" whereby activities, kinship terms, themes, or whatever are organized and rendered meaningful to the members of the society. The *function* of such a structure is the contribution it makes, through its interaction with other elements in the social system, to the maintenance of that system.

Essentially, a structural-functional analysis of a social system is an attempt to define the nature of the enduring forms of relationships within a society—its structure—with reference to the "rules" or principles of social organization on which these relation-

Figure 2. A Trobriand Islander grooming his hair in preparation for the *kula* festivities, in which he will entertain his trading partner. Ceremonial exchange is essential to this prestige economy, and vigorous participation establishes a man's name and his sense of worth. **Figure 3** (right). A map of the *kula* ring.

ships are based, and to show how these sets contribute to the maintenance of society as a whole—their functions.

Social anthropologists have differed in their assessments of the kinds of functions they find significant in the activities of the members of a society. Bronislaw Malinowski, one of the earliest of the so-called functionalists in anthropology, emphasized two tenets. The first is that all the elements of a society are interdependent. In this view, society forms a coherent, interrelated whole in which each part affects every other part, and Malinowski termed these mutual effects "integral functions." The second is that each institution in a society fulfills certain basic human psychological or biological needs, such as those for adequate nutrition, protection from the harshness of the environment, and sex and reproduction.

In the course of becoming organized to fulfill these basic needs, a society necessarily shapes the responses of its members in such a way that certain "derived needs" are created in them that must also be fulfilled.

These derived needs are based on biological needs and come from the necessity for people to meet their biological requirements in the ways customary in their society rather than in any of the many other possible ways. Thus, hunger is a basic need, but what, how, when, and where one learns to eat can be such potent derived needs that people will starve in the presence of perfectly nutritious foods because such foods do not meet the requirements instilled by cultural conditioning.

Malinowski's view is that any set of social practices is explainable by determining its contribution to either basic or derived needs, and such social and psychological contributions are what he means by "functions." His approach emphasizes the similarity of all societies in terms of the functional interrelatedness of their parts and the need-fulfilling character of the institutions of that society. This view of functionalism, however, does not account very well for the important differences that exist among various societies. It is difficult, for instance, to account for the differences between matrilineal and patrilineal kinship systems when both can be considered as functioning to fulfill the same basic needs—sexual satisfaction, care of the young, socialization, and so on.

Malinowski's analysis of the *kula*, in his book *Argonauts of the Western Pacific*, is the classic example of his brand of functional analysis.

THE *KULA* RING
A fleet of canoes, laden with red shell necklaces, approaches an island just off the southeastern tip of New Guinea. When it is sighted, the inhabitants of a nearby village rush to the beach, bearing armloads of white shell bracelets. Once the canoes are beached a feast begins, during which the necklaces (*soulava*) are exchanged for the bracelets (*mwali*) in an elaborate ceremony. For the next few weeks, almost the entire village participates in a series of rituals and feasts.

Eventually, however, the visitors depart for home, taking with them their newly acquired cargo of bracelets. And some months later, after appropriate magic has been performed, a party of men from the village sets out on a canoe voyage of its own, in this instance to an island lying in the direction opposite that from which the bearers of the red necklaces had come. Their intention is to trade the necklaces for white shell bracelets.

The participants in this curious Melanesian trade relationship refer to it as the *kula*. In brief, it can be described as the continuous flow of goods—bracelets and necklaces—around a rough circle of islands, with the bracelets always moving clockwise and the necklaces moving counterclockwise (Figure 3). It is this circular pattern that gave rise to the concept of the *kula* "ring."

At first glance, the *kula* might appear to be simply an economic relationship wherein goods are exchanged according to a rather rigid formula. But Malinowski considered the ramifications of the *kula* to be of profound significance to the several participating societies and perceived that economic considerations were among the least important of these. Most of his data came from the Trobriand Islands, which form an integral part of the "ring." Like most Melanesians, the Trobrianders are sedentary horticulturalists. They are nearly self-sufficient, although some trade with inland farmers and coastal fishermen is necessary. Their participation in the *kula* does not have much effect one way or another on their physical well-being, however, even though some "economic" goods are always traded along with the necklaces and bracelets.

What is more important, Malinowski suggests, is the degree to which the *kula* binds all concerned into a cohesive social unit. All trading is done on an individual basis. Each man has at least two trading partners and the relationship established between such partners is in many cases stronger than that

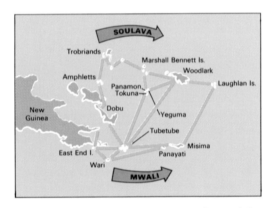

between close kinsmen. Thus, what might appear to be purely an economic relationship actually involves a host of very different sentiments.

This extra-economic aspect of the *kula* is perhaps most clearly evident in the complex of rituals and myths associated with it. There is an elaborate cycle of myths explaining its origins, and most of the behavior relating to the necklace-bracelet exchange has strong magic and religious implications. Even the flow patterns have their mythical bases, and each location within the "ring"— from Kiriwina, the principal island of the Trobriand group, to Wari, the southernmost island—has its local myths and legends. Most of the Trobriand *kula* myths are based on relations with the inhabitants of the island of Dobu, the originators of the *soulava*. The content of these myths typically includes details of noteworthy voyages, participation in them by clan ancestors, and conflicts between Trobriand and Dobuan villages. The magic surrounding the *kula* is complex. Much of it relates to the canoes and their construction and the preparation of an expedition. And a good part of the magic centers on beautification, on making oneself attractive to one's trading partner.

Malinowski did not view the *kula* as a haphazard form of exchange, but rather as a system based on myth, traditional law, and magic rites. All its primary transactions are

Figure 4. Launching of the *kula* canoe. *Kula* trading persists in spite of long European contact and the coexistence of a cash economy. This persistence reflects the continuing wide economic gap between native and European standards of living in the face of which native self-esteem still depends on the older prestige economy. It persists also because its older functions of social integration and the stimulation of production of all native commodities are still necessary.

public and ceremonial and are made according to established rules. And it is not practiced whimsically: the *kula* occurs periodically, at prescribed dates, and is followed along definite trade routes that lead to fixed meeting places. In sociological terms, even though the *kula* is transacted between tribes of quite different language and culture, it is based on a fixed and permanent status, on a partnership binding together some thousands of individuals. In characterizing the relationship that develops among trading partners, Malinowski pointed out that the partnership is a lifelong relationship that implies various mutual duties and privileges and constitutes an intertribal relationship on a grand scale.

The *kula* can thus be perceived as a complex of behavioral patterns, many of which might at first glance appear quite disconnected. Among other things, it involves food preparation for the feasts, performance of a variety of magic rituals, and the development of what amounts to a pattern of fictive kinship (the trading partner relationship) as well as the exchange of goods.

Malinowski analyzed two sets of functions of the *kula*. First, he asked how its various elements unite into an integrated whole. He found that each element of the *kula* functions to maintain the institution itself. It is a functionally interrelated pattern wherein the essence of Trobriand and other societies involved can be discerned. Without benefit of functional analysis, even at the relatively simplistic level developed by Malinowski, explanation of this pattern might never have emerged.

His second question was what basic human needs the institution serves. Here Malinowski suggested that there are universal needs for display and prestige. Thus, the individuals involved derive prestige from their generous behavior during the *kula* exchange and are continually provided with opportunities to display their wealth by sharing it with others, by feasting, or by participating in the *kula* exchange itself. Malinowski pointed out that the high value placed on the intrinsically nonutilitarian necklaces and bracelets is similar to the high value Britishers place on the Crown jewels and that both sets of objects function to fulfill the need for display.

A third type of function, about which Malinowski was not explicit, also emerges from his analysis of the *kula* complex. The *kula* serves to mobilize and symbolize the major social relationships of Trobriand society. Kinsmen are called upon to contribute goods for trading and feasting. Trade is carried on between various local communities in order to achieve the proper amounts of goods necessary for the preliminary feasts and for the *kula* expedition itself. And all the local people gather for feasting and canoe racing prior to the expedition, at which time prestige accrues to the chiefs, who make the greatest display of goods at the feast and who *always* win the canoe races. The result is that the importance of local ties is symbolized and reinforced through the mobilization and use of this broad range of social relationships *within* the local area in preparation for carrying on the trade with people *outside* the local areas.

A. R. Radcliffe-Brown, Malinowski's contemporary and chief rival as foremost British social anthropologist of their time, used a quite different concept of function. His approach and that of his followers is often called *structural-functionalism* as distinguished from Malinowski's functionalism. His emphasis is on social function—the contribution a particular institution makes to the maintenance of the society of which it is a part. With this approach, it is possible to account for some of the differences between societies, inasmuch as the social *function* of an institution will vary with the particular *structure* of the institution itself and the structure of the society in which it is located. This is in direct contrast to Malinowski's emphasis on the generalized *psychologi-*

Figure 5. Some kinship terms of the Thonga.
Figure 6 (right). A young girl emerges in her
"coming out" dress from the seclusion that
follows the onset of puberty among many of the
matrilineal valley and plateau Thonga of southern
Zambia. Among the chiefdoms that practice
seclusion, the emergence serves as an elaborate
initiatory ritual with much beer drinking,
drumming, and dancing.

cal functions of the institutions he describes.
The structural-functional approach is illustrated in the following two studies.

THONGA KINSHIP TERMS

Among the Thonga as well as several other
South African Bantu-speaking tribes, a curious relationship exists between a man and
his maternal uncle (or, as anthropologists
are apt to term him, his "mother's
brother"). When his nephew is sick, the
uncle performs sacrifices on his behalf. His
nephew is permitted a great degree of freedom in the relationship with his maternal
uncle. He may, for example, eat food that
has been prepared for his uncle's meal, an
act that ordinarily would result in disciplinary action. When the uncle offers a sacrifice
to his ancestors, his nephew is allowed to
steal and consume offerings of the meat or
beer. Indeed, at his mother's brother's funeral, he is expected to steal the sacrifice
that has been made on his late uncle's behalf. In short, the behavior surrounding the
relationship between these two kinsmen is
highly distinctive and does not conform to
the general pattern of Bantu kinship relations. What makes this relationship even
more distinctive is the fact that the Thonga,
like most southern Bantu, are patrilineal
(tracing descent from father to son), which
excludes the mother's brother from his
nephew's clan and which would thus seem
to remove him from the immediate circle of
kinsmen among whom one might expect a
degree of familiarity.

In "The Mother's Brother in South Africa,"
one of the classic contributions to the discipline, Radcliffe-Brown sought to explain this
role relationship. And here we move to a
somewhat more sophisticated level of analysis than that offered by Malinowski in the
kula.

In rejecting the then-popular thesis that
the special character of the relationship between the mother's brother and the nephew
stemmed from an earlier period in the

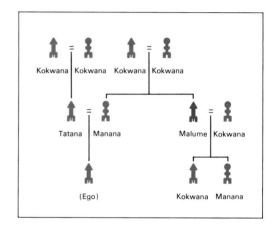

development of society when matrilineal institutions supposedly predominated, Radcliffe-Brown pointed out that this relationship has a number of structural correlates
that might not be immediately recognizable.
Among the Thonga and all the other tribes
that define the relationship in this fashion,
the behavior considered appropriate between a man and his father's sister is dia-
metrically opposite that permitted between
a man and his mother's brother. It is characterized by a great deal of respect on the part
of the nephew for his aunt, and any and all
familiarity between the two is strongly
frowned upon. The father's sister's word is
"law" as far as her nephew is concerned,
and to a marked degree the relationship
parallels the typical relationship between a
boy and his father. A second correlate is the
semantic character of the term used to designate mother's brother, regardless of the
particular words used by a particular people. One good example of this is the Thonga
term *malume*, where the stem *ma-* means
"mother" and the suffix *-(l)ume* can be rendered as "male" or "masculine." And the
term for father's sister is usually translata-
ble as "female father."

As a "female father" and as a member of
her nephew's clan, the father's sister is quite
concerned with the socialization process.

She clearly represents the generation of elders and is immediately concerned with her nephew's comportment, which, as Radcliffe-Brown suggests, is in character in a strongly patrilineal community. Because the mother's brother is necessarily excluded from the clan into which his sister has married, he therefore plays little part in his nephew's socialization. These distinctions mean that the maternal uncle is an outsider as far as his nephew's *clan* is concerned and has no immediate claims upon the latter's respect and obedience.

Yet no society is ever *totally* patrilineal—or matrilineal, for that matter—and a man will necessarily have certain hereditary ties to his mother's clan even if they are minimal when compared to those that bind him to his father's clan. From the boy's viewpoint, the mother's brother is the chief male representative of his mother's clan, the male equivalent of mother, as the kinship term suggests. It follows, then, that the relationship between a boy and his mother, which is typically a warm and affectionate one, will be extended to her nearest male kinsman—her brother. Indeed, the solicitude shown by a maternal uncle for his nephews can be seen in the fact that a portion of the *lobola* (bride price), which is paid in cattle, is given over to a girl's mother's brother. He in turn keeps the cattle in reserve, so to speak, for his sister's children, especially for her son. Thus, if the latter needs an extra cow or two to pay the *lobola* for *his* intended bride, the uncle is obligated to help.

Radcliffe-Brown concluded that there is a strong tendency for individuals in primitive society to merge into the group to which he or she belongs. With respect to kinship, there is a tendency to extend to all members of a group a certain type of behavior that originated in a relationship to one particular member of the group. The tendency in the Thonga tribe would appear to be one of extending to all members of the mother's group (either family or lineage) a certain

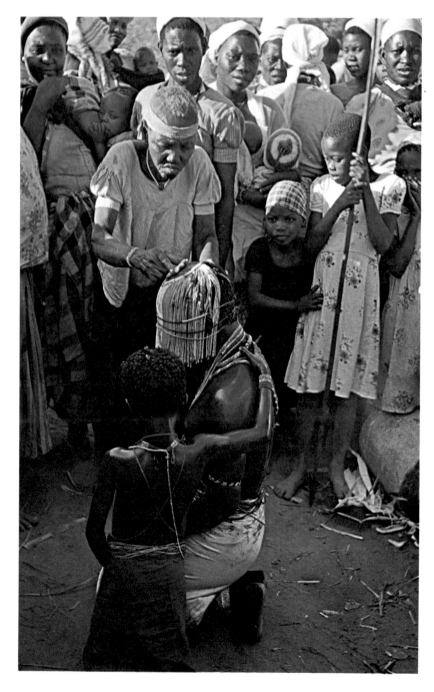

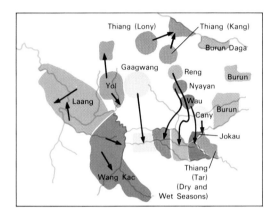

Figure 7. Each year the Nuer must migrate from their wet season villages to their dry season cattle camps, sometimes of necessity crossing the territories of rival political groups. The forms of political organization help to prevent the occurrence of attacks and disputes during such migrations. (After E. E. Evans-Pritchard, *The Nuer.* Oxford, England: The Clarendon Press).

behavior pattern that derives from the special pattern appearing in the behavior of a son toward his mother. He expects care and indulgence from his mother, and he looks for the same sort of treatment from the people of his mother's group. And yet he owes obedience and respect to his paternal kin. The patterns pertaining to the father and the mother are thus generalized and extended to the kin on the one side and on the other.

In short, the British anthropologist suggests that one cannot understand the special character of the relationship between a man and his mother's brother without reference to the nature of the descent system, the linguistic terms used, the institution of the *lobola*, and, perhaps most importantly, the character of the mother-son relationship. All these matters form integral pieces of a much larger mosaic. As in the case of most major research efforts in social anthropology, this mosaic was assembled systematically from the observation of diverse individual behavioral acts (in this instance, much of the basic ethnographic work had been done by Henri Junod, upon whose descriptive accounts of the Thonga as well as other South African people Radcliffe-Brown drew extensively), such as the gift of a cow to a kinsman and the stealing of food set out for a sacrifice—acts that in themselves might seem wholly unrelated.

Radcliffe-Brown's structural-functional interpretation of this most important aspect of southern Bantu social organization remains one of the high points in the history of social anthropology. It demonstrates rather effectively some of the basic operational procedures in this kind of analysis.

NUER KINSHIP AND POLITICS

The Nuer, a people of the southern portion of what is now the Republic of the Sudan, were described some years ago by E. E. Evans-Pritchard in *The Nuer.* Like most of their neighbors, the Nuer subsist principally on the products of their herds and on crops of millet and maize, which they cultivate during the extended rainy season. During the dry season, which lasts approximately half the year, they move their cattle almost continuously from pasture to pasture, dwelling in cattle camps of varying size.

Socially, the Nuer are a classic example of what social anthropologists have frequently termed a "lineage segmented" society, inasmuch as there is a set of increasingly comprehensive kin groups based on the patrilineal principle. These groups range from the localized family, or minimal lineage, to the clan, which may include more than 5,000 people. Marriage is patrilocal, the bride coming to live with her husband's family.

The Nuer are a fierce, proud, warlike people who value their individuality highly. In fact, they will fight to the death to avenge what Westerners might consider a minor insult, and they relish nothing better than to engage in warfare against other Nuer or neighboring groups of Dinka. On the surface, Nuer social life seems to be remarkably fluid and lacking in organization. A man is a member of his father's lineage by birth, but he may decide to move away from his father's village and live elsewhere. Furthermore, the wet-season village units may break up during the dry season and coalesce with other groups in the dry-season cattle camps. There is no formal political authority at or above the village level. In the absence of a government and a formalized legal system, how is it that individuals and groups can settle disputes and retain such a high degree of freedom of movement?

One would think that people would fear for their lives each time they leave their village. And yet the people not only retain their relatively great autonomy but also coalesce in large groups for purposes of mutual defense or to attack other groups. In fact, in the years preceding their conquest by the British, the Nuer were in a process of territorial expansion at the expense of their neighbors, the Dinka. The general problem Evans-Pritchard set out to solve was how the Nuer are able to act effectively in large groups in the absence of formal legal and governmental structure—how they maintain sufficient social cohesion to prevent a kind of anarchistic state of warfare among small groups from destroying the freedom of movement necessary to their economic well-being, as well as protect the individual dignity and independence they value so highly. He found that, to a large extent, these ends are attained through the institutions of territorial and lineage organization.

Each Nuer is a member of an agnatic lineage (one that traces descent through the males). A minimal lineage consists of the descendants through three to five generations of a single male and is usually localized in one household or several households clustered together within a village. This cluster of households is called a hamlet. Thus, the minimal lineage is usually a localized group that functions as an economic unit within a village. As time passes and the lineage grows in size, some of its members may decide, for various reasons, to move to a different part of the village or to a different village. In this case, *fission* is said to occur within the lineage. Although the members of the two parts of the lineage no longer live together, they still recognize a

Table 1. Nuer Lineage—Territorial Organization

Territorial Group Tribe	Lineage Group Clan
Primary tribal sections	Maximal lineages
Secondary tribal sections	Major lineages
Tertiary tribal sections	Minor lineages
Village communities	Minimal lineages

Source: After E. E. Evans-Pritchard, *The Nuer* (Oxford, England: Clarendon Press), 1940.

blood relationship, and eventually they come to think of themselves as two separate minimal lineages that together form a minor lineage.

There are usually five steps in this process of lineage *segmentation:* clan, maximal lineage, major lineage, minor lineage, minimal lineage. Clans sometimes include thousands of individuals and are typically spread over a large area of Nuerland. Also, a number of lineages from different clans may be mixed together in any one village. It is obvious that the closest and most crucial kinship relationships are within the minimal lineage, and the most distant and least important ones are those between members of different maximal lineages of the same clan. It is forbidden to marry within the clan, and sexual relations within the clan are considered to be incestuous. One function of these groups is that they provide a large, widely dispersed network of social ties between individuals—ties that provide for hospitality, mutual aid and protection, and so on. A man can find fellow clan members almost anywhere he goes. In addition, the minimal lineage functions as the basic economic unit in Nuer society, inasmuch as the members of the minimal lineage are dependent upon each other for their very survival.

The Nuer also have a territorial system that is segmented and directly parallel to the lineage segments (see Table 1). A tribal territory is subdivided into several primary sections that are in turn subdivided into several secondary sections, then further subdivided into several tertiary sections that are made up of a number of village communities. Each tribal territory is thought of as belonging to a given clan, and different sections of the tribal territory belong to different lineages of the clan, as outlined in Table 1. Although in a formal sense these "dominant" clans and lineages are the "owners" of the land, they do not have exclusive rights to its use, nor do they form an aristocracy in the usual sense. People from other lineages and clans may move into and live in a given lineage's territory. As a matter of fact, the members of the dominant lineage usually form only a small proportion of the inhabitants of any given area. Although they receive a certain formal respect in some situations, the dominant lineages do not necessarily have any greater voice in village affairs than do any other individuals. In addition, there is no centralized authority at any level of the territorial system.

Within a village, there is usually a close relationship among all the inhabitants based on cognatic or affinal kinship (relationships of blood kinship or of kinship through marriage), even though several lineages may reside there. People moving into a village attempt to establish a close relationship with the dominant lineage, through either intermarriage or adoption into it. Thus, in the absence of a governmental structure, the institution of the dominant clan functions to produce a coherent set of ties between people at the local level and, to a lesser extent, at each of the levels of territorial organization. People can use their kin ties to ease their move into a new community. Once there, they can cement their relationships in the community through intermarriage or adoption, and the problem of achieving flexibility of movement with a minimum of personal danger is thus partly solved. The processes of intermarriage and adoption within a village usually produce a situation in which people are so closely related to each other

that they must seek marriage partners from outside the village. Therefore, kinship ties with other surrounding communities are produced, and tribal solidarity is reinforced by the bonds of kinship. These bonds are strongest at the village level and weakest at the tribal level.

Evans-Pritchard defined the Nuer tribes in terms of the following characteristics: each tribe (and each segment within it) has a name; there is a feeling of unity among members of the same tribe (or section); the tribe has a distinct territory, which is in turn subdivided by sections; the members of a tribe feel a moral obligation to unite in warfare against other tribes and against neighboring people; and there is a moral obligation to settle feuds and other disputes by arbitration within the tribe.

This last characteristic is in many ways the most important. If a man is killed, his kinsmen are obligated to avenge his death by killing the killer; the kinsmen of the killer have the obligation of supporting him against the avengers. Similarly, each of the opponents in a dispute may call upon his kinsmen for support. But as we have seen, most or all of the people in a village and many people in neighboring villages are kin, and because of the broad network of lineage ties, a blood feud or dispute may involve kinsfolk in many parts of the tribal territory. Clearly, disputes within villages must be settled quickly in order to maintain the sort of unity necessary for economic cooperation among villagers, for disputes could rend the village into hostile factions. Thus, there is a great deal of pressure within the local group to settle disputes by arbitration.

In the case of disputes between inhabitants of neighboring villages, however, the need for amicable settlement is not as strong, and the more geographically removed the disputants are from each other, the less pressure there is to reach a settlement. Beyond the level of the tribe, there is no such obligation. In fact, tribes are more

Figure 8. Daily life among the Nuer, showing the final marriage ox being brought in (above), an artificial watering place, and a homestead and cattle camp. The payment of bride price to compensate the bride's family is widespread in Africa. In numerous societies around the world, people practicing this custom would find it extremely difficult to understand the traditional European custom of dowry, in which the bride's family makes payment to the groom's.

or less in a continual state of warfare, only occasionally cooperating in order to raid the Dinka. Within the tribe, disputes function to mobilize kinsmen and tribal sections that are in opposition to one another. Thus, if a man from village A kills a man in neighboring village B, there will be tension and possible conflict between the two villages. The greater the necessity of cooperation between the villages for economic well-being or the more serious the disruption caused by the dispute, the more pressure there will be on the disputants to settle their differences by arbitration—for example, by the payment of cattle by the killer's kin as compensation to the victim's kin for the life of the dead man. If two members of different tribal sections come into conflict—for instance, if a man from village X in primary section A kills a man from village Z in primary section B— then much larger groups mobilize. Because there is much less contact and less need for cooperation between people in these groups, the need for arbitration will be felt much less strongly, and the dispute may continue for some time. As long as the dispute is within a single tribe, however, there will be some feeling that it should be settled by arbitration.

The significance of disputes, then, is that they function to mobilize and define the ties that link members of territorial sections. In so mobilizing them, a dispute emphasizes the importance of these ties for the well-being of the people and thus serves to maintain the territorial organization. Kinship and territorial segments function to order relationships among individuals and to inhibit the growth of disputes and blood feuds to the extent necessary to ensure the well-being of individuals within the society. On the other hand, the disputes themselves are necessary in order to mobilize and validate the segmentary groups, thus ensuring their endurance. In this manner, the Nuer are able to achieve sufficient social cohesion to prevent a state of constant, anarchistic warfare

of individual against individual and small group against small group and, at the same time, to allow for a great deal of individual autonomy.

The Nuer political and lineage systems, like the *kula* and the mother's brother relationship in South Africa, serve as the focus of a wide variety of specific behaviors, many of which might initially appear to be unrelated. A structural-functional analysis reveals their interrelationships and shows their importance in ordering and maintaining Nuer social life.

THE OEDIPUS MYTH

The next example of structural analysis, Lévi-Strauss' interpretation of the Oedipus myth, differs from the preceding analyses in that it does not involve generalizations based on first-hand observations in a community. Instead, it involves a search for the underlying structure or *deep structure* of a narrative that originated in a society long since vanished: classic Greece. Nevertheless, the Greeks preserved their thoughts in extensive writings, so the Oedipus myth can be approached *as if* it had been recorded by a field worker, and the method used in its interpretation can be—and has been—applied in the interpretation of myths and folktales characteristic of living communities.

Lévi-Strauss has suggested that the only way to isolate the basic structure of a myth is to assemble as many variants of it as possible, to disregard the specific temporal or linear sequences of events it contains, and to reorganize these events in terms of the logical relationships among them. Expressed graphically, the result is a series of columns, each of which constitutes a "bundle of relationships," as Lévi-Strauss terms it, abstracted from the several variants concerned. The true structure of a myth is formed, he asserts, by the interrelationships among the several columns or "bundles." It is in terms of the unfolding sequence of columns, rather than in the character

of the "plot," that the fundamental meaning of a myth can be understood. As the relationships among the columns generally unfold in what amounts to a dialectic pattern (that is, a series of structural oppositions punctuated by a resolution of sorts), Lévi-Strauss suggests that the primary function of most myths, including the Oedipus myth, is *to provide a framework for the mediation of inherent conflicts and contradictions that cannot be resolved in the real world.* Edmund Leach, who in 1961 attempted to apply Lévi-Strauss' method to an analysis of Genesis I–IV, stated that a myth provides a "logical" model the human mind can use to evade unwelcome contradictions. For instance, one contradiction is that human beings cannot enjoy life without suffering death; another is that rules of incest conflict with a doctrine of unilineal descent. The myth functions to "mediate" contradictions so that they will appear less final than they really are and thus more acceptable.

In applying this method to the Oedipus myth, Lévi-Strauss sums together the several known versions—for example, the Homeric and the Sophoclean versions—and reorganizes their contents into four bundles of columns (see Figure 9). The first of these columns includes such logically related, albeit nonjuxtaposed, events as the rape of Cadmus' sister, Europa, by Zeus (Cadmus was the founder of the Theban house and an ancestor of Oedipus); Oedipus' marriage to his mother, Jocasta; and Antigone's burial of her brother, Polynices, despite official prohibition (Antigone and Polynices were offspring of Oedipus).

The common denominator here is what Lévi-Strauss calls the "overrating of blood relations." He saw the relations between close kinsmen, such as that between Oedipus and Jocasta, as more intimate than they should have been according to social conventions. The second column in the analysis includes the incident wherein the Spartoi kill one another; Oedipus kills his father,

Figure 9. Structural components of the Oedipus myth. In the first vertical column, Cadmus seeks his sister Europa, ravished by Zeus; Oedipus marries his mother Jocasta; and Antigone buries her brother Polynices despite official prohibition. In the second vertical column, the Spartoi kill one another; Oedipus kills his father Laius; and Eteocles kills his brother Polynices. The third column shows Cadmus slaying the dragon and Oedipus slaying the Sphinx. Finally, grouped into the fourth column are Labdacos (=lame), Laius (=left-sided), and Oedipus (=swollen foot). The columns contain equivalent terms in the structure of the myth, whereas the horizontal relations between columns indicate their logical relations.

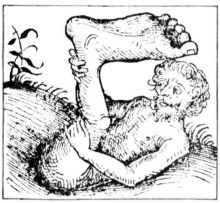

Laius; and the death of Polynices at the hands of his brother, Eteocles. Here, the logical relationship is termed an "underrating of blood relationships," wherein close kinsmen kill one another in what amounts to an inversion of the previous column. The third column, which includes Cadmus' slaying of the dragon and Oedipus' killing of the sphinx, refers to monsters being slain. Monsters such as the dragon and the sphinx are *chthonic* beings that would deny or abort the birth of mankind, and this column refers to what Lévi-Strauss terms the "denial of the autochthonous origin of man." Finally, the fourth column includes the similarity in meaning of the names Oedipus ("swollen-foot"), Laius ("left-sided"), and Labdacos ("lame"), Oedipus' grandfather, all of which refer to difficulties in walking straight and standing erect. Citing evidence from other regions and other times, including Pueblo and Kwakiutl mythology, Lévi-Strauss suggested that chthonic figures generally have difficulty walking erect at the moment they emerge from the earth. But this disability is in itself a sign of autochthonous origin, and thus the column in question refers to "the persistence of the autochthonous origin of man."

The relationships among the columns are such that the fourth column (persistence of autochthony) is to the third column (denial of autochthony) as the first column (overrating of blood relations) is to the second (underrating of blood relations). In 1967, Lévi-Strauss suggested that, although these two relationships cannot be connected, they are identical because they are both self-contradictory in a similar way. He also suggested that the Oedipus myth relates to the inability of a culture to find a satisfactory transition between the belief that mankind is autochthonous and the knowledge that humans are actually born from the union of man and woman (viviparous reproduction). He concluded that the problem could not be solved, but that the Oedipus myth still provided a logical tool relating the original problem (born of one or born from two?) to the derivative problem (born from different or born from same?). A correlation of this type indicates that the overrating of blood relations is to the underrating of blood relations as the attempt to escape autochthony is to the impossibility to succeed in doing so. He concluded that although experience contradicts theory, social life still validates cosmology by its similarity of structure. Thus, cosmology is true.

This is an example of the structural analysis of myth as practiced by Lévi-Strauss. His approach, however, is by no means univer-

Figure 10. Medieval conceptions of monsters living in the then-uncharted regions of the world. Such mythic monsters of the distant make the proximate, by contrast, seem less monstrous, almost human.

sally accepted. Indeed, many anthropological folklorists have suggested that it is something of a "conjuring trick." Yet conjuring trick or not, despite its "bugs"—not the least of which is how to isolate truly intersubjective categories or bundles—this method may eventually prove to be a most important addition to the social anthropologist's methodological armory. If applied judiciously, structural analysis is capable of yielding some valuable and otherwise not readily available insights into the workings of that most complex of complex phenomena, the human mind—and, by extension, of the social systems it conceives.

THE ABSTRACTION PROCESS

The foregoing examples of structural analysis, although different from one another in many respects, share one thing in common. They all involve a process of abstraction that begins with phenomenal reality. As far as Malinowski, Radcliffe-Brown, and Evans-Pritchard are concerned, this reality consists of observed social behaviors; in the example just discussed, it consists of the several surviving texts of the Oedipus myth that, one must assume, were originally set down by individuals. Furthermore, the abstraction process involves a number of fairly specific steps, which move logically from immediate categories to underlying structures.

Before considering these steps, however, a word or two must be said about the nature of anthropological versus lay observation. At the outset, it was suggested that the social anthropologist is fundamentally in the same position as the tourist who would make sense out of his impressions of another culture. But there is a difference between the casual observations of a tourist and the systematic observations of a trained anthropological field worker. When an anthropologist begins his field work (or begins to analyze the text of a myth, for that matter), he necessarily brings to bear a set of rubrics and categories not ordinarily used by the

layman. For example, by virtue of his training he is already conditioned to look for behaviors that relate to such phenomena as kinship, magic, and economics.

Unlike the layman who takes up residence in a society other than his own, the social anthropologist is a trained observer who records systematically his impressions of as many aspects of the target society as are relevant to his purpose. Moreover, he may very well utilize statistical and other procedures, such as the taking of a census, the administration of a projective test, or the recording of genealogies, that the casual visitor would not be expected (or trained) to use. Once he has recorded his observations, the abstraction process begins. It should be emphasized that this process does not occur only upon completion of the field experience, but is almost always an ongoing one. Typically, each day's observations are subjected to analysis as soon as possible—in the field worker's hut or tent before he retires for the night.

The first step is to organize specific *behaviors* into immediate *categories*. In the case of the *kula* ring, this would mean a search for a common denominator or pattern underlying specific performances, no two of which will be identical. Having done this, the next step in the abstraction process is to look for consistent relationships among the several patterned behaviors. Again, in the case of the *kula* this would involve the construction of a more inclusive category wherein certain types of feasting, magical rituals, and myths are seen as linked to one another and to the exchange pattern. The result is a delineation of a common structure, or *institution*, that includes several immediately distinct albeit patterned behaviors, such as exchanging necklaces for bracelets, preparing canoes for voyages, eating certain types of foods, and performing specified acts of magic. In the process of abstracting the existence of institutions, the anthropologist must seek to determine the

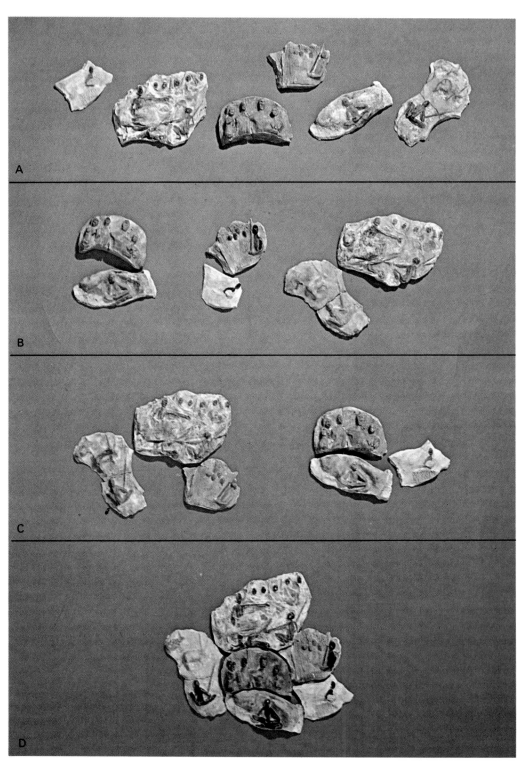

ways in which its several components are articulated. It is not enough to merely list a series of linked traits; rather, full delineation of the nature of an institution is achieved only when the relevant *functional* relationships are understood. For example, in order to understand the full import of the *kula*, Malinowski had to understand the extent to which the trading partner relationship functions to determine certain magical attitudes toward beauty. The same thing can be said for Radcliffe-Brown's understanding of the role of the mother's brother among the Thonga; this sort of understanding was not fully possible until the functional relationship between joking behavior and the

Figure 11. As the anthropologist studies the stream of events in a culture (A), he abstracts the terms, forms, and relations that he will use to piece together the larger cultural patterns and institutions. On some level of detail, no two events are physically, precisely alike. Their equivalence that makes it possible to place them into classes of events (as represented by sections B and C) is formal — that is, the equivalence depends on the internal criteria, applied by members of the culture, and on the external criteria, developed in cross-cultural research and applied by the anthropologist. The interrelationship of this inner and outer perception (D) produces the anthropologist's valid understanding of patterns and institutions.

kinship category in question had been delineated. Similarly, Evans-Pritchard's interpretation of the Nuer age-sets is predicated upon an understanding of the several functional relationships involved—for example, the extent to which deferential behavior is a function of the degree to which one set is removed from another in the cycle.

After the structural and functional characteristics of given institutions (or myths) have been brought to light, the final step, one not fully discussed in the previous examples, is to ascertain the ways in which these several institutions articulate to form an overall social system or structure. Once again, a process of abstraction is involved. This time, the several institutions become equivalent to the several patterned behaviors from which individual institutions are abstracted; certain institutions may be grouped into clusters as a result of their functional relationships. The last step is the delineation of a system—or institutions and clusters of institutions—as economic, political, familial, and religious systems. At the same time, one must search for common principles that cut across the several subsystems and their component institutions and that link them together into a more-or-less coherent whole. Thus, it is common to find a similarity between the attitudes and values in family relations and those in the marketplace, between those characterizing the relationships between a religious practitioner and his following, and those governing the relationships between the dramatis personae of a myth. These common values, or themes, tie the several patterned behaviors, institutions, and subsystems together. They may, in retrospect, be manifest in even the most mundane and immediately observable behavioral situations, but it is often difficult if not impossible to delineate them until some form of abstraction process is attempted.

It should be emphasized that these several phenomena are in the best sense of the term *abstractions* in that they are necessarily removed from observable reality; they are but devices—metaphors, if you will—that serve to organize observed reality, and they do not have any existential reality in themselves. This is often misunderstood, even by some anthropologists, who sometimes come to assume implicitly that the categories and functional relationships they have abstracted actually exist in some form or another. Indeed, largely as a reaction to this tendency toward reification, a whole school of contemporary ethnologists (with the exception of Lévi-Strauss, the scholars whose work was reviewed earlier are all classical functionalists) has come to the conclusion that the only truly relevant categories are those that are meaningful to the natives themselves. Nevertheless, as long as the investigator does not confuse the models that result from his abstractions with reality per se, much can be said for the use of objective categories such as pattern, institution, and social structure. For one thing, without such categories—unreal as they may be in the absolute sense—effective comparison of cultures is exceedingly difficult.

In sum, social anthropology involves at least four levels of abstraction from observed behavior: the level of *patterned behavior*, abstracted from a series of observations of individuals interacting with one another and with their environment; the level of *institution*, abstracted from a set of linked patterned behaviors; the level of *subsystem* (or *system*), abstracted from a set of linked and interrelated institutions; and the level of *social system* (or *social structure*), abstracted from the interrelationships that are found among the several institutions and subsystems. There is, beyond this, one more level or step, involving the abstraction of a general principle of or hypothesis about human culture from a comparison of several social systems, a hypothesis wherein such variables as population, ecology, and overall level of technological and sociocultural complexity are brought to bear.

Language

26

It is interesting that the speech sounds made by children from different cultures are not distinguishable from one another until children approach the end of their first year of life; only then do variations begin to emerge and become increasingly patterned after the adult speech used in their respective cultures. The implication is that children are not taught their "first" language: they discover it on their own because they have the biological capacity to do so. Of all the animals, man alone has certain unique, inborn capacities to discover and create the rules and abstract structures that account for his linguistic behavior. And yet, given the universal nature of language in general, how do we account for the tremendous variation in *languages*, the particular structures that are unique to particular groups of men? This question is a concern of cultural anthropology.

Anthropologists know that language is more than just another part of culture. Unlike religion, for example, or law, or political structures, language is central to culture in that it permeates all other parts, provides a system of symbolization for them, and even provides the major means by which the rest of culture is learned. Many skills, such as cooking, basketry, or driving a car, could be learned without the use of language simply by watching and seeing how they are performed. But it is clearly impossible for social, legal, and religious systems to be transmitted from one generation to another without the use of a language. A community of deaf-mutes, deprived of all substitutes for language such as writing or an elaborate gesture system, would surely not be able to continue its cultural existence.

Here we find one of the reasons for the special importance of language in cultural anthropology. Because people invariably depend on language for the use and the transmission of the rest of their culture, it follows that almost all of the significant institutions, customs, practices, habits, and artifacts of a culture will be reflected in the vocabulary of the language. A good dictionary of a language can therefore be taken quite literally as an index to the culture, and a study of the vocabulary can yield insights into the way the culture functions.

An illustration of this fact can be seen in one aspect of the difference between the Western American culture of the nineteenth century and the urban American culture of today. To the Western cowboy, the horse was at least as important as the automobile is to us. And he used such words as mare,

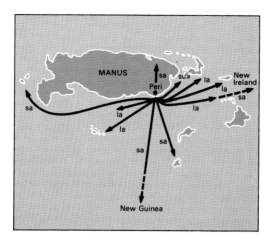

stallion, gelding, sorrel, and piebald very much as we use such words as convertible, station wagon, sedan, hot-rod, and dune buggy.

A more detailed illustration can be given by an account of one anthropologist who did field work with the Paipai Indian tribe of Baja California. The subject of his research was the adaptation of these Indians to their environment—the way in which they managed to survive by finding wild plant foods, fish, and game in different areas at different times of the year. The anthropologist eventually decided that the Indians derived their subsistence from four ecological zones—the mountains, the foothills, the desert, and the seashore—each of which provided its particular food products at various seasons. Meanwhile, the anthropologist's wife, a linguistics specialist, had been studying the Indian language. When she attempted to elicit the Indian words for the four ecological zones identified by her husband, she found that two different terms were given for what we call "desert." Upon further questioning, she found out that the Indians in fact had no single term for this ecological zone but insisted upon a distinction between what in English might be called "high desert" and "low desert." Furthermore, this linguistic distinction was by no means arbitrary. The two kinds of desert were in fact different food zones for the Indians, and their survival depended on being in the right zone at the right time. This investigation of the Indian vocabulary led to an important revision of the anthropologist's ecological description, in that he came to recognize five zones instead of four. The result was not his own arbitrary classification but rather one that reflected the Indians' own categorization of their universe.

Anthropologists also give great importance to language in their study of culture because people learn most of the elements of their culture primarily through the medium of language. It has been argued that the television age has substituted visual images for words and that increasingly the thoughts and actions of individuals will be determined more by visual images, with their more direct impact on the brain, than by the more subtle influences of language. Although this argument may be valid, it is as yet unproven. In either case, visual images will not totally displace language. So far as anthropology is concerned, the vital element in the process of learning through language is that whatever structure is inherent in the grammar and vocabulary of a particular language is likely to act as a filter for all the knowledge an individual acquires through the medium of language, whether his experience is of the natural world or of the culture that he acquires in his formative years.

To put the same point another way, it is the grammar and words he uses that may determine to a large extent how a person will think and act. This possibility has given rise to hypotheses, especially those of Benjamin Whorf, about the degree to which arbitrary classifications inherent in language may influence habits of perception and of reasoning—hypotheses that may amount to a theory of linguistic determinism of thought. For example, English grammar treats words for time the same as words for material objects, so that we are led naturally to such concepts as "saving *time*" and "*time* is money." And these concepts in turn cause us to overemphasize such concepts as *speed* and *hurrying*—both well-known characteristics of Western civilization.

In counterbalance to linguistic determinism, it is apparent that both language and thought change over time. New ideas, new modes of thought press for expression, and where the available or everyday words and structures of a language do not suffice, new words or modifications of structure may be created, adapted, or borrowed. Islands of formal discourse—the calculi of kinship reckoning in all societies, or of poetics or

Figure 2 (left). In English we have the one verb *to go*; the Manus language, however, requires a choice among three verbs that are selected according to direction and distance and that also imply vertical motion. Thus, *sa* is to go up; *sua* is to go down; and *la* implies motion that is neither up nor down. A person leaving Peri village would use *la* for general coastwise travel, but as he approaches the limits of the archipelago he would use *sa*. As the direction of departure approaches a right angle to the coast he would use *sa* for shorter and shorter distances. The north coast is considered to be "down" from the south coast; thus *sua* must be used. If we map the verbs against place names around and beyond Manus, we would plot the conceptual topography of an elongated saucer-world. Of course just as we use *uptown* and *downtown* metaphorically, the Manus do not expect to coast down the sloping sea wall of their saucer, but the metaphor may reflect the increased danger to the voyager as he departs more sharply or more distantly from his familiar coastline. Figure 3 (below). Islands of formal discourse. All languages contain some special modes of discourse. Their purpose may be to increase or decrease ambiguity or to control access to meaning.

mathematics and logic—may be developed that overcome some of the limitations of ordinary language. It has been argued that the language of the Hopi Indian centers on events and processes and that English centers on things and relations among them, and that therefore the Hopi is more oriented to understanding, say, Einstein's theories than an English speaker. But Einstein's theories can be only approximated in any speech—whether it be Hopi or English—because they actually are pure mathematics. Language, at a given moment of its history, acts as a system of constraints and a priori categories, and the production of an enormous number of new utterances is possible within this system. But change and evolution of culture and thought indicate that language is also a medium capable of being transformed in order to better express new meanings and modes of thought. Rather than focusing on the limitations *versus* the potentials of language structure, the issue is perhaps dissolved by seeing these two aspects as necessary to each other.

Still another factor that makes language especially important to the study of culture is the fact that linguistics has enjoyed a success in analyzing language that surpasses the achievements of scholars studying other varieties of cultural phenomena. It has even been suggested that, of all the subdisciplines of anthropology, linguistics alone has succeeded in identifying basic units of structure, of types that are universal to all societies and at the same time objectively verifiable within particular societies. Such units are those known to linguists as *phonemes* and *morphemes*. Every language has its own characteristic sounds, and these sounds as distinguished from one another in particular languages are known as phonemes. They may be vowels or consonants—a long or a short *a*, a *t*, or an *s*. Morphemes are the basic units in the grammar or structure of a language. They may be words or parts of words—*and* and *it*, for example, or the verbal suffixes *-ing* and *-ed* or the plural

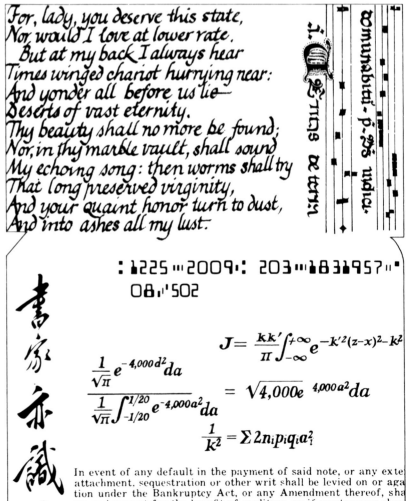

$$J = \frac{kk'}{\pi} \int_{-\infty}^{+\infty} e^{-k'^2(z-x)^2 - k^2}$$

$$\frac{\frac{1}{\sqrt{\pi}} e^{-4{,}000d^2} da}{\frac{1}{\sqrt{\pi}} \int_{-1/20}^{1/20} e^{-4{,}000a^2} da} = \sqrt{4{,}000e}\ ^{4{,}000a^2} da$$

$$\frac{1}{k^2} = \Sigma\, 2n_i p_i q_i a_i^2$$

In event of any default in the payment of said note, or any exte attachment, sequestration or other writ shall be levied on or aga tion under the Bankruptcy Act, or any Amendment thereof, sha an assignment for the benefit of creditors, or if mortgagors shou mortgagors will deliver the Chattels to mortgagee. Mortgagee n out legal process, enter any premises wherein the Chattels may sold as a unit or in parcels. Unless Chattels are perishable or t sold on a recognized market, mortgagee will give to mortgagor day on or after which any private sale or other disposition of C mortgagor or be deposited in the United States mail, registere vided in Section 9504(3) of the Uniform Commercial Code. The repairing and selling Chattels and less the expense of liquidat hereunder. The surplus remaining shall be paid to mortgagors unsatisfied. Mortgagee may take possession of any other propert porarily for the mortgagors without any responsibility or liabilit

Acceptance of any payments after maturity or waiver or condon of any other subsequent breach or default. No waiver of or char note shall be binding on the mortgagee unless evidenced by a wri Mortgagors waive the benefit of all homestead and other exempt

suffix -es. Whereas phonemes distinguish morphemes from one another, the morphemes have syntactic and semantic functions.

The recognition of such units in the study of language permits highly systematic, formal accounts, not only of the structure of a language at a given time but also of the way in which a language changes through time, and the way in which one language is related to another. The progress that has been made along these lines has raised the hope that comparable units might be identified for other aspects of culture, and that "grammars" of, say, music, law, and religion might be developed on the analogy of linguistic grammars—and even that a grammar for a culture as a whole could be an eventual possibility. The possibilities of such an achievement, however, must be evaluated in terms of some of the structural characteristics of language.

LANGUAGE STRUCTURE

Possibly the most important concept in linguistic analysis is the recognition of a difference between two levels of language, which Noam Chomsky has called *surface structure* and *deep structure*. Essentially, surface structure is the overt aspect of linguistic behavior, the level that is most obvious to the ear. Deep structure, on the other hand, represents the psychological level underlying this obvious linguistic behavior. It contains the basic units that the speaker of a language unconsciously selects to convey his message before he encodes them into the physical noises of speech.

Examples of the difference between the physical aspect of surface structure and the psychological aspect of deep structure may be drawn from two Spanish sounds that have similar-sounding counterparts in English. These may be transcribed phonetically as the stop [d], as in *día* (day), and the fricative [th], as in *nada* (nothing). The surface phonetics of English contain comparable sounds: the stop [d], as in *day*, and the

fricative [th], as in *they*. At the superficial level, English and Spanish are alike in that they differentiate between these two sounds. An examination of deep structure, however, demonstrates that the two languages are not at all the same. In English, the difference between the sounds [d] and [th] can be used to create a difference of *meaning* between utterances; in Spanish this is never done. Spanish speakers are not even aware that there is a difference that they can produce at will. They unconsciously obey a general rule stating that only [d] will occur at the *beginning* of an utterance and only [th] will occur *medially* between vowels. This example illustrates what is meant in saying that the difference between [d] and [th] are phonemic in English but nonphonemic in Spanish.

It is clear that the difference between [d] and [th] in English is relevant not only on the surface but also in the deep structure; the distinction between the two sounds is what keeps the word *day* separate from *they* in speech. This particular difference is readily perceived or produced by English speakers. A study of English and Spanish at the surface level could not reveal these distinctions, for we can get at deep structure only in terms of the meanings that native speakers associate with speech behavior—or, when we are ourselves native speakers of the language being studied, by bringing to the surface our intuitions of our own speech.

Examples of the difference between surface and deep structure may also be drawn from grammar. Surface structures often are misleading, for they may show very similar patterns in cases where the deep structures are radically different. A classic pair of sample sentences is *John is eager to please* and *John is easy to please*. The two sentences have very similar surface structures, differing only in the identity of the adjective in the middle. But the relationship between words within each of the two sentences is quite distinct. In the first sentence, *John* is the logical subject of the verb *please:* the

Figure 4. This illustrative sentence is ambiguous in that two or more readings are possible. The sentence itself lies at the surface, beneath which differing syntactic interpretations lead us to cut and group the words differently. Descriptive grammars start with utterances found in speech and attempt to analyze them into their constituents. Generative grammar begins with semantic intention and the simplest nuclear sentences. It progressively elaborates these through the application of rules of substitution and transformation until the actual communicable utterance is selected. In the first interpretation of this sentence, *flying* is the subject of the predicate *can be dangerous;* in the second, *planes* is the subject.

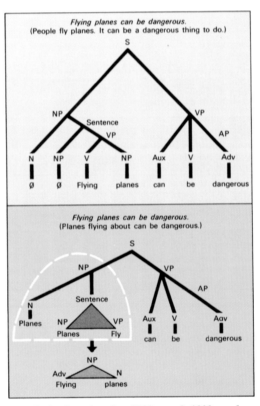

sentence implies that John is eager to please someone. In the second sentence, *John* is evidently the object of the verb *please:* the sentence means that it is easy for someone to please John. These two paraphrases correspond roughly to the difference in deep structure between the two sentences—a difference that is clearly much greater than anything observable from the surface structure.

In an even more extreme case, it is possible for two different deep structures to have identical surface structures, a phenomenon known as an ambiguous sentence. Consider Chomsky's famous example: *Flying airplanes can be dangerous.* Here, the deep structure can be interpreted as meaning that airplanes flying about can be dangerous or that the flying of airplanes can be dangerous, and the recognition and possible resolution of such ambiguities is part of our psychological equipment as native speakers of English.

It is the function of a grammar to account for just such implicit knowledge that a native speaker has of his language—to account for the possible deep structures that may exist and for the modifications that must be made on those deep structures in order to produce the surface structures of speech. The rules relating deep structures and surface structures are currently called transformations and have given their name to *transformational grammar,* the school of linguistic analysis now dominant in the United States. This school, which was given its impetus by the work of Chomsky, has emphasized the difference between deep and surface structures and the importance of the transformational rules relating these two levels.

SEMANTICS

In this century, linguists have often deliberately avoided semantic considerations, or the study of the meaning of what is communicated. This attitude seems to derive from the behaviorist approach fashionable among psychologists in the 1920s and 1930s, when it was considered desirable to avoid constructs, such as meaning, that could not be directly observed in behavior. In 1933, the prominent linguist Leonard Bloomfield defined the meaning of a linguistic form as the situation in which the speaker utters it and the response it evokes from the hearer. This definition removed much of the investigation of meaning from the province of linguistics, for it seems to imply a model of linguistic function with only two parts: the linguistic form and the associated linguistic events. A more satisfactory model was provided some 2,000 years ago by the Hindu philosopher Patanjali, when he suggested the idea of concentrating separately on the word, the meaning, and the object (or event), which are mixed up in common usage. The relationships between words and meanings and

Figure 5. Normalized foci of basic color terms in twenty languages, as reported by Brent Berlin and Paul Kay in their study of the evolutionary implications concerning the manner in which color terms are added to a language. Numerals appearing in the top chart refer to the number of languages in the sample of twenty that encode the corresponding basic color category. The societies representing the seven evolutionary stages are, from top to bottom in the smaller graphs, Jalé, Tiv, Ibibio, and Ibo (left-hand column), and Tzeltal, Plains Tamil, Malayalam, and English (right-hand column). The large color chart depicts all the stimulus chips used in this research study. (After Brent Berlin and Paul Kay, *Basic Color Terms: Their Universality and Evolution.* Los Angeles and Berkeley: The University of California Press, 1970.)

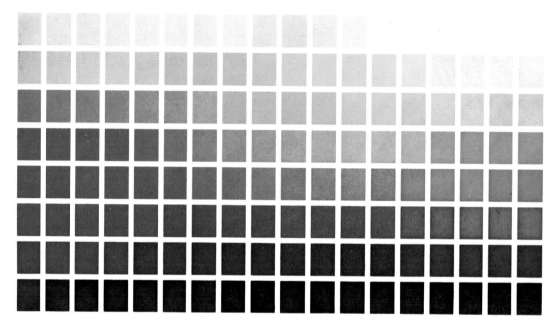

between words and objects are usually arbitrary. (The rare exception here would be cases where the word is made to resemble some aspect of the meaning or object as in onomatopoeia—with bees buzzing, cannons booming, and wet shoes squishing.)

At this point, the concept of deep structure versus surface structure becomes applicable not only to linguistic form but also to *content*—not only to language itself but to the things that are talked about. The nonlinguistic universe, too, may be said to appear to the human observer as having a surface structure, an overt physical manifestation that, in all its infinite diversity, is the topic of study in the physical and biological sciences. Men in all cultures attempt to bring order to the enormously varied appearances of the reality they live in by categorizing their environments. They do this by grouping ranges of variation into systems of classification, usually by giving names, that can be manipulated and stored in the mind and communicated to others. In certain striking cases, the natural world in fact presents a continuum of infinite gradation between

phenomena, as in the spectrum of colored light. But every culture treats the spectrum not as the continuum that it is but as a set of discrete entities. The number and exact identity of the colors recognized varies from culture to culture in ways that are superficially arbitrary but that may have an important relation to environmental adaptation.

This potential relationship is the subject of a research project conducted recently by Brent Berlin and Paul Kay. They have questioned the widely accepted belief that the way color is classified in the world's languages is totally arbitrary. They initially collected data from twenty languages of various linguistic origins, but this number later grew to 100. Their first step was one of defining what a "basic color term" actually is—in this case, simple words (for example, red, green, as opposed to reddish, greenish), primary (scarlet is not primary because it is a kind of red), and widely applicable (blond is not, for it is limited to hair and furniture).

Figure 5, which is a reproduction of the stimulus that was employed in the actual research, is superimposed with a composite,

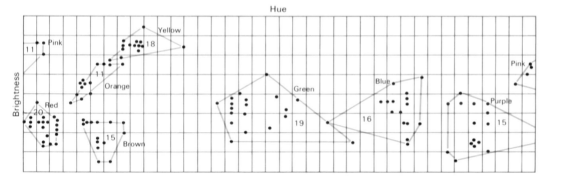

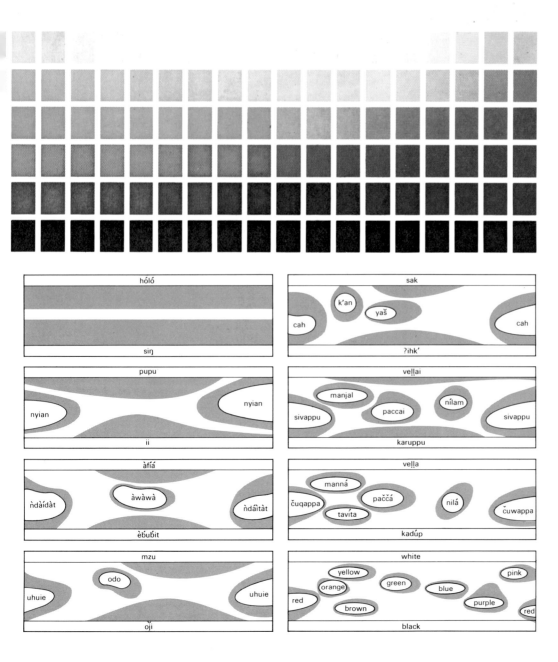

Table 1. Evolutionary Stages of Culture as Implied by Color Codification

Stages of Development	Number of Basic Color Terms	Perceptual Foci Encoded in a Basic Color Term*
I	2	BLACK, WHITE
II	3	BLACK, WHITE, RED
IIIa	4	BLACK, WHITE, RED, GREEN (extends into blue)
IIIb	4	BLACK, WHITE, RED, YELLOW
IV	5	BLACK, WHITE, RED, GREEN, YELLOW
V	6	Black, white, RED, green, YELLOW, blue
VI	7	Black, white, RED, green, YELLOW, blue, brown
VII	8–11	Black, white, red, green, yellow, blue, brown, purple, pink, orange, gray

* Capital letters indicate maximum extension of a term at any one point; lowercase letters indicate a term has been reduced in its extension to that which it has in the seven-stage system.
Source: After Brent Berlin and Paul Kay, *Basic Color Terms: Their Universality and Evolution* (Berkeley and Los Angeles: University of California Press), 1970.

compiled for all languages, of the centers (or foci) of all basic color terms. The composite clearly shows a striking similarity in the way focal points cluster in a few areas of the spectrum. In fact, it shows there are exactly eleven foci of basic color categories from which the color terms of any given language are always drawn. The set of color terms that each language derives from these eleven categories is not a chance selection but results from an evolutionary process by which color terms are added to a language in a definite order. The implication is that if we know the number of terms a culture has for categorizing color, we can predict to a large extent what color categories they cover. Berlin and Kay consider that this order reflects the actual temporal sequence in which color terms come to be encoded in all languages; it thus had important evolutionary implications in the development of color vocabulary. One obvious conclusion is that the order reflects a fixed sequence of evolutionary stages through which any language must pass as its color vocabulary becomes expanded over time. There are just two evolutionary sequences:

$$\left.\begin{array}{c}\text{white} \\ \text{black}\end{array}\right\} \rightarrow \text{red} \rightarrow \text{green} \rightarrow \text{yellow} \rightarrow \text{blue} \rightarrow \text{brown} \rightarrow \left\{\begin{array}{l}\text{gray} \\ \text{pink} \\ \text{orange} \\ \text{purple}\end{array}\right.$$

$$\left.\begin{array}{c}\text{white} \\ \text{black}\end{array}\right\} \rightarrow \text{red} \rightarrow \text{yellow} \rightarrow \text{green} \rightarrow \text{blue} \rightarrow \text{brown} \rightarrow \left\{\begin{array}{l}\text{gray} \\ \text{pink} \\ \text{orange} \\ \text{purple}\end{array}\right.$$

It now appears possible to suggest at least seven evolutionary stages in the develop-

ment of basic color terms, as the data from the representative cultures in Figure 6 illustrate. These stages are listed in Table 1.

The researchers have observed also that the languages possessing few basic color terms—as indicated by the stages depicted in Figure 5—are invariably spoken by people who have relatively limited levels of economic and technological development. On the other hand, languages with full color lexicons are usually spoken in the more complex societies. It need not be assumed that languages with few color terms represent degenerate systems, however, because groups with limited basic color lexicons appear in every continent, and these groups have quite varied individual culture histories. Instead, the logical assumption is that these simple systems accurately reflect the first stages of abstract color naming that must have been characteristic of early man. (Here, *abstract* is used in the sense of being generally applicable and not recognizably tied to a particular thing; for example, using the word for "blood" as a word for "red.") From an evolutionary view concerned with environmental adaptation, it can be argued that abstract color terms are, in effect, relatively unimportant concepts in societies close to nature and that numerous and highly specific distinctions of meaning are more important to encode linguistically in such groups. Berlin and Kay's initial evidence shows that several languages exhibiting early stages of basic color lexicons have highly complex "secondary" color vocabularies, or words that can deal with colors even if they do not name the colors per se. The adaptive mechanisms involved are not

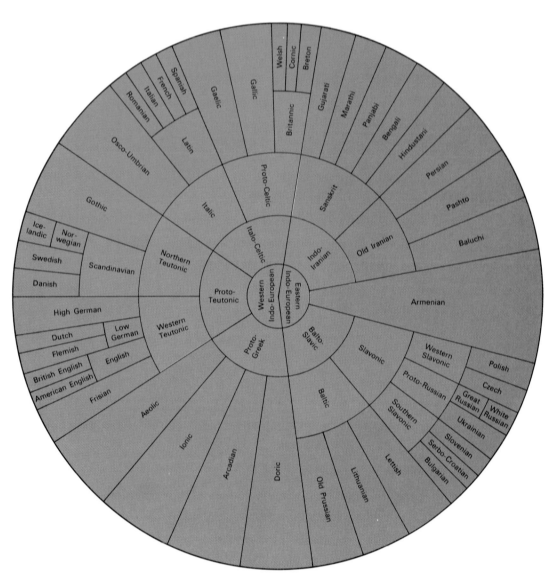

yet understood, but it is likely that the presence of numerous highly concrete secondary color terms in languages spoken by primitive societies is a reflection of the need of such groups to develop a direct and maximally efficient means of talking about the natural environment. Likewise, the development of abstract color terms appears to be related to other developments in the lexicon of a language whose community of speakers becomes progressively large and more diversified over time.

It is just this sort of categorization that we may call the deep structure of a culture, insofar as this structure embodies the psychologically relevant world in which the members of the society live, and this structure may be taken as the goal of ethnographic description. Culture is not to be equated with the collection of objects or instances of behavior in which its surface structure is manifest, but rather it must be considered a body of knowledge that is shared by the members of a society and that conditions their behavior. The deep structure of culture is, in part, revealed through

analysis of the vocabulary of the associated language. The meaning relationship may then be seen as the link between linguistic and cultural deep structures. In other words, one promising approach to the anthropologist's task of understanding culture is to consider culture in terms of being a semantic system.

HISTORICAL LINGUISTICS

In the broadest sense, historical linguistics refers to any study of language change through time. In a narrower sense, however, it refers to the tracing of historically documented linguistic changes, as opposed to comparative linguistics, in which the comparison of related languages can be used to extrapolate into the past and reconstruct prehistoric stages. The comparative approach is of particular interest to anthropological investigations of prehistory, as the following example of linguistic reconstruction illustrates.

In 1786 William Jones, a British scholar in India, announced that Sanskrit, the ancient language of India, showed a stronger affinity

Figure 7 (left). Linguistic borrowing as well as cultural diffusion is evident in this trio of advertisements for a popular soft drink from Tehran, Tijuana, and Ahmedabad. In the lower photograph, a scribe earns his living by preparing letters and documents for illiterate people. Figure 8 (right). Several languages are juxtaposed in this Chinese restaurant sign in Mexico.

in both the roots of verbs and the forms of classic Greek and Latin grammar than could possibly have been produced accidentally. Jones considered this affinity to be so strong that no scholar could examine all three without sensing a common source, which perhaps no longer existed. The common source to which Jones referred, the language now called proto-Indo-European, did indeed exist in prehistoric times but was never documented in writing. By comparing historical languages from Europe all the way to India, however, it is possible to reconstruct the phonology, grammar, and vocabulary of this proto-language with considerable accuracy. Again, the vocabulary of a language provides an index to the associated culture; the reconstructed lexicon of proto-Indo-European thus permits reasonable hypotheses not only about how our proto-Indo-European ancestors lived but also about where they lived (somewhere in eastern Europe) and how they reached their historical locations.

Methods of comparative linguistic reconstruction are even more valuable when we turn to the historic study of preliterate cultures, such as those of the American Indian. There is no written evidence for the history

of these cultures before the time of European contact, and studies of the pre-Columbian cultures must usually be based on such indirect evidence as that provided by archaeology. But linguistic reconstruction can add an immense amount of information that would never be recoverable through archaeological findings. Linguistic evidence alone shows that the Navajo and Apaches of the American Southwest are in fact close kinsmen to other tribes in northwestern California and to a still larger group of tribes in the subarctic area of Alaska and northwestern Canada. It is linguistic evidence that demonstrates the subarctic zone was the original home of this Athapaskan linguistic family, and this evidence makes possible the reconstruction of features of their prehistoric culture. Similar linguistic research shows that the Paiute of Nevada are akin to the Hopi of Arizona and to the Aztecs of central Mexico within the Uto-Aztecan family.

Another case in point may be taken from research on India. At the time when speakers of Sanskrit first entered the Indian subcontinent from the northwest, a high civilization already flourishing in the Indus Valley used a non-Indo-European language written in a script that until recently resisted decipherment. The linguistic affiliation of this Indus Valley civilization thus remained a mystery for many years. It has now been shown that the oldest Sanskrit texts, dating from a time when Sanskrit speakers had only just penetrated the Indus Valley, already contained loan words from the Dravidian linguistic family that is centered today in southern India. These loan words lead to a strong hypothesis that the Indus Valley civilization was in fact Dravidian-speaking. Most recently, this hypothesis has received strong new support from scholars who have shown that the Indus Valley script can be usefully deciphered in terms of proto-Dravidian forms, as reconstructed by the methods of comparative linguistics. Linguistic findings have thus lent support to the conviction that a Dravidian high culture ex-

isted in both northern and southern India in remote times and that the developing Sanskrit culture, which came to dominate northern India, must have incorporated many linguistic and nonlinguistic elements of the proto-Dravidian culture that preceded it there.

LANGUAGE AND SOCIETY

All the types of study mentioned so far treat each language as a unified whole. But another type of research that has recently acquired importance focuses attention on the variation that exists within languages or within multilingual speech communities.

For example, variations in the use of words are commonly found to be correlated with one or more socially defined factors, such as the social identity of the speaker, the person he addresses or the person referred to, and the social context in which communication takes place. It is apparent in our own society, for instance, that different types of English are used in black communities as compared to white communities and that similar differences of English usage exist between groups of different education, occupation, religion, and so on. In some of the world's societies, such linguistic differences are even more sharply marked. In India, to take an extreme case, the strict social stratification of the caste system has its linguistic counterpart in the existence of sharply defined caste dialects. In all such situations, the study of the covariance between linguistic diversity and social structure has now come to be recognized as the new field of sociolinguistics. The findings of this field are applicable, from the synchronic viewpoint, to the diagnosis and analysis of social encounters, and, from the historical viewpoint, to the examination of the ways in which linguistic patterns and social systems each change under the influence of the other.

Especially complicated and interesting instances of sociolinguistic diversity are to be found in multilingual communities. Such communities are found in American society, especially in areas of Mexican-American and of Puerto Rican concentration. Again, however, there is even more complexity in India, where sixteen vernacular languages are legally recognized—most of them with their own unique writing systems—in addition to dozens of important nonstandard languages, plus Sanskrit and Persian as languages of religious and cultural tradition, and English as a major language of education, administration, and communication between areas. Where an educated city dweller in the United States may use four different styles of English in the context of home, business, school, and church, his Hindu counterpart may well use four different languages in corresponding circumstances. Clearly, sociolinguistic variation may encompass any degree of linguistic difference.

The aim of the anthropological linguist is, essentially, to account for what people know about their linguistic usage, within the framework of human culture. From the viewpoint of formal structure, emphasis is on the native speaker's knowledge of what constitutes a grammatical sentence. From the viewpoint of semantics, emphasis is on his knowledge of what makes sense, in terms of the limitations of his physical and cultural world. And finally, from the sociolinguistic viewpoint, emphasis is on the speaker's knowledge as to the appropriateness of a given dialect, style, or language under specific social conditions. Man's linguistic and cultural behavior is governed by rules founded in the inherited structures of his brain and elaborated by the processes of learning: the goal of the linguist is to bring these rules to the level of awareness.

Thus far, he has shown that the structure of language reveals, in part, the deep structure of human experience, itself shaped by the deep structures of culture. Similarly, he has used language to penetrate the enigmas of human societies long since vanished, as well as to trace the structure of modern society through the variation of its many languages.

Art and Society

27

Art is an act of creation and the entire universe is its province. It can grow out of relationships between humans; it can be drawn from visible sights of the earth, the sky, and the sea; it can depict the activities of imagined gods and how they relate to men. The potential subject matter and the ways in which the subject matter is treated are unlimited. Moreover, no culture is precisely the same as another culture, and no individual artist is precisely the same as other individual artists. Clearly art by its very nature is infinitely varied. Yet by looking at art comparatively, anthropologists show that art does tend to follow certain patterns and to serve similar functions in many societies.

CONCEPTS OF ART AND ARTISTS

To most of us, the word "art" usually conjures up the idea of entertainment. A novel may have an uplifting theme and a movie might point a moral, but to the average person a movie or novel—or a television show or concert or exhibition of paintings—serves primarily as a way to pass time pleas-

antly. But to us the word also implies a specific type of entertainment, one connected with creativity and beauty, just as our use of the word "artist" implies an individual performing a specific type of creative activity that involves at least some element of aesthetic satisfaction.

This view of art and artists reflects the specialization that is one of the most striking characteristics of modern industrial societies. Even in the cultural history of the West, the idea of art has not always been so restricted. The basic meaning, going back to the Roman *ars*, is a skill or competence at performing some activity, such as dancing, carpentry, or architectural designing, that is not instinctive. In the Middle Ages, the meaning shifted slightly to emphasize forms of scholarly learning such as rhetoric, mathematics, and literacy in general. And in seventeenth-century Europe and eighteenth-century England, art as an exclusively aesthetic skill came to be differentiated from purely utilitarian skills, and a distinction arose between artists and artisans. The modern American usage of the term "art" is really

short for "fine art," in which emphasis is more on form than on meaning or content. Meaning may be present, but it is secondary to the manner in which it is conveyed.

In other societies, however, both art and artists have been viewed quite differently. Early China was also a society with a considerable degree of division of labor, and its people had a general word for art—*yi-shu*, meaning any kind of learned skill. But within this category, the distinctions made reflected Chinese tastes and the nature of their social system. The gentry engaged in poetry, calligraphy, and painting, all of which were considered to be the highest forms of art, whereas the professionals practiced what was viewed as the less prestigious architecture, sculpture, seal making, pottery, paper cutting, and so on. The distinction was made between those who created the art forms rather than between the relative merit of the art forms themselves, a distinction somewhat analogous to the one Americans use to categorize artists and craftsmen. The individual creators of the high arts were considered as eminent as their creations, but the professionals who created even such highly regarded objects as scrolls and painted pottery were considered as inconsequential as their place in the social hierarchy.

The members of far less specialized societies may not even have a word or concept for art. For instance, among the Eskimo all men are hunters, and all man-made objects are lumped together as *sanasimajanga* ("that which has been made"), irrespective of utility or aesthetic considerations. Unless a society sustains specialists in the arts, its concept of art usually will not be differentiated from its concept of all other manufactures and creative events. This does not necessarily mean that aesthetic considerations are absent, but rather that they are considered less important than the content or meaning of the art form. Certainly in simpler societies the importance of art as entertainment is reduced. In fact, it is very often

intimately bound up with the running of society and the maintenance of social order, teaching not only facts and history but also morals and ideals.

How does the anthropologist approach the study of art in view of the existing conceptual diversity? Some guidelines have already been established. Franz Boas long ago emphasized the skill aspect of art, indicating that when technical treatment has reached a certain standard of excellence and when control of the process involved is such that typical forms are produced, the process is called art, with the judgment of perfection being essentially aesthetic. This approach, although helpful, emphasizes form rather than meaning or content. Other investigators have stressed aesthetic impact rather than technical perfection, but their definitions tend to be too far removed from the anthropological context.

A more recent definition by Adrian Gerbrands provides a better perspective. He states that when a creative member of a society personally interprets his society's values through matter, movement, or sound in such a way that the resultant forms comply with his society's standards of beauty, this creative process and the creations themselves are called art. Gerbrands emphasizes the creativity of the individual as well as the beauty of his creation and at the same time recognizes that the production of art is related to the society's standards and is never merely a personal affair of self-gratification.

Whatever the circumstances, whatever the type of society, the artist or craftsman does not create in a vacuum. His work must comply with the standards of beauty, or of utilitarianism, that are accepted in his society. Art is therefore one kind of *expressive culture*, just like other forms of expressive culture, including mythology and religion. This definition implies that the idea of what art is or should be exists between the artist and the society with which he shares his views. Art in this sense cannot exist outside society or it will lose its meaning and become merely the plaything of the creator. In other words, an artist may seek to move outside the existing standards of his society through the manipulation of art, but recognition of what he is trying to do is possible only when it can be related in some way to the cultural understanding of his audience.

ART STYLES AND THEIR COMPONENTS

Societies tend to show aesthetic and cultural preferences for styles of art forms that continue to give satisfaction to classes within a society, to a whole society, or even to a number of related societies. Such styles involve meanings and techniques that have become accepted and handed down from generation to generation as standards of excellence and propriety. Because of this continuity, art historians and anthropologists find the concept of style useful for tracing the history and diffusion of aesthetic and cultural influences. For one example, in isolated societies that have been subject to few disturbing outside influences, styles may appear to be fairly stable over long periods of time. In preindustrial civilizations, for another, styles reflect national integrity and generally change only when outside influences are strong or when the internal social and political order begins to change.

Form and Meaning

Styles can be viewed as continuities of form and cultural meaning, lasting only as long as the culture lasts. Form is the obvious feature to observers from other societies, but meaning within most societies is usually more important than aesthetic considerations, and the strength of the relationship between art and aesthetics will depend on the producing society's concern with it.

Meaning in art is both overt and covert. In eighteenth- and nineteenth-century Europe, hunting scenes were a popular theme for artists, but they tended to be obvious representations of the pleasurable activities of a leisured class. Other hunting scenes in history and prehistory may have connoted wish

fulfillment or a kind of imitative magic, and the meaning in many cases is not obvious nor the portrayal true to life.

One common world-wide technique that artists use is to let the audience fill out the scene by using the part that is represented to stand for the whole. In Australia, for example, an audience may know by shared convention that drawing a certain kind of track signifies an emu, whereas another track might signify a snake or lizard. These productions may be thought of as *signs*, representing an element that has a necessary connection with the total object or event being depicted, just as in American society the sign of a pointing hand signifies direction.

Symbols are more subtle and culturally specific, and they differ further from signs in that there is, at least overtly, no necessary connection between the symbol and what it

is meant to convey. The symbols that are chosen to represent other objects are purely arbitrary. The letters and words used in language are examples of such arbitrary symbols, for they possess only the meaning that is arbitrarily assigned to them. Symbolism is a common, universal phenomenon in the arts, and the audience cannot know what the meanings of symbols are without having learned them, most commonly by growing up in and sharing the culture of the creator.

Symbolism is often complicated and esoteric, perhaps understood by only a small segment of the society, such as the elders or members of an elite, educated class. For instance, a cross may be purely pictorial or it can represent a crucifixion. During the first century it also came to possess a special symbolic meaning for the small band of people who were called Christians. Later, for millions of people around the world, the cross came to possess further symbolic

Figure 4 (left). "The Adoration of the Magi," a fifteenth-century painting by Fra Angelico and Fra Fillipo Lippi that is highly charged with Christian symbolism. For instance, the ox and the ass symbolize Isaiah's prophecy "the ox knows its owner and the ass his master's crib"; the peacock represents immortality, and the markings on its tail signify the all-seeing eye of the Church; the Magi's gifts of gold convey the idea of kingly power, frankincense is a recognition of the divine, and myrrh is a portent of suffering and death. Symbolism may be representational or abstract. In the first case, the object or event the symbol represents should be apparent from the form of the symbol itself. In the second case, the relation between a symbol and its referent is conventional, in that the symbol is one side of a code to which the viewer must have a key. Figure 5 (right). The "Venus" of Willendorf. Such prehistoric figurines appear throughout the world and over broad expanses of time.

meaning, involving the ideas of death and rebirth, self-abnegation, and the victory of spirit over matter. In other places, a cross has come to symbolize colonial oppression and the forced imposition of alien beliefs.

Symbolism of various kinds is also used to reinforce the more obvious conventional signs and representations. The Asmat of New Guinea, who were headhunters until recently, used three symbolic colors. Black signified human hair, or the head to be hunted; red signified blood and enhanced the hunt; and white signified the ashes of ancestors whose deaths had to be avenged by the killing of more enemies. These colors were further used to embellish more recognizable symbols such as the praying mantis —an apt symbol for headhunting, inasmuch as the female mantis eats the male's head during copulation. Thus, all these symbols contributed to the Asmat's central shared concern for headhunting and were dependent upon and integrated with their general belief system.

Use and Function

In addition to giving consideration to form and meaning, anthropologists view art in terms of its use and function. The function of an art form may be differentiated from its actual use. The "use" is the specific purpose for which the art form is produced, but to determine the function it is necessary to examine the art object or event in relation to the rest of society. Clearly, people know how things in their society are put to use, but the actual social functions of a cultural phenomenon are not always perceived by them. These functions can often be isolated only by the anthropologist who, standing outside the society, can see its various parts objectively and in perspective and can comprehend how art forms serve, for example, to sustain group integration (as patriotic songs do for some groups and protest songs do for others), to delineate and maintain the social hierarchy (as jewels and distinctive clothing do), to express social relationships

(as various emblems such as rings do), or to promote social change (as the emotional presentation of a group's suffering does). Clearly, the implicit functions underlying observable art can be quite complex.

THE PREHISTORIC ARTS

For most of man's time on earth, his only record is "written" in his surviving artifacts and bones. This prehistoric era came to an end some 5,000 years ago in the Middle East with the discovery of the means for setting down accounts with symbols. Nevertheless, it survived until a generation or two ago in some remote areas of the world, such as parts of the Amazon basin or the central arctic region of northern Canada.

Although man as a craftsman and tool maker is known to have existed for at least 2 million years, the earliest things discovered that can be confidently identified as art forms date back only 40,000 or 50,000 years. It is possible that early man may have developed artistic traditions, such as body painting, tattooing, sand drawing, dancing, and poetry, about which modern man will never know. The long tool-making traditions have been well traced, but the stone implements found in prehistoric assemblages are usually recognized as primarily utilitarian, not aesthetic. Using the Boasian "standard of excellence," we might well judge many stone tools as beautiful, but the aesthetic judgment would be made by us, not by the early creator and his audience—and there is no way to speculate about his judgment or theirs.

Cave Arts

The earliest and best-known types of what we might call prehistoric art come from the caves of southeastern France, Spain, and other areas around the Mediterranean, and they include both pictorial and geometric etchings and paintings. One of the earliest forms, associated with the Aurignacian period (about 30,000 B.C.), consists of a tangled series of three parallel lines etched on

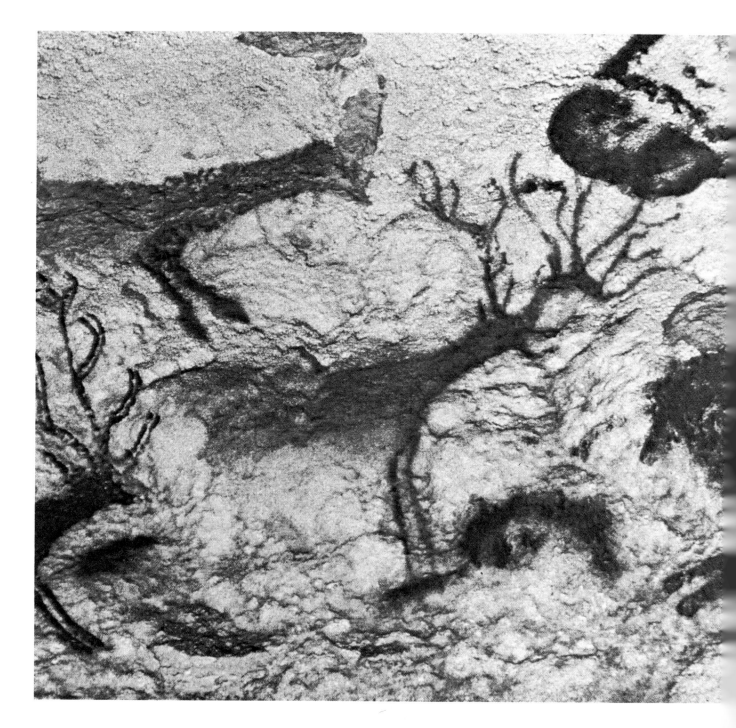

Figure 6. Reindeer painted on the walls of a cave at Lascaux, France. Figure 7 (right). Early Indian petroglyph from southern California. In primitive societies, objects and their representations were believed to be effectively connected. To represent was to manipulate, create, or increase in number the thing represented. The aesthetic quality of the symbol was probably considered to enhance the efficiency of the mystical connection.

cave walls. The curves of these obviously nonutilitarian lines have so far defied understanding. The archaeologist cannot determine whether they are actual representations of something with which people today are unfamiliar or whether they are abstractions or symbols. They may well be nothing more than imitations of the scratchings of the three-toed sloths that inhabited the caves.

These enigmatic lines are found together with later, recognizable forms, but other nonrepresentative forms were produced throughout the 20,000-year period when the cave arts flourished. During this period, there seems to have been a general trend from purely two-dimensional renderings into reliefs and three-dimensional sculpturing. But this trend is not absolute, for some of the earliest pieces from this period consist of small, portable sculptures, often stylized female figurines.

Overwhelmingly, animals constitute the subject matter of this cave art. Human figures and geometric forms make up less than one-sixth of the items. The earlier renderings tended to be simple outlines in monochrome. Within 10,000 years, however, such outlines eventually became filled in, and the scratchings around natural rock formations developed into relief sculptures. Toward the end of the Magdalenian, the second 10,000-year period, there appeared what by our standards were the most magnificent of all the cave art forms. Polychrome was used in the paintings, the reliefs became filled out even more, and all the forms were imbued with a naturalism and movement that few artists today can match. These late Magdalenian arts ceased about 10,000 B.C. and have no continuity with later arts of the same regions.

One of the easiest guesses that can be made about the function of these art forms is that early men decorated the walls of their caves for pleasure and that the figures they produced amounted to no more than art for its own sake. The emphasis of this explanation is on aesthetics. A more common and widely accepted explanation is that these representations of animals and hunting scenes were somehow associated with wish fulfillment, the power of imitative magic, or fertility rituals. This view is supported by comparisons with the art of recent and contemporary hunting people such as the Pygmies of the Congo, the Bushmen in South Africa, and some American Indian groups—art that is known to be associated with such cultural phenomena. Moreover, the presence of human forms, usually portrayed as hunters but occasionally depicted in poses imitating animals, supports such interpretations.

Rock Engravings

Well-made tools of great antiquity are found almost everywhere, but art is another matter. It is likely that only a bold carving or well-protected cave painting could have survived through the millenniums. Other creations, even of ivory or bone, disintegrate after a few centuries unless they are well protected, and soft woods, skins, basketry, and textiles last only a few years. In protected places in Africa, North America, and Australia, some etchings, sculptures, and paintings have survived from prehistoric times. In South Africa, there is an abundance of rock paintings, mainly of human and animal scenes, that were probably created by hunting and pastoral societies. They resemble European cave arts in some general ways, as in the progression from monochrome to polychrome, in the emphasis on animals, and in conventional treatments of the human figure. It is fairly certain that these rock paintings are no more than a few thousand years old at the most. Some are thought to have been made as recently as the seventeenth century, inasmuch as their creation and creators alike are remembered in stories that are still passed down through the generations.

In Australia, too, there are quite recent cave paintings and rock etchings. In the

Figure 8 (left). Whistling jar, a musical instrument from Peru. Figure 9 (right). Arm panel from the throne of Thut-mose IV. In religious art, the invisible is made visible and its existence validated. The conjunction of men and gods is made concrete and familiar, and the artist is creator in both realms. Abstract symbols such as the ankh used here or the cross of the Christians are nuclei around which such rich accretions of meaning develop that the symbol itself may be perceived and used as having great power.

north and southeast, the styles tend to be naturalistic or at least symbolic of well-known mythological phenomena, whereas in the southwest the designs are more geometric. In some regions, however, the two styles do overlap. Some of the etchings are thought to be 4,000 years old, but, as in South Africa, these prehistoric arts merge into the historic and recorded arts that were being produced when Europeans first came to Australia and spread from the coast into the hinterland.

There are also many rock engravings in North America, particularly in the less-populated areas in the West and Southwest. These engravings tend to be schematic and often symbolic, and, as with the arts of most hunters and gatherers, men and animals constitute the principal subject matter. These rock arts are of no great age and can be related to the historically recorded artistic endeavors of the American Indians.

Other societies made greater use of geometric and repetitive designs and decorations that undoubtedly were intended to evoke aesthetic pleasure from their audience. But the marked emphasis on design and repetitiveness could also signify an abundance of crops or numbers of people, as these elements did in the painted pottery of the agricultural Pueblo Indians of New Mexico. This association may explain why agricultural people with larger and denser populations tend to make more use of the geometric and abstract visual arts than do hunting and gathering people, who tend to concentrate on representing, or at least symbolizing, individual people and animals.

THE ARTS OF CIVILIZATION
The earliest art styles of the world's first civilizations usually evolved out of the prehistoric art styles first developed by the agricultural societies that were indigenous to the areas. In Peru, for instance, there are sequences of sculpture and pottery over several centuries that lead to the arts of the Incas. And in Egypt, the arts of the earliest dynasties are recognizably similar to those

of the Gebel el Arec site of Upper Egypt. As civilizations became increasingly complex, however, such art styles acquired a character of their own under the influences of the new social, political, and religious orders that were emerging to lead and to control the growing populace.

Art and the Rural-Urban Dichotomy
As people moved to the growing centers of civilization a dichotomy developed between city and rural life, and inside the cities the development of more complex economies and a more complex division of labor led to the creation of social hierarchies, complete with elite groups at the top. The elite groups developed their own art forms, usually characterized as the "high arts," and these arts generally spread throughout the entire region controlled by the center of civilization. Inevitably, art traditions tended to reflect the tastes of the ruling classes, and the symbols of their art appeared everywhere and were understood by everyone throughout the area. Occasionally, a form of high art carried over to adjacent but politically autonomous civilizations as happened, for example, when Buddhism spread throughout the whole of southern and eastern Asia over a period of several centuries.

Folk arts, on the other hand, were more likely to be local expressions, but they still were related to the high arts in two ways. First, peasant and lower-class art forms were crude imitations of the forms and styles of the art of the elite, sharing and identifying with the overriding symbolism of the civilization as a whole. In this relationship, folk art was influenced by the high art through what has been described as the "trickle-down effect." A second relationship occurred when one civilization overran or engulfed other, less powerful ones having different cultural traditions, as happened when the Spaniards conquered the Indians of Mexico and much of South America, imposing Catholicism and other aspects of Spanish culture as they went. In this situation, local traditions often persisted for several centuries but were concurrently influenced by the art of the conquerors, and the admixture created a totally new form of regional art. Although many of the conventions and symbols of the hybrid art were widely accepted, others possessed only local meaning and were not fully understood either by the ruling class or by people of other regions who were subjects of the same civilization.

Art and the Influence of Religion

Most commonly, the high arts of civilization were inseparable from the central belief systems and values of the elite. It was the ruling classes who patronized the arts in preindustrial civilizations, and they naturally determined the form that art should take, making it serve both their beliefs and their political ambitions. In most of these societies—among the Maya and in medieval Europe, in Japan and ancient Egypt—the leadership either was the exclusive domain of a priestly group or was heavily influenced by religion. Most of the art expressed the dominant concern of these societies with religious and supernatural beings. In ancient Egypt, where the kings held power with the aid of the priestly class and the ruler himself was deemed a god, almost all the art and architecture concerned the relations between the gods and men. When Christianity spread throughout Europe, converting people of many different countries and backgrounds, its art promoted adherence to this religious faith. Indeed, in the Byzantine Empire and throughout southern Europe, there was almost no art but Christian art during the Middle Ages.

Religion was an important source of the power by which the leaders ruled and by which conformity to their rule was enforced and sanctioned. The intensification of religious feeling and commitment through sculpture, painting, architecture, song, and ritual was essential for the maintenance of the religiously based governments that

brought order to these larger societies. Whereas the aesthetics were those of the elite, the content and symbolism had to be understood by the bulk of the society. In Byzantium and medieval Europe, where the Christian symbolism was well known to the people, emphasis was placed on the traditional meanings of the subject matter—such as episodes from the Passion Cycle—rather than on the invention or originality of the creator. This process was carried to an extreme in the Byzantine Empire. Not only were the artists anonymous, they also had to paint all their art forms in precisely the same style, following instructions laid down by the Church. And in western Europe, the men who built the great Gothic cathedrals of the late Middle Ages worked in such anonymity that even the names of the principal architects for the most part go unremembered.

Some of these great civilizations arose and then collapsed, leaving little continuity with their descendants, as was the case with the Maya and ancient Egypt. Others in Europe and in China carried on their high traditions with more continuity into the present era.

The arts and culture of ancient Greece have had the most lasting effect, forming much of the basis of European artistic traditions down to the present day.

The Greek people based their early arts on the styles of the already existing civilizations of Crete and Mycenae and were further influenced by the art of Egypt and Persia, nations with which the enterprising Greeks traded. They developed traditions of their own, however, many of which have endured for more than 2,000 years. First came an intense concern with naturalism, expressed in the sculpture of "ideal" forms of the human body. These sculptures, such as the "Venus de Milo" or the "Discus Thrower," have been held up as models of human and artistic perfection in the West. This fast-developing tradition soon came to include portraiture of real people rather than of ideal people or gods, something hinted at earlier in Egyptian art and developed to a greater degree in the later Roman arts.

Perhaps even more important than the degree of technical perfection achieved was the philosophical concern that the Greeks had with their own art. They wrote and argued about it and may be said to have invented the disciplines of art history and art criticism. They saw the conflict between the artist's search for perfection and the "lagging tastes" of the masses. They also were probably the first to identify the individual artist and take the creator out of the realm of anonymity that was and still is characteristic of other traditions and periods. The Greek concepts were admired and elaborated upon by the Romans, who carried them throughout much of the Western world.

Early Directions in Western Art

It is in the well-recorded history of western Europe that the development of art forms in their changing social and cultural context can be most clearly traced. In painting and in sculpture, the Renaissance represented the high point in Christian religious art.

Figure 10 (left). Tracing the growing naturalism in Greek art from 600 B.C. to its full expression in 1 B.C. In the Egyptian art that preceded it, experimentation was suppressed by the despotic state and by the powerful priesthood that came to reduce all art and intellect to conformed patterns. This suppression was in fact an extension of the Eastern concern with domination by the supernatural, a development fed by conditions of human misery that turned the masses toward enduring what Goethe called the "inner universe" — the universe controlled by the priesthoods. In India where Buddhism prevailed, the triumph was complete. The controlled artistic expression of the supernatural was calm and overwhelming, and man was insignificant in its presence. Greek art is all the more remarkable for its emergence amidst these prevailing abstractions of humanity, for it expresses the spirit of men at ease in the natural world. The influence of its combining of spirit and flesh touched even the despotic states of ancient India and Rome (Figure 11, below) and has reached over time to shape the art traditions of the West.

After the sixteenth century the power of the Church declined radically, and the Church was replaced as the principal patron of the arts by men of wealth and leisure. The waning power of the Church was reflected in the arts, which shifted from emphasis on religious figures and stories to purely secular subjects. Although the styles remained representational, they became artificial and genteel, as the court art of Fragonard vividly portrays. As trade increased and more distant explorations were undertaken, other art forms became fashionable, particularly the high arts of China and Japan, which achieved great popularity among those grown rich in the industrial revolution. Although folk art and primitive art were known about, they were still considered the products of inferior beings.

Until well into the nineteenth century, naturalism continued to be considered the highest form of visual art—a view maintained by the somewhat sterile academic schools that continued to dominate the standards of taste for most of the patrons of the arts. During the nineteenth century, however, this attachment to traditional standards was challenged. Photography emerged to challenge the artists, for it could "represent" as well as, or probably better than, any human creator. Moreover, the furious pace of industrialization produced a concurrent reaction against modern life, and these two factors provided the impetus for artistic experiments, both in technique and in content, that led eventually to the creation of the style called cubism.

Some artists, most notably Paul Gauguin, experimented with an idea that had recurred throughout history—that of the "noble savage." The complexities of European life led Gauguin and others to search for simpler and perhaps stronger ways of expressing themselves, and they thought they found their answer in the exotic but neglected world of primitive society.

One group of French artists was struck by the deliberate distortions of natural forms

Figure 12. "The Dream," by Henri Rousseau. Western artists were influenced not only by the forms of primitive art but by the notion of primitivism itself. Here, Rousseau strives for this quality. The influence of primitive art on the Western tradition may reflect one of the main differences between the two. The Western artist is eclectic, drawing upon all the world's traditions and using them in his striving to innovate. The traditional primitive artist, in contrast, draws from a much narrower range of source forms.

that they saw in some African carvings and masks that had been collecting dust in museums for several decades. They considered these forms to be a valuable break from the conventions of academic art, and along with other inspirations derived from the sciences —especially crystallography—they transformed the African ideas into new forms of painting and sculpture. At first the artists concentrated on reproducing African art forms ("art negre," as it was called), but, interestingly enough, they soon discovered that the African art was as conservative within its own traditions as the schools they themselves had left behind.

THE PRIMITIVE ARTS

The art of people outside the influence of the well-known civilizations historically has been referred to as primitive art, a term that grew out of the ethnocentrism characteristic of eighteenth- and nineteenth-century Europe. Today the term is still in use, but it is applied without pejorative connotations.

As the French artists eventually realized, primitive arts are all essentially conservative, in that adherence to traditional forms and techniques is considered more important than creativity. Originality is rare because the art forms usually are important in the functioning of the society, and for that reason the members of the society must be able to share in the traditional understandings of what the art forms mean. Among the Northwest Coast Indians, for instance, painted masks are used in the winter ceremonies to reenact important myths or stories, and the audience must be able to recognize the performer through the shared conventions of the mask he wears. Similarly,

Figure 13. Above, a Maori carver working with the highly elaborate, decorative style of his tradition. Such traditional arts are generally so distinctive that the expert would rarely fail to correctly assign a work of art to the society that produced it. Below, Australian bark painting. The Australian artist frequently depicts both external and internal details, as if with x-ray vision. The figures may depict a totemic species.

where tribal history and religious knowledge is to be passed from generation to generation, as in the initiation ceremonies of the Australian aborigines, the standard depictions of important events and beings are adhered to as closely as possible.

This does not mean that primitive art styles do not change. Even when the artist believes he is doing exactly what his predecessors did before him, he may have no way of checking. In some societies models are rarely used as a guide, and individual and perhaps unintended variation keeps creeping in. In the case of the Asmat, enormous ancestor poles are carved and erected outside the men's houses for use at funerals. After a few weeks, the poles are thrown away to rot in the tropical forest, so that when the next death occurs the carver must rely not on models but on memory alone.

Even in societies with the simplest division of labor there may be specialists in the arts. Among the Pende, an African tribe, there are carvers who specialize in making statuettes for the chiefs and headmen. Among the Chokwe, a society with a similar level of social organization, everyone believes he is an artist and equally capable of making the complex masks used in initiation rites. It is only in large societies with a more specialized division of labor that full-time specialists are found who are able to make a living from their art.

In the contemporary world, primitive societies are no longer isolated entities, and their activities and even art production have been modified considerably by outside influences and by increasing commercialization and urbanization. These arts have followed one of three main paths. In some areas, the local people still concentrate on producing art for their own use, although frequently they employ new techniques and materials. The Maori of New Zealand, for instance, now use metal tools and modern paints in making their traditional wood carvings. Other primitive people, such as the bark painters of Aarnhem Land in Australia, have

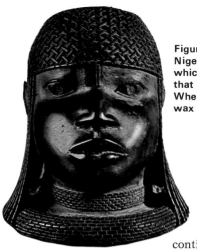

Figure 14. This example of Benin sculpture from Nigeria was created by the lost-wax method, in which molten bronze is poured into a clay mold that has been shaped around a wax carving. When the bronze is poured into the mold, the wax melts and is replaced by it.

continued to follow traditional styles but aim their production at an outside market. Still other primitive societies, such as the Kamba of Kenya, never did much wood carving until they saw the possibility of sale to Europeans; they now concentrate on producing such carvings as souvenirs and their motive is purely commercial. The Kamba, moreover, in trying to make their art look "African," have borrowed designs from other tribes. They have even set up shops with production lines in order to fill orders from the American market.

In still other cases, previously isolated groups have been encouraged by contacts with the outside world and have come to produce new kinds of art superior in quality to anything they produced before. A striking example is that of the Eskimo of northern Canada, who have been encouraged since World War II to produce soapstone carvings and, more recently, lithographic prints that rival any produced in the West. Similarly, the Kombe of Tanzania now produce imaginative and striking wood carvings, whereas previously their work had been quite ordinary and relatively unimportant even within their own culture.

Art does not necessarily cease to be art just because it is made for money or because it is created for a wider audience. In American society alone, most artists certainly hope to make a profit in addition to satisfying their aesthetic ambitions. It is just that the influence of the market on non-Western arts can become particularly strong when the entire livelihood of a society comes to depend on continuing sales. In some primitive societies, for example, people who have settled down to produce art for a livelihood are better off than those who perform the more menial occupations that conquering civilizations tend to reserve for subject people. Navajo jewelers are more respected than ordinary herdsmen or laborers. Namatjira, the Australian aborigine who took up watercolor painting, became so well known that his fame caused the Australian government to clarify the status of all aborigines, and he himself was granted the legal status of a white man. And a few Eskimo have become so well known for their art that they travel abroad and often meet heads of state. Other Eskimos, however, have come to believe that the market demands something particularly "Eskimo" of them and have suppressed some of their own artistic taste, thinking they would avert financial failure. It is ironic that the affluent of the Western world have increasingly developed a taste for the arts of primitive society, thereby creating these and other situations in which the production of art has been encouraged for reasons quite foreign to the ambitions of the creators themselves.

FOLKLORE, MUSIC, AND DANCE

The study of *folklore* developed out of amateur studies of popular antiquities and literature. The term itself was not invented until 1846, and controversy still continues on what should be the proper content of the subject. Some people believe that the term "folklore" should refer only to oral and traditional topics, whereas others would include non-verbal phenomena such as superstitions, gestures, and even cartoons. In the nineteenth century, folklorists concentrated on the historic and geographic nature of their subject, much as art historians had concentrated on folk arts, and the emphasis was on finding the original archetype of a folk tale and then tracing the spread and variations of it through time and space. In the present century, folklorists have also concerned themselves with the oral literature of non-literate people around the world and with the unwritten sayings of literate members of the world's civilizations. But they have also expanded the scope of their study by becoming more concerned with the symbolism and functions of folklore.

Like some other arts, folklore serves not only to provide entertainment but also to perform more serious functions. For exam-

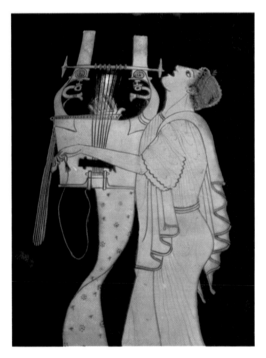

Figure 15. Painting of Orpheus on a Greek amphora (about 490 B.C.). The song as sound is an ephemeral event. Its persistence as form before the invention of musical notation depended on the performer's memory. Through long chains of performers, songs have persisted for millenniums, changing as they moved from culture to culture in time and space, yet retaining a tenuous continuity of expression.

ple, Victorians wrote "Cautionary Tales" to teach morality to their children, and in Nigerian courts both accuser and plaintiff make adroit use of proverbs in order to promote their cause and discredit their opponent. Folklore can serve other functions as well. Normally it tends to be conservative, but occasionally folklore can serve as an agent of social change. This has happened in the Soviet Union and in Communist China, where new folk tales, folk songs, and dramas tell of the downfall of the rich, the overthrow of capitalism, and the rise of the poor classes. Such simple and easily understood media serve to strengthen a government by uniting a tremendous number of people, both literate and nonliterate, in a common cause.

In either its vocal or its instrumental form, *music* has probably always existed in human culture. And in music, too, distinctions can be made between folk art, primitive art, and the art of high civilizations. Throughout the world, the wind and string instruments and particularly the drums are used most widely. But instruments usually call for more skill than song, and the players are more likely to be specialists. Because of the need for specialization, instruments are not found everywhere and, where they are present, they are often subordinate to song and dance.

Song is universal and embraces a great variety of melodic themes, although the basic forms may be few. The musical forms tend to be simple and therefore easy to remember and to sing. The stanza, a common but not quite universal form, contains four lines at the most, and few songs have been found that extend further than one and one-half octaves in range. Like most early arts, folk songs tend to be anonymous and traditional, with variations expanding on common themes. Many folk songs and primitive songs tend to be associated with group activities, particularly those celebrations of annual or life cycle events that bring the group together and emphasize its unity and

shared beliefs. In this way, song reinforces social solidarity in much the same manner that more complex forms of music tie together the affluent classes of Western society, as when people gather on such occasions as the opening night of an opera season. In primitive societies, singing can also serve more immediately practical purposes. Some people sing to their animals in order to sooth them and facilitate milking or handling. And the Congo Pygmies of the great tropical forests sing as they travel in order to announce their coming and so reduce the risk of startling a dangerous animal.

There has been a close relationship between folk music and the music of the upper classes. Many verbal and musical themes have trickled down from the upper classes and remain popular in folk music long after they have been discarded by the classes that invented them. But, as with other arts during the past century, influences have also

Figure 16. The dance blends form, color, and time. Here, the costume of this Shaguna dancer amplifies and lends variety to the moving pattern of his body.

436   **Culture in Its Infinite Variety | VII**

moved in the opposite direction: many composers, from Shubert to Bartók and Dvořák to Enesco, have used anonymous folk melodies as inspiration for their own work.

Like music, *dance* is universal and ranges from total group participation to often specialized performances. Among literate people, dance may constitute a form of visual entertainment, involving specialized choreographers and performers. In primitive societies, dances are less varied in form and more conservative in tradition than in industrial societies. They are usually repeated at social events, and often they serve functions of profound social importance.

In southern Italy, for example, the tarantella was danced by people who suffered psychosomatic afflictions, supposedly inflicted by tarantula bites. In northern England, a very different form of dance, the Morris dances, were originally symbolic reenactments of battles that soon became reinterpreted as the battles of the seasons to displace one another. They were danced to increase fertility at spring rituals. In some primitive societies, dances were often performances of characters who represented important gods or powers of the universe. The dances expressed relationships between the gods themselves and between the gods and mankind. The purpose of such dances was to renew the power of the gods, but they also served to teach the uninitiated the essential nature of the universe and the proper relation between gods and men.

ART AS A CULTURAL MAP

In many respects, all art constitutes a kind of cultural map, a guide that can be used to help explain the cultural make-up of a society. In the rituals and ceremonies of some societies, going back to an earlier example, the art forms express the relationships between men and supernatural beings. In other societies, the rituals function to express the proper order and relationships of all the groups within the society. Even the procession at a British coronation represents, with almost diagrammatic accuracy, the relationships that supposedly exist not only between the different classes of English society, but also between Britain and other members of the Commonwealth, and foreign nations.

All art tends to possess the theme of rhythm or repetitiveness, most obviously in the cases of music and dance, but also in the more subtle decorative arts. A special form of rhythm is symmetry, a common worldwide theme that probably derives both from nature and from man's seeming preference to make order out of chaos, and it is often possible to see how the structure of a society is revealed in the use made of repetitive or symmetrical design. The designs in egalitarian societies, for instance, are characterized by empty spaces, whereas the designs in hierarchical societies tend to be filled in. Symmetrical designs and figures without enclosures are more characteristic of egalitarian societies, and asymmetry and closed figures indicate the existence of a hierarchical social order. Egalitarian societies tend to stress the repetitive design of similar elements, whereas hierarchical societies stress the repetition of dissimilar elements.

There is probably an underlying association between certain art forms and certain periods in history as well. Romanticism seems to flourish in periods of social and political change, as it did in the period that began with the French Revolution and continued until the European revolutions of the 1840s. Classicism, in contrast, tends to dominate art forms in authoritarian societies when economies are static and views of the world and of human nature are rigid, as under the Roman and Byzantine empires.

On many levels, then, the arts reflect the character of individuals and of societies. Whether among primitive or complex societies, rich groups or poor, all people practice art and have done so throughout history. The arts are, in effect, an essential and recurrent part of the humanity of man.

Kinship Systems

28

The Nayar of Malabar have a family system that must seem extraordinary to the unprepared Western observer. Before she reaches adolescence, every Nayar girl is supposed to go through a ceremony of marriage and any girl who does not suffers a disgrace from which she may never fully recover. But after the ceremony the girl may never see her "husband" again, and it is extremely unlikely that he will ever share her bed. When she matures, the Nayar girl settles in her own hut near the huts of her brothers and takes lovers from the Nambudiri Brahmins, a rich and exclusive caste of priestly land owners who live nearby. Nayar girls tend to have several lovers, so when a Nambudiri goes to visit his mistress in the evening, he sticks his spear in the ground outside her hut. If he finds her alone when he arrives, he goes inside. If he finds a spear already stuck outside the hut, he goes off, to return another night.

The Nambudiri men are the biological fathers ("genitor") of the children born to the Nayar women, but that is as far as the relationship goes. The Nayar children are brought up entirely by their mothers and by their mother's brothers, who play the role of social fathers ("pater"). Curious as it might seem, the Nayar system of family relationships—or kinship, as anthropologists usually refer to the subject—is actually well adapted to the particular circumstances of these two parts of the society and it benefits both sides. On one side, the Nambudiri have remained rich by observing a rule that forbids the division of their estates. In each family only the eldest son marries, and he marries a Nambudiri girl. The younger sons are not allowed to marry or to have children, but by taking Nayar mistresses they are at least allowed to satisfy their sexual drive. The Nambudiri men are content with the relationship because they can satisfy their sexual desires and still retain control over their estates, free from the squabbles that would follow the birth of too many claimants.

On the other side, the Nayar find the system to be advantageous because it allows them to maintain complete control over their children without interference from any outsiders. Because the Nayar mother's brother is pater but not genitor, the child is kept under the control of the maternal brother and sister without incest. Inasmuch

Figure 2. This diagram depicts independent nuclear families that are not extended into unilineal groups. In this and all other kinship diagrams in this chapter, the arrow symbols represent males and the rounded symbols, females. Double lines show marriage bonds; single lines indicate descent and sibling relationship. In this particular photograph, descent lines are directly connected to marriage ties in order to define the nuclear family.

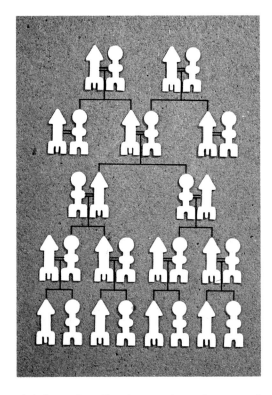

as Nambudiri lovers are genitor rather than pater, the family estate is not fragmented, and celibacy is not required of the younger brothers.

The only victims of the system are the Nambudiri women who are not taken in marriage by the eldest sons, for they are not allowed to marry outside their own group. They live in a state of strict seclusion. If they go out of their houses, their bodies must be completely enveloped in clothing and their faces hidden under an umbrella. Even the lucky few who do get married cannot attend their own weddings or make any other public appearance but must be replaced by a Nayar girl.

These impositions are not general characteristics of the Muslim world. But in terms of its practical consequences, the Nayar system works efficiently and can stand as an example of human ingenuity and adaptability.

THE FUNCTIONS OF KINSHIP

Kinship was the subject of Lewis Henry Morgan's *Systems of Affinity and Consanguinity*, one of the classic works that established the science of anthropology, and kinship has remained a principal subject of anthropological inquiry for good reason. The bonds between kin are potentially the most fundamental of all social bonds and they perform at least two functions that are essential to the perpetuation of society.

Kinship serves to provide continuity between generations. All societies must arrange for their children to be cared for, disciplined, and educated, and they must also arrange for the transmission of property, social position, and, sometimes, of special knowledge or political power from one generation to the next. The *family* is by far the most important social group in many societies, and it is the kinship system that determines the make-up of the family—in other words, how new members are recruited into the family (by birth, for exam-

ple), how the offspring are brought up, and how inheritance and succession are regulated. From this point of view, kinship systems can be regarded as *vertical* systems of organization that order relationships between generations and thereby perpetuate societies and their cultures over time.

Kinship serves a second essential function. Families are immensely important in many societies, and the social order is regulated primarily through systems in which the separate families are linked to one another by ties established through marriage between their members. These marriage-based ties are called affinal relationships, and they can unite large numbers of people from the families of the husband and wife, inasmuch as the links unite otherwise separate members of the same generation. These bonds may be referred to as *horizontal* systems of organization, and they, too, are determined by the particular circumstances of a society.

THE DESCENT ASPECT OF KINSHIP

Descent systems, one aspect of vertical organization, are the ways in which different societies have organized family succession and inheritance. In the United States, the principal descent unit is the *nuclear family*, consisting of the father or husband, the mother or wife, and their children. In most instances, members are recruited into the family by being born to their parents, and inheritance passes vertically from parents to children, usually with little deference to sex or birth order. This system strikes Americans as natural, partly because they are used to it and partly because it operates along the simplest biological lines. But it is important to remember, from an anthropological point of view, that kinship deals with *social* relationships rather than with *biological* relationships, although the two usually overlap. It is not merely the existence of biologically based ties that makes a kin relationship; rather it is how society actually regards the facts of biological relatedness.

At first glance, it might seem that the relationship between parents and children is based on the unavoidable facts of reproduction and birth. Even though there is the possibility of adoption, whereby a child becomes the social and legal equivalent of a "born" offspring, there are limits to how extensively adoption can be employed. A look at the cross-cultural record again illustrates the range of human ingenuity in avoiding the facts.

In some societies, such as those found in Samoa and ancient Ireland, children were commonly farmed out to foster parents, and the basic responsibilities of suckling and training children were carried out by women who were not the progenitive mothers. In many societies, the blood relationship between a father and his illegitimate children may not be recognized. In the Trobriand Islands and among some Australian aborigines, the existence of a biological relationship between *any* man—whether married to the mother or not—and his child is denied, for intercourse is not believed to have any role in conception. In other societies, such as those of Japan and the United States, a man may adopt a child to whom he is not biologically related and make him his legal heir.

Among the Nuer of the Sudan, a dead man can have children, for a man earns the right to his wife's children by paying cattle for her, and even when he dies he is regarded as the social father of any children his wife may conceive by other men. Among the Nuer, it is even possible for a woman to be a father. If she has enough cattle, the Nuer woman can buy a wife and then get some man to father the pseudo-wife's children, who will inherit her property and her name. In other societies, even the true biological relationship between parents and children goes largely unrecognized.

Even with all the variation as to how they are composed, descent groups are the most prevalent form of kinship and all are based on a relationship between people who share a common ancestor. There is the *clan*, in which a group of people are descended from a real or supposed (fictive) ancestor. The ancestor may be a historic human being from whom all the members trace descent or even a mythological person or animal from whom descent is claimed even if it cannot be demonstrated. Very often the operating unit of the kinship system is a group smaller than a clan, called the *lineage*, that consists only of people who can trace actual descent from a known ancestor. Lineages, even more often than clans, are *corporate groups* in the sense that they act as a body by owning impartible land, by being collectively responsible in law for their members, and by following the same patterns of cultural behavior.

MATRILINEAL SYSTEMS

Despite their different notions of the nature of biological relationships, all societies view the mother-child relationship as a basic unit in the social system, together with the tie between siblings (children of the same mother). This unit of a woman and her children must be protected, provisioned, and

Figure 3. The nuclear family is again shown by the combination of marriage, descent, and sibling bonds. The colored lines indicate matrilineal descent groups. Three matrilineages are shown in magenta, green, and black (which is depicted discontinuously as it intermarries with the first two). Here, the nuclear family is now divided; the parents are derived from different matrilineages and the children inherit lineage membership from the mother.

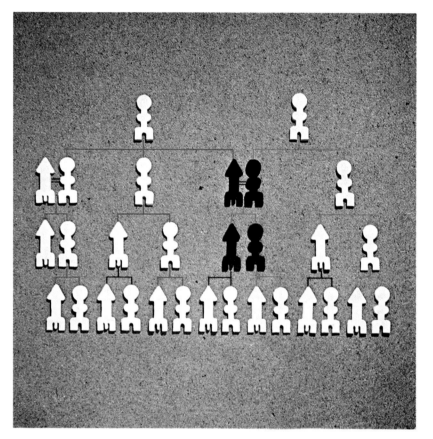

They share inheritance from their parents, they worship the same ancestral gods, and they are members of the same lineage. It might therefore seem natural that they should remain together after they have grown up, with the brothers playing the role of fathers to their sisters' children and the children themselves inheriting the position and property from their mothers' brothers and so keeping these possessions within the mother-based family, without letting outsiders get control of any part of it through marriage.

Continuity and the Incest Tabu

Before the brother-sister system can operate, outsiders must be brought into it, for all societies function under an incest tabu that forbids brothers to mate with their sisters. Men must be brought in from other families if the sisters are to become impregnated. It is possible for a brother to allow his sister to become impregnated while retaining absolute control over her and surrendering nothing to her mate or mates. Some systems, notably the Nayar, have come close to achieving this arrangement, but this system is unusual. More commonly, the sister is loaned out to another man, who gains rights to her sexual and economic services but not to her reproductive services. With this system, the ensuing children belong to the brother. They are his heirs and successors, not the heirs and successors of their father. They may be brought up in their father's village, if the kinship system is such that the wife goes to live in her husband's house. But when the children reach adolescence they will return to their mother's village, where they will inherit property from her brothers, and it is this village that they will always regard as their home. Their own father is more concerned with his sister's children, who will inherit *his* property. This solution to the continuity problem is called matriliny and such a kinship system is matrilineal (see Figure 3). For purposes of inheritance

controlled, and it is the men of the society who have the primary responsibility for performing these functions. But which men? To Americans the answer is obvious: it is the man who is responsible for conceiving the children. But it is possible to approach the issue from a quite different direction, as the Nayar do. To them, the next basic family unit after the mother-child unit is not the relationship between the man and wife but that between brother and sister.

This point of view is in fact perfectly reasonable. From birth, brothers and sisters are used to living together. Being members of the same basic family unit, they trust each other more than they trust any outsiders.

Figure 4. Trobriand children belong to a matrilineage and will inherit from their mother's brother rather than from their father. Matriliny tends to be distributed over large, contiguous areas. It is found in many of the Melanesian islands, whereas it is almost totally lacking on the mainland of New Guinea. Matrilineal societies are also found in Central Africa.

and succession, the most important kinship links are traced through the mother, or females, not through the father, or males.

The Trobrianders follow the matrilineal form of kinship, and they can be used to illustrate some of the problems associated with it. When a Trobriand couple marries, the woman normally goes to live with her husband in his village. When they have children, he is the one who exercises daily control over them. But the husband is made to pay for the rights to his wife's sexual services and for the economic services—and pleasure—he derives from his children until they reach maturity and must leave his home. He must pay a certain amount of food to his wife's parents and to her brothers, a situation many men resent even though they in turn receive food from men who marry their sisters. And this resentment is only one of the difficulties.

Tension and the Mother's Brother

As is common in matrilineal systems, the mother's brother tends to be a figure of authority and respect, and his position causes a certain amount of tension between him and his sister's sons, tension exacerbated by the fact that the sons will inherit their uncle's property and status when he dies. Additional tension is created when the brother exerts his authority over his married sisters. Between husband and wife, however, the relationship is usually affectionate and tender. Moreover, unlike the situation that exists in many other societies, the relationship between father and son is free of the bitterness stemming from the son's resentment of his father's discipline—and from the father's resentment of the fact that his son is awaiting his death, whereupon the son will inherit his property. Because the relationship between Trobriand fathers and sons tends to be warm and relaxed, however, its limitations can be a source of bitterness. A man may resent the food payments that must be made to his

wife's brother and he may resent the control her brother exerts over her. He resents far more the fact that his property and status will be inherited not by his son, whom he loves, but by his sister's son, whom he may detest and who may detest him for the same reasons that are found in the father-son conflicts in other societies. He knows that no matter how hard he works he cannot pass on any of his inheritance to his sons. He can give his sons gifts, but when he does he provokes the bitter resentment of his sister's sons, who must stand by helplessly and watch their cousins being given what they believe is rightly their own.

In *Crime and Custom in Savage Society*, Bronislaw Malinowski described the kind of problem the matrilineal system can breed. To'uluwa was a rich and powerful chief who lived in the capital village of Omarakana with several wives and their children, including his favorite son, Namwana Guya'u. A number of his nephews who were his heirs apparent also lived in the village, which was, according to the Trobriand system, their real home. It was not, of course, Namwana Guya'u's real home, and resentment grew between Namwana Guya'u and his cousins, especially the second oldest, Mitakata.

The resentment exploded into a family feud when Mitakata appeared as the defendent in a court case and it was Namwana Guya'u's testimony that convicted him and put him in prison. When the news reached the village, pandemonium broke loose. Although Namwana Guya'u was the chief's son and lived in the village, he was considered nothing more than a stranger there, for his true home was the village of his mother's people; Omarakana was really the home of his cousins, his father's nephews. To'uluwa shut himself up in his hut, fearful of what would happen to his favorite son who, by attacking Mitakata, his cousin, had outraged law and propriety. The kinsmen of the imprisoned Mitakata seethed with anger, and when night fell no one appeared in the central place; even the chief and his wives and their families remained indoors. Then Bagido'u, the eldest brother of the imprisoned man and heir apparent to the chief, emerged from his hut and in a loud voice accused his cousin of having lived off the food of the village to which he did not really belong and then of turning on his cousins, the true sons of the village. "We do not want you to stay here," he shouted. "This is our village. You are a stranger here. Go away. We chase you away. We chase you out of Omarakana."

Before the night was over, Namwana Guya'u had left Omarakana and settled in his own village, a few miles away. For several weeks his mother and his sister wailed for him as if they were mourning for the dead. Even the chief, To'uluwa, remained in his hut for three days, and when he came out he looked, as Malinowski described him, older and stricken with grief. All his interest and all his affection were for his favorite son, but he could do nothing to help him. Under the matrilineal system his nephews were his heirs. It was to them that the village and the chiefdomship belonged. They had acted in accordance with their rights and all the affection of fatherhood could do nothing to hold them back. Within a year after the expulsion, Namwana Guya'u's mother had died, an event probably hastened by her grief, and two years later Namwana Guya'u was still living in his own village aloof from his father's kinsmen. The relationship between the two lineages had been irreparably damaged.

Despite the bitterness revealed in this classic study, matrilineal societies do not have some of the strains and tensions that are characteristic of patrilineal and other kinds of societies. No social arrangement really is without sources for quarrels and hatred. The matrilineal system is common among American Indians, in the Pacific Islands, and in a wide belt running from east to west across Central Africa, so there can be no question that the system works well enough

to hold the society together. Still, it does possess disadvantages, and the drawbacks inherent in the matrilineal system may help to explain why the patrilineal system tends to be more widespread.

PATRILINEAL SYSTEMS

In the patrilineal system, a man gains absolute control over his wife at the expense of her brothers, and inheritance and succession are traced through the father, or males, not through the mother, or females (see Figure 5). From the structural point of view, the main problem in the patrilineal system is that the man must detach his prospective wife from her relationship with her own father and brothers and gain control over her in order to gain absolute rights over her children. Also, there are usually problems for the woman, who must go to live among "strangers" (her husband's kin), and her standing among them usually depends entirely on her role as wife and mother.

In most patrilineal societies, the man makes some form of payment for his bride, usually referred to as *bridewealth*. It may consist of quantities of food or, as is most common among African patrilineal groups, a certain predetermined number of cattle, such as the forty cows that a Nuer bridegroom pays for his bride. The payment of bridewealth does not mean that a man buys his wife in the sense that a slave owner buys a slave. It is rather a payment in recognition of receiving her sexual and economic serv-

ices and for the rights to her children, all of which will be lost to her own lineage and transferred instead to the lineage of the bridegroom's father. Although her children will belong to her husband's patrilineage, however, she will always be a member of her father's group.

In a patrilineal system, marriage and legitimacy are usually more important and are surrounded by more sanctions than they are in matrilineal systems, where—theoretically at least—marriage is unnecessary and illegitimacy impossible. Under the Nuer system of marriage, for instance, the bridewealth is paid by the bridegroom's patrilineal kin because he usually has not accumulated enough cattle of his own at the time he marries. The cattle are paid out over a period of time, and the last payment is made at about the time the first child of the marriage is born. These payments, together with certain ceremonials, constitute the marriage process. Without the payment of bridewealth, a marriage among the Nuer is not socially recognized. Moreover, the cattle that are received are distributed among three different groups—the bride's immediate kin on both sides, her father's closest kin, and her mother's closest kin (these "close kin" are mainly related patrilineally)—all of whom may use the cattle to help pay bridewealth for wives for their own sons. The Nuer also have a complicated system for determining just how many cattle must be returned if a woman insists on leaving her

husband, or if a woman dies before she bears children, or if a woman is unable to bear children. And if a woman leaves her husband but does not get a divorce and has an affair with another man, it is the husband who has the rights to the children she bears "in the bush," as the Nuer describe it.

The complex arrangements that attend marriage among the Nuer are fairly typical of patrilineal societies, in which great care is taken to delimit and guarantee the husband's rights. But clearly a system such as that of the Nuer is more than just a way to bring men and women together. Patriliny not only ties together a man, a woman, and their children, it also unites the immediate patrilineage relationships centering on the bridewealth. This unity between lineages persists after payments are completed, and the members of the two groups retain obligations to avoid mutual hostilities as long as the children of the marriage—and even *their* children—live.

UNILINEAL AND DOUBLE DESCENT

In both matrilineal and patrilineal societies, descent from the founder is traced in one line only—whether the male or the female—and such groups are called *unilineal descent groups*. As social units these groups have certain advantages, the major ones being that they perpetuate themselves through birth and do not overlap. Membership is unambiguous, and ownership, rights, duties, and legal position vis-a-vis everyone in the society are neatly defined for any individual. By knowing the descent group to which a stranger belongs and the nature of the relationship between his group and another's, everyone immediately knows how to treat one another.

Lineages and clans can have many functions beyond simple family recruitment. They may, for example, be exclusively religious groups or political units. They may exist only to regulate marriage. Or they may be primarily units of economic production.

Because the functions of the groups can vary, it is possible for any society to have both matrilineal and patrilineal descent groups operating within it, and a few actually do have both. For example, in one such society there are matriclans that base rituals and ceremonies on the matrilineal relationships and patriclans that control the way in which food production is organized. In such *double descent systems*, every individual is a member of both a patrilineal group through his father and a matrilineal group through his mother. For each situation he behaves as he would in a simple unilineal system, except that he is playing more roles. A male is both a father and a husband in his patrilineal group and a brother and a maternal uncle in his matrilineal group. In the former role, he is concerned with his rights over his wife and his own sons; in the latter, with his rights over his sister and her sons. Actually, in double descent systems a person is born with membership in two descent groups and a close relationship with two others—his father's matrilineal group and his mother's patrilineal group.

AMBILATERAL DESCENT
Western society, together with others in Micronesia, Ethiopia, the arctic, and elsewhere, does not have unilineal descent of any kind. Kin related through the father are not differentiated from kin related through the mother, with respect to rights, duties, group membership, or any other aspect. In such societies, there are no lineages or clans, inasmuch as there is no possible basis for such unilineal groupings, equal weight being accorded kin on both sides. In fact, there are no enduring kin groups beyond the husband-wife-unmarried children constellation, and unlike the situation in unilineal societies, this group is dependent on the strength of the marriage along for its continuation.

A partial exception to the absence of kin-based groupings is the existence in some societies of the *kindred*. This is made up of

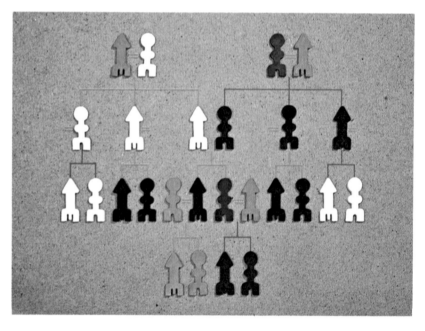

Figure 7. Double descent, in which some rights, statuses, and resources are inherited through females while others are inherited through males. For example, among the Manus, clan membership is inherited through the father along with primary rights in land and fishing resources, whereas membership in matrilineages marked by food tabus and certain spiritual powers are inherited through females. In this diagram, the matriline of descent is represented by color of the symbols; patrilines are indicated by line colors (blue and magenta). Here, there would be an intersection of two patrilines with three matrilines (yellow, white, and brown).

all the people related to a given individual. Except for full siblings—and only then if their relatives by marriage are excluded—everyone has a kindred that is different from the kindred of any other individual. Unlike unilineal groups, kindreds do overlap and are not discrete: a given person belongs to a number of kindred. In fact, he belongs to as many as the number of sibling sets to which he traces kinship, and he shares membership in each of these sets with some—but not all and not the same—of his relatives. In Western society, the kindred is a social category and not a group: although its members can be traced and identified, they do nothing as a total group and have no clear identity. In some societies, kindreds do act as groups, and Ward Goodenough and others have recently made important advances in understanding how these are formed and how they operate.

In the United States and most of Europe, surnames are taken from the father, and wives take their husband's names, but such

practices should not becloud the ambilateral character of this descent system. Not only is there an absence of kin groups beyond the nuclear family, there is also an absence of any difference in status between the father's brother and the mother's brother. In unilineal societies, these relatives and many others are in very different positions to their brother's and their sister's children, respectively. In American society they are simply "uncles."

THE ALLIANCE ASPECT OF KINSHIP

In unilineal systems, the primary concern has been the issue of vertical organization, or how kinship systems serve to pass traditions and property from one generation to the next. But unilineal kinship systems also organize society horizontally by establishing how marriages can be made between different descent groups—in other words, by establishing how women form alliances within the society through bonds based on marriage between the separate lines of kin.

Exogamy and the Incest Tabu

The basic factor that lies behind affinal relationships is the rule of exogamy, which requires that a member of one descent group marry a member of some other descent group. It is closely related to the incest tabu that forbids close relatives to mate with one another. The rule of exogamy and the incest tabu are not necessarily the same things, for it is socially acceptable in some societies for a man and a woman to mate even though they are not allowed to marry. In most societies, however, exogamy and the incest tabu are related in that the relationship between the two activities of mating and marriage is a close one, and normally societies prohibit any man from mating with a woman he is not permitted to marry.

Almost all societies, for example, forbid a brother to mate with his sister, a father to mate with his daughter, or a mother to mate with her son. It is true that in some socie-ties, such as that of the Aztecs or that of Egypt under the Pharaohs, brother-sister marriages were not only permitted but required among the ruling families. So far as is known, however, such brother-sister marriages have been confined exclusively to members of ruling groups and they have never been encouraged, or even permitted, among those outside the ruling class. Beyond the close parent and sibling ties, the incest tabu or marriage regulations vary. Cousins may or may not be able to marry cousins, and uncles and aunts may or may not be able to marry nephews or nieces. Until quite recently, the Anglican Church forbade a man to marry his deceased wife's sister.

On the whole, in nonindustrial societies these regulations extend over more kin relationships than they do in Western society, largely because kinship in these groups plays a more important role, and relationships are therefore extended to cover situations that are structured by economic, legal, special interest, and casual relationships in Western societies. A father's brothers may be called by the same kin term as the father and treated, in effect, as auxiliary fathers, and this relationship may be extended to father's brother's sons and on to *their* sons. Similarly, a mother's sisters can be regarded as auxiliary mothers, and the children of these mother's sisters and father's brothers may be treated as biological brothers and sisters and called by the same terms. Father's sisters and mother's brothers and their children may also be grouped together with parents and siblings, but in unilineal societies, such grouping presents problems because they will belong to different kin groups. Although father's brother's and mother's sister's children are almost always excluded as sexual partners and spouses, this restriction does not always hold true for the children of father's sisters and of mother's brothers. These latter kin are called cross-cousins, and in some societies mar-

Figure 8 (left). Limestone relief from the temple of Hathor at Tarraneh, representing Ptolemy I offering incense to the goddess Hathor (about 305-280 B.C.). Ptolemy I was one of the few documented participants in sibling marriage in Dynastic times. Figure 9. In this photograph, a patrilineal society is selected to represent a distinction between cross-cousins and parallel cousins. In a unilineal society, the children of a brother and the children of his sister will belong to two different descent groups. Such children are cross-cousins. In contrast, parallel cousins are related through siblings of the same sex. In many such societies, given the rule that lineages are exogamous, there is the possibility that one might marry one's cross-cousin inasmuch as he or she belongs to another lineage.

riage between them is allowed. In a relatively few societies, cross-cousin marriage is preferred to other marriages and in still fewer societies it is required (Figure 9).

Effect of Exogamic Restrictions

So far as marriage is concerned, the functional effect of exogamic restrictions is to force men to look for wives not only outside their immediate family circle but outside whatever the society regards as the descent group. The result is that different descent groups are forced into relations of affinity with each other in order for their members to marry and reproduce. The presence of some kind of rules forbidding incest between close relatives and marriage between whatever is defined as the members of the same descent groups is universal, and several explanations have been advanced to account for them.

One possibility, as widely accepted as any and suggested by Malinowski, is that the incest tabu serves to preserve close blood relationships—between father and daughter, mother and son, and brother and sister—from the potentially disruptive effects of sex. According to this theory, a man grows up trusting his parents and his siblings and is emotionally close to them. He can confidently expect these relationships to sustain him all his life. But sex is disruptive. It breeds possessiveness, jealousy, and often hatred. In order to keep these disruptive elements from contaminating and even destroying valuable blood relationships, people developed incest tabus, thereby insulating their closest blood relationships against the disruptiveness of sexual passion.

In Malinowski's view, the rules of exogamy are an extension of this same principle. If a man marries his sister and later finds living with her so intolerable that he is forced to leave, he will have broken his bonds not only with a wife but also with a sister and endangered his ties not with a replaceable mother-in-law and father-in-law

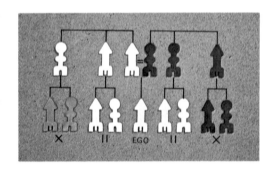

but with his own parents. But if a man marries someone outside his own descent group, he can always leave her and his ties to his blood kin will not be weakened in any way.

Intermarriage and Social Unity

The explanation of preserving close blood relationships is consistent with another theory that has generally been accepted as the basis for the incest tabu and, more importantly, for the obligation to marry outside the group. In most nonindustrial societies, a man's most trusted friends, confidants, and coworkers are fellow members of his clan or lineage. He is likely to regard everyone outside this group as potentially dangerous and possibly even as an active rival or enemy, as is the case among the Sarakatsani of Greece or the Osko-Shavente of Bolivia. However, the members of one descent group do not live by themselves. In every society having exogamous descent groups, there is more than one group and the lineages and clans must find some way to coexist with other clans. If the members of any descent group are to avoid living in a state of permanent fear of the members of all other groups at all times, they must somehow make friends with them or at least avoid being enemies.

The most obvious and effective method of achieving this understanding is intermarriage, which not only has the effect of placing wives as hostages inside other descent groups but also leads to the birth of

Figure 10. A bride from a north coast Manus village, adorned with bride wealth of native currency—dog's teeth and shell beads. Marriages in many primitive societies, aside from the nuclear families they establish, form a bond between the entire descent groups of the bride and groom. From betrothal in infancy through marriage in Manus, the birth of children and all other family events are marked by large ceremonial exchanges between these two groups. Marriage provides the cross-cutting ties that link together descent groups, which provides continuity through time. Figure 11 (right). A series of marriages based on brother-sister exchange.

offspring in whom both groups have a protective interest. Indeed, in many societies the children of intermarriage serve as vital intermediaries in restoring the peace when relations are strained or broken. If, for example, a man of lineage A murders a man of lineage B, the members of lineage B might be tempted to take revenge by murdering a member of lineage A and thus starting a feud which would end all peaceful relations between the two lineages. But suppose that the sisters of the men of lineage B are married to men of lineage A, and their children

are therefore the children of men of lineage A. There will be strong pressure on the men of lineage B not to attack the men of lineage A (their sisters' husbands and their nieces' and nephews' fathers) or, if a feud does develop, to bring it to an end as quickly as possible.

There is a great deal of evidence to show that the desire to establish friendly relations with potentially hostile groups is responsible for the practice of exogamy. Very often the men of a lineage draw their wives from precisely the same group that they regard as their most dangerous rivals or feared enemies. This practice has been demonstrated indirectly by the terms of address some people use for one another. Terms of address, and especially kinship terms, are viewed by many anthropologists as invaluable indicators of social relationships. For example, a boy might call his sister by the name X. He may call his parallel cousin (the daughter of his father's brother or his mother's sister) by the term Y. And what term does he use for his cross-cousin? He might call her by the term X or he might call her by the term Y. If he calls his cross-cousin by a different term, however, then it is at least possible that he is permitted to marry her. Using the same kind of reasoning, it is possible to deduce that lineages also tend to marry into groups they fear. For example, the members of a descent group in the Trobriand Islands refer to members of groups they marry into by the word "tabu," which carries with it the implication of something that is either forbidden or to be feared.

Reciprocal Exchange

From the viewpoint of any particular descent group, exogamy has its disadvantages. It may help to reduce the danger from a potentially hostile group, but it also means that a descent group will relinquish its claim on some of its women and their children. Compensation is provided in various ways. The Nuer provide it by the payment of bride-

wealth, so that the loss of women and the right to their children is balanced by the receipt of cattle. Another method is the setting up of positive rules of marriage to ensure that women lost to a group in one generation are returned to it in the next generation.

The rule that underlies exogamy is only a negative rule. It simply states: *Thou shalt not marry a member of thine own descent group.* Suppose there is added to it a positive rule dictating that a member of one descent group *must* marry a member of certain other groups. Then reciprocal relationships of affinity (relationship through marriage) will exist between the groups that will be perpetuated over the generations. The groups will function as reciprocal "suppliers" and "consumers" of women on a regular basis. Consider the aforementioned rule that a man must marry his cross-cousin. Marriage to a parallel cousin is rare, because parallel cousins (the children of two brothers or two sisters) are necessarily members of the same descent group, whether it be patrilineal or matrilineal. But as noted earlier, cross-cousins are necessarily members of different descent groups. Now consider the implications of marriage between cross-cousins. When a brother and a sister take spouses, their children belong to different descent groups. But if these children (who are cross-cousins) then marry each other, they reunite their parents with a new tie between the descent groups and they are thus associated by birth and marriage.

Such a system of cross-cousin marriage can therefore be regarded as a form of direct reciprocal exchange between two family groups. The same result can be achieved equally well by the custom, also very common, of exchanging sisters: *I give my sister to another man who in exchange gives his sister to me, and the children of our marriages then exchange sisters in the same way.* Both unrestricted cross-cousin mar-

riage and the exchange-of-sisters marriage produce the same result: a continuing reciprocal exchange between the members of two descent groups, a constant feeding back of spouses in a closed system of perpetual affinal relationships. The result of these systems is that the descent group retains control of its daughters and their children (or its sons and *their* children if the society is matrilineal) and also of any property or statuses that are inherited, because all its members and their possessions will constantly be returned to the descent group involved.

The exchange system of spouses can also be elaborated so that it covers more than two descent groups. At this point the systems can become rather difficult to follow, but they are important because in some societies they lie at the root of the whole social organization. Consider what happens in a society in which a man may marry one cross-cousin but not the other. Suppose, for example, the marriage rules state that a man may marry only his mother's brother's daughter and not his father's sister's daughter. Such a prohibition effectively precludes any direct exchange of spouses between two groups, because what it really means is: *If I give my sister to you, I cannot take your sister in return.* The rule precludes a direct exchange of women between two descent groups and therefore forces them to engage in a wider network of ties: *Instead of exchanging sisters with another man, my group will give our women to his group generation after generation, and we will get women from a third group.* This rule can then be extended between pairs of descent groups to make up whole chains of alliances, so that with marriage to the mother's brother's daughter, descent groups are bound to each other in perpetuity—with each being wife givers to particular lines and wife takers from other lines. Lineage A gives wives to lineage B, which gives wives to lineage C, which gives wives to lineage D

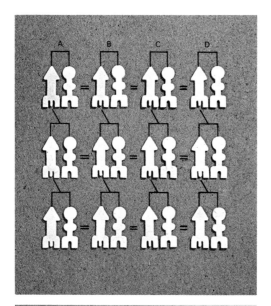

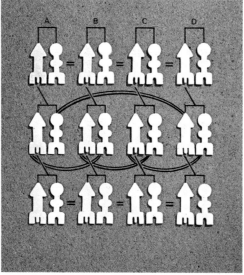

Figure 12. The two forms of asymmetrical cross-cousin marriage. Above is the matrilateral form (highly idealized) in which each man marries his mother's brother's daughter. The rule of exchange among the four lineages, in which A gives wives to B, B to C, C to D, and D to A (not shown), is the same in each generation. Below is the patrilateral form in which each man marries his father's sister's daughter. The result is quite different from the matrilateral case, in that two different rules of exchange among the lineages apply in alternating generations.

The exogamy rule forces every descent group to look outside its own ranks for wives and for husbands, and a systematic exchange arrangement ensures a regular supply of spouses. When one descent group gives a wife to another group, it does not have to rely on luck to get a wife in exchange because its alliance with other similar groups guarantees a wife in return. The result is that all the groups involved become dependent on one another, and this marriage system provides a basic structure of interdependent parts that organize the whole society.

From the society's point of view, the exchange of women between descent groups creates a situation rather like that created by the division of labor in which each group of workers performs a specialized task. Suppose that one group of people specializes in fishing, another in raising vegetables, and a third in building houses. Each group is dependent on the other two groups for an exchange of goods and services in order to survive. It exchanges its own excess, which it cannot and does not want to consume, for the goods it needs but does not produce. In essence, the exchange of spouses serves a similar purpose. Every descent group "produces" women that it cannot "consume" and it therefore exchanges them for women that it needs but cannot produce.

But why exchange women rather than goods and services? The answer lies in the fact that it is usually the most technologically simple societies, such as the Australian aborigines, that have the most complicated marriage exchange rules. In a technologically simple society, the division of labor has not proceeded very far by definition, and each group of people will tend to produce exactly the same goods as every other group. This is the situation that Emile Durkheim characterized as one in which unity must come from *mechanical solidarity*, because in it there can be no interdependency created by interdependent economic specialization.

and so on, and the system can be enlarged to embrace a considerable number of descent groups. When marriage to the father's sister's daughter is required, the results are quite different even though, like marriage to mother's brother's daughter, it is a form of unilateral cross-cousin marriage. With marriage to the cross-cousin on the father's side, groups establish a relationship in which one generation A gives wives to B, but in the next generation B gives wives to A. In the third generation, however, the situation is the same as the first and once again A gives wives to B (see Figure 12).

When two descent groups exchange women, the system is considered symmetrical, and when one group gives wives to a second group and takes wives from a third group, the system is considered asymmetrical. Regardless of which form a system takes, the underlying rationale seems clear.

Every group is economically self-sufficient, so there can be no exchange of goods and services to help integrate the society in the manner that such exchanges integrate people in highly specialized industrial societies such as the United States. Durkheim called this latter kind of unity *organic solidarity*. But the need for integration of some kind still exists in the technologically undifferentiated societies, and it is satisfied by the exchange of women. Through marriage alliances, self-sufficient and potentially hostile groups are welded together to form a wider society. It has been claimed that the circulating, or asymmetrical method, has greater potential for such purposes and this would explain why it usually operates in large populations. The direct or symmetrical system of marriage exchange seems to be confined to fairly small populations.

KINSHIP AND SOCIAL STRUCTURE

In economically homogeneous societies, systems of descent and marriage exchange form the basis of the social structure, and this kinship foundation explains why anthropologists have expended so much effort in trying to comprehend its various permutations and combinations. The study of kinship, in fact, forms an important basis for the *structural approach* to the understanding of social systems.

The question of which group takes wives and which group gives wives may be associated with other elements in the social structure. Among the Kachins of Burma, a man will do everything possible to avoid marrying into a class beneath him, and he will also seek to make the maximum profit out of the marriage of his daughters. A Kachin man who is a commoner will try to marry the daughter of a Kachin chief. But in return for this improvement in his status, he must pay a bride price, which often takes the form of working for his father-in-law. By doing so, he acquires the status of associating with a family of higher rank but pays for

it by becoming, in effect, a kind of feudal retainer. In this situation, it is the wife-giving family that occupies the superior position. In contrast, among certain Chinese groups a dowry is given with the wife, so that the marriage payments are made by the wife givers to the wife receivers. Usually it is the woman rather than the man who is transferred from a family of lower standing to a family of higher standing. In her husband's house, she is the least privileged of all the members and the dowry goes with her in order to improve her lowly position. Among these Chinese groups, it is the wife receivers who occupy the higher status. In both societies, as among many others, marriage not only serves to join different descent groups together but also forms part of an elaborate system of exchanges—of wives and husbands, of consumer goods, of political rights, and of relative status.

Political Systems

29 Despite his torn shirt and patched trousers, the village chief looked imposing and dignified as he told the people of his village that he had received orders from the government requiring that the villagers build roads. The people listened quietly as he explained that the new roads would make it possible for trucks and cars to come to the village and would aid the development of the entire nation. After the meeting was over, a number of people came up to an anthropologist who was present and half-jokingly suggested that he build the roads by himself inasmuch as his Land-Rover was the only car in the village. Other villagers not so jokingly muttered about the pointlessness of building roads, the time away from the fields the work would take, and the difficulty of cutting roads into the hard East African clay. Despite the muttering, the whole village turned out for the road building and in a few months of weekly work an impressive amount had been done with hoes, muscle, and sweat.

In a way, there is nothing very remarkable about this scene and the road building that resulted from it. People had been told about a government order, they received the order quietly and without enthusiasm, but nevertheless they had done what was asked of them. Virtually no one in the village saw any real benefit coming to himself from the roads, and they all would have preferred to spend the time and energy the construction required on their own fields and gardens. But they did the government work anyway. In other societies people pay taxes, fight in wars, and obey laws and regulations of all sorts with which they do not agree and with which they may, in fact, sharply disagree. What is remarkable about this behavior is that it happens.

BEHAVIOR AND PUBLIC GOALS

How are people brought to do things they do not really want to do? Why, for example, do they build roads when they see no need for roads and would rather spend their time in ways other than working on them? Political anthropology focuses on such questions, which concern sources of conformity with unappealing orders. It also focuses on all the behavior that concerns deciding upon and implementing public goals. In the East African village scene, the public goal—road building—was decided upon by officials who did not live and work in the village. But a study of how they reached their decision—

Figure 2. Greek Athenian war figures, in contrast with the peaceful proceedings of an Emir's court in the Sudan (Figure 3 right). The state provides a means of peaceful settlement of disputes within a polity. Where a superordinate state does not exist, as between nations, violence is often seen as the only recourse.

and how the individuals who made the decision attained their positions that made it their right and duty to make such decisions —would also be within the scope of political anthropology. This scene fits into political anthropology in another way. The village chief displayed public power by the very act of announcing that government orders had come to him, and the people's quiet attention to his announcement and their carrying out of the directive he told them about are evidence of that power. The attainment and use of public power is another area of concern for political anthropology. Public power is a special kind of public goal, in that it is sought in all societies and because it is involved in one way or another in the decisions about public goals of other kinds and in their implementation and use. It can thus be said that the core of political anthropology is a concern with behavior centered around public goals and that the interest in how power is attained and used is part of this concern.

Going back to the village and its roads, we might have been tempted to say that the people implemented the goal of road building because they saw that it had benefit for them, but clearly they did not believe that the roads would do anything for them. The other explanation that comes easily to mind is that they built the roads because "they had to." But this explanation is hardly more satisfactory than the first. There were no police in the village—in fact, the nearest police were a difficult forty miles away—and although the village chief had the power to take anyone who failed to work on the roads before the village court for disobedience, he could not very often do so because his "name would be broken" and he would cease to be an effective chief.

During the months of road work there was only one incident in which the village court was invoked against anyone, and in this case several women were fined for missing a day on the project. Significantly, the village court has no power—and makes no effort—to enforce its decisions. It merely tries to get those involved to agree to them. If the women had refused to agree that they had done wrong, nothing would have been done about their refusal and there would have been no fine. Can it be said that they were forced to agree they had done wrong—and that the chief's limited ability to take people before the court was enough to conclude that the villagers all worked on the road because "they had to" in the sense that the women provided an example for all the others of what would happen if one refused to cooperate? This would be piling one unsound conclusion on top of another.

The problem of why the people worked on the road begins to appear in its true complexity. It is tempting to say that there is no alternative to obeying the government order to do the work, but at least in the strict sense this is not true. The worst that can happen to someone who refuses is that he will be brought to court, and this occurrence is not too likely because of the chief's fear for his "name." Even if he is brought before the court, its decision will not affect him unless he agrees to the sentence. It is hardly an accurate representation of this situation to say that the people have no alternative, although clearly even the mild threat of a court that does not enforce its decisions is an element in understanding the situation.

LEGITIMACY AND COERCION

A central issue that arises from considering the villagers' willingness to work on the roads is the question of what constitutes coercion and how effective it really is in achieving public goals. The villagers were clearly not coerced in any obvious and straightforward way, but it is equally clear that they did not do the road work because they wanted to. This kind of situation is common in most societies. We find people doing things connected with achieving or maintaining public goals, or refraining from

doing them when restraint is what advances the goal. Such behavior occurs even though they do not really desire the goal and even though force or other kinds of coercion are rather unlikely to be applied to them if they do not comply—and even when coercion, if applied, does not appear very formidable. Most Americans do not like paying their income tax, and not a few fail to see any substantial benefit to themselves in paying it. There are, of course, people who refuse to pay it and others who use various means to pay less that the law requires of them, but most people most of the time pay at least as much as they should, even when the chances of being caught if they do not are fairly remote and even when the punishment if they are caught is not too likely to be very great. Where is the coercion in this situation and how does it work?

Achieving Compliance

Approaching the problem from an extreme view, a moment's examination reveals that no one can be forced to do anything. The most those who are willing to apply coercion can do is make compliance with their wishes more attractive than the consequences of refusing to comply. In the final resort they can say, "Do what we want or we will kill you." It is always possible to say to this, "All right, kill me." Although such ultimate defiance is not common, history abounds with examples of it. Contrary to the popular saying, death is certain but taxes—and any other acceptance of the power of others—are not.

The most extreme coercion, then, is by no means certain of success. This uncertainty is not the only problem in its use. It is also very expensive. If half of a group must spend its time watching and punishing the other half, the ability of the group to get anything done is sharply reduced. Moreover, there is the difficulty recognized in the ancient Latin question *Quis custodiet ipsos custodes?* ("Who watches the watchers themselves?"). Somewhere along the line, there must be a substantial number of people who see something directly or indirectly beneficial to themselves in connection with the public goal being sought or maintained. But how can this apply to the road work in the East African village where the people say there is no benefit to them in the roads? The answer to this comes in the fact that they *do* see benefit to themselves in obeying their chief. By working through the chief, the government above the village level is able to get cooperation from the villagers even on projects that the villagers do not view as directly beneficial. For most of the people, the *legitimacy* of the office of village chief is enough to bring them to comply with particular directives he issues even when these directives have little or no intrinsic appeal in them.

One way of understanding "legitimacy" is to view it as very broad expectations people have about what will come to them from the object with legitimacy. This "object" can be an individual such as the particular man who is village chief (or president or party leader). It can equally well be an office—as distinct from its occupant at a given time—such as that of chief, president, or party leader or a connected series of offices such as the government of a state or nation. It can even be a set of procedures or rules such as "the law" or "the democratic (or any other) system." Whatever the object of legitimacy, those who grant the legitimacy expect it to deliver vague but important things to them at some time in the future. These expectations may be along the lines of making an orderly and peaceful life possible or they may have to do with the attainment of some ideal state such as preserving a heritage, establishing heaven on earth, or bringing "social justice."

Nonspecific Legitimacy

What all these sorts of expectations have in common is that they are not very specific, with respect to either what exactly is to be delivered from the source of legitimacy or when it is to be delivered. The absence of specificity gives the object of legitimacy a good deal of scope for the exercise of power, because it is not necessary for every public goal connected with the object to have any immediate or obvious benefit for those who grant the legitimacy. They go along because, in the long run, they feel that the totality of what comes from the object of legitimacy will be to their benefit even if particular instances are not obviously or immediately beneficial.

Specificity of Coercion

Given this view of legitimacy, it is fruitful to look at coercion as also being a kind of expectation people have, but one that is highly specific as to what will happen and when it will happen. We have already considered the most extreme form of coercion ("Do it or we will kill you") and that is certainly specific enough, but less dramatic forms of coercion are also highly specific. For example, the virtual certainty that one will be generally thought of as a troublemaker and a difficult person if one disobeys the village chief works together with the widely shared legitimacy granted his office to bring people to perform the road work in the East African village. If the chiefly office did not have legitimacy for most people, there would be little general feeling that those who flaunted its authority were behav-

ing undesirably and the coercion would not be effective. It is thus important to keep in mind that legitimacy and coercion are often intimately connected in bringing about general willingness to cooperate for the attainment of public goals.

In fact, legitimacy and coercion are best understood as the two ends of a single continuum rather than as two qualitatively different things. They are both types of expectations people have, and they differ only in their degree of specificity. This difference is a vitally important one, because the less specific the expectations, the freer the legitimate object is to make demands without providing immediate or clear-cut "pay-offs." When a government is accepted as the one most likely to bring about some desirable but vague condition, such as "the good life," it can ask a great deal of its people—including things they do not particularly want to do—without producing much that is directly and immediately beneficial because the people see ultimate benefit coming to them from what they do. All of it has some kind of connection in their minds with achieving the distant goal of a "good life."

Of course, there are limits on such demands, and even the most legitimate official, office, government, or set of procedures must produce some benefits if its legitimacy is to be maintained. It is probably true that both legitimacy and coercion are always jointly involved in any such political activity, but the balance can be heavily on one side or another, with most conformity and cooperation coming from one source rather than the other. From current evidence, it appears that the part played by legitimacy in maintaining relatively stable and enduring political processes of all kinds is probably greater for most of the people involved in these processes than the part played by coercion, but it is essential to remember that the two bases for political activity are very closely connected.

LOCI OF LEGITIMACY AND COERCION

In studying politics, anthropologists are interested not only in the balance of legitimacy and coercion but also in their loci. On the one hand, there is a government (whether of a village, a tribe, or a nation) that is itself legitimate to the majority of the people whom it governs in the sense that the people broadly expect benefits to come to them from the type of political system they have. On the other, there is a government that, as an organization of political positions, has legitimacy for very few of its citizens but where some particular individual is the focus of legitimacy. The stability, endurance, and means of operation of these two political situations would be very different, and the ability of individuals to act outside the governmental framework in pursuit of public goals would also differ greatly.

DISPUTE SETTLEMENT

Related closely to the concern with the locus of legitimacy and of coercion is an interest in their source. The chiefly office in the East African village under consideration gains its legitimacy—or most of it—from the role any chief plays in the settlement of disputes. In the tribe of which the villagers are members, the Bena of Tanzania, there are no dependable internal methods for settling disputes among kinsmen and neighbors, and the more serious the dispute, the less likely it will be settled within the network of kin and neighborhood ties. As in all human groups, disputes arise among people who live and work closely together, and if they are to continue their relationships these disputes must be settled in some way. The maintenance of amicable relations is highly valued among the Bena, so that the settle-

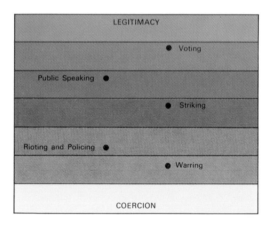

ment of disputes takes on even greater than usual significance in this society. The settlement of the most difficult disputes is achieved through the village chief's court, and the connection of the office with this vital activity and with the values stressing the resumption of peaceful and cooperative relations imparts to it a legitimacy. In other words, there is the feeling that it is the source of "good things," broadly construed, which makes it possible for the occupants of the office to gain compliance with the orders passed down to them from higher authorities.

Legitimacy is always rooted in the values of the people who grant it, and the East African case where dispute settlement is the key source of legitimacy is only one of the many possible ways that connections between values and political offices, officials, or rules and regulations are secured. Among the Tolai of New Britain in Melanesia, political offices are almost always held by "big men" who achieve their positions as "big men" through the successful manipulation of the shell money used by the members of this society. Through shrewd participation in clan rituals and funerals, where the shell money is collected and distributed, these men become wealthy. Because they become wealthy, they command the support and respect of their fellow-men. Although Tolai is

Figure 6. The legitimacy of a specific figure — in this example, the king (center) — may come from his villager's view of his qualities, from his position as an occupant of a respected office, or from his relationship to a positively evaluated government. Figure 7 (right). Cree Indian. The traditional chiefdomship in the setting of a modern nation creates a role conflict that is difficult to resolve. The chief must mediate between the differing expectations of his people and the government.

an egalitarian society and all men are thought to be fundamentally equal, Richard Salisbury, who has studied these people, has indicated that the ability the "big men" have shown as financial manipulators justifies their positions of power in the eyes of their fellow-men.

In this group there is a Horatio Alger ideology, which holds that men rise to wealth through their own personal efforts and abilities and that the ability to accumulate money (in this society shell money) is an indication of virtue, wisdom, and general worth. Thus, through the award of offices to wealthy men and through the view that they most clearly exemplify the society's values concerning personal ability and virtue, legitimacy is attached to office holders through the broad expectation that they are the individuals who are most likely to perform wisely and well. The broad expectations of office holders among the Tolai can be summed up as follows: The best test of a man's ability and wisdom is how successful he is in getting money. And if those with a great deal of money are the occupants of political offices they will carry out the duties of these offices with the same skill and judg-

ment they showed in getting rich. It is therefore clear that all sorts of "good things" can be expected from them.

THE ORGANIZATION OF POLITICS

So far, the discussion has centered on the sorts of politics that concern the activities involving chiefs, presidents, kings, or other political officials. But politics is not limited to these activities only. Political behavior is defined here as referring to all behavior centering around public goals, and all societies have politics. But it is not true that all societies have distinctly political statuses or positions. Power is never uniformly distributed in social groups, and it is always true that some people will have more than others, but this distribution need not be permanently fixed or recognized in enduring positions such as chief, headman, or some other title and office.

Many hunting and gathering bands do not have political officials of any kind. Even though some men—usually because of their ability, experience, and seniority—have more ability to influence such public goals as moving the group to another area for better hunting or planning a cooperative hunt, they have neither a formal position or title nor any power beyond the legitimacy they personally command to bring anyone to follow their advice. The absence of formal political statuses has often confused outsiders who first meet groups without leadership positions and who believe, in their ethnocentric innocence, that every group has some kind of a "chief." Treaties and agreements have been negotiated with men thought to be political leaders from these groups even though these men had no more right to commit the groups they came from than any other group member. When other members of these groups paid no attention to the agreements made by those who represented themselves as "chiefs," or who were assumed to have such positions, the outsiders often took this as a sign of the deceitful-

ness and savagery of the groups. In fact, the people had been behaving in accord with their own political system.

Societies without formal political statuses are not limited to small hunting and gathering bands. The famous studies of E. E. Evans-Pritchard among the Nuer of the Sudan in East Africa describe and analyze politics in a group having more than 200,000 members but not having any formal political statuses. In Nuer society, the most important public goals concern the settlement of dis-putes and the protection and enlargement of the cattle herds that form a vital part of the economy and that also play an enormous role in almost every other sphere of life—from personal prestige to kinship, marriage, and religion. The attainment of most public goals in this society involves fighting or the threat of fighting. When men wish to enlarge their herds, they often organize raiding parties to seize animals from other tribes or from other sections of their own tribe. When one person has a dispute with another, the

Figure 8. Segmentary opposition. (After E. E. Evans-Pritchard. *The Nuer.* Oxford, England: Clarendon Press.) Figure 9 (right). Bakuba king from the Kasai Province of the Belgian Congo. The Bakuba are one of the many African peoples who had hereditary kingship. The king was both a living symbol of the state and a technician in the art of resolving and containing conflict.

settlement of the dispute ultimately rests on a fight or the threat of a fight, and this behavior exists whether the dispute concerns women, property, personal honor, or debts.

Fission and Fusion

Among these warlike people, the number of spearmen who can be mobilized will determine the safety of their herds, the outcome of a dispute, or the success of a raid. This condition means, in turn, that the solidarity of social groups (how surely the members of a group will come to the aid of a fellow member) and the clarity of assignment to them is the crucial dimension in Nuer politics. It would be a relatively uncomplicated matter if the Nuer were simply divided into small kinship groups entirely separate from one another but internally united throughout the year. Such an arrangement, however, not only is inimical to some Nuer goals (such as large-scale cattle raids requiring more fighters than a single, small kin group could provide) but also is contrary to the requirements of the ecology of their region. During the wet season, the people and their cattle live in small kin-based groups on ridges in the otherwise flat and flooded terrain. In the dry season, these small groups must combine around the relatively few year-around water sources where the cattle can get pasturage. Both their goals and physical survival demand that they live in small groups part of the time but that these groups combine into larger groups at other times. Permanent division into bandlike kin groups is thus impossible. What is required is a means of coordinating the separation (fission) and combination (fusion) of a large number of people over many hundreds of square miles.

Segmentary Opposition

The basic mechanism by which the required fission and fusion takes place is what Evans-Pritchard calls segmentary opposition.

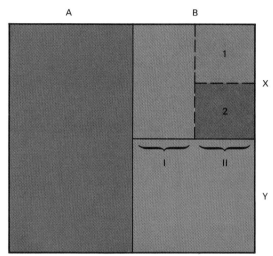

The basic unit of Nuer political organization is the settlement, which is composed of men who trace relationship to a single patrilineal lineage together with the wives and children of these men. Within this basic unit, internal fighting is avoided by strong social pressures and its members are committed to mutual defense and assistance. When a dispute involves members of two different but related settlements, only the two settlements involved will provide men for the threatened or actual fight that serves to end the dispute. Should a dispute involve settlements that are not closely related, other settlements would come into it on each side until groups of the same structural level opposed one another. What this means is that in a dispute, help would be forthcoming for each party based on relatives drawn from ties as many generations back on one side as on the other. The further back ties are traced, the larger the group, so that when distantly related settlements quarrel, quite large groups are involved in the fighting or threatened fighting that ensues.

In Figure 8, cell 1 and cell 2 represent individual settlements, and when they quarrel no one else is involved. If, however, settlement 1 were to engage in a dispute with a settlement from I, 2 would join with 1 against the joined settlements of I. Similarly, if any settlement from X were to quarrel with any settlement from Y, all of X would act together against all of Y. And were any settlement of B to act against any settlement of A, the settlements of X would combine with those of Y against all those of A. Thus, enemies in one kind of situation are allies in another in a completely unambiguous way. People are assigned to sides on the basis of closeness of relationship without any involvement of political officials, which in fact are nonexistent in this society. The attainment of such public goals as those of the Nuer is accomplished entirely without any "kings," "chiefs," or "headmen," despite the fact that large numbers of people are involved. This goal is attained by having more closely related groups join together against more distantly related ones in the rather involved way just discussed. Almost paradoxically, the opposition between parts or segments leads to unity among other segments, with the scope and content of the unity varying according to context and goal.

Michael Smith has shown that segmentation of the sort found in Nuer politics is characteristic of all politics whether in groups having political statuses or not. Real understanding of many political processes and organizations requires an analysis that reveals the relevant segments and how they are separated from and united with one another. Max Gluckman's pioneering studies have brilliantly illuminated the crucial role of opposition as a unifying force in a wide variety of political settings.

CONFLICT, REBELLION, AND REVOLUTION
In the framework of politics, as defined here, Gluckman has shown that although the members of a society may seek particular goals that bring them into conflict with one another, this very conflict may serve ultimately to unite the entire social system. Perhaps his most well-known application of this insight concerns the effect of rebellion

on the continuation of the office of a king. He has shown that rebellions, whether actual wars or as ritual expressions, direct the discontent and hostility that is always present against the particular man who occupies the office of king—but in the very act of doing so reaffirm the importance of the kingship as an office. When rules of succession to the kingship are unclear—and in many societies they are—the death of the reigning king can lead to a civil war that rends the society and sets brother against brother. Each side in these conflicts is supporting its own candidate for the kingship, but they affirm the importance of the office by the act of fighting for it. Thus, once the succession is settled, there is a new basis for broad unity (the contending sides having been united internally by their mutual opposition) in the resumption of operation of the office whose significance has just been demonstrated by the shedding of blood.

Gluckman does not maintain that all conflict leads to enhanced unity or that there is no such thing as revolution (which differs from rebellion in that it denies the virtue and propriety of the political system itself and not just the worthiness of the men who hold office at a given time). A general statement of his important views that goes beyond offices and office holders to basic social processes is found in his book *Order and*

Rebellion in Tribal Africa. In it he states first that quarrels arise between men because they live together in a society. Each society has customs that mold the form these quarrels will take. To some extent, these customs also direct and control the quarrels through conflicts of allegiance, so that despite rebellion, the same social system is reestablished over broader areas of community life and through longer periods of time. Gluckman believes this happens because of rebellion. He does not mean to imply that the forces are always perfectly balanced, so that no change occurs or no state breaks up, but rather that such processes work through elaborate institutional arrangements, which have clearly evolved over time. He thus suggests that they inhibit quarrels from destroying the system, even though they cannot always prevent that destruction.

Divide and Cohere

Gluckman's overall position is that in politics and the rest of social life, men are divided in some contexts and united in others, and that this alternating separation and unification leads to the perpetuation of the political, and more broadly the social, system. He makes clear that "divide and rule" is not just the Machiavellian trickery of conquerors and exploiters but also a general political and sociological principle that he calls divide and cohere. In some contexts, individuals are united with the members of their families in opposition to the demands and interests of other families; in other contexts, the family is divided by competition for the resources (material and emotional) commonly held by the family, with the individuals being united with others from other families who are in the same position (for example, sons with sons against fathers). In some settings, villagers are united with one another in opposition to their chief and other political authorities, and in others they unite with their chief in pursuit of common goals in competition with other villagers and their chiefs. In these examples and many others that could be cited, the kind of opposition at the heart of the main political process among the Nuer operates to bring solidarity out of conflict and competition, just as it does in rebellion. Sometimes the forces do not balance and the system changes, perhaps through revolution, but the fact that societies last as long as they do despite the presence of strong internal divisions, conflict of interest, and division of loyalty argues powerfully for the validity of Gluckman's divide and cohere principle.

When the System Fails

None of this discussion is meant to imply that the world today is the best of all possible worlds and that political tensions and struggles always work out "for the best" or, for that matter, work out at all. An example of their failure to do so comes from the Cree Indians of Canada, although similar examples could be taken from other parts of the world.

Among the modern Cree, there is conflict between the traditional Cree expectation associated with the "good man" who may counsel but never coerce and the Canadian government's expectations of a chief that he must gain compliance with their orders. The chiefs, who are appointed by the national

Figure 10 (left). The July days in Petrograd. Machine gunners call upon the Putilov workers to support the action against the provisional government. Figure 11 (below). In many societies in the New Guinea highlands, warfare is the result of an unresolved conflict that escalated through a series of violent retaliatory actions. Neighboring local groups frequently form alliances against an enemy from another district. Often these alliances are highly unstable and contingent upon temporary political exigencies of the participating groups. Dance festivals and reciprocal prestations of pigs and other valuables consolidate an existing alliance and symbolize its unity in opposition to a common enemy.

government, have an impossible task. To the extent that they meet the government's requirements of them, they put themselves outside the definition of being a "good man" in the eyes of the people with whom they must work, and to the extent that they meet their people's requirements for being a "good man" they move outside the government's requirements that they bring compliance with its orders. If the people agreed or could be brought by counsel to agree with government orders, the chief could easily meet both sets of requirements, but the people do not usually agree with what the government wants them to do and the government usually will not change its requirements to meet the people's interests. The result is that public goals of all kinds among the Cree are rarely formulated and even more rarely achieved, and the men who serve as chief are politically impotent.

MODERN POLITICAL ANTHROPOLOGY

The Cree example may suggest that political change, including political disintegration, is a new feature of some or many parts of the world and that there was a "pure" era before the present chaotic one when stability, order, and the continuity of individual and group life were supreme. In fact, of course, this is not so. Archaeologists and historians have helped to show that no system lasts forever and that every system, during its course as an identifiable entity, undergoes highly significant alterations. The tensions, struggles, and conflicts to which Gluckman calles attention are features of human social life—not *modern* social life, but *human*. There is, then, nothing qualitatively different about the things observed and experienced in the world of today.

The Rate of Political Change

It may be, however, that there are quantitative differences between the kinds of political processes encountered now and those found in at least some other periods. It is quite possible that more human groups are moving more quickly through political and, more generally, social developments now than in, say, the period ending with World War II. It is very difficult to measure such things and determine whether there is a real difference between the rate at which events are occurring currently as opposed to some earlier period or only a difference in awareness of what is occurring. But if this trend is present, as it seems to be, it is important to recognize both that contemporary political developments are different from the politics of other periods and that this difference is one of *rate* and not of *kind*. This may be the age of widespread and rapid political change, but it surely is not uniquely the age of political change.

In response to the perception that public goals are not as eternally fixed in societies as they sometimes seem to be and that the means of determining, striving for, and utilizing these goals are more flexible and open to manipulation than they once were thought of as being, political anthropologists have been emphasizing some concepts found in the earlier writings in the field more than others and developing new ones as well. They are also applying their concepts and comparative perspective to types of political activity—for example, Fred Bailey's stimulating study of the politics of committees and studies being carried out by a number of researchers on the politics of ghettos in the United States—which anthropologists had not often considered seriously before.

Focus on Case Studies

One emphasis that has appeared in the research of a number of political anthropologists is a concern with the mobilization of resources by individuals and groups to maximize their own advantages and achieve their own, as opposed to "general," ends. Victor Turner's pathbreaking book *Schism and Continuity in an African Society* dramatically portrays the struggles of a man, Sandambu, who has been called "the Hamlet of anthropology" because of his foredoomed struggles to become a village headman against a socially and culturally determined fate that granted him too meager resources to achieve his desired end. This study shows both the possibilities that are open for the manipulation of a society's relevant resources for political ends and the limitations there are on such manipulation. To be a headman in a village of the group Turner studied, the Ndembu of what is now Zambia, one had to belong to the strongest segment of the village's main matrilineage and have many sisters' sons to call on for assistance. Sandambu had neither of these, and, lacking them, his good works availed him nothing. Instead of becoming headman he was temporarily exiled from the village.

What Turner's work does is to reveal the workings of the system as a whole through careful examination of highly detailed case studies ("social dramas" is his term for these). This approach not only provides the basis for a particularly fine-grained understanding of political processes but focuses our attention on the suppleness of even a highly traditional system and underlines the continuous developments that take place in the system.

Politics and Game Theory

Fredrik Barth's approach is quite different from Turner's, but he shares with Turner a concern for the details of the operation of the system rather than the more global sort of characterization that was common in earlier studies. In his study of the Yusufzai Pathans of Pakistan, Barth uses game theory, developed by John von Neumann and Oskar Morganstern, to understand how Pathan political groups are formed. The "rules" of the Pathan "game of politics" come from the features of their patrilineal lineage organization and its assignment of rights to community property. Within the limits of these rules, individuals (in fact brothers who act together) make strategic choices aligning them with other individuals into groups that act together, and against other similarly formed groups, in pursuit of public goals. The choices people make, which Barth views as dictated by their seeking personal advantage within the confines of the "rules" as they apply in particular situations, are seen as the basis for the solidarity of the society's political groups.

Political Conflict Groups

The formation of political groupings, including those outside the framework of traditional kinship, neighborhood, and—in India and Ceylon—caste networks, has been of considerable interest to political anthropologists in recent years. Although there is a good deal of disagreement as to how the term "faction" should be used, it can generally be said to be a political conflict group (thus in political processes involving this sort of grouping there must be at least two groups in order for conflict to arise) that need not be based on traditional interpersonal ties and that may endure only for the

period of time during which a particular conflict for a public goal lasts. Ralph Nicholas stresses the role of leaders in recruiting these groups and the general lack of commitment and loyalty to the groups by their members. Nicholas presents the important hypothesis that factions will be the characteristic form of political groups whenever new resources are being brought into a relatively poor area from a relatively rich one. Thus, if the national government of India is giving scholarships to young people in rural areas, the struggle for control of these scholarships in those areas will be between groups that cut across traditional alignments and are formed around leaders. If his hypothesis proves to be true, it will be an important contribution to the understanding of the politics of development at the local level, for much of development involves just the sort of movement of resources with which Nicholas is concerned.

Modern political anthropology clearly retains the interest in group structure described earlier in Evans-Pritchard's study of the Nuer, and it draws on the structural tradition stemming from Emile Durkheim through A. R. Radcliffe-Brown and, more recently, Meyer Fortes, and it builds on their discoveries and insights. But it has developed new interests and new conceptual tools that fit it more closely to the rapidly changing political arrangements anthropologists encounter in most parts of the world.

Economics and Anthropology

30

A fundamental, although often unappreciated, assumption found in Western and particularly American society is that the purpose of work is to accumulate money or the goods money can buy. The rich man is a success; the poor man is a failure. This assumption is, in large part, an inheritance of the Protestant ethic, which Max Weber examined in his classic work, *The Protestant Ethic and the Spirit of Capitalism.* As Weber pointed out, Protestants—particularly the Calvinists of the sixteenth and seventeenth centuries—believed that some people were the elect, destined by God's choice for eternal salvation, whereas the rest must endure without it. The decision as to who were the elect and who were not was entirely arbitrary, determined by God, and no individual could influence his own eternal destiny, however much he might struggle to do so.

But how did a person find out if he was one of the elect, chosen by God? If he was, then whatever enterprise he engaged in would prosper and thus material prosperity would demonstrate his superiority in visible ways. Inasmuch as Protestantism developed at a time and in countries where commerce and industry were beginning to flourish, the idea that one's spiritual superiority should be demonstrated in visible ways coincided with a widespread impetus toward economic progress. The result was that acquisition of wealth and the hard work required to achieve it came to be accepted as an indication—indeed the principal indication—of spiritual superiority.

This association of ideas can still be found in Western economic thought. It came to be taken for granted that the acquisition of wealth was the natural and proper aim of any "normal" man—such was the perspective of the classic economists who saw the profit motive as the basis for everything that came under the heading of economic activity. People worked to make money. They operated by a system of rational choices—such as buying at the lowest possible price and selling at the highest possible price. A great deal of the classic economist's efforts were devoted to showing that even when people diverge from these basic rules, as in situations where the market is controlled by one organization (monopoly) or by a few organizations (oligopoly), the people concerned are nevertheless attempting to maximize their profits.

THE CONCEPT OF ECONOMIC CHOICE

During the past few years, the assumption that the profit motive is inherently good has come under severe attack. In the United States, a main element of the dissent expressed by today's generation of students has been the questioning of such assumptions, and the newspapers regularly report on debates over the consequences of single-minded dedication to the acquisition of money and material goods—intense and unrelenting competition, for example, or the impersonal character of the corporate empire. It has even become fashionable to ask if making money is a particularly admirable motive or even sufficient justification for labor that has no other justification, or if hard work is in itself any more virtuous than easy work or no work at all.

It has also been pointed out that many conventional assumptions are inadequate as explanations of the ways in which people actually behave. A professional golfer who spends an afternoon practicing may be said to be working to maximize his profits. But what about the amateur golfer who spends his afternoon in precisely the same way, practicing just as diligently? A market gardener and a housewife who gardens may be doing exactly the same thing, but their motives are quite different. Clearly, the distinction between activity that is productive and activity that is unproductive cannot be satisfactorily explained in purely economic terms.

Moreover, the very idea that the economic actions of people are governed only by the desire to maximize profits does not meet the facts. John D. Rockefeller and Andrew Carnegie, for example, amassed great fortunes and then spent much of the latter part of their lives giving their fortunes away, a mode of behavior that has since become fashionable among many highly successful businessmen. Their motives may have been noble in that they perhaps felt the need to help the less fortunate, or perhaps they merely wished to soothe their consciences or appear virtuous or enhance their status. In any case, it is apparent that they were governed by considerations far more complicated than the simple desire to make money. Or consider the successful Cree Indian hunter who distributes his caribou meat to less successful hunters. To his way of thinking, the rewards in prestige associated with this act far outweigh the personal gain in material goods were he to retain the meat for his own consumption. It is thus equally apparent that the assumption about economic choices being entirely "rational"—in other words, profit-oriented—is, at best, an oversimplification.

In reality, men and women in different cultures make many varied choices in allocating their resources of material goods, of their own labor, and of the assistance to be obtained from their fellow-men in order to satisfy the multitude of ends that are open to them, and this is the realm of economic anthropology. As a branch of social anthropology, it pays particular attention to the various social devices that can be used to enlist the collaboration of others and to the way in which established social relationships affect the choices that men and women make. It also pays more attention than does traditional economics to the nonmonetary commodities that enter into the calculation of individuals. But its central concern is one of understanding choice making in other cultures, where circumstances differ widely from those customarily treated by economists and where money tends to be less than a universal yardstick for measuring value.

The first nineteenth-century accounts of other cultures tended to ignore the fact that choice does exist. Anthropologists believed

that primitive man was bound by his technology and culture to follow resignedly the actions of his forefathers and his contemporaries, and only "civilization" has permitted him any choice. A description of the technology and the social norms for economic behavior was considered sufficient analysis. Although perceptive observers such as F. R. Barton and Richard Thurnwald clearly described choice making in such activities as long-distance trading voyages in Papua or bride-wealth negotiations in the Philippines, few analysts followed their lead. Even Bronislaw Malinowski, who in 1922 followed Barton in describing a similar Papuan trading system, perpetuated the view of the uncalculating "primitive." Malinowski had turned his attention on the *kula* exchange system, which is described in the chapter "Structural-Functional Analysis." He argued that much of the behavior he observed was not rational, inasmuch as rationality would be interpreted by an economist in terms of maximizing yields. It was based rather on seeing reciprocity as the ideal: "I do things today so that you will reciprocate tomorrow, and I myself reciprocate what you did yesterday." In this way everyone was supposedly forced to continue doing what their fathers and their neighbors did, and everything worked smoothly as long as civilization did not disrupt reciprocity. Although this Rousseau-like view of the Trobriand Islander was contradicted by much of his own data that actually showed failures of reciprocity and unequal distributions of rewards, Malinowski's study dominated the

thinking in economic anthropology for many decades. And some anthropologists still assert that people in nonmonetary societies have no choices.

Although it is difficult for a city-living, money-using observer to appreciate the range of choices open to the Trobriand Islander, the fact remains that such a range does exist. Consider the subsistence farmer, for another example. We might initially view farming as a choice between growing certain standard crops and starving. The technology of cultivation does seem to determine entirely what is done. In fact, however, every subsistence farmer has to make a range of decisions, and a look at an Amerindian farmer in Guyana will illustrate the principles involved.

CHOICES IN SUBSISTENCE FARMING

The Wapisiana farmer of Guyana lives on open, grassy savanna that is unsuitable for agriculture. Although he gains some subsistence by hunting and fishing and even by raising a few cattle, he lives primarily on food crops grown on patches cleared in the margins of the nearby tropical forests. Every year he must select new patches for clearing, for the debris that is burned during the clearing process adds nutrients to the soil, which in turn gives excellent yields of the most prized crops of green vegetables and bananas in addition to the staple crop of cassava.

His choice is between several alternatives. He may continue cultivating previously cleared plots, but these give lower crop yields as the soil nutrients are depleted. Although he is spared the work of felling trees, the amount of work he must expend in controlling the regrowth of forest saplings in the clearings increases steadily. If he decides to clear forests, he must consider how much work is involved in clearing different areas of forest and he must balance the work involved in clearing each with the quality of the soil, the drainage, and the prevalence of

Figure 3. Slash-and-burn agriculture in the New Guinea Highlands. The edge of this Siane garden, planted first about nine months before, is being recultivated. Unlike the "hot burn" required in Guyana, the fire is employed merely to remove waste roots. Figure 4 (right). Informal relations within the Jamaican marketplace.

crop-damaging insects or monkeys. Untouched virgin forest would give extremely high crop yields but would require much time in clearing; previously cultivated areas where, after thirty years, trees have grown to about one foot in diameter need the least work for the most soil fertility; younger trees are closely spaced, have difficult undergrowth, and indicate low soil fertility; sloping land with red soil gives ideal drainage and good growth but may be difficult to clear. Clearing a new area of virgin forest, although hard work, would also bring more land into the pool of previously cleared areas from which his village would be able to reclaim patches in thirty years' time. Whatever he chooses, he must consider the time taken to walk from home to work in each garden and from old gardens to new gardens.

The result is that each farmer makes intricate calculations, balancing advantages and disadvantages in different ways. Moreover, his decisions are also affected by his personal circumstances. A village headman, or *tushau*, may opt for clearing virgin forest. A good hunter may look for a site near the edge of the forest that will give low yields and thus require little work, which will leave him more time for hunting. A man with a growing family that can help with the work

may be able to pick an ideal site fairly deep in the forest. Labor costs, crop yields, and how spare time can be put to use all influence actual decisions. Even changes in the availability of fish or game, or the attractions of living in a village where there is a school, may have far-reaching effects. Farmers of this sort, as they consciously make economic choices, are constantly adapting their behavior to changes in their life situation, and the picture that shows them as "slaves to tradition" is inaccurate. In the language of economists, they are trying to optimize their behavior under conditions of highly imperfect knowledge and considerable uncertainty. A Western economist, faced with similar decisions, would use a computer and techniques of linear programming; a Wapisiana farmer uses rules of thumb and does a good job with them. Studying these local "rules of thumb" is a major part of economic anthropology, for which the term "ethnoeconomics" can be applied.

ETHNOECONOMICS AND MARKETING

Although a Wapisiana farmer uses rules of thumb, he nevertheless is making choices—and rational choices at that. But again, what constitutes "rational"? The anthropologist, in attempting to comprehend the ethnoeconomics of people in other cultures, must recognize that what is rational depends on one's objectives. The classic economist had a very clear idea of what constituted rational economic behavior, based on his assumption that the objective of all decisions was the maximizing of profits, and nothing else. He devised a pattern of what to expect when buyers and sellers came together, each with a full knowledge of market conditions and each making independent decisions. Everyone would sell at the highest price he could get and buy at the lowest, irrespective of all other considerations. The only exceptions were those imposed by purely economic considerations. For example, a company that commanded a monopoly over the market

would sell *all* its products at a lower price rather than sell *some* of its products at the highest price it could command, or a group of companies might agree to fix their prices at a level different from that which would be determined by the normal supply-and-demand curve. But despite these variations, the classic economists assumed that decisions would be determined rationally because of the profit motive and that prices would settle at the level where the number of marginal sellers would exactly balance the number of marginal buyers.

Anthropologists discovered, however, that the groups they were studying often refused to fit into the pattern expected by the economist. They encountered peasants who did not bargain. They encountered others who insisted on selling goods in the marketplace even though they could get better prices on their way to the market. But could this behavior be called irrational? The answer, given in another perspective, is that it is not. To some people there are considerations that outweigh in importance the short-run maximizing of profits. For example, the Jamaican traders described by Margaret Katzin in 1960 minimize competition by agreeing on prices that will yield a steady profit to everyone, and few of them attempt to compete by cutting their prices for retail customers. Given their objectives, their marketing system is completely logical.

Jamaicans classify traders generally into "country people" or "growers," "country higglers," and "town higglers," with some sub-

types. The growers sell their own produce in local markets and occasionally come to Kingston, the capital, but they sell most of their produce to the country higglers who tour the countryside at midweek, building up a load that they then carry to Kingston to sell at the weekend markets. They, in turn, sell much of their loads wholesale to town higglers who sell at retail from stalls in the public marketplaces. Country higglers also sell at retail but generally prefer an assured quick wholesale profit to the greater retail profit which carries with it the risk of sitting long hours with goods spread out and tempting thieves.

Each trader calls the people from whom she buys and sells her customers. She retains her customers by always being regular in both buying and selling, by concentrating on four or five commodities for which she becomes a dependable source of supply or demand, and by giving appropriate recognition to customers in the form of "brawta" (bonuses in kind) or of generous units—counting 120 oranges as only 100 "in case the load mash." People at all levels know the retail prices in the marketplace. They do not bargain with customers but agree to trade with them at prices that will allow each trader a fair mark-up. Credit arrangements are common, and if retail prices change unexpectedly, there will be retroactive and friendly adjustment of intermediate prices so that no one operates at a loss. As Jamaicans say, "Poor folk got to help each other." As Katzin says, traders rationally try to max-

Figure 5 (left). Rationing is the allocation of scarce resources on the basis of some social criterion. When the criterion is status, the rationed goods may become desired more as tokens of prestige than for their own utility. Figure 6. The strong attraction of status symbols is evident from the amount of trouble someone is going to in order to travel by limousine in an area where there are few roads.

imize their long-term gains, often at the cost of short-term profits, by cementing long-term relationships. They are prepared, in other words, to suffer short-term losses in order to keep their customers happy. Although this custom may conflict with standard United States practice—where retailers respond to increased wholesale prices by charging more even for goods already in stock—it is not necessarily "irrational," especially in a situation where the people involved know one another and know they will be trading with one another for some time.

Clearly, an ethnoeconomic system based on long-term relationships is not necessarily "irrational." In fact, as D. G. Norvell and M. K. Thompson showed in 1968, the Jamaican ethnoeconomic system is in harmony with M. L. Greenhut's formal economic model of the spatially perfect market. To understand this model, we must assume, in addition to the assumptions of the classic economist, that there is only so much "space" in a market. Traders, or firms, will compete among themselves for this space as well as with customers for prices, so that the actions of each seller will be taken into account by other sellers and such features as described by Katzin will emerge. In the economist's language, these features are an unorganized oligopoly made up of many firms of varied sizes that earn profits consistent with their state of uncertainty; the presence of a "kinky oligopoly demand curve"; and rigid prices that do, however, become flexible with high demand. At that time, the space limitations on the market become unimportant. This language is far removed from that of "customers" and "brawta" and "helping other poor folk," but both languages need to be understood and need to be used in different contexts.

The economic anthropologist, given a knowledge of how traders calculate in terms of preserving lasting relationships, can predict many other sorts of behavior that would then occur and relate the economic choices

to other aspects of behavior. One illustration of how the principle of economic choice implies a whole complex of other behavior is provided by Mary Douglas' 1967 analysis of rationing, and what is associated with it.

CEREMONIAL ECONOMICS

Basically, the principle behind rationing is that when all individuals need a good that exists in limited quantity, it may be more equitable to limit everyone's access to that good, so that no one may completely deprive anyone else by taking what he needs. The classic example is that of shipwrecked sailors in a lifeboat who find that their water supply is limited. The amount of water allotted to each individual might depend either on the status of each sailor—the captain, for example (assuming he did not relish the idea of going down with his ship), might demand more water than a member of his crew. Or rationing might depend on performance of specific actions—for example, those who can take a turn at rowing will be given more water. The rationed commodity then serves to mark status divisions: the amount of water that each person receives indicates his status.

Usually the division of goods preserves the existing hierarchy, but it may also create a new one. At this level, once the question of status has been introduced, the desire for a good becomes a desire not only for the commodity itself but also for the status that access to the rationed commodity can confer. During World War II, when gasoline was rationed, it was a great convenience to have access to greater quantities of it. But access to more gasoline also conferred status, inasmuch as it showed that the fortunate individual was considered important. Similarly, an American who drives an expensive car or lives in an expensive home is liable to do so not only because his car or his house provides actual physical comfort but because possession of them gives him greater status as well. But such commodities are also rationed. Driving a Rolls-Royce confers more status than driving a Chevrolet only because everyone cannot afford a Rolls-Royce: no one achieves greater status by drinking more water than the person next door.

This issue of rationing or status is of great importance in understanding the ceremonial "economics" found in the small-scale societies in Melanesia, North America, and Africa. These goods can be considered analogous to the gasoline coupons used in wartime Britain, although here the "coupons" are mainly shells, fur robes, or cattle. They circulate rapidly in these societies, produce little, but are of intense concern to everyone. Richard Salisbury showed in 1962 that the commodity these goods confer upon the participants is "free-floating power." Inasmuch as these ceremonial economic systems react rapidly to changes in the number of "coupons"—or to changes in society—they are extremely important regulatory devices. In fact, the analysis of how such systems work can give insights into the working of modern, centrally controlled rationing systems that conventional economic analyses do not.

One example of this sort of system was described by Marcel Mauss in his classic work *The Gift* and he refers to it as gift exchange. In theory, gift exchanges are voluntary but in fact they are obligatory; they

are reciprocities in effect that constitute the fulfillment of contracts. Moreover, they are ways of competing for and establishing status and superiority. The best-known example is that of the potlatch of the American Indians of the Northwest Coast. These Indians were hunters and fishermen who inhabited an extremely rich environment that enabled them to accumulate large surpluses of food. During the spring they dispersed to engage in hunting, gathering, and fishing, and in the winter they collected in towns, spending much of their time in an intense round of social contacts, visits, and feasts.

The potlatch, or ceremonial feast, was held on all important occasions between families, between clans, or between tribes, and it consisted of exchanges of gifts that were characterized by extreme rivalry for status and were often accompanied by violence. As Mauss described it, the themes of credit and honor are basic to an understanding of the potlatch. A person's honor as well as the honor of his lineage was bound up with the amount of food and other goods that he could afford to distribute or even—a supreme sign of his status—destroy. Every chief was obliged to potlatch on a number of occasions in order to maintain a minimum of respect from his own people and command their obedience. When he potlatched another chief he had to show that he was favorably regarded by his ancestral spirits and possessed great fortune, and it was by potlatching that he demonstrated the extent of his fortune.

A failure to potlatch not only involved him in acute loss of prestige but also involved the loss of favor of the ancestral spirits of his lineage. A chief, therefore, tried to demonstrate his superiority by heaping gifts on his rival. The rival was then obligated to reciprocate, preferably with even larger and grander gifts. In accepting an invitation, a chief was in effect accepting a challenge—he was committing himself to outdo the potlatcher on a future occasion—and it was as impossible to refuse an invitation to a potlatch as it would have been for a seventeenth-century French nobleman to refuse a challenge to a duel.

The results of contact with Western society, which has increased the number of goods available for potlatching, have been described by Helen Codere. Potlatching increased at a geometric rate. So did the number of status positions, even though the population decreased because of disease. The late nineteenth century was a period of cultural florescence, when nearly everyone had a title. Potlatching, which is seen to be a rationing system for allocating prestige, provided a way of converting material affluence into cultural achievement.

ENTREPRENEURSHIP
Systems of rationing bring out a distinction between the cultural rules that are apparently set, but are, in fact, a framework of ground rules that individuals try to manipulate in order to achieve their personal goals. This emphasis on the individual maneuvering within a set of ground rules—or entre-

preneurship, as it is called—has been particularly stressed in the work of Fredrik Barth. His 1967 analysis of the Sudanese society of Darfur shows this phenomenon clearly in relation to a common cultural phenomenon—that particular goods are defined as being usable only in certain forms of activities, or given in exchange for only a limited number of other goods. Thus in Darfur, tomatoes and wheat are crops that people say are grown exclusively for cash sale. Cattle, tended by the owner's family, are supposedly kept only as a reserve of savings, to be sold only when the owner gives a feast or makes a pilgrimage to Mecca. Millet, the main crop, is used either as food for the grower's family or to brew beer for feasts. And feasts are held either to bring prestige to the giver or to reward workers who help cultivate fields or build houses.

If these cultural rules were followed, each household by its own hard work would gradually increase its wealth as it produced more than it consumed and as its children grew up and were able to tend more cattle. As stocks of millet built up, beer parties could be given and labor recruited to farm larger areas and grow more millet. Eventually older families could convert their wealth into prestige by feasting younger families or into religious merit by spending the proceeds from cattle sales on pilgrimages to holy places.

But some people bend the cultural rules. They try to buy millet outside Darfur for cash (none is for sale in Darfur) and use it for beer parties, so that they can cultivate large areas of land. Instead of using this land to grow millet, however, they grow cash crops of tomatoes and wheat, export them, and import more cheap millet, and so on. "Conversions" of this kind, from one form of exchange to another, are the mark of the entrepreneur and can bring high returns. Barth does not discuss the problem of how far cultural rules can be bent before they change, but presumably if workers feel they

Figure 7. Berti village life at the time of L. Holý's field work. Although economic change is contributing to the rise of entrepreneurship and strain on traditional social relationships among the Darfu, many of the traditional skills are still being practiced.

are being exploited by beer parties, or if other farmers feel the entrepreneurs are taking too much land, then the rules will change. In the meantime, the entrepreneurs are adding to Darfur welfare by importing cheap millet and reallocating labor to the most productive tasks.

Perhaps the most striking set of cultural rules that provide a framework for individual manipulation are those that accompany the emergence of centralized states and that define a certain set of goods as "nationally strategic goods." In 1957, Karl Polanyi introduced anthropologists to the study of this field with his work *Trade and Markets in the Early Empires.* The state, by accumulating taxes (in labor, goods, cash, or obligations of service) can use them to produce specialist goods and to engage in long-distance trade where individuals could not. The goods thus produced and the exotic commodities obtained in trade form the category of nationally strategic goods. They are used to reward state officials in a process of redistribution.

Within this form of exchange there tends to be a range of organizations—the specialist workers organized as state bureaucrats or in guilds, trade carried out in terms of fixed equivalents rather than fluctuating prices, and special enclave ports of trade where interstate trading can occur but foreign trad-

ers can be isolated from contact with the internal economy of the other state. Yet individual exploitation of the rules is always present in the form of black markets, trading on the side for nonstrategic goods, or production for private customers—and equally ever-present are the state attempts to make the rules work by more rigid controls and more severe punishments.

Polanyi arrived at his generalizations by considering ancient Mesopotamian and Greek societies and then comparing them with the Aztecs at the time of the Spanish conquest and with West Africa during the eighteenth-century slave trade. Yet the analysis given above could apply equally well to crop marketing boards in newly independent African countries or to the aerospace and nuclear industries of the major world powers. Economic anthropology, in short, although based on data that seem strange to the citizens of a large industrial country, nevertheless has implications for them as well.

ECONOMICS AND SOCIAL CHANGE

Despite its implications for the large industrial nation, the most obvious application of the work of economic anthropologists is in their studies of the changes occurring around the world as small-scale and primarily agricultural societies become part of much larger national systems, as they relate to urban centers, and as they diversify their activities to include the range of manufacturing, service, white-collar, and professional occupations. Typically, where the economist analyzes these changes as they appear at the national or macrolevel in capital investment budgets or gross national product, the economic anthropologist is interested in what these changes involve at the personal, local, or microlevel.

The economic anthropologist is interested in such effects of change as how peasants in Guatemala react to the wage-work opportunities when a factory is located in their

Figure 8. This neighborhood market in one of the slums of Mexico is an example of small-scale entrepreneurship. Families with the desire to own their own business set up small shops hoping to improve their economic well-being. They usually are able to continue in business on a low profit margin, however, without realistic prospect of expansion.

town, or how the perceptions of peasants who become entrepreneurs differ from those of peasants who do not. He studies how nobles in Bali, shorn of the political offices that once involved financing such ceremonial industries as gong making, began organizing bus companies and ice-making plants, or how a technological change such as introducing steel tools in New Guinea altered time expenditures and eventually the structure of local society, or how the news of technological innovations spreads among peasants in Colombia.

A major problem that constantly occurs in situations of economic change is how to get large-scale businesses operating in societies where the extended family may have been the largest economically productive unit. One economic approach, which can be analyzed in terms of so-called Horatio Alger principles, is to encourage individual entrepreneurs to start small businesses. Then, with such help as government loans, they can gradually build up industrial empires. With the personal drive for individual profit as the motivating force, production will flourish and the entire society will benefit.

But despite some notable individual successes, the statistically normal pattern of large business development in developing countries—and probably in the United States as well—has not been the steady build-up of small private firms. In Japan, the entrepreneurs worked from the start for noble family corporations, called *daibatsu*. Here, the motivation was not personal profit but the expansion of the corporate estate and with it the well-being of the family dependents. Even today, the relationship between corporations and workers in Japan and the structure of ownership of Japanese industry

bears strong evidence of this principle. An economist basing his advice on Japanese experience would recommend different measures than would a Horatio Alger devotee.

Economic anthropologists working in New Guinea have described how small organizations of this type have emerged independently. Local people without knowledge of the complexities of Western business ideology have tried to organize for themselves, using modern technologies. The goal has been to satisfy local demands for widespread well-being, rather than to amass personal profits for a few. The emerging enterprises differ from Western "businesses" but are called *bisnis* in pidgin English. A *bisnis* typically involves a group of people subscribing small amounts to some named entity that they feel they "belong to" or that is "theirs." The entity may have a village name, a clan name, or a "personal" name. For example, a group of Tolai men of several clans set themselves up as *ToVurmatana* ("Mr. Mixup") to form a copra-marketing agency in the early 1950s; *IaMinat* ("Mrs. Death") is a group of women from several clans in one village that has built up a *bisnis*, successively marketing eggs and chickens, bulking copra and manufacturing lime, operating a taxi-truck service, and buying land.

The subscribers clearly distinguish between what is "of the *bisnis*" and what is personal to individuals. They feel their subscriptions are no longer personally owned but are part of the *bisnis*. The life, health, and growth of "their" *bisnis* is a matter of personal pride, and they expect that profits will be used to make the *bisnis* grow. A *bisnis* should not distribute profits. It should exist perpetually, and future generations should be able to point with pride at the founders who set it up and fostered it—just as Americans presumably continue to point with pride to their ancestors who set up the great American corporations.

Nevertheless, the subscribers to a *bisnis* certainly expect to benefit from it. They expect a *bisnis* to provide personal returns to its members and involve its members in its operations rather than provide any distribution of profits. In "Mrs. Death," members and nonmembers pay the same rates for hiring the taxi-truck, although members do have priority. The personal return to the women of the village is that by owning a vehicle and having a paid driver on call, they have their own ambulance service to carry women in labor three miles to the hospital without charge. *Namasu*, a Lutheran-sponsored trading company, is now the largest native-owned company in New Guinea, but many subscribers are disappointed with it because it has distributed dividends from profits. They feel that dividend distribution is a sign that the company is about to collapse and that "their" company has somehow been taken away from them because it does not provide all the services of transporting goods from remote areas to market that they would expect a *bisnis* to provide. They feel it has been taken over by Europeans who operate a business, not a *bisnis*.

The New Guinea *bisnis*, aimed at building up a corporate estate and providing benefits for members, is clearly functional in producing development. It mobilizes monetary capital from wide groups, and it enables underemployed labor of *bisnis* members to be invested in growth. It also rewards the individual who sparks a successful *bisnis* not with money but with the prestige of being a "big man" and a leader of his group. It pyramids assets, as a growth company should, but more importantly, it ensures that corporations are responsive to the well-being of the people whom they affect.

A village-owned mine, such as the one in Fiji that Cyril Belshaw described in 1965, cannot help but point to how mining activities affect local farming. A copra-marketing *bisnis* composed of copra producers must balance the possibly competitive alternatives of lowering marketing costs but increasing producers' costs by buying at centralized points, or increasing the return to growers but making marketing more expensive by collecting produce at the farms. A local project is evaluated in terms of its impact on the whole local economy, the employment it will provide, the investment, and the services it will produce rather than in terms of whether nonlocal owners will make a profit. An economic anthropologist advising on how to produce Japanese-style corporations would thus stress the need to strengthen the power of locally formed corporations over their assets, to make their registration (and hence their power to invoke court action) much simpler, and to teach the bookkeeping skills appropriate to growth companies, not those of nonexpanding firms. Member control over corporate activities is already implicit in the New Guinea organizations whereas the problems of community involvement in the environmental changes produced by industry or of worker involvement in management are only now being faced by North American organizations.

This, then, is another example of the general aims of economic anthropology—to understand the principles underlying the various attempts that people around the world have made to solve for themselves the problems of allocating resources to meet needs, not only for food, housing, employment, and leisure but for security and a meaningful involvement in and control over their own lives. The store of technological knowledge already available in the world is enough to provide plenty for all. There is considerable knowledge of how to organize production in a monetary economy to ensure that enough material goods are produced. Knowledge of how to distribute those goods and how to meet people's needs for security and participation in their own destinies is still woefully lacking. Economic anthropology, while seeking for knowledge of how people have reached solutions in other environments, may well provide insights for suggesting answers to our own problems.

Religion

31

Among the Yao of Southeast Africa, the village headman is ritually "killed" by a blow on the head that leaves him unconscious. First, however, he is warned of the dangers a headman faces, such as the threat of outside enemies and the conflicts within his village. After he is struck down by one of the ritual leaders, he is dressed as a corpse and sprinkled with flour from a sacrificial basket and later brought to life ceremonially. During a subsequent period of seclusion, he is lectured by other leaders in the village on the duties of his office and is subjected to (and passes) a test whereby he is judged good or bad on the basis of whether or not he vomits human flesh served to him. Finally, the people are called upon to vouch their unswerving loyalty to him.

Each year, at the time of the Renewal of the Sacred Arrows, an entire Cheyenne tribe gathers near a good stream, where there is abundant forage for their horses, to renew symbolically their vitality. The arrows the Cheyenne use are regarded as gifts from supernatural beings, and without them they will not succeed in the hunt or in war. Despite all their efforts, the specter of starvation

walks through the Cheyenne camp. Although their braves are impeccably skilled warriors, they are defeated and the Cheyenne are killed, scalped, or taken into captivity.

The Nyoro of Africa know that a sorcerer is a man who can kill people. He kills them by blowing medicine in their direction, by hiding it on the path where people walk, or by putting it in food or water. Anyone might be a sorcerer, practicing his art against those who steal from him, against people who are richer than he is, or against people he just doesn't like, or envies, or quarrels with.

It is difficult, at first, to comprehend the relationship of these diverse rituals. Yet all are patterns of behavior whereby societies work—in large part unwittingly—to minimize the problems of day-to-day living and to give their members the means to cope with the crises that stem from the unexpected and unexplainable. The Yao, in temporarily reversing their culturally defined standards of behavior—in this case, trust in their headman to guide them through danger —tend to emphasize and reinforce the importance of these standards. These inaugural rites symbolize the death of the headman

and his rebirth into a new social position. The Cheyenne must cope with a harsh environment, and without some expression of hope for a better life they might well be unable to continue their struggle. And the Nyoro have devised their own explanation of why some people sicken and die, and why some remain healthy, in order to dispel the uncertainties of living. Their interpretation of the cause of diseases also suggests positive courses of action for their cure.

Dispelling such uncertainties is one of the major concerns of religion everywhere. Some of the forms religion takes may appear naïve, others bizarre, others quite sophisticated, but religion beneath its external dress is essentially much the same for all mankind.

RELIGIOUS UNIVERSALS

In studying religion, anthropologists have normally started with the assumption that all varieties of mankind are so similar biologically that the variation in religious behavior throughout the world has little to do with racial or other physical variations. Another enduring view is that religion is part of culture, the man-made part of the universe, and therefore a creation of man.

In the anthropological view, man has created gods in his own image, rather than the reverse. For beyond the limits of every society's knowledge of the natural world and the technology that society has developed to come to terms with it, certain events remain unexplained. The technical knowledge of early man was not enough to explain, for instance, why the hunt would be successful one day and a failure the next, why some stars appeared to fall from the sky, or why death could come suddenly to seemingly healthy people. He interpreted such unpredictable events on the basis of whether they benefited or threatened him personally—an *anthropocentric* view, in which he considered himself the center of the universe. As a further example, even within the vast store of knowledge and technology of today's complex societies, which among them has an explanation for the origins of the solar system? Although they might include astronomy, physics, and geology in their explanation of the natural world, complex societies, too, have limits beyond which their existing body of knowledge fails.

Man has devised religion—a symbolic expression of human life that interprets the universe and provides motives for human action. His gods and witches, ghosts and devils are symbols that everywhere represent *supernatural* forces beyond the realm of the natural world, and all are responses to what Max Weber has called the problem of meaning. It is not that people in different cultures deny natural explanations of misfortune. Consider an Azande who happens to be sitting beneath a large, wooden grainery, one of the few sources of shade in his hot environment. And suppose the structure happens to fall on him and crush him. The Azande can reason that the ever-present termites ate through the wood and caused the grainery to collapse—but why did it collapse on that particular man, at that particular time? Although they do not deny natural explanations, where such explanations are available, the Azande and other societies as well need ones that are more emotionally satisfying. And his religious practices such as prayer or sacrifice are ways he has invented to bring explanation within his control, or at least within reach of his understanding.

Religious symbols and practices vary among societies, and religion in this sense may be considered *ethnocentric*, as reflecting the unique culture and experiences of each society. The Pygmies of the Congo, for instance, live as hunters and gatherers in the tropical forest and do not worship gods of the sea; and although some modern Americans might claim divine power to locate underground petroleum, they do not claim the aboriginal American Indian power to "charm" antelopes. Man has arbitrarily at-

Figure 2 (left). The Aztec god pantheon: corn, rain, and earth interpreted in stone. Figure 3 (below). Print from Captain Cooke's voyages to the South Seas. The complex system of tabus revolving around the notion of *mana* in Hawaii rapidly disintegrated when the king one day decided he did not possess any supernatural powers. Dismounting from his litter, he walked about touching things, and when the many dreaded catastrophes associated with the tabu did not materialize, the commoners ceased to believe in the system.

tached special religious significance to the objects and events that are the most important to him in the particular natural and cultural environment in which he lives.

Expressions of the Supernatural

In all historically known societies, supernatural forces are conceived in two distinct forms, referred to by anthropologists as personified and impersonal power. These two forms may coexist in the beliefs of any society, although the emphasis given one may greatly overshadow the other.

Personified power is an attribute of supernatural beings, such as gods or demons, that operates at their will or direction. Supernatural beings may bring rain or good crops, or abundant game, or they may cause sickness, starvation, and other misfortunes. They are the creation of men and very often are remarkably like him, possessing the full range of human emotions. They socialize with man in various ways, and share his qualities of character. Like man, they may be benevolent or malevolent, joyous or dour, moral or immoral, powerful or weak, loving or hateful, wise or foolish, or they may alternate between these opposing characteristics and exhibit different traits at different times. Because they resemble powerful human beings, these supernatural beings are usually approached in ways traditionally used to approach human superiors. They are given reverential treatment through prescribed acts of worship or other forms of deference that closely resemble the behavior of ordinary men to kings or princes.

Impersonal power is a force, usually invisible, that may permeate the entire universe or be found in only certain objects and places. It may be possessed by gods, men, and natural forces and substances, or it may be called into operation by magic without the intervention of supernatural beings. It is used to explain the characteristics of trees, stones, and rivers, or to explain one man's success in battle over another. It may be

analogous with the properties of objects, such as coldness or warmth, hardness or softness, the bite of acids, and toxic or therapeutic properties of certain plants and minerals. Regardless of how it is acquired, impersonal power may be manipulated like objects to help or to harm. In some societies, such as in various aboriginal tribes of the Great Plains, impersonal power might be bought, sold, given away, or bequeathed.

The most familiar example of impersonal power in anthropological writings is the *mana* of Melanesia and Polynesia. In Polynesia *mana* was both personified and impersonal. In aboriginal Hawaii the gods and all human individuals were thought to possess some *mana*, but the amount an individual could hold was proportional to his position in the social hierarchy: the higher the status, the more the *mana*. Ways of gaining *mana*, such as eating the eye of a fallen enemy, also existed. Like electricity, it could flow through conductors, animate or inanimate. *Mana* was the key to success, but it was also dangerous. The king of Hawaii was so saturated with it that many precautions had to be taken to prevent this communicable power from flowing from him to common people: wherever his feet trod or his shadow fell, the ground became dangerous to commoners, and when traveling away from the royal compound he was transported by special bearers so that his feet would not touch the ground. A complex of *tabus*, a Polynesian word meaning prohibited things, protected people from the danger of *mana*.

Elsewhere in the world, many other societies held similar ideas about supernatural power. Among various western Indian tribes of North America, for example, this power could be highly specialized. Visions ranging from simple dreams to hallucinations brought on by fasting and self-torture were signs that an individual had received power. This power might be general, perhaps assuring success in warfare or any other endeavor; it might be highly specialized, perhaps imparting the ability to cure sickness or to "charm" antelopes—that is, so they could be hunted successfully—or perhaps giving the possessor immunity from the bites of rattlesnakes or from the danger of bullets. Among modern Western societies, ideas of impersonal power do not stand out prominently but many nevertheless exist, as in the traditional Christian beliefs of power inherent in the cross and in holy water, and in the relics of saints.

The difference between personal and impersonal forms of power naturally affects the way people behave toward them. Man sometimes approach supernatural beings with force or threats of force, especially when hospitable overtures have failed to bring desired results. An old European custom, still observed in Brazil, was to punish saints by tying up their statues and throwing them into the open fields under the hot sun when prayers for rain were not granted. An impersonal power may be accumulated, safeguarded, manipulated, and regarded with the kind of respect extended to any powerful substance, but it is not worshiped.

Magic Versus Religion

Anthropologists have often distinguished magic from religion, but frequently have treated both subjects under the heading of supernaturalism. Magic is said to consist of

ideas and acts that imply control by man over the supernatural, whereas religion implies control over man by the supernatural. The French sociologist Emile Durkheim drew a distinction primarily on the basis of organization, arguing that true religion always operates through an institution—a church in one form or another—whereas magic is the work of individuals operating essentially on their own.

In contrast to the religious view of a universe controlled by unpredictable supernatural powers, magic is based on the concept that the universe can be explained in terms of an orderly relationship between cause and effect, and therefore can be controlled by certain mechanical formulas that exploit this effect. Like recipes for making cakes, these formulas assure results, provided the correct formulas are used and conditions are favorable. Magic also tends, more frequently than prayer or any other behavior directed toward supernatural beings, to be the act of individuals rather than groups. It is performed when the need arises rather than at fixed intervals, and it tends to be rather less emotional in nature, often involving a professional-client relationship between the skilled performer and the client who wishes to use magic.

Magic may control either impersonal forces or supernatural beings. Rites of magic may be part of complexes of ritual acts that include or emphasize prayers, or worship, or sacrifice, or they may be used alone as a way to achieve desired ends. Most acts of magic involve ideas of connection or sympathy between things, and for this reason they were given the names of sympathetic magic and contagious magic by the early British anthropologist James Frazer. *Sympathetic magic* operates on the principle that what is simulated or imitated will actually occur; it symbolically represents such desired things and events as rain, bountiful crops, pregnancy, successful childbirth, and the killing of game animals. In *image magic,* a variation of sympathetic magic that is often harmful in intent, the performer hopes to inflict pain, sickness, or death on enemies by symbolically wounding or killing dolls or other images made to represent them.

Contagious magic rests on the idea that things once in contact remain forever in contact. One example is *exuvial magic,* which makes use of organic castoffs of the human body such as hair, fingernail cuttings, excreta, and umbilical cords. Whatever symbolic act is performed upon these exuviae will befall the human beings from which they came. A classic case is that of the Arapesh, described by Margaret Mead. The Arapesh are a peaceful, rather passive people who inhabit the mountains inland from the coast of northern New Guinea and they live in dread of aggressive neighbors who live on the plains. Their overriding fear is that some enemy will steal a piece of their castoffs and deliver it to a plains sorcerer. If this happens the victim is forever in the power of the sorcerer who can, at will, cause his vic-

tim to sicken and die. Whenever an accident befalls an Arapesh, he automatically attributes it to his castoffs having been delivered into the hands of a plains sorcerer.

THE ORIGINS OF RELIGION

Archaeological evidence dating back to the late Paleolithic shows that ideas of supernaturalism are very ancient. There are well-preserved cave paintings, drawings, and sculpture from this era in Europe, and they appear to be forms of image magic depicting wounded or dying animals of the chase, pregnant animals, and pregnant women. And later archaeological sites throughout the world show many similarities in religious behavior, as in the apparently widespread practices of burials, making offerings to supernatural beings, and building edifices used for religious ceremonies. Pioneer scholars attempted to infer the circumstances leading to these many similarities. The main thrust of their studies of religion naturally tended to follow the anthropological trend of the day. Nineteenth-century anthropologists laid heavy stress on evolutionary theory, and their early attempts to explain religion followed the same path.

The Evolutionary Explanation

The best known of these evolutionary explanations was offered by the British anthropologist Edward Burnett Tylor, who saw *animism,* which he defined as belief in spiritual

Figure 6 (below). A Chinese ancestral shrine from the village of Hang Mei, near Hong Kong. Figure 7 (right). It has often been said that, as the level of technology in a society increases, the degree of dependency on religion and magic decreases. Durkheim's theory of the sacred and profane behavior in fact has not been disproved.

thinks of as inanimate phenomena seemed to have a life of their own. Boulders fall, volcanoes erupt, the sun sets and the moon rises, and clouds seem to move with a will of their own.

When all such phenomena had been endowed with souls, the animistic view of the world was complete. It was followed in many cases by an emphasis on ancestor worship, in which ghosts of deceased forebears became increasingly the focus of ritual and cult. As civilization advanced and social hierarchies developed in human societies, the stage of polytheism also developed, in which well-defined spirit beings or gods, each possessing a personality of its own, presided over orders of phenomena rather than specific events. Finally, the most powerful of the gods came to assume more and more of the functions of his fellow divinities, and the last stage appeared—monotheism, in which the entire universe is ruled by one all-powerful god. Evolutionary theories such as this were generally abandoned about the turn of the century as being unverifiable speculation that could not be supported by information on individual societies.

Totemism

In *The Elementary Forms of the Religious Life* (1912), Emile Durkheim suggested what has since become recognized as the classic functional interpretation of the origin of religion. Durkheim proposed that only elements of crucial importance to a society will become a symbolic part of its religion, a concept that emerged from his examination of the practices of Australian aborigines.

Australian *totemism*, as in the religion of the desert Arunta, showed him how man, nature, and the supernatural can be interwoven by religion. In the territory of an Arunta band are sacred places, called totem centers, in which a particular species of animal or plant abounds and the spirits of Arunta dead reside. When one of these spirits enters the body of a woman, a child is

beings, as the foundation of all religions. The earliest spirit being was the soul, the concept of which originated in attempts to explain dreams and hallucinations wherein the dreamer finds himself in contact with persons long dead or when the dreamer sees himself in places far away from where he actually is, and doing things he cannot do while in an ordinary, wakeful state. It was, Tylor suggested, only a short step from the concept of the individual soul to the concept of a universe filled with souls, for in a very real sense man lives in what appears to be an animate universe. Animals are close analogues to human beings; they are born, they sleep, they eat, they die. To a lesser degree, the same holds true of plants. Yet to a prescientific community, even what man now

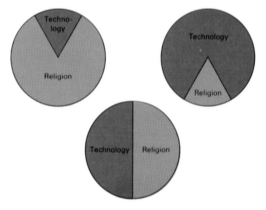

conceived. The child is considered a reincarnated ancestor, related to the totem center of the ancestral spirit. The Arunta whose spirits come from the same totem center are members of an exclusive cult who see that all members observe specific restrictions on procuring and eating the special plant or animal of the totem center. Ceremonies are performed by the cult to ensure the well-being of its particular totem plant or animal. The totem religion closely links the members of the cult to their environment, to the animal and plant life they depend upon for subsistence.

Durkheim saw the beginning of religion in the group ritual of totemism, for he regarded the culture of the Arunta as the simplest in the world, and he used their culture as an approximation of primordial conditions. He viewed such Arunta totems as the kangaroo and wallaby as symbolic representations of the societies having such totems, and he believed the rites centering on these totems consisted of society worshiping itself. The communal beliefs and ritual acts of totemism thus served to unite the society into one moral community. Durkheim's ideas of the origins of religion long ago were discarded, but his ideas of the social significance of religious beliefs and acts are still discernible in functionalist studies.

Man's everyday dependence on religion, as many anthropologists later pointed out, is inversely proportional to the level of technological development of his society. In primitive societies the sacred has much to do with everyday activities, whereas in large, technologically advanced societies the sacred holds comparatively little sway. In urban areas of Europe and America, for example, religion is usually seen only during special formal occasions.

Psychoanalytic Explanation
Another and very different interpretation of the origin of religion was suggested by the psychoanalyst Sigmund Freud with his myth of the Oedipus complex. This myth describes how in the primeval band a group of sons, jealous of their father's control over their mother, united and killed the father. Then, as atonement for this act of murder, they took to worshiping the figure of the father as God the Father. Today, Freud's idea of primordial social organization is regarded by anthropologists as unsound. But his interpretation can be seen as an ethnocentric version of the origin of religion, based on the patriarchal Viennese society of his youth—a projection illustrating the anthropological view that supernatural beings and acts are projections of men and their particular social circumstances.

The Functionalist Explanation
Today anthropologists are seldom concerned with the question of the origin of religion, having turned instead to the roles it plays in society. They have come to view religion as a tool for survival, integrated as a part of the cultural system or the social system, stating these relationships as *functions* of religion. Early functionalist studies of religion centered on the relationship between religion and the social order, especially as exemplified by A. R. Radcliffe-Brown, who drew many of his ideas from the earlier sociologist Emile Durkheim. The pioneer functionalist Bronislaw Malinowski used psychological as well as sociological views of the significance of religion, including in his interpretation of its functions the relationships of religion to the psychological state of the individual. Based on the assumption that culture as a system must be composed of congruent parts and that incongruency or malfunction leads to change or breakdown, a fourfold set of terms describing functions was developed and remains in current use. Functions were labeled as *positive*, contributing to the maintenance of society and the individual, or *negative*, contributing to the disruption or breakdown of society or the individual; and as *manifest*, having goals or effects that are

known to the people concerned and are usually the motives for following customs, and latent or *implicit* functions, concerning those effects of beliefs and acts that generally go unrecognized by the members of society and can be deduced only by scholars.

For example, the belief that illness is caused by intrusion of a spirit into the body has a positive and implicit function of providing an interpretation of an event that, if unexplained, might otherwise be highly demoralizing to society and to the invalid. The manifest function of the religious rites employed to cure the patient is to drive out the intrusive spirit. The mobilizing of social action for such rites is socially integrative and psychologically satisfying, and these are implicit functions of which the participants are usually unaware. The rites may also have psychotherapeutic value unknown to the participants; for example, when such rites require rest and the use of heat therapy, massage, and emetics to drive out the spirit, they may be practical and effective treatments as well. On the other hand, the interpretation of the cause of illness can inhibit the devising of more efficient therapy, and this interpretation thus has a negative effect.

Functionalist studies of religion have served especially to point out relationships that exist between religion and the social order. Close attention has been given to establishing the identities and relationships of participants in religious events, what they actually do, what social values are stated or are represented symbolically in ritual acts, and when the acts are performed. Studies along these lines have been criticized because they emphasize relations or functions at a fixed point in time and thus deal inadequately with change. Nevertheless, early functionalist studies made substantial contributions to the literature, and their decline in recent years is undoubtedly due in part to the fact that they successfully achieved their objectives. Certain early functionalist studies of rites of passage, for example, are po-

tential blueprints that could be used with change only in details to interpret rites of passage of other societies.

RELIGION AND SOCIAL CONTROL

In the Western world, where Christianity and Judaism have prevailed, religion is recognized for its moral value and in fact is often defined as a moral code. Beginning with Tylor, however, anthropologists have held that the frequent connection between religion and morality, as important and functional as it may be, is not necessarily an inherent relation. All human societies have *moral codes*, or ideas of proper and improper human relations, and such codes are essential to the workings of society. But cross-cultural studies of primitive and non-primitive societies point out that relationships between religion and morality vary enormously. In certain societies, for example, an individual's moral conduct may have no bearing on supernatural rewards or punishments, either during his life or after it. The afterworld to which an individual's soul is consigned after death might depend on the nature of his funeral, or, according to the ancient Aztec, on his sex and occupation in life.

In some societies, important moral values are thought to be supernaturally sanctioned, but in primitive societies many of the strongest supernatural sanctions are made against violation of tabus that have no readily discernible moral significance. The tabus surrounding the king of aboriginal Hawaii were important in maintaining the social scheme, but the individual who accidentally and innocently violated a tabu was subject to the same supernatural punishment as a deliberate transgressor. Part of the problem in understanding the relationship between religion and morality is that concepts of morality differ from one society to another. It is possible to regard the tabus of Polynesia as moral issues—at least, they worked to preserve the social status quo—but many

Figure 8. The medium in a Manus seance was usually an old woman who had a deceased male child. His ghost carried messages between her and the dead. In any major illness, the medium along with diviners attempted to find the sins of the living for which they had been stricken by the ghosts.

other examples may be given of values that are considered extremely important but not supernaturally sanctioned.

The Manus of Melanesia provide an excellent illustration of how a religious system can govern individual conduct. The Manus have neither productive land nor a manufacturing economy of their own. They live by fishing and trading with neighboring tribes, serving as middlemen between other groups by transporting the artifacts of one for trade with the others. Although at first glance their religion might seem to be highly individualistic, it serves well to hold the people together.

Personified Power and the Manus

The basic element in Manus religion is the belief in the spirits of dead ancestors. Each spirit supposedly dwells in the house it once inhabited, and it manifests itself in the skull of the body it left behind. The skull, which is preserved in carved wooden bowls over the door, is the focus of the spirit's power. It guards the house and those who inhabit it, and also supervises their morals. It lives, thinks, and behaves like a living man, even going so far as to marry and have children in the spirit world.

Every household has its own personal ghost, who is addressed as "Sir Ghost." Each Sir Ghost protects his wards and brings them luck and wealth, but he also punishes them for moral transgressions. To any one householder, the personal Sir Ghosts of individuals of other households are merely ghosts in general, and ghosts in general are malevolent. But his own Sir Ghost is expected to protect him from them.

Manus Oracles and Social Harmony

The essential element in any person's spiritual or religious life is his soul-stuff. Ghosts may take a person's soul-stuff out of maliciousness, or an individual's own Sir Ghost may take it as a punishment for sin. If a piece of an individual's soul-stuff is stolen he

Figure 9. Azande from Africa. The study of witchcraft among these people by E. E. Evans-Pritchard is one of the classics in anthropology. Shown below is an Azande making preparation for the poison oracle, a form of witchcraft that is employed only when disputes cannot be settled by less extreme means.

will fall ill, and if it is not eventually returned, he will die. Recovery from illness comes when the lost soul-stuff is returned, and this can be achieved by the performance of certain acts of expiation. The regaining of soul-stuff must be achieved through oracles, either diviners or mediums, who are people who communicate with the supernatural. A diviner can obtain "yes" or "no" answers from a man's Sir Ghost by casting two small pieces of bone attached by a cord over his shoulder so that one lands on the chest and the other on his back. An itch on the right side constitutes a "yes" answer, and an itch on the left side constitutes a "no." The role of medium is played by women who have lost a male offspring, and his ghost acts as her intermediary to convey messages to and from the spirit world.

When a person falls ill, he assumes that the spirit responsible is a ghost, and he or one of his relatives will seek out one of the oracles to discover the cause in a public ceremony of divination. The people serving as oracles are usually older individuals, and they are usually shrewd. They may have an idea of who has been doing what and with whom, and under the act of communication with the ghosts involved, they may bring the whole issue out into the open. The sick person is put under pressure to confess any moral transgressions that may have led to the resentment of the ghosts, either his own or those of some other family. In the latter case, the other family is pressed to admit the involvement of the ghosts of their household and to accept expiation or help remove the grievance on which their ghost acted, perhaps unknown to themselves. If they do not cooperate and the ill person dies, public opinion may hold them responsible for the death of the victim.

There are obviously flaws in this system and means of escape are provided for failures. The sick person may not recover even after his alleged sin has been wiped out. If this happens, the sickness is attributed to

other causes, such as unknown malicious bush spirits. Indeed, if the oracle believes that the disease in question will probably prove fatal, she is less likely to attribute it to other village families, inasmuch as this could cause irreparable strain between members of the group through constant suspicion of murder. Such strains do arise from time to time and occasionally lead to splits or estrangement among the lineages of the village.

Infant mortality in Manus is very high, and to search for a causative sin whenever a child falls seriously ill would soon overtax the normal moral system that would require a sin to account for each death. This strain is avoided by attributing a child's illness to black magic, sometimes coming from the mother's kin, who may have some disagreement with her. The remedy for the illness is exorcism of the infant by a magician in what is called a rite of pregnancy. Very often, this rite is performed as a matter of course soon after birth, and is actually almost a rite of passage. Another explanation commonly used for the death of infants is that the death is brought on by a curse imposed by some member of the father's matrilineage.

Morality and the Manus Ghosts
Accusations that other people have caused a person injury obviously reflect personal rivalries, resentments, and hatreds, and by

providing a means of testing these accusations and resolving conflicts, the Manus ghost system acts to promote a degree of social harmony in a generally atomistic society. The religion reflects this social atomism, in that it is essentially a cult of the household and secondarily a cult of the collective ghosts of small lineages. Each cult is paralleled by, but is not joined to, those of other households and lineages. At the same time, the religious system also works to prevent other forms of antisocial behavior, through the interpretation of each illness or misfortune as ghostly punishment for sin, leading to pressure for confession and rectification.

The most common sin is loose sexual behavior, although many other things such as failure to pay a debt or to repair a house are also sins. In Manus society, almost anything remotely sexual that occurs outside of marriage is sinful; even seeing a person's sexual parts accidentally when they are exposed in sleep or by falling down ranks as a sin. The punishment for such an offense is illness or some other misfortune, inflicted by the sinner's Sir Ghost. The remedy is confession and expiation, and here the element of social control enters, for the innocent may be struck down as well as the guilty. If a boy and girl have illicit relations, the consequent illness may strike in the boy's house, in the girl's house, or in whatever house the transgression took place. It is then perfectly possible that someone innocent of any wrongdoing may be struck down by illness and the effect of the moral sanction is therefore to make everyone in the society interested in the transgressions of everyone else, and anxious to prevent them.

WITCHCRAFT

Whether or not witchcraft constitutes a form of religion in the strict sense has been much debated, but there is no questioning the importance of the role it plays in many primitive societies. Beliefs in witchcraft are seen by anthropologists to serve implicitly as social sanctions for two reasons. Those who are accused of witchcraft and become subject to the worldly and supernatural punishments for its performance are often people thought to be antisocial: they are the mean-looking, mean-acting, or otherwise socially disruptive people whose behavior departs from norms. In this same respect, the targets of witchcraft are usually those people who in various ways are also social nonconformists.

Witchcraft Substance of the Azande

The role of witchcraft in society was analyzed and explained by Evans-Pritchard in his classic study *Witchcraft, Oracles and Magic Among the Azande*, which demonstrated how witchcraft serves as a system of morals.

The Azande believe that witchcraft power is a physical substance in the body of a witch that enables his soul to embark on errands to harm other men. The witch practices a form of incorporeal vampirism by removing the soul of his victim and so causing a slow, wasting disease, which can produce death. But the witch performs no rite and uses no bad medicine. Essentially, witchcraft is a psychic act that bridges the distance between the person of the witch and the person of his victim, even though the originator may not voluntarily desire to bewitch the victim. His jealousy or envy may cause the witchcraft substance in his body to act even without his knowing that it is happening. It is this involuntary aspect of witchcraft that distinguishes it from *sorcery*, which basically is a pseudoscience that is always purposefully mobilized. Unlike sorcery, witchcraft may be considered an inborn characteristic of an individual; it is not, like chemistry, something that can be learned.

Witchcraft substance, sometimes described by the Azande as a "round hairy ball with teeth," is inherited. It is transmitted from parent to child, all the sons of a male witch

Figure 10. Azande administering *benje* to a fowl as part of the poison oracle, a ritual that serves to help in maintaining social order in their society by preventing open arguments and disruption among group members.

and all the daughters of a female witch being witches. Because witchcraft substance is organic, its presence can be determined by a post-mortem investigation. The presence or absence of witchcraft substance is determined by the physical appearance of the intestines. (Evans-Pritchard suggests that this evidence proving a person to be a witch is probably caused by some intestinal disease.)

The close kin of a dead person—especially if the deceased is believed to be a notorious witch—might ask for an autopsy in an attempt to establish that they themselves are not witches. Otherwise, an Azande really is not much interested in knowing who is a witch, for there is a strong likelihood that anyone might be a witch. But he is interested in knowing whether at a particular moment somebody is bewitching him. He does not sense that he is being bewitched and is therefore going to suffer a misfortune; rather, his suspicions are aroused only when a misfortune occurs. The Azande accept everyday annoyances as being witchcraft much as we accept such annoyances as being bad luck, and with the same bad humor. But when he believes witchcraft is causing a protracted illness or ruining his crop, he attempts to discover who is responsible. A witch, it is believed, launches his attacks when motivated by hatred, envy, greed, or jealousy. Therefore, the victim first reviews the list of those who are likely to feel such emotions toward him, and then sets about trying to discover who is actually the guilty person.

The Poison Oracle

The Azande cannot, or at least do not, perform operations on living persons in order to determine whether their intestines contain witchcraft substance. If decisions cannot be reached, or if the problem is too difficult to solve, they may appeal finally to what they call the poison oracle. At considerable difficulty a powdered red poison, known

as benje, is prepared from forest creepers, and under proper ritualistic conditions it is mixed with water and forced into the beaks of domestic fowls, which are compelled to swallow it. A supposedly impartial questioner then addresses the poison as if it were an animate being. Speaking in a respectful tone, the questioner marshals all the evidence, recites the history of the case, and then instructs the fowl to die if the name of the man brought up is in fact a witch. A different fowl is used as each name is mentioned, and, according to Evans-Pritchard, death seems to strike the fowls almost at random.

There are obvious variables, such as the amount of the dose, the strength of the poison, and the age of the chicken, but in practice, these seem irrelevant to whether the chicken lives or dies. The Azande themselves have absolute confidence in the poison oracle but if pressed to explain how it can know who is a witch and who is not, an Azande will simply reply that its soul can see.

Functions of Azande Witchcraft

Despite the generalized anxiety it causes, the operation of witchcraft among the Azande serves ingeniously if not consciously to maintain the social order. It provides an explanation for what would otherwise be unexplainable and hence, potentially disruptive. It also provides a means of dealing with misfortunes that otherwise might produce active conflict. When someone suffers a misfortune he cannot retaliate against the responsible witch, or the person he believes responsible, until he has consulted the oracle and also has received permission from the ruling prince to take action, which calls for acts of expiation from the witch. As long as the accused and the victim observe the established forms of behavior, an incident can be closed without disruptive hostility.

Witchcraft therefore functions to prevent open argument and subsequent social difficulties. It also helps to preserve the stratification of Azande society. Lesser people do not accuse their princely rulers or nobles of witchcraft—matters are so arranged that those who dare to make such accusations pay a severe penalty. But between people of the same level witchcraft serves to maintain equality. Repeated good fortune or the acquisition of more than normal amounts of wealth are often construed as the result of witchcraft; thus, afraid of being called witches, individuals rarely aspire to outdo their neighbors.

Moreover, witchcraft comprises a set of moral judgments. It helps to reinforce ideas of what is good and what bad, and also who is good and who is bad. Because it is the people whose behavior conflicts with the social norms who are most likely to be accused, witchcraft helps make all Azande conform with accepted standards of behavior. Witchcraft tends also to be equated with the sentiments that provoke it, such as envy, greed, and hatred, precisely the sentiments that are socially condemned. A jealous man will be suspected of witchcraft by those of whom he is jealous; so he will try to avoid suspicion by curbing his jealousy. Or alternatively, those of whom he is jealous may be witches and may try to injure him for being jealous; so he will curb his jealousy for fear of being bewitched. Either way, the sanctions against witchcraft act in practice as sanctions against feelings and forms of behavior harmful to the society, and so help to preserve peace and harmony among its members.

RITUAL OF REVERSAL

Religious practices can also serve as a form of safety valve when the norms of everyday behavior are temporarily displaced by behavior that in one way or another reverses the everyday practices. These are called rituals of reversal and are institutionalized ceremonies common to many societies. These reversals range from acts with no evident moral or social significance, such as wearing headgear or other clothing back-

ward, to allowing sexual license, lewdness, obscenity, theft, insults, and assault. Rites of this kind occur on fixed occasions that are often annual events, but they may also occur at funerals or weddings, or be part of still other ritual observances. In some African societies, sons-in-law and mothers-in-law are allowed or expected to insult each other, and commoners deride kings; in other societies, males and females don each other's clothing and perform satirical burlesques of the opposite sex. No world-wide survey has yet been made of the frequency of these customs, but it is clear that they were formerly common at least among many societies of Africa, North America, and India, and in the Western world traces of them remain in the customs of Mardi Gras and Carnival.

As with witchcraft and many other practices of supernaturalism that appear to be socially disruptive, the positive function of rites of reversals is not readily obvious. All these rites, whether morally significant or insignificant, relate to the occasions on which they are performed; their significance otherwise is multiple and varied. Reversals that appear to express social conflict between inferiors and superiors—such as between commoner and king, or wife and husband—have been given the name "rituals of rebellion" by Max Gluckman. These are not acts of anarchic revolt but are orderly events that begin and end at fixed times and follow firm rules. Gluckman interprets them to be acts of symbolic rebellion but not as acts of revolution—they express resentment or hostility against individuals of higher social status, but they do not question the institutions of kingship, marriage, or any other similar feature of the social order. They are thus institutionalized forms of aggression that function as safety valves and, because they end with a return to everyday behavior, as reverse affirmations of standard values. The symbolism of rituals of reversal sometimes very clearly affirms the standard behavior. Among the aboriginal Swazi of Africa, rites in which commoners berated the king ended with a song that is the equivalent of the "Star-Spangled Banner" in the United States.

CYCLICAL AND NONCYCLICAL RITES
Most societies also practice *cyclical rites*, which are intended to help guarantee the performance of events essential to existence. Sometimes the rites are supposed to perform an economic function, to ensure a satisfactory harvest perhaps, or a successful fishing season, and such rites are normally practiced at fixed intervals. When the rites concern economic activities such as farming or hunting, they are often closely connected with seasonal changes and relate to such events as ground breaking, planting, or harvest. American Indians of northwestern America, for example, held first-fruits rites at the beginning of the annual run of salmon, and horticultural tribes of the eastern United States held similar rites when corn was ready for the harvest.

Rites of this sort are of equal importance to all members of the society. Others relate to individuals and are normally noncyclical. The most important are the *rites of passage*, which serve to ease the transition of individuals from one status to another. They were first described and interpreted in a famous work, *Rites of Passage* (1909), by the sociologist Arnold van Gennep. He devoted most of his analysis to rites connected with birth, initiation into adulthood, marriage, and death. Characteristically, as van Gennep noted, these rites fall into three distinguishable segments, which he described as separation, transition, and reincorporation. In each rite, the individual is first separated from his old status, often by being physically isolated in a special room or in a hut set apart from ordinary living quarters. During the period of transition, he must follow behavior that is not customary. Finally, he is returned to normal life in his new status by ritual observances that carry with them the assurance that he is socially accepted in his new position.

Much of the anthropological study of these rites has been aimed at understanding why rites are well developed in some societies and poorly developed in others. The obvious answer lies in the relative importance of the events that are celebrated and the individuals upon whom they center. Almost all societies have rites marking marriage and death. But the degree of their importance or unimportance has not always been obvious, and

Figure 12. Initiation rite in Australia. It is clearly a rite of passage from one status to another, a cultural phenomenon that is characteristically found in most societies. The transition is marked by a period of seclusion and instruction during which the novitiate is removed from profane contacts until a final ritual episode returns him to the living in his new status.

anthropologists have commonly looked to the social order to gain understanding.

Among matrilineal societies, for example, wedding ceremonies are often minor affairs. In these societies, the important kin group consists of matrilineal relatives, and the husband may be economically unimportant to his wife and children. If the marriage does not endure, the social group of mothers, their children, their brothers, and their other matrilineal relatives can continue quite efficiently. Another view, based on the theories of Freud, stresses the correlation, in coming-of-age ceremonies for males, between well-developed rites that include circumcision and other forceful symptoms of change, and the social order that creates during childhood a strong emotional tie between mother and son. This tie would be socially disruptive if allowed to continue, and the principal function of the coming-of-age ceremony is therefore to underline the break between mothers and sons.

RELIGIOUS MOVEMENTS

Religious activity often becomes heightened in societies that are undergoing marked cultural changes and social disruption. Hundreds of primitive societies that have experienced demoralizing contact with European cultures have responded with organized religious movements. These activities have sometimes been accompanied by warfare and nonreligious acts of rebellion against dominance, but they often attempt to improve conditions of life by wholly supernatural means.

Essentially, these religious movements are attempts to marshal the strength of the threatened society, and they have therefore been given the name of *revitalization movements* by Anthony Wallace. Among the most important have been the Ghost Dance movements of the American Indians in California and in the Great Plains during the late nineteenth century, which were highly ritual complexes that, through appeal to the supernatural, sought to bring back the good old days.

Possibly the best known of all revitalization movements are the Cargo cults of Melanesia. Although this name is ordinarily restricted to movements of the twentieth century, similar religious activities go back to the nineteenth century, following the white man's seizure and control of the islands. The greatest development occurred during and after World War II, when contact with soldiers and other bearers of Western culture was intensified. Cargo cults are based on the idea that cargo—the food, clothing, and equipment carried in ships or airplanes—are really gifts of the gods and ancestors who must be influenced to favor man with the desired objects. The Melanesians of these cults have sometimes believed that the cargo is meant for them but is being appropriated by the white man, who changes the addresses of the shipping crates and "lures" planes away from their destination by building irresistibly impressive airfields. The cultists have built pseudo-runways and wooden plane decoys on the mountaintops in an attempt to lure the planes back.

Like other forms of religious movements, the Cargo cults are attempts at self-help, through ritual and the seeking of supernatural intervention, but they also have been regarded as signs of social disruption. Once exposed to the wealth, power, and knowledge of the white colonists, traders, and missionaries, the Melanesians feel overwhelmed and seek instant wealth and parity through magical and religious means.

RELIGION IN ADVANCED SOCIETIES

In the past few decades, the anthropological study of religion has placed increasing emphasis on the functions served by religion in advanced societies. Early in the twentieth century, the German sociologist Max Weber produced a classic study in which he held that a close connection existed between the Protestant ethic and the development of capitalism in the West. This study, like other studies of societies in Japan and Africa, has demonstrated that religion can provide forceful motivation toward material achievement. It is no doubt true that in modern, highly complex societies, religion does not occupy as prominent a place as it does among more primitive societies, such as the Australian aborigines or the people of Melanesia. It is true, also, that belief in the supernatural has declined in modern industrial societies, with their strong emphasis on scientific interpretations of the universe. Still, even in the West very large numbers of people continue to believe in the existence of supernatural beings possessed of more-than-human power. Through membership in certain churches, religion continues to provide social bonds and continues to provide the most widely accepted rationale for moral codes.

Social and Cultural Change

32

What would Thomas Jefferson's reaction be if, restored to life, he were asked to compare Washington, D.C., with the Washington of his own day? At first, he probably would be bewildered by the mass of buildings, the thousands of automobiles, the planes overhead. He would no doubt be confused by the sheer size of the federal buildings and the number of government workers, and he might well wonder what so many thousands of people can find to do.

Still, given Jefferson's intelligence, it is probable that he would quickly comprehend the scene around him. He would perceive that the cars and the planes are merely complex devices for moving men from one place to another, thus performing the same function as the horse. He would recognize that the huge federal bureaucracy is an expansion of the already swelling bureaucracy of his own time, the ultimate realization of his greatest fears. Under the modern trappings, he would surely soon identify the ancient struggles for power between political parties, between State Department and military agencies, between House and Senate, and

between Congress and the Presidency that marked his own period in the White House. And if he were to attend a briefing at the State Department, he would probably grasp quickly that the position of the United States as a world power has really been a progression from his own Louisiana Purchase.

THE PARADOX OF SOCIAL CHANGE

Beneath the radical transformation that has occurred in the United States—or in any other society, for that matter—a fundamental paradox is inevitably imposed by the passing of time: a paradox that combines continuity with change. The rate of change varies enormously. Until recently, some Australian aborigines lived essentially as their ancestors did thousands of years ago, whereas in the past fifty years the rate of technological change in the West has been so rapid that means of production and transportation, of cleaning house and cooking meals, are now changing at a speed once reserved for changes in women's fashions. But, concurrent with any change that may be imposed on a society, there must be some continuing degree of social order. People must be brought together into groups, roles must be assigned to individuals, conflicts must be minimized so that necessary work can be done and existence made somewhat safe, and the entire organization must be cycled so that the ways of one generation can be passed on to the next as part of its survival apparatus.

Change, however widespread and rapid, cannot be chaotic if a society is to survive. For brief moments in history—as in times of revolution—chaos may seem to reign. When regarded in perspective, however, social change can be seen to occur not adventitiously or whimsically but in a regular and patterned way.

EVOLUTIONARY THEORIES

In the fourth century B.C., Aristotle perceived that there seemed to be an order and rhythm in history, and he maintained that societies go through stages of democracy, oligarchy, and tyranny. The theory that history goes through recurrent cycles was also advanced by the fourteenth-century Arab historian Ibn-Khaldun. He found that sedentary, agrarian states were vulnerable to the incursions of nomadic warriors, falling under their sway in periods of dissolution and going through the same cycle of conquest as the warriors settled and became increasingly decadent rulers themselves. There are elements of a similar *cyclical theory* in Gibbon's history of the Roman empire and Toynbee's universal history, and other modern scholars have found that the theory has also applied to the historical relationship between the Chinese and the Mongols.

The exploration of the world that began with the Portuguese voyages of the fifteenth century set the stage for the view that historical changes do not occur in cycles but evolve in an orderly manner from the simple to the more complex. In Africa, Polynesia, and the Americas, people were discovered who lived quite differently from the Europeans of the period. The most striking distinc-

tions were that their technology was in some ways comparatively simple and their social life far less complex. The simplicity of their life style led certain philosophers, notably Jean Jacques Rousseau, to consider these people as living in a state of nature, without government or the amenities of modern civilization—and therefore as representing a way of life that all men must once have lived. Rousseau may have been mistaken about the absence of a civil order, but some anthropologists believe he was right in viewing the societies of contemporary primitive men as approximate relics of life in the past —the essential premise of all the theories of social evolution that were to follow.

Social Evolutionism

In the early nineteenth century, the development of a long-range perspective of human history was encouraged by the rise of the study of organic evolution. The biological theories of evolution did not in themselves spawn social evolutionism (both approaches grew apace in the same period), but they did provide direction for the social theorists. The most famous of the social evolutionists was Lewis Henry Morgan, who in *Ancient Society* outlined what he thought to be the three principal stages of history: savagery, barbarism, and civilization, as was described earlier in the chapter entitled "Developing Sociocultural Views." Morgan worked on the quite modern premise that there are no substantial mental differences between populations that would account for their differing cultures or their relative degrees of advancement. He believed that all human

Figure 2 (left). Christopher Columbus greeting New World aborigines. Figure 3 (below). Portrait of the last Tasmanians. The intrusion of white culture and the ensuing wars and disease contributed to the extinction of nearly 1,200 Tasmanians in less than a century. The last member died in 1888.

institutions evolved in the same order, with each stage having its prerequisite in the preceding stage. Although the details were occasionally altered by particular circumstances, cultural evolution on the whole proceeded onward to its inevitable conclusions. It had a single direction and it went through a single sequence of forms, a *unilinear evolution,* so to speak. Morgan's evolutionary system was essentially a taxonomy that he thought unfolded over time, but his taxonomy—and therefore his evolutionary interpretation—was at fault because it lacked the unifying theory of the dynamics of cultural growth.

Historical Materialism

Morgan's theories were to play an unanticipated part in the development of political thought. Karl Marx read *Ancient Society* with great interest and he and his associate Friedrich Engels used it as the foundation for their *Origin of the Family, Private Property, and the State.* They radically altered the theories Morgan had advanced, however. Morgan had used material criteria for his evolutionary stages but he did not make any effort to argue systematically that these criteria caused the various changes he described. Marx and Engels believed that all the characteristics of a culture are determined by material considerations—principally by its economic organization—and they attempted to fit Morgan's scheme into their theory of historical materialism.

They viewed the early condition of man as one of primitive communism in which each member of a society contributed what he could and received what he needed. The great change, according to Marx and Engels, came with the development of private property, which split societies into classes and ended with the growth of the state as a device, run by the propertied classes, to maintain control over all members of the state. The state, classes, and property were thus not permanent and unalterable but transitory phenomena, constituting what

Marx considered to be the intermediate period of human existence—the product of conflict between different groups. But he believed that this phase would eventually be replaced by a withering away of all government and all divisions among men, leading to a return to the struggle against nature and the pursuit of man's true, individual interests.

The Factor of Borrowing

Theories of unilinear evolution, with their view of social forms unfolding in a universally consistent pattern, fell into disrepute by the end of the nineteenth century. The main problem was they were ideal and arbitrary constructs that could not accommodate the increasing volume of data that was being assembled. The work of Edward Tylor, a contemporary of Morgan, was still fundamentally unilinear but it represented an advance on Morgan's cultural evolutionism. Tylor maintained that society progressed in a unilinear fashion because ideas emerged in a consistent and supposedly natural order, but he also recognized that social evolution did not proceed in a straightforward fashion like biological evolution. Biologically, when a species diverges from its individual line, it can no longer interbreed with other species, and thus one species cannot genetically influence the form of another. But societies continually borrow ideas, techniques, and social patterns from one another. Such borrowing is one of the most important sources of social change, for it enables a society to skip stages of any hypothetical evolutionary process and also to combine institutions that supposedly do not fit together in any ideal, abstract scheme.

The Rise of Functionalism
During the period between the two world wars, the evolutionary perspective was almost totally supplanted, especially in England, by the new developments associated with A. R. Radcliffe-Brown and Bronislaw Malinowski. Radcliffe-Brown, however, paid some deference to evolutionism, following the lead of Emile Durkheim.

In *The Division of Labor*, Durkheim had advanced an evolutionary interpretation of certain aspects of society. He made a distinction between two basic modes for achieving social solidarity. One is found in primitive societies in which the great majority of the people perform similar tasks—hunting, fishing, growing yams, or tending sheep. He described this situation as one of *mechanical solidarity*, by which persons and groups are distinguished from one another by a few basic principles and held together by their essential similarity. Durkheim contrasted primitive societies with more highly developed societies, in which a specialization of labor occurs and people perform many different kinds of jobs. Durkheim described this second means of achieving unity as *organic solidarity*, a phrase intended to draw a comparison between society and an animal organism, in which the various parts of the body are interdependent. The solidarity of society arises from this interdependence; for example, in the United States a doctor, a farmer, an automobile mechanic, and an accountant may all be dependent on the services of one another by virtue of their distinctiveness. In this evolutionary view, societies progressed from a primitive condition of unity based on common beliefs and activities to a more complex condition marked by the development of new interdependent social forms created by an increasing division of labor.

Radcliffe-Brown accepted this view of evolutionism, calling it a process of growth in complexity and gross size of social units. But he was interested more in how the various interdependent and interrelated elements in a society function together as parts of a quasi-organic whole. Unlike the evolutionists concerned with society changing over a period of time (diachronic studies), Radcliffe-Brown focused on society as it exists at any one time (synchronic studies). Malinowski took a somewhat different attitude. He evaluated behavior—hunting, fishing, magic and ritual, family life, building canoes, or raising crops—in terms of what function each form of behavior served in the fulfillment of human needs rather than looking at the functions as parts of an interrelated, organic whole. In its own way, Malinowski's approach was as functional and as synchronic as Radcliffe-Brown's and paid little attention to the element of evolution as a way of interpreting social behavior.

Universal Cultural Evolution
In the United States, evolutionary theory came under attack from a group of historical-minded anthropologists led by Franz Boas, whose views will be considered later.

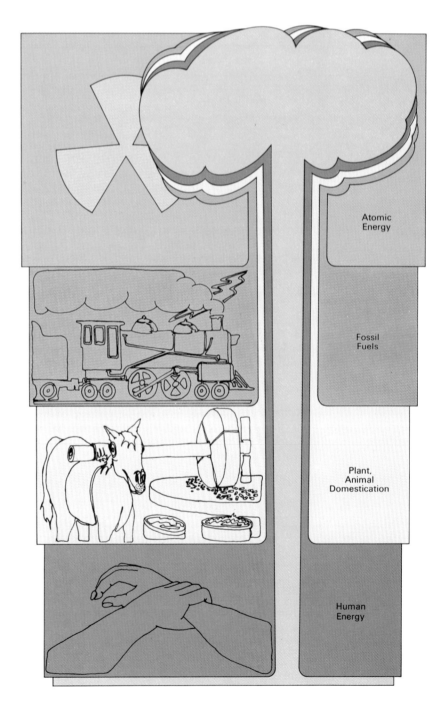

Figure 4. An interpretation of the energy revolution concept, where universal human progress is viewed in terms of an accelerating increase in the amount of energy per capita used. Although some societies may advance technologically more rapidly than others, the element of diffusion works to unify the course of cultural evolution.

Atomic
Energy

Fossil
Fuels

Plant,
Animal
Domestication

Human
Energy

It is enough to say for the moment that their criticism was so effective that theories of social and cultural evolution became respectable again only during the 1940s, largely through the work of Leslie White and Julian Steward.

It is White's emphasis on economic determinants that sets him apart from the older evolutionists. He believes that the critical factor in evolution was man's growing control over forms of energy, measured in terms of productivity and the principal forms of energy used in productive processes. According to White, the major steps in human progress can be associated with the steady improvement in the forms of energy used, starting with simple hunting implements and proceeding through the domestication of plants and animals to control of wind and water power, the steam engine, and, more recently, atomic energy. Each of these moves has been accompanied by increases in productivity, growth in population, evolution of greater social complexity, and more centralized, comprehensive means of social control. These are indeed universal movements, and White's scheme is universal in that it applies not to any particular culture but to human culture viewed as a whole. Periods of retrogression, occasionally referred to as Dark Ages, do occur, but they are only temporary setbacks in the course of man's growing domination of his environment. And despite the fact that some societies progress faster than others, the mechanics of diffusion, or the spread of culture, tend to iron out the differences and so make the course of cultural evolution unitary.

White tends to look upon the course of human progress as an increasing quantity of symbols, knowledge, tools, and techniques, all disembodied from the particular circumstances of time and place. This view reflects his *superorganic* approach to culture, the approach first advanced by Herbert Spencer, later by Emile Durkheim, and most fully by Alfred Kroeber. This approach emphasizes that culture can never be explained merely by biology and psychology. White carried this premise further, arguing that culture causes further changes in culture and that the individual as such is of minimal importance in culture change. The specific events historians see as causes of human behavior are merely manifestations of social transformation. White's evolutionism is thus an interpretation of the development of culture rather than an approach to history as the word "history" is usually understood. The activities of individual people and the influence of their environments may be important for an understanding of the short-range history of a particular society, but cultural evolution is a steady and persistent process that, in both time and space, transcends the finite and ephemeral lives of individuals or even of societies and nations. Human technological advances are inevitable and determined by prior developments. They are not the possessions of certain individuals or societies but are the product and the legacy of all mankind.

White's theories are open to the same kind of charges made against the older evolutionists, for he paints a panorama of human progress extending from the age of stone tools to the advent of nuclear fission. Most anthropologists would accept that technological progress is a condition for the further development of culture, but, putting aside the question of individual creativity, what are the social conditions for technological advance? Why do such advances occur in some societies but not in others, and how does the scheme apply to one specific society when it is stated in terms of general laws that supposedly apply universally?

Multilinear Evolution

Because White's scheme has been thought inadequate for explaining differences between one society and another, many anthropologists have turned to the writings of Steward. He rejects universal or unilineal evolutionism on the grounds that it is an ideal construct that, however handsome, has limited use as a tool of social analysis. In its place, he offers a theory of multilinear evolutionism, which states that social and cultural evolution can take many different directions through a distinctive sequence of institutional forms. There is not, however, a different evolutionary line for each society. Steward believes that a comparison of societies and their history will show that many have gone through the same processes of change induced by similar causes. Essentially, multilinear evolutionism is a method for discerning causality in human affairs.

Like White's, Steward's theory is based on certain ideas about the factors that determine the make-up of different cultures. Whereas White depends on a general concept of energy control, Steward believes that the principal factor lies in the relationship between the natural environment, the society's technology, and the patterns of work. His theory of *cultural ecology* states that the social forms of production in a society are determined by the body of tools and knowledge used to exploit a particular environment. Steward's theory is significant as a theory of causality rather than as an evolutionary scheme. As we have seen, such evolutionary schemes have exhibited a fatal tendency either to overspecify the forms that society took in the past, thereby presenting highly speculative and arbitrary pictures of social evolution, or to be so broad and general as to lack content. White's ideas on energy control and Steward's concept of cultural ecology produced explanatory concepts for the dynamics of development that were lacking in the nineteenth-century formulations, and they provide modern anthropologists with valuable tools for analyzing cultural and social change.

DIFFUSION AND INNOVATION

Many of the early evolutionists attributed the recurrence of customs and institutions among different societies to the fact that these societies had independently reached similar evolutionary stages of development, but obviously this approach to assessing a society's evolutionary status becomes unworkable when the factor of intercultural borrowing is taken into account. One nonevolutionary anthropologist, Ralph Linton, estimated that no more than 10 percent of the cultural items in any society is derived from the inventiveness of its members and that the other 90 percent is borrowed—the result of diffusion.

In a reflection on the "100 percent American," Linton wrote of a day in the life of the average citizen, proud of the "uniqueness" of American society. He awakens in a bed first designed in the Near East and modified in northern Europe before it came to America. He tosses back covers made of cotton (domesticated in India), of wool (from sheep domesticated in the Near East), or of silk (used first in China). Linton goes on to describe the American's clothes (patterned after clothes first used in the Asian steppes) and his shoes (originally from Egyptian leather tanning methods and Mediterranean design).

After dressing, he looks out a window of Egyptian-invented glass to see that it is raining and then puts on overshoes made of rubber, first used by Central American Indians, and takes out an umbrella, invented in Southeast Asia. His breakfast is an international adventure, for he uses Chinese-derived earthenware plates, a medieval Italian fork, a spoon of Roman style, and a knife of steel, first alloyed in India. He eats a Persian-domesticated cantaloupe, drinks coffee that originated in Ethiopia, and eats a boiled egg as well, thanks to the ancient people of Southeast Asia who first domesticated the hen. He then reads the news, printed (German) on paper (Chinese) with a script that is a descendant form of ancient Semitic writing. As he ponders reports from foreign places he will, if he is an upright citizen,

thank a Hebrew deity in an Indo-European language that he is 100 percent American.

The Idea of Culture Circles

One diffusionist theory of universal history was presented by Wilhelm Schmidt and his associates in Germany and Switzerland. According to *Kulturkreislehre* (the study of culture circles), diffusion did not occur through the spread of discrete and isolated customs and artifacts but rather through the transmission of whole bundles, or circles, of items. The items were not shown to be functionally connected with one another, however, and they had the peculiarity of traveling over tremendous distances in the minds of the adherents of the school. For example, one culture circle encompassed West Africa and Indonesia and another united New Guinea and the South American rain forests. The problems of how culture was transmitted over such long distances and of why the circles skipped over the intervening societies did little to dampen the enthusiasm of these scholars, who had substituted hunches and impressions for careful examination.

Synchronous Development

A more cautious approach to culture history had its beginnings in the United States under Franz Boas and his students. They rejected limited inquiry into whether or not diffusion could be stipulated and mapped, favoring instead critical inquiry into how it occurs and what impact borrowing has had on the recipient culture. Boas was well aware that cultural resemblances did not necessarily prove that diffusion had taken place, for it was always possible for societies independently to develop similar artifacts or forms of behavior or social institutions. The Mayan pyramids, for example, need not have been borrowed from Egyptian models. There is, after all, nothing unique about the idea of constructing monuments for religious purposes, and consideration must be given to the fact that, to early builders, the possibili-

Figure 5. Although Thor Heyerdal has established that primitive crafts may have drifted or sailed across the Pacific and Atlantic, most anthropologists, taking into account available cultural, archaeological, and linguistic evidence, consider the pyramid-building civilizations of Egypt and Mesoamerica to have been parallel independent developments.

ties for such construction were limited to very few shapes. In short, there are only a given number of possibilities for the solution of a given problem, and it would place a low premium on human creativity to assume that each invention or cultural innovation could be developed once and only once.

In fact, the occurrences of synchronous yet independent inventions in human history are well documented. Among the more recent were the independent development of calculus by Newton (1671) and Leibnitz (1676), and the biological theory of natural selection by Darwin and Wallace (1858), logarithms by Napier (1614) and Burgi (1620), and photography by Daguerre and Niepce and by Talbot (1839). And it seems indisputable that agriculture was invented independently in the New World and Old World and that there were probably at least three independent centers of domestication in the eastern hemisphere.

Stimulus Diffusion

The diffusion of an idea may be seen as an event that merely accelerated what was already inevitable, just as the time for calculus had come when Leibnitz and Newton invented it. Had they not done so, some other mathematician of the time eventually would have hit upon the idea because the prerequisite mathematical knowledge was already present and the then-current problems in theoretical mechanics made the invention of calculus necessary.

Social institutions, too, can develop independently in similar situations. An example may be found in unilineal descent, which refers to kin groups composed of only relatives traced through the father and his male ancestors and their male descendants (patriliny) or through the mother and her female ancestors and their female descendants (matriliny). It is found most commonly in societies that possess either simple agriculture or a highly productive hunting economy. In such economies, there is usually a certain level of population density combined with a scarcity of natural resources, so that the society involved has a need for some form of corporate grouping to control the rights and duties of individuals and regulate access to resources and political authority. Unilineal descent groups need not invariably appear under these conditions and they may be found under different circumstances; few cultural elements are ever determined by one single cause. Nevertheless, unilineal descent groups generally do tend to be associated with simple agriculture or a highly productive hunting economy, and so the presence or absence of unilineal institutions cannot be explained as a simple result of historical borrowing. They must be functional for the particular culture involved.

Cultures are not infinitely spongelike, and often there are substantial impediments to diffusion. Just as there must be some basis for borrowing in the recipient culture, so also do cultural factors militate against some new element from outside, as many applied anthropologists and others who are working on development programs in the preindustrialized world have found. Birth control programs provide one example of cultural resistance. Most Americans regard limitations on family size as both logical and desirable, largely because of the costs of raising and educating children, and they tend to assume that other people should be equally rational. But in preindustrialized nations, children are often valuable additions to the work force, and a large family may be a source of prestige and political power. A man without sons may be viewed as a poor and weak man, and in some societies birth control is irrational no matter how rational it may seem to outsiders worried about the population explosion.

Syncretism

Even when diffused items are accepted, they commonly undergo transformation of form and meaning that make them acceptable

Figure 6. As a religion is transferred from one cult to another, it becomes, in effect, a new religion that is translated into the cultural idiom of the new converts. All religions bear within them survivals of their ancestral origins. Syncretism, the process that blends imported concepts with native beliefs, is aided by the many parallelisms in religious beliefs of diverse cultures. The elements of the Mundurucú myths on the origin of sex and on the Fall from a work-free Paradise through the violation of tabu are in many ways similar, for example, to the myths of Oceania.

emotionally and intellectually to a borrowing society. This kind of reinterpretation, in which the new and the old become fused, has been given the name "syncretism." The process has been observed wherever diffusion takes place and it constitutes a major factor in culture change. It can be seen, for example, in middle America, where native religious specialists sacrifice chickens in front of Christian crosses placed on top of sacred mountains as part of a ritual to cure the sick. Diffusion is not a simple process of mechanical acceptance of items borrowed from other societies but a dynamic interaction in which new forms are created, incorporating elements both from the borrowing and the giving cultures and producing results that differ from both.

THE MUNDURUCÚ OF BRAZIL

The processes of change can be illustrated by examining how change in one aspect of a culture brings about readjustments in the entire social system. The Mundurucú Indians of Brazil were studied in 1952 and 1953 by the anthropologists Robert and Yolanda Murphy. The Mundurucú live today in the upper reaches of the Tapajós River, one of the southern tributaries of the Amazon River. They have been in contact with colonial Portuguese and later Brazilian society since the end of the eighteenth century, but the remoteness of their homeland has protected them from sudden disruptions of their tradition. Change has been inexorable, but slow and orderly.

At the time of their first contact with the "civilized" world, the Mundurucú were a warlike people whose headhunting forays against other Indians and Portuguese colonials were well known in the Amazon basin. They lived in permanent villages of 250 to 500 people near the headwaters of streams tributary to the Tapajós. These villages consisted of a number of dwellings, occupied by extended families, and a men's house for male-centered rituals. The men's house also served as a dormitory for village bachelors and for newly wed males making the temporary but obligatory "bride service" to their fathers-in-law. Permanent residence after marriage was patrilocal, and the grooms and their brides returned to the groom's father's villages after about a year of service with the bride's father. Each Mundurucú village was the seat of one or more patrilineal clans that were in turn parts of two patrilineal and exogamic groups called moieties, which between them included all the kin groups in the society. Marriages were regulated by this division, which effectively split the society and thus provided reciprocal exchange of women for brides.

The Mundurucú economy was simple but adequate. The men fished and hunted, and the women did most of the farming and all the household work. The men made clearings in the forest for their crops, and the women cultivated and processed the main crop, manioc, into flour and cakes. Garden vegetables were supplemented by wild fruits gathered by both men and women. The division of labor between males and females was otherwise quite strict, and within each sex there was extensive economic cooperation.

Although the Portuguese were at first attacked by the Mundurucú, they soon capitalized on intertribal enmities and enlisted the warriors as mercenaries. As more whites came into the Amazon, this association with the Mundurucú provided the basis for trade relationships. By the mid-nineteenth century, trading for manioc flour and hides was thriving, and with the rubber boom in the latter part of the century, the Mundurucú became part-time rubber tappers. The rubber boom also brought missionaries, and by 1914 a permanent mission staffed by German Catholic priests was established in the area, and in 1941 the Brazilian government had set up a post of the Indian Protection Service. Despite these contacts, the non-Indian population of the upper Tapajós River was still

quite small in the early 1950s. There were a few missionaries, a few Indian Service functionaries, the traders in their scattered stores, and a widely dispersed population of Brazilian rubber tappers. The collapse of the market for wild rubber in 1914 and again at the end of World War II, coupled with the fact that travel into the region could be accomplished only in small boats on a dangerous river, allowed the Mundurucú to maintain a large part of their aboriginal culture almost intact.

Aspects of Diffusion

All Mundurucú villages show the far-reaching effects of diffusion upon their material culture. Trade in hides and rubber provides the Indians with an income that, however small, nevertheless revolutionized their technology. The manufacture and use of stone axes is remembered only remotely, and the clearing of forests for gardens is done today only with steel axes. One can surmise that the greater efficiency of steel axes enabled the Mundurucú to make larger gardens and raise the surplus manioc crops that they traded to the whites over a century ago. The yield from this trade in turn enabled them to buy other items, which further changed their way of life. The inventory of any Mundurucú household also includes steel knives, scissors, and machetes; in fact, not a single cutting tool of aboriginal manufacture can be found. Bows and arrows are still used, but about one-third to one-half of the men own some kind of firearm.

All the Indians own clothes, although they may not wear them continually. Each woman has a cotton slip and dress, and the men have cotton pants and shirts. Until quite recently, women went completely nude and the men dressed in bark belts and genital covers of palm leaf; to this day, most Mundurucú men wear a bark belt and the genital sheath under their shirts and pants. The men now cut their hair in Brazilian style. The women are avid collectors of orna-

ments, perfumes, and whatever finery they acquire from the local whites, but they also paint their bodies with native vegetable dyes and make bracelets and necklaces of local woods and nut shells.

The aboriginal Mundurucú house was oval with bark walls and a steep thatch roof. Today's dwellings display various blends of this style with local Brazilian architecture. The layout of the villages has changed as well, for the dwellings of most Mundurucú settlements now follow a haphazard arrangement unlike the circular village plans of times past. Of the remaining Mundurucú settlements, only six have men's houses. The men's houses are now domitories for *all* the men of the village, however, because no adult males live in the dwellings with their wives and children.

Religion has been affected by the catechization of both the missionaries and pious Brazilians. The Mundurucú, however, show an amazing ability to respond simultaneously to both Christian concepts and their native beliefs, and they also blend them in the process of syncretism. God, for example, is equated with the mythological creator Karusakaibö and Satan with the Yuruparí, a class of malignant forest and water spirits. Biblical stories have been rendered freely into an idiom and setting intelligible to the Mundurucú. The Mundurucú version of the Garden of Eden concerns a man and a woman, Adjun and Eva, who live in a land where there is no work. But there was also no sex in this land until a snake came to Adjun and told him in precise and graphic terms what uses should be made of a woman. Adjun was horrified, for he had been placing medicine on Eva's vagina in the belief that it was a wound. The snake reassured him that sex was harmless and pleasurable, and people have been enjoying it ever since. Sex was thus a splendid innovation. The actual downfall of man has a different theme. In those days, the Mundurucú say, axes worked by themselves, and man did not have to cut down trees to make his gardens. Adjun was warned, however, that he must not look at the axes when they were chopping. His curiosity overcame him and he spied on the axes, whereupon they fell useless to the ground and all the trees turned hard, as they are today. Work was man's condemnation for this transgression, but there is curiously a moral that is in common with the Biblical version—that human misery is promoted by human curiosity and the quest for knowledge, which is perhaps a parable for our times as well.

Effects on Society and Economy

One of the effects of diffusion is the transplanting of tools from culture to culture, a process that may cause profound disturbances in the recipient society. Steel axes and knives, for example, apparently increased agricultural productivity among the Mundurucú, which had further consequences for social life. But it must not be assumed that such an increase is an automatic result of improved tools, for the change depends on the existence of a *need* for food production above the normal requirements of the population. Anthropologists have been able to study the effects of the steel ax in other parts of South America and also in New Guinea, and instances were found in which the time saved in garden clearing was not devoted to making larger gardens but to ceremonial activity or to leisure. The critical element for increased production among the Mundurucú was the existence of outside markets for their crops. The Indians were able to translate their improved efficiency into the superior tools and weapons with which they had become acquainted and which they now sought avidly.

One result of the increased agricultural activity was the heightened importance of female labor. Although historic information for nineteenth-century Mundurucú society is incomplete, it can be hypothesized that fathers grew reluctant to lose their married daughters after the period of bride service because of their contribution in growing manioc and processing it into flour. Moreover, this work requires cooperation among the women, and it may well have been more expedient to keep together a group of women and their daughters, who would be able to work closely together. Whatever actually transpired in this period, the result was a shift from patrilocality to a mode of residence that was predominantly matrilocal. The residential core, formerly a group of males related in the male line, became a group of women related in the female line.

There are still patrilineal clans, but the male members—through whom clan membership is derived—commonly marry women of other villages and move into regular residence with their in-laws. This fractionates and disperses clan membership so thoroughly that a village of a hundred people may include men of from fifteen to twenty clans. The clans today do little more than provide a web of fraternal ties that crosscuts all the Mundurucú villages, for they have little other minimal obvious function. Marriage is still regulated by the moiety division, but kinship and neighborliness no longer overlap. Every Mundurucú now has rather diffuse ties with his fellow villagers and with his clan members in several villages.

Another effect of the change in residence was the shift in function of the men's house to a dormitory for all the adult males rather than just for bachelors and men in bride service. Presumably, bride service simply became indefinitely extended, and the in-marrying males stayed in the men's house as a preferable alternative to the perils and frictions of close contiguity with their in-laws. The arrangement is somewhat unusual, even in the exotic literature of anthropology. It works perfectly well, however, for the men take their principal meals at the men's houses and snack and drink in the dwellings with their wives and children. Sexual rela-

Figure 7. A Mundurucú of the Amazonian basin in Brazil, as he appeared at the time of Robert and Yolanda Murphy's studies in 1952 and 1953. The traditional Mundurucú life way is rapidly becoming altered under economic pressures that arise from their own desires for the marvelous goods of the white man as well as knowledge of new markets in outside cultures.

tions revolve around nothing more complicated than a furtive walk across the village at night or a conjugal stroll in the forest.

It can be argued that influence from the outside world caused the Mundurucú to become a little more different from the Europeans in the case of the men's house and agricultural expansion, but the subsequent trade in wild rubber is forcing a readjustment in the direction of Western society. The exploitation of wild rubber represents an ecological change without modification of the actual physical environment. The collection of rubber from trees was known to the Mundurucú before outside contact, but they had little use for the product. The development of a market for rubber thus changed the trees from occasionally useful parts of the natural setting into an important and scarce resource.

Rubber collecting is essentially solitary work, unlike the cooperative labor in hunting, fishing, and farming. Not only does it individuate work but it forces people to live apart from one another. Because the trees are thinly distributed, one man may exploit a stretch of river valley extending for a few miles upstream and downstream from his house. Some men travel by canoe to more distant rubber tree areas each morning, but the rubber collectors tend to live in single-family isolation or with one or at most two other families.

Most Mundurucú collect rubber along the banks of the larger rivers only during three or four months of the dry season, returning to their villages for the balance of the year. Even for these people, the work separates them from close dependence on the community. They live in small groups for part of the year and exploit a natural resource that becomes, in effect, the private property of the man who works it. If a man decides to devote greater effort to rubber tapping, he usually finds it inconvenient to return to the village and may plant a garden near his rubber-collecting residence. There is thus a steady drift of people from the traditional villages of the interior to life in the small hamlets or single houses located on the larger rivers.

The breakdown of Mundurucú cooperation in labor and of collectivism in ownership of resources is promoted by rubber collection, but it is being promoted by other sources as well. The introduction of the hook and line makes solitary fishing more profitable, and firearms have weakened the need for the cooperation characteristic of bow and arrow hunting. And the Mundurucú no longer must band together for self-defense—or offense— because both depopulation through disease and pacification by the authorities have eliminated warfare. All the essential ties that bound the group together are weakening, and the people know it.

It is inevitable that the Mundurucú will one day lose their traditional community life completely and merge with the backwoods Brazilian population, itself a mixture of European, African, and Indian strains. The grinding force that has led them to this condition has been essentially economic. Their social system is being ground to pieces between their own desires for the new, the efficient, and the gaudy and the restless reach for markets and resources of an insatiable foreign economy.

Change in the Modern World

33 The emergence of the Western industrial and scientific revolutions opened an era in which man's cultures and social orders have changed more rapidly and extensively than in any other period in human history. And the basic processes of culture change—innovation, diffusion, acculturation, cultural growth, and the development of social institutions in response to changing circumstances and needs—are occurring simultaneously throughout the world at an astounding rate. No human group—not even the most remote settlement of Eskimo in Hudson's Bay, the most backward peasant village in India, the Pygmies in the most inaccessible region of the African rain forest—has been able to avoid change. And most people are confused, bewildered, and overwhelmed by processes of change so swift that each succeeding generation appears a stranger to the one that preceded it.

Although contemporary processes of change are unique in many ways, the basic processes and mechanisms of change are the same as those that have occurred throughout history. The changes affecting Mexican peasants moving from rural villages into urban centers can be compared with the changes affecting rural migrants from Nile villages into Cairo. Contemporary urbanization can be measured against the changes that began with rising civilizations in Mesopotamia, Egypt, India, China, and Peru thousands of years ago that first began to attract villagers from the rural hinterlands. Ultimately, such comparative studies reveal the regular processes of change. It is this knowledge that enables the anthropologist to help plan for the future.

RATE OF INNOVATION AND DIFFUSION

Innovation or invention has always occurred in human societies because all men have the ability to innovate, but the *rate* has varied in time and in place as a result of factors that inhibit or encourage inventiveness. Generally speaking, the larger the cultural inventory a society possesses, the more likely its members will create new cultural material. Men are more likely to innovate when they are in effective communication with other members of their society and when they are exposed to ideas from many different cultures. Members of a small, isolated society such as

Figure 2. This graph shows the general trend in the rate of innovation over the course of human existence. Over the long span of hominid evolution, the curve rose only slightly. A point of inflection occurs somewhere about 9000 B.C., with the increase in population following the agricultural "revolution" and subsequent urban development. The exponential acceleration continues toward an unimaginable future. Figure 3 (right). A glimpse into the political and social change that has taken place in China from the beginning of the period of extensive contact with the West. Above, the Old Court. In the center sequence, the capture of Chinkangfoo during the Opium War in 1842; Sun Yat sen; and Chang Kai-shek. Finally, a Chinese Communist rally at Peking.

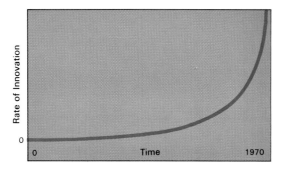

a Pacific island group or an Eskimo village will innovate at a slower average rate than a cosmopolitan citizen of the United States or the Soviet Union. And innovations are more likely to appear during periods of political and social uncertainty than they are in stable societies. Moreover, people are more likely to innovate in societies that are future-oriented and that interpret history as a progressive movement than they are in conservative and past-oriented societies such as traditional Egypt or India.

Under the influence of the Western idea of progress, people everywhere have now come to value change and to look for the ideal society in the future instead of in a past "Golden Age." This value orientation encourages and rewards change. Also, in the contemporary world, the development of transportation and communication facilities such as the airplane, radio, television, and the tremendously increased amount of printed material has given contemporary man access to more cultural materials than ever before, and this has increased the number of new raw materials upon which innovation is based.

Diffusion of cultural elements within a population and the passing of elements between cultures have also been intensified by increased travel and contacts between people and, again, by faster and more effective communications. Several thousand years ago, it took centuries for such innovations as the bow and arrow and pottery to spread; to-day diffusion is almost instantaneous. Paris-dictated dress styles and American popular songs appear almost instantaneously in downtown Tokyo and Hong Kong, and technological advances in German automobiles quickly appear on Japanese automobiles imported into the United States.

THE PROCESS OF ACCULTURATION

Acculturation results from prolonged contact between two societies in which one or both cultures subsequently change. It has been an important feature of culture change throughout man's history, but its pace has accelerated since the fifteenth and sixteenth centuries, when the spread of new cultural materials from Western societies to the non-Western world began in earnest. Because of their superior technology, Western imperialist countries precipitated economic, technological, political, social, and cultural transformation in every country in the world. Non-Western people often became colonies of the dominant Western nations or had their political autonomy seriously compromised. The Western powers used their military and political power to exploit economically the non-Western countries. Exploitation has commonly been accompanied by attitudes of social and cultural superiority, including the notions that Western countries are the most advanced nations in the evolutionary process and all other countries are "backward" or "underdeveloped." Western ethnocentrism frequently has been expressed in racism as well, the implication being that the supposed social and economic backwardness of non-Western societies is due to some biological inferiority. Every other society in the world has had to cope with the threat to its self-respect, cultural pride, and political independence constituted by contact with Western nations.

The story of Western contact with China, although unique in many ways, exemplifies problems commonly experienced by many traditional societies in their efforts to adapt

to Western pressures. The Chinese traditionally considered themselves the only civilized people in the world and were tremendously proud of their cultural achievements. In their initial contact with Western merchants and traders in the fifteenth century, they had assumed a posture of confident superiority. By the mid-nineteenth century, Western pressure increased and the Chinese were defeated repeatedly by European countries, as in the Opium War. They were badly shaken and frantically sought the changes necessary to protect themselves. At first, the Chinese wanted to retain Chinese culture and merely adopt weapons and other useful material

aspects of Western culture. Like people before and after them, however, the Chinese discovered that to adopt Western technology and its accompanying industrial apparatus meant a change in many more aspects of their society.

By the end of the nineteenth century, Chinese reformers attempted to abolish the old Chinese governmental and educational systems and introduce modern Western institutions. The old Chinese dynasty fell in 1912, and under the leadership of Sun Yat-sen the Chinese tried to import Western parliamentary democracy. This alien system could not be grafted onto the ancient

Chinese agrarian bureaucratic society, and during the remainder of the twentieth century China experienced political anarchy and economic disruption. The Chinese were unable to unify their country, and Western countries exploited this weakness, turning China into a semicolonial country. Ultimately, the Chinese Communist movement achieved power in 1949 and, in iconoclastic fashion, finally rejected the old Chinese spirit as they sought to modernize their country with a communist formula adapted to Chinese needs as a blueprint for modernization and development.

The Chinese experience, in general terms, has been repeated hundreds of times by the people of Africa and Asia as they have tried to react to the trauma of Western contact. Some people, including some American Indian tribes, have had their way of life and even their zest for living shattered by Western pressures; still others, including the Indians of California and the Tasmanians, have been annihilated. Most of the people of Asia and Africa lost their independence and were transformed under colonialism. Only a few countries in the world, such as Japan, have been able to change and adapt rapidly enough to protect their independence and meet the Western countries on equal terms. And even the Japanese have had to radically change their culture and their institutions.

One of the important themes of the history of the past fifty years has been the reaction of non-Western people against Western encroachments. Throughout history, when a society is threatened with the destruction of its way of life, *revitalization movements* arise in which people try to create a more viable and meaningful society better adapted to changed circumstances. Among sophisticated societies, revitalization movements have taken such forms as the passive-resistance movement in India led by Mahatma Gandhi. When revitalization movements have taken more violent political overtones, they have become anticolonial revolutionary movements—the Cuban, Chinese, Vietnamese, and Algerian conflicts fall into this category. But in every case, the major aim has been to throw off Western dominance, to revitalize the threatened society, and to make it more suitable to the modern world.

THE PROCESS OF MODERNIZATION

Modernization is a term that refers to the process of change through which traditional societies attempt to adapt themselves politically, economically, and culturally to the requirements of the contemporary world. It is a combination of Western influence with the efforts of the elites of the emerging nations of the "Third World."

Political development refers to attempts by the elite to create new nation-states, usually modeled on those of the West. The new political systems take different forms, depending on the nature of their traditional political institutions and their experience under colonial rule. India's political system, for example, was strongly influenced by the British model. Latin American politics most often take the form of military dictatorships. Still others, such as China, were originally patterned after the Soviet Union's communist state organization but are still in the process of evolving an enduring form of political organization.

A world political system consisting of nation-states and their interrelations is a Western concept. China, for example, had no such notion in their traditional political theory—they were cultural chauvinists but not nationalists. Attempts to build modern states in tribal Africa by combining different tribes under the same national political system have sometimes led to disaster, as witnessed by the civil war in Nigeria and earlier strife in the Congo. Once a state framework has been established, the governments of new nations try to mobilize the citizenry through ideological appeals. Nationalism is the cornerstone of most new ideologies, along with some form of socialism. There are many

problems involved in building a modern nation on a tribal or peasant base that is linguistically and culturally diverse. The political elite are successful to the extent that they are able to erect a new political framework, to mobilize the masses of their populations, and to develop their society in the face of such problems as lack of capital, overpopulation, and lack of education and skills. An important element in their success is in the creation of a modern administrative bureaucracy that can overcome tribal and ethnic loyalties, inefficiency, and corruption that exists in a social milieu where treating people according to who they are and where they stand in society have been traditionally stressed.

The exposure of peasant and tribal people to the material goods and higher living standards of European countries has led to unrest and popular demand for change. *Economic development* is as important as political development to the modernization of societies. It involves the building of a modern industrial and commercial economy with an accompanying growth in per capita income. However, basic changes in the political and social systems are necessary prerequisites to what Walter Rostow called the take-off period of economic development. An entrepreneurial elite, a group capable of leading economic development, must come into existence and guide the process of economic change.

The new elites have various social origins in the different non-Western countries. It was the lower Samurai class that led the economic development of Japan. In China, the entrepreneurial elite consists of government bureaucrats, who may be regaining their position after being discredited during Mao Tse-tung's cultural revolution. And in other countries, entrepreneurs have come from the military or the merchant class. The elite group must raise the social overhead capital to build the transportation, communications, educational, and other facilities necessary as a framework for economic growth. The capital needed for investment in heavy industry comes from foreign aid, commerce, or internal savings squeezed from the peasantries that form the bulk of the population in most emerging nations. If the process goes smoothly, it can lead to a take-off into sustained economic growth and eventually to the economic maturity characteristic of the West and Japan.

The difficulties that developing countries must face in their attempts to modernize are myriad, and failures to attain desired rates of development are at least as common as successes. Overpopulation and a high rate of population growth absorb economic gains as fast as they are made, and available capital is usually insufficient to finance economic growth. The competition from established industrialized nations of the West prevents industrial development or leads to foreign control of industrial enterprises. The failure to modernize rapidly enough leads to discontent and results in political instability, which sets back the process of development even further. All these obstacles have made the road to economic modernization among most Third World countries a rocky one, indeed.

Industrialization, whether introduced by Western capitalists or by indigenous entrepreneurs, has been one of the main forces changing traditional cultures. Everywhere people are leaving their rural villages to find jobs in the industrial and commercial establishments of cities. The peasant of southern Italy migrates into northern Italy and Germany to find jobs, the African tribesman moves from his village to work in the copper mines, and the Indian peasant is forced by limited land and a growing family to seek a job in Bombay or Calcutta. Throughout the world, *urbanization*—the changes in social and cultural patterns resulting from movement into urban milieus—is another force that is changing traditional societies. Traditional cities have always existed in societies in such places as China, India, and West Africa, but with industrialization they change in type as they become centers for new trade and industry and centers of modern Western cultural influences.

Modernization tends to uproot people from their villages and tribes. Although traditional kinship and family ties initially help them find jobs, offer them security, and help if they fail to succeed in the city, ultimately the geographic and social mobility of modern urban society leads to the breakdown of kinship ties, and extended families and small nuclear family patterns characteristic of the West become more common. This pattern of change is aided by the very different economic realities of city life and by attitudes of non-Western people who seek to emulate the more prestigious family patterns of Western societies and reject older kinship and family patterns as "feudal" or old-fashioned.

Yet rural peasant and tribal people play a crucial role in the modernizing of new nations. They ultimately have to be educated in the skills necessary for industrial labor force, and they must be motivated to fill new types of jobs in industry and commerce. In many countries, the capital necessary for industrialization must come from rural peasantries. Rural people are therefore the targets of much propaganda effort by the new governments—exhorted by nationalism and other ideologies to work hard and sacrifice to bring about the modernization of their countries and at the same time asked to change their traditional patterns of life so that they are in accord with modern standards.

Traditional peasant societies in Asia, Africa, the Middle East, and Latin America have been changed beyond recognition. Village communities, once semi-isolated and semi-independent from their wider society, have their independence lessened as modern governmental bureaucracies extend their power and influence down to the local level.

Figure 5. Signs of modernization in the village of Hang Mei, a pattern of change that is affected by the economic influence of city life and by increased knowledge of patterns from the West.

The old cultural diversity of traditional people is lessening as Westernized urban culture extends throughout rural populations. And the old fatalism characteristic of many of the world's peasants is slowly changing as these people find economic opportunity and social and geographic mobility in the world outside their traditional villages.

THE VILLAGE OF HANG MEI

Hang Mei is a village in Hong Kong's rural New Territories, located in one of the last British colonies on the southernmost tip of the Chinese mainland. The ancestors of the Tangs, the lineage of the village, settled in this area as early as the twelfth century, and their descendants have inhabited the village ever since. Until this century, many were peasant farmers growing two crops of rice a year in the favorable tropical climate of southern China. Some of their ancestors passed the imperial civil service examinations at various times in the past and left wealthy ancestral estates, the income from which is still shared by their descendants. The major events of their social life took place in the context of the traditional Chinese extended family that consisted, when economic circumstances permitted, of an old couple together with their married sons and their grandchildren living together under the same roof. For protection and economic support, they relied on their lineage brothers who lived in the same village and in adjoining villages. Much of their life took place within the context of family, lineage, and village. The social horizon of most villagers extended little beyond the nearby market town where they sold their surplus agricultural produce for the few necessary goods, such as silk and oil, that they themselves did not produce.

When the Portuguese established their colony at Macao in the sixteenth century and later when other "foreign devils" began to trade along the southern coast of China, it is likely that the Hang Mei villagers heard about them and it is possible that they even participated in trade, but these possibilities are shrouded in the past. In 1841, after the Chinese defeat in the Opium War established Britain's authority to flood China with the destructive drug, the British forced the Chinese government to cede to them the island of Hong Kong as a secure base from which they could engage in the China trade. As Hong Kong grew in population in the latter part of the nineteenth century and became an important British colony, the villagers of Hang Mei on the mainland thirty miles away must have been increasingly affected by the activities of the colony. Even with its Western culture and its growing commerce, however, Hong Kong did not begin to strongly affect the lives of Hang Mei villagers until 1898. That year, as a result of imperialist wars, Britain forced the Chinese government to lease several hundred square miles of rural Chinese countryside on the mainland to them for a period of ninety-nine years. This area was designated the New Territories. The Tangs and other Chinese villagers, who by this time hated the "foreign devils"—particularly the British for the humiliations they were heaping on their country—raised a peasant force to resist the British takeover of their villages. They had no chance against a trained and disciplined army, and they were defeated and incorporated into the British colony.

In the seventy-odd years since 1898, particularly the years following World War II, the impact of the modern world has affected the villagers with increasing intensity and has drastically transformed the economic, cultural, and social fabric of their lives.

After the British took over the New Territories, they built roads and a railroad out into the rural hinterland of the colony. Eventually, as urban areas of the colony grew in size and as industry and commerce developed, the villagers' economic patterns became changed beyond recognition. Agriculture has become increasingly commercialized, and most village agriculturalists now consider rice cultivation as unprofitable and are growing vegetables for the urban market. They are no longer traditional peasants but farmers who engage in agricultural enterprises as a business and who sell all their produce on the market. Their traditional farm technology, which had not changed basically for a thousand years, is rapidly disappearing. Human and animal manure fertilizers have been replaced by chemical fertilizers from Japan, Germany, and the United States. Modern insecticides have increased vegetable yields, and traditional hand- and foot-operated water wheels have been replaced by gasoline pumps. The farmers can be seen in their vegetable plots, smoking American cigarettes, wearing Panama hats and khaki shorts, and listening to

their Japanese-manufactured transistor radios. Their working lives are totally dominated by their concern with market prices and their activities in the vegetable and pig-raising cooperatives introduced by the Hong Kong government after World War II.

Most of the villagers have abandoned agricultural occupations, working instead in market towns, urban shops, and factories. Young men and women now regularly go to work in the exciting milieu of the city before they marry, and many leave the village permanently. The villagers now working in the urban areas are suburbanites who share many features with Americans who live on the suburban fringes of United States cities. Most of them probably would have taken up permanent residence in the city if it were not for the nearness of their village to the city, the frequent and inexpensive bus service, and the better living conditions they enjoy in the suburbs.

Almost all the villagers, whether vegetable growers or factory workers, now enjoy a much higher standard of living than in traditional times. Increased wealth has enabled them to buy all the gadgets of industrial civilization—radios, sewing machines, clocks, contemporary furniture, and electric fans. In the village stores, they can purchase sanitary napkins, canned goods, and other merchandise imported from all over the world. The clothing styles of the younger generation are almost universally Western in character. And the village now enjoys electricity, running water, and telephones.

The culture of the village is bifurcated into the traditional patterns followed by the older generation and the Westernized urban Chinese patterns adhered to by the younger people. Most young people have received a modern education, and their world view is quite different from their parents'. Some of the young men have collections of Western popular music and wear only Arrow shirts. The entire village, particularly the young people, regularly attend the motion picture

Figure 6. Modernization has often meant Westernization — a trend that may be disturbing or abhorrent to the nationalism that accompanies this process. Tradition may be sacrificed to the need for competence in the wider world in which formerly traditional peoples are now inextricably involved. Apparent assimilation, however, may be tempered by persisting values affecting modes of social relations.

theaters in the market town and see recent Hollywood productions as well as Chinese pictures made in Hong Kong or imported from Communist China.

The young people have gained economic independence from their work outside the family and they have been strongly influenced by Western notions of romantic love. Now they choose their own marriage partners instead of having them chosen by their parents, as was the traditional practice. The village and the lineage have become less important in their lives, and their important ties are now with friends and co-workers outside the community. Many young people are contemptuous of the magical and religious patterns of the older generation. In all these ways, the villagers of Hang Mei have been and are now being affected by the influences of the modern world. Although their experience since 1949 has been quite different from their fellow villagers just two miles away in Communist China, they, too, are proud of the China that has been revitalized by the Communist Revolution in which peasant villagers like themselves played a crucial part. Now they are modern men who meet Westerners on even terms and are no longer ashamed of being Chinese.

No one village can truly represent in microcosm the changes that have taken place in China, let alone all the tribal and peasant villages in the non-Western world. Yet the *kinds* of changes that have been experienced by the villagers of Hang Mei over the past century have been experienced everywhere. The process of change stimulated by the emergence of modern industry and science in western Europe 200 years ago has not yet run its course. Even while Western countries were changing the rest of the world, they themselves have not stood still. The rate of change even in American society, in social and cultural patterns as well as in technology and science, shows no sign of decreasing. Like the Hang Mei villagers of Hong Kong, even Americans are increasingly regarded as strangers by their younger generations.

Contributing Consultants

G. Berreman

H. Bleibtreu

C. L. Brace

R. Braidwood

W. Bright

Gerald Berreman was graduated with honors from the University of Oregon and later received his doctorate in anthropology from Cornell University. His research interests in caste and intergroup relations as well as in sociocultural change have led him to the Aleutians and to India, where he lived among the Paharis and observed their life ways. He is now professor of anthropology at the University of California, Berkeley, and has also served as vice-chairman and acting chairman of the Anthropology Department there. Dr. Berreman also has been president of the Southwestern Anthropological Association and is a member of the Ethics Committee of the American Anthropological Association. He recently was granted a Fulbright-Hays fellowship for advanced research in India on urban organization. He is the author of an ethnographic study, *Hindus of the Himalayas*.

Hermann K. Bleibtreu was awarded his doctorate in anthropology from Harvard University in 1964 and presently is associate professor of anthropology at the University of Arizona. He is editor of *Evolutionary Anthropology*, which is a reader in human biology. Dr. Bleibtreu was co-author of the book *Human Variation* and has published numerous articles in journals in anthropology.

C. Loring Brace, an eminent physical anthropologist at the University of Michigan, was graduated from Williams College and went on to obtain his doctorate in anthropology from Harvard University. He has participated in numerous expeditions into France, Yugoslavia, and East and South Africa. He has authored numerous publications, the most well known of which are *Stages of Evolution* and *Man's Evolution: An Introduction to Physical Anthropology*, the latter being co-authored with M. F. Ashley Montagu. Dr. Brace holds membership in the American Anthropological Association, the American Association of Physical Anthropologists, and the International Association of Biological Anthropologists. He also is a fellow of the American Association for the Advancement of Science and an associate of *Current Anthropology*. For relaxation, Dr. Brace spends some of his free moments in his household's resident zoo, with its collection of more than 175 animals of assorted varieties.

Robert Braidwood, one of the few anthropologists to be elected to the National Academy of Sciences, currently is Oriental Institute Professor of Old World Prehistory and professor in the department of anthropology at the University of Chicago. He was graduated from the University of Michigan and received his doctorate in archaeology from the University of Chicago. Interested in the development of village society in the Old World, Dr. Braidwood has conducted field research in Iran, Turkey, Iraq, and Syria. He is a fellow of the American Academy of Arts and Sciences and the American Philosophical Society. Dr. Braidwood also is a member of the American Anthropology Association, the International Union of Prehistoric and Protohistoric Sciences, and the Conference on Asian Archaeology of New Delhi. He has contributed to several field reports on late prehistoric sites in the Near East, including the Plain of Antioch and Iraqi Kurdistan, is author of *Prehistoric Men*, and coeditor of the authoritative *Courses Toward Urban Life*.

William Bright did his undergraduate and graduate work in general linguistics at the University of California, Berkeley. A grammar of the Karok Indian language of northwestern California· earned him his doctorate in 1955. During the next two years, Dr. Bright taught and conducted research in India that resulted in a grammar of Kanarese. In 1959 he joined the Department of Anthropology at the University of California, Los Angeles, where he is now professor of linguistics and anthropology. He has been abstracts editor and review editor of the *International Journal of American Linguistics*, and since 1966 he has served as editor of *Language*, the journal of the Linguistic Society of America. His continuing interests are in languages of aboriginal America and of India, in ethnolinguistics, and in sociolinguistics.

J. Deetz

R. Carmack

M. Coe

I. DeVore

M. Diaz

Robert Carmack, a professor of anthropology at the University of California, San Diego, holds a doctorate in anthropology from the University of California, Los Angeles. He has received numerous grants to conduct field work, principally in Guatemala, and has participated in the Latin American studies programs for the Peace Corps, the UCLA Latin America Center, and Arizona State University. His interests range from the study of Latin American societies, especially Mexico and Guatemala, to a broader research perspective in social anthropology and in methods and theory in anthropology. Recent and forthcoming publications include monographs on the prehistoric Quiche Maya state and politics in a Guatemalan peasant society. Dr. Carmack is a member of many scholarly societies, including the American Anthropological Association, the Royal Anthropological Institute of Great Britain and Ireland, and the Instituto Nacional de Antropología e Historia de Guatemala.

Michael Coe received his doctorate from Harvard University in 1959. He is professor of anthropology at Yale University. His interests in ethnology have taken him to Taiwan, and his interests in archaeology have led to extensive field research in Mexico, Guatemala, British Honduras, and Costa Rica, and in Tennessee and Wyoming. Dr. Coe, who presently is adviser to the Robert Woods Collection of Pre-Columbian art at Harvard University, has authored numerous authoritative publications derived from his field research, including his books *The Jaguar's Children: Pre-Classic Central Mexico, The Maya,* and *America's First Civilization.*

James Deetz, an anthropologist well known for his authoritative research into the seventeenth-century American colonies, is presently serving as professor of anthropology at Brown University as well as assistant director of Plymouth Plantation. He received his doctorate in anthropology from Harvard University and later went on to do extensive field work in California, the Great Plains, and New England. He is currently interested in archaeological methods and theory and has authored numerous publications, including his book *Invitation to Archaeology* and *The North American Indians,* for which he was coauthor.

Irven DeVore, associate professor of anthropology at Harvard University, was graduated with honors from the University of Texas. In 1962 he received his doctorate in anthropology from the University of Chicago. His interests in primate behavior have taken him twice to the savannas of Kenya, where he has studied the behavior and ecology of baboons. He also has spent several summers in the Kalahari, working among the Bushmen of that region. He is the recipient of several grants and has served on the Advisory Committee on Primate Research Centers for the National Institute of Mental Health. Dr. DeVore currently is consulting for the Danforth Foundation and Education Development Center, and much of his work has been incorporated into a fifth-grade course entitled "Man, A Course of Study." Three of his well-known books include *Primate Behavior: Field Studies of Monkeys and Apes* and *Man the Hunter,* for which he was editor, and *The Primates,* which he coauthored.

May Diaz, an associate professor of anthropology at the University of California at Berkeley, received her doctorate from the same institution in 1961. She has authored several authoritative accounts of peasant societies, including *Tonalá: Conservatism, Responsibility, and Authority in a Mexican Town,* and was coeditor of *Peasant Society: A Reader.* Other works include a paper on the social structure of the Swedish village of the nineteenth century and a related paper on the political process in rural Sweden during that era.

R. Fox

S. Garn

W. Goldschmidt

N. Graburn

Robin Fox was graduated with honors from the University of London in 1953, specializing in social anthropology and social philosophy. He spent two years at Harvard University (which, he claims, was an accident: he meant to go to Cornell and become a philosopher) and in New Mexico, studying the Pueblo Indians. This research led to his doctorate from the University of London and later to his book *The Keresan Bridge: A Problem in Pueblo Ethnology*. After teaching for several years in England, Dr. Fox returned to America and founded the Department of Anthropology at Rutgers, The State University, where he is now chairman of the department. Among his publications are papers on incest, witchcraft and curing, Pueblo baseball, and factionalism, as well as his delightful and authoritative book *Kinship and Marriage: An Anthropological Perspective*. He has appeared frequently in television broadcasts and has given numerous public lectures. He is a member of many scholarly societies and a fellow of the Royal Anthropological Institute, the Zoological Society of London, and the American Anthropological Association. Currently his interests center on the implications of research in animal—particularly primate—behavior for an understanding of human evolution and behavior. For relaxation he enjoys good conversation, some English poets, and the Spanish guitar.

Stanley Garn is a fellow of the Center for Human Growth and Development at the University of Michigan and professor of health development in the school of public health. Educated at Harvard College and Harvard University, and with research training at the Massachusetts Institute of Technology and the Massachusetts General Hospital, he has long investigated the interactions of nutrition and genetics in tissue growth and aging. He has done field work in the Aleutians and in Central America, and has had a major role in nutritional surveys here and abroad. Dr. Garn has published over 350 scientific papers and books, including *Human Races, Culture and the Direction of Human Evolution*, and *Growth and Loss of Cortical Bone*. He is associate editor of *Human Biology*, advisory editor of *Clinical Orthopedics*, past president of the American Association of Physical Anthropologists, and a fellow of numerous other scientific associations. His avocations include the culture of succulents, including *Lithops*, and macrophotography.

Walter Goldschmidt is professor of the Anthropology Department at the University of California, Los Angeles. He was graduated with honors from the University of Texas and later received his doctorate in anthropology at the University of California, Berkeley. His extensive field work in the United States, both of Indian tribes and modern society, Africa, and Europe has formed the basis for his many respected and important publications on culture, society, and human behavior. Among his theoretical and methodological books are: *Comparative Functionalism: An Essay on Anthropological Theory*, *Kambuya's Cattle. The Legacy of an African Herdsman*, and *Man's Way: A Preface to the Study of Human Society*. Dr. Goldschmidt is a past editor of *American Anthropologist* and is now president of the American Ethnological Society as well as director of the Culture and Ecology of East Africa Project. He is also a fellow of the American Anthropological Association, a founding fellow of the African Studies Association, and a member of many other professional societies.

Nelson Graburn was graduated with honors from Cambridge University, England, and went on to study at Canada's McGill University and at the University of Chicago, receiving his doctorate from the latter institution in 1963. Now associate professor of anthropology at the University of California, Berkeley, Dr. Graburn's interests in the Eskimo and Indians of North America have led him to Baffin Island, the Ungava Peninsula, and other regions of the Canadian Arctic. A frequent lecturer on acculturation problems in complex and tribal societies, he has given several papers concerning the effect of the acculturation process on art. He has authored several articles and books, including *Eskimos Without Igloos*.

J. Honigmann

L. Klein

W. LaBarre

C. S. Littleton

D. Mandelbaum

R. Murphy

John Honigmann received his doctorate from Yale University in 1947 and at present is professor of anthropology at the University of North Carolina. He began his field work among the Athapaskan Indians of British Columbia, later doing applied anthropology among the Cree Indians of Ontario. Dr. Honigmann spent two summers at Great Whale River, Quebec, in a study of the Eskimo. Further ethnographic research was conducted in West Pakistan, in England during World War II, and in Austria during the 1960s. In 1963 Dr. Honigmann returned to the upper regions of North America under a National Science Foundation grant, this time to study the Eskimo in the Baffin Island town of Frobisher Bay and later the Athapaskan and Eskimo in the Mackenzie Delta town of Inuvik. His extensive research has led to numerous publications, the most recent being *Personality in Culture* and *Eskimo Townsman.*

Lewis Klein received his master of arts degree in anthropology from the University of California, Berkeley. He presently is acting assistant professor at that institution and is working toward his doctorate. He began his study of spider monkeys at the Fleischaker Zoo in San Francisco and then went on to study their behavior and ecology in their natural habitat. As a result of his field work in the tropical forests of Colombia east of the Andes, he already is contributing important new data to the field of primatology.

Weston LaBarre, an internationally known authority on cultural anthropology, was graduated *summa cum laude* from Princeton and received his doctorate with honors from Yale University in 1937. He has lived twice in South America, twice in the Caribbean, traveled twice across Africa, and lived two years in China, India, and Ceylon, besides living in twenty countries of Europe studying prehistoric caves and ethnographic art. He has also studied fifteen North American Indian tribes. A research intern in the Menninger Clinic, Dr. LaBarre received the Roheim Award "for distinguished contributions to psychoanalysis and the social sciences." During World War II he was a parachuter for the Office of Naval Intelligence and the Office of Strategic Services, and later was attached to the Staffs of Commander Destroyers and Commander-in-Chief, Atlantic Fleet. Now the James B. Duke professor of anthropology at Duke University, he is affiliated with a number of learned societies, here and abroad. He is editor of over fifty books in the *Landmarks in Anthropology* series. He has written six books and over 100 scholarly articles, appearing in seven languages, in both anthropology and psychiatry. His major books are *The Peyote Cult, The Human Animal,* and *The Ghost Dance.*

C. Scott Littleton is associate professor of anthropology and chairman, Department of Sociology and Anthropology, at Occidental College. He received his doctorate in 1965 from the University of California, Los Angeles. A specialist in myth, religion, and folklore, Dr. Littleton has done extensive research in comparative Indo-European mythology. He is also concerned with linguistics and with the extent to which linguistic models can be applied in the analysis of extralinguistic social and cultural phenomena. He is the author of the book *The New Comparative Mythology* and of several articles that have appeared in professional journals. In 1959 he did field research among the immigrant East Indian communities of California.

David Mandelbaum is professor of anthropology at the University of California, Berkeley. He was graduated from Northwestern University and went on to obtain his doctorate in anthropology from Yale University. Dr. Mandelbaum is a recognized authority on the ethnology of South Asia and Southeast Asia. He has been a Fulbright fellow, a Guggenheim fellow, a fellow of the Center of Advanced Studies for the Behavioral Sciences, and a senior fellow of the American Institute for Indian Studies. Among his recent publications are *Society in India* and *The Teaching of Anthropology,* of which he was an editor.

Robert Murphy, chairman of the Department of Anthropology at Columbia University, is a widely recognized authority on the Indians of Brazil. He received his doctorate in anthropology from Columbia University in 1954. He has been a fellow of the Social Science Research Council, a Ford Foundation Area research fellow,

E. Norbeck

J. Potter

J. Robinson

J. Sackett

R. Salisbury

and a Guggenheim fellow. Dr. Murphy's numerous articles in scholarly journals relate primarily to social change and acculturation, kinship systems, and structural theory. Two of his well-known books are *Headhunter's Heritage: Social and Economic Change Among the Munducurú Indians* and *Munducurú Religion.*

Edward Norbeck, a well-known authority on the societies of Japan and Hawaii, is professor of anthropology and sociology at Rice University. He studied Oriental civilizations, languages, and literature at the University of Michigan, receiving his doctorate in anthropology from that institution in 1952. The recipient of numerous research grants, Dr. Norbeck conducted extensive ethnographic field work in Japan for several years, focusing on kinship and social structure, cultural change and evolution, and religious practices and beliefs. He has authored and edited more than seventy-five publications including six books, the most well known of which are his *Religion in Primitive Society* and *The Study of Personality: An Interdisciplinary Approach.* He is a member of many learned societies, including the American Anthropological Association, the American Association for the Advancement of Science, and the Japanese Society for Ethnology. He is listed in numerous biographical books such as *Who's Who in America, American Men of Science,* the *International Directory of Anthropologists,* and *Creative and Successful Personalities of the World.*

Jack Potter was graduated with honors from the University of California, Berkeley, and, following graduate work in anthropology at the University of Chicago, went on to obtain his doctorate in anthropology at Berkeley. He is the recipient of a Woodrow Wilson National Fellowship and a Ford Foundation Foreign Area Training Fellowship. During the period from 1961 to 1963, Dr. Potter did extensive field work in Hong Kong's New Territories, which is described in his book *Capitalism and the Chinese Peasant: Social and Economic Change in a Hong Kong Village.* Presently he is associate professor of the Anthropology Department at the University of California, Berkeley.

John Robinson received his doctorate in zoology from the University of Capetown, South Africa, and shortly thereafter became scientific assistant to the vertebrate paleontologist Robert Broom of the Transvaal Museum, Pretoria. During his field work, which began under Broom's guidance, he helped recover more than 300 australopithecine specimens and a few specimens of *Homo erectus* as well as the first stone industry found in situ with very ancient hominid remains. He was assistant director of the Transvaal Museum until 1963. He became professor of anthropology and zoology at the University of Wisconsin in 1967. Dr. Robinson is a past president of the South Africa Biological Society and was a founder of the South African Museum of Science and Industry, later becoming a member of its board of trustees. He has published over ninety scientific papers and books.

James Sackett attended Lawrence College in Wisconsin as an undergraduate and received his doctorate in anthropology from Harvard University. His continuing interest in paleolithic archaeology has led to field work primarily in France. At present Dr. Sackett is an associate professor of anthropology at the University of California at Los Angeles. He has been the recipient of foundation awards and has published many articles in scholarly journals.

Richard Salisbury is chairman of the Department of Sociology and Anthropology at McGill University in Canada. He studied at Cambridge University in England, where he was an open scholar and a Strathcona research scholar, and at Harvard University and the Australian National University, receiving his doctorate from the latter institution in 1957. Dr. Salisbury has spent several years in New Guinea and Guyana, studying the Siane, Tolai, and Wapisiana tribes and more recently the Bougainville copper and Mackenzie bauxite mines there. He has served as president of the Northeastern Anthropological Association and presently is president of the Canadian Sociology and Anthropology Association, and he is a member of the International Editorial Advisory Board for the journal *Ethnology* and of the Social Science Research Council of Canada, as well as many other scholarly associations. Dr. Salisbury has published numerous authoritative articles and books, the most recent of which is *Vunamami: Economic Transformation in a Traditional Society.*

T. Schwartz

E. Service

E. Simons

J. Steward

W. Sturtervant

Theodore Schwartz was graduated from Temple University and went on to obtain his doctorate from the University of Pennsylvania in 1958. In 1953 and 1954, he did field research among the Manus and other people of the Admiralty Islands of Melanesia. His authoritative monograph on Cargo cults, *The Paliau Movement in the Admiralty Islands*, appeared in 1962. Dr. Schwartz taught at the University of Michigan and the University of Chicago and was a research fellow of the American Museum of Natural History. From 1958 to 1961, he and his wife, Dr. Lola Romanucci Schwartz, carried out a study of a Mexican village. Following this field work, he spent two years as a postdoctoral fellow at the University of Paris and then returned to the Admiralty Islands for more than three years of further field work. During this time, Dr. Schwartz made several trips into the remote and relatively unacculturated regions of New Guinea. Since 1966, he has been senior specialist at the East West Center of the University of Hawaii, has taught at the University of California, Los Angeles, and is now associate professor of anthropology at the University of California, San Diego.

Elman Service, well known for his ethnological field work in Paraguay, Mexico, and the American Southwest, presently is professor of anthropology at the University of California, Santa Barbara. He was graduated from the University of Michigan and went on to study at the University of Chicago and Columbia University, receiving his doctorate from the latter institution in 1950. Several of his authoritative books are *Cultural Evolutionism: Theory in Practice*, *The Hunters*, *Profiles in Ethnology*, and *Tobati: Paraguayan Town*.

Elwyn Simons, one of the outstanding authorities on human paleontology, is professor of geology at Yale University and curator of vertebrate paleontology for the Peabody Museum. Dr. Simons was graduated from Rice University and later received his doctorate from Princeton University. Awarded a Marshall scholarship, he went on to study at Oxford University, England, and received a doctor of philosophy degree from that institution. Dr. Simons has led numerous expeditions into regions of Wyoming, collecting deposits representative of the Paleocene and

Eocene epochs, and has recovered deposits from field sites in England, France, Spain, Egypt, Arabia, East Africa, and India. He has written numerous important articles for scholarly journals, dealing primarily with the primates of all epochs of the Tertiary. He was assisted in the preparation of his contribution to this book by Ian Tattersal and Peter Ettel, graduate students at Yale University.

Julian Steward, a figure of international stature in cultural anthropology, has recently retired from the University of Illinois. He was elected to the National Academy of Science and was chosen to membership in the Center for Advanced Study, University of Illinois. He received his doctorate in anthropology at the University of California, Berkeley, in 1929. Between 1926 and 1938 he did field research among the Shoshonean Indians of the Great Basin, the Hopi, the Carrier, and several other North American tribes. During these years he developed the concept of cultural ecology. Subsequently, as a member of the Bureau of American Ethnology, Smithsonian Institution, he founded the Institute of Social Anthropology, whose staff conducted cooperative research in Mexico, Colombia, Peru, and Brazil. Meanwhile, he edited the seven-volume *Handbook of South American Indians*. He conducted research on contemporary Puerto Rico while on the staff of Columbia University and as a member of the staff at the University of Illinois, he directed comparative studies of recent culture change in Africa, East Asia, and Latin America. One of his major works, *Theory of Culture Change: the Methodology of Multilinear Evolution*, which sets forth recurrent cross-cultural regularities in cultural evolution, was honored with the Viking Fund Medal, the American Anthropological Association's top award.

William Sturtevant is curator of North American anthropology in the Smithsonian Institution. He was graduated from the University of California, Berkeley, and went on to receive his doctorate from Yale University in 1955. He has done field work in Burma and in various eastern North American Indian communities, and his current interests are still centered on the ways of life of the latter people. He holds membership in various professional societies and is author of several important publications, including "Studies in Ethnoscience" in *The American*

M. Swartz

B. Trigger

C. Valentine

R. Woodbury

Anthropologist; Significance of Ethnological Similarities Between Southeastern North America and the Antilles; and "Spanish-Indian Relations in Southeastern North America" and "Anthropology, History, and Ethnohistory," both articles appearing in the journal *Ethnohistory.*

Marc Swartz studied at Washington University, St. Louis, and received his doctorate from Harvard in 1958. His first field work was a study of the race riots in Cicero, Illinois, in 1952. His next field research took place in Truk Atoll in Micronesia, where he did a study of behavior among kinsmen. This latter research formed the basis of his doctoral dissertation and a number of articles in various anthropological journals. Dr. Swartz also worked among the Bena of southwestern Tanzania, studying social organization, village politics, and cultural dynamics. The results of this study have been published in a series of articles and in two books he edited, *Political Anthropology* (with Victor W. Turner and A. Tuden) and *Local Level Politics.* His current research interests continue in the areas of politics, kinship, social organization, and cultural dynamics. Dr. Swartz is currently professor of anthropology at the University of California, San Diego. He was a student fellow of the Social Science Research Council and project director for the National Institutes of Health. He is a fellow of the American Anthropological Association, the Royal Anthropological Institute, the African Studies Association, and the African Studies Association of the United Kingdom.

Bruce Trigger is professor of anthropology at McGill University, in Canada. He obtained his bachelor's degree from the University of Toronto and his doctorate in anthropology from Yale University. His publications include four books, *History and Settlement in Lower Nubia, The Late Nubian Settlement at Arminna West, Beyond History: The Methods of Prehistory,* and *The Huron: Farmers of the North,* as well as numerous articles dealing with Sudanese prehistory, Iroquoian ethnohistory, and archaeological theory. He is a fellow of the Royal Anthropological Institute, the American Anthropological Association, and Sigma Xi.

Charles Valentine, research professor of anthropology at Washington University, studied at the University of Pennsylvania and received his doctorate in anthropology from that institution in 1958. He was the recipient of both a Fulbright scholarship to the Australian National University and a Mellon postdoctoral fellowship to the University of Pittsburgh. His interest in intergroup relations and culture change led to field work in New Guinea and later to research in the black community of Seattle, Washington. For the past ten years, Dr. Valentine has been a participant-observer within the American civil rights movement and recently has been studying intergroup relations and social change in the northern urban United States. He has contributed numerous articles to scholarly journals and is the author of the book *Culture and Poverty* and of the chapter "Making the Scene, Digging the Action, and Telling It Like It Is" in the book *Afro-American Anthropology.* He is a fellow of the American Anthropological Association and a member of the American Association for the Advancement of Science.

Richard Woodbury, one of the prominent figures in American archaeology, is professor and chairman of the Department of Anthropology at the University of Massachusetts. He was graduated with honors from Harvard University, did graduate work at Columbia University, and received his doctorate from Harvard. He has participated in numerous archaeological expeditions in Guatemala, Mexico, and throughout the United States, studying prehistoric human ecology, primitive farming, and water control in arid lands. Dr. Woodbury recently was curator of North American anthropology of the Smithsonian Office of Anthropology. He has published over 100 authoritative books and papers, including *Societies Around the World, The Ruins of Zaculeu, Guatemala,* and "Archaeology: The Field," in the *International Encyclopedia of the Social Sciences.* Currently he is editor for the New World, *American Journal of Archaeology,* and is a former editor of *American Antiquity.* He is listed in *American Men of Science, Who's Who in America,* and the *Dictionary of International Biography.*

Selected Bibliography

1

Beals, Ralph L., and Harry Hoijer. *An Introduction to Anthropology*. 3rd ed. New York: Macmillan, 1965.

Cohen, Yehudi A. (ed.). *Man in Adaptation*. 2 vols. Chicago: Aldine, 1968.

Fried, Morton H. (ed.). *Readings in Anthropology*. 2nd ed. 2 vols. New York: Crowell, 1968.

Gajdusek, D. C., and Vincent Ziga. "Kuru: Clinical, Pathological, and Epidemiological Study of an Acute, Progressive, Degenerative Disease of the Central Nervous System Among the Natives of the Eastern Highlands of New Guinea," *American Journal of Medicine*, Vol. 26 (1959).

Hammond, Peter B. (ed.). *Cultural and Social Anthropology: Selected Readings*. New York: Macmillan, 1964.

———. *Physical Anthropology and Archaeology: Selected Readings*. New York: Macmillan, 1964.

Hoebel, E. Adamson. *Anthropology*. 3rd ed. New York: McGraw-Hill, 1966.

Keesing, Felix M. *Cultural Anthropology: The Science of Custom*. New York: Holt, Rinehart and Winston, 1958.

Kroeber, Alfred L. *Anthropology: Race, Language, Culture, Psychology, Prehistory*. Rev. ed. New York: Harcourt, Brace & World, 1948.

Kroeber, Alfred L., and T. T. Waterman (eds.). *Source Book in Anthropology*. New York: Johnson Reprint Corporation, 1965.

LaBarre, Weston. *The Human Animal*. Chicago: Phoenix Books, 1968.

Titiev, Mischa. *The Science of Man*. New York: Holt, Rinehart and Winston, 1954.

———. *Introduction to Cultural Anthropology*. New York: Holt, Rinehart and Winston, 1959.

Wasson, R. Gordan. *Soma: Divine Mushroom of Immortality*. New York: Harcourt, Brace & World, 1968.

2

Black, Davidson. "Sinanthropus pekinesis," *Science*, New Series Vol. 69 (June 1929).

Boas, Franz. *The Mind of Primitive Man*. New York: Macmillan, 1911.

Brace, C. L., and Ashley Montagu. *Man's Evolution: An Introduction to Physical Anthropology*. New York: Macmillan, 1965.

Darwin, Charles. *On the Origin of Species*. Cambridge, Mass.: Harvard University Press, 1964.

Dubois, Eugene. *Pithecanthropus erectus, eine Menschenahnliche Ubergangsform von Java*. Djakarta: Landes Druckerei, 1894.

Hulse, Frederick. *The Human Species*. New York: Random House, 1963.

Leakey, L. S. B., P. V. Tobias, and J. R. Napier. "A New Species of the Genus Homo from Olduvai Gorge," *Nature*, Vol. 202 (1964).

Leakey, Richard. "In Search of Man's Past at Lake Rudolf," *National Geographic*, Vol. 137 (1970).

Lyell, Charles. *The Geological Evidences of the Antiquity of Man*. London: Murray, 1863.

Schaller, George. *The Year of the Gorilla*. Chicago: University of Chicago Press, 1964.

Schoetensack, Otto. *Der Unterkiefer des Homo heidelbergensis aus den Sanden von Mauer bei Heidelberg*. Leipzig: n. pub., 1908.

Van Lawick-Goodall, Jane. *My Friends, the Wild Chimpanzees*. Washington, D.C.: National Geographic Society, 1967.

3

Benedict, Ruth. *Patterns of Culture*. Boston: Houghton Mifflin, 1959.

Chomsky, Noam. *Language and Mind*. New York: Harcourt, Brace & World, 1968.

Conklin, Harold. *Hanunoó-English Vocabulary*. Berkeley: University of California Press, 1953.

Durkheim, Emile. *The Division of Labor in Society*. G. Simpson (tr.). New York: Macmillan, 1933.

Freud, Sigmund. *Totem and Taboo*. James Strachey (tr.). New York: Norton, 1950.

Goodenough, Ward. "Cultural Anthropology and Linguistics," in D. Hymes (ed.), *Language in Culture and Society*. New York: Harper & Row, 1964.

Harris, Marvin. *The Rise of Anthropological Theory*. New York: Crowell, 1968.

Harris, Zellig. *Mathematical Structures of Language*. New York: Interscience Publishers, 1968.

Kroeber, Alfred L., and Clyde Kluckhohn. *Culture: A Critical Review of Concept and Definitions*. Cambridge, Mass.: Harvard University Press, 1952.

Kroeber, Alfred L., and Talcott Parsons. "The Concept of Culture and of Social System," *American Sociological Review*, Vol. 23 (1958).

Lévi-Strauss, Claude. *Structural Anthropology*. C. Jacobson (tr.). New York: Basic Books, 1963.

Littleton, C. Scott. *The New Comparative Mythology: An Anthropological Assessment of the Theories of Georges Dumezil*. Berkeley and Los Angeles: University of California Press, 1966.

Lounsbury, Floyd. "A Formal Account of Crow and Omaha-Type Kinship Technologies," in Ward Goodenough (ed.), *Explorations in Cultural Anthropology*. New York: McGraw-Hill, 1964.

Malinowski, Bronislaw. *Argonauts of the Western Pacific*. New York: Dutton, 1922.

Radcliffe-Brown, A. R. *Structure and Function in Primitive Society*. New York: Free Press, 1965.

Redfield, Robert. "The Folk Society," *The American Journal of Sociology*, Vol. 52 (1947).

Rousseau, Jean Jacques. *The Social Contract*. G. D. H. Cole (tr.). New York: Dutton, 1938.

Steward, Julian H. *Theory of Culture Change*. Urbana: University of Illinois Press, 1955.

Thomsen, Christian. *A Guide to Northern Antiquities*. London: n.pub., 1848.

Tylor, Edward Burnett. *Primitive Culture*. 7th ed. New York: Brentano's, 1924.

Wallace, Anthony. *Culture and Personality*. New York: Random House, 1961.

Weidenreich, Franz. *Apes, Giants, and Man*. Chicago: University of Chicago Press, 1946.

White, Leslie A. *The Evolution of Culture*. New York: McGraw-Hill, 1959.

4

Binford, L. R., and S. R. Binford. *New Perspectives in Archeology*. Chicago: Aldine, 1968.

Clark, J. G. D. *Archaeology and Society: Reconstructing the Prehistoric Past*. New York: Barnes & Noble, 1960.

Deetz, James. *Invitation to Archaeology*. New York: National History Press, 1967.

———. *The Dynamics of Stylistic Change in Arikara Ceramics*. Urbana: University of Illinois Press, 1965.

Dorsey, George. *Traditions of the Arikara*. Washington D.C.: Carnegie Institution of Washington, 1904.

Heizer, Robert F. *A Guide to Archaeological Field Methods*. Palo Alto, Calif.: National Press, 1958.

Heizer, Robert F., and Frank Hole. *An Introduction to Prehistoric Archeology*. New York: Holt, Rinehart and Winston, 1965.

Taylor, Walter W. *A Study of Archeology*. Carbondale: Southern Illinois University Press, 1967.

Wheeler, R. E. M. *Archaeology from the Earth*. New York: Pelican, 1956.

5

Carpenter, C. R. *Naturalistic Behavior of Nonhuman Primates*. University Park: Pennsylvania State University Press, 1964.

DeVore, Irven (ed.). *Primate Behavior: Field Studies of Monkeys and Apes*. New York: Holt, Rinehart and Winston, 1965.

Eimerl, Sarel, and Irven DeVore. *The Primates*. New York: Time-Life, 1965.

Eisenberg, J. F., and Robert Kuehn. "The Behavior of *Ateles Geoffroyi* and Related Species," *Smithsonian Miscellaneous Collections*, Vol. 151 (1966).

Jay, Phyllis C. (ed.). *Primates: Studies in Adaptation and Variability*. New York: Holt, Rinehart and Winston, 1968.

Morris, Desmond (ed.). *Primate Ethology*. Chicago: Aldine, 1967.

Southwick, Charles H. (ed.). *Primate Social Behavior*. Princeton, N.J.: Van Nostrand, 1963.

Wagner, H. O. "Freilandbeobachtungen an Klammeraffen," *Zeit. f. Tierpsychol.* Vol. 13 (1956).

6

Berger, Peter L. *Invitation to Sociology: A Humanistic Perspective*. Garden City, N.Y.: Doubleday, 1963.

Evans-Pritchard, E. E. *The Nuer*. New York: Oxford University Press, 1940.

Firth, Raymond. *We, the Tikopia*. London: Allen and Unwin, 1936.

Osgood, Cornelius. *Ingalik Material Culture*. New York: Oxford University Press, 1940.

Shils, Edward A. "Social Inquiry and the Autonomy of the Individual," in D. Lerner (ed.), *The Human Meaning of the Social Sciences*. New York: Meridian Books, 1959.

Whorf, Benjamin Lee. *Language, Thought and Reality: Selected Writings of Benjamin Lee Whorf*. John B. Carroll (ed.). Cambridge, Mass.: MIT Press, 1956.

7

Benton, Michael (ed.). *The Social Anthropology of Complex Societies*. New York: Praeger, 1966.

Berger, Bennett M. "Soul Searching: Review of Urban Blues by Charles Keil," *Trans-Action*, Vol. 4 (1967).

Blauner, Robert. "Black Culture: Myth or Reality," in Norman E. Whitten and John Szwed (eds.), *Afro-American Anthropology: Contemporary Perspectives*. New York: Free Press, 1970.

Cleaver, Eldridge. *Soul on Ice*. New York: McGraw-Hill, 1968.

———. *Eldridge Cleaver: Post-Prison Writings and Speeches*. New York: Random House, 1969.

Ellison, Ralph. *Shadow and Act*. New York: Random House, 1964.

Glazer, Nathan, and Daniel P. Moynihan. *Beyond the Melting Pot: The Negroes, Puerto Ricans, Jews, Italians, and Irish of New York City*. Cambridge, Mass.: MIT and Harvard University Press, 1963.

Gluckman, Max,, and Fred Eggan. "Introduction," in Michael Banton (ed.), *The Social Anthropology of Complex Societies*. New York: Praeger, 1966.

Hannerz, Ulf. *Soulside: Inquiries into Ghetto Culture and Community*. Stockholm: Almqvist and Wiksell, 1969.

Johnson, Norman J., and Peggy R. Sanday. *Cultural Variations in an Urban Poor Population*. Carnegie-Mellon Action Project, Research Report 1.

Keiser, R. Lincoln. *The Vice Lords: Warriors of the Streets.* New York: Holt, Rinehart and Winston, 1969.

Leacock, Eleanor (ed.). *The Culture of Poverty: A Critique.* New York: Simon and Schuster, 1970.

Lewis, Oscar. *La Vida: A Puerto Rican Family in the Culture of Poverty—San Juan and New York.* New York: Random House, 1966.

Liebow, Elliot. *Tally's Corner; A Study of Negro Street Corner Men.* Boston: Little, Brown, 1967.

Mitchell, J. Clyde. "Theoretical Orientations in African Urban Studies," in Michael Banton (ed.), *The Social Anthropology of Complex Societies.* New York: Praeger, 1966.

Schulz, David A. *Coming Up Black: Patterns of Ghetto Socialization.* Englewood Cliffs, N.J.: Prentice-Hall, 1969.

Stewart, William. "Nonstandard Speech Patterns," *Baltimore Bulletin of Education,* Vol. 43 (1966).

Suttles, Gerald D. *The Social Order of the Slum: Ethnicity and Territory in the Inner City.* Chicago: University of Chicago Press, 1968.

Valentine, Charles A. *Culture and Poverty: Critique and Counterproposals.* Chicago: University of Chicago Press, 1968.

————. *The Deficit Model of Afro-American Psychology as a Self-Fulfilling Prophecy in Externally Controlled Ghetto Institutions.* Paper presented at the Annual Meetings of the American Psychological Association (1969).

Valentine, Charles A., and Betty Lou Valentine. *Ethnographic Study of Complex Sociocultural Fields from Multiple Participant-Observational Perspectives.* Paper presented at the Annual Meetings of the American Anthropological Association (1969).

Whitten, Norman E., and John Szwed (eds.). *Afro-American Anthropology: Contemporary Perspectives.* New York: Free Press, 1970.

Wolfe, Alvin, et al. "The Soulard Area: Adaptations by Urban White Families to Poverty," mimeographed. St. Louis: Washington University, 1968.

8

Bleibtreu, Hermann K. *Evolutionary Anthropology: A Reader in Human Biology.* Boston: Allyn & Bacon, 1967.

Brace, C. L., and M. F. Ashley Montagu. *Man's Evolution: An Introduction to Physical Anthropology.* New York: Macmillan, 1965.

Buettner-Janusch, John. *Origins of Man.* New York: Wiley, 1966.

Cohen, Yehudi A. *Man in Adaptation.* 2 vols. Chicago: Aldine, 1968.

Downs, James F., and Hermann K. Bleibtreu. *Human Variation: An Introduction to Physical Anthropology.* Beverly Hills, Calif.: Glencoe Press, 1969.

Fried, Morton H. *Readings in Anthropology.* 2nd ed. New York: Crowell, 1968. Vol. I.

Hammond, Peter B. *Physical Anthropology and Archaeology: Selected Readings.* New York: Macmillan, 1964.

Harrison, G. A., J. S. Weiner, J. M. Tanner, and N. A. Barnicot. *Human Biology: An Introduction to Human Evolution, Variation and Growth.* Oxford, England: Clarendon, 1964.

Hulse, Frederick S. *The Human Species: An Introduction to Physical Anthropology.* New York: Random House, 1963.

Korn, Noel, and Fred W. Thompson. *Human Evolution: Readings in Physical Anthropology.* 2nd ed. New York: Holt, Rinehart and Winston, 1967.

Kraus, Bertram S. *The Basis of Human Evolution.* New York: Harper & Row, 1964.

Lasker, Gabriel Ward. *The Evolution of Man.* New York: Holt, Rinehart and Winston, 1961.

Laughlin, W. S., and R. H. Osborne. *Human Variation and Origins: An Introduction to Human Biology and Evolution.* San Francisco: Freeman, 1949.

McKern, Thomas W. *Readings in Physical Anthropology.* Englewood Cliffs, N.J.: Prentice-Hall, 1966.

Sheldon, W. H., S. S. Stevens, and W. B. Tucker. *The Varieties of Human Physique.* New York: Hafner, 1940.

Simpson, G. G. *Life of the Past.* New Haven, Conn.: Yale University Press, 1953.

9

Altmann, Stuart A. (ed.). *Social Communication Among Primates.* Chicago: University of Chicago Press, 1967.

Buettner-Janusch, John, et al. "The Relatives of Man: Modern Studies of the Relation of the Evolution of Nonhuman Primates to Human Evolution," *Annals,* Vol. 102 (1962).

Harrison, Barbara. *Orang-Utan.* London: Collins, 1962.

Imanishi, Kinji, and Stuart A. Altmann (eds.). *Japanese Monkeys.* Edmonton, Alberta, Canada: Stuart A. Altmann, 1965.

Jolly, Allison. *Lemur Behavior.* Chicago: University of Chicago Press, 1966.

Kummer, Hans. *Social Organization of Hamadryas Baboons: A Field Study.* Chicago: University of Chicago Press, 1968.

Napier, J. R., and N. A. Barnicot (eds.). *The Primates.* The Proceedings of the Symposium of the Zoological Society of London, No. 10. London: The Society, 1963.

Napier, J. R., and P. H. Napier. *A Handbook of Living Primates.* New York: Academic Press, 1967.

Reynolds, Vernon. *The Apes.* New York: Dutton, 1967.

————. *Budongo, An African Forest and Its Chimpanzees.* Garden City, N.Y.: Natural History Press, 1965.

Schaller, George B. *The Year of the Gorilla.* Chicago: University of Chicago Press, 1964.

————. *The Mountain Gorilla: Ecology and Behavior.* Chicago: University of Chicago Press, 1963.

Schrier, Allan M., Harry F. Harlow, and Fred Stollnitz (eds.). *Behavior of Nonhuman Primates: Modern Research Trends.* 2 vols. New York: Academic Press, 1965.

Starck, D., R. Schneider, and J. J. Kuhn (eds.). *Neue Ergebnisse der Primatologie.* Stuttgart, Germany: Gustav Fischer Verlag, 1967.

Van Lawick-Goodall, Jane. "The Behavior of Free-Living Chimpanzees in the Gombe Stream Reserve," in J. M. Cullen and C. G. Beer (eds.), *Animal Behaviour*. London: Bailliere, Tindal and Cassell, 1968. Part III, Vol. I.

———. *My Friend, the Wild Chimpanzees*. Washington, D.C.: National Geographic Society, 1967.

Washburn, S. L., Phyllis C. Jay, and Jane B. Lancaster. "Field Studies of Old World Monkeys and Apes," *Science*, New Series Vol. 150 (1965).

10

Clark, W. E. Le Gros. *History of the Primates: An Introduction to the Study of Fossil Man*. 5th ed. Chicago: University of Chicago Press, 1966.

Black, Davidson. *Fossil Man in China*. China Geological Survey Memoir Series A, no. 11, 1933.

Broom, Robert. *Finding the Missing Link*. 2nd ed. London: Watts, 1951.

Napier, J. R., and P. H. Napier. *A Handbook of Living Primates*. New York: Academic Press, 1967.

Simons, E. L. "A Critical Reappraisal of Tertiary Primates," in John Buettner-Janusch (ed.), *Evolutionary and Genetic Biology of the Primates*. New York, Academic Press, 1963. Vol. I.

———. "The Early Apes," *Scientific American*, Vol. 217 (December 1967).

———. "The Early Relatives of Man," *Scientific American*, Vol. 211 (July 1964).

11

Bishop, W. W., and J. D. Clark. *Background to Evolution in Africa*. Chicago: University of Chicago Press, 1967.

Clark, W. E. Le Gros. *The Fossil Evidence for Human Evolution*. 2nd ed. Chicago: University of Chicago Press, 1964.

Day, M. *Guide to Fossil Man*. Cleveland: World Publishing, 1965.

Dart, Raymond, and Dennis Craig. *Adventures With the Missing Link*. New York: Viking Press, 1959.

Dubois, Eugene. *Pithecanthropus erectus, eine Menschenahnliche Ubergangsform von Java*. Djakarta: Landes Druckerei, 1894.

Ellefson, J. O. "Territorial Behavior in the Common White-Handed Gibbon, *Hylobates lar Linn*," in Phyllis Jay (ed.), *Primates*. New York: Holt, Rinehart and Winston, 1968.

Goodman, M. "Serological Analysis of the Phyletic Relationships of Recent Hominoids," *Human Biology*, Vol. 35 (1963).

Hall, K. R. L. "Tool-Using Performances as Indicators of Behavioral Adaptability," *Current Anthropology*, Vol. 4 (1963).

Kortlandt, A., and M. Kooj. "Protohominid Behavior in Primates," Symposium of the Zoological Society of London, Vol. 10 (1963).

Leakey, L. S. B. "A New Fossil Skull from Olduvai," *Nature*, Vol. 184 (1959).

Lorenz, K. *On Aggression*. New York: Harcourt, Brace & World, 1966.

Marks, P. "Preliminary Note on the Discovery of a New Jaw of *Meganthropus*," *Indonesian Journal of Natural Science*, Vols. 1, 2, and 3 (1953).

Oakley, K. P. "Tools Makyth Man," *Antiquity*, Vol. 31 (1957).

Robinson, J. T. "The Genera and Species of the Australopithecinae," *American Journal of Physical Anthropology*, Vol. 12 (1954).

Schoetensack, Otto. *Der Unterkiefer des Homo heidelbergensis aus den Sanden von Mauer bei Heidelberg*. Leipzig: n.pub., 1908.

Tobias, P. V. *Olduvai Gorge: The Cranium and Maxillary Dentition of Australopithecus (Zin Janthropus) Boisei*. London: Cambridge University Press, 1967. Vol. II.

Van Lawick-Goodall, Jane. "A Preliminary Report on Expressive Movements and Communication in the Gombe Stream Chimpanzees," in Phyllis Jay (ed.), *Primates*. New York: Holt, Rinehart and Winston, 1968.

Von Koeningswald, G. H. R. *Meeting Prehistoric Man*. London and New York: Thames and Hudson, 1956.

Weidenreich, Franz. *Apes, Giants, and Man*. Chicago: University of Chicago Press, 1946.

12

Brace, C. L. *The Stages of Human Evolution: Human and Cultural Origins*. Englewood Cliffs, N.J.: Prentice-Hall, 1967.

Brace, C. L., and M. F. Ashley Montagu. *Man's Evolution: An Introduction to Physical Anthropology*. New York: Macmillan, 1965.

Coon, Carleton S. *The Origin of Races*. New York: Random House, 1962.

Howell, F. Clark. *Early Man*. New York: Time-Life, 1965.

Morris, Desmond. *The Naked Ape: A Zoologist's Study of the Human Animal*. New York: McGraw-Hill, 1967.

Washburn, S. L. "Tools and Human Evolution," *Scientific American*, Vol. 203 (September, 1960).

Weiner, J. S., and B. G. Campbell. "The Taxonomic Status of the Swanscombe Skull," in C. D. Ovey (ed.), *The Swanscombe Skull*. London: Royal Anthropological Institute, 1964.

13

Allison, Anthony. "Aspects of Polymorphism in Man," *Cold Springs Harbor Symposia on Quantitative Biology*, Vol. 20 (1955).

Blumberg, B. (ed.). *Proceedings of the Conference on Genetic Polymorphisms and Geographic Variations in Disease*. New York: Grune & Stratton, 1961.

Garn, Stanley M. *Human Races*. 2nd ed. Springfield, Ill.: Thomas, 1969.

———. *Readings on Race*. 2nd ed. Springfield, Ill.: Thomas, 1968.

——— (ed.). *Culture and the Direction of Human Evolution*. Detroit: Wayne State University Press, 1964.

Keusch, G. T., et al. "Lactase Deficiency in Thailand: Effect of Prolonged Lactose Feeding," *The American Journal of Clinical Nutrition*, Vol. 22 (1969).

Neel, J. (ed.). *Biomedical Challenges Presented by the American Indian.* Washington, D.C.: Pan American Health Organization, 1968.

Pauling, Linus. *The Chemical Bond.* Ithaca, N.Y.: Cornell University Press, 1967.

Schaumburg, H. H., et al. "Monosodium L-Glutamate: Its Pharmacology and Role in the Chinese Restaurant Syndrome," *Science*, Vol. 30 (1969).

Sinsheimer, Robert. *Book of Life.* Reading, Mass.: Addison-Wesley, 1967.

United States Department of Health, Education and Welfare. *Genetics and the Epidemiology of Chronic Diseases.* Public Health Service Publication 1163. Washington, D.C.: Government Printing Office, 1965.

Watt, Kenneth. *Ecology and Resource Management; A Quantitative Approach.* New York: McGraw-Hill, 1968.

14

Barnett, Homer G. *Innovation, the Basis of Culture Change.* New York: McGraw-Hill, 1953.

Binford, L. R., and S. R. Binford. *New Perspectives in Archeology.* Chicago: Aldine, 1968.

Coe, Michael. *The Maya.* New York: Praeger, 1966.

Hole, Frank, and Robert F. Heizer. *An Introduction to Prehistoric Archeology.* New York: Holt, Rinehart and Winston, 1965.

Libby, Willard. *Radiocarbon Dating.* Chicago: University of Chicago Press, 1955.

Meggers, Betty J. (ed.). "Functional and Evolutionary Implications of Community Patterning," in Robert Wauchope (ed.), *Seminars in Archaeology: 1955.* Salt Lake City, Utah: Society for American Archaeology, 1956.

Phillips, P., J. A. Ford, and J. B. Griffin. *Archaeological Survey in the Lower Mississippi Alluvial Valley 1940–1947.* Cambridge, Mass.: Harvard University Press, 1951.

Steward, Julian H. *Theory of Culture Change.* Urbana: University of Illinois Press, 1955.

Willey, G. R., and P. Phillips. *Method and Theory in American Archaeology.* Chicago: University of Chicago Press, 1958.

15

Augusta, Josef, and Zdenek Burian. *Prehistoric Man.* New York: Tudor, 1961.

Bordaz, Jacques. "First Tools of Mankind," *Natural History*, Vol. 68 (1959).

Bordes, François. The Old *Stone Age.* New York: McGraw-Hill, 1968.

———. "Mousterian Cultures in France," *Science*, Vol. 134 (1961).

Braidwood, R. J. *Prehistoric Men.* Glenview, Ill.: Scott, Foresman, 1967.

Butzer, Karl W. *Environment and Archeology: An Introduction to Pleistocene Geography.* Chicago: Aldine, 1964.

Clark, Grahame. *The Stone Age Hunters.* New York: McGraw-Hill, 1967.

Coles, John M., and Eric Higgs. *Archeology of Early Man.* New York: Time-Life, 1961.

Dart, Raymond, and Dennis Craig. *Adventures With the Missing Link.* New York: Viking Press, 1959.

Howell, F. Clark. *Early Man.* New York: Time-Life, 1965.

Lee, Richard B., and Irven DeVore (eds.). *Man the Hunter.* Chicago: Aldine, 1968.

Leakey, M. D. "Preliminary Survey of the Cultural Material from Beds I and II, Olduvai Gorge, Tanzania," in Walter W. Bishop and J. Desmond Clark (eds.), *Background to Evolution in Africa.* Chicago: University of Chicago Press, 1967.

Macgowan, Kenneth, and Joseph A. Hester, Jr. *Early Man in the New World.* Rev. ed. Garden City, N.Y.: Doubleday, 1962.

Oakley, Kenneth P. *Frameworks for Dating Fossil Man.* Chicago: Aldine, 1964.

Pfeiffer, John E. *The Emergence of Man.* New York: Harper & Row, 1969.

———. *The Search for Early Man.* New York: American Heritage, 1963.

Smith, Philip E. "The Solutrean Culture," *Scientific American*, Vol. 211 (1964).

Ucko, Peter J., and Andree Rosenfeld. *Palaeolithic Cave Art.* London: World University Library, 1967.

16

Binford, L. R. "Post-Pleistocene Adaptations," in L. R. Binford and S. R. Binford (eds.), *New Perspectives in Archeology.* Chicago: Aldine, 1968.

Braidwood, R. J. *Prehistoric Men.* Glenview, Ill.: Scott, Foresman, 1967.

Braidwood, R. J., and G. R. Willey. *Courses Toward Urban Life.* Chicago: Aldine, 1962.

Braidwood, R. J., Halet Cambel, and P. J. Watson. "Prehistoric Investigations in Southeastern Turkey," *Science*, Vol. 164 (1969).

Chang, Kwang-chih. *The Archaeology of Ancient China.* Rev. ed. New Haven, Conn.: Yale University Press, 1968.

Davies, O., H. J. Hugot, and D. Seddon. "The Origins of African Agriculture," *Current Anthropology*, Vol. 9 (1968).

Flannery, K. V., and Michael D. Coe. "Social and Economic Systems in Formative Mesoamerica," in L. R. and S. R. Binford (eds.), *New Perspectives in Archeology.* Chicago: Aldine, 1968.

Hole, Frank. "Evidence of Social Organization from Western Iran, 8000–4000 B.C.," in L. R. and S. R. Binford (eds.), *New Perspectives in Archeology.* Chicago: Aldine, 1968.

Mellaart, J. *Earliest Civilizations of the Near East.* New York: McGraw-Hill, 1965.

Pickersgill, B. "Plant Domestication in Peru," *American Antiquity*, Vol. 34 (1969).

Rodden, R. J. "An Early Neolithic Village in Greece," *Scientific American*, Vol. 212 (1965).

Ucko, Peter J., and
G. W. Dimbleby. *The Domestication and Exploitation of Plants and Animals.* Chicago: Aldine, 1969.

Wright, H. E., Jr. "Natural Environment of Early Food Production North of Mesopotamia," *Science,* Vol. 161 (1968).

17

Adams, Robert M. *The Evolution of Urban Society: Early Mesopotamia and Prehispanic Mexico.* Chicago: Aldine, 1966.

Chang, Kwang-chih. *The Archaeology of Ancient China.* Rev. ed. New Haven, Conn.: Yale University Press, 1968.

Childe, V. Gordon. *What Happened in History.* Harmondsworth, England: Penguin Books, 1942.

Coe, Michael D. *The Maya.* New York: Praeger, 1966.

———. *Mexico.* New York: Praeger, 1962.

Covarrubias, Miguel. *Indian Art of Mexico and Central America.* New York: Knopf, 1957.

Daniel, Glyn. *The First Civilizations: The Archaeology of Their Origins.* New York: Crowell, 1968.

Frankfort, Henri. *The Birth of Civilization in the Near East.* Garden City, N.Y.: Doubleday, 1956.

Hawkes, Jacquetta, and Leonard Woolley. *Prehistory and the Beginnings of Civilization.* New York: Harper & Row, 1963.

Lanning, Edward P. *Peru Before the Incas.* Englewood Cliffs, N.J.: Prentice-Hall, 1967.

Oppenheim, A. Leo. *Ancient Mesopotamia: Portrait of a Dead Civilization.* Chicago: University of Chicago Press, 1964.

Piggott, Stuart (ed.). *The Dawn of Civilization.* New York: McGraw-Hill, 1961.

Polanyi, Karl, C. M. Arsenberg, and H. W. Pearson. *Trade and Market in the Early Empires.* New York: Free Press, 1957.

Rowe, John H. *Chavín Art: An Inquiry into Its Form and Meaning.* New York: Museum of Primitive Art, 1962.

Sahlins, Marshall. *Tribesmen.* Englewood Cliffs, N.J.: Prentice-Hall, 1968.

Sanders, William T., and Barbara J. Price. *Mesoamerica: The Evolution of a Civilization.* New York: Random House, 1968.

Trigger, Bruce G. *Beyond History: The Methods of Prehistory.* New York: Holt, Rinehart and Winston, 1968.

Willey, G. R. *An Introduction to American Archaeology.* Englewood Cliffs, N.J.: Prentice-Hall, 1966.

Wittfogel, Karl A. *Oriental Despotism: A Comparative Study of Total Power.* New Haven, Conn.: Yale University Press, 1957.

18

Cressey, G. B. *Asia's Lands and Peoples.* New York: McGraw-Hill, 1944.

Dobyns, Henry F. "Estimating Aboriginal Population: An Appraisal of Techniques With a New Hemispheric Estimate," *Current Anthropology,* Vol. 7 (October 1966).

Drucker, Philip. *The Northern and Central Nootkan Tribes.* Washington, D.C.: Smithsonian Institution, 1951.

Elkin, A. P. *The Australian Aborigines: How to Understand Them.* Sydney and London: Angus and Robertson, 1954.

Jenness, Diamond. *Indians of Canada.* Ottawa, Canada: National Museum of Canada, 1932.

Kroeber, Alfred L. *Cultural and Natural Areas of Native North America.* Berkeley: University of California Press, 1939.

Lattimore, Owen. *Inner Asian Frontiers of China.* New York: American Geographical Society, 1951.

Levine, Morton H. "Prehistoric Art and Ideology," *American Anthropologist,* Vol. 59 (December 1957).

Malinowski, Bronislaw. *Argonauts of the Western Pacific.* New York: Dutton, 1922.

Montagu, Ashley. *The Concept of the Primitive.* New York: Free Press, 1968.

Rattray, R. S. *Ashanti.* New York: Oxford University Press, 1923.

Spencer, Baldwin, and F. J. Gillen. *The Arunta.* New York: Macmillan, 1927.

Spencer, Robert. *An Ethno-Atlas.* Dubuque, Iowa: W. C. Brown, 1956.

Stefansson, Vilhjalmur. *My Life With the Eskimos.* Rev. ed. London: G. G. Harrap, 1924.

Steward, Julian H. *Basin-Plateau Aboriginal Sociopolitical Groups.* Washington, D.C.: Smithsonian Institution, 1938.

Steward, Julian H., and Louis Faron. *Native Peoples of South America.* New York: McGraw-Hill, 1959.

19

Chambers, J., and P. J. Madgwick. *Conflict and Community.* London: G. Philip, 1968.

Diaz, May N. *Tonala: Conservatism, Responsibility and Authority in a Mexican Town.* Berkeley and Los Angeles: University of California Press, 1966.

Diaz, May N., and Jack M. Potter. "Introduction: The Social Life of Peasants," in Jack M. Potter, May N. Diaz, and George M. Foster (eds.), *Peasant Society: A Reader.* Boston: Little, Brown, 1967.

Erasmus, Charles. "Culture Structure and Process: The Occurrence and Disappearance of Reciprocal Farm Labor," *Southwestern Journal of Anthropology,* Vol. 12 (1956).

Foster, George M. "What Is Folk Culture?," *American Anthropologist,* Vol. 55 (1953).

———. "The Dyadic Contract: A Model for the Social Structure of a Mexican Peasant Village," *American Anthropologist,* Vol. 63 (1961).

———. "The Dyadic Contract in Tzintzuntzan, II; Patron-Client Relationship," *American Anthropologist,* Vol. 65 (1963).

———. "Peasant Society and the Image of Limited Good," *American Anthropologist,* Vol. 67 (1965).

———. *Tzintzuntzan: Mexican Peasants in a Changing World.* Boston: Little, Brown, 1967.

Kroeber, Alfred L. *Anthropology: Race, Language, Culture, Psychology, Prehistory.* Rev. ed. New York: Harcourt, Brace & World, 1948.

Lerner, Daniel. *The Passing of Traditional Society.* New York: Free Press, 1958.

Mintz, Sidney W. "Pratik: Haitian Personal Economic Relationships," *Proceedings of the Annual Spring Meetings of the American Ethnological Society,* 1961.

Potter, Jack M. "Introduction: Peasants in the Modern World," in Jack M. Potter, May N. Diaz, and George M. Foster (eds.), *Peasant Society: A Reader.* Boston: Little, Brown, 1967.

Redfield, Robert. *Peasant Society and Culture: An Anthropological Approach to Civilization.* Chicago: University of Chicago Press, 1956.

Wolf, Eric. *Peasants.* Englewood Cliffs, N. J.: Prentice-Hall, 1966.

———. "Closed Corporate Peasant Communities in Meso-America and Central Java," *Southwestern Journal of Anthropology,* Vol. 13 (1957).

———. "Aspects of Group Relations in a Complex Society: Mexico," *American Anthropologist,* Vol. 58 (1956).

———. "Types of Latin American Peasantry: A Preliminary Discussion," *American Anthropologist,* Vol. 57 (1955).

20

Bensman, Joseph, and Arthur Vidich. *Small Town in Mass Society.* Rev. ed. Princeton, N.J.: Princeton University Press, 1968.

Caudill, William A. *The Psychiatric Hospital as a Small Community.* Cambridge, Mass.: Harvard University Press, 1958.

Djamour, Judith. *Malay Kinship and Marriage in Singapore.* New York: Humanities Press, 1965.

Fallers, L. A. *The King's Men: Leadership and Status in Buganda on the Eve of Independence.* New York: Oxford University Press, 1964.

Firth, Raymond. *We, the Tikopia.* 2nd ed. Boston: Beacon Press, 1963.

Furnivall, J. S. Colonial Policy and Practice. New York: New York University Press, 1956.

Gann, Lewis, and Peter Duignan. *Burden of Empire.* New York: Praeger, 1967.

Gans, Herbert. *The Urban Villagers; Group and Class in the Life of Italian-Americans.* New York: Fress Press, 1962.

Goldschmidt, Walter. *Exploring the Ways of Mankind.* New York: Holt, Rinehart and Winston, 1960.

Harding, F. C., and R. A. Bottenberg. "The Effect of Personal Characteristics on the Relationship Between Attitude and Job Performance," *Journal of Applied Psychology,* Vol. 45 (1961).

Henry, Jules. *Culture Against Man.* New York: Random House, 1963.

Kelly, Isabel. *Folk Practices in North Mexico.* Austin: University of Texas Press, 1965.

Lewis, Oscar. *Five Families; Mexican Case Studies in the Culture of Poverty.* New York: Basic Books, 1959.

———. *La Vida; A Puerto-Rican Family in the Culture of Poverty— San Juan and New York.* New York: Random House, 1966.

Liebow, Elliot. *Tally's Corner; A Study of Negro Street-Corner Men.* Boston: Little, Brown, 1967.

Nelson, Lowry. *The Mormon Village.* Salt Lake City: University of Utah Press, 1952.

Powdermaker, Hortense. *After Freedom.* New York: Russell & Russell, 1966.

Rattray, R. S. *Ashanti.* Oxford: Clarendon Press, 1923.

Redfield, Robert. *Tepoztlan, a Mexican Village.* Chicago: University of Chicago Press, 1930.

Schneider, David. *American Kinship.* Englewood Cliffs, N.J.: Prentice-Hall, 1968.

Stein, Maurice. *The Eclipse of Community.* Princeton, N.J.: Princeton University Press, 1960.

Sudnow, David. *Passing On: The Social Organization of Dying.* Englewood Cliffs, N.J.: Prentice-Hall, 1967.

Tylor, E. B. *Primitive Culture.* 7th ed. New York: Brentano's, 1924.

21

Geertz, Clifford. "The Growth of Culture and the Evolution of Mind," in Jordan M. Scher (ed.), *Theories of the Mind.* New York: Free Press, 1962.

Hymes, Dell H. (ed.). *Language in Culture and Society: A Reader in Linguistics and Anthropology.* New York: Harper & Row, 1964.

Kluckhohn, Clyde. "The Scientific Study of Value, and Contemporary Civilization," *Proceedings of the American Philosophical Society,* Vol. 102 (1958).

Kroeber, Alfred L. *Anthropology: Race, Language, Culture, Psychology, Prehistory.* Rev. ed. New York: Harcourt, Brace & World, 1948.

Mandelbaum, David G. "Cultural Anthropology," in David L. Sills (ed.). *International Encyclopedia of Social Sciences.* New York: Macmillan, 1968. Vol. I.

Mead, Margaret. *Anthropology: A Human Science: Selected Papers 1939–1960.* Princeton, N.J.: Van Nostrand, 1964.

Murdock, George P. *Social Structure.* New York: Macmillan, 1949.

Radcliffe-Brown, A. R. *Structure and Function in Primitive Society.* New York: Free Press, 1965.

Redfield, Robert. *The Little Community: Viewpoints for the Study of a Human Whole.* Chicago: University of Chicago Press, 1955.

Sahlins, Marshall D., and Elman R. Service (eds.). *Evolution and Culture.* Ann Arbor: University of Michigan Press, 1960.

Steward, Julian H. *Theory of Culture Change.* Urbana: University of Illinois Press, 1955.

White, Leslie A. *The Evolution of Culture.* New York: McGraw-Hill, 1959.

Wolf, Eric R. *Anthropology.* Englewood Cliffs, N.J.: Prentice-Hall, 1964.

22

Benedict, Ruth. *Patterns of Culture.* Boston: Houghton Mifflin, 1959.

Davenport, William. *Jamaican Fishing: A Game Theory Analysis.* New Haven, Conn.: Yale University Publications in Anthropology, 1960.

Evans-Pritchard, E. E. *The Nuer.* New York: Oxford University Press, 1940.

Gruber, Jacob W. *Ethnographic Salvage and the Shaping of Anthropology.* Paper presented at the Annual Meetings of the American Anthropological Association (November, 1968).

Hsu, Francis K. *The Study of Literate Civilizations.* New York: Holt, Rinehart and Winston, 1969.

Keesing, Felix M. *Cultural Anthropology: The Science of Custom.* New York: Holt, Rinehart and Winston, 1958.

Kluckhohn, Clyde. "Universal Categories of Culture," in Alfred L. Kroeber (ed.), *Anthropology Today: An Encyclopedic Inventory.* Chicago: University of Chicago Press, 1953.

Lévi-Strauss, Claude. "Anthropology: Its Achievements and Future," *Current Anthropology,* Vol. 7 (1966).

Lowie, Robert H. *Primitive Society.* New York: Liveright, 1947.

Murdock, George Peter, et al. *Outline of Cultural Materials.* New Haven, Conn.: Human Relations Area Files, 1961.

23

Benedict, Ruth. *Patterns of Culture.* Boston: Houghton Mifflin, 1959.

Bruner, Jerome S., Rose R. Olver, and Patricia M. Greenfield. *Studies in Cognitive Growth.* New York: Wiley, 1966.

DuBois, Cora. *The People of Alor.* Cambridge, Mass.: Harvard University Press, 1960.

Erikson, Erik. *Identity; Youth and Crisis.* New York: Norton, 1968.

Field, Peter B. "A New Cross-Cultural Study of Drunkenness," in David J. Pittman and C. R. Snyder (eds.), *Society, Culture, and Drinking Patterns.* New York: Wiley, 1962.

Freud, Sigmund. *Civilization and Its Discontents.* Joan Riviere (tr.). London: Hogarth, 1957.

Fromm, Erich. *The Sane Society.* New York: Holt, Rinehart and Winston, 1955.

Gorer, Geoffrey. *The American People.* Rev. ed. New York: Norton, 1964.

Hallowell, A. Irving. *Culture and Experience.* Philadelphia: University of Pennsylvania Press, 1955.

Honigmann, John J. "Psychological Anthropology," *The Annals of the American Academy of Political and Social Science,* Vol. 383 (1969).

Horton, Donald. "The Functions of Alcohol in Primitive Societies," *Quarterly Journal of Studies on Alcohol,* Vol. 4 (1943).

Kardiner, Abram. "The Concept of Basic Personality Structure as an Operational Tool in the Social Sciences," in Ralph Linton (ed.), *The Science of Man in the World Crisis.* New York: Columbia University Press, 1945.

Leighton, Alexander H. *My Name Is Legion.* New York: Basic Books, 1959.

Lewis, Oscar. *La Vida; A Puerto-Rican Family in the Culture of Poverty—San Juan and New York.* New York: Random House, 1966.

Malinowski, Bronislaw. *The Father in Primitive Society.* New York: Norton, 1955.

Mead, Margaret. *Coming of Age in Samoa.* New York: William Morrow, 1928.

———. "Socialization and Enculturation," *Current Anthropology,* Vol. 4 (1963).

Parker, Seymour. "The Wiitiko Psychosis in the Context of Ojibwa Personality and Culture," *American Anthropologist,* Vol. 62 (1960).

Roheim, Geza. *Magic and Schizophrenia.* New York: International Universities Press, 1955.

Sapir, Edward. "The Emergence of the Concept of Personality in a Study of Cultures," *Journal of Social Psychology,* Vol. 27 (1934).

Spindler, George D. *Sociocultural and Psychological Processes in Menomini Acculturation.* Berkeley: University of California Press, 1955.

Wallace, Anthony F. C. *The Modal Personality Structure of the Tuscarora Indians.* Washington D.C.: Smithsonian Institution, 1952.

Whiting, John W. M., and I. L. Child. *Child Training and Personality.* New Haven, Conn.: Yale University Press, 1953.

24

Adams, Robert McCormick. *The Evolution of Urban Society: Early Mesopotamia and Prehistoric Mexico.* Chicago: Aldine, 1966.

Alihan, Milla Aissa. *Social Ecology.* New York: Columbia University Press, 1938.

Ardrey, Robert. *African Genesis.* New York: Dell, 1961.

Benedict, Ruth. *The Chrysanthemum and the Sword.* Boston: Houghton Mifflin, 1946.

Brown, Carol Osman. "Barbed Wire, the Fence That Tamed the West," *Arizona Highways,* Vol. 45 (October 1969).

Dyson-Hudson, N. *Karimojong Politics.* Oxford, England: Clarendon, 1966.

Fleming, Donald. "On Living in a Biological Revolution," *Atlantic Monthly,* Vol. 223 (February 1969).

Goldschmidt, Wallace. "Theory and Strategy in the Study of Cultural Adaptability," *American Anthropologist,* Vol. 67 (1965).

Helm, June. "The Nature of Dogrib Socioterritorial Groups," in Richard B. Lee and Irven DeVore (eds.), *Man the Hunter.* Chicago: Aldine, 1968.

Hiatt, L. R. "Ownership and Use of Land Among the Australian Aborigines," in Richard B. Lee and Irven DeVore (eds.), *Man the Hunter.* Chicago: Aldine, 1968.

Kroeber, Alfred L. *Handbook of the Indians of California.* Washington, D.C.: Smithsonian Institution, 1925.

Manners, Robert (ed.). *Process and Pattern in Culture.* Chicago: Aldine, 1964.

Muller, Hermann. *Studies in Genetics.* Bloomington: Indiana University Press, 1962.

Murphy, Robert F., and Julian H. Steward. "Tappers and Trappers: Parallel Process in Acculturation," *Economic Development and Cultural Change,* Vol. 4 (1956).

Steward, Julian H. *Theory of Culture Change.* Urbana: University of Illinois Press, 1955.

———, et al. "Cultural Ecology," in *International Encyclopedia of the Social Sciences.* New York: Macmillan, 1968. Vol. IV.

White, Leslie A. *The Evolution of Culture.* New York: McGraw-Hill, 1959.

Winter, Edward H., and Thomas O. Beidelman. "Tanganyika: A Study of an African Society at National and Local Levels," in J. H. Steward (ed.), *Contemporary Change in Traditional Societies.* Urbana: University of Illinois Press, 1967. Vol. I.

Woodburn, James. "Stability and Flexibility in Hadza Residential Groupings," in Richard B. Lee and Irven DeVore (eds.), *Man the Hunter.* Chicago: Aldine, 1968.

25

Evans-Pritchard, E. E. *The Nuer.* New York: Oxford University Press, 1940.

Junod, Henri. *The Life of a South African Tribe.* New Hyde Park, N.Y.: University Books, 1962.

Leach, Edmund R. "Lévi-Strauss in the Garden of Eden: An Examination of Some Recent Developments in the Analysis of Myth," *Transactions of the New York Academy of Sciences,* Vol. 23 (1961).

Lévi-Strauss, Claude. *Structural Anthropology.* Claire Jacobson and Grundefest Schoepf (trs.). New York: Basic Books, 1963.

Littleton, C. Scott. "Lévi-Strauss and the 'Kingship in Heaven': A Structural Analysis of a Widespread Theogonic Theme," *Journal of the Folklore Institute* (in press).

Malinowski, Bronislaw. *Argonauts of the Western Pacific.* New York: Dutton, 1922.

Radcliffe-Brown, A. R. "The Mother's Brother in South Africa," in *Structure and Function in Primitive Society.* New York: Free Press, 1965.

Tyler, Stephen A. (ed.). *Cognitive Anthropology.* New York: Holt, Rinehart and Winston, 1969.

26

Bright, William (ed.). *Sociolinguistics.* The Hague, Holland: Mouton, 1966.

Bloomfield, Leonard. *Language.* New York: Holt, Rinehart and Winston, 1933.

Chomsky, Noam. *Syntactic Structures.* The Hague, Holland: Mouton, 1957.

———. *Aspects of the Theory of Syntax.* Cambridge, Mass.: The MIT Press, 1965.

Whorf, Benjamin Lee. *Language, Thought and Reality: Selected Writings of Benjamin Lee Whorf.* John B. Carroll (ed.). Cambridge, Mass.: MIT Press, 1956.

27

Beier, U. *Contemporary Art in Africa.* New York: Praeger, 1968.

Boas, Franz. *Primitive Art.* New York: Dover, 1955.

Drucker, Philip. *The Indians of the Northwest Coast.* New York: McGraw-Hill, 1955.

Dundes, A. (ed.). *The Study of Folklore.* Englewood Cliffs, N.J.: Prentice-Hall, 1965.

Fischer, J. L. "Art Styles as Cultural Cognitive Maps," *American Anthropologist,* Vol. 63 (1961).

Gerbrands, A. A. (ed.). *The Art of the Asmat, New Guinea.* New York: New York City Museum of Primitive Art, 1962.

Graburn, N. H. H. "Art and Acculturative Processes,"

International Social Science Journal, Vol. 21 (Fall, 1969).

Grand, P. M. *Prehistoric Art.* Greenwich, Conn.: New York Graphic Society, 1967.

Heizer, R. F., and M. A. Baumhoff. *Prehistoric Rock Art of Nevada and California.* Berkeley and Los Angeles: University of California Press, 1962.

Herzog, George. "Song," in M. Leach (ed.), *Standard Dictionary of Folklore, Mythology and Legend.* New York: Funk & Wagnalls, 1950. Vol. II.

Hsu, Francis K. "Rethinking the Concept 'Primitive,'" *Current Anthropology,* Vol. 5 (1964).

Kavolis, V. *Artistic Expression: A Sociological Analysis.* Ithaca, N.Y.: Cornell University Press, 1968.

Kurath, G. P. "Dance," in M. Leach (ed.), *Standard Dictionary of Folklore, Mythology and Legend.* New York: Funk & Wagnalls, 1950. Vol. I.

Lee, S. E. *A History of Far Eastern Art.* New York: Abrams, 1964.

Munro, T. *The Arts and Their Interrelations.* New York: Liberal Arts Press, 1949.

Swinton, G. *Eskimo Sculpture.* Toronto: McClelland and Stewart, 1965.

Turnbull, C. *The Forest People.* New York: Simon and Schuster, 1961.

28

Fortes, Meyer. "Descent, Filiation, and Affinity," *Man,* Vol. 59 (1959).

———. "The Structure of Unilineal Descent Groups," *The American Anthropologist* Vol. 55 (1953).

———. "Time and Social Structure," in *Social Structure: Essays Presented to A. R. Radcliffe-Brown.* New York: Oxford University Press, 1949.

Fox, Robin. *Kinship and Marriage.* Baltimore: Pelican Books, 1967.

Freeman, D. "The Concept of the Kindred," *Journal of the Royal Anthropological Institute,* Vol. 91 (1961).

Goodenough, Ward. *Property, Kin, and Community on*

Truk. New Haven, Conn.: Yale University Press, 1951.

Lewis, I. M. "Problems in the Comparative Study of Unilineal Descent," in Michael Banton (ed.), *The Relevance of Models for Social Anthropology*. London: Tavistock Publications, 1965.

Murdock, G. P. *Social Structure*. New York: Macmillan, 1949.

Radcliffe-Brown, A. R. *Structure and Function in Primitive Society*. New York: Free Press, 1965.

Radcliffe-Brown, A. R., and D. Forde (eds.). *African Systems of Kinship and Marriage*. New York: Oxford University Press, 1950.

Romney, A. K., and P. J. Epling. "A Simplified Model of Kariera Kinship," *American Anthropologist*, Vol. 60 (1958).

Schneider, David, and Kathleen Gough (eds.). *Matrilineal Kinship*. Berkeley and Los Angeles: University of California Press, 1961.

29

Bailey, Fred. *Tribe, Caste, and Nation*. Manchester, England: Manchester University Press, 1960.

Banton, Michael (ed.). *Political Systems and the Distribution of Power*. New York: Praeger, 1965.

Barth, F. "Segmentary Opposition and the Theory of Games: A Study of Pathan Organization," *Journal of the Royal Anthropological Institute*, Vol. 89 (1959).

Evans-Pritchard, E. E. *The Nuer*. New York: Oxford University Press, 1940.

Gluckman, Max. *Politics, Law, and Ritual in Tribal Society*. Chicago: Aldine, 1965.

Salisbury, Richard. "Politics and Shell-Money in New Britain," in M. Swartz, V. Turner, and A. Tuden (eds.), *Political Anthropology*. Chicago: Aldine, 1966.

Smith, M. G. "On Segmentary Lineages," *Journal of the Royal Anthropological Institute*, Vol. 86 (1956).

Swartz, Marc (ed.). *Local Level Politics*. Chicago: Aldine, 1968.

Turner, Victor. *Schism and Continuity in an African Society*. Manchester, England: Manchester University Press, 1957.

Von Neuman, John, and Oskar Morgenstern. *Theories of Games and Economic Behavior*. Princeton, N.J.: Princeton University Press, 1947.

30

Barnett, H. E. "The Nature of the Potlatch," *American Anthropologist*, Vol. 40 (1938).

Barth, F. "Economic Spheres in Darfur," in R. W. Firth (ed.), *Themes in Economic Anthropology*. London: Tavistock Publications, 1967.

Barton, R. F. "Ifugao Economics," *University of California Publications in American Archaeology and Ethnology*, Vol. 15 (1922).

Belshaw, C. S. *Traditional Exchange and Modern Markets*. Englewood Cliffs, N.J.: Prentice-Hall, 1965.

Bohannan, P. J., and G. Dalton. *Markets in Africa*. Evanston, Ill.: Northwestern University Press, 1962.

Carneiro, Robert. "Slash-and-Burn Agriculture: A Closer Look," in A. F. C. Wallace (ed.), *Men and Cultures*. Philadelphia: University of Pennsylvania Press, 1960.

Codere, Helen. *Fighting With Property*. Seattle: University of Washington Press, 1966.

Douglas, M. "Primitive Rationing," in R. W. Firth (ed.), *Themes in Economic Anthropology*. London: Tavistock Publications, 1967.

Finney, B. "Big-Fellow Man Belong Business in New Guinea," *Ethnology*, Vol. 4 (1968).

Greenhut, M. L. *Micro-Economics and the Space Economy*. Scott, Foresman, 1963.

Hagen, E. E. *On the Theory of Social Change*. Homewood, Ill.: Dorsey Press, 1961.

Katzin, Margaret. "The Business of Higglering in Jamaica," *Social and Economic Studies*, Vol. 9 (1960).

Norvell, D. G., and M. K. Thompson. "Higglering in Jamaica and the Mystique of Pure Competition," *Social and Economic Studies*, Vol. 17 (1968).

Polanyi, K., C. M. Arensberg, and H. W. Pearson. *Trade and Markets in the Early Empires*. New York: Free Press, 1957.

Sahlins, Marshall. "Exchange Value and the Diplomacy of Primitive Trade," *Proceedings of the American Ethnological Society, Spring Meetings*, 1965.

Salisbury, Richard. "Ethnographic Notes on Wapisiana Agriculture," in *Ethnographic Notes on Amerindian Agriculture*. Montreal, Quebec: McGill University Savanna Research Project Series No. 9, 1968.

———. "Trade and Markets," in David L. Sills (ed.), *International Encyclopedia of the Social Sciences*. New York: Macmillan, 1968. Vol. XVI.

Thurnwald, Richard. *Economics in Primitive Communities*. New York: Oxford University Press, 1932.

Wilbert, J. *The Evolution of Horticultural Systems in Native South America*. Caracas: Sociedad de Ciencias Naturales, 1961.

31

Ellis, W. *Polynesian Researches*. London: Fisher, Son, and Jackson, 1831.

Evans-Pritchard, E. E. *Witchcraft, Oracles, and Magic Among the Azande*. Oxford, England: Clarendon, 1958.

Frazer, James G. *The Golden Bough*. Abridged ed. New York: Macmillan, 1922.

Fortune, R. F. *Manus Religion: An Ethnological Study of the Manus Natives*. Philadelphia: American Philosophical Society, 1935.

Freud, Sigmund. *Totem and Taboo*. James Strachey (tr.). New York: Norton, 1950.

Gluckman, Max. *Rituals of Rebellion in South-East Africa*. Manchester, England: University of Manchester Press, 1954.

Goode, William J. *Religion Among the Primitives*. New York: Free Press, 1951.

Malinowski, Bronislaw. *Magic, Science, and Religion and Other Essays*. New York: Free Press, 1948.

Mead, Margaret. *The Changing Culture of an Indian Tribe*. New York: Capricorn Books, 1966.

Mooney, James. "The Ghost Dance Religion and the Sioux Outbreak of 1890," *Bureau of American Ethnology Fourteenth Annual Report, 1892–1893* (1896).

Norbeck, Edward. *Religion in Primitive Society*. New York: Harper & Row, 1961.

Radcliffe-Brown, A. R. *Structure and Function in Primitive Society*. New York: Free Press, 1965.

Turner, Victor W. *The Forest of Symbols*. Ithaca, N.Y.: Cornell University Press, 1967.

Tylor, Edward Burnett. *Primitive Culture*. 7th ed. New York: Brentano's, 1924.

Van Gennep, Arnold. *The Rites of Passage*. Chicago: University of Chicago Press, 1960.

Wallace, Anthony F. C. "Revitalization Movements," *American Anthropologist*, Vol. 58 (1956).

Weber, Max. *The Protestant Ethic and the Spirit of Capitalism*. Talcott Parsons (tr.). London: George Allen and Unwin, 1930.

32

Eggan, Fred. *The American Indian: Perspectives for the Study of Social Change*. Chicago: Aldine, 1966.

Herskovits, Melville. *Acculturation: The Study of Culture Contact*. New York: J. J. Augustin, 1938.

Linton, Ralph. *The Tree of Culture*. New York: Knopf, 1961.

Malinowski, Bronislaw. *Argonauts of the Western Pacific*. New York: Dutton, 1922.

Mead, Margaret. *New Lives for Old*. New York: New American Library, 1961.

Murphy, Robert F. *Head-hunter's Heritage*. Berkeley and Los Angeles: University of California Press, 1960.

Radcliffe-Brown, A. R. *Structure and Function in Primitive Society*. New York: Free Press, 1965.

Redfield, Robert. *The Primitive World and Its Transformations*. Ithaca, N.Y.: Cornell University Press, 1953.

Schmidt, Wilhelm. *The Origin and Growth of Religion*. 2nd ed. H. J. Rose (tr). London: Methuen, 1935.

Steward, Julian H. *Theory of Culture Change*. Urbana: University of Illinois Press, 1955.

Tylor, Edward Burnett. *Primitive Culture*. 7th ed. New York: Brentano's, 1924.

White, Leslie A. *The Evolution of Culture*. New York: McGraw-Hill, 1959.

33

Almond, Gabriel, and James Coleman (eds.). *The Politics of Developing Areas*. Princeton, N.J.: Princeton University Press, 1960.

Arensberg, Conrad M., and Arthur H. Niehoff. *Introducing Social Change*. Chicago: Aldine, 1964.

Breese, Gerald. *Organization in Newly Developing Countries*. Englewood Cliffs, N.J.: Prentice-Hall, 1966.

Foster, George M. *Traditional Cultures and the Impact of Technological Change*. New York: Harper & Row, 1962.

———. *Tzintzuntzan: Mexican Peasants in a Changing World*. Boston: Little, Brown, 1967.

Geertz, Clifford, and Lloyd Fallers (eds.). *Old Societies and New States: The Quest for Modernity in Asia and Africa*. New York: Free Press, 1963.

Halpern, Joel M. *The Changing Village Community*. Englewood Cliffs, N.J.: Prentice-Hall, 1968.

Lloyd, Peter C. *Africa and Social Change*. Baltimore: Penguin Books, 1967.

Moore, Wilbert E. *The Impact of Industry*. Englewood Cliffs, N.J.: Prentice-Hall, 1965.

Redfield, Robert. *A Village That Chose Progress: Chan Kon Revisited*. Chicago: University of Chicago Press, 1950.

Rostow, W. W. *The Stages of Economic Growth*. Cambridge, England: Cambridge University Press, 1960.

Schurmann, Herbert Franz. *Ideology and Organization in Communist China*. Berkeley and Los Angeles: University of California Press, 1966.

Srinivas, M. N. *Social Change in Modern India*. Berkeley and Los Angeles: University of California Press, 1966.

a

Abbevillian. In Europe, a transitional phase of the lower Pleistocene characterized by the use of crude hand axes. In Africa, the Chellean is the comparable period.

acculturation. The process by which the culture of a society that is in prolonged contact with another society subsequently changes.

acephalus society. A society in which there are no formal political offices of statuses.

Acheulean. In Europe and Africa, a phase of the Lower Pleistocene characterized by the use of often elegant hand axes and a full complement of fairly standardized flake tools.

Adapis. An Eocene prosimian, probably the forerunner of the modern lemur, distinct from archaic mammals because of its greater brain size and frontality of the eyes.

adaptation. A biological response of an organism to environmental stress. Also, a cultural response of a society or a psychological response of an individual to pressure for change.

adenine. A nucleotide base of the DNA molecule.

Aegyptopithecus. A primitive Fayum ape, possibly the basal ancestor of the dryopithecines from which the first hominids may have evolved.

Aeolopithecus. A small Fayum primate with distinctive dentition.

affinal relationships. All relationships through marriage, including systems by which separate families are linked to one another by ties established through marriage between members.

age-area theory. The view that inventions and innovations flow evenly in an outward wavelike pattern from an assumed cultural center toward the periphery of a culture area. In this view, the more widely distributed the trait, the older it is.

agriculturists. People who use a system of cultivation involving plows and, usually, draft animals and, in its more complex forms, large-scale and centrally controlled systems of terracing and irrigation.

alleles. Two or more alternative forms in a single gene that represents differences in the chemical effect of the gene. The combination of alleles present at a specific position on the chromosome dictates what effect that position will have on cell functioning.

Alorese. People of the southwest Pacific islands of Alor.

ambilateral descent. A system in which descent is traced equally through the father and mother and their kin without respect to sex. The only kin grouping here is the kindred.

Amphithecus. A late Eocene fossil primate in Burma that may have been a primitive ape.

anagenesis. An evolutionary process in which a species evolves into another species by gradually undergoing genetic change over time. See also *cladogenesis.*

Andean area. The culture area encompassing Peru, southern Ecuador, western Bolivia, and northernmost Chile. See also *Mesoamerica.*

animism. A belief that spirit beings inhabit most natural objects.

anthropocentricism. A view of the universe with man as the center and focus of the occurrences within it.

Anthropoidea. The higher primates, classified as New World monkeys, Old World monkeys, and apes and man.

anthropological sampling. A research method whereby members of a society being studied are classified by their position in the social stratification and then their responses are related systematically to one another in order to obtain a view of the general characteristics of that society and culture.

anthropology. The scientific study of man based on the comparative analysis of and subsequent generalizations about his physical and behavioral characteristics.

anthropometrics. The statistical measurement of the outside dimensions of the human body.

Anuak. A pastoral people living in the Sudan.

apes. Large anthropoids that evolved in the Miocene and now represented by the gorilla, chimpanzee, orangutan, and gibbon.

Apidium. An Oligocene primate bearing unmistakable resemblances to modern Old World monkeys.

Apache. Indian tribes of Athapaskan stock found in the American Southwest.

applied anthropology. The study of the combined social and psychological relationships involved in a given institution that will affect and be affected by changes in existing patterns of behavior made for economic or administrative purposes.

Arapesh. A people of the mountains of eastern New Guinea.

arboreal. Adapted to life in the trees.

archaeology. The study of man's past on the basis of the tangible remains of his activities and of the surviving effects of these activities.

art. The process whereby individuals personally interpret their society's values through matter, movement, or sound in

Glossary of Anthropological Terms

such a way that their interpretations can be understood within the framework of their society's standards of beauty or utilitarianism.

artifact. Any surviving material object, such as tools and sculpture, from cultural traditions of the past.

Arusha. A people with an agricultural base who live in northern Tanzania; closely related to the pastoral Masai.

Asian zone. The cultural zone that includes the Chinese, Hindu, Buddhist, and Muslim culture areas.

associational principle. The concept that particular goals may be achieved to the benefit of all by joining together many individuals into a voluntary association.

Athapaskan. A linguistic subdivision of the Nadene language group; the Athapaskan-speaking Indians found primarily in the southwestern United States and northwest Canada.

atlatl. A spear-throwing implement.

Aurignacian. The Upper Paleolithic period in Europe following the Mousterian.

australopithecines. A nontechnical term referring to members of, or hominids closely related to, the genus *Australopithecus*, the immediate ancestors of the pithecanthropines.

Australopithecus. A genus of ancient plains-dwelling manlike apes evolving in the direction of man.

autochthonic. Of the earth.

Aztec. A society that became the most powerful of all the Mesoamerican civilizations by A.D. 1500.

baboons. Large, heavily built monkeys that live in cohesive social groups in the savannas of East and Central Africa.

backed flakes. Hand-held flake tools with an edge that is blunted so that pressure can be exerted on the opposite edge without cutting the hand.

band. A territorially based and simply organized social group economically dependent upon hunting and gathering.

basic personality structure. A widely shared individual adaptive process, governed by the manner in which a particular society's customary modes of thought and behavior prepare its members to meet demands of the outer world and their internal biological drives.

behavioral anthropology. The detailed examination of particular facets of behavior of institutions, not as corporations but as patterned modes of action.

bifaces. Hand tools with retouch applied to both the upper and lower faces.

biometrics. The statistical analysis of the people of the world, especially in terms of disease, birth, death, and growth.

biospecies. A subpopulation of a new species that comes to live in a totally new environment, adapting to the extent that gene flow with the originating population cannot occur because of the ensuing genetic diversity. See also *cladogenesis.*

bisnis. In New Guinea, the pidgin English term for a small-scale enterprise whose goal is not to amass personal profit but to satisfy local demands for widespread well-being of the people who make up the enterprise.

blade tools. Flat, thin tools with parallel sides.

borer. A pointed tool with an end similar to a twist drill.

brachiation. Locomotion by swinging from the arms from one branch to another, as performed by the gibbon.

Branisella. The oldest South American monkey known, dating from Early Oligocene.

bridewealth. A payment of food, cattle, or other objects of value made by a bridegroom to his bride's family; a common practice in patrilineal societies and present in some matrilineal groups, especially in Africa.

Buganda. One of the kingdoms of what is now Uganda in East Africa.

burin. A cutting and grooving tool made by removing one or more long retouch spalls from the end of a flake to fashion a chisel edge.

Bushmen. A nomadic hunting and gathering people of South Africa having very small stature and other distinctive physical characteristics.

caches. Concealed storage places for provisions or possessions.

carnivore. A flesh-eating mammal, as judged by its dentition.

caste stratification. A hierarchical system of social organization with each group assigned a ranked status and all individuals required to marry a person from the group into which they were born.

Çatal Hüyük. Developed village-farming level site in Anatolia noted for its impressive degree of cultural elaboration. (Turkish *hüyük* refers to a mound built up by village life at the same place over the generations.)

celts. Chisellike implements probably used as axes or hoes, or both.

cenotes. Naturally formed water wells.

Cenozoic. The period beginning about 65 million years ago and including the Paleocene, Eocene, Oligocene, Miocene, and Pliocene epochs.

ceremonial economics. The study of systems where limited goods are "rationed" so that no one may deprive another by taking what he needs, and where the desire for the rationed commodity becomes a desire for the status that access to it can confer.

Chavín. The first period of Andean prehistory dating from about 1000 B.C. to 200 B.C. See also *Huari; Inca.*

Chellean. In Africa, a phase of the Lower Pleistocene characterized by the use of crude hand axes.

chimpanzee. An ape that lives in groups in dense tropical forest regions of Africa.

chinampa. The "floating garden" region in the southern part of the Valley of Mexico.

chopper. A core tool consisting of a nodule from which a few flakes have been detached to form a rough and somewhat straight cutting edge.

Chou. The period of Chinese culture following the Shang period, characterized by a power struggle, the appearance of China's principle philosophers (Confucius and Lao-tzu), and the discovery of a method for casting iron.

Choukoutien. An Acheulean site near Peking that yielded a large collection of *Homo erectus* specimens, all of which were lost during World War II.

chromosomes. The chainlike structures within the nucleus of the cell that carry genes, the basic units of inheritance.

chronospecies. The situation arising from genetic incompatibility between an original species and a descendant form of it that prevents further interbreeding. See also *anagenesis.*

chthonic. Of the underworld; infernal.

civilization. A level of cultural development characterized by large population centers, formalized organizations based on specialized division of labor, and classes and statuses based more on economic standing than on kinship and heredity.

Clactonian. A form of tool industry found in northern Europe and dating from the Lower Paleolithic.

cladogenesis. The evolutionary process by which a subpopulation isolated from its originating population by some barrier that prevents further gene flow adapts to its new environment and new conditions, so that the two become genetically diverse. See also *biospecies.*

clan. An exogamous, unilineal descent group that shares a common ancestor, who may be real or fictive, to whom ties are asserted but cannot be traced genealogically.

classical evolutionism. Theories concerned with the idea that all societies or some aspect of society in general must progress through specific stages of development.

cleaver. A bifacial hand tool that ends in a straight cutting edge rather than a point.

cloning. The concept of mass-producing genetically identical individuals.

Clovis. A type of spearpoint.

compadrazgos. An institution in Latin America involving a close relationship between two people (who refer to each other as "compadres") who are not related by ties of blood but voluntarily enter into the relationship when one partner acts as godfather or godmother at the christening of the other's child.

comparative linguistics. The comparative study of related languages in order to extrapolate into the past to reconstruct prehistoric stages.

component. In archaeology, a term used to indicate how many times a given site has been occupied in archaeologically separable periods.

consanguinity. A socially, not biologically, based belief in family membership based on common descent.

control pit. An excavation pit dug near a site in order to verify the nature of the soils and deposits in an undisturbed state.

cooperative work party. A form of labor exchange in which relatives and neighbors participate in such reciprocal activities as harvesting, mowing, or house building.

core tools. Tools made by striking off one or more flakes of a nodule, or core, of rock. See also *flake tools.*

Cro-Magnon. Man of modern form who inhabited western Europe during the Upper Paleolithic, between 35,000 and 10,000 years ago. Named after a site in southwestern France where the first specimen was found.

cross-cutting ties. A force for unity and for settling disputes and exercising social control in which family ties and intermingled loyalties and allegiances are brought to bear, so that the ties uniting people in some situations affect their behavior in other situations where they are separated.

crossing over. During meiosis, the random breaking, exchanging of parts, and recombining of chromosomes.

cultural anthropology. The study of human behavior, and its products, from the perspective of the knowledge, meanings, and values shared by the members of human groups and transmitted from generation to generation by learning.

cultural ecology. The study of the structure of social groups and their interactions as they exploit various environments by means of particular technologies.

cultural patterning. The relation of sometimes disparate aspects of behavior into discernible interrelations.

cultural relativism. The idea that behavior in a society should be judged intellectually, not morally, in terms of the society's own cultural values in order to gain an understanding of the behavior of its people according to their own, rather than external, standards.

culture. All the socially learned and transmitted patterns of behavior, mutual expectations, common understandings, and values an individual shares with others of his group.

culture area. A classification of related human groups within a large geographic region; the term that is used for a collection of groups having similar social structures, economies, religions, and artistic and technological styles as a result of dependency on similar natural conditions and a long history of intergroup contact, possibly beginning with common membership in a single ancient group.

culture of poverty. The theory that each social class has its own life style and that people in the lowest strata are kept poor by their own culture, which is adapted to their adverse conditions in the short run but tends to perpetuate poverty in the long run.

cunieform. Hieroglyphic script characterized by wedge-shaped indentations, developed by the Mesopotamians.

cyclical rite. Rituals performed at regular intervals to ensure that events essential to existence will run smoothly, as in agricultural planting and harvest rites.

cytogenetics. The direct microscopic study of chromosomes.

cytosine. A nucleotide base of the DNA molecule.

d

daibatsu. In Japan, noble family corporations concerned not with personal profit but with expansion of the corporate estate and the well-being of the family dependents.

dendochronology. The dating of wood or charcoal fragments from prehistoric sites by boring into types of trees that show variations in ring width as a response to broad climatic fluctuations, then matching the fragment against the master ring sequence chart for a given region.

deoxyribonucleic acid (DNA). One of three chemical substances forming the chromosome. Heredity instructions carried by a gene are coded in the arrangement of the nucleotide bases along the strands of the DNA molecule (or molecules).

diffusion. The spread of customs and institutions among different societies as a result of intercultural borrowing.

direct reciprocity. The giving of goods, services, and aid in return for other goods, services, and aid either of the same or different kinds.

DNA. See *deoxyribonucleic acid.*

Dogrib. An Athapaskan people of northern Canada who lived primarily by hunting.

Dolichocebus. A monkey of the Late Oligocene, known from the earliest monkey skull found in South America.

dominant alleles. Masking alleles that cover the effect of other alleles, preventing them from expression in heterozygous combination. See also *recessive alleles.*

double descent system. A social system in which every individual is a member of both a patrilineal group through his father and a matrilineal group through his mother.

Dryopithecus. A genus of Miocene and Pliocene primitive apes probably ancestral to the hominids.

dyadic contract. In societies lacking corporate structure, an informal structure that binds together two individuals rather than larger groups, maintained and expressed through continuing exchanges of goods and services.

dynamics of status. The description of social class; commonly used in community studies.

e

East Rudolf. Archaeological site in Kenya containing evidence for tool use perhaps 2,500,000 years ago.

ecology. The study of the adaptations of all features to the physical environment and to one another within a given territory.

economic anthropology. The study of the principles underlying the ways people solve for themselves the problems of producing and distributing goods to meet basic needs and to give meaning to and control over their own lives.

economic choice. The theory that people in different cultures make many varied choices in allocating their resources of material goods, of their own labor, and of the assistance to be obtained from others in order to satisfy the multitude of ends that are open to them.

effective population size. The percentage of the total number of individuals in a population who actually carry out reproduction of that population.

egalitarian society. A social organization operating on the principle that all of its members are given equal prestige and equal responsibility in the functioning of that system.

endogamy. The rule that all members of a group must marry only within that group.

entrepreneurship. Individual maneuvering within a framework of cultural ground rules in order to achieve personal goals.

Eocene. An early Cenozoic period, lasting from about 50 million years ago.

ethnic group. People who conceive of themselves and are regarded by others as belonging together by virtue of common ancestry, real or fictive, and a common cultural background.

ethnocentrism. The preoccupation with one's own culture, which usually leads to a judging of all groups but one's own as inferior.

ethnoeconomics. The study of how local peoples consciously make economic choices, trying to optimize their behavior under changing and uncertain life conditions.

ethnography. The study and description of the way of life of a particular group of people.

ethology. The study of animal behavior.

exogamy. The rule stating that a member of one descent or residential or status group must marry a member of some other such group.

f

fission. The division of a group into several new groups, either permanently or temporarily.

flake tool. A tool made from flakes broken off of rock cores. See also *core tool.*

flint. A fine-grained homogeneous rock used in making tools during the Paleolithic.

Fontechevade. A site in France where fossil hominid skull fragments have been found.

functionalism. The view of society as being composed of parts that all make some kind of contribution, through interaction with other parts, to the maintenance of society as a whole and to the individual's welfare.

fusion. The division of a group into several new groups, either permanently or temporarily.

g

gamete. A sex cell produced in the testes or the ovaries.

Ganj Dareh. Developed Natufian site near Kermanshah, Iran.

gene flow. The evolutionary force that can influence the physical make-up of a population when genes move from one population to another.

gene pool. Of the species, the total collection of genes available to man. Of individual groups, the genetic variations characteristic of members of a given breeding population.

genes. Together with the chromosomes, the basic units of heredity.

genetic drift. Changes in gene frequency that have nothing to do with selective advantages or disadvantages of a gene but rather are attributable to oscillations between generations due to chance alone.

genotype. The genetic material that exists in a cell but that is not necessarily manifest in an individual. See also *phenotype*.

geologic dating. Dating of prehistoric cultural materials on the basis of the geologic deposits in which they are found.

gibbon. The smallest of the apes, and the only true brachiator.

gift exchange. As a formal arrangement, a system of centrally controlled giving and receiving wherein reciprocities constitute the fulfillment of contracts and the means to compete for and establish status.

Gigantopithecus. A fossil primate for which hominid affinities have been claimed.

gorilla. An African anthropoid; the heaviest extant primate.

guanine. A nucleotide base of the DNA molecule.

h

Hacilar. Southwest Asia site containing an aceramic level of cultural development.

hand ax. A relatively sophisticated core tool consisting of a nodule whose cutting edge continues around all or most of its border.

herbivore. An animal that eats only vegetation, as judged by its dentition.

heterozygote. A hybrid that contains a nonidentical gene pair for a certain trait. See also *homozygote*.

hierarchical societies. Those groups in which the people are stratified into classes or statuses having differential prestige and power.

hieroglyphics. The stylized picture writing originated in Egypt.

higglers. In Jamaica, traders who minimize competition by agreeing on prices that will yield a steady profit to everyone.

historical linguistics. Any study of language change through time, especially the tracing of historically documented linguistic changes.

holistic. In anthropology, an approach to the study of a culture that proceeds from the assumption that every part of it is related to every other part.

hominid. A true human form, either prehistoric or extant.

Homo. The genus to which all forms of man belong.

Homo erectus. Presapient hominids distributed throughout the Old World and who stand between *Australopithecus* and modern man.

Homo sapiens. The species to which all modern human forms belong; literally, "man the wise."

homozygote. An organism that contains an identical gene pair for a certain trait. See also *heterozygote*.

Horatio Alger ideology. A set of principles underlying economic and political systems; the view that men rise to wealth through their own personal efforts and abilities and that the ability to accumulate money is an indication of virtue, wisdom, and general worth.

horizon. In archaeology, a set of traits that links various cultures over a broad area in a brief timespan.

horticulturists. Those who cultivate with the simplest tools, such as digging sticks and hoes.

Huari. The second of three horizons that integrate Andean prehistory; it flourished around A.D. 500. See also *Chavín; Inca.*

i

ideology. The characteristic forms of knowledge that a culture makes available to all its members; a general interpretation of reality in terms of a combination of values or preferences and objective descriptions of events.

impersonal power. An invisible force that permeates the universe and that can be possessed by gods, men, and natural substances or that may be called into being by magic. See also *personified power*.

Inca. An Andean civilization that flourished around A.D. 1400; the third of the three horizons that integrate Andean prehistory. See also *Chavín; Huari.*

incest tabu. The rule forbidding close relatives to mate with one another. Which relatives are included under the rule varies widely from society to society.

indirect reciprocity. Distribution of goods in which each person contributes according to this ability and each person receives the benefits according to his need.

institutional ethnology. The study of cultural institutions (factories, hospitals, schools) as social systems.

institutions. Sets of roles established or constituted in society in which particular functions are performed, such as family, education, religion, law, and politics.

interpluvial. In climatic terms, a warm, dry period separating wet periods.

j

joking relationships. A means to alleviate potentially disruptive relationships by an exaggerated amount of horseplay, such as the traditional relationship in some societies between members of different clans.

judicial authority. Legal power to adjudicate disputes, determine guilt in crimes, and set punishments.

k

kindred. A descent group made up of all the people related to a given individual; found in societies where there is no unilineal kin-based grouping. When individuals by marriage are included, every individual has a unique kindred.

kinship. Socially, not biologically, defined relationships serving to provide continuity between generations and to regulate various aspects of the social order.

kula ring. The ceremonial economic exchange of shell necklaces and bracelets among a number of Melanesian societies.
kuru. A degenerative neurological disease found among natives in the remote New Guinea mountains.

l

language. An abstract system of word meanings and syntactic structures that provides a system of symbolization for all of culture.
language, deep structure of. The psychological level underlying the surface structure of language, including the basic units that the speaker unconsciously selects to convey his message before he encodes them into the physical noises of speech.
language, surface structure of. The overt aspects of linguistic behavior; the level most obvious to the ear.
langur. A large Asiatic monkey.
law. A system of relatively formalized and enforceable rules governing various aspects of behavior in all cultures.
legitimacy. In political anthropology, the broad expectations people have about what will come to them from the individual, the office, or the rules or law to which they comply.
Limnopithecus. A gibbonlike fossil monkey of the Miocene in East Africa.
lineage. A unilineal kinship group smaller than a clan, consisting only of people who can trace actual descent from a known ancestor.
linguistic determinism. The theory that the arbitrary classifications inherent in language may influence habits of perception and of reasoning.
linguistics, comparative. The comparison of related languages for the purpose of extrapolating into the past and reconstructing prehistoric languages.
linguistics, historical. The study of language change through time. Specifically, the tracing of historically documented linguistic changes.
lobola. A southern Bantu term meaning "bride wealth."
locus. In genetics, a position on a chromosome occupied by a gene.

Lothagan. Archaeological site in Kenya indicating hominid forms may date from about 5 million years ago.

m

Magdalenian. The final culture level of the Upper Paleolithic Age in Europe.
magic. The conscious control and manipulation by individual men of the supernatural through innate abilities or learned techniques.
Mallaha. Open-air site in northern Israel containing an interesting Natufian inventory.
malume. A Thonga word meaning "male mother" and referring to mother's brother.
mana. In Melanesia and Polynesia, a supernatural force that both gods and individual men could possess.
manuports. Unmodified rocks that were deliberately carried into cultural sites but whose functions are unknown.
Maori. A tribal people of New Zealand.
marmoset. A small, primitive South American monkey.
Masai. A warlike, pastoral tribal people of East Africa.
matriliny. A type of unilineal kinship that, for purposes of inheritance and succession, traces the kinship line only through the mother and her female forbears.
Maya. A civilization that developed in the lowlands of Yucatán and northern Guatemala and flourished about A.D. 300.
mechanical solidarity. The binding together of human groups by consensus. Present when the division of labor is minimal and everyone shares the same activities, interests, and values. See also *organic solidarity.*
mediator. A go-between for disputing parties.
meiosis. The process of somatic cell division whereby each pair of chromosomes in a cell separates and one member of each pair is drawn into each gamete.
melanin. A dark pigment in the skin and hair of man and certain animals.

Mendelian population. A community of interbreeding individuals that is reproductively isolated from other individuals of the same species.
Mesoamerica. The area comprising much of central and all of southern Mexico, Guatemala, British Honduras, and parts of Honduras and El Salvador.
microenvironment. The physical features of a small geographic territory, including its exploitable resources and limitations.
microlith. A small geometrically shaped stone blade, probably used as a point or barb for projectile weapons.
middlemen. Cultural brokers who mediate relationships between clients and patrons and who form a channel of communication between two major sectors of society—for example, the elite and the peasants.
Mindel. In archaeology, the second European glacial period, extending from about 500,000 to 450,000 years ago.
Miocene. A Cenozoic period, lasting from about 25 to 15 million years ago.
mitosis. Cell division in which the two daughter cells are identical to the parent cell in chromosomal content.
moieties. Units that divide societies organized in this way into distinct halves, usually on the basis of clans, each of which belongs to one moieties and not the other.
monopoly. A situation in which a market is controlled by one organization.
monotheism. The belief that the universe is created and governed by one all-powerful being.
moral code. A set of social ideas concerning what human actions are proper or improper, right or wrong.
morpheme. In speech, the smallest sound unit having a lexical or grammatical meaning. See also *phoneme.*
morphology. The scientific study of body shape, form, and composition using techniques of comparative anatomy, physiology, and biochemistry.
Mousterian. Culture level of the Middle Paleolithic, lasting from the Third Interglacial through the Fourth Glacial period.

Mundurucú. A South American tribe in advanced stages of acculturation.

Mureybit. Site in Syria containing material traits typical of the earliest farming villages.

mutation. A point change in the DNA code that can occur mechanically, regardless of possible function or usefulness.

mutation rate. The rate of alteration in the basic chemistry of a gene.

mwali. White shell bracelets exchanged in the Melanesian *kula* ring.

n

national character. The generalized delineation of the world view, ethos, and patterns of behavior of the people who share a culture and belong to the same group.

nationally strategic goods. The goods accumulated by the state (labor, cash, obligations, or service) and used to produce specialist goods and to engage in long-distance trade.

Natufian. In archaeology, a term used to designate early level of cultural development; foreshadowed inventories of early farmers in the Near East.

natural selection. Any environmental force that promotes reproduction of certain members of the population who carry certain genes at the expense of all other members.

Navajo. Indian tribes of Athapaskan stock found in the American Southwest.

Neanderthal man. Designation for an ancestral form of *Homo sapiens* that is associated with Mousterian culture and lived through the middle part of the Pleistocene.

Necrolemur. A prosimian of the Eocene Epoch.

neontology. A term used to denote all those aspects of the study of evolution that do not involve the fossil record.

notch. A flake tool with a concave beveled edge.

Notharctus. A prosimian primate of the Eocene Epoch.

nuclear family. A descent unit consisting of the father or husband, mother or wife, and their children.

Nuer. A pastoral and agricultural group that lives in the southern portion of the Republic of Sudan.

o

occipital lobe. The area of the cerebral cortex that is concerned with vision.

Oceania. The cultural zone that contains the culture areas of Micronesia, Polynesia, Malaysia, Melanesia, and Australia.

Oldowan tradition. A Lower Paleolithic cultural level characterized by pebble tool industries.

olfaction. The sense of smell.

Oligocene. A Cenozoic period, lasting from about 35 to 25 million years ago, in which early apes appeared in Egypt and ancestral Old World monkeys appeared.

Oligocene. *A Cenozoic period,* primate of the Oligocene Epoch, some remains of which have been found in the Fayum.

oligopoly. A situation in which a market is controlled by more than one organization.

Olmec. The first known civilization in Mesoamerica, lasting from about 1500 B.C. to A.D. 300.

omnivore. An animal that eats both meat and vegetation, as judged by its dentition.

oracle. A person who supposedly can communicate directly with the supernatural and who transmits what he learns from such communication to others.

orangutan. An anthropoid ape found in Borneo and Sumatra.

Oreopithecus. A fossil primate of the Late Miocene and Early Pliocene.

organic solidarity. The binding together of human groups through a sense of common purpose based on complementary and mutually dependent relationships, present when the division of labor is elaborate. See also *mechanical solidarity.*

osteometrics. The metric measurement and anatomical comparison of the skeletons of extant and nonextant populations.

p

Paharis. The inhabitants of the lower Himalayan area of India; meaning "of the mountains."

Paiute. Indian tribes found in California, Nevada, Utah, and Arizona.

Paleocene. The first period of the Cenozoic, lasting from about 70 to 50 million years ago.

Paleolithic. The archaeological stage encompassing the time-span from the Lower Pleistocene until about 10,000 years ago. Also known as the Old Stone Age.

paleontology. The study of the life forms that existed in the past.

palynology. The scientific study of pollen and spores, used by anthropologists in the determination of prehistoric climates.

Paranthropus. A genus of prehistoric woodland herbivore more closely related to the apes than to man. See also *Australopithecus.*

Parapithecus. A Fayum primate bearing resemblances to modern Old World monkeys.

parietal lobe. The area of the cerebral cortex that is concerned with hearing.

participant-observer. One who studies a culture by living within it for a period of time.

pastoralists. Those who gain a livelihood by herding animals.

patriliny. A type of unilineal kinship that, for purposes of inheritance and succession, traces the kinship lines only through the father and his male forbears.

Périgord. A region of southwestern France where prehistoric hunting settlements extended for hundreds of yards and sometimes involved permanent habitation.

personified power. Power belonging to supernatural beings, such as gods or demons, which they operate at their will or direction. See also *impersonal power.*

Peyotists. American Indians who belong to the Peyote cult, a revitalization movement, which involves the eating of portions of the peyote plant in religious ceremonies.

phenotype. The genetic characteristics that are manifest in an individual and can be measured.

phoneme. The smallest significant sound unit in a language. See also *morpheme.*

physical anthropology. The study of man's evolution as a biological and cultural being.

Draws on medicine, health research, archaeology, primatology, paleontology, human genetics, serology, osteology, and other disciplines.

pibloktoq. A mental disorder found among Eskimo women.

pick. A core tool consisting of a nodule that is flaked into a heavy pointed form.

pithecanthropines. A nontechnical term referring to certain nonextant varieties of early hominids nearly indistinguishable from modern man from the shoulder down but varying importantly in skull shape. Term was derived from the wrongly applied genus name *Pithecanthropus;* pithecanthropines are now considered of the genus *Homo erectus.*

Pithecanthropus erectus. An early hominid, now generally included in the genus *Homo erectus.*

Pleistocene. The last 1 million to 500,000 years of geologic history.

Plesiadapis. A prosimian of the Paleocene Epoch.

Pliocene. A Cenozoic period, lasting from about 15 million to 2 million years ago, in which prehuman primates and apes of modern type appeared.

Pliopithecus. A gibbonlike fossil monkey of the Miocene in Europe.

plural society. A political unit in which different groups have different systems of basic institutions and different cultures.

political behavior. All behavior centering around public goals and the distribution and use of public power.

political system. That part of the organization of a society within which political behavior occurs.

polygenic trait. A trait that is controlled by more than one gene pair.

polymers. Molecules of similar structure that are joined together.

polymorphism. The presence of more than one allele for a given locus in a given population.

Pondaungia. A fossil primate of the Late Eocene in Burma that may have been a primitive ape.

population. In genetics, all those individuals who share the same gene pool.

population genetics. The study of the relations between the distribution of genes and the distribution of individual differences in trait expression in Mendelian populations.

potlatch. A ritual feast given by Northwest Coast Indians in the United States in which there was competition to establish who could give away the most lavish gifts and destroy most of his own property.

potsherds. Pottery fragments.

prehensile tail. In primatology, tails adapted for seizing or grasping, especially by wrapping around an object.

prehistory. The period of mans' existence preceding the advent of written records.

primary institutions. The customary modes of thought and behavior that act on a child early in life, such as maternal care and parental discipline; all the attitudes of society, both permissive and restrictive, that affect the formation of the child's personality. See also *secondary institutions.*

primate. The highest order within the mammalian class, including lemurs, tarsiers, monkeys, apes, and man.

primatologist. One who studies the zoological order of man and his primate relatives.

Propliopithecus. A small Fayum primate that may have been a primitive ape.

prosimians (pre-monkeys). A suborder of primates that includes tarsiers and lemurs.

Pseudoloris. A prosimian primate of the Eocene Epoch.

psychological anthropology. The branch of anthropology concerned with studying the role of such personality characteristics as motivation in affecting social institutions and cultural complexes and vice versa.

Pueblo Indians. A farming society of the southwest United States.

quadrumanous. Four-handed.

quadruped. An animal having four feet.

quinoa. A type of high-altitude cereal grown in the Andean cultures.

quipu. A cord used in an involved method employed by the Incas to keep accounts with knots, based upon numeration.

races. Mendelian populations that differ in the relative frequencies of various alleles in their gene pools.

Ramapithecus. A very early hominid, possibly an ancestor to *Australopithecus.*

rationing. The equitable distribution of goods that are limited in supply.

Recent Epoch. The interglacial period that began around 9000 B.C. and has continued to the present.

recessive alleles. The alleles that are masked by other alleles covering the same effects. For some genes, if both alleles are recessive the heterozygote will show a form of the trait intermediate between the homozygous forms. See also *dominant alleles.*

religion. Man's symbolic expressions that provide emotionally satisfying meaning to the unexplainable through reference to the supernatural.

retouch. A secondary chipping phase in the construction of tools.

revitalization movements. Religious movements that attempt to introduce new strength into threatened or declining practices and beliefs in a society that is undergoing marked cultural changes and social disruption.

Rh factor. A substance that is present in the red blood cells of most higher animals and in the majority of humans and that is inherited according to Mendel's genetic laws. Rh incompatibility between mother and father may affect a child at birth.

ribonucleic acid. One of three chemical substances making up the chromosomes.

ribosomes. The bodies in the cytoplasm of a cell that synthesize proteins.

Riss glacial period. The third European glacial period, extending from about 250,000 to 125,000 years ago.

rite of passage. A ceremony or ritual that serves to ease the transition of individuals from one status to another, most commonly connected with birth, initiation into adulthood, marriage, and death.

rituals of reversal. Religious practices in which the norms of everyday behavior are temporarily displaced by behavior that in one way or another reverses the everyday practice.

Rorschach inkblot test. A type of projective test in which inkblots are used as stimuli.

S

sanasimajanga. An Eskimo word for both aesthetic and utilitarian productions meaning "that which has been made."

Sanskrit. An ancient literary language of India.

savanna. A climatic zone characterized by grasslands with scattered tree growth.

scrapers. Flake tools that carry a straight or curved beveled edge executed in unifacial retouch. The bevel may continue almost all the way around the tool or it may be restricted to one edge.

secondary institutions. Modes of behavior that serve as society's means for compensating, rationalizing, denying, or vicariously gratifying blocked impulses. Secondary institutions include magic, ideology, and art. See also *primary institutions.*

segmentary opposition. In societies that are divided into segments such as that of the Nuer, the unity of any one segment in opposition to an opposing segment of equal magnitude or scope.

semantics. The scientific study of the meaning of words.

seriation. The dating of cultural artifacts based on the assumption that the popularity of a particular style or type of artifact tends to increase from its initial introduction, reach a maximum, and eventually decline.

serology. The calculation of gene frequencies in a gene pool through examination of blood samples from individuals in the population.

shaman. A religious specialist supposedly endowed with supernatural powers that enable him to perform extraordinary feats.

Shoshoni. A hunting-gathering people that inhabited the North American Great Basin.

siblings. Children of the same mother.

signs. Representations of objects or activities having an intrinsic connection with that which is being signified. See also *symbols.*

Sinanthropus pekinensis. A type of fossil man found near Peking in China that is now considered of the same species as *Homo erectus.*

social anthropology. The study of human behavior and institutions from the perspective of existing social relationships and systems of interpersonal and intergroup ties and cleavages, and the consequences of these relationships, ties, and cleavages.

social character. The set of motivating conditions shared by most members of a society that serves as an instrument for maintaining that society.

social death. The carrying on of appropriate social behavior before, during, and after the biological death of a person.

social differentiation. The separation of "classes" based on economic condition, length of residence, social prestige, political power, life style, kinship connection, or a combination thereof.

social fact. The concept of a power over members of society that functions to unify and control individual behavior. This power becomes manifest when it takes the form of coercion exercised over an individual through certain sanctions or when it is used to suppress individual efforts to violate these sanctions.

social personality. The psychological profile of a people or society. Also known as modal personality.

sodalities. Nonresidential common-purpose groups.

Solutré. A prehistoric site in France of a mound of thousands of fossil horses that apparently were stampeded over a cliff.

somatology. The characterization and classification of human body form.

song duel. A kind of trial-by-combat used by Eskimo in settling disputes. Both plaintiff and defendant attempt to outperform the other in singing insultingly about his opponent in order to earn to applause of the jury and thus win the case.

sorcery. Basically a pseudoscience purposefully mobilized against a victim. Distinguished from witchcraft, which can be involuntary and is innate rather than learned.

soulava. Red shell necklaces exchanged in the Melanesian *kula* ring.

speciation. The genetic divergence of a species into two new populations that thereafter are unable to interbreed.

species. A population that is distinct genetically, morphologically, and behaviorally from all other populations.

Steinheim. A fossil hominid skull found in western Germany, believed to be 150,000 years old. It is believed to be either *Homo erectus* or *Homo sapiens.*

stratigraphy. Analysis of geologic (or cultural) deposits in terms of discernible layers. A chronology of the cultures that occupied a site can be determined from the relative positions of the layers.

styles. In art, meanings and techniques that have become accepted as standards of excellence and propriety and that promote social identification.

subculture. A group within a culture that either does not hold all of the beliefs and values of the larger culture or accords them different emphasis.

supernatural. That which is unexplainable in terms of the natural world.

superorganic. The term for cultural manifestations as distinguished from the inorganic and the organic phenomena in the universe; it asserts a realm for cultural phenomena entirely separate from that of psychological and biological phenomena.

Swanscombe. Pieces of the back of a fossil hominid skull found in England, used as evidence that *Homo sapiens* is an older species than was previously thought.

Tell us what you think

All over the country, today's students are taking an active role in the quality of their education. They're telling administrators what they like and what they don't like about campus communities. They're telling teachers what they like and what they don't like about courses.

This response card offers you a unique opportunity to tell a publisher what you like and what you don't like about his book.

Student Response Card

We care about your opinion of *Anthropology Today*. It took us a lot of time and effort to produce, and the best we could do at the time went into it. But we know it can be improved. Any textbook can be improved. What we don't know is where you think the improvements should be made. What are your general impressions?

Term Used_____ Date_____

Name_____ School_____

Address (good for three months)_____

City_____State_____Zip_____

☐ Would you be willing to give us additional guidance? If so, please check this box, and we'll send you a detailed questionnaire about the book that takes about half an hour to fill out. (In return for serving us as a consultant in the evaluation of *Anthropology Today*, we'll offer you—free—your choice from a selection of books in the Psychology Today Book Club.)   **2nd Printing   Q113**

symbols. Arbitrary representations of objects or activities. See also *signs*.

synoecism. The process by which adjacent towns and villages unite to form larger integrated economic and political units.

t

tabu. That which is forbidden, or to be feared; any restraint or prohibition with a supernatural sanction attached to it.

talisman. An object that has supposed supernatural powers of effecting unusual happenings and guarding against evil.

Tamaulipas. An excavation site in the Tehuacan Valley of Mexico.

temporal lobe. The area of the cerebral cortex that is concerned with vocalization.

Teotihuacán. A civilization that developed in the Valley of Mexico, in which modern Mexico City is located, and that dominated most of Mesoamerica between the time of Christ and A.D. 600.

Tell es-Sultan (Jericho). Site in the valley of the Dead Sea noted for its size, architecture, and obsidian artifacts.

Terre Amata. An early Acheulean site on the French Riviera.

Tetonius. A prosimian primate of the Eocene period.

Thematic Apperception Test (TAT). A projective test in which the subject is required to make up stories about ambiguous pictures.

theocratic states. Societies that are governed by a priestly class.

Thonga. A South African Bantu-speaking tribe.

thymine. A nucleotide base of the DNA molecule.

tipi. A conical-shaped dwelling usually made of skins stretched over upright poles.

Toltec. A militaristic Mexican civilization that flourished after the Maya, around A.D. 900.

Torralba. An Acheulean site in central Spain.

totemism. A belief system involving the origin of kin groups that interweaves man, nature, and the supernatural based on the elements of crucial importance to a society, such as some aspect of the environment, an animal, or a plant, any of which may be viewed as the founding ancestor of a clan or lineage.

touf. Loaded sun-dried bricks used architecturally in Developed Natufian cultures.

traditions. Major blocks of cultural development.

transformational grammar. The school of thought that emphasizes the difference between deep and surface structures and the importance of the rules relating these two levels.

transhumance. The system of cyclical movements between different regions at various seasons necessary for the year-around care of domesticated animals.

tribe. A constellation of groups of kinsmen who identify themselves and are identified by others as a distinct group.

trickle-down effect. The influence of the elite art of a civilization on the peasant and lower-class art.

Trobrianders. Natives of the Trobriand Islands in Melanesia.

tundra. Treeless plains of the arctic, marshy in the summer and frozen in the winter.

typology. The classification of artifacts or other objects according to the presence or absence of various characteristics.

u

uniformitarianism. The theory that, unless there is evidence to the contrary, events that occurred in the past will have happened in the same way similar events happen now.

unilineal descent groups. Kin groups formed on the basis of either matrilineal or patrilineal descent.

urban anthropology. The study of complex societies in terms of problems of ethnic minorities, urban deterioration, and popular discontent.

v

varves. Thin deposits in calm glacial lakes that show by color and texture the material laid down each season.

Vertezöllös. A site in Hungary dating from the Mindel glacial period.

w

wiitiko. A psychosis prevalent among the Cree-Ojibwa Indians in which the patient became obsessed with cannibalism.

witchcraft. A supposed inborn characteristic of an individual that is brought into being either voluntarily or involuntarily, to harm other men. See also *sorcery*.

working floor. A place where tools were made by early men.

Würm glacial period. The fourth European glacial period, extending from about 75,000 to 25,000 years ago.

y

yi-shu. An early Chinese word for art, meaning any kind of learned skill.

Yir Yoront. A primitive Australian tribe.

z

ziggurat. A hill or platform made of sun-dried bricks atop which Sumerian temples were built.

zygote. A cell formed when a female gamete (ovum) is fertilized by a male gamete (sperm).

Index

a

socialization, 362–363
 discipline in, 363
 Freudian theories, 359–360
 and technology, 363
society, definition of, 40, 340
sodality, 285
Solomon Islanders, 7
Solutré, 231, 372
Solvieux, *209*
soma, search for, 17–21, *20*
somatology, 127–128
sorcery, 491
soulava, 390
space-time framework, 204–205
spears, 375
 atlatls, 374
 clovis, 263
 multipronged, 375, *377*
speciation, 120
Speke, J. H., 312
Spencer, Herbert, 39, 274, 372, 503
spider monkey, *64*, 65–75, *73*, *74*
 prehensile tail use, 74–75, 155
 social behavior, 72–74
Spindler, George, 365
spy, 24
squirrel monkey, *69*
state, rise of, 251–253
status, dynamics of, 306,
Stefansson, Vilhjalmur, 286
Stein, Maurice, 306
Steinheim, 27, *27*, 182–184
Sterkfontein, *162*, 164, 173
Steward, Julian, 44, 45, *45*, 46, 49, 205, 207, 370, 372, 379, 504
Stirling County, 366–367, *366*
stratigraphy, 211–212, 218
structural-functional analysis, 389–390, 393, 403–405, *404*
structuralism, 332–334, 453
Sudan, emir's court, *454*, *457*
Sudnow, David, 309
Sumer, *252*, 255
Sun Yat sen, *515*
supernaturalism, 286–287, *335*, 482–484
 impersonal power, 483
 magic, 484–485
 personified power, 483
Swanscombe, 27, *27*, 182
Swartkrans, 173
sweat baths, 13, *13*
sweat glands, *120*, 180
symbiosis, *135*, 138, 290, *291*
symbolism, 423–425, *424*, *429*
synchronic study, *334*
syncretism, *506*, 507–508, 509–510
synoecism, 254

t

tabu, 321, *483*, 484
Tacitus, 33–34, *34*
Taiwanese, *188*
talismans, 484, *485*

Tarsius, 153
Tasmanians, 379, *501*, 516
Taung, *22*, 164
Tchambuli, 356
technology, and environmental adaptation, 370, 371
Tell es-Sultan (Jericho), *237*, 244, 246, 253
Teotihuacán, 266, *382*
Ternefine, *27*, 173
Tetonius, 153
Thematic Apperception Test (TAT), *364*, 365
thermoluminescence of pottery, 213
Third World, 315, 516, 518
Thompson, M. K., 474
Thomsen, Christian, 24, 34, 205
Thonga, 394–396, *394*, *395*
Thurnwald, Richard, 471
Tiahuanaco, 269
Tobias, Phillip, *25*
Togo, *336*
Tolai, 459, 460
Toltec, 267, 269
tool traditions, 219–220, *219*, *220*
Tonga, monarchs of, *314*
Torralba, 225, *225*
totemism, 287, 486–487
tradition (archaeology), 215, 220
transformational grammar, development of, 47
tree shrew, 149
trephining, 130–131, *131*
trickledown effect, 297–298, *297*, 428
Trobrianders, *120*, *206*, *388*, *390*, *392*, 441, 443, 471
Tuareg, *15*, *521*
Turnbull, Colin, 372
Turner, Victor, 466–467
twin studies, 128
Tylor, Edward Burnett, 36–38, *36*
 on religion, 37, *37*, 485–486, 488
 on social evolution, 501–502
 on social reform, 303, 318, 319
type categories, 59–61, 214
typology, human, 119

u

uniformitarianism, 23
unilinear evolution, 36, 336, 500–501
Ur, 255–256, *256*
urbanization, *91*, 299–301, *301*, 320–321, 478–479, 518
Uruk, White Temple at, 255

V

Valentine, Betty Lou, 89
Valentine, Charles, 89, 318–319
Vallonet, 221
Van Gennep, Arnold, 495
varves, 212
Venus figurines, 233, *245*, *425*, 427, 430
Verteszöllös, *27*, 224, 225
vervet, *140*
Vidich, Arthur, 306
village farming, developed, 247–248
village farming, primary, 245–247

W

Wallace, Anthony, 42
Wapisiana, 471–472
Warner, W. Lloyd, 305, 306
Washburn, Sherwood, 180
Watson-Crick model, 110
weaponry, evolution of, *372*
Weber, Max, 370, 469, 482
Weidenreich, Franz, 172
Weiner, J. S., 182
White, Leslie, 44, 45, 372, 503–504, *503*
Whiting, John, 366
Willendorf, Venus of, *425*
Wissler, Clark, 38, 304
witchcraft, 491–494
Withers, Carl, 305
Wittfogel, Karl, 252, 381
Wolf, Eric, 291, 337
Wolfe, Alvin, 96
working floor, definition of, 27
writing systems, 255, *255*, 257, 260, 261, 264, *264*, 265, 269, *408*
Würm, 228, 229, *229*, 231

Y

Yao, 481–482
Yir Yoront, 320
Yangshao culture, 262, *262*
Yoruba, *366*, 367

Z

Zarzian, 243, 244
Zawi Chemi Shanidar, 244, 245
Zdansky, Otto, 171
Ziggurat, 255
Zinjanthropus. See australopithecines; *Paranthropus*
Zorbaugh, Harvey, 304
Zulu, *280*, 281
Zuñi, 40, 277, 329, 348
zygote, 110–111, *112*, *113*, 117

HORIZONS IN THE STUDY OF MAN I
Netsilik Eskimo at winter sea-ice camp.
Film Studio, Education Development Center.

1 The Science of Man
1. Astronaut White floating in zero gravity of space. National Aeronautics and Space Administration. 2. William Davenport. 3. Paul Slick, after C. Scott Littleton. 4. Wayne McLoughlin. 5. European Art Color Slides, Peter Adelberg, Inc. 6. (Above), Bob Broder, University of Arizona; (lower left) F. E. Patterson, U.S. Geological Survey; (lower right) University of Arizona. 7. Armstrong/Fountain Graphic Art. 8. The Bettmann Archive, Inc. 9. Marc Riboud, Magnum. 10. Stan Solleder. 11. Terry Lamb. 12. Editorial Photocolor Archives. 13. The Bettmann Archive, Inc. 14. The Granger Collection. 15. Hiram L. Parent from National Audubon Society. 16. David Chivers.

2 Studies of Man the Animal
1. Cast of the Taung child skull. John T. Robinson. 2. (Above) The Granger Collection; (middle) Collection Musée de L'Homme; (below) collection Musée de L'Homme. 3. Karl Nicholason. 4. (Above) Anonymous; (middle) courtesy of the American Museum of Natural History; (below right) Phillip V. Tobias, Head, Department of Anatomy, University of the Witwatersrand, Johannesburg. 5 and 6. Karl Nicholason. 7. Armstrong/Fountain Graphic Art. 8. Karl Nicholason. 9 and 10. Joyce Fitzgerald. 11. Stan Solleder.

3 Developing Sociocultural Views
1. Sepik River native, Melanesia. Wayne McLoughlin. 2. The Bettmann Archive, Inc. 3. Musée de L'Homme. 4. The Bettmann Archive, Inc. 5. Armstrong/Fountain Graphic Art and Paul Slick. 6. (Above) Historical Pictures Service, Chicago; (below) The Granger Collection. 7. Terry Lamb. 8. Gerrie Blake. 9. Culver Pictures. 10. Historical Pictures Service, Chicago. 11. Museum of Man, San Diego, California. 12. George Pressler, Photophile. 13. Wayne McLoughlin. 14. Monkmeyer Press Photos. 15. Armstrong/Fountain Graphic Art. 16. Bruno Barbey, Magnum. 17. Wayne McLoughlin. 18. Armstrong/Fountain Graphic Art. 19. Paul Slick and Donna Levitt. 20. Armstrong/Fountain Graphic Art.

WHAT THE ANTHROPOLOGIST DOES II
L. S. B. Leakey at Olduvai Gorge. Ian Berry, Magnum.

4 Case Study: Digging Up the Past
1. Recovering an American Indian skull. Bob Van Doren. 2. Thomas Gilcrease Institute, Tulsa, Oklahoma. 3. Armstrong/Fountain Graphic Art. 4 and 5. James Deetz; River Basin Surveys, Smithsonian Institute; and Midwest Archaeological Center, National Park Service. 6. Larry Leach. 7 through 9. James Deetz; River Basin Surveys, Smithsonian Institute; and Midwest Archaeological Center, National Park Service. 10. John Dawson. 11. Karl Aldana.

5 Case Study: Primates in the Field
1. Spider monkey, Colombia, South America. Dorothy and Lewis Klein. 2. Armstrong/Fountain Graphic Art. 3 through 11. Dorothy and Lewis Klein.

6 Case Study: In the Remote Village
1. Children of Sirkanda, India. Gerald Berreman. 2. Armstrong/Fountain Graphic Art. 3 through 9. Gerald Berreman.

7 Case Study: In a Complex Society
1. Afro-American in the United States. Burke Uzzle, Magnum. 2. (Above) Reynold Hernandez; (middle left) Photo Trends; (middle right) Magnum; (below) Reynold Hernandez. 3. Armstrong/Fountain Graphic Art, after Charles A. Valentine. 4. Builder Levy. 5. Armstrong/Fountain Graphic Art, after Charles A. Valentine. 6. David DaSilva. 7. Armstrong/Fountain Graphic Art, after Charles A. Valentine. 8. Builder Levy. 9. Armstrong/Fountain Graphic Art, after Charles A. Valentine. 10. Builder Levy. 11 and 12. Armstrong/Fountain Graphic Art, after Charles A. Valentine. 13 and 14. Builder Levy.

THE EVOLUTION OF MAN III
Child and orangutan. Bob Van Doren.

8 Methods in Physical Anthropology
1. Doctors in Kerala. Marilyn Silverstone, Magnum. 2. Armstrong/Fountain Graphic Art. 3 through 6. Bob Kinyon, Millsap and Kinyon. 7 and 8. Armstrong/Fountain Graphic Art. 9. Lester Bergman and Associates. 10. Wayne McLoughlin. 11. Robert L. Carneiro, American Museum of Natural History. 12. Otto Lang, Photophile. 13 and 14. Armstrong/Fountain Graphic Art. 15. Bob Van Doren and Armstrong/Fountain Graphic Art. 16. John T. Robinson. 17. George Rodger, Magnum. 18. Reynold Hernandez.

Credits and Acknowledgments

9 Primate Social Behavior
1. Female baboon and infant, Nairobi Park. Irven DeVore. 2. K. Kawanaka. 3. (Above left). Stuart Altmann, University of Chicago; (above right) Irven DeVore; (below) Stuart Altmann, University of Chicago. 4. (Above) Irven DeVore; (lower left) K. Kawanaka; (middle right) Bob Van Doren; (below right) David Chivers. 5. Irven DeVore. 6. Armstrong/Fountain Graphic Art. 7. (Above) Stuart Altmann, University of Chicago; (below) David Chivers. 8 through 11. Irven DeVore. 12. Stuart Altmann, University of Chicago. 13. Junichiro Itani.

10 Prehuman Primates
1. *Dryopithecus africanus* skull from Kenya. Courtesy the British Museum of Natural History; Elwyn L. Simons. 2. Karl Nicholason. 3 and 4. Armstrong/Fountain Graphic Art. 5. D. E. Russell and Donald Baird; courtesy Elwyn L. Simons. 6. Karl Nicholason. 7. Bob Van Doren. 8. John Dawson. 9 and 10. A. H. Coleman; courtesy Elwyn L. Simons. 11. Karl Nicholason. 12. T. F. Walsh; courtesy Elwyn L. Simons. 13 and 14. A. H. Coleman; courtesy Elwyn L. Simons.

11 Presapient Hominids
1. Excavations at Sterkfontein, South Africa. John T. Robinson. 2. Karl Nicholason. 3 through 6. John T. Robinson. 7. Karl Nicholason. 8. John T. Robinson. 9. Karl Nicholason. 10. Gordon W. Gahan, © 1970 National Geographic Society. 11. John T. Robinson. 12. (Above) Courtesy of the American Museum of Natural History, the Geological Survey of China, and Franz Weidenreich. 13. Phillip V. Tobias, Head, Department of Anatomy, University of the Witwatersrand, Johannesburg. 14. Armstrong/ Fountain Graphic Art. 15. Karl Nicholason.

12 *Homo Sapiens*
1. Site at Mount Carmel, where Neanderthal forms have been recovered. Arthur J. Jellinek. 2 and 3. Karl Nicholason. 4. The Summer Institute of Linguistics, Inc. 5. Collection Musée de L'Homme, Paris. 6. Karl Nicholason. 7. Armstrong/Fountain Graphic Art. 8. and 9. Karl Nicholason.

13 Modern Man
1. Street scene in Taiwan. Reynold Hernandez. 2. Armstrong/Fountain Graphic Art. 3. Eve Arnold, Magnum. 4. Wayne McLoughlin. 5. Marilyn Silverstone, Magnum. 6. U.S. Department of Agriculture. 7. Don Hesse, the Summer Institute of Linguistics, Inc. 8. Armstrong/Fountain Graphic Art. 9. Lester Bergman and Associates. 10. Arthur Tress, Photo Trends. 11. Darrel Millsap, Millsap and Kinyon. 12. G. Phillip Smith.

THE ARCHAEOLOGICAL RECORD IV
Saqqara, tomb of Zoser in Egypt.
Ray Weiss, Photophile.

14 Methods in Archaeology
1. Tegucigalpa, Honduras. Kay Frishman, Nancy Palmer. 2. Collection Musée de L'Homme. 3. Wayne McLoughlin. 4. Carol Randall. 5. George J. Gumerman, Prescott College; and U.S. Geological Survey, Prescott Research Unit, Water Resources Division. 6. James Sackett. 7. Thomas Gilcrease Institute, Tulsa, Oklahoma. 8. John Veltri. Courtesy Michael L. Katzev, Oberlin College. 9. MGM Documentary Department. 10. John Dawson. 11. Armstrong/Fountain Graphic Art.

15 Paleolithic Culture
1. Rock shelter near Les Eyzies, France. Elliott Erwitt, Magnum. 2. Armstrong/Fountain Graphic Art. 3. Reynold Hernandez. 4. Armstrong/ Fountain Graphic Art. 5. John Dawson. 6. H. B. S. Cooke, Dalhousie University, Nova Scotia. 7. John Dawson. 8. Courtesy Museum and Laboratory of Ethnic Arts and Technology, UCLA. 9. L. G. Freeman. 10. John Dawson. 11. Karl Nicholason. 12. Collection Musée de L'Homme. 13. Courtesy Museum and Laboratory of Ethnic Arts and Technology, UCLA. 14. Armstrong/Fountain Graphic Art. 15. European Art Color Slides, Peter Adelberg, Inc. 16. Courtesy Museum and Laboratory of Ethnic Arts and Technology, UCLA. 17. Karl Nicholason.

16 Beginnings of Domestication
1. Excavations at Abou Gosh in Israel. Jean Perrot, and Centre de Recherches Préhistoriques Français de Jérusalem and Mission Archéologique Français en Israël. 2. John Dawson. 3. Armstrong/Fountain Graphic Art. 4 and 5. John Dawson. 6 and 7. Prehistoric Project, The Oriental Institute, University of Chicago; Courtesy Robert J. Braidwood. 8. John Dawson.

9. Prehistoric Project, The Oriental Institute, University of Chicago; Courtesy Robert J. Braidwood. 10. Armstrong/Fountain Graphic Art. 11. Jean Perrot, and Centre de Recherches Préhistoriques Français de Jérusalem and Mission Archéologique Français en Israël. 12. John Dawson. 13. John Dawson, after The Oriental Institute, University of Chicago; Courtesy Charles A. Reed. 14. Prehistoric Project, The Oriental Institute, University of Chicago; Courtesy Robert J. Braidwood. 15. Armstrong/Fountain Graphic Art. 16. Terry Lamb.

17 The Rise of Civilization
1. Mukteswar Temple, India. C. A. Peterson, Rapho Guillamette. 2. Karl Nicholason. 3. The Metropolitan Museum of Art, gifts of Mrs. Khalil Rabensu and Norbert Schimmel, 1959. 4 and 5. Armstrong/Fountain Graphic Art. 6. The Metropolitan Museum of Art, gift of Matilda W. Bruce, 1907. 7. By courtesy of the Trustees of The British Museum. 8. The Metropolitan Museum of Art, Museum Excavations, Rogers Fund, 1930. 9. Armstrong/Fountain Graphic Art. 10. (Above) Elliott Erwitt, Magnum; (below) The Metropolitan Museum of Art, gift of the Egyptian Exploration Fund, 1901, and Rogers Fund, 1919. 11 and 12. Armstrong/Fountain Graphic Art. 13. Courtesy Chase Manhattan Bank, Money Museum. 14. The Metropolitan Museum of Art, the Harris Brisbane Dick Fund, 1949. 15. Freer Gallery, Smithsonian Institute, Washington, D.C. 16. Armstrong/Fountain Graphic Art. 17. John Dawson. 18. Michael Chatfield. 19. Armstrong/Fountain Graphic Art. 20. John Dawson. 21. Harry Crosby, Photophile. 22. Organization of American States. 23. Museum of the American Indian, Heye Foundation. 24. Organization of American States. 25. Bodleian Library Color Filmstrip.

EMERGENCE OF CONTEMPORARY SOCIETY V
Aborigines in Arnhemland. Photographic Library of Australia.

18 Primitive Societies
1. Hunter in New Guinea. Wayne McLoughlin. 2. Armstrong/Fountain Graphic Art. 3. Film Studio, Education Development Center. 4. Harry Crosby, Photophile. 5. Robert L. Carneiro, American Museum of Natural History. 6. Wayne McLoughlin. 7. Japan National Tourist Organization. 8. H. B. S. Cooke, Dalhousie University, Nova Scotia. 9. Stanley Washburn. 10. Wayne McLoughlin. 11. Irven DeVore.

19 Peasant Societies
1. Threshers in Mexico. Harry Crosby, Photophile. 2. The Metropolitan Museum of Art, Rogers Fund, 1922. 3. Armstrong/Fountain Graphic Art. 4. Ron Himes, The Summer Institute of Linguistics, Inc. 5. The Metropolitan Museum of Art, Rogers Fund, 1919. 6. Armstrong/Fountain Graphic Art. 7. Otto Lang, Photophile. 8. Courtesy *Artes de Mexico*. 9. The Bettmann Archive, Inc. 10. Michael Chatfield. 11. Otto Lang, Photophile.

20 Complex Societies
1. Festival at Gokalasheni, India. Marilyn Silverstone, Magnum. 2. Jane Latta, Bethel Agency. 3. Triangle Color Lab. 4. Armstrong/Fountain Graphic Art. 5. Carl Jaffe. 6. Marc Riboud, Magnum. 7. Reynold Hernandez. 8. Otto Lang, Photophile. 9. George Rodger, Magnum. 10. The Granger Collection. 11. David Beal, Photo Media Ltd. 12. R. Lloyd Jones. 13. Charles Harbutt, Magnum. 14. Collection of Merton D. Simpson Gallery, Inc. 15. Culver Pictures. 16. Gordon Menzie, Photophile. 17. J. Toussaint.

THE STUDY OF SOCIETY AND CULTURE VI
Houseboats in the Philippines. Don Hesse, The Summer Institute of Linguistics, Inc.

21 Methods in Cultural Anthropology
1. Vanishing life way; Netsilik woman of the Arctic. Film Studio, Education Development Center, Inc. 2. Diego Rivera, National Palace, Mexico City, D.F. 3. Wide World Photos. 4. Armstrong/Fountain Graphic Art. 5. Theodore Schwartz, Courtesy American Museum of Natural History. 6. Michael Lowy. 7. (Above left) Ray Weiss, Photophile; (above right) David Lyon, Magnum; (below) Otto Lang, Photophile. 8. Armstrong/Fountain Graphic Art and Paul Slick. 9. Peter Furst. 10. Peace Corps.

22 Ethnographic Field Work
1. Village woman of India. Gerald Berreman. 2. Gerald Berreman. 3. The Summer Institute of Linguistics, Inc. 4. Gerald Berreman. 5. Ray Weiss, Photophile. 6. Film Studio, Education Development Center. 7. Terry Lamb.

23 The Psychological Perspective
1. Bushman mother and child, Africa. Irven DeVore. 2. Wayne McLoughlin. 3. Armstrong/Fountain Graphic Art. 4. Hugh Wilkerson. 5. Dr. Block Color Reproductions. 6. (Above) Ray Weiss, Photophile; (below) Marcia Keegan. 7. Armstrong/Fountain Graphic Art and Paul Slick. 8. Bruno Barbey, Magnum. 9. Otto Lang, Photophile. 10. Museum of the American Indian, Heye Foundation. 11. Pertti J. Pelto and Robert J. Maxwell. 12. Armstrong/Fountain Graphic Art, after John Honigmann. 13. Margaret Mead.

24 Cultural Ecology
1. Australian aborigines making spears. Jeff Carter, Photographic Library of Australia. 2. Armstrong/Fountain Graphic Art. 3. Reynold Hernandez. 4. Armstrong/Fountain Graphic Art. 5. John Dawson. 6. M. G. Froelich. 7. Photographic Library of Australia. 8. Karl Nicholason. 9. Wayne McLoughlin. 10. Stanley Washburn. 11. Museum of Man, San Diego, California. 12. The Bettmann Archive, Inc. 13. (Above) G. Phillip Smith; (middle) Jim Flores, Los Angeles; (below) J. Toussaint. 14. Bob Mosher, Photophile. 15. Dr.

Block Color Reproductions. 16. George Rodger, Magnum. 17. Philip Jones Griffiths, Magnum. 18. Otto Lang, Photophile

25 Structural-Functional Analysis
1. Observing the *kula* festivities, Trobriand Islands. Wayne McLoughlin. 2. Wayne McLoughlin. 3. Armstrong/Fountain Graphic Art. 4. Wayne McLoughlin. 5. Armstrong/Fountain Graphic Art. 6. Phillip V. Tobias, Head, Department of Anatomy, University of the Witwatersrand, Johannesburg. 7. Armstrong/Fountain Graphic Art. 8. Courtesy E. E. Evans-Pritchard and Pitt-Rivers Museum, University of Oxford. 9. Terry Lamb. 10. Collections of The New York Public Library; Astor, Lenox, and Tilden Foundations. 11. Paul Slick.

CULTURE IN ITS INFINITE VARIETY VII
Gathering in Kabul, Afghanistan. Carl Jaffe.

26 Language
1. Elements of Western language systems diffusing into Melanesia. The Summer Institute of Linguistics, Inc. 2. Armstrong/Fountain Graphic Art. 3. Terry Lamb. 4. Armstrong/Fountain Graphic Art. 5. University of California Press, Los Angeles and Berkeley. 6. Armstrong/Fountain Graphic Art. 7. (Above) J. Toussaint; (middle) Reynold Hernandez; (below) G. Phillip Smith. 8. Reynold Hernandez.

27 Art and Society
1. Eskimo sculpting. Nelson Graburn. 2. The Metropolitan Museum of Art, Fletcher Fund, 1947, The A. W. Bahr Collection. 3. Larry Leach. 4. National Gallery of Art. 5. Vienna Museum of Natural History, European Art Color Slides, Peter Adelberg, Inc. 6. European Art Color Slides, Peter Adelberg, Inc. 7. Armstrong/Fountain Graphic Art. 8. Courtesy Metropolitan Museum of Art, The Crosby Brown Collection of Musical Instruments, 1889. 9. The Metropolitan Museum of Art, The Theodore M. Davis Collection. Bequest of Theodore M. Davis, 1915. 10. The Metropolitan Museum of Art, Fletcher Fund, 1932. 11. (Above) The Metropolitan Museum of Art, Rogers Fund, 1920; (below) The Metropolitan Museum of Art, Rogers Fund, 1914. 12. Museum of Modern Art. 13. Wayne McLoughlin. 14. Museum of Primitive Art, Elizabeth Little. 15. The Metropolitan Museum of Art, The Fletcher Fund, 1956. 16. Larry Leach.

28 Kinship Systems
1. Members of a matrilineage in Melanesia. Wayne McLoughlin. 2 and 3. Joyce Fitzgerald, after Marc Swartz. 4. Wayne McLaughlin. 5.

Joyce Fitzgerald, after Marc Swartz. 6. Theodore Schwartz, Courtesy American Museum of Natural History. 7. Joyce Fitzgerald, after Marc Swartz. 8. Courtesy, Museum of Fine Arts, Boston. 9. Joyce Fitzgerald, after Marc Swartz. 10. Theodore Schwartz, Courtesy American Museum of Natural History. 11 and 12. Joyce Fitzgerald, after Marc Swartz. 13. Burt Glinn, Magnum.

29 Political Systems
1. Emir's court in the Sudan of Africa. Larry Leach. 2. The Metropolitan Museum of Art, Fletcher Fund, 1925. 3. Larry Leach. 4. Wide World Photos. 5. Armstrong/Fountain Graphic Art. 6. Bonnie Hernandez. 7. Thomas Gilcrease Institute, Tulsa, Oklahoma. 8. Armstrong/Fountain Graphic Art. 9. Otto Lang, Photophile. 10. The Bettmann Archive, Inc. 11. Klaus Koch. 12. Alan Mercer.

30 Economics and Anthropology
1. Peruvian market scene, Costa Manos. Magnum. 2. Jamaica Tourist Board Photo, Courtesy Sontheimer and Company, Inc. 3. R. F. Salisbury. 4. Jamaica Tourist Board Photo, Courtesy Sontheimer and Company, Inc. 5. Culver Pictures. 6. Otto Lang, Photophile. 7. L. Holý, Courtesy Jiřana Svobodova, in charge of the Institute for Ethnology, Prague, Lazarská 8, CSSR. 8. Reynold Hernandez.

31 Religion
1. Participant in an Australian corroboree. Photographic Library of Australia. 2. John Dawson. 3. Culver Pictures. 4. Paul Ganster, Photophile. 5. Ernst Haas, Magnum. 6. Jack Potter. 7. Armstrong/Fountain Graphic Art. 8. Terry Lamb. 9 and 10. Courtesy E. E. Evans-Pritchard and Pitt-Rivers Museum, University of Oxford. 11. Harry Crosby, Photophile. 12. The Summer Institute of Linguistics, Inc.

32 Social and Cultural Change
1. Acculturated Australian aborigine. David Beal. 2. The Bettmann Archive, Inc. 3. Photographic Library of Australia. 4. Armstrong/Fountain Graphic Art. 5. (Above) Jane Latta; (below) Gordon Menzie, Photophile. 6. Terry Lamb. 7. Robert Murphy.

33 Change in the Modern World
1. Western paraphernalia in Africa. Larry Leach. 2. Armstrong/Fountain Graphic Art. 3. (Above) Dr. Block Color Reproductions; (middle left) Culver Pictures; (center) Culver Pictures; (middle right) Wide World Photos; (below) Marc Riboud, Magnum. 4. Copyright © 1970, Gary Yanker. From *Prop Art* by Yanker, published by Darien House, Inc., New York City. 5. Jack Potter. 6. Marc and Evelyne Bernheim, Rapho Guillamette.

Cover sculpture by L. Burry.
Design by Reynold Hernández.
Photograph by John Oldenkamp.

Anthropology Today Book Team
Richard L. Roe, *Publisher, Social Sciences*
Cecie Starr, *Editor*
Paul Bailiff, Gladys Rysman, *Editorial Assistants*
Diana Vennard, *Editorial Coordinator*
Reynold Hernández, *Designer*
Catherine Flanders, *Associate Designer*
Barbara Blum, *Director of Production*
Robert E. Hollander, *Production Manager*
Sheridan Hughes, *Production Assistant*

CRM Books
Richard Holme, *Publisher*
Richard L. Roe, *Publisher, Social Sciences*
John H. Painter, *Publisher, Life and Physical Sciences*
Genevieve Clapp, Phillip M. Whitten, *Associate Publishers*
Jacquie Hyatt, Charlotte van Andel, *Editorial Coordinators*

Jean Smith, *Editorial Director*
Charles B. Jackson, *Managing Editor*
Arlyne Lazerson, Michael McKean, *Senior Editors*
Jacquelyn Estrada, Johanna Price, Cecie Starr, *Editors*
Martha Rosler, *Associate Editor*
Lee Massey, *Promotion Editor*
Carolyn Hultgren, Beth Lanum, Cynthia MacDonald, Susan Orlofsky, Sandra Powell, JoAn Rice, Roberta
    Savitz, Ray Seavers, *Editorial Assistants*
Cindy Lyle, Evelyn Shapiro, *Promotion Editorial Assistants*
Elaine Kleiss, *Editorial Coordinator*

Rick Connelly, *Marketing Director*
John Ochse, *Sales Manager, Western Region*
Dave Ratliff, *High School Products Manager*
Carol Walnum, *College Sales Supervisor*
Ann Bradley, Eloise Comer, Gail Dedman, Mona Drury, Connie Rogers, Delle Willett, *College Sales
    Coordinators*
Denise Willett, *Research Coordinator*
Debbie Benner, Marti Rice, *Staff*
Frederic Squires, *Operations Manager*
Sharon Broad, Charlotte Downey, Nancy Kinzer, Patti Stumpf, Sue Trevitchick, Colnlin Underwood,
    Operations Coordinators
Kathy Quinn, *Customer Services Coordinator*

Barbara Blum, *Director of Production*
Robert E. Hollander, *Production Manager*
Catherine Hunink, *Production Supervisor*
Patricia Bouchard, *Production Associate*
Joyce Couch, *Promotion Production Supervisor*
Phyllis Bowman, Sheridan Hughes, Vicki Wing, *Production Assistants*
Vickie Self, *Production Coordinator*

Tom Suzuki, *Director of Design*
Leon Bolognese, *Art Director*
John Isely, *Promotion Art Director*
Donald Fujimoto, *Senior Designer*
Catherine Flanders, Reynold Hernández, *Designers*
Sally Collins, Pamela Morehouse, Dale Phillips, *Associate Designers*
Linda Higgins, Paul Slick, *Assistant Designers*
Richard Carter, Kurt Kolbe, Ron Mertz, *Staff*
Ken Melton, *Design Operations Supervisor*
Lois Wynn, *Operations Assistant*

Nancy Hutchison, *Rights and Permissions Supervisor*
Janie Fredericks, Mary Whiteside, *Assistants*

Lynn D. Crosby, *Office Manager*
Cathy Harding, Rochelle Pinnell, *Assistants*

Officers of Communications Research Machines, Inc.
Nicolas H. Charney, *Chairman of the Board*
John J. Veronis, *President*
Richard Holme, *Vice-President*
James B. Horton, *Vice-President*
Paul Lazarus III, *Vice-President*
Walter C. Rohrer, *Vice-President*

This book was set in Linotype Aster and manufactured by Kingsport Press, Inc., Kingsport, Tennessee.
Display type is Univers #75 and captions are set in Univers #65, both supplied by Central Typesetting,
    Inc., San Diego, California.
Transparencies were processed and assembled by Robert Crandall Associates, New York, New York.
Text paper is Glatcotext Web, furnished by Perkins & Squier Company, New York, New York.
Endsheets are Schlosser Multicolor.